DICTIONARY OF AMERICAN HISTORY

DICTIONARY OF
AMERICAN HISTORY

INDEX

DICTIONARY OF
AMERICAN HISTORY

JAMES TRUSLOW ADAMS
Editor in Chief

R. V. COLEMAN
Managing Editor

INDEX

NEW YORK

CHARLES SCRIBNER'S SONS

1940

Advisory Council

Foreword

THERE are 6425 separate articles in the *Dictionary of American History*, each covering a definite aspect of American history. These articles are arranged alphabetically, under captions to which the average user of the work would most naturally turn, and cross references are inserted where varying captions are in common use. Thus, the separate articles are easily found and references to them do not appear in this Index.

However, in related articles, by different scholars and under different captions, there are, frequently, additional facts or interpretations. These related articles are indicated by the symbol ^{q} (*quod vide*, "which see"), and are thus brought to the reader's attention. But for finding the elusive reference or subject or name an Index is essential.

The editors recommend that the user of the work first turn to the text for a separate article on the subject desired. If, having found such an article, and having followed through the pertinent cross references, additional material is desired, then the Index should be consulted. For example, in the text (Volume IV, pp. 13–15) there is a thousand-word article on the Monroe Doctrine, by Professor Dexter Perkins; the Index lists references to this subject in twenty-six other articles by other scholars.

Again, the reader may not find a separate article on the exact subject desired. In that case, reference to the Index may bring to light, in one or more articles dealing with related subjects, the information wished.

Finally, in tracing the part which a particular person played in the events dealt with in the various articles, the Index will be useful. No biographical sketches, as such, appear in the *Dictionary of American History*; that has been done in the *Dictionary of American Biography*, to which the reader is referred for connected biographical material. Nonetheless, the present Index will enable the reader to trace, through

Foreword

the significant events of American history, the activities of each of the men and women who had a part in making that history.

Since phrasing the captions for the Index has sometimes called for a different approach from that used in determining the captions for the body of the work, the user is warned against accepting the caption in the body of the work as necessarily the phrasing in the Index. Where practicable, the phrasing has been identical, but if not readily found in the Index, a different phrasing should be tried; in fact, all phrasings should be tried. Particularly where a subject admits of more than one phrasing, all ways should be tried; for example, if Separation of Powers is not found under "Separation," it should be looked for under "Powers." Again, subjects which might be prefixed by such words as "Federal" or "National" or "American" should be tried both under those headings and without those headings.

The wordings of the sub-headings have been phrased, in most cases, with a view to showing the relationship of the subject indexed to the article in which the reference will be found. This policy has been followed both because, in general, the significance of the reference lies in its relationship to the article in which it appears and because such phrasing helps materially in locating the reference on the page.

Where more than one reference occurs under a general heading, the sub-headings are listed serially, by volume and page. Inasmuch as this otherwise useful arrangement sometimes results in the separation of identically worded or closely related references, the editors recommend that the user do not assume that having found one reference to the subject desired, there may not be others farther along under the same general heading. Also, it should be noted that the sub-headings are phrased to connect with the leading caption, and not with the sub-heading just preceding.

So far as possible, uniformity of policy has been preserved, but where it has appeared that greater usefulness will be attained by departing from uniformity, usefulness has been the first consideration.

THE EDITORS

Dec. 5, 1940

DICTIONARY OF
AMERICAN HISTORY

INDEX

[The Foreword, on pages vii and viii, constitutes a guide
for the use of this Index, and should be carefully read.]

A

Abbe, Cleveland, and weather forecasts, V, 430

Abbot, Abiel, establishes a free public library, III, 272

Abbot, Charles Greeley, secretary of the Smithsonian Institution, V, 102

Abbot, Downing & Co., II, 2

Abbott, Emma, and the opera, IV, 178

Abbott, Jacob, travel stories by, I, 363

Abbott, Lyman, and evolution, II, 231; theological writings, V, 261

Abbott, Samuel Warren, and vital statistics, V, 382

Abbott, W. H., and early pipe lines, IV, 276

Abenaki Indians, and Algonquins, I, 48; in Dummer's War, II, 175; form confederacy, II, 320; massacre at Haverhill, Mass., III, 17; Jesuit missions among, III, 175; and King Philip's War, III, 210; as refugees from King Philip's War, III, 211; in King William's War, III, 211; at Pemaquid, IV, 239; attack on Salmon Falls, V, 17; attack on York, Me. (1692), V, 507

Abercrombie, Fort, Sibley returns to, II, 106

Abercromby, James, fails to reach Fort St. Frederic, II, 93; expedition against Ticonderoga (1758), III, 229; and colonial rangers, IV, 416; operations at Ticonderoga (1758–59), V, 268

Abilene, Kans., railroad reaches, I, 33; cattle market opened at, I, 326; Chisholm Trail leads to, I, 368; as cow town, II, 79

Abittibi Indians, I, 48

Abnaki, The. See Abenaki

Abolition Movement, and antislavery societies, I, 58; and use of the mails, I, 85; and compensated emancipation, II, 205; and the Emancipator, II, 206; and the doctrine of equality, II, 223; and free Negroes, II, 332; and the Garrison mob, II, 372; literature, II, 377; and immediatism, III, 72; and the Kansas-Nebraska Act, III, 197; and the Lovejoy riots, III, 310; and mobs and riots, IV, 3; and New England Antislavery Society, IV, 99; and the Pearl case, IV, 237; and peculiar institution, IV, 238; and antislavery petitions, IV, 257; begun by Garrison and Weld, IV, 363; and secession, V, 51; in South Carolina, V, 125

Abraham, Heights of, Wolfe scales, II, 343

Abraham Lincoln: A History, written by John G. Nicolay and John Hay, I, 190

Abraham Lincoln, Fort, Custer's expedition sets out from, I, 195; the Far West carries news of Custer's annihilation to, II, 244; and Little Big Horn battle, III, 284

Abreú, Ramon, and El Crepúsculo de la Libertad, IV, 127

Abruzzi, Duke of, polar expedition of, IV, 293

Abstract of Title, III, 243

Academies, and education, II, 185; and high school, III, 30; replace the Latin School, III, 250; and private schools, V, 41; in the Old South, V, 122; and education of women, V, 480

Academy of Natural Science, IV, 47

Acadia, and the Penobscot region, II, 346; National Park, IV, 218; and Port Royal, IV, 315; fall of, in Queen Anne's War, IV, 389; ceded to Great Britain by treaty of Utrecht, V, 354

Acadians, expelled from Nova Scotia, I, 298; in Charleston, S. C., I, 343; and "Evangeline," II, 230; settle at Pointe Coupée, IV, 292

Accident Insurance, III, 131

Accidents. See Workmen's Accident Compensation

Ackia, Battle of, I, 360; II, 110; V, 280

Acoma, as a mesa, III, 379; Chamuscado expedition to, IV, 500

I

Acosta, Bert, wins air trophy, **I**, 36

"Acres of Diamonds," lecture by R. H. Conwell, **III**, 260

Act Concerning Religion, **III**, 348

Act for the Impartial Administration of Justice, **I**, 408; **III**, 147

Ad Valorem Duties, **II**, 102, 180

Adaes, fortified by Aguayo, **I**, 34

Adair v. U. S., and Coppage v. Kansas, **II**, 57; and the yellow-dog contract, **V**, 504

Adam, Robert B., library of, **I**, 212

Adams, Abigail, and feminism, **II**, 265; and the White House, **V**, 459; and the woman movement, **V**, 477

Adams, Alvin, and express business, **I**, 9

Adams, C. F., and the *Alabama*, **I**, 40; and the *Bermuda* admiralty case, **I**, 179; publishes life of John Adams, **I**, 190; Civil War diplomacy, **I**, 391; nominated by Free Soil party, **II**, 334; and the Liberal Republican party, **III**, 269; and the *Trent* affair, **V**, 321

Adams, Fort (Miss.), Freeman's expedition leaves, **II**, 339; established, **II**, 428; Loftus Heights becomes site of, **III**, 294

Adams, Henry, author of *Life of Albert Gallatin*, **I**, 190

Adams, Herbert, sculptor, **I**, 124

Adams, James, and the *Wilmington Courant*, **IV**, 126; first printer in Delaware, **IV**, 345

Adams, James Truslow, and political writings, **IV**, 303

Adams, John, and Anglo-American relations, **I**, 74; and British debts, **I**, 240; elected Vice-President, **I**, 280; elected President, **I**, 281; and the drafting of the Declaration of Independence, **II**, 120; signer of the Declaration of Independence, **II**, 123; and the Definitive Treaty of Peace (1783), **II**, 129; and the Dutch bankers' loans, **II**, 178; selects motto, *E Pluribus Unum*, **II**, 180; lends moral support to the Embargo, **II**, 208; and the Federalist party, **II**, 264; and the Fourth of July, **II**, 318; and Franco-American relations, **II**, 328; and the Jefferson-Burr election dispute, **III**, 170; recommends judicial reform, **III**, 189; and Marbury v. Madison, **III**, 341; and the midnight judges, **III**, 395; and Miranda's intrigues, **III**, 414; philosophical thought and writings, **IV**, 263; and the Plan of 1776, **IV**, 282; political writings of, **IV**, 302; and presidential exemption from subpœna, **IV**, 334; and presidential title, **IV**, 334; and the President's message, **IV**, 336; and republican form of government, **IV**, 453; and the American Revolution, **IV**, 465; and financing the Revolution, **IV**, 471; and the spoils system, **V**, 147; and state constitutions, **V**, 166; and the Boston Massacre trial, **V**, 323; and the Vice-Presidency, **V**, 366; and "whitewash," **V**, 461; and "the wise, and good and rich," **V**, 475; and the X Y Z affair, **V**, 498

Adams, John Quincy, and the abolition movement, **I**, 3; and Adams-Onís Treaty, **I**, 9; and the antislavery movement, **I**, 86; defends Jackson in Arbuthnot and Ambrister case, **I**, 98; elected President (1824), **I**, 282; defeated (1828), **I**, 282; and corrupt bargain charges, **II**, 63; and the Democratic party, **II**, 136; and the Embargo, **II**, 208; and treaty of Ghent, **II**, 387; and disarmament agreement on Great Lakes, **II**, 415; and Hispanic American wars of independence, **III**, 32; and internal improvements, **III**, 137; and recognition of Latin-American Republics, **III**, 250; bitter opponent of Masonry, **III**, 352; and the Monroe Doctrine, **IV**, 13; and the National Republican party, **IV**, 62; and the *National Journal*, **IV**, 128; and astronomical observatories, **IV**, 156; and oratory, **IV**, 180; and the panic of 1819, **IV**, 208; contests gag rule, **IV**, 256, 257; and secession, **V**, 51; and annexation of Texas, **V**, 251; and Perry's mission to Venezuela, **V**, 359; and the War of 1812, **V**, 406

Adams, Robert, and dime novels, **II**, 146

Adams, Samuel, and Boston Committee of Correspondence, **I**, 223; and Boston Tea Party, **I**, 224; as brewer, **I**, 236; promotes committees of correspondence, **I**, 437; signer of the Declaration of Independence, **II**, 123; and liberalism, **III**, 269; organizes resistance in Massachusetts, **III**, 356; and natural rights, **IV**, 66; and oratory, **IV**, 179; and political theories, **IV**, 300; and political propaganda, **IV**, 358; and Revere's ride, **IV**, 463; and the Massachusetts Circular Letter, **IV**, 466

Adams, Thomas S., and the Wisconsin Idea, **V**, 474

Adams, William H., publishes the *Kansas Weekly Herald*, **IV**, 126

Adams Act (1906), **I**, 25

Adams Express Company, robbery of, **V**, 303; carries mail, **V**, 308

Adams-Onís Treaty, and annexation of territory, **I**, 79; and the Arbuthnot and Ambrister case, **I**, 98; and state boundaries, **I**, 226; makes Florida part of United States, **II**, 287, 288; and the Florida boundary, **II**, 290; and foreign policy, **II**, 303; and Greer County dispute, **II**, 425; and recognition of Latin-American Republics, **III**, 250; and the Long expedition, **III**, 298; and Louisiana boundaries, **III**, 309; and the Mexican boundary, **III**, 382; and the Oregon Question, **IV**, 184; Spain signs, **V**, 57; and Spanish-American relations, **V**, 135; and territorial claims of the United States, **V**, 246; and annexation of Texas, **V**, 251; and western boundary

of Louisiana, V, 252; and West Florida contro-versy, V, 437

Adamson Act, and railroads, IV, 408; establishes legal work day for railway employees, V, 387

Addams, Jane, and peace movements, IV, 235; and Hull House, V, 109; and the Women's Peace party, V, 395

Adding Machine, I, 259

Addison, William H., and sea fencibles, V, 47

Adena Mound Culture, III, 391

Aderholt, O. F., killed in Gastonia riots, II, 374

Adjusted Compensation, I, 210

Adjutant General, duties of, I, 115

Adkins v. Children's Hospital, and minimum-wage laws, III, 408; and *stare decisis*, V, 161; and minimum wages, V, 387; and West Coast Hotel Co. v. Parrish, V, 436

Administrative Agencies, and justice, I, 11; and the delegation of powers, II, 133; and emer-gency legislation, II, 210; as quasi-judicial agen-cies, IV, 387; and tyranny, V, 337

"Admiral's Map," III, 339

Admiralty Cases, and the judiciary, III, 185

Admiralty Courts, as prize courts, IV, 352; during the Revolution, IV, 471; and royal colonies, IV, 504

Admission of States, V, 172

Adobe House, and building materials, I, 250; and the pioneers, IV, 275

Adobe Walls, and the Cheyenne Indians, I, 355; Santanta in battle of, V, 31

Adult Education, promotion of, II, 188; and the lyceum movement, III, 316

Adulteration, and patent medicine, IV, 222; and Pure Food and Drug Acts, IV, 383

Adultery, and sex relations, V, 61

Adventists. *See* Millerism

Adventurers, and New Plymouth colony, IV, 111

Advertising, and consumer protection, II, 44; false, reduced by Federal Trade Commission, II, 264; and magazine publishing, III, 323; and newspapers, IV, 125; and patent medicine, IV, 222; and price maintenance, IV, 340; and Pure Food and Drug Acts, IV, 383; and trade jour-nalism, V, 298; and trade-marks, V, 299; and yellow journalism, V, 505

Aero Club of America, I, 36

Ætna Insurance Company, III, 129

African Company, Royal, V, 91, 94

"African Iron," in the triangular trade, V, 296

African Methodist Episcopal Church, IV, 83

African Methodist Episcopal Zion Church, IV, 83

Agamenticus, and Gorges in Maine, II, 401

Agassiz, Alexander, and Calumet and Hecla Mine, I, 276; Swiss origin, V, 215

Agassiz, Louis, in Latin America, III, 248; early science lecturer, III, 260; and museums, IV, 47

Aged, homes for the, IV, 260

Agg, John, editor of the *National Journal*, IV, 128

Agramonte, Aristide, and yellow fever, V, 505

Agrarian Movement, I, 81

Agricultural Adjustment Act, and government control, I, 32; and cotton control, I, 156; de-clared unconstitutional, I, 261; as emergency legislation, II, 210; and the farm bureau, II, 245; and Hoosac Mills Case, III, 44; and in-terstate commerce laws, III, 144; and the Su-preme Court, III, 184; and Rickert Rice Mills v. Fontenot, IV, 482; grants subsidy to farmers, V, 195; and the Thomas Amendment, V, 264

Agricultural Adjustment Administration, and the agrarian movement, I, 22; and congressional regulation, II, 17; and delegation of powers, II, 133; as pump-priming agency, IV, 96; and price fixing, IV, 339; and taxation, V, 227

Agricultural Banks, I, 157

Agricultural Colleges, and the Morrill Act, IV, 27

Agricultural Credit Corporations, and the Recon-struction Finance Corporation, IV, 428

Agricultural Credits Act of 1923, and banking, I, 157; creates intermediate credit banks, III, 136; and the War Finance Corporation, V, 403

Agricultural Experiment Stations, I, 25; II, 78, 171, 253, 255, 371; V, 102

Agricultural Extension, provided by Smith-Lever Act, V, 102

Agricultural Fair, I, 26, 174

Agricultural Marketing Act, II, 246; enactment of, II, 250; and the Federal Farm Board, II, 257

Agricultural Museum, farm periodical, II, 248

Agricultural Papers, and advertising, I, 16

Agricultural Production, and Federal taxing power, V, 232

Agricultural Societies, and agricultural educa-tion, I, 25; established, I, 27; and Department of Agriculture, I, 30; formation of, I, 32; and diversification, II, 154; and farmers' institutes, II, 253

Agriculture, and crop failures, II, 91; and farm machinery, II, 247; control of, II, 250; and the industrial revolution, III, 118; as colonial in-dustry, III, 119; and changes in rural life, IV, 508, 509

Agriculture, Department of, and agricultural so-cieties, I, 26; and air photography, I, 35; and office of dry land agriculture, II, 171; estab-lished, II, 296; and fire control, II, 308; takes over supervision of work of Four-H clubs, II, 316

Aguayo, San Miguel de, re-establishes San Fran-cisco de los Tejas, V, 24

Aguinaldo, Emilio, captured by Funston, II, 357; and the Philippine insurrection, IV, 262

Air Brake, I, 8

Air Commerce, Bureau of, I, 432

Air Commerce Act of 1926, I, 37

Air Conditioning, grew from brewing installation, I, 236; and electricity, II, 195; and refrigeration, IV, 437

Air Corps Reserve, and army peace-time work, I, 111

Air Mail, and airways, I, 37; and aviation, I, 143; and Civil Aeronautics Act, I, 381; contracts, I, 439; inauguration of, IV, 320

Air Transport Companies, mail subsidies granted to, V, 195

Aircraft Carriers, of United States fleet, II, 284; and warship, V, 412

Airplanes, and aviation, I, 142; and growth of democracy, II, 135; Congress authorizes construction of, II, 148; and freight shipments, II, 341; invention of the, III, 149; and munitions, IV, 45; and transportation and travel, V, 309; construction of, during the World War, V, 492

Airway Traffic Control, I, 37

Airways, and Civil Aeronautics Act, I, 380; and international communications, I, 439; at Guam, II, 427

Aitken, Robert, publishes first American Bible in English, I, 182

Aix-la-Chapelle, Treaty of, and French claims in Ohio, II, 343; ends King George's War, III, 210; and Louisburg, III, 304

Akron, name given to the airship ZRS–4, II, 149

Alabama, and repudiation of state debts, IV, 457; organized, and admitted, V, 249; and West Florida, V, 436

Alabama, sinking of (1864), I, 390; and the Confederate navy, II, 8; and *Kearsarge,* III, 202; and prizes, IV, 353

Alabama Claims, arbitration of, I, 96; and proposed annexation of Canada, I, 300; and Civil War diplomacy, I, 392; arbitration of, IV, 89; and the Treaty of Washington (1871), V, 416

Alamance, Battle of, and the Granville Grant, II, 412; and the Regulators of North Carolina, IV, 440

Alamo, massacre at the, IV, 447; at Fort Sam Houston, V, 20; Santa Anna takes, V, 257

Alarcón, Hernando de, discovers the Colorado River, I, 427

Alaska, territorial expansion in, I, 128; and expansion, II, 234; an incorporated territory, III, 127; and our interests in the Pacific, IV, 196; Russian Orthodox Church makes first appearance in, IV, 511; and territorial claims of the United States, V, 247; organized as a territory, V, 249

Alaska, Purchase of, and territorial expansion, I, 79; and "manifest destiny," III, 332; and the Pribilof Islands, IV, 338; and seal fisheries, V, 49

Alaska Boundary Question, and Anglo-American relations, I, 77; and Canadian-American relations, I, 300

Alaska Commercial Company, leases seal islands, V, 49

Alaska-Juneau Lode Mine, II, 396

Alaska Packers Association, II, 297

Alaska-Treadwell Lode Mine, II, 396

Albany, granted charter, II, 160; Dutch merchants at, II, 179; and the fur trade, II, 361; founded, III, 55; emigrants settle at, IV, 107 f.; as a frontier post, V, 302

Albany (N. Y.) *Argus,* as political organ, IV, 128

Albany Congress (1754), I, 421; and covenant chain, II, 77; and Treaty of Easton, II, 183; DeLancey presides over, IV, 115; and the Susquehannah Company, V, 211

Albany Evening Journal, and anti-Masonic movements, I, 82; as a political órgan, IV, 128

Albany Regency, established by Van Buren, III, 319; and the *Albany Argus,* IV, 128

Albemarle, and the Cape Fear River settlements, I, 306

Albemarle Point, first permanent settlement of South Carolina, V, 125

Albemarle Sound, settlements along, IV, 144

Albright, Samuel J., founder of the *Dakotah Democrat,* IV, 127; first printer of South Dakota, IV, 346

Alcott, A. Bronson, and Concord Group, II, 2; and experiment at Fruitlands, II, 354; and "Peter Parley," IV, 255

Alcott, Louisa M., edits *Merry's Museum for Boys and Girls,* I, 363

Alden, John, arrest of, III, 204; and Plymouth Rock, IV, 290

Alder Gulch, discovered by Bill Fairweather, II, 236

Aldine, and wood engraving, V, 482

Aldrich, Nelson W., and tariff, IV, 229

Aldrich, Thomas Bailey, author of *The Story of a Bad Boy,* I, 363

Aldrich-Vreeland Act, Congress passes, I, 157; and appointment of National Monetary Commission, IV, 61

Aldworth, Robert, and Monhegan Island, IV, 9; and Pemaquid, IV, 239, 240

Alemany, Joseph, Dominican bishop, II, 159

Aleutian Islands, Cook's voyages through, II, 55; United States purchases, IV, 195

Alexander, Robert, and the Oise-Aisne operation, IV, 167

Alexander, William. *See* Stirling, Earl of

Alexanderson, E. F. W., and wireless telegraphy, V, 472

Alexandra, The, and the Alabama Claims, I, 40

Alexandria, occupied by Banks in the Red River campaign, IV, 430

Alfalfa, Spanish origin of, V, 138

Alfred, The, purchased by the Continental Navy, IV, 471

Alfriend, Frank H., editor of the *Southern Literary Messenger,* V, 130

Algeciras Conference, and isolation, III, 163; and Madrid Conference, III, 322; and the Perdicaris affair, IV, 253; and treaties, V, 318

Alger, Andrew and Arthur, settle Dunstan, V, 3

Alger, Horatio, books of, I, 363

Algernourne, Fort, and Fortress Monroe, IV, 12

Algiers, and the Barbary Wars, I, 162; United States declares war on, II, 119; treaties with, V, 316

Algonquin Indians, and Abenaki, I, 1; Arapaho, a branch of the, I, 94; the Blackfeet as members of, I, 197; and the canoe, I, 305; and the Cheyenne Indians, I, 355; and food getting, II, 294; Fox Indians, a tribe of, II, 319; houses of, III, 111; Lake Champlain as thoroughfare for, III, 229; attack Maine, III, 326; and *Midewiwin,* III, 395

Alibamon Indians, Jesuit missions among, III, 175

Alien and Sedition Acts, and the Federalist party, II, 264; and tyranny, V, 337; and Virginia-Kentucky Resolutions, V, 376

Alien Land Law of California, I, 271

Alien Property Custodian, and confiscation of property, II, 16; and patents, V, 492

Aliens, deportation of, II, 139; as voters, V, 383

Alison, Francis, and life insurance, III, 129

All American Canal, I, 428

Allbrights, The, rifle makers, IV, 483

Alleghany, The, American merchantman, threatened by Algiers, I, 162

Alleghenies, Freighters of the, II, 3

Allegheny Portage Railway, and *Hit or Miss,* III, 35; completed, IV, 243; tunnel on the, V, 329

Allegheny Transportation Company, IV, 166, 276

Allegiance, and expatriation, II, 234; and impressment of seamen, III, 81; and international law, III, 141; and political theories, IV, 300

Allen, Capt., and group migration, III, 397

Allen, Ethan, captured by British, I, 297; and free thinking, II, 340; and "Great Jehovah," II, 414; and the Green Mountain Boys, II, 422; and Haldimand negotiations, III, 4; and Onion River Land Company, IV, 174; philosophical thought and writings, IV, 263; as prisoner of war, IV, 348; and capture of Ticonderoga (1775), V, 267, 362 f.

Allen, H. W., joins Shelby's Mexican expedition, V, 68

Allen, Henry T., commander of American Forces in Germany, I, 116

Allen, Horatio, and railroad gauges, IV, 402

Allen, Ira, and the Green Mountain Boys, II, 422; and Onion River Land Company, IV, 174

Allen, Samuel, buys the Mason title, III, 351

Allen, Thomas, editor of the *Madisonian,* II, 403

Allen, William, uses phrase "fifty-four forty or fight," II, 271

Allen's Farm, Battle of, and the Peninsular Campaign, IV, 241

Allgeyer v. Louisiana, IV, 254

Alliance, The, and the Bergen prizes, I, 179; only vessel owned by Navy after Revolution, II, 282; frigate, IV, 77; in the American Revolution, IV, 471

Alligator, Seminole chief, V, 476

Allison, W. B., and the Bland-Allison Act, I, 198

Allouez, Claude, builds mission house on Chequamegon Bay, I, 351; establishes mission of St. Marc, II, 319; visits Green Bay, II, 422; at Great Village of the Illinois, III, 69; establishes Jesuit missions, III, 174; visits the Mascouten, III, 350; labors and dies at Fort St. Joseph, V, 10; addresses the Indians at Sault Ste. Marie pageant, V, 35; reaches Lake Superior, V, 205

Allston, Washington, painter, I, 123

Almanac Calculated for New England, I, 51

Almanacs, and advertising, I, 16; and colonial newspaper, I, 420; *Farmer's,* II, 252; *New England,* IV, 98; *Poor Richard's,* IV, 307; printing of, IV, 344

Almshouses, and pauperism, IV, 226; and philanthropy and benevolence, IV, 260

Alsop, Richard, one of the Hartford Wits, III, 15

Alta California, and the Anza Expedition, I, 87

Altgeld, John Peter, and government by injunction, II, 402; and the Haymarket riot, III, 20

Alton, Ill., prison camp at, IV, 347

Altoona, The, and steamboat racing, V, 178

Aluminum, development of, III, 118

Amadas, Philip, and Raleigh's patent, IV, 413

Amalgamated Association of Iron, Steel and Tin Workers, III, 43

Amalgamated Copper Company, I, 71; II, 348

Amalgamated Iron and Steel Workers, strike of, V, 180

Amalgamationists, II, 25

Amana Community, as a communistic experiment, I, 440; and group migration, III, 397

Amangual, Francisco, and Texan-Santa Fé expedition, V, 251

Ambassadors, and the Constitution, II, 36; and foreign service, II, 306; V, 163

Ambrister, Robert, Jackson captures, I, 98

Ambrose Light, The, case of, I, 176

Amelia Island, center of slave smuggling, V, 92

Amendments to the Constitution, in Barron v. Baltimore, I, 165; and Bill of Rights, I, 184; and Article Five, II, 38; proposal of, II, 90

America, The, figurehead on, **II**, 272; ship-of-the-line, **V**, 75, 411

America, The, and yacht racing, **V**, 499

American Academy of Arts and Sciences, **III**, 256

American Agriculturist, farm periodical, **II**, 248

American and Foreign Christian Union, **IV**, 65

American Anthropological Association, **III**, 257

American Antiquarian Society, **I**, 212, 330; **III**, 33

American Anti-Slavery Society, and emancipation, **II**, 204; and gag rule, **II**, 365; and the *Liberator,* **III**, 270; and right of petition, **IV**, 257; as propagandist agency, **IV**, 359

American Archives, by Peter Force, **II**, 300

American Art Association, **I**, 211

American Association for the Advancement of Science, **III**, 257

American Association of Advertising Agencies, **I**, 19

American Association of Engineers, **II**, 216

American Bankers Association, **III**, 287

American Bar Association, and law schools, **III**, 252; and uniform state laws, **V**, 170; and the World Court, **V**, 485

American Bible Society, **I**, 181, 214; **III**, 417

American Board of Commissioners for Foreign Missions, **III**, 103, 417

American Boy, magazine, **I**, 363

American Bridge Company, **V**, 348

American Chemical Society, **III**, 257

American Civil Liberties Union, **IV**, 359

American Colonization Society, and abolitionist literature, **I**, 3; and emancipation, **II**, 204; and Liberia, **III**, 270; and proslavery, **IV**, 363

American Cotton Oil Trust, **V**, 326

American Council of Learned Societies, **III**, 257

American Crisis, title of series of essays by Thomas Paine, **V**, 271

American Dictionary of the English Language, **II**, 146

American Economic Association, **III**, 257

American Electric Company, **II**, 375

American Emigrant Company, and immigrant labor, **III**, 73

American Engineering Council, **II**, 216

American Expeditionary Forces, and the Army General Staff, **I**, 115; and army supply, **I**, 119; and demobilization, **II**, 134; and military roads, **III**, 402; and the militia, **III**, 404; and Officers' Reserve Corps, **IV**, 158; in the World War, **V**, 491

American Express Company, and Wells, Fargo & Co., **V**, 433

American Farm Bureau Federation, and agrarian movement, **I**, 22; promotes co-operatives, **II**, 57; formed, **II**, 244; maintains lobbies, **III**, 287; as a pressure group, **IV**, 337

American Farmer, **I**, 27; **II**, 248

American Federation of Labor, and Boston police strike, **I**, 223; and boycotting, **I**, 232; and Buck Stove and Range case, **I**, 246; and campaign of 1924, **I**, 291; and communism, **I**, 440; and Congress of Industrial Organizations, **II**, 20; and Danbury Hatters' case, **II**, 108; demands repeal of the Eighteenth Amendment, **II**, 190; formation of, **II**, 336; and the Industrial Workers of the World, **III**, 118; and the injunction, **III**, 124; and passage of the Clayton Act, **III**, 144; and Knights of Labor, **III**, 215; formation of, **III**, 219; and labor parties, **III**, 223; organized, **III**, 224; endorses the La Follette party, **III**, 227; maintains lobbies, **III**, 287; and the McNamara case, **III**, 367; and Populism, **IV**, 313; as a pressure group, **IV**, 337; and propaganda, **IV**, 358; and the railroad strikes of 1886, **IV**, 405; and railway shopmen's strike of 1922, **IV**, 410; and steel strikes, **V**, 180; and craft unions, **V**, 344; and the United Mine Workers, **V**, 346; and Western Federation of Miners, **V**, 443

American Female Guardian Society, **IV**, 20

American Folk Lore Society, **III**, 102

American Friends Service Committee, **IV**, 386; **V**, 488

American Fur Company, and Fort Assiniboine, **I**, 130; and Astoria, **I**, 133; and Fort Benton, **I**, 178; and Cabanne's Post, **I**, 264; post at La Pointe, **I**, 351; and Chouteau and Company, **I**, 369; and the Columbia Fur Company, **I**, 429; and rise of John Jacob Astor, **II**, 311; and the fur trade, **II**, 360, 362, 363; and Green River, **II**, 423; sends out the Illinois Fur Brigade, **III**, 70; and Indian trade, **III**, 110; and Fort John, **III**, 177; and Fort Kiowa, **III**, 213; purchases Fort Laramie, **III**, 245; and liquor, **III**, 282; and Mackenzie's treaty, **III**, 321; and Minnesota, **III**, 410; and Missouri River fur trade, **III**, 431; and abandonment of Fort William, **IV**, 29; joined by North West Company, **IV**, 147; and Pacific Fur Company, **IV**, 195; and Prairie du Chien, **IV**, 328; and the Red River of the North, **IV**, 431; and Red River cart traffic, **IV**, 431; maintains post at Sault Ste. Marie, **V**, 34; protected by Fort Snelling, **V**, 106; merges with Southwest Fur Company, **V**, 133; and Fort Union, N. Dak., **V**, 341; and founding of Astoria, **V**, 415; and western merchants, **V**, 445; and the *Yellowstone,* **V**, 506

American Girl, magazine, **I**, 364

American Historical Association, sets up the Public Archives Commission, **I**, 103; and government publications, **II**, 405; and historical societies, **III**, 33; and learned societies, **III**, 257

American Home Missionary Society, and Congre-

gationalists, **II**, 17; and the Illinois Band, **III**, 69; and the Iowa Band, **III**, 153; and churches, **III**, 417; and American religion, **IV**, 442

American Horse, defeated at Slim Buttes, **V**, 87; surrenders, **V**, 98

American Humane Association, **V**, 112

American Indian Mission Association, **III**, 103

American Institute at La Paz, **III**, 248

American Institute of Chemical Engineers, **II**, 216

American Institute of Electrical Engineers, **II**, 216

American Institute of Laundering, **III**, 115

American Institute of Public Opinion, **V**, 21

American Journal of Railway Appliances, **V**, 298

American Labor Union, **IV**, 174

American Land Company, **III**, 240

American Law Institute, fosters restatement of the law, **III**, 251

American League against War and Fascism, **V**, 395

American Legion, demands repeal of the Eighteenth Amendment, **II**, 190; maintains lobbies, **III**, 287; as a propaganda organization, **IV**, 359; and soldier vote, **V**, 117; as veterans' organization, **V**, 365

American Legislators' Association, **V**, 175

American Library Association, *Bulletin,* **III**, 34; formed, **III**, 272

American Machinist, trade journal, **V**, 298

American Magazine, **III**, 323; **IV**, 258

American Medical Association, **III**, 257, 369; **IV**, 222

American Messenger, **I**, 51

American Meteorological Society, **V**, 271

American Mineralogical Society, **III**, 117

American Miners' Association, **I**, 404

American Minerva, edited by Noah Webster, **IV**, 123

American Missionary Association, **II**, 17; **III**, 417

American Museum of Natural History, **III**, 248; **IV**, 47

American Nettie Mine, **V**, 25

American Numismatic Society, **IV**, 48

American Oriental Society, **III**, 257

American (Know-Nothing) Party, and the Bedini riots, **I**, 173; in campaign of 1856, **I**, 284; in campaign of 1860, **I**, 285; and Constitutional Union party, **II**, 44; opposes homestead movement, **III**, 42; and intolerance, **III**, 147; and nativism, **IV**, 65; as a political party, **IV**, 296; and secret societies, **V**, 53; as a third party, **V**, 262

American Pathfinders, anti-Catholic organization, **IV**, 66

American Peace Society, maintains lobbies, **III**, 287; formed, **IV**, 233; and propaganda, **IV**, 359; as an antiwar organization, **V**, 395

American Philological Association, **III**, 257

American Philosophical Association, **III**, 257

American Philosophical Society, and industrial research, **III**, 117; founded, **III**, 256; **IV**, 258; and Wistar parties, **V**, 475

American Prison Association, **IV**, 348

American Protective Association, **III**, 285; **IV**, 65, 443

American Protestant Association, **I**, 323

American Protestant Society, **IV**, 65

American Protestant Vindicator, anti-Catholic paper, **IV**, 65

American Psychological Association, **III**, 257

American Railway Engineering Association, **II**, 216

American Railway Express Company, and air mail, **I**, 143; Wells, Fargo merge with, **V**, 434

American Railway Union, and the Debs case, **II**, 116; and use of injunction, **III**, 123; and the Pullman strike, **IV**, 381; and Social Democratic party, **V**, 106

American Red Cross, and ambulance companies, **I**, 54; and sale of Christmas seals, **I**, 371; and philanthropy and benevolence, **IV**, 261

American Relief Administration, **II**, 297; **V**, 487

American Republican Party, organized by nativists, **IV**, 65; and the Philadelphia riots, **IV**, 259

American Revolution. *See* Revolution, American

American-Scandinavian Foundation, and foreign exchange students, **V**, 192

American School Peace League, **IV**, 235

American Sheet Steel Company, **V**, 348

American Smelting and Refining Company, **V**, 25, 101

American Social Hygiene Association, **IV**, 365

American Society for the Judicial Settlement of International Disputes, **IV**, 235

American Society of Civil Engineers, **II**, 215

American Society of Equity, and agrarian movement, **I**, 22; promotes co-operatives, **II**, 57; and tobacco co-operatives, **V**, 275

American Society of Mechanical Engineers, **II**, 215

American Standards Association, **V**, 4

American Steel and Wire Company, **V**, 348

American Steel Founders Case, **III**, 124; **IV**, 266

American Steel Hoop Company, **V**, 348

American Student Union, **V**, 511

American Sugar Refining Company, and sugar trust, **V**, 201; and U. S. v. E. C. Knight Co., **V**, 348

American Sunday School Union, and distribution of the Bible, **I**, 181

American System, and free trade, **II**, 334; Clay's, **III**, 137; Clay pleads for, **IV**, 203

American System, of interchangeable parts, **III**, 133, 148

American Telegraph and Cable Company, **I**, 434

American Telephone and Telegraph Company,

stockholders, **I**, 310; and patents, **IV**, 223; and employment, **V**, 236; as holder of the Bell patent, **V**, 239

American Temperance Union, **V**, 240

American Tin Plate Company, **V**, 272, 348

American Tobacco Case, and trust-busting, **V**, 326

American Tobacco Company, and the Sherman Antitrust Law, **V**, 70; organized, **V**, 274

American Tract Society, **I**, 181; **IV**, 20

American Union against Militarism, **V**, 395

American Weekly Mercury, makes earliest printed reference to a lottery, **III**, 303; founded by Andrew Bradford and John Copson, **IV**, 127

American Youth Congress, **V**, 511

Americanization, and assimilation, **I**, 130; and Catholicism, **I**, 323; and growth of democracy, **II**, 136; and the social settlement, **V**, 109

America's Cup, and yacht racing, **V**, 499

Ames, A. A., and political rings, **IV**, 485

Ames, E. S., and theological writings, **V**, 261

Ames, Fisher, and "the wise, and good and rich," **V**, 475

Ames, John G., and government publications, **II**, 405

Ames, Nathaniel, and the almanac, **I**, 52

Ames, Oakes, and Crédit Mobilier, **II**, 84; and the Union Pacific Railroad, **V**, 343

Ames, Oliver, and Crédit Mobilier, **II**, 84

Ames, Winthrop, and "little theater" movement, **III**, 286

Ames Building, introduces skeleton construction, **V**, 88

Amherst, Jeffery, forces Bourlamaque to blow up Fort St. Frederic, **II**, 93; drives French from Lake Champlain, **III**, 229; **IV**, 18; in the French and Indian War, **IV**, 115; at Fort Ontario, **IV**, 191; and Rogers' Rangers, **IV**, 416; leads army against Ticonderoga, **V**, 268; in Vermont, **V**, 362

Amherst College, **II**, 17; **V**, 191

Amish Mennonites, **III**, 373

Amman, Jacob, **I**, 68

Ammann, O. H., and bridges, **I**, 237

Amnesty, and the case of Jefferson Davis, **II**, 112; and pardon, **IV**, 214; and pardon brokers, **IV**, 215; and Reconstruction, **IV**, 426

Amoskeag Company, **IV**, 102

Ams, Charles M., and the open-top can, **I**, 304

Amundsen, Roald, and Northwest Passage, **IV**, 151; attempts to reach the Pole by aeroplane, **IV**, 293

Amusements, and the circus, **I**, 377; and leisure, **III**, 264; and motion pictures, **IV**, 31; and the shooting match, **V**, 76; and the theater, **V**, 259

Anaconda Copper Mining Company, **II**, 57; **V**, 101

Anadarkho Indians, and Fort Belknap, **I**, 175

Anæsthesia, and dentistry, **II**, 138; first public demonstration of, **III**, 51; and surgery, **III**, 369; C. H. Long's work in, **V**, 123

Anarchiad, produced by the Hartford Wits, **III**, 15

Anarchists, case of 1886, and unlawful assembly, **I**, 130; and the Haymarket riot, **III**, 20; ineligible for naturalization, **IV**, 67

Anchor Line, and steamboat navigation, **V**, 179

Ancient, Fort, **IV**, 34

Andaste Indians, and the Iroquois league, **III**, 159

Anderson, Alexander, and wood engraving, **V**, 482

Anderson, Bill, guerrilla band of, **II**, 428

Anderson, C. H., and battle of Spotsylvania Courthouse, **V**, 150

Anderson, Gen., and the Philippine insurrection, **IV**, 261

Anderson, John, builds blockhouses near Big Moccasin Gap, **I**, 184

Anderson, Joseph Reid, agent of the Tredegar Iron Company, **V**, 319

Anderson, Maxwell, playwright, **II**, 166

Anderson, Orvil, and the stratosphere, **V**, 187

Anderson, R. H., and battles at Sailor's Creek, **V**, 5; and battle on Santa Rosa Island, **V**, 30

Anderson, Robert, and Fort Sumter, **V**, 52, 203

Anderson, Sherwood, and fiction, **II**, 270

Anderson Galleries, **I**, 211

Anderson Zouaves, **V**, 514

Andersonville Prison, **I**, 136, 175; **II**, 8

Andover Theological Seminary, **V**, 261

André, John, and Arnold's betrayal, **I**, 119; and King's Ferry, **III**, 212; and the Mischianza, **III**, 415; as a spy, **V**, 145

Andrée, S. A., attempts to reach the Pole in a balloon, **IV**, 293

Andrew Doria, The, purchased by the Continental Navy, **IV**, 471

Andrew Jackson, The, clipper ship, **I**, 307, 402

"Andrew Marvel," pseudonym for William Goddard, **IV**, 127

Andrews, John, and cruise of the *Saginaw's* gig, **V**, 5

Andrews, John Bertram, and industrial hygiene, **III**, 64

Andrews, Samuel, original stockholder of Standard Oil Company, **V**, 156

Andros, Edmond, annexes Connecticut to his Dominion of New England, **II**, 22; and the Ipswich protest, **III**, 153; as royal governor of the Dominion of New England, **III**, 355; and inauguration of Dominion of New England, **IV**, 98; and quitrents, **IV**, 390; seizes St. Castin's trading house, **V**, 6; as governor of York's proprietary, **V**, 508

"Andy Gump," dispute over rights to, **I**, 431

Angelus v. Sullivan, and the draft, **II**, 164

Anglican Church, established, **I**, 371; and the Great Awakening, **II**, 413; and intolerance, **III**, 147; and the formation of the Revolutionary party, **IV**, 443; and the old regime in Virginia, **V**, 375

Anglo-American Relations, and the Bayard-Chamberlain Treaty, **I**, 169; and the doctrine of continuous voyage, **II**, 142; and Erskine's agreement, **II**, 227

Animal Shelters, **V**, 112

Ann McKim, The, Baltimore clipper, **I**, 151, 402

Annals of Congress, **II**, 21; **III**, 182

Annapolis Convention, **I**, 47; **II**, 47, 49

Annapolis Royal, English name for Port Royal, **IV**, 315

Annexation, and imperialism, **III**, 78

Annuities, and old age, **IV**, 170

Antarctica, Palmer's discovery of, **IV**, 201

Anthony, Susan B., feminist leader, **II**, 266; reform lecturer, **III**, 260; and woman suffrage, **V**, 478

Anthony Burns, by C. E. Stevens, **I**, 3

Anthracite, and bituminous coal, **I**, 192; Delaware, Lackawanna and Western Railroad carries, **II**, 131; Delaware and Hudson Canal carries, **II**, 132; substituted for charcoal, **III**, 155

Antietam, battle of, **III**, 350; tardiness of McClellan after, **IV**, 324

Anti-Federalists, and Genêt's mission, **II**, 377

Anti-Masonic Party, in campaigns of 1832 and 1836, **I**, 283; originator of convention system, **II**, 52; and intolerance, **III**, 147; and the Morgan trials, **IV**, 23; inaugurates the national nominating convention, **IV**, 137; as a political party, **IV**, 296; earliest third party, **V**, 262; joins with the Whigs, **V**, 455

Anti-Monopoly Party, **I**, 287; **V**, 262

Antinomian Controversy, and fast days, **II**, 254; and the Gortonites, **II**, 402; and New Haven Colony, **IV**, 103; and establishment of Portsmouth, **IV**, 477

Anti-Rent Agitation, and New York land speculation, **IV**, 116

Anti-Saloon League, and the Eighteenth Amendment, **II**, 190; and intolerance, **III**, 147; maintains lobbies, **III**, 287; and local option, **III**, 290; as a pressure group, **IV**, 337; and prohibition, **IV**, 357; as a propaganda organization, **IV**, 359; and the W. C. T. U., **V**, 479

Antislavery Movement, and the Bible, **I**, 181; and gag rule, **II**, 366; and the Garrison mob, **II**, 372; and the *Liberator*, **III**, 270; and the Oberlin movement, **IV**, 155; and the churches, **V**, 97

Antislavery Newspapers, **I**, 3; **II**, 206

Antislavery Petitions, **IV**, 257

Antislavery Sentiment, **V**, 95

Antislavery Societies, **I**, 2, 3

Antisyndicalist Laws, and the I. W. W., **III**, 119; in the states, **V**, 215

Antitrust Laws, and the Democratic party, **II**, 137; and attempts to abolish privilege, **IV**, 351; and trusts, **V**, 327

Anza, Juan Bautista de, his expedition, **I**, 275, 278; **II**, 370; and horses, **III**, 48; founds a *presidio* at San Francisco, **V**, 23; in command of Tubac, **V**, 328

Apache Indians, in Arizona, **I**, 104; at Camp Grant, **I**, 279; driven out by the Comanche, **I**, 430; Fort Bliss established as protection from, **II**, 204; and Geronimo's campaigns, **II**, 385; and Goodnight Loving Trail, **II**, 400; and the horse, **III**, 92; and the Indian Country, **III**, 97; placed on reservations, **III**, 108; and Mangas Coloradas wars, **III**, 331; and Medicine Creek Council, **III**, 370; New Mexico exposed to attacks of, **IV**, 107; was with, ended with capture of Geronimo, **IV**, 107; capture the Oatman girls, **IV**, 155; and the Pima Indians, **IV**, 272; on the Great Plains, **IV**, 281; and Rubí's tour, **IV**, 505; and Santa Fé Trail, **V**, 29; and scouting on the plains, **V**, 46; held prisoners at Fort Sill, **V**, 79; and Fort Stanton, **V**, 158; at Fort Sumner, **V**, 202; and Texas missions, **V**, 252; and Fort Union, N. Mex., **V**, 341; and water holes, **V**, 421

Apalache, Moore commands expedition into, **I**, 144

Apalache Missions, **II**, 380

"Apostle to the Indians," John Eliot, **IV**, 330

Appalachees, Fla., DeSoto spends first winter of his expedition at, **II**, 141

Appalachian Coal Case, **V**, 327

Appeal of the Independent Democrats, **III**, 197

Appeals from Colonial Courts, and judicial review, **III**, 182; and the Privy Council, **IV**, 351

Appleby, John F., and the development of the reaper, **IV**, 419

Applegate, Jesse, and wagon trains, **V**, 389

Applegate's Cutoff, and the Great Basin, **II**, 414

Apples, dried, **II**, 169

Appleton, James, and prohibition in Maine, **III**, 327

Appleton, John J., and American claims on Naples, **IV**, 52

Appointment, Council of, abolished in New York, **IV**, 117

Appomattox, and the Confederacy, **II**, 12; Lee surrenders at, **IV**, 481

Apportionment, Congressional, **II**, 18; and the Constitution, **II**, 31; and the Convention of 1787, **II**, 51; of congressional districts, **II**, 153; and taxation, **V**, 226

Apprenticeship, and education, **II**, 185; and industrial education, **III**, 114; and labor in the colonies, **III**, 221

Appropriations, Committee on, **IV,** 314; and the Speaker of the House, **V,** 142

Aquarium, in New York, **I,** 168

Arabic Case, and the *Sussex* case, **V,** 211; and the World War, **V,** 491

Aranjuez, The Convention of, and diplomacy of the Revolution, **IV,** 470

Arapaho Indians, and Algonquins, **I,** 48; Fort Bascom a protection against, **I,** 165; barter at Bent's Fort, **I,** 179; confederated with the Cheyennes, **I,** 355; sign treaty with Indian Commission, **III,** 95; and the Indian Country, **III,** 97; land cessions, **III,** 100; placed on reservations, **III,** 108; and Jesuit missions, **III,** 175; and treaty of Fort Laramie (1851), **III,** 245; and Medicine Creek Council, **III,** 370; and Oklahoma openings, **IV,** 169; on the Great Plains, **IV,** 281; and the Platte Bridge fight, **IV,** 286; and prospectors, **IV,** 364; and the Red River Indian War, **IV,** 431; attacked at Sand Creek, **V,** 27; and Fort Sedgwick, **V,** 55; placed on the Wind River Reservation, **V,** 497

Arbitration, Industrial, and railroad brotherhoods, **IV,** 400; as function of War Labor Board, **V,** 403. *See also* Mediation, Industrial

Arbitration, International, in Anglo-American relations, **I,** 77; and Olney-Pauncefote treaty, **IV,** 172; and peace conferences, **IV,** 232; clauses in treaties, **IV,** 234; and treaties, **IV,** 501; embodied in Jay's Treaty, **V,** 316

Arbor Day, **V,** 320

Arbuckle, Matthew, founds forts Gibson and Towson, **IV,** 168

Arbuthnot and Ambrister, execution of, **V,** 57; and Spanish-American relations, **V,** 135

Arc Lamps, **III,** 277

Archaeology, and Folsom culture, **II,** 294

Archbald, Robert W., and Court of Commerce, **I,** 432; impeachment of, **III,** 76

Archbold, John D., and Standard Oil Company, **V,** 157

Archer, Branch T., and financing the Texas revolution, **V,** 253

Archer, Gabriel, leader in the Jamestown settlement, **V,** 372

Archery, **I,** 70

Architect of Federal Buildings, under the Treasury Department, **V,** 314

Architecture, and lighting, **III,** 277; Spanish influence on, **V,** 138; influenced by the World's Columbian Exposition, **V,** 495

Archives, as history sources, **III,** 33

Arctic Expeditions, **II,** 421

Areas, and representation, **IV,** 451

Argall, Samuel, names Delaware Bay, **II,** 132; and sack of Mount Desert, **III,** 326; **IV,** 35; destroys settlement at Port Royal, **IV,** 315; and the

Potomac River, **IV,** 324; and the Virginia Company of London, **V,** 377

Argentinian Meat, **III,** 249

Argonne, American army at, **V,** 492

Arikara Indians, attack Ashley's expedition, **I,** 128; and Leavenworth expedition, **III,** 258; Lewis and Clark reach towns of, **III,** 266; and Little Big Horn battle, **III,** 284; and Missouri River fur trade, **III,** 431; and scouting on the plains, **V,** 46

Arizona, organized, and admitted, **V,** 249

Ark, The, **I,** 423; **III,** 348

Arkansas, and repudiation of state debts, **IV,** 457; organized, and admitted, **V,** 249

Arkansas, The, ironclad ram, **I,** 167; **V,** 367

Arkansas Gazette, started by William Edward Woodruff, **IV,** 126

Arkansas Indians, Jesuit missions among, **III,** 175

Arkansas Post, commanded by Couture, **II,** 76; capture of, **III,** 425; and Santa Fé Trail, **V,** 29

Arkansas Route, caravan traffic along, **I,** 312

"Arkansas Traveler," and the fiddle, **II,** 270

Arks, **I,** 80; **IV,** 491

Arkwright Machinery, effects on cotton, **II,** 67; introduced by Samuel Slater, **III,** 174; and the linen industry, **III,** 281; the loom, **III,** 320; and manufacturing, **III,** 336; installed at Pawtucket, **IV,** 229

Arlington House, and U. S. v. Lee, **V,** 349

Armaments, and national defense, **II,** 126; naval, **IV,** 71

Armand, Marquis de la Rouërie, commissioned in the Revolutionary Army, **IV,** 473

Armat, Thomas, builds first crude machine for projecting pictures on a screen, **IV,** 31

Armed Merchant Ships, and "little group of willful men," **III,** 285

Armed Merchantmen, in the World War, **V,** 491

Armed Neutrality of 1780, **IV,** 283, 470

Armenian Churches, **IV,** 187

Arminian Magazine, first denominational periodical in America, **IV,** 445

Arminianism, and frontier preaching, **II,** 353; and theological writings, **V,** 261; develops in the Western Reserve, **V,** 446

Armistice, World War, **V,** 492

Armour, Philip D., rise of, **II,** 312; and meat packing, **IV,** 199

Armour Packing Company, and the Beef Trust cases, **I,** 173; and stockyards, **V,** 184

Arms, Right to Bear, and the Bill of Rights, **I,** 186; and U. S. v. Cruikshank, **V,** 348

Armstrong, Edwin H., and wireless telegraphy, **V,** 472

Armstrong, Fort, treaty signed at, **I,** 194; **III,** 100

Armstrong, John, builds Fort Raystown, **I,** 172; and Forbes expedition, **II,** 298; and Kittanning

campaign, **III**, 214; builds Fort Loudon, **III**, 304; raids Kittanning, **IV**, 219

Armstrong, John, and battle of Bladensburg, **I**, 198; author of the Newburgh Addresses, **IV**, 121; and capture of York (Toronto), **V**, 507

Armstrong, William W., chairman of joint committee on insurance investigation, **III**, 132

Army, General Staff, development of, **I**, 115; and the Army school system, **I**, 118; and military intelligence, **III**, 400; Corps, created in War Department, **V**, 402

Army, Revolutionary, organized, **IV**, 467

Army, The United States, and the Constitution, **II**, 33; and national defense, **II**, 126; and the National Guard, **IV**, 60; recruiting of, **IV**, 428; *see also* Regular Army

Army and Navy Register, and the destruction of the *Maine,* **IV**, 447

Army Contracts, **I**, 111

Army Engineers. *See* Engineers, The Corps of

Army Industrial College, a General Service School, **I**, 118

Army of Occupation, and German-American debt agreement, **II**, 382; and the Wadsworth agreement, **V**, 386

Army of the Philippines, **V**, 365

Army on the Frontier, and Indian treaties, **III**, 96

Army School System, **I**, 114

Army Supplies, on the frontier, **I**, 117

Army Supply Posts, **IV**, 322

Army Uniforms, **V**, 340

Army War College, establishment of, **I**, 118; and military intelligence, **III**, 400

Arndt, Charles C. P., shot by James Vineyard, **I**, 129

Arnold, Alfred, establishes a little theater, **III**, 286

Arnold, Benedict, and André, **I**, 73; and Burgoyne's invasion, **I**, 255; and invasion of Canada, **I**, 297; and battle of Ridgefield, **II**, 108; in second battle of Freeman's Farm, **II**, 339; and burning of New London, **IV**, 106; at Valcour Island, **IV**, 471; in the Revolutionary War, **IV**, 476; raid on Richmond, **IV**, 482; and battle of Ridgefield, **IV**, 483; in the Southern campaigns (1780–81), **V**, 129; and capture of Ticonderoga, **V**, 267; and battle of Valcour Island, **V**, 355; and Yorktown campaign, **V**, 509

Arnold, Ripley A., Fort Worth built under command of, **II**, 310

Arnold, Samuel, and Lincoln's assassination, **III**, 280

Arnold Arboretum, **IV**, 47

Arnold's (Jacob) Tavern, **IV**, 28

Aroostook, and potato growing, **IV**, 323

Aroostook War, and Northeast boundary, **IV**, 147

Arosaguntacook Indians, **I**, 48

Arrest, Arbitrary, during the Civil War, **I**, 386; and the Corning letter, **II**, 60; during the Civil War, **V**, 399

Arrest, Freedom from, as colonial privilege, **IV**, 350

Arriola, reaches Pensacola Bay, **IV**, 249

Arrowsmith's Map, **V**, 283

Arroyo Hondo, and Louisiana boundaries, **III**, 309; **V**, 252

Arsenals, Baton Rouge, **I**, 167; and munitions, **IV**, 44; and ordnance, **IV**, 182

Art, and the miniature, **III**, 408

Art Journal, and wood engraving, **V**, 482

Arthur, Chester A., and the Presidency, **IV**, 333; wins Vice-Presidential nomination, **V**, 154; demands a thorough rehabilitation of the Navy, **V**, 412

Arthur, Gabriel, journeys of, **IV**, 81; visits Tennessee, **V**, 242

Arthurdale Subsistence Homestead Colony, **V**, 195

Article Ten, and the Lodge Reservations, **III**, 293

Articles of Confederation, and state coinage, **I**, 410; and Committee of the States, **I**, 435; and the Confederation, **II**, 13; and ratification of Constitution, **II**, 28; framing and ratification of, **II**, 47; and the Convention of 1787, **II**, 50; dual government under, **II**, 171; and Federal state relations, **II**, 263; and the judiciary, **III**, 184; and Pennsylvania-Connecticut boundary dispute, **IV**, 246; as instrument of union, **IV**, 469; and taxation, **V**, 225; and the Decree of Trenton, **V**, 322; and the name United States of America, **V**, 347; Maryland refuses to ratify, **V**, 444

Articles of War, and military law, **III**, 401

Artillery, and munitions, **IV**, 45

Artillery Instruction, School of, begun at Fortress Monroe, **I**, 118

Arver v. U. S., and the draft, **II**, 164

Asbury, Francis, and Methodist Episcopal Church, **I**, 376; **III**, 380; and religious periodicals, **IV**, 445; organizes Sunday School, **V**, 204

Ascension, Fort, original name of Fort Massac, **III**, 354

Ash Hollow, battle of, **I**, 355; **III**, 11; **V**, 86

Ashburner, Charles E., and city manager plan, **III**, 289

Ashby Gap, **IV**, 221

Ashe, John, at Briar Creek, **I**, 236

Ashley, Edward, establishes trading post at Castine, **I**, 321

Ashley, James M., Radical Republican, **IV**, 395; and the Thirteenth Amendment, **V**, 264

Ashley, William Henry, on the Colorado River, **I**, 427; fur trading ventures of, **II**, 235; and Green River, **II**, 423; and the Leavenworth expedition, **III**, 258; and the Platte River Trail,

IV, 286; and the Rocky Mountain Fur Company, **IV**, 498; and Jedediah Strong Smith, **V**, 101; and topographic mapping, **V**, 283; and trappers' rendezvous, **V**, 310

Ashurst-Sumners Act, and prison industries, **IV**, 347

Asiento, and Royal African Company, **I**, 19; and Queen Anne's War, **IV**, 389; and the slave trade, **V**, 91; granted by treaty of Utrecht, **V**, 354

Askin, John, fur trader, **III**, 111

Aspen, silver camp at, **II**, 138

Aspinwall, William, and introduction of vaccination, **V**, 355

"Assarigoa," governor of Virginia called, **IV**, 173

Assembly, Right of, and the Bill of Rights, **I**, 185; and the Constitution, **II**, 39; and U. S. v. Cruikshank, **V**, 348; in time of war, **V**, 399

Assenisipia, Jefferson's proposed state, **III**, 173

Assessments, Political, and the spoils system, **V**, 147

Assessors, Board of, and county government, **III**, 288

Assimilation and Americanization, **I**, 67

Assiniboine Indians, trade with, **I**, 130; and Duluth's explorations, **II**, 175; and Mackenzie's treaty, **III**, 321; and Fort Union, N. Dak., **V**, 341; depend upon wild rice for their food supply, **V**, 464

Assistants, and colonial assemblies, **I**, 416; and the General Court, **II**, 375; claim negative voice, **IV**, 81

Associate Reformed Church, and home missionary societies, **III**, 417; and foreign missions, **III**, 417

Associated Press, and news reporting, **IV**, 122

Associates, and the trading company, **V**, 301

Association of Iron and Steel Electrical Engineers, **I**, 8

Association of Land-Grant Colleges and Universities, **I**, 25

Associations, and Provincial Congresses, **IV**, 368; and the American Revolution, **IV**, 466; and Revolutionary committees, **IV**, 474; enforce boycott on English imports, **V**, 232; and trade in tea, **V**, 233; and Trade with the Enemy Acts, **V**, 300

Assumption, Fort, built at Chickasaw Bluffs, **I**, 359; soldiers assembled at, **I**, 360; built on site of Memphis, **III**, 372; built by the French, **V**, 242

Assumption, Mission of the, **III**, 174

Assumption and Funding of Revolutionary Debt. *See* Debt, Public

Assumption of Risk Doctrine, **II**, 212

Astor, John Jacob, and Alaska, **I**, 42; and the American Fur Company, **I**, 61; and Astoria, **I**, 133; sells Western Department, **I**, 369; achieves first great fortune, **II**, 311; and the fur trade, **II**, 360, 363; **III**, 111; and land speculation, **III**, 239; and the New York Public Library, **III**, 272; organizes the Pacific Fur Company, **IV**, 195; and the Protective War Claims Association, **IV**, 366; organizes the Southwest Fur Company, **V**, 133; founds Astoria, **V**, 415

Astor, Mrs. William, and the Four Hundred, **II**, 316

Astor Overlanders, traverse the Platte River Trail, **IV**, 286

Astor Place Opera House, **IV**, 178

Astor Place Riots, **I**, 130; **IV**, 3

Astoria, the *Albatross* reaches, **I**, 46; post on the Columbia River, **I**, 430; establishment of, and the Oregon Question, **IV**, 184; and the Pacific Fur Company, **IV**, 195; and territorial claims of the United States, **V**, 246; and the *Tonquin*, **V**, 281; as frontier trading post, **V**, 302; founded, **V**, 415

Astoria Expedition, crosses Big Horn Mountains, **I**, 184

Astorians, Lisa races with the, **II**, 235; visit Green River Valley, **II**, 423; on the Oregon Trail, **IV**, 185; on Snake River, **V**, 106; and South Pass, **V**, 128

Astronomical Diary and Almanac, **I**, 52

Astrüp, Eivind, and Peary's polar expeditions, **IV**, 237

Atchison, D. R., and sack of Lawrence, **III**, 253; and repeal of the Missouri Compromise, **III**, 429

Atchison, Topeka and Santa Fé Railroad, and Albuquerque, **I**, 46; buys half interest in Atlantic and Pacific Railroad, **I**, 135; and the Chisholm Trail, **I**, 368; and the building of the Denver and Rio Grande Railway, **II**, 139; reorganization of, **IV**, 449; and rail transportation, **V**, 309; and Whipple's expedition, **V**, 456

Atherton v. Atherton, **V**, 174

Athletics, taken up by colleges, **V**, 149

Atkin, Edmund, appointed superintendent of Indian Affairs, **III**, 104

Atkins, Samuel, and the almanac, **I**, 51

Atkinson, Fort, flour mill constructed at, **I**, 118

Atkinson, Fort, treaty of 1853 and Indian policy, **III**, 106

Atkinson, Fort (Council Bluffs), and the Leavenworth expedition, **III**, 259; serves as military encampment, **IV**, 80

Atkinson, Fort (Kans.), or Fort Mann, **III**, 333

Atkinson, Henry, and Black Hawk War, **I**, 145, 195; and the Magee-Kearny expedition, **III**, 324; commands the Yellowstone River Expedition, **V**, 506

Atkinson, Samuel C., first to publish the *Saturday Evening Post*, **V**, 33

Atlanta, The, Congress authorizes construction of, **II,** 283; one of the vessels of the White Squadron, **V,** 460

Atlanta Campaign, and Army of Tennessee (C.), **V,** 241; and Army of the Tennessee (U.), **V,** 242

Atlanta (Ga.) *Constitution,* and pot likker and corn pone, **IV,** 322

Atlantic and Pacific Railroad, **I,** 46

Atlantic and Pacific Tea Co., **II,** 412

Atlantic and Pacific Telegraph Company, **V,** 447

Atlantic Monthly, "Battle Hymn of the Republic" printed in, **I,** 168; and the *Biglow Papers,* **I,** 184; and magazine publishing, **III,** 323

Atlantic Neptune, atlas, **III,** 341

Atlas Portland Cement Company, **V,** 348

Atocha, Col., and the Mexican War, **III,** 386

Atrocity Stories, as Civil War propaganda, **I,** 385; and Parson Brownlow's book, **IV,** 219; and Spanish-American relations, **V,** 135; World War, **V,** 491

Attainder, and the Constitution, **II,** 34; in Cummings v. Missouri, **II,** 98; and the Garland Case, **II,** 372; and colonial punishments, **IV,** 383

Attakullakulla, Cherokee chief, **I,** 176; represents Cherokees as to Donelson's Line, **II,** 160; and the Sycamore Shoals treaty, **V,** 215

Attorney General, and the Department of Justice, **III,** 191

Atwater, W. O., and farmers' institutes, **II,** 253; publishes food pamphlet, **II,** 296

Atwood, Charles B., architect, **I,** 101

Atwood, William, appointed chief justice of New York, **I,** 419

Atzerodt, George A., and Lincoln's assassination, **III,** 280

Aubry, Charles Philippe, erects Fort Massac, **III,** 354

Auburn Prison System, **IV,** 348

Auctions, and the slave trade, **V,** 93

Audit Bureau of Circulations, **I,** 18

Audubon, John James, as painter, **I,** 123; author of *Birds of America,* **II,** 235; and civilization of the Old South, **V,** 123; drawing of the wild turkey cock, **V,** 331

Audubon Societies, establish bird sanctuaries, **I,** 190

Aughwick, and Braddock's Expedition, **I,** 233; and Kittanning campaign, **III,** 214; Logstown Indians remove to, **III,** 295

Augur, Camp, early name for Fort Washakie, **V,** 412

Augusta, occupation of (1778), **IV,** 477

Augusta *Constitutionalist,* southern newspaper, **V,** 123

Aull, James, supplies Fort Leavenworth, **IV,** 322; western merchant, **V,** 445

Auraria, discovered by Green Russell, **II,** 236

Aurora Community, **I,** 181

Aury, Luis, and the Amelia Island affair, **I,** 54; leader of Galveston pirates, **II,** 368

Aury-Lafitte Pirates, **IV,** 278

Austin, Ann, and the Quakers, **IV,** 386

Austin, Moses, and the Austin colony, **I,** 139; and the Rio Grande, **IV,** 486; develops lead mining methods, **V,** 9; and colonization of Texas, **V,** 251

Austin, Stephen F., and the Austin colony, **I,** 139; and the battle of Concepcion, **II,** 1; and the Rio Grande, **IV,** 486; and colonization of Texas, **V,** 251; and financing the Texas revolution, **V,** 253

Austin, The, and the Texas navy, **V,** 256

Australian Ballot, **I,** 149

Austria, treaties with, **V,** 318

Autobiography, written by Benjamin Franklin, **I,** 189

Automatic Car Coupler, **I,** 8

Automatic Machinery, in manufacturing, **III,** 336

Automobile, and American Automobile Association, **I,** 58; and amusements, **I,** 71; as a factor of crime, **II,** 88; and engineering, **II,** 215; and Ford Motor Company, **II,** 300; freight carried by, **II,** 341; and installment credit, **III,** 127; and internal improvements, **III,** 139; takes the place of interurban electric lines, **III,** 145; invention of the, **III,** 149; and leisure, **III,** 264; manufacture of, **III,** 320; and railroads, **IV,** 408; and Federal road building, **IV,** 495; and good roads movement, **IV,** 496; and rubber, **IV,** 504; and sex relations, **V,** 62; and touring, **V,** 286; widens trading areas, **V,** 297; and transportation and travel, **V,** 39; affects the wayside markets, **V,** 428

Automobile Racing, at county fairs, **II,** 74

Autossee, Red Sticks defeated at, **II,** 86

Avery, Ephraim K., murder trial of, **V,** 323

Avery, Robert, starts first nursery in Iowa, **IV,** 154

Avilés, Pedro Menéndez de. *See* Menéndez

Awa Tsira, develops school in water colors, **III,** 93

Awakening, Second, and revivals, **IV,** 464

Ayaville, battle of, **I,** 144

Ayer, E. E., collector of Americana, **I,** 212; **III,** 273

Ayllón, Lucas Vásquez de, **I,** 57, 361; **V,** 125

B

Babbitt, Almon W., and Deseret, **II,** 140

Babcock, O. E., and annexation of Dominican Republic, **II,** 158

Babcock, S. M., devises butterfat test, **II,** 104

Baca, Jesús María, printer of *El Crepúsculo de la Libertad,* **IV,** 127; first printer of New Mexico, **IV,** 346

Bach Festivals, at Bethlehem, IV, 48

Bache, William, and silhouettes, V, 78

Bachelder, John, patents a sewing machine, V, 61

Bacheller, Irving, and newspaper syndicates, IV, 123

Bachelor, Samuel, improves the loom, III, 301

Bachelors, taxing of, III, 346

Back Country, cattle in the, II, 77; or Piedmont region, IV, 268; and the pioneers, IV, 274; and rivers, IV, 491

Backus, Elijah, and Blennerhassett Island, I, 199

Bacon, C. E., and higher criticism, III, 31

Bacon, Henry, architect of Lincoln's Memorial, I, 101

Bacon's Castle, architecture of, I, 99

Bacon's Rebellion, the Andaste Indians in, I, 72; Jamestown burned during, III, 167; colonial militia in, III, 404; and colony of Virginia, V, 372; and the West, V, 435

Bad Axe, battle of, I, 195; IV, 489

Badger, Joseph, portraitist, I, 123

Badin, Stephen T., resident missionary at Pokagon Village, IV, 292

Badlands, Sully attacks Indian camp located in, II, 107; and the Messiah War, III, 380

Baer, George F., and anthracite strike of 1902, I, 80

Baffin, William, and Baffin Bay, IV, 151

Bagby, George William, editor of the Southern Literary Messenger, V, 130

Baha'ism, and Oriental cults, IV, 187

Bailey, Francis, and first known publication of title "Father of His Country," II, 254; starts Freeman's Journal, II, 339

Bailey, Gamaliel, and the Ohio State Antislavery Society, IV, 165; becomes sole editor of The Philanthropist, IV, 260

Bailey, James A., and the three-ring circus, I, 377

Bailey, Theodorus, commands the store ship Lexington, III, 266

Bailey v. Alabama, IV, 252

Bailey v. Drexel Furniture Company, and stare decisis, V, 161

Bailhache, W. H., and the Illinois State Journal, IV, 129

Bain, Alexander, patents the chemical telegraph, V, 238

Bainbridge, William, and the Barbary wars, I, 163; and the Constitution-Java engagement, II, 30; and the George Washington, II, 379; and capture and burning of the Philadelphia, IV, 259

Baird, Spencer Fullerton, and the Smithsonian Institution, V, 102

Baja (Lower) California, III, 311

Baker, Daniel, establishes Fort Saginaw, V, 4

Baker, E. D., killed in battle of Ball's Bluff, I, 150

Baker, E. M., marches against the Piegan Indians, IV, 268

Baker, Edward L., and the Illinois State Journal, IV, 129

Baker, George F., and the Pujo Committee, IV, 380

Baker, George Pierce, experimental theater of, III, 286

Baker, Lafayette C., Civil War spy, V, 146

Baker, Newton D., orders building of cantonments, I, 296; and the World War, V, 491 f.

Baker, Ray Stannard, "The Railroads on Trial," IV, 38

Baker Island, annexed by the U. S., IV, 195

Balboa, Vasco Nuñez de, I, 57

Baldwin, Abr., signer of the Constitution, II, 39

Baldwin, Frank D., and the wagon train charge, V, 388

Baldwin, Joseph, writer, V, 123

Baldwin, Loammi, designs stone docks, II, 156

Baldwin, Matthias, locomotive builder, IV, 406

Baldwin, Theron, organizer of the Illinois Band, III, 69; member of the Yale Band, V, 500

Baldwin, Thomas Scott, builds first dirigible for the government, II, 148

Baldwin Locomotive Works, III, 292

Ball, Ephraim, and the development of the reaper, IV, 419

Ballads: "Joe Bowers," III, 177; and mountain people, IV, 37

Ballinger, Richard A., and conservation movement, II, 27; suggests naval oil reserves, IV, 71

Ballinger-Pinchot Affair, and "standpatters," V, 158

Balloons, at county fairs, II, 74; helium used in, III, 24; ascend to the stratosphere, V, 187

Ballot, use of, II, 193; party emblems on, II, 209; Massachusetts, III, 356; used in voting, V, 383

Ballou, Adin, and creation of Hopedale Community, III, 45; and formation of the New England Non-Resistance Society, IV, 234

Ballou, Hosea, and the Universalists, V, 350

Ball's Bluff, and the Confederacy, II, 11

Baltimore, Lord, and the controversy over ownership of Delaware lands, II, 130; and Maryland, III, 348; and Pennsylvania-Maryland boundary dispute, IV, 247; granted Maryland, IV, 362

Baltimore Affair, and the Itata incident, III, 164; and the Quinteros Bay episode, IV, 390

Baltimore and Ohio Railroad, tries out the Aeolus, I, 19; and internal improvements, III, 138; and Latrobe's Folly, III, 251; "Tom Thumb" locomotive makes first run on, III, 292; and railroad rate wars, IV, 403; and railroad strike of 1877, IV, 404; financing and construction of, IV, 406; installs streamlined trains, V, 188; and "Tom Thumb" locomotive, V, 279;

and rail transportation, V, 308; and Wheeling, W. Va., V, 455

Baltimore Clipper, development of, I, 150; and War of 1812, I, 402

Baltimore Riot, and writing of "Maryland! My Maryland!", III, 350

Baltimore Weekly Museum, first Sunday newspaper, IV, 125

Balzac v. People of Porto Rico, III, 127

Bancroft, Edward, as a spy, V, 145

Bancroft, George, book collection, I, 213; establishes United States Naval Academy, IV, 68

Bancroft, H. H., book collection, I, 212

Bandits, II, 88

Bangs, Platt & Co., book auctions, I, 211

Bangs, Samuel, first printer of Texas, IV, 346

Bangs-Merwin, book auctions, I, 211

Bank Deposits, insurance of, II, 256; and the gold standard, II, 398

Bank Failures, and banking, I, 157; and crisis of 1933, I, 158; and the panic of 1857, IV, 208; and the panic of 1907, IV, 210; and specie payments, V, 144

Bank for International Settlements, established by the Young plan, V, 510

Bank Note Reporters, and wildcat banks, I, 161

Bank Notes, and banking, I, 156; and currency, II, 99; as cause of inflation, III, 120; as paper money, IV, 212

Bank of Massachusetts, second bank founded in the United States, I, 156

Bank of Mutual Redemption, V, 164

Bank of New York, third bank founded in the U. S., I, 156

Bank of North America, built by Benjamin Latrobe, I, 100; founded by Robert Morris, I, 156; and credit, II, 84; government corporation, II, 402

Bank of Pennsylvania, formed with aid of state funds, II, 402

Bank of the United States, deposits of, I, 153; founding of, I, 156; branches of, I, 158; and internal improvements, I, 211; and campaign of 1832, I, 283; and credit, II, 84; taxed by Crow-Bar law, II, 92; notes of, II, 99; foreign investments in, II, 302; government corporation, II, 402; validity of, upheld by Marshall, III, 79; and interest laws, III, 133; and the Bonus Bill (1816), III, 137; and Jacksonian Democracy, III, 165; and liberal construction, III, 268; and McCulloch v. Maryland, III, 364; and money power, IV, 9; hostility toward, in Ohio, IV, 160; and Osborn case, IV, 189; and the panic of 1819, IV, 208; and paper money, IV, 213; and pet banks, IV, 255; and profiteering, IV, 355; and removal of deposits, IV, 448; and the Republican party (Jeffersonian), IV, 454; and

repudiation of state debts, IV, 456; and the stock market, V, 182; and strict construction, V, 189; and the Whig party, V, 455

Bankers' Panic of 1907, I, 47

Bankhead Cotton Act, and governmental control of agriculture, I, 32

Banking, branch, I, 158; and clearing houses, I, 397; and the Edge Act, II, 185; and the Federal Reserve system, II, 261; free system of, II, 331; and Glass-Steagall Act, II, 391; and Jacksonian Democracy, III, 165; Louisiana Specie Reserve, III, 307; and the National Monetary Commission, IV, 61; and the panic of 1893, IV, 209; and safety fund system, V, 4; Suffolk Banking System, V, 198

Banking Act of 1933, and creation of Federal Deposit Insurance Corporation, I, 157; II, 256; and interest laws, III, 134; and money power, IV, 9; and Wall Street, V, 393

Banking Act of 1935, I, 157

Banking Crisis of 1933, and Reconstruction Finance Corporation, I, 157; and issue of Federal Reserve bank notes, II, 262; and Federal expropriation of gold, II, 393; and specie payments, V, 144

Bankruptcy, and the Constitution, II, 33; and imprisonment for debt, II, 117; and mortgages, IV, 29; act of 1934, IV, 449; and Sturges v. Crowninshield, V, 192; and "whitewash," V, 461

Banks, and government ownership, II, 404; and the panic of 1837, IV, 208; postal savings, IV, 319; and the Reconstruction Finance Corporation, IV, 428; and the stock market, V, 182. *See also* National Banking System

Banks, N. P., directs Bayou Teche expedition, I, 170; and battle of Cedar Mountain, I, 330; and battle of Pleasant Hill, IV, 287; besieges Port Hudson, IV, 315; and the Red River campaign, IV, 430; defeated in battle at Sabine Crossroads, V, 1; and the Army of Virginia, V, 374; and battle of Winchester, V, 470

Bannack, gold found at, IV, 16

Bannock War, Paiute Indians take part in, IV, 200

Baptist Home Mission Society, III, 417

Baptists, and Brown University, I, 244; and colleges, I, 413; and the Disciples of Christ, II, 149; as dissenters, II, 151; and evangelism, II, 230; and frontier preaching, II, 353; and the Great Awakening, II, 413; and the Great Revival, II, 419; and Indian missions, III, 103; and mountain people, IV, 37; and Reconstruction, IV, 428; and religion, IV, 442; and religious liberty, IV, 445; and revivals, IV, 464; oppose slavery, V, 97; and colonial law, V, 203; and Sunday Schools, V, 204; open a theological seminary, V, 261; in the Western Reserve, V, 446

Baraboo *Republican,* and newspaper syndicates, **IV,** 123

Baranoff, Alexander, and Alaska, **I,** 42

Barataria, pirates of, **IV,** 278; center of slave smuggling, **V,** 92

Barbara Fritchie Incident, **II,** 330

Barbary Pirates, and the Mediterranean Fund, **III,** 371

Barbary Wars, and Decatur's cruise, **II,** 119; and the Derna expedition, **II,** 140; Navy in, **IV,** 77; and tribute, **V,** 325

Barbecue, and frontier oratory, **II,** 353; and rodeos, **IV,** 499

Barbed Wire, and cattle drives, **I,** 326; and cow custom, **II,** 79; and the end of the cowboys' fenceless empire, **II,** 80; and the fence war, **II,** 266; and frontier transition, **II,** 351; and open range cattle period, **IV,** 178; and Osage hedge, **IV,** 189; and the Great Plains, **IV,** 282; and fencing of public lands, **IV,** 373; and extinction of the buffalo and cattle, **V,** 463; and the windmill, **V,** 470

Barber-Surgeons, and the practice of dentistry, **II,** 138

Barbier v. Connolly, equal protection of law in, **II,** 222

Barbour, John S., and the Readjuster Movement, **IV,** 419

Barbour Scholarships, for foreign exchange students, **V,** 191

Bard, Samuel, writes on diphtheria, **II,** 221

Bargemen, and rivermen of the Ohio, **IV,** 490

Barges, for river navigation, **IV,** 489

Bark Fibers, Indians skilled in use of, **III,** 87

Barker, James Nelson, dramatist, **II,** 166

Barley, and rotation of crops, **II,** 154

Barlow, Joel, one of the Hartford Wits, **III,** 14; and American hymns, **III,** 65; agent of the Scioto Company, **V,** 44

Barlowe, Arthur, and Raleigh's patent, **IV,** 413

Barnard, Frederick A. P., as president of Columbia College, **I,** 429

Barnard, George, and Torreys' Trading Post, **V,** 285

Barnard, George G., and the Tweed Ring, **V,** 333

Barnard, George Grey, sculptor, **I,** 124

Barnard, Henry, lecturer, **III,** 260; attends librarians' conference, **III,** 272; and educational reform, **V,** 39

Barnard College, **V,** 480

Barnard's Trading Post, **V,** 302

Barnburners, and the Free Soil party, **II,** 333; and Hunkers, **III,** 60; as a political party, **IV,** 296

Barnes, Albert, heresy trial of, **III,** 27

Barney, Joshua, in battle of Bladensburg, **I,** 198; commands the *Hyder Ali,* **III,** 62; in battle of Bladensburg, **V,** 417

Barn-raisings, **I,** 174

Barnum, Phineas T., and amusements, **I,** 70; and the three-ring circus, **I,** 377; manages Jenny Lind's tour of America, **III,** 280; and Madison Square Garden, **III,** 322

Barnum's Museum, **IV,** 47

Barnwell, John, builds Fort King George, **III,** 209; in the Tuscarora War, **V,** 332

Barracks, at army posts, **I,** 118

Barrancas, Fort, surrenders to the Confederates, **IV,** 250

Barreiro, Antonio, editor and publisher of *El Crepúsculo de la Libertad,* **IV,** 127

Barrett, Theodore H., and battle of Palmito Ranch, **IV,** 201

Barron, James, duels with Decatur, **I,** 198; and the *Chesapeake-Leopard* incident, **I,** 354; duels with Decatur, **II,** 174

Barron, Samuel, relieves Preble in the Barbary Wars, **I,** 162

Barrows and Company, begin operating first successful pipe line, **IV,** 276

Barry, John, and the frigate *Alliance,* **I,** 51; commands the *Lexington,* **III,** 266; and frigate *Alliance,* **IV,** 77; and the *United States,* **V,** 347

Barry, Philip, playwright, **II,** 166

Barsimon, Jacob, first Jew seen in New Amsterdam, **III,** 176

Barter, "Rattlesnake Dick," stagecoach robber, **V,** 153

Bartholdi, Frederic Auguste, conceives Statue of Liberty, **V,** 176

Bartholdt, Richard, and the "peace bloc" in Congress, **IV,** 235

Bartholet, Louis, establishes trading camp at Kansas City, Mo., **III,** 196

Bartleson, John, and immigration to California, **I,** 269

Bartlett, C. E., journalist, **V,** 123

Bartlett, Josiah, signer of the Declaration of Independence, **II,** 123

Bartlett, Paul, sculptor, **I,** 124

Bartlett, Robert A., and Peary's polar expeditions, **IV,** 237, 293

Barton, Benjamin Smith, and gardening, **II,** 371

Barton, Clara, organizes the American Red Cross, **IV,** 429

Barton, Enos M., and the Western Electric Company, **V,** 441

Barton, James L., and diplomacy, **III,** 415

Barton, William, designs reverse side of United States seal, **V,** 49

Bartram, John, botanist, **I,** 225; establishes first botanical garden, **II,** 371

Bartram, William, botanist, **I,** 225; travels of, **II,** 235

Baruch, Bernard, appointed chairman of the War Industries Board, **V,** 403

Base-Burner, introduced, III, 23

Base Lines, and survey of public lands, IV, 373

Baseball, as an amusement, I, 70; as organized sport, V, 149

Basketball, introduction of, V, 149

Basketry, and Indian art, III, 93

Bass, Charles Cassedy, and malaria, III, 329

Bass, Sam, commemorated by folk singer, I, 148; bandit, I, 152; train robber, V, 303

Bassett, Richard, signer of the Constitution, II, 39

Bassett Town, Washington (Pa.) named, V, 415

Bateau, use of, in Arnold's attack on Quebec, I, 120; introduced by the French, III, 423; and the Missouri River fur trade, III, 431; for river navigation, IV, 489; in transportation, V, 306

Bates, Elisha, buys *The Philanthropist*, IV, 260

Bates, Jacob, displays feats of horsemanship, I, 377

Bathtubs, and plumbing, IV, 289

Baton Rouge, battle of, I, 105; and opening of the Mississippi, III, 419; and Spanish-American relations, V, 135; captured by Spaniards, V, 139; and annexation of West Florida, V, 436

Batteries, Floating, II, 284

Battery "D," 5th Field Artillery, present name of Hamilton's Battery, I, 113

Battery Wagner, attack on, V, 388

Battleships. *See* Warships

Bauman, Matthias, starts the Newborn, IV, 121

Baxter, Elisha, governor of Arkansas, I, 243

Baxter, Thomas, and Dutch war of 1653, IV, 479

Baxter, W., Jr., invents electric elevator, II, 201

Bay Psalm Book, I, 182, 213; III, 64

Bay State Shoe and Leather Company, IV, 354

Bayard, James A., and treaty of Ghent, II, 387; and the War of 1812, V, 406

Bayard, Thomas F., first ambassador, I, 54

Bayley, Richard, and epidemics, II, 221

Baylor, John R., seizes southern New Mexico, IV, 107

Baynton, Wharton and Morgan, and the Black Boys, I, 193; and the fur trade, II, 361; III, 110; and Sideling Hill, V, 77; and western land schemes, V, 443

Beachy, Lincoln, sets altitude record, I, 142

Beacon Hill, I, 222

Bead Work, and Indian art, III, 93

Beadle and Adams, and dime novels, II, 147

Beal, Fred E., and Gastonia riots, II, 374

Beales, John Charles, and the English colony on the Rio Grande, IV, 486

Beall's Raid, I, 298; III, 178; IV, 150

Bean, William, and settlement of Tennessee, V, 242, 420

Bear Flag Revolt, I, 271, 275; III, 18

Bear Mountain Bridge, III, 55

Bear Skins, Indians trade in, III, 109

Beard, Charles A., and political writings, IV, 303

Beasley, Daniel, and massacre at Fort Mims, III, 405

Beaubien, Carlos, and the Maxwell land grant, III, 361; secures Sangre de Cristo grant, V, 27

Beaubien, Narciso, and Sangre de Cristo grant, V, 27

Beauchamp, John, and the Waldo patent, V, 391

Beauharnois, Charles de, sends force to Crown Point, II, 93

Beauharnois, Fort, building of, II, 320; French outpost in Minnesota, III, 410

Beaujeu, Capt., at Fort Duquesne, I, 233

Beaumarchais, Pierre A. C. de, and Franco-American Alliance, II, 326; and origin of Hortalez et Cie, III, 50; and diplomacy of the Revolution, IV, 470; and financing the Revolution, IV, 471; and foreign volunteers in the Revolutionary Army, IV, 473; and profiteering in the Revolution, IV, 475

Beaumont, Andrew, and the Copperheads of 1840, II, 58

Beaumont, William, pioneer study of the stomach, III, 369, 394; V, 13

Beauregard, P. G. T., becomes a general, I, 110; at Bull Run, I, 250; at Drewry's Bluff, II, 169; and the Dutch Gap Canal, II, 179; and Army of Mississippi, III, 419; and Fort Sumter, V, 203

Beaver, as money, II, 99, 100; and hat industry, II, 358; and the Kennebec trading post, III, 204; hat industry, colonial restrictions of, III, 335; destruction of, by settlement, V, 462

Beaver, The, Astor ship, I, 133

Beaver Islands, and the Strangite Kingdom, V, 187

Beaver Trade, Indian, III, 109

Beavers, Tony, and tall stories, V, 186

Becknell, William, and Santa Fé Trail, I, 312; II, 236; IV, 107; V, 30, 219, 389

Beckwith, E. G., and government railroad surveys, IV, 405

Beckwith, George C., and peace movements, IV, 234

Bedford, Fort, and Forbes expedition, II, 299

Bedford, Gunning, Jr., signer of the Constitution, II, 39

Bedford Cut Stone Case, III, 124

Bedinger, Henry, and Rumsey's steamboat, IV, 507

Bee, B. E., at Bull Run, I, 251

Beecher, Catherine, encourages college training for women, V, 477, 480

Beecher, Henry Ward, and abolition, I, 3; and free thinking, II, 340; lecturer, III, 260; pulpit orator, IV, 180; and religious periodicals, IV, 446; revivalistic preacher, IV, 464; and theological writings, V, 261; and the Tilton suit, V, 323

Beecher, Lyman, evangelist, **II**, 230; heresy trial of, **III**, 27; revivalistic preacher, **IV**, 464; sermons on temperance, **V**, 59; and the temperance movement, **V**, 240

Beecher Island Fight, Arapaho participate in, **I**, 94; and the Cheyenne Indians, **I**, 355

Beecher's Bibles, **V**, 64

Beef, and rotation of crops, **II**, 154

Beekman's Tract, **III**, 55

Beer, drinking of, **II**, 170

Beers, Clifford Whittingham, and mental hygiene, **III**, 64

Beers, Ethelind Eliot, and "All Quiet along the Potomac," **I**, 50

Beers, Henry P., *Bibliographies in American History*, **III**, 34 f.

Beet Sugar, **I**, 228; **II**, 421

Behel, Jacob, and the development of the reaper, **IV**, 419

Beidler, John X., and vigilantes, **V**, 368

Beissel, Conrad, and communities, **I**, 440; leader in the founding of Ephrata, **II**, 220

Belasco, David, playwright, **II**, 166

Belcher, Jonathan, and Masonry, **III**, 351

Belcourt, G. A., builds first church in North Dakota at Pembina, **IV**, 240

Belgian American Educational Foundation, **V**, 191

Belknap, Fort, and the Goodnight Loving Trail, **II**, 400

Belknap, Fort, Reservation, Assiniboines moved to, **I**, 130

Belknap, Jeremy, founds first historical society, **III**, 33; climbs and names Mt. Washington, **IV**, 36

Bell, Alexander Graham, and the American Telephone and Telegraph Co., **I**, 66; provides for founding of Volta Bureau for the deaf, **II**, 115; invents the telephone, **III**, 148; patents the telephone, **IV**, 223; invents the telephone, **V**, 239; and the Western Electric Company, **V**, 441

Bell, J. R., and Long's explorations, **III**, 300

Bell, John, nominated for President, **I**, 285; and Committee of Thirteen, **I**, 436; Constitutional Union party candidate, **II**, 44

Bell, Robert, bookseller, **I**, 211

Bell, Tom, "gentleman highwayman," **V**, 153

Bell Telephone Company, **I**, 66

Bellamy, Edward, political writings of, **IV**, 302

Bellamy, George A., and social settlements, **V**, 109

Belleau Wood, American army at, **V**, 492

Bellerive, St. Ange de, and Missouri, **III**, 426

Bellestre, Marie François Picoté, at Pickawillany, **IV**, 266

Bellevue, Fort, **III**, 322

Bellevue, Nebr., trading post, **IV**, 80

Bellevue Hospital, **III**, 50

Belligerency, and Confederate states, **II**, 9; and foreign policy, **II**, 303; and freedom of the seas, **II**, 338; and Geneva conference, **II**, 377; and liability of private property to capture, **III**, 76; and international law, **III**, 141; and Declaration of London, **III**, 296; and neutral rights, **IV**, 87; and neutrality, **IV**, 89; and Neutrality Act of 1939, **IV**, 91; and Declaration of Paris (1856), **IV**, 216; and prize courts, **IV**, 352; and retaliation in international law, **IV**, 461; and the submarine in international law, **V**, 192; and visit and search, **V**, 381

Bellomont, Earl of, and colonial plans of union, **I**, 420; and kerosene oil, **III**, 207; administration of, **IV**, 114; and land speculation in New York, **IV**, 115; and piracy, **IV**, 278

Bellows, George, painter, **I**, 123; lithographer, **I**, 124

Bellows, Henry W., and the Protective War Claims Association, **IV**, 366; president of United States Sanitary Commission, **V**, 28

Bellows Falls Canal, and locks, **III**, 292

Belmont, August, rise of, **II**, 311

Belmont, Wis., dead city, **II**, 114

Beltrami, Giacomo C., in Minnesota, **III**, 411; on the *Virginia*, **V**, 374

Ben Hur, written by Lew Wallace, **I**, 180

Benavides, Alonso de, missionary in New Mexico, **IV**, 107

Bendix Transcontinental Speed Dash, **I**, 36

Benet-Mercie Machine Guns, **III**, 319

Benezet, Anthony, attacks slavery, **V**, 94

Benjamin, Judah P., and flight of Confederate Cabinet, **II**, 5

Benjamin, Park, and cheap books, **I**, 213

Benjamin Packard, last American Cape Horner in existence, **I**, 307

Bennett, Floyd, polar flight of, **IV**, 293

Bennett, James Gordon, co-founder of Commercial Cable Company, **I**, 434; and the cheap press, **III**, 353; publisher of the New York *Herald*, **IV**, 123; and polar cruise of the *Jeannette*, **IV**, 292; and yellow journalism, **V**, 505

Bennett, John, and children's books, **I**, 363

Bennington, Battle of, and Burgoyne's invasion, **I**, 255; Green Mountain Boys in, **II**, 422; and Number 4, **IV**, 154; and Burgoyne's invasion, **IV**, 476; and Vermont, **V**, 362 f.

Benoist, François M., of Lisa & Co., **III**, 283

Benson, A. C., takes possession of Howland's Island, **III**, 54

Benson, Simon, devises a cigar-shaped raft of logs, **III**, 314

Benson, William S., first appointee as Chief of Naval Operations, **IV**, 71

Bent, Charles, killed by Indians of Taos, **V**, 219

Bent, Charles and William, barter with trappers and Indians, **II**, 236, 362

Bent, William, and the Cheyenne Indians, **I**, 355

Benteen, F. W., and Little Big Horn battle, **III**, 284

Benton, Caleb, and the New York and Genesee Company, **IV**, 117

Benton, Fort (at the mouth of the Big Horn), **V**, 302

Benton, Thomas Hart, and the American Fur Company, **I**, 61; duels with Charles Lucas, **II**, 174; opposes Indian factory system, **II**, 239; advocates the Graduation Act of 1854, **II**, 407; and the homestead movement, **III**, 42; and repeal of the Missouri Compromise, **III**, 429; and Missouri Pacific Railroad, **III**, 430; and money, **IV**, 7; and oratory, **IV**, 180; political writings of, **IV**, 302; and the Webster-Hayne debate, **V**, 431

Bentonville, Terry's Texas Rangers at, **V**, 249

Bent's Fort, and the Arkansas River route, **I**, 107; and Fort Bernard, **I**, 180; created, **I**, 426; and Town of Kansas, **III**, 196; as a frontier trading post, **V**, 302

Berceau-Boston Engagement, **IV**, 73

Berckmanns, J., starts nursery in Georgia, **IV**, 154

Berdan, Hiram, commands First Regiment of United States Sharpshooters, **V**, 64

Berger, Victor, and Social Democratic party, **V**, 107, 110

Bergh, Henry, organizes the Society for the Prevention of Cruelty to Animals, **V**, 112; organizes Society for the Prevention of Cruelty to Children, **V**, 112

Bering, Vitus, and Alaska, **I**, 42; discovers the Aleutian Islands, **I**, 47

Bering Sea, seal fisheries, **V**, 49

Bering Sea Fur-Seal Question, and Canadian-American relations, **I**, 300

Berkeley, George, and Yale University, **V**, 500

Berkeley, John, Lord, and Long Island, **III**, 299; joint proprietor of New Jersey, **IV**, 104; original proprietor of New Jersey, **IV**, 105; and New Jersey, **IV**, 362; and West Jersey, **V**, 437; York leases New Jersey to, **V**, 508

Berkeley, William, and Bacon's rebellion, **I**, 145; defied by Cecil Calvert, **III**, 349; suppresses Nuthead's printing press, **IV**, 345; and colony of Virginia, **V**, 372

Berkman, Alexander, and anarchists, **I**, 72

Berkshire Agricultural Society, **I**, 26; **II**, 73

Berle, A. A., Jr., and Brain Trust, **I**, 234

Berlin, Treaty of, and German-American debt agreement, **II**, 382; ends war between the United States and Germany, **V**, 364

Berlin Decree, and the Embargo, **II**, 207; and Orders in Council, **IV**, 180

Berliner, Emil, produces the gramophone, **IV**, 264; and the telephone, **V**, 239

Bermuda Admiralty Case, and continuous voyage, **II**, 142

Bermuda Company, **V**, 301

Bermuda Hundred, Army of the James bottled up at, **III**, 166

Bernard, Francis, receives Mount Desert Island, **IV**, 35

Bernhardt, Sarah, stars in *Queen Elizabeth,* **IV**, 32

Berry, G. L., and American Labor party, **I**, 62

Berthold, Bartholomew, and Chouteau and Company, **I**, 369

Berthold, Fort, Sully marches to, **II**, 107; refuge of survivors from Five Villages, **II**, 280

Berthoud, James, and Tarascon, Berthoud and Company, **V**, 220

Bertron, S. R., and the Root mission to Russia, **IV**, 501

Bessemer Steel, and bridges, **I**, 238; rise of, **II**, 312; invented, **III**, 156; introduction of, **III**, 337; patents, **IV**, 223; and plow making, **IV**, 287; used in rail making, **IV**, 410

"Best Friend of Charleston," first locomotive built in the United States for actual service on a railroad, **III**, 292

Bethania, founded by the Moravians, **V**, 500

Bethany College, founding of, **II**, 149

Betharaba, founded by Moravians, **IV**, 22; **V**, 500

Bethlehem, Pa., begun by the Moravians, **IV**, 22

Bethlehem Steel Company, and armor plate, **I**, 109; and munitions, **IV**, 45

Betty Lamps, for lighting, **III**, 276

Beveridge, Albert J., and oratory, **IV**, 180; and the Pacific Ocean, **IV**, 196; leads revolt against the Payne-Aldrich Tariff Bill, **IV**, 356

Beverwyck, **I**, 44; **II**, 179

Biard, Pierre, Jesuit missionary, **III**, 174

Bible, The, as best seller, **I**, 180; and colonial newspapers, **I**, 420; and the Gideon Society, **II**, 389; and higher criticism, **III**, 30; and religion, **IV**, 443; revision of the, **IV**, 463; as early schoolbook, **V**, 40

Bible Commonwealth, and theocracy in New England, **V**, 260

Bibliographies, as history sources, **III**, 35

Bicameral Legislature, and the Connecticut Compromise, **II**, 23; and the city council, **II**, 71; and the "Sow Case," **V**, 134

Bicycling, as an amusement, **I**, 70; and good roads movement, **IV**, 496; and organized sports, **V**, 149

Biddle, James, and the *Hornet-Penguin* engagement, **III**, 46; governor of Naval Home, **IV**, 70

Biddle, Nicholas, becomes president of Second Bank of United States, **I**, 155; and rechartering of the Bank of the United States, **I**, 156

Bidlack-Mallarino Treaty of 1846, and Panama Canal, **IV,** 204; and the Panama revolution, **IV,** 207

Bidwell, John, and emigration to California, **I,** 269; **II,** 236; and Sequoia trees, **V,** 58

Bienville, Jean Baptiste le Moyne, Sieur de, builds Fort Assumption, **I,** 359; and Chickasaw-French War, **I,** 360; and Fort Condé, **II,** 3; and the settlement of Côte des Allemand, **II,** 67; and D'Artaguette's defeat, **II,** 110; plants first permanent French colony on Gulf coast, **III,** 305; builds Fort Assumption, **III,** 372; founds Natchez, **III,** 420; on the Mississippi River, **III,** 424; and Biloxi, **III,** 425; and Mobile, **IV,** 1; establishes Fort Rosalie, **IV,** 56; and the Natchez Indians, **IV,** 57; founder of New Orleans, **IV,** 109, 188; seizes Pensacola, **IV,** 249; and Fort Rosalie, **IV,** 502; attacks Indians at Ackia, **V,** 280; said to have built Fort Toulouse, **V,** 286

Big Bear Markets, **V,** 205

Big Bonanza, discovery of, **I,** 444

Big Bone Lick, **III,** 275

Big Business, and the holding company, **III,** 37

Big Elk, and Indian oratory, **III,** 103

Big Foot, and the Messiah War, **III,** 380; and battle of Wounded Knee, **V,** 495

Big Four Railroad, **IV,** 118

Big Four Railroad Brotherhoods, **III,** 225; **IV,** 400

Big Hole River, Chief Joseph victorious at, **IV,** 129

Big Mound, Sibley defeats Indians at, **II,** 106

Big Pasture Lands, opening of, **IV,** 169

Big Springs Convention, and Kansas Free-State party, **III,** 196; and the Kansas struggle, **III,** 198

Big Track, chief of the Great Osage Indians, **IV,** 189

Bigelow, Erastus B., and carpet manufacture, **I,** 318; and the loom, **III,** 301

Bigelow, Horatio, editor of the *Texas Republican,* **IV,** 127

Bigelow, Jacob, and use of drugs, **II,** 171

Bigelow, John, and Civil War diplomacy, **I,** 391

Bigelow, Maurice Alpheus, and social hygiene, **III,** 64

Biggs, Hermann Michael, and hygiene, **III,** 64; and tuberculosis, **V,** 328

Biglow Papers, **I,** 85

Bilateral Conventions, and treaties with foreign nations, **V,** 318

Bilbo, Theodore G., and agrarian movement, **I,** 22

Bill of Rights, and amendments to the Constitution, **I,** 55; and Barron v. Baltimore, **I,** 165; billeting prohibited in, **I,** 187; and civil liberties, **I,** 381; and protection of civil rights, **I,** 382; and common law, **I,** 439; and the Consti-

tution, **II,** 39; and enumerated powers, **II,** 220; and Federal-state relations, **II,** 263; and the judiciary, **III,** 185; and personal liberty, **IV,** 254; and right of petition, **IV,** 256; and postal power, **IV,** 319; Virginia Declaration of Rights as a model for, **V,** 378

Billeting, and the Constitution, **II,** 39

Billings, John Shaw, and medical bibliography, **III,** 369; introduces mechanical aids in counting statistical data, **V,** 382

Billings, Josh, humorous lecturer, **III,** 260

Billings, Warren K., and the Mooney case, **IV,** 19

Billings, William, hymn writer, **III,** 65

Bills of Credit, and the Confederation, **II,** 13; and the Continental Congress, **II,** 47; and Craig v. Missouri, **II,** 83; Continental Congress issues, **II,** 85; and Continental currency, **II,** 100; and public debt, **II,** 117; as fiat money, **II,** 269; and inflation, **III,** 120; and legal tender, **III,** 261; as paper money, **IV,** 212; issued to finance the Revolution, **IV,** 470

Bills of Rights, State, and reserved power of the people, **IV,** 458

"Billy Boy," song, **II,** 293

"Billy in the Low Ground," fiddle tune, **II,** 270

Billy the Kid, bandit leader, **II,** 88

Biloxi, Charlevoix taken ill at, **I,** 345; and Fort Maurepas, **III,** 360; founded by Iberville, **III,** 420; French at, **III,** 424

Biloxi, Fort, founding of, **II,** 346

Bimeler, Joseph Michael, and the Zoar Society, **V,** 514

Bimetallism, and Anglophobia, **I,** 78; and the Bland-Allison Act, **I,** 198; and *Coin's Financial School,* **I,** 412; defended by leaders of free coinage movement, **II,** 89; establishment of, **II,** 157; abolished, **II,** 332; and coinage, **IV,** 7; and silver legislation, **V,** 80; and the Silver Republican party, **V,** 82; and the Thomas Amendment, **V,** 264. *See also* Sixteen to One

Binding Twine, in the development of the reaper, **IV,** 419

Bingham, Caleb, author of *American Preceptor,* **V,** 40

Bingham, George Caleb, painter, **I,** 123

Bingham, Hiram, and missionary activity in the Pacific, **III,** 415

Bingham, Hiram, leads expedition to Peru, **III,** 248

Bingham, Robert W., advocates co-operative marketing of tobacco, **V,** 276

Bingham, William, and Lancaster Pike, **III,** 233

Binny and Ronaldson, type foundry of, **IV,** 346

Biograph Company, **IV,** 32

Biological Survey, Bureau of, establishes bird sanctuaries, **I,** 190

Birch Coulee, defeat at, **V,** 86

Birch Seal, and the Green Mountain Boys, **II,** 422

Bird, Henry, invades Kentucky, **I,** 191; and British plan of campaign in West in 1780, **I,** 240

Bird, Robert Montgomery, dramatist, **II,** 166

Bird, William, and the Hopewell Iron Works, **III,** 45

Bird-Lore, magazine published by Audubon Society, **I,** 137

Bird Sanctuaries, maintained by Audubon Societies, **I,** 137

Bird Woman, **II,** 280; **III,** 266

Birds of America, written by John James Audubon, **II,** 235

Birkbeck, Morris, establishes the English Settlement, **II,** 217

Birney, James G., and abolition movement, **I,** 2; and campaign of 1840, **I,** 284; candidate of the Liberty party, **III,** 272; and the Matilda Lawrence case, **III,** 359; editor of *The Philanthropist,* **IV,** 260

Birney, Mrs. Theodore, co-founder of the National Congress of Mothers, **IV,** 215

Birth Control, and the family, **II,** 242; and sex relations, **V,** 62

Birth of a Nation, greatest financial success in film history, **IV,** 32

Birth Rate, and population, **IV,** 311

Bishop, Bridget, acquitted of witchcraft, **V,** 475

Bishop, Henry, sets "Home, Sweet Home" to music, **III,** 40

Bishop, Stephen, first official guide of Mammoth Cave, **III,** 329

Bishop Hill Colony, **I,** 440; **II,** 114; **V,** 214

Bissell, Emily P., and Christmas seals, **I,** 371

Bissell, George H., and the oil industry, **IV,** 166

Bissell, Israel, brings news of the battle of Lexington to New York, **IV,** 120

Bit, and coinage names, **I,** 411

Bituminous Coal, used in blast furnaces, **III,** 155

Black, G. V., and dentistry, **II,** 138

Black, J. W., takes first aerial photograph, **I,** 35

Black, James, nominated for President by the Prohibition party, **IV,** 357

Black, Jeremiah S., and the Alta Vela claim, **I,** 52; and the peace movement of 1864, **IV,** 233

Black, Samuel W., territorial governor of Nebraska, **IV,** 80

Black and Tan Convention, **III,** 420

Black Ball Line, and merchant marine, **III,** 375; and sailing packets, **IV,** 198; inaugurated, **V,** 73

Black Boys, and Baynton, Wharton and Morgan, **I,** 170; gain Fort Bedford, **I,** 173; fire upon Fort Loudon, **III,** 304; attack at Sideling Hill, **V,** 77

Black Codes, and the Civil Rights Act, **I,** 381; and Code Noir, **I,** 407; for freedmen, **II,** 335; enacted by Mississippi, **III,** 420; and Reconstruction, **IV,** 425

Black-Connery Thirty-Hour Bill, **II,** 239

Black Fish, Shawnee chief, **I,** 216

Black Hawk, leader of Sauk and Fox in Bad Axe battle, **I,** 145

Black Hawk Purchase, **III,** 100

Black Hawk War, and decline of Fort Crawford, **II,** 83; brings troops back to Fort Dearborn, **II,** 115; Fox Indians in, **II,** 319; and Fort Howard, **III,** 54; and first Indian cession of Iowa land, **III,** 152; U. S. Rangers in, **IV,** 416; and Sauk Indians, **V,** 33; Fort Winnebago during, **V,** 471; and Wisconsin, **V,** 473; and battle of Wisconsin Heights, **V,** 474

Black Hills, and robberies, **I,** 152; Borglum sculptures at, **I,** 220; discovery of gold in, **II,** 106, 396; and Little Big Horn battle, **III,** 284; discovery of gold in, **V,** 87; and stage holdups, **V,** 153

Black Hills Gold Rush, and oxen, **IV,** 194

Black Hills War, **I,** 195

Black Horse, Comanche leader, **I,** 248

Black-Horse Cavalry, or the Regulators, **IV,** 439

Black Jack, and border war, **I,** 220

Black Kettle, band destroyed, **III,** 96; Custer destroys camp of, **V,** 420

Black Rock, and Great Lakes naval campaign of 1812, **II,** 416; Americans defeated at, **IV,** 130

Black Tom Explosion, **V,** 400

Blackfeet, The, and Algonquin family, **I,** 48; attack Henry's expedition at Great Falls, Mont., **I,** 128; trade with, **I,** 130; enemy of the Crow Indians, **II,** 92; on Green River, **II,** 423; and horses, **III,** 48; and Mackenzie's treaty, **III,** 321; and Manuel's Fort, **III,** 335; attack fort at Three Forks of the Missouri, **III,** 428; and Missouri River fur trade, **III,** 431; in Montana, **IV,** 16; and St. Louis Missouri Fur Company, **V,** 13

Blacklisting, and labor, **III,** 219; opposed by National Association of Manufacturers, **IV,** 58

Blackman, Capt., and group migration, **III,** 397

Blacksmiths, in iron manufacture, **II,** 309

Blackstock's Plantation, battle at, **II,** 218

Blackstone, William, settles Cumberland, R. I., **IV,** 477

Blackstone Canal, and locks, **III,** 292

Blackwell, Antoinette Brown, ordained to the ministry, **V,** 478; receives theological degree, **V,** 481; ordained to the ministry, **V,** 482

Blackwell, Elizabeth, first woman to receive a medical degree in modern times, **V,** 478; and opening of medical schools to women, **V,** 480; first licensed woman physician in the United States, **V,** 481

Bladensburg, Battle of, and burning of Washington, **V,** 417

Bladensburg Duelling Ground, **II,** 174

Blaine, James G., and Burchard Incident, I, 254; and campaign of 1876, I, 286; in campaigns of 1880, 1884, 1888, I, 287; and Garfield-Conkling controversy, II, 372; and the Mugwumps, IV, 39; author of the Mulligan letters, IV, 40; and Pan-American conferences, IV, 202; and peace conferences, IV, 232; and reciprocity, IV, 422; and Bering Sea seal fisheries, V, 50; and reciprocity agreements with South America, V, 123; as Speaker of the House, V, 142; and commercial treaties, V, 315

Blair, Francis Preston, Sr., editor of the Washington *Globe*, II, 392, 403; and Hampton Roads conference, III, 7; member of the "Kitchen Cabinet," III, 213; and the peace movement of 1864, IV, 233; journalist, V, 123

Blair, Frank, nominated for Vice-President, I, 286

Blair, James, and William and Mary College, V, 467

Blair, John, signer of the Constitution, II, 39

Blair, Montgomery, and the Universal Postal Union, IV, 322

Blair v. Williams, IV, 170

Blake, Eli Whitney, invents rock breaker, III, 9

Blake, George A. H., establishes Fort Massachusetts, III, 354

Blake, Katherine Devereux, and peace caravans, IV, 231

Blakelock, Ralph, painter, I, 123

Blakely, Johnston, commander of the *Wasp*, V, 420

Blanchard, Jean Pierre, makes first balloon ascent in America, I, 149

Bland, Richard, and the colony of Virginia, V, 373; alumnus of William and Mary College, V, 467

Bland-Allison Act, and purchase of silver, I, 252; revives coinage of silver dollar, II, 99; and the silver dollar, II, 157; and mortgages, IV, 29; and silver legislation, V, 80

Blast Furnaces, and forges, II, 309; and the iron and steel industry, III, 155; and early iron industries, III, 156, 158

Blaumiler, Joseph, and Zoar Community, I, 440

Blavatsky, Helena P., and theosophy, IV, 187; V, 262

Blease Movement, and Tillmanism, V, 270

Bleeding Kansas, and the sack of Lawrence, III, 253

Blennerhassett, Harman, and Burr Conspiracy, I, 199, 257

Blessing of the Bay, built for John Winthrop (1631), V, 72

Blimps, II, 148

Blind, The, and the American Bible Society, I, 58; Federal aid for, II, 255; social legislation for, V, 108; and social security, V, 108

Blind Tiger, I, 217

Bliss, Fort, established at El Paso, II, 204; and Sibley's operations on the Rio Grande, IV, 485

Bliss, George, and the Michigan Southern Railroad, III, 393

Bliss, T. H., and the World War Peace Conference, V, 490

Blizzard of 1886, and the cattle industry, IV, 86, 178

Blizzards, I, 29; prevent electors from meeting and voting, II, 73; and the range cattle industry, II, 79; and Texas longhorns, III, 300

Block, Adrian, explores Connecticut coast and river, II, 21; first to note Fishers Island, II, 277; explores the coast of Rhode Island, IV, 477

Blockade, and the *Amy Warwick* admiralty case, I, 71; and Anglo-American relations, I, 74; and armed neutrality, I, 108; of the Confederacy, I, 110; causes decline of foreign trade, I, 147; and belligerents, I, 176; and the Civil War, I, 383, 386, 390; and Civil War diplomacy, I, 392; and Civil War munitions, I, 393; of the Confederacy, II, 5, 8, 10; and cotton money, II, 70; and the doctrine of continuous voyage, II, 146; and foreign policy, II, 303; and freedom of the seas, II, 338; and international law, III, 141; paper, and Latin-American relations, III, 249; and Declaration of London, III, 296; off the Mississippi Deltas, III, 421; and the Confederacy, IV, 78; and neutral rights, IV, 88, 89; and Orders in Council, IV, 180; and Declaration of Paris (1856), IV, 215; and the *Peterhoff* admiralty case, IV, 255; defined in Declaration of Paris (1856), IV, 283; and prize courts, IV, 352; and retaliation in international law, IV, 462; of the Confederacy, V, 18; and the *Springbok* admiralty case, V, 150; and the submarine in the Civil War, V, 193; of southern ports, and Trade with the Enemy Acts, V, 300; in War of 1812, V, 404, 406; and the World War, V, 490

Blockade Runners, and the Alabama Claims, I, 40; Civil War, and the Bahama Islands, I, 146; and Civil War diplomacy, I, 392; and the Confederacy, II, 8; and Fort Fisher, II, 277; use Mobile, Ala., IV, 1; North Carolina, IV, 145; at St. Marks, V, 13; and the stone fleets, V, 185

Blommaert, Samuel, promoter of New Sweden Company, IV, 113; patroonship of, IV, 226; and Zwaanendael Colony, V, 515

Bloodgood, Abraham, designs a floating battery, II, 284

Bloody Angle, battle of, V, 150

Bloody Island Duelling Ground, II, 174

Bloody Marsh, battle of, III, 173; V, 126

Bloody Run, battle of, IV, 306

Bloody Shirt, in campaigns of 1868, 1872, 1876, I, 286; and presidential campaigns, I, 296

Bloomery Forges, and early ironmaking, **III**, 158

Bloomingdale Asylum, **III**, 125

Bloudy Tenent of Persecution, by Roger Williams, **IV**, 263

Blount, Fort, **II**, 98

Blount, James H., executive agent, **II**, 232; and Hawaii, **III**, 18

Blount, William, signer of the Constitution, **II**, 39; and Holston treaty, **III**, 39; and the Muscle Shoals speculation, **IV**, 47; and the Southwest Territory, **V**, 133; as governor of Tennessee, **V**, 243

Blue Eagle, and codes of fair competition, **I**, 408

Blue Laws of Connecticut, **II**, 21

Blue Licks, **III**, 275

Blue Licks, battle of, **III**, 88, 205

Blue Mountains, and the Oregon Trail, **IV**, 186

Blue Ridge Gap, **IV**, 221

Blue Ridge Mountains, Ashby's Gap in, **I**, 127; Batts-Fallam expedition crosses, **I**, 168

Blue Sky Laws, and government regulation, **II**, 406; or the Publicity Acts, **IV**, 378

Blue Swallowtail Line, and sailing packets, **IV**, 198

Blunt, J. G., and battle at Prairie Grove, **IV**, 329

Blynman, Richard, and Cape Ann, **I**, 306

Board, Cornelius, builds first furnace of the Sterling Iron Works, **V**, 181

Boards of Trade, and Chambers of Commerce, **I**, nial agent, **I**, 415; and colonial councils, **I**, 418; and the judiciary, **I**, 419; and colonial plans of union, **I**, 420; and British colonial policy, **I**, 422; based on Lords of Trade and Plantation, **III**, 302; and restrictions of colonial manufactures, **III**, 335; and Mitchell's map, **III**, 431; and the Privy Council, **IV**, 351; and Proclamation of 1763, **IV**, 353; and royal colonies, **IV**, 504; and the Vandalia Colony, **V**, 357

Boards of Trade, and Chambers of Commerce, **I**, 337

Bobtail Gold Mine, **II**, 396

Body of Liberties, **II**, 356; **IV**, 30

Boehm, Martin, joint founder of the Church of the United Brethren, **V**, 345

Boelen, Jacob and Henricus, silversmiths, **V**, 82

Bog Iron, **II**, 309; **III**, 155, 157

Bogardus, A. H., and the Wild West show, **V**, 464

Boggs, Lilburn W., issues order against the Latter-day Saints, **IV**, 26, 449

Bogle, W. Y., and the open-top can, **I**, 304

Boies, Horace, Democratic governor of Iowa, **III**, 153

Boilerplate, and newspaper syndicates, **IV**, 123

Bois de Belleau, and the Aisne Defensive, **I**, 38

Boisbriant, Pierre Duqué, and Kaskaskia, **III**, 199

Boise, Fort, established, **III**, 66

Boise, Idaho, mint at, **I**, 129

Boker, George, dramatist, **II**, 166

Bolivar, Simon, and Pan-Americanism, **IV**, 203; and the Panama Congress (1826), **IV**, 206

Boll Weevil, **II**, 91

Bolon, A. J., and the Yakima Indian wars, **V**, 500

Bolter, James, and accident insurance, **III**, 131

Bombing Plots, of the "reds," **IV**, 433

Bonanza Kings, and Denver, **II**, 138

Bonanza Wheat Farming, **I**, 29

Bond, Thomas, co-founder of the Pennsylvania Hospital, **IV**, 247

Bond Issues, Corporate, **II**, 63

Bonds, Government, and banking, **I**, 157; and national banks, **I**, 160; during Civil War, **I**, 388; five-twenties, issue of, **II**, 280; and Liberty Loans, **III**, 271

Bonham, M. L., at Bull Run, **I**, 251

Bonhomme Richard, captures *Serapis*, **IV**, 77

Bonner, Robert, and magazine publishing, **III**, 323

Bonnet Carré Spillway, **IV**, 109

Bonneville, speed tests made at, **I**, 139

Bonneville, B. L. E., conducts wagon train across South Pass, **I**, 312; and the fur trade, **II**, 362; and Fort Howard, **III**, 54; on the Oregon Trail, **IV**, 185; takes wagons over South Pass, **V**, 128; follows Sublette's cut-off, **V**, 192; and topographic mapping, **V**, 283; takes wagon through South Pass, **V**, 389; and the J. R. Walker expedition, **V**, 392; and western exploration, **V**, 442; leads first fur-trading expedition into Wyoming, **V**, 496

Bonneville Dam, and the Dalles, **II**, 107; and the Federal Power Commission, **II**, 261; administrator of, **III**, 135; and water power, **V**, 423

Bonney, William H. (Billy the Kid), and the Lincoln County War, **III**, 278

Bonpland, Aimé, surveys and maps the Pacific coast, **III**, 341

Bonus, and American Legion, **I**, 62; and privileged groups, **IV**, 350; and soldier vote, **V**, 117; and state debts, **V**, 168

Bonus Bill, provisions of (1816), **III**, 137

Bonuses, and industrial relations, **III**, 116

Bonython, Richard, begins settlement north of Saco River, **V**, 3

Booger Red, and the rodeo, **IV**, 499

Boole, Ella A., president of the W. C. T. U., **V**, 479

Boomers, in Oklahoma, **IV**, 168, 169

Boone, Daniel, and Big Moccasin Gap, **I**, 184; hero of the Bluegrass Country, **I**, 205; founds Boonesborough, **I**, 216; and Charleston, W. Va., **I**, 344; passes through Cumberland Gap, **II**, 96; early explorer, **II**, 235; and Filson's map, **II**, 274; hunter, **III**, 60; comes to Kentucky, **III**, 204; and expansion into Kentucky, **III**, 235;

and salt licks, **III**, 275; long hunter, **III**, 298; and "men of the western waters," **III**, 373; turns back at Powell's Valley, **IV**, 326; cuts a wagon trail in Kentucky, **IV**, 494; as early surveyor, **V**, 210; employed to make a reconnoissance of the Kentucky country, **V**, 215; and the Wilderness Road, **V**, 465

Boone, Israel, **I**, 216

Boone, Nathan, and Fort Kearny, **III**, 200

Boone's Gap, and the Great Trading and War Path, **II**, 420

Boonesborough, Anglo-Saxon government organized at, **I**, 205; and Jemima Boone episode, **I**, 215; settlement of, **II**, 96; and Cumberland settlements, **II**, 97; siege of, **III**, 205; located at a salt lick, **III**, 275; and the Transylvania Company, **V**, 310; settlement of, **V**, 450; and the Wilderness Road, **V**, 465

Boot and Shoe Industry, growth of, **III**, 148

Boot Hill, graveyard of the cow towns, **II**, 79; in Dodge City, **II**, 156

Booth, Ballington, establishes the Volunteers of America, **V**, 20

Booth, John Wilkes, shoots Lincoln, **III**, 279; and *"sic semper tyrannis,"* **V**, 77

Booth, Sherman, and Ableman v. Booth, **I**, 2

Bootlegging, and Anti-Saloon League, **I**, 84; and "hi-jackers," **I**, 152; and crime, **II**, 88; and the Eighteenth Amendment, **II**, 190; and padlock injunctions, **IV**, 200

Borah, W. E., and the Kellogg Pact, **IV**, 233; leads fight against World Court, **V**, 485

Borax, product of Death Valley, **II**, 116

Borden, Gail, and condensed milk, **I**, 304; **II**, 105, 297

Borden, Lizzie, murder trial of, **V**, 323

Border Forts, in Anglo-American relations, **I**, 74; and British debts, **I**, 240; evacuation of, **I**, 299; **II**, 241; **III**, 110, 169, 391, 394; **IV**, 159; **V**, 440

Border Ruffians, and the Emigrant Aid movement, **II**, 211; and the Kansas struggle, **III**, 198

Border Slave State Convention, **I**, 442; **V**, 52

Border States, and Civil War, **I**, 386; in the Confederacy, **II**, 3, 10; and compensated emancipation, **II**, 205; and the Emancipation Proclamation, **II**, 205; do not secede, **V**, 52; during the Civil War, **V**, 131; Unionist sentiment in, **V**, 344; and the westward movement, **V**, 452

Border War, and Missouri, **III**, 427; and popular sovereignty, **IV**, 309

Borglum, Gutzon, sculptor, **I**, 124; colossal sculptures of, **I**, 195

Borgne, Lake, American fleet defeated on, **IV**, 110

Borneo, treaties with, **V**, 317

Borough, as a political subdivision, **IV**, 299

Bosque Redondo, Fort Sumner established at, **V**, 202

Bosses, and party machines, **III**, 318

Boston, evacuation of, **I**, 127; and coast defense, **I**, 405; city directory appears in, **II**, 148; siege of (1776), **IV**, 476; siege of, and capture of Ticonderoga, **V**, 267; siege of, and Washington's eight months army, **V**, 418

Boston, The, Congress authorizes construction of, **II**, 283; one of the vessels of the White Squadron, **V**, 460

Boston and Albany Railroad, **IV**, 118

Boston and Lowell Railroad, construction begun on, **IV**, 406

Boston and Providence Railroad, building of, **IV**, 406

Boston and Western Land Company, **III**, 240

Boston Athenæum, **I**, 124; **IV**, 47

Boston-Berceau Engagement, **IV**, 73

Boston Cooking School Cook Book, **I**, 180

Boston Ephemeris, **IV**, 99

Boston *Gazette,* publishes John Dickinson's "Liberty Song," **V**, 350

Boston Manufacturing Company, **II**, 68; **III**, 301

Boston Massacre, benefit of clergy in, **I**, 178; and British troops, **V**, 290; and famous trials, **V**, 323

Boston Museum of Fine Arts, **I**, 124

Boston Navy Yard, **II**, 156; **IV**, 79

Boston News-Letter, **I**, 16, 222, 420; **IV**, 123, 127

Boston Port Act, **I**, 132, 408; **II**, 307; **III**, 147; **IV**, 467

Boston Public Library, architecture of, **I**, 101; begins special library for the blind, **I**, 200; and book collections, **I**, 212; founded, **III**, 272

Boston Society of Civil Engineers, **II**, 215

Boston Society of Natural History, **IV**, 47

Boston Tea Party, and the Coercion Acts, **I**, 408; and the Intolerable Acts, **III**, 147; and the American Revolution, **IV**, 467

Bostwick, J. A., & Company, **V**, 156

Botanists, early, **II**, 371

Botetourt County, creation of, **I**, 139

Boudinot, E. C., and boomer movement, **I**, 215

Boudinot, Elias, and the American Bible Society, **I**, 58; and the Miami Purchase, **III**, 390

Boudinot, Elias, editor of the *Cherokee Phoenix and Indian Advocate,* **V**, 59

Boulder (Hoover) Dam, and the Colorado River aqueduct and projects, **I**, 428; for flood control, **II**, 285; and government ownership, **II**, 404; compact, **III**, 144; and water power, **V**, 423

Boundary Waters Treaty, **V**, 317

Bounties, military, **I**, 111, 210, 387; **II**, 163, 217; fishing, **II**, 277; and mercantilism, **III**, 374; military, **III**, 402; and mobilization, **IV**, 2; for naval stores, **IV**, 72; and the Navigation Acts, **IV**, 74; military, **IV**, 472; and salt, **V**, 18; military, and state debts, **V**, 168; military, and volunteers, **V**, 382; for exterminating wolves, **V**, 477

Bounty Jumping, and profiteering, **IV,** 355

Bouquet, Henry, enlarges and strengthens Fort Raystown, **I,** 173; and Forbes expedition, **II,** 299; and battle of Grant's Hill, **II,** 411; builds Fort Ligonier, **III,** 277

Bouquet's Expedition, and Bushy Run, **I,** 258; follows the Great Trail, **II,** 421; and Indian council at Niagara, **IV,** 130; and Bushy Run, **IV,** 229; and Pennsylvania, **IV,** 243; and Fort Pitt, **IV,** 279; and Pontiac's War, **IV,** 306; and Raystown Path, **IV,** 418

Bourbon Whiskey, **II,** 151

Bourgmont, Étienne Veniard de, and French exploration, **II,** 345; establishes Fort Orleans, **II,** 363; explores Missouri, **III,** 426; uses the name Nebraska for the Platte, **IV,** 80; builds Fort Orleans, **IV,** 188

Bourlamaque, forced to blow up Ft. St. Frederic, **II,** 93

Bourne, Randolph, and youth movements, **V,** 511

Bourne, Richard, and the Praying Indians, **IV,** 330

Bout, and the Petition and Remonstrance of New Netherland, **IV,** 256

Boutwell, G. S., among the leaders of the Radical Republicans, **IV,** 395

Bowdoin, James, governor during Shays' rebellion, **V,** 66

Bowen, Daniel, and wax portraits, **V,** 426

Bowen, J. S., and battle at Port Gibson, **IV,** 314

Bowers, Henry F., founds the American Protective Association, **I,** 64

Bowery, site of Stuyvesant's farm, **II,** 353

Bowery Boys, battle Dead Rabbits, **IV,** 3

Bowie, James, and the Alamo, **I,** 41; and the Sandbar Duel, **V,** 27; perishes in the Alamo assault, **V,** 257

Bowie, Walter, Confederate spy, **V,** 146

Bowles, Samuel, as newspaper editor, **IV,** 123

Bowles, William A., and Forbes purchase, **II,** 299; burns the Panton, Leslie store in St. Marks, **V,** 13; and Spanish-Indian relations, **V,** 140

Bowlin, James B., and the Paraguay expedition, **IV,** 213

Bowman, Isaiah, and the Inquiry, **III,** 124

Bowne, Borden P., and religious thought and writings, **IV,** 447; **V,** 261

Bowyer, Fort, as coast defense, **I,** 405

Boxer-Enterprise Action, **II,** 219

Boxer Rebellion, and good will of China, **I,** 366; and Far Eastern policy, **II,** 243; and foreign policy, **II,** 305; and indemnities, **III,** 84; and American policy toward Manchuria, **III,** 330; and the Peking Congress, **IV,** 239

Boycott, and the American Federation of Labor, **I,** 60; and industrial arbitration, **I,** 95; and Buck Stove and Range case, **I,** 246; and Dan-

bury Hatters' case, **II,** 108; and labor unions, **III,** 225; opposed by National Association of Manufacturers, **IV,** 58; and Norris-LaGuardia Anti-Injunction Law, **IV,** 143; and restraint of trade, **IV,** 460; and strikes, **V,** 190; and Truax v. Corrigan, **V,** 325

Boyd, Belle, Confederate spy, **V,** 146

Boyd, John P., and battle of Chrysler's Field, **I,** 371

Boydton Plank Road, and siege of Petersburg, **IV,** 256

Boyle, Hon. Robert, philanthropy of, **V,** 467

Boylston, Zabdiel, pioneer of epidemiology, **II,** 221; and inoculation, **V,** 100

Boys' Life, magazine, **I,** 364

Bozeman, John M., opens Bozeman Trail, **II,** 236

Bozeman Pass, **IV,** 222

Bozeman Trail, Fort Connor established on, **II,** 24; Fort Phil Kearny principal military post on, **III,** 200; Sioux agree to opening of, **III,** 245; and Powder River campaign, **IV,** 326; and Red Cloud War, **IV,** 429; and Sioux wars, **V,** 86; opening of, and Wyoming, **V,** 496

Brace, Charles Loring, and the Children's Aid Society, **IV,** 260

Brackenridge, H. H., author of *Modern Chivalry,* **II,** 270; and the *Pittsburgh Gazette,* **IV,** 124

Brackenridge, Henry M., and western exploration, **V,** 442

Bradbury, John, and western exploration, **V,** 442

Braddock's Expedition, departure from Alexandria, **I,** 47; and Aughwick, **I,** 138; and Fort Augusta, **I,** 138; and the building of Fort Cumberland, **II,** 96; and Fort Duquesne, **II,** 177; and French and Indian War, **II,** 342; Logstown Indians join, **III,** 295; and the battle of the Monongahela, **IV,** 11; uses Nemacolin's path, **IV,** 12; and Penn's Creek massacre, **IV,** 242; utilizes the Potomac Valley, **IV,** 325; and wagon manufacture, **V,** 388; and Charles de Langlade, **V,** 473

Braddock's Road, and the Alleghenies, **I,** 51; and Cumberland Road, **II,** 97; as a military road, **III,** 402; and mountain passes, **IV,** 221; and the westward movement, **V,** 450

Bradford, Andrew, printer, **I,** 213; and magazine publishing, **III,** 323; co-founder of the *American Weekly Mercury,* **IV,** 127; produces the *American Magazine,* **IV,** 258

Bradford, John, publishes *The Kentucke Almanac,* **III,** 204; brings press into Kentucky, **IV,** 124; and the *Kentucke Gazette,* **IV,** 126, 345

Bradford, William, and Monhegan Island, **IV,** 9; considered author of *Mourt's Relation,* **IV,** 38; made governor of New Plymouth Colony, **IV,**

112; and the Pilgrims, **IV,** 271; and Thanks-giving Day, **V,** 259

Bradford, William, printer, **I,** 213; publishes first newspaper in New York City, **IV,** 118; founder of the *New-York Gazette,* **IV,** 127; and the first paper mill, **IV,** 212; and printing in America, **IV,** 345 f.

Bradley, Joseph P., and the Electoral Commission, **I,** 286; and the Supreme Court Packing Bills, **V,** 208

Bradstreet, Simon, a founder of Cambridge, **I,** 277

Bradstreet Company, **III,** 374

Bradstreet Expedition (1758), success of, **II,** 299; and capture of Fort Frontenac, **II,** 349

Bradstreet Expedition (1764), and siege of Fort Detroit, **II,** 143; and Indian Council at Niagara, **IV,** 130; and Pontiac's War, **IV,** 306; and Sandusky, **V,** 27

Brady, Fort, erected, **V,** 14

Brady, Mathew B., and photography, **IV,** 265

Bragg, Braxton, becomes a general of the Confederate army, **I,** 110; and the Chattanooga campaign, **I,** 348; and battle of Chickamauga, **I,** 359; retreats through Cumberland Gap, **II,** 96; and invasion of Kentucky, **III,** 205; and battle of Missionary Ridge, **III,** 416; and the Army of Mississippi, **III,** 419; and capture of Munfordville, **IV,** 40; and battle of Murfreesboro, **IV,** 46; and battle of Perryville, **IV,** 254; and the Army of Tennessee, **V,** 241; and the Tullahoma campaign, **V,** 329

Braille, American, **I,** 200

Brailsford v. Georgia, **II,** 379

Brainerd, David, attempts to Christianize the Indians, **III,** 103

Brainerd, John, and Praying Indians, **IV,** 330

Braislin, W. C., sale of Americana, **I,** 213

Branding, as a colonial punishment, **IV,** 382

Brandy, and the Indian, **III,** 91

Brandywine, battle at, **IV,** 476

Brant, Joseph, leads Indians in Cherry Valley massacre, **I,** 353; in the Revolution, **III,** 88; and Lochry's defeat, **III,** 291; raids Minisink, **III,** 410; and battle of Oriskany, **IV,** 188; conversion of, **IV,** 330

Brattle, Thomas, and astronomical observatories, **IV,** 156

Bratton, John, and battle of Wauhatchie (1863), **V,** 425

Braud, Denis, and printing in America, **IV,** 345 f.

Braxton, Carter, signer of the Declaration of Independence, **II,** 124

Bray, Thomas, establishes parochial libraries, **III,** 272

Brazil, and the *Wachusett* affair, **V,** 386

Brearley, David, signer of the Constitution, **II,** 39

Breathitt County, and Hargis-Callahan-Cockrill feud, **III,** 10

Breckinridge, John C., attacks Baton Rouge, **I,** 167; nominated for President, **I,** 285; and flight of Confederate Cabinet, **II,** 5; and the land speculation, **III,** 240; and battle at Marion, **III,** 344; in battle of New Market, **IV,** 106; and siege of Port Hudson, **IV,** 315

Breckinridge, William C. P., sued for breach of promise, **V,** 324

Breda, Treaty of, and Castine, **I,** 321; and Maine, **III,** 326; returns Penobscot to the French, **IV,** 249

Breen Mine, **III,** 374

Breidenbaugh, C. F., launches the showboat *Theatorium,* **V,** 77

Brent, Charles, and Missouri Fur Company, **V,** 13

Brent, Margaret, feminist, **II,** 265

Brevoort, J. C., book collector, **I,** 212

Brewer, D. J., and Kansas-Colorado water rights litigation, **III,** 196; and Pollock v. Farmers Loan and Trust Co., **IV,** 303

Brewery Workers, and craft unions, **V,** 344

Brewing, **II,** 170

Brewster, Jonathan, in charge of Plymouth Trading Post, **IV,** 291

Brewster, William, and the Pilgrims, **IV,** 270

Brewster & Company, **IV,** 355

Briand-Kellogg Pact (Pact of Paris, 1928), and Anglo-American relations, **I,** 77; and international arbitration, **I,** 97; and Far Eastern policy, **II,** 243; adoption of, **III,** 142; and isolation, **III,** 163; and the Sino-Japanese controversy, **III,** 256; and the Monroe Doctrine, **IV,** 15; and neutrality, **IV,** 90; and nonrecognition, **IV,** 140; framing of, **IV,** 232; and treaties with foreign nations, **V,** 318

Briar Creek, patriots lose at, **II,** 379

Bribery Law (1918), enactment of, **II,** 64

Brice, Calvin S., and campaign of 1888, **I,** 288

Brick, in American architecture, **I,** 99; imported, **I,** 249; erection of first house of, **III,** 167

Bridger, Fort, and caravan traffic, **I,** 312; and the Great Basin, **II,** 414; and Marcy's march, **III,** 342; and the Mormon Trail, **IV,** 24; and the Oregon Trail, **IV,** 186; and the Overland Trail, **IV,** 193; as frontier trading post, **V,** 302; and first permanent settlers in Wyoming, **V,** 496

Bridger, James, mountain man, **I,** 128; discoverer of Great Salt Lake, **II,** 235; mountain man, **II,** 362; discovers the Great Salt Lake, **II,** 419; mountain man, **IV,** 37; scout, **V,** 46; and Ashley's expeditions, **V,** 310; explores Wyoming, **V,** 496

Bridger's Pass, Ashley crosses by, **I,** 128; discovery of, **IV,** 222; and stagecoach lines of greater Southwest, **V,** 152

Bridges, suspension, **I,** 243; Eads, **II,** 180; Golden

Gate, **II**, 399; Latrobe's Folly, **III**, 251; steel, **III**, 337; and railroads, **IV**, 407; toll, **V**, 278; and travel, **V**, 306

Bridges, John, and the Wawayanda patent, **V**, 426

Bridgman's Fort, attacked, **V**, 361

Briggs, Ansel, elected governor of Iowa, **III**, 152

Briggs, C. A., convicted of heresy, **III**, 28; and higher criticism, **III**, 31

Briggs Map, **III**, 340

Brigham, Clarence S., Bibliography of American Newspapers (1690–1820), **III**, 34

Bright, Francis, founder of Charlestown, Mass., **I**, 345

Brigs, as warships, **V**, 411

Brine Wells, and the oil industry, **IV**, 166

Brinkerhoff, Jacob, and the Wilmot Proviso, **V**, 470

Brinley, George, and book collecting, **I**, 212

Brisbane, Albert, introduces Fourierism to America, **II**, 317; and the socialist movement, **V**, 110

Bristol (York), Maine, settled, **I**, 20

Bristol, Mark, in Turkey, **IV**, 76

Bristow, Benjamin H., and the Whiskey Ring, **V**, 457

British Debts, and alien property, **I**, 50; and Anglo-American relations, **I**, 74; and Border Forts, **I**, 219; and the Definitive Treaty of Peace, **II**, 129; and Jay's Treaty, **III**, 169; and Ware v. Hylton, **V**, 408; and Border Forts, **V**, 440

British Plan of Campaign in the West (1780), **I**, 191

Brockenbrough, John, and the *Richmond Enquirer*, **IV**, 129

Brockway, Zebulon, and the Elmira Reformatory, **IV**, 348, 436

Broderick, David, duels with David S. Terry, **II**, 174

Brodhead, Daniel, and abandonment of Fort Laurens, **III**, 251; and second treaty of Fort Stanwix, **V**, 159; and Sullivan-Clinton campaign, **V**, 202

Bronco, and the cow horse, **III**, 46

Bronson v. Rodes, **IV**, 455

Brook Farm, as a communistic experiment, **I**, 441; experiment in transcendentalism, **II**, 114; experiment in Fourierism, **II**, 317; and religion, **IV**, 442; and the socialist movement, **V**, 110; and transcendentalism, **V**, 304; and distribution of wealth, **V**, 429

Brooke, Fort, and the Dade massacre, **II**, 103

Brooke, John M., on the designing board of the *Virginia*, **IV**, 414

Brooke, John R., institutes reforms in Cuba, **II**, 94

Brooke, Lord, and designation "Lords and Gentlemen," **III**, 301

Brooklyn, The, wooden screw sloop, **V**, 99

Brooklyn, The, in battle of Mobile Bay, **II**, 108

Brooklyn, The, and blockade and battle of Santiago, **V**, 31

Brooklyn Bridge, opening of, **IV**, 119

Brooklyn Institute, **I**, 124; **III**, 316

Brooklyn Navy Yard, **II**, 156

Brooklyn Rapid Transit Corporation, **V**, 197

Brooks, Elisha, and the Kanawha salt works, **III**, 194

Brooks, James, and the Crédit Mobilier, **II**, 85

Brooks, John F., organizer of the Illinois Band, **III**, 69

Brooks, P. S., assault upon Sumner, **III**, 198

Brooks, Phillips, pulpit orator, **IV**, 180; and religious thought, **IV**, 446; and theological writings, **V**, 261

Broom, J., signer of the Constitution, **II**, 39

Brother Jonathan, **III**, 181

Brotherhead, William, and Americana, **I**, 214

Brotherhood of Locomotive Engineers, and Burlington Strike, **I**, 256

Brotherhood of Railway Trainmen, **III**, 225

Brough, John, defeats Vallandigham as governor of Ohio, **IV**, 161; and the Union Democrats, **V**, 342; Vallandigham conducts unsuccessful campaign against, **V**, 355

Broughton, Samuel, and Little Nine Partners' patent, **III**, 285

Broughton, W. R., and the Columbia River, **I**, 430

Brown, Albert G., and popular sovereignty, **IV**, 309

Brown, Antoinette. *See* Blackwell

Brown, B. Gratz, nominated for Vice-President, **I**, 286; and the Liberal Republican party, **III**, 269

Brown, Camp, early name for Fort Washakie, **V**, 412

Brown, J. G., painter, **I**, 123

Brown, Jacob, in battle of Chippewa, **I**, 367; attacked at French Creek, **II**, 344; and Lundy's Lane, **III**, 315; and the Niagara campaigns, **IV**, 130; repulses British attack, **IV**, 159; and operations at Sackett's Harbor, **V**, 2; in War of 1812, **V**, 405

Brown, John, receives first deed drawn up in Maine, **III**, 203; buys land from Chief Samoset, **IV**, 239

Brown, John, and burning of the *Gaspee*, **II**, 373

Brown, John, sent to Canada by Massachusetts (1775), **I**, 297; and the Diamond Island fight, **II**, 145; **III**, 230; and capture of Ticonderoga (1775), **V**, 267

Brown, John, and the battle of Black Jack, **I**, 195; and Potawatomie massacre, **I**, 220; and

the Coppoc case, **II**, 58; and Harpers Ferry raid, **III**, 12; avenges the raid on Lawrence, **III**, 198; and the Potawatomie massacre, **III**, 253; and the battle of Osawatomie, **IV**, 189; and the Potawatomie massacre, **IV**, 323; uses Sharps rifles in Harpers Ferry raid, **V**, 64

Brown, John, Jr., and prohibition in Kansas, **III**, 195

Brown, John Carter, book collector, **I**, 212; and land speculation, **III**, 240; library of, **III**, 273

Brown, Joseph C., and topographic mapping, **V**, 283

Brown, Joseph E., and states' rights in Confederacy, **II**, 12; and Georgia, **II**, 380; nonslaveholder, **IV**, 141; and states' rights during Civil War, **V**, 176

Brown, Joseph R., attacked at Birch Coulee, **I**, 190

Brown, Maurice, and the "little theater" movement, **III**, 286

Brown, Moses, and land speculation, **III**, 240; and the cotton mill at Pawtucket, **IV**, 478

Brown, Noah, builds the *Walk-in-the-Water*, **V**, 392

Brown, Postmaster General, and the Southern Overland Mail, **V**, 130

Brown, Rear Admiral, and the Quinteros Bay episode, **IV**, 390

Brown, W. A., and theological writing, **V**, 261

Brown, W. W., and the Bellevue War, **I**, 176

Brown, William, issues earliest published pharmacopœia in the United States, **II**, 171

Brown, William Henry, and silhouettes, **V**, 78

Brown Settlement, and the Watauga Association, **V**, 421

Brown University, **I**, 212; **II**, 185, 413; **IV**, 478

Brown v. Maryland, enunciates original-package doctrine, **IV**, 187

Brown v. U. S., **V**, 398

Browne, Carl, and the Commonweal of Christ, **II**, 82

Browne, R. C., inventor of the mine, **IV**, 148

Browne, Robert, and Brownists, **I**, 244

Browne, Thomas, forms the Florida rangers, **II**, 291

Brownists, Separatists dubbed, **V**, 58

Brownlow, William G., and the Parson's book, **IV**, 219; Reconstruction governor of Tennessee, **V**, 243; and Union sentiment in the South, **V**, 343

Brown's Hole, **III**, 37

Brownson, Orestes, and religious periodicals, **IV**, 445

Brownsville Riot, and Negro soldiers, **IV**, 85

Brûlé, Etienne, and Lake Huron, **III**, 61; and Lake Ontario, **IV**, 175; first white man to reach Sault Ste. Marie, **V**, 34; probable discoverer of

Lake Superior, **V**, 205; and topographic mapping, **V**, 282

Brundage, Hiram, founder of the *Daily Telegraph*, **IV**, 128; first printer of Wyoming, **IV**, 346

Brunner, Edmund de S., and adult education, **I**, 14

Brush, Charles F., brings out arc lamp and electric dynamo, **II**, 197

Brutus, The, and the Texas navy, **V**, 256

Bruyere, Fabry de, and the Mallet brothers, **III**, 329

Bryan, Charles W., nominated for Vice-Presidency, **I**, 291

Bryan, William Jennings, supported by Anti-Imperialists, **I**, 82; an advocate of bimetallism, **I**, 189; Democratic nominee for Presidency (1896), **I**, 288; defeated for Presidency, **I**, 290; and Cross of Gold speech, **II**, 91; and free silver, **II**, 333; and the Gold Democrats, **II**, 395; and the phrase, "He kept us out of war," **III**, 21; reform lecturer, **III**, 260; resigns as Secretary of State, **III**, 315; as candidate for Presidency (1896), **III**, 395; and oratory, **IV**, 180; and Philippine independence, **IV**, 261; and the Populist party, **IV**, 314; and Scopes trial, **V**, 45; resigns as Secretary of State, **V**, 491

Bryan-Chamorro Treaty, and Central American Court of Justice, **I**, 333; and the leasing of the Corn Islands, **II**, 60; brings fiscal aid to Nicaragua, **IV**, 131; and Nicaraguan Canal project, **IV**, 132

Bryan Treaties, with foreign nations, **V**, 318

Bryan Treaty Model, and international arbitration, **I**, 97; and conciliation, **II**, 2; Gondra Treaty modeled upon, **IV**, 232

Bryan's Station, heroism of women at, **V**, 151

Bryant, Sturgis & Co., and hide and tallow trade, **III**, 29

Bryant, William Cullen, and bookshops, **I**, 214; and American hymns, **III**, 65; as newspaper editor, **IV**, 123; and the socialist movement, **V**, 110

Bryant's Minstrels, and "Dixie," **II**, 156

Bryce, James, and the Waterways Treaty, **V**, 425

Bryce National Park, **IV**, 218

Bryn Mawr College, **V**, 480

Bubble Act of 1720, and land banks, **III**, 234

Bubonic Plague, **II**, 150

Bucareli Conference, and mixed claims commissions, **I**, 63; and the Mexican Oil controversy, **III**, 384

Buccaneers, and the logwood trade, **III**, 295

Buchan, David, polar expedition of, **IV**, 292

Buchanan, Franklin, commands the *Virginia* (*Merrimack*), **III**, 378; in battle of Mobile Bay, **IV**, 1; first superintendent of United States

Naval Academy, **IV,** 68; and the *Tennessee,* **V,** 243

Buchanan, James, contemplates purchase of Alaska, **I,** 43; elected President, **I,** 284; and the Covode investigation, **II,** 77; and expatriation, **II,** 234; and the Mexican War, **III,** 385 f.; vetoes Morrill Act, **IV,** 27; and the Ostend Manifesto, **IV,** 190; and policy of recognition, **IV,** 424; and secession of Southern states, **V,** 51; and Anderson's move to Fort Sumter, **V,** 203

Buchanan, John, editor and proprietor of the *Montana Post,* **IV,** 127

Buchmanism, and religion, **IV,** 443; as youth movement, **V,** 511

Buck Stove and Range Company Case, **I,** 232; **III,** 124, 220

Buckaroo, origin of term, **II,** 81

Buckley and Weeks, rolling show of, **I,** 377

Bucklin, Joseph, and burning of the *Gaspee,* **II,** 373

Buckner, S. B., and the Gold Democrats, **II,** 395; and "Unconditional Surrender," **V,** 337

"Buckshots," or "Molly Maguires," **IV,** 6

Buddhism, **IV,** 187

Budget, Bureau of the, **V,** 314

Budget and Accounting Act (1921), **I,** 93, 444

Budget System, and "pork barrel," **IV,** 314

Buel, Jesse, author of the *Cultivator,* **II,** 248

Buell, Abel, and type manufacture, **IV,** 346; map of, **V,** 283

Buell, D. C., original commander of Army of the Cumberland, **II,** 96; and invasion of Kentucky, **III,** 205; and battle of Perryville, **IV,** 254; and battle of Shiloh, **V,** 71

Buell, David, and silver smelting, **V,** 81

Buell, George, and the Red River Indian War, **IV,** 431

Buena Vista, and the Mexican War, **III,** 386

Buena Vista Oil Reserve, **IV,** 71

Buenaventura River, and Frémont's explorations, **II,** 414

Buenos Aires, Pan-American conference at (1910), **IV,** 202

Buenos Aires Peace Conference (1936), and "The more abundant life," **I,** 5; and Mexican relations, **III,** 385; action taken at, **IV,** 231 f.

Buerger, Leo, and medicine, **III,** 370

Buffalo, on the Great Bend of the Arkansas, **I,** 106; Cíbola as, **I,** 375; extinction of, and the six shooter, **I,** 429; and the cow country, **II,** 78; Indians hunt the, **II,** 107; on the Great American Desert, **II,** 178; as trail makers, **II,** 421; and hide and tallow trade, **III,** 29; and the Indian, **III,** 87; as trail makers, **III,** 103 f.; destruction of, **IV,** 178; on the Great Plains, **IV,** 281; and roads, **IV,** 493; destruction of, **V,** 463

Buffalo, N. Y., and Erie Canal, **II,** 226

Buffalo Academy of Science, **IV,** 47

"Buffalo Bill," nickname for William F. Cody, **V,** 464

Buffalo Bill's Wild West Show, **IV,** 499

Buffalo Chips, as fuel, **II,** 243

Buffalo Creek, Treaty of (1802), and Indian land cessions, **III,** 100

Buffalo Grain Pool, **IV,** 307

Buffalo Hides, Indians trade in, **III,** 109

Buffalo Horn, Chief, in the Bannock War, **I,** 161

Buffalo Hunters, **II,** 156; **III,** 60; **IV,** 240

Buffalo Robes, in the Red River cart traffic, **IV,** 430

"Buffalo Skinners," occupational ballad, **I,** 148

Buffington, L. S., and skyscrapers, **V,** 88

Buffington Island, battle at, **IV,** 23

Buford, Abraham, and battle of Waxhaws, **V,** 426

Buford, Abraham, and the Cherokee Trail, **I,** 353

Buford, Fort, site of Fort Mortimer, **IV,** 29; and Fort Union, N. Dak., **V,** 341

Buford, Jefferson, and the Emigrant Aid Movement, **II,** 211

Buggy, supersedes the chaise, **I,** 319

Buhl Foundation, **II,** 314

Buick Motor Company, **I,** 140

Building and Loan Associations, and the Reconstruction Finance Corporation, **IV,** 428

Bulfinch, Charles, architect, **I,** 100; and the Capitol at Washington, **I,** 311; enlarges Faneuil Hall, **II,** 243

Bull, Dixie, captures Pemaquid, **IV,** 239

Bull, Ole, establishes Oleana, **IV,** 171

Bull, Thomas, and regicides in New England, **IV,** 438

Bull Boats, on the Colorado River, **I,** 427; on the Mississippi, **III,** 423; for river navigation, **IV,** 489

Bull-Moose Party, formation of, **IV,** 454

Bull Run, First Battle of, **I,** 111, 197; **II,** 11; **IV,** 173, 324

Bull Run, Second Battle of, **IV,** 317; **V,** 374

Bull-Whackers, or mule-skinners, **IV,** 40; and overland freighting, **IV,** 192; and wagon trains, **V,** 389

Bullard, R. E., and the Meuse-Argonne offensive, **III,** 381; and the Oise-Aisne operation, **IV,** 167

Bullfrog Mining District, **IV,** 479

Bullion, and the Assay offices, **I,** 129; and currency, **II,** 100; and the silver dollar, **II,** 157; market ratio, **IV,** 7; and seigniorage, **V,** 55

Bullitt, Alexander, editor of *The Republic,* **II,** 404

Bulloch, J. D., and the *Alabama,* **I,** 40; Confederate agent, **II,** 5; and the Confederate navy, **II,** 8; and Laird rams, **III,** 228

Bullock, Leonard H., and the Transylvania Company, **V,** 309

Bullock, Rufus B., impeached, **III**, 41

Bunau-Varilla, Philippe Jean, and the Panama revolution, **IV**, 206

Bunbury, M. Simmones, and sea fencibles, **V**, 47

Bundling, and sex relations, **V**, 61

Bunker Hill, and siege of Boston, **I**, 222; casualties in Central Burying Ground, Boston, **I**, 223; and the command, "Don't fire till you see the white of their eyes," **II**, 161; Lafayette at fiftieth anniversary of the battle of, **III**, 227; Monument Association, **III**, 351; and the American Revolution, **IV**, 467, 476; entrenchment at, **V**, 321; fought by Washington's eight months army, **V**, 419

Bunker Hill and Sullivan Mine, **III**, 254

Bunting v. Oregon, **V**, 387

Bunyan, Paul, and tall stories, **V**, 186

Burd, Fort, erected at Redstone Old Fort, **IV**, 433

Burd, James, and Forbes expedition, **II**, 298; and battle of the Loyalhanna, **III**, 312

Bureaucracy, and delegation of powers, **II**, 133

Burgess, Edward and W. Starling, American naval architects, **V**, 499

Burgess, John W., political writings of, **IV**, 302

Burgesses, House of, and representative government, **IV**, 452

Burgh, Albert Coenraets, patroonship of, **IV**, 226

Burgoyne's Invasion, and the battle of Bennington, **I**, 178; and campaign of 1777, **I**, 239; and Convention Army, **II**, 49; and the Diamond Island fight, **II**, 145; and the abandoning of Fort Edward, **II**, 189; and surrender of the British, **II**, 326; and Freeman's Farm battles, **II**, 339; and surrender of the British, **III**, 31; and Lake Champlain area, **III**, 230; and the McCrea murder, **III**, 364; defeated, **IV**, 476; and surrender of the British, **V**, 32; and Ticonderoga, **V**, 268

Burke Act (1906), and Indian land policy, **III**, 90; and Indian citizenship, **III**, 95

Burley Association, and tobacco co-operatives, **V**, 276

Burlingame Treaty of 1868, and Chinese Exclusion, **I**, 366

Burlington Company, and western land schemes, **V**, 443

Burnet, William, and colony of New York, **IV**, 115; and Oswego, **IV**, 190; and the Palatines, **IV**, 201

Burnett, Peter H., and wagon trains, **V**, 389

Burnham, D. H., architect, plans a new Chicago and San Francisco, **I**, 101; and Washington, D. C., **V**, 413

Burnham and Root, architects of the Rookery and the Monadnock block, **V**, 87

Burning, as a colonial punishment, **IV**, 382

Burning Spring, and natural gas, **II**, 372

Burns, Lucy, and woman suffrage, **V**, 478

Burns, Tommy, prize fighter, **IV**, 353

Burns, William J., detective agency of, **II**, 228; exposes Oregon land frauds, **IV**, 183

Burnside, A. E., at Antietam, **I**, 81; at Bull Run, **I**, 251; and the battle of Fredericksburg, **II**, 330; issues General Order No. 38, **II**, 376; commander in chief of Grand Army of the Republic, **II**, 407; and siege of Knoxville, **III**, 216; besieges Fort Macon, **III**, 321; and the Mud March, **IV**, 39; commands the Army of the Ohio, **IV**, 162; and the capture of Roanoke Island, **IV**, 497; and battle of South Mountain, **V**, 128; and battle of Spotsylvania Courthouse, **V**, 150; and Vallandigham incident, **V**, 355

Burnside Rifle, **IV**, 483

Burnt Corn Attack, and massacre at Fort Mims, **III**, 405

Burr, Aaron, alleged to have plotted treason at Blennerhassett House, **I**, 199; his squaw, **I**, 279; and campaigns of 1796 and 1800, **I**, 281; and Jefferson election dispute, **III**, 170; and party machines, **III**, 318; and Miranda's intrigues, **III**, 414; and martial law in New Orleans, **IV**, 110; organizes the Manhattan Company, **IV**, 119; courts the widow Prevost at the Hermitage, **IV**, 214; held prisoner at Fort Stoddert, **V**, 184

Burr, Aaron, Sr., and the Presbyterians, **IV**, 332

Burr Conspiracy, and the Blount conspiracy, **I**, 204; and writ of habeas corpus, **I**, 208; presaged by Cox insurrection, **II**, 82

Burr-Hamilton Duel, **II**, 174

Burr Trial, and presidential exemption from subpœna, **IV**, 334; and treason, **V**, 313

Burritt, Elihu, peace advocate, **I**, 197; lecturer, **III**, 260; and peace movements, **IV**, 234

Burrow, Rube, train robber, **I**, 152

Burrowes, Thomas H., and Buckshot War, **I**, 246

Burrows, J. M. D., and contract for Fort Snelling, **IV**, 322; western merchant, **V**, 444

Burt, Francis, territorial governor of Nebraska, **IV**, 80

Burt, William A., inventor of the typewriter, **III**, 148; and the solar compass, **V**, 116; and the typewriter, **V**, 336

Burton's Texas Rangers, as horse marines, **III**, 48

Bus Transportation, trade magazine, **V**, 298

Bushnell, C. S., and the *Monitor*, **IV**, 10

Bushnell, David, and Battle of the Kegs, **III**, 202; invents first practical submarine, **V**, 194; invents the torpedo, **V**, 284

Bushnell, Horace, and religious education, **IV**, 444; and religious thought and writings, **IV**, 446; **V**, 261

Bushrangers, **II**, 74

"Bushrod (Richard) and his Associates," represent Western Merchants, **II**, 161

Bushwhacking, in Kansas, **II**, 428

Bushy Run, battle of, **I**, 229; **IV**, 229

Business, and corporations, **II**, 62; public control of, **IV**, 376; big, and trust busting, **V**, 326

Business Cycle, and the panic of 1893, **IV**, 209; and relief, **IV**, 440

Bussey Institution, **I**, 25

"Buster Brown," comic character, **I**, 431

Busti, Paul, and Holland Land Company, **III**, 38

Bute, Fort, established on Iberville River, **III**, 65

Butler, Andrew P., and Brooks-Sumner Affair, **I**, 244

Butler, B. F., supplied with Gatling guns, **I**, 393; sets up doctrine of Negroes as contraband, **II**, 47; and the Dutch Gap Canal, **II**, 179; and exchange of prisoners, **II**, 232; and the bombardment of Fort Fisher, **II**, 277; nominated by Greenback party, **II**, 424; and capture of Hatteras Inlet, **III**, 17; and impeachment trial of Andrew Johnson, **III**, 77; and Army of the James, **III**, 166; enlists Negroes in the Civil War, **IV**, 84; and capture of New Orleans, **IV**, 110; and the Sanborn contracts, **V**, 26; and Soldiers and Sailors Conventions, **V**, 117

Butler, Camp, as prison camp, **I**, 279; **IV**, 347

Butler, Edward, and political rings, **IV**, 485

Butler, Elizur, and Worcester v. Georgia, **V**, 484

Butler, Henry, and showboats, **V**, 76

Butler, John, at Fort Niagara, **IV**, 130; and the Niagara Company, **IV**, 130; and battle of Oriskany, **IV**, 188; and the Wyoming massacre, **V**, 210. *See also* Butler's Rangers

Butler, M. C., and battle of Drewry's Bluff, **II**, 169

Butler, Pierce, signer of the Constitution, **II**, 39

Butler, Pierce, in West Coast Hotel Company v. Parrish, **V**, 436

Butler, Pierce Mason, and "It's a damn long time between drinks," **IV**, 145

Butler, Richard, and Hot Water battle, **III**, 51; and Indian treaty at Pittsburgh (1775), **IV**, 280

Butler, Robert, commands garrison at Fort Miami, **III**, 389

Butler, Zebulon, and the Wyoming massacre, **V**, 497

Butler Brothers, and mail-order houses, **III**, 325

Butler's Rangers, and the Cherry Valley massacre, **I**, 353; and the Wyoming massacre, **V**, 497

Butte des Morts, battle at, **II**, 320; treaty of, **V**, 5

Butter, and dairy industry, **II**, 105; and rotation of crops, **II**, 154

Butterfield, Daniel, and Black Friday (1869), **I**, 194

Butterfield, John, and the Overland Mail, **IV**, 306; **V**, 103; and the Southern Overland Mail, **V**, 130, 152, 254

"Butternuts," term used to describe Democrats opposed to Lincoln's war policy, **II**, 57

Buttrick, John, and battle on North Bridge (1775), **III**, 267

Buying Power Theory, **IV**, 455

Byam, Ezekiel, manufactures loco foco matches, **III**, 359

Byers, William Newton, publishes the *Rocky Mountain News*, **IV**, 126; Colorado printer, **IV**, 345

Byllynge, Edward, and New Jersey, **IV**, 104; **V**, 437

Byrd, James, and Forbes expedition, **II**, 298

Byrd, Richard E., polar flight of, **IV**, 293

Byrd, William, I, obtains tracts of land around Richmond, **IV**, 482; and the old regime in Virginia, **V**, 375

Byrd, William, II, as book collector, **I**, 212; names Dismal Swamp, **II**, 151; and the old regime in Virginia, **V**, 375

Byrne, Stephen, and the Holy Name Society, **III**, 40

C

Cabanne, Jean Pierre, and Chouteau and Company, **I**, 369

Cabet, Etienne, and Icaria, **III**, 66; and the socialist movement, **V**, 110

Cabeza de Vaca, Alvar Nuñez, walks from Pensacola Bay to Gulf of California, **I**, 57; *conquistadore*, **II**, 25; journey of, **IV**, 54; probably first white man to see New Mexico, **IV**, 106; and Texas, **V**, 252; and the Zuñi Indians, **V**, 515

Cabinet, appointments and senatorial confirmation, **II**, 15; and the Constitution, **II**, 36; and Convention of 1787, **II**, 51; and the Federal Government, **II**, 259; and Revolutionary committes, **IV**, 475; and the Vice-Presidency, **V**, 366

Cable, G. W., and fiction, **II**, 270

Cable Law, and naturalization, **IV**, 67; and citizenship of married women, **V**, 479

Cables, Atlantic, **I**, 135; laid by Commercial Cable Company, **I**, 434; and international communications, **I**, 439; laid by the *Great Eastern*, **II**, 414; transpacific, and the Midway Islands, **III**, 395; development of, **V**, 74; and the Yap mandate, **V**, 503

Cabot, John, discovers North America, **I**, 56; explores American coast, **IV**, 150

Cabot, Sebastian, and coastal maps, **III**, 340

Cabot, The, purchased by the Continental Navy, **IV**, 471

Cabrillo, Juan Rodríguez, explores California, **I**, 270; discovers Santa Catalina Island, **I**, 322

Cacique, **I**, 329

Caddo Indians, and Fort Belknap, **I**, 175; attack Parker's Fort, **IV**, 217; and Spanish post on the Red River, **IV**, 430

Cadillac, Antoine de la Mothe, Sieur, and Crozat grant, **II**, 93; and Fox-French Wars, **II**, 319; founds Detroit, **II**, 416; at Michilimackinac, **III**, 394; establishes Fort Pontchartrain du Detroit, **IV**, 305; investigates lead-producing area, **V**, 9

Cadillac Motor Company, **I**, 140

Cadore Letter, and Napoleon's Decrees, **IV**, 52

Cadotte, Jean Baptiste, at Chequamegon Bay, **I**, 351

Cadwalader, Thomas, and medicine, **III**, 369

Cahokia, Franciscans labor at, **II**, 325; and the fur trade, **II**, 363; and attack on St. Louis (1780), **V**, 11

Cahokia Indians, and the Algonquin family, **I**, 48; and the Illinois, **III**, 71

Cahokia Mounds, **IV**, 34

Cahuenga Capitulation, **I**, 271; **V**, 24

Cairo, The, gunboat, **II**, 180

Cajon Pass, **IV**, 221

Calash, and colonial vehicles, **V**, 359

Calaveras, and dead cities, **II**, 114

Caldwell, Charles S., and founding of Louisville Medical Institute, **III**, 369

Caldwell, James, barnstormer, **I**, 164

Caldwell, Kans., becomes famous because of trail-driver patronage, **I**, 326; as a cow town, **II**, 79

Caledonia, The, in battle of Lake Erie, **II**, 224

Calhoun, Fort, constructed, **IV**, 12

Calhoun, John C., and the "Address of the Southern Delegates," **I**, 10; and Bonus Bill, **I**, 211; elected Vice-President, **I**, 282; and the cotton kingdom, **II**, 70; and the Democratic party, **II**, 136; and the Eaton affair, **II**, 183; Jackson's hostility to, **II**, 264; and Fort Hill letter, **II**, 310; and Indian removal, **III**, 107; and the Bonus Bill, **III**, 137; and the Nashville Convention, **IV**, 55; and natural rights, **IV**, 66; and the *Washington Republican,* **IV**, 128; his *Exposition,* and nullification, **IV**, 153; and oratory, **IV**, 180; and Jackson's toast, "Our Federal Union, etc.," **IV**, 191; and the peculiar institution, **IV**, 238; and political theories, **IV**, 301; political writings of, **IV**, 302; defends slavery, **IV**, 363; and proslavery literature, **IV**, 364; and the Rip Raps contract scandal, **IV**, 486; and the soundness of slavery, **V**, 123; advocates principle of concurrent voice, **V**, 124; and the Southern Rights movement, **V**, 131; and state sovereignty, **V**, 173; and distribution of surplus revenue, **V**, 209; and Bonus Bill, **V**, 209; and the Tarpley letter, **V**, 224; and Virginia-Kentucky Resolutions, **V**, 376; and the War Department, **V**, 402; as a leader of the War Hawks, **V**,

403; his *Exposition,* and the Webster-Hayne debate, **V**, 432; plans the Yellowstone River expedition, **V**, 506

California, acquisition of, **I**, 128; Republic of, erected, **I**, 171; discovered by Cabrillo expedition, **I**, 266; emigrants to, follow the Canadian River, **I**, 302; and Compromise of 1850, **I**, 442; and Escalante-Domínguez expedition, **II**, 227; gold discovered in, **II**, 393; conquest of, **III**, 201; and the J. R. Walker expedition, **V**, 392; and discovery of the Big Trees, **V**, 392; Big Trees and Yosemite National Park, **V**, 509

California Doctrine, and irrigation, **III**, 160

California Electric Light Company, **II**, 197

California Fruit Canners Association, **II**, 297

California Fruit Growers Exchange, **I**, 379

California Gold Rush, and bandits, **I**, 152; and Fort Bernard, **I**, 180; and clipper ships, **I**, 402; and the Great American Desert, **II**, 140; and gold mining, **II**, 396; and New Mexico, **IV**, 107; and overland companies, **IV**, 192; and overland freighting, **IV**, 192; and the Great Plains, **IV**, 282; and rivers, **IV**, 491; and development of roads, **IV**, 495; and growth of San Francisco, **V**, 23; and Sutter's Fort, **V**, 212; and vigilantes, **V**, 368; and wagon trains, **V**, 389; and the westward movement, **V**, 451

California Gulch, lead deposits discovered at, **III**, 254

California Institute of Technology, **V**, 44

California Missions, **I**, 275; **III**, 175

California Trail, Grattan massacre on, **I**, 127; and Kansas City, Mo., **III**, 196; and water holes, **V**, 421

Californian, started by Colton and Semple, **IV**, 126

Call of the Wild, written by Jack London, **I**, 180

Callaway Girls, **I**, 215

Caller, James, and battle of Burnt Corn, **I**, 257

Calomel, and yellow fever, **V**, 504

Calumet and Hecla Corporation, **II**, 57

Calumet Dance, **III**, 97

Calvert, Benedict, renounces the Roman Catholic faith, **III**, 349

Calvert, Cecil, and Maryland, **III**, 348

Calvert, Charles, disputes Penn's claims to Maryland, **III**, 349

Calvert, George, and Maryland, **III**, 348. *See also* Baltimore, Lord

Calvert, Leonard, and Maryland, **III**, 349

Calvinism, and Arminianism, **I**, 108; and the Baptists, **I**, 161; and the Edwardian Theology, **II**, 189; and change to social Christianity, **II**, 340; and frontier preaching, **II**, 353; and philosophical thought and writings, **IV**, 263; and Puritanism, **IV**, 384; and American religion, **IV**, 442; and religious thought and writings, **IV**,

446; and the Synod of Dort, **V**, 215; and theological writings, **V**, 261; and the Westminster Confession, **V**, 448

Calvo Doctrine, and concessions, **II**, 1; and non-intervention, **IV**, 139

Cambridge Agreement, and the Great Migration, **II**, 418

Cambridge Ephemeris, **IV**, 99

Cambridge Platform, and Calvinism, **I**, 277; and church union movements, **I**, 373; and Congregationalists, **II**, 16; and the Saybrook Platform, **V**, 37; and the Westminster Confession, **V**, 448

Camden, Battle of, **IV**, 477; **V**, 129

Camden and Amboy Railroad, **IV**, 105, 406

Cameron, A. S., & Company, **IV**, 355

Cameron, Alexander, represents Cherokees, **II**, 160

Cameron, Simon, and Civil War contracts, **I**, 391

Cameron-Quay-Penrose Machine, **II**, 64; **IV**, 244

Caminetti, Anthony, commissioner general of immigration, **III**, 163

Cammock, Thomas, and settlement of Saco Bay, **V**, 3

Camp, Walter, and football, **II**, 298; **V**, 149

Camp Bird Gold Mine, **II**, 396; **V**, 25

Camp Chase, and atrocity stories, **I**, 136; and the Northwest Conspiracy, **IV**, 150, 347

Camp Douglas, Copperheads charged with plotting release of prisoners from, **II**, 58; and Northwest Conspiracy, **IV**, 150; as prison camp, **IV**, 347

Camp Jackson, capture of, **IV**, 339

Camp Meeting, evolution of the, **I**, 143; at Cane Ridge, **I**, 304; brings religion to frontier family, **II**, 243; and frontier preaching, **II**, 353; and hymn writing, **III**, 65; and the Leatherwood God, **III**, 258; and loneliness, **III**, 297; and frontier missions, **III**, 418; and the protracted meeting, **IV**, 367; and religion, **IV**, 442, 444

Campaign Expense Act of 1910, **I**, 293

Campaign Investigating Committee, **I**, 294

Campaign of 1800, Jefferson elected in, **II**, 136; and Jefferson-Burr election dispute, **III**, 170; and western democracy, **V**, 435

Campaign of 1824, and election of the President, **II**, 192; and National Republican party, **IV**, 62; congressional caucus used for the last time in, **IV**, 137

Campaign of 1828, and the political rally, **IV**, 414

Campaign of 1840, Liberty party in, **III**, 272; and the political rally, **IV**, 414; and stump-speaking, **V**, 192; Whig slogan, **V**, 273; and the Whig party, **V**, 455

Campaign of 1844, and the Raleigh Letter, **IV**, 412; and the term "roorback," **IV**, 501; and the Whig party, **V**, 456

Campaign of 1852, and Free Soil party, **II**, 334

Campaign of 1856, and Raleigh Conference of Southern Governors, **IV**, 412

Campaign of 1860, and the "Wide-awakes," **V**, 462

Campaign of 1864, and Loyal Publication Societies, **III**, 312

Campaign of 1868, keynote of, **III**, 264

Campaign of 1872, and Greenback Movement, **II**, 423

Campaign of 1876, and election of the President, **II**, 192; and elections, **II**, 194; and Reconstruction, **IV**, 426; and the Wormley conference, **V**, 495

Campaign of 1888, and free trade, **II**, 334

Campaign of 1892, and the McKinley tariff, **III**, 366

Campaign of 1896, and the Dingley tariff, **II**, 147; and the political rally, **IV**, 414

Campaign of 1912, and the Progressive Movement, **IV**, 356

Campaign of 1916, and the Progressive Movement, **I**, 250; and the World War, **V**, 491

Campaign of 1928, and religion, **IV**, 443; and the Solid South, **V**, 118

Campaign of 1936, and radio in politics, **IV**, 398; and the United Mine Workers, **V**, 346

Campaign Resources and Uses, legislation dealing with, **II**, 64; and political assessments, **IV**, 295; and publicity laws, **IV**, 379

Campaign Slogans, **V**, 98

Campaign Songs, **I**, 280

Campaigns, Political, and party platforms, **IV**, 285

Campbell, Alexander, and the Disciples of Christ, **II**, 149; frontier religious leader, **IV**, 444; and Rice debates, **IV**, 480; and the Baptists, **V**, 446

Campbell, David, and Joplin lead mining district, **III**, 181

Campbell, H. W., carries on private experiments in dry farming, **II**, 171

Campbell, Hugh, attempts to treat with Indians of the Illinois, **III**, 68

Campbell, J. A., and Hampton Roads conference, **III**, 7

Campbell, John, publisher *Boston News-Letter*, **I**, 223; **IV**, 123, 127

Campbell, John, agent for the Illinois and Wabash Company, **III**, 69; at Falls of the Ohio, **IV**, 162; lays out Pittsburgh, **IV**, 280

Campbell, John B., and battle of Mississinewa, **III**, 419

Campbell, Robert, descends the Yukon River, **V**, 512

Campbell, Robert, establishes Fort Laramie, **III**, 245; and Ashley's expeditions, **V**, 310

Campbell, Thomas, and the Disciples of Christ, **II**, 149

Campbell, William, and battle of King's Mountain, **III**, 212

Canada, proposed cession of, **I**, 40; fisheries dispute with, **I**, 41; Arnold's attack on, **I**, 120; and expansion, **II**, 233; and Fenian raids, **II**, 267; invasion of and Indian activities, **III**, 88; and International Joint Commission, **III**, 140; reciprocity with, **IV**, 422; attempts to invade, during the Revolution, **IV**, 476; treaties with, **V**, 317; and the War Hawks, **V**, 403; demand for, and the War of 1812, **V**, 405

Canadian-American Reciprocity Treaty, and the fisheries question, **II**, 277

Canadian-American Relations, and the Bayard-Chamberlain Treaty, **I**, 169

Canadians, as political exiles, **IV**, 295

Canal Zone, **IV**, 205; **V**, 247

Canals, and agriculture, **I**, 27; and aqueducts, **I**, 93; and the Baltimore and Ohio Railroad, **I**, 150; Chesapeake and Delaware Canal, **I**, 354; Chesapeake and Ohio Canal, **I**, 354; and growth of cities, **I**, 378; Delaware and Hudson Canal, **II**, 132; Dutch Gap Canal, **II**, 179; Erie Canal, **II**, 225; Federal aid for, **II**, 255; Gallatin's Report on, **II**, 367; and government ownership, **II**, 404; Illinois and Michigan Canal, **III**, 69; Indiana State Canals, **III**, 113; and the industrial revolution, **III**, 118; as internal improvements, **III**, 136; James River and Kanawha Canal, **III**, 166; and locks, **III**, 292; Louisville and Portland Canal, **III**, 310; Middlesex Canal, **III**, 395; and mill streams, **III**, 404; Ohio State Canals, **IV**, 165; and the panic of 1837, **IV**, 208; in Pennsylvania, **IV**, 243, 245; and the public domain, **IV**, 370; and railroads, **IV**, 407; and state debts, **IV**, 456; influence on public roads, **IV**, 495; St. Marys Falls Ship Canal, **V**, 14; Santee Canal, **V**, 31; South Carolina Canal, **V**, 126; and state debts, **V**, 168; and the stock market, **V**, 183; and the General Survey Act of 1824, **V**, 209; and domestic trade, **V**, 292; and shifts in trade routes and centers, **V**, 299; and transportation and travel, **V**, 307; Union Canal, **V**, 342; and the urban drift, **V**, 352; Wabash and Erie Canal, **V**, 385; and wagoners, **V**, 390; and water power, **V**, 422; as inland waterways, **V**, 425; Welland Canal, **V**, 433

Canby, E. R. S., and the surrender of the Confederate armies, **I**, 385; and the Modoc War, **IV**, 4; and operations on the Rio Grande, **IV**, 485; and battles of Tule Lake, **V**, 329; and battle of Valverde, **V**, 356

Cancer, **II**, 150

Cancer Institute Act of 1937, **III**, 22

Candles, for lighting, **III**, 276; and the whaling industry, **V**, 452

Candy Industries, **II**, 105

Cane Ridge Revival, **II**, 419

Canfield, Richard, American gambler, **II**, 369

Cannibalism, practised in Aztalan, **I**, 144; in Donner Party, **II**, 161; and Port Royal (S. C.), **IV**, 315; on Smoky Hill Trail, **V**, 103

Canning Industry, and drying fruits and vegetables, **II**, 169; and food packing, **II**, 297; and fruit growing, **II**, 354; and glass, **II**, 391; and the tin can, **V**, 271

Cannon, as munitions, **IV**, 44

Cannon, Joseph G., and powers of the Speaker, **II**, 18; as floor leader, **II**, 287; as Speaker of the House, **V**, 142

Cannonism, and "Standpatters," **V**, 158

Canoes, birch-bark used for, **I**, 190; Indians instruct colonists in use of, **III**, 88; on the Mississippi, **III**, 424; and water routes, **IV**, 316; for river navigation, **IV**, 489; in transportation, **V**, 306; *voyageurs* employed by fur companies to paddle, **V**, 385

Canonchet, joins King Philip's War, **III**, 210

Cantigny, American Expeditionary Forces at, **I**, 59; **V**, 492

Cantino, Alberto, map of, **III**, 340

Canton, trade with, **I**, 128; **II**, 55

Canton Island, under United States jurisdiction, **IV**, 195

Cape Ann, and the Dorchester Company, **II**, 162

Cape Cod, discovered by Champlain (1605), **I**, 57

Cape Cod Canal, **I**, 303; **IV**, 488

Cape Fear, settled, **IV**, 144

Cape Horn, and clipper ships, **I**, 402

Cape May, as a summer resort, **IV**, 460

Capen House, architecture of, **I**, 99

Capital, and credit, **II**, 84; and United States as creditor nation, **II**, 85; and the decline of thrift, **V**, 266; and the triangular trade, **V**, 297

Capital, controversy concerning location of national, **I**, 132; location of, and the Public Credit Act, **IV**, 369

Capital Punishment, electrocution as, **II**, 200; hanging as, **III**, 7; and humanitarianism, **III**, 59; lethal gas as, **III**, 265; and colonial punishments, **IV**, 382

Capital-Stock Tax, **V**, 227

Capitalism, and socialism, **V**, 110; and distribution of wealth, **V**, 429

Capitol, early architecture of, **I**, 100

Capitol Syndicate, forms XIT ranch, **V**, 154

Capone, Al., and lawlessness, **III**, 253; racketeer, **IV**, 395

Capper-Ketcham Act (1928), and agricultural education, **I**, 25

Capper-Volstead Act of 1922, for farm relief, **II**, 249

Capt. Jack, and the Modoc War, **IV**, 4

Caracas, mixed commission at, **V**, 359

Card Playing, I, 69

Cardinal, Jean, and Galena-Dubuque mining district, II, 367; at Prairie du Chien, IV, 328

Cardis, Louis, and the Salt War, V, 19

Cardozo, Albert, and the Tweed Ring, V, 333

Care, Henry, and rights of Englishmen, IV, 484

Carey, Mathew, and book publishing, I, 213; and epidemiology, II, 221

Carey Act of 1894, and irrigation, III, 161; and reclamation, IV, 423

Carey's Atlas, V, 283

Caribbean Area, and foreign policy, II, 305; and imperialism, III, 79; marines in, III, 343; and Spanish-American War, V, 137

Caribbean Policy, and the Gulf of Mexico, III, 389; and the Monroe Doctrine, IV, 14; and nonintervention, IV, 139

Carillon, Fort, established, III, 229; as Fort Ticonderoga, V, 268; and Vermont, V, 361

Carleton, Guy, and Rouse's Point boundary controversy, IV, 503

Carleton, James H., and Mangas Coloradas' surrender, III, 331; in New Mexico, IV, 107

Carleton College, and Congregationalists, II, 17

Carlisle, J. G., as Speaker of the House, V, 142

Carlisle, Lord, and Peace Commission of 1778, IV, 231

Carlisle, Pa., arsenal at, I, 122

Carlisle Indian School, founded, III, 86

Carlotta, Confederate colony of, V, 68

Carlsbad Caverns National Park, IV, 218

Carmack, Edward W., shot by Robin Cooper, I, 129

Carmack, George, and the Klondike rush, III, 214; as a prospector, IV, 364

Carncross and Dixey Minstrels, popularize songs, V, 120

Carnegie, Andrew, benefactions and gifts of, I, 177; rise of, II, 312; gives to libraries, III, 273; and Mesabi Iron Range, III, 379; and philanthropy, IV, 260; and the United States Steel Corporation, V, 348

Carnegie Company, and the Homestead strike, III, 43; and consolidations, III, 156; and steel strikes, V, 180

Carnegie Corporation, and adult education, I, 14; endowment of, II, 314; finances the American Law Institute, III, 251; supports National Research Council, IV, 62

Carnegie Endowment for International Peace, II, 314; IV, 235

Carnegie Foundation, endowment of, II, 314; and medical professorships, III, 369

Carnegie Institute of Technology, V, 44

Carnegie Institution of Washington, and foreign archives, I, 103; endowment of, II, 314; and guides to foreign archives, III, 34; publishes

Estabrook's report on the Jukes, III, 189; started rather than National University, IV, 64; and restoration of St. Augustine, V, 6; and Washington, D. C., V, 413

Carolina, and the Albemarle Settlements, I, 46; as a proprietary province, IV, 362

Carolina Proprietors, and Margravate of Azilia, I, 144; granted the Bahama Islands, I, 146; remove Culpeper, II, 96; and the Granville Grant, II, 412; grant to, IV, 144; and Port Royal, IV, 316; grant to, V, 125

Carolinas, Sherman's march through, V, 242

Caroline, Fort, building of, II, 288; destroyed by the Spaniards, IV, 315; and founding of St. Augustine, V, 6; captured by Spanish, V, 126

Caroline, The, and the McLeod case, III, 366

Carondelet, Baron, and the McGillivray Incident, III, 365; and Spanish-Indian relations, V, 140

Carondelet, Fort, erected by the Chouteaus, I, 370

Carondelet, The, gunboat, II, 180; in capture of Island Number Ten, III, 161

Carpenter, C. C., and boomer movement, I, 215; Oklahoma squatter, IV, 169

Carpenter, S. D., and the development of the reaper, IV, 419

Carpetbaggers, and freedmen, II, 335; and the Black and Tan Convention, III, 420; and Radical rule in the South, IV, 395; and Reconstruction, IV, 426 f.; and Scalawags, V, 37; and Democratic party in the Solid South, V, 118

Carr, Eugene A., crushes the Cheyennes under Tall Bull, V, 420

Carr, Robert, demands surrender of New Amstel, IV, 95

Carrell, Alexis, awarded Nobel prize in medicine, III, 370

Carriages, and colonial vehicles, V, 358

Carrier, Willis H., invents an improved air washer, I, 34

Carrington, H. B., and the Fetterman massacre, II, 268; builds Fort Phil Kearny, III, 200; begins erection of forts on Bozeman Trail, III, 245; and Fort Reno (Wyo.), IV, 448

Carrizal, Pershing at, III, 388

Carroll, Charles, on mission to Montreal, I, 297; signer of the Declaration of Independence, II, 124; seeks to win Canada to the American cause, III, 230

Carroll, Daniel, signer of the Constitution, II, 39

Carroll, James, and yellow fever, V, 505

Carroll, John, and the beginning of Catholic ecclesiastical legislation in Baltimore, I, 151; and Catholicism, I, 323; Catholic bishop, II, 159; seeks to win Canada to the American cause (1776), III, 230

Carroll, John, painter, **I**, 123

Carson, Kit, early guide, **II**, 236; mountain man, **II**, 362; as hunter, **III**, 60; appointed to Indian Commission, **III**, 95; and Kearny's march to California, **III**, 201; contacts the Mohave Indians, **IV**, 4; mountain man, **IV**, 37; punishes the Navaho Indians, **IV**, 68, 107; scout, **V**, 46; at Taos, **V**, 219; and battle of Valverde, **V**, 356

Carson, Moses B., and Missouri Fur Company, **V**, 13

Carson Pass, **IV**, 221

Cartagena, attack on (1740), **III**, 173

Carte de la Louisiane, by Delisle, **V**, 282

Carter, James G., advocates consolidation of schools, **V**, 41

Carter, Robert, and the old regime in Virginia, **V**, 375

Carter v. Carter Coal Company, **II**, 428

Carteret, George, gets East Jersey, **II**, 182; joint proprietor of New Jersey, **IV**, 104; original proprietor of New Jersey, **IV**, 105; and New Jersey, **IV**, 362; receives East Jersey, **V**, 438; York leases New Jersey to, **V**, 508

Carteret, Philip, admitted to Elizabethtown Associates, **II**, 202; appointed governor of New Jersey, **IV**, 104; and councils of the New Jersey proprietors, **IV**, 105

Carter's Valley, and battle of Long Island Flats, **III**, 299

Cartier, Jacques, explorations of, **I**, 57; and maps, **III**, 340; and New France, **IV**, 100; discovers the St. Lawrence River, **IV**, 150; explores St. Lawrence River, **V**, 10

Cartoons, Nast's, **IV**, 55

Cartwright, Peter, frontier preacher, **I**, 376

Carver, John, first governor of New Plymouth Colony, **IV**, 112; and the Pilgrims, **IV**, 271

Carver, Jonathan, sets out to find Northwest Passage, **II**, 320; and Minnesota, **III**, 410; visits Prairie du Chien, **IV**, 328; arrives at the Falls of St. Anthony, **V**, 6; describes Sauk Indian village, **V**, 33 f.

Carver, W. F., and the Wild West show, **V**, 464

Casco, Treaty of, ends King Philip's War, **III**, 211

Case, Jerome I., and the threshing machine, **II**, 248; **V**, 266

Casein, chief protein of milk, **II**, 105

Casement, Dan, and bluestem pastures, **I**, 206

Casey, Joseph J., and *Hening's Statutes,* **III**, 26

"Casey Jones," ballad, **I**, 148; **II**, 293

Casimir, Fort, erected, **IV**, 55

Cass, G. W., wheat farm, **I**, 208

Cass, Lewis, and the American Fur Company, **I**, 61; and Butte des Morts Council, **I**, 263; candidate for President, **I**, 284; and the Chicago treaties, **I**, 358; and Compromise of 1850, **I**, 442; and Lake Superior copper, **II**, 57; and

"fifty-four forty," **II**, 271; Van Buren's votes prevent election of, **II**, 334; becomes ex-officio superintendent of Indian Affairs, **III**, 91; and liquor in the fur trade, **III**, 282; in Minnesota, **III**, 411; and popular sovereignty, **IV**, 309; and treaty of Prairie du Chien, **IV**, 329; negotiates treaty of St. Marys, **V**, 14; advocates squatter sovereignty, **V**, 96; and the Winnebago War (1827), **V**, 471

Cass and Butler Almanac, **I**, 52

Cassatt, Mary, painter, **I**, 123

Castaño de Sosa Explorations, and Texas, **V**, 252

Castigator, **I**, 3

Castillo Explorations, and Texas, **V**, 252

Castine, Baron, and Penobscot, **IV**, 249

Castine, Me., and dead cities, **II**, 114; and the Penobscot Expedition, **IV**, 249

Castle Square Opera Company, **IV**, 178

Castle Thunder, Confederate prison, **II**, 8

Castle William, as fortification, **II**, 311; erected on Governors Island, **II**, 406

Castration, as a colonial punishment, **IV**, 383

Caswell, Fort, and battle of Long Island Flats, **III**, 299

Cat Nation. *See* Erie Indians

Cataract, The, steamboat race of, **V**, 178

Catawba Indians, and Congress of Augusta (1763), **I**, 138; and the Shawnee, **V**, 65; and the Virginia Indian Company, **V**, 379; and Great Warriors Path, **V**, 408

Catfish Camp, Washington (Pa.) as, **V**, 415

Cather, Willa, and fiction, **II**, 270

Catholic Church, and Americanism, **I**, 67; and the Baltimore Councils, **I**, 151; and birth control, **I**, 191; and colleges, **I**, 413; and the Sacred Congregation de Propaganda Fide, **II**, 16; and the Dominicans, **II**, 159; and the Eucharistic Congress at Chicago, **II**, 229; and the Faribault plan, **II**, 244; and intolerance, **III**, 147; and Irish immigration, **III**, 154; and frontier missions, **III**, 418; and nativism, **IV**, 64; and Oregon missions, **IV**, 184; and the Paulists, **IV**, 226; and religion, **IV**, 442; and Trappist monasteries, **V**, 312

Catholic University of America, **I**, 324

Catholic World, established by the Paulists, **IV**, 226

Catlin, George, and the Indian, **II**, 235; on board the *Yellowstone,* **V**, 506

Catskill Aqueduct, **V**, 330

Catt, Carrie Chapman, and woman suffrage, **V**, 478

Cattle Associations, and rodeos, **IV**, 499

Cattle Brands, and rustlers, **I**, 327; and cow custom, **II**, 79; and open range cattle period, **IV**, 177; and rodeos, **IV**, 499

Cattle Drives, and army posts, **I**, 118; on the Chis-

holm Trail, **I**, 368; and growth of cow towns, **II**, 79; and fencing laws, **II**, 266; and Goodnight Loving Trail, **II**, 400; and the Long Drive, **III**, 298; and Missouri, Kansas and Texas Railway, **III**, 427; and open range cattle period, **IV**, 177; and stampedes, **V**, 155; and trail drivers, **V**, 302; from Wichita, **V**, 461

Cattle Industry, and the Atchison, Topeka and Santa Fé Railroad, **I**, 134; and barbed wire, **I**, 163; and Dodge City, **II**, 156; and food, **II**, 294; and the Great Plains, **IV**, 282; and the Southwest, **V**, 133; and stockyards, **V**, 184; Texas leads in, **V**, 255; and destruction of the buffalo, **V**, 463

Cattle Pastures, **I**, 206

Cattle Range, cowboys as citizens of, **II**, 81

Cattle Trails, and Ogallala, **IV**, 159

Caucus, Congressional, and campaign pledges, **I**, 292; and election of the President, **II**, 191; and the nominating system, **IV**, 137; and the notification speech, **IV**, 153; and the Presidency, **IV**, 333; and direct primary, **IV**, 341

Caucus, Party, selects Speaker of the House, **V**, 142

Caucus, Primary, as method of nominating candidates, **IV**, 137

Cavaliers, as political exiles, **IV**, 295

Cave-in-Rock, river pirates at, **I**, 152; Mason Band at, **III**, 351

Cavendish, Fort, later name of Fort de Chartres, **I**, 347

Cavendish, Lord, and the Virginia Company of London, **V**, 377

Cayuga Indians, one of the Five Nations, **II**, 279; of the Iroquois League, **III**, 159; and treaty of La Famine, **III**, 226; and Sullivan-Clinton campaign, **V**, 202

Cayuse War, caused by the Whitman massacre, **V**, 461

Cazenove, Theophile, and the Holland Land Company, **III**, 38

Caziques, and Fundamental Constitutions of Carolina, **I**, 316

Cease and Desist, orders to, **II**, 264

Cedar Creek, attack at, and Sheridan's ride, **V**, 69

Cedar Post, established, **III**, 431

Cellophane, and the rayon industry, **IV**, 418

Céloron de Bienville, expedition of, **II**, 342, 344; **III**, 295; **IV**, 12; and discovery of the Ohio River, **IV**, 162; expedition of, **IV**, 165, 266, 316; **V**, 359

Celotex, uses cane fiber, **V**, 200

Cement, used in locks, **III**, 292

Cemetery Ridge, and battle of Gettysburg, **II**, 386

Censorship, **II**, 337; **III**, 400; **V**, 492

Census, Bureau of, **I**, 432; and Congress, **II**, 18;

and Department of the Interior, **III**, 134; transferred to the Department of Commerce, **III**, 135; under Department of State, **V**, 162; and vital statistics, **V**, 381

Centennial Exposition, and architecture, **I**, 100; and manufacturing, **III**, 337; "Spirit of '76" exhibited at, **V**, 146

Centinel of Freedom, one of the first newspapers in Newark, **IV**, 121

Centinel of the North-Western Territory, **IV**, 124, 127; **V**, 44

Central American Court, and Bryan-Chamorro Treaty, **I**, 245

Central-American Peace Conferences, **IV**, 232

Central Bank for Co-operatives, **II**, 245

Central Canal, **III**, 114

Central Overland, California and Pikes Peak Express, **III**, 258; **IV**, 193, 510

Central Pacific Railroad, and development of California, **I**, 274; and internal improvements, **III**, 138; subsidies granted to, **V**, 195; and rail transportation, **V**, 309; and the Union Pacific, **V**, 342

Centralization, and the Civil War, **I**, 389; trend toward, in Federal-state relations, **II**, 263; and Slaughter House cases, **V**, 89; and state government, **V**, 170; and U. S. v. Lanza, **V**, 349

Century Dictionary, **II**, 146

Century Magazine, **III**, 323

Century of Progress Exposition, **I**, 356; **V**, 464

Cerro Gordo, battle of, **II**, 134; **III**, 386

Certificates of Purchasing Agents, **IV**, 471

Chaboillez, occupies Pembina, **IV**, 240

Chain Gangs, **II**, 53

Chain Stores, and the distribution of merchandise, **II**, 152; Five-and-Ten-Cent stores as, **II**, 279; and price maintenance, **IV**, 340; and the Robinson-Patman Act, **IV**, 497; and super markets, **V**, 205

Chaise, The, makers of, **I**, 319; in travel, **V**, 306; and colonial vehicles, **V**, 359

Chalmers, Lionel, and epidemics, **II**, 221

Chamber of Commerce of the United States, **IV**, 358

Chamberlin, Clarence, flies the Atlantic, **I**, 143

Chambers, Joseph, establishes government factory at St. Stephens, **V**, 15

Chambers, Thomas, settles Kingston, N. Y., **III**, 213

Chambersburg, Pa., burning of, **V**, 68

Chambly, Fort, capture of, **I**, 297; **IV**, 481; **V**, 9

Chamizal Tract, and the Mexican boundary, **III**, 383; and rivers in American diplomacy, **IV**, 492

Champion v. Ames, **III**, 304

Champlain, Samuel de, explorations of, **I**, 57; passes site of Crown Point, **II**, 93; explorations of, **II**, 344; on the Great Lakes, **II**, 415; and

Lake Huron, **III**, 61; and the gun, **III**, 92; mentions Isles of Shoals, **III**, 162; and Lake Champlain, **III**, 229; visits Maine, **III**, 326; map by, **III**, 340; describes Monhegan Island, **IV**, 9; lands in New Hampshire, **IV**, 101; and Nicolet's explorations, **IV**, 133; and Lake Ontario, **IV**, 175; and the St. Croix settlement, **V**, 7; and topographic mapping, **V**, 282; discovers Vermont, **V**, 361

Champlain Canal, and the Hudson River, **III**, 55

Chamuscado, Francisco Sánchez, explorations of, **IV**, 106; and the Rodríguez expedition, **IV**, 500

Chancellorsville, as a trench battle, **V**, 321

Chanco, saves Jamestown in the Great Massacre, **II**, 418

Chandler, John, and battle of Stoney Creek, **V**, 185

Chandler, W. W., and refrigerator cars, **IV**, 437

Chandler, Zachariah, member of Committee on the Conduct of the War, **I**, 436; among the leaders of the Radical Republicans, **IV**, 395

Chandler Act of 1938, revises bankruptcy statutes, **I**, 159

Channing, William Ellery, and the abolition movement, **I**, 3; and Concord Group, **II**, 3; transcendentalist, **II**, 340; and the Massachusetts Peace Society, **IV**, 233; and philosophical thought and writings, **IV**, 263; and religious periodicals, **IV**, 445; and religious thought and writings, **IV**, 446; and theological writings, **V**, 261; and the Unitarians, **V**, 344

Chanute, Octave, and gliding experiments, **I**, 142

Chaparral, and drouths, **II**, 170

Chaperonage, and manners, **III**, 334

Chapin Mine, **III**, 374

Chaplin, Charles S., introduced to the screen by Mack Sennett, **IV**, 32

Chapman, J. Wilbur, revivalist, **IV**, 464

Chapman, John (Johnny Appleseed), **I**, 90

Chapman, William, and showboats, **V**, 76

Chapman, William S., and land speculation, **III**, 240

Chapman's *Drawing Book,* woodcuts in, **V**, 482

Chapultepec, battle of, **III**, 386

Charbonneau, Toussaint, interpreter of Lewis and Clark expedition, **III**, 266

Chariot, for travel, **V**, 306

Charity, and unemployment, **II**, 136; private, **IV**, 260

Charity, The, lands three Devon cows, **II**, 103

Charity Organization Movement, **IV**, 227, 260; **V**, 109

Charity Schools, **II**, 186; **V**, 39

Charles, Fort, taken by the Indians, **IV**, 240

Charles, Joseph, founder of the *Missouri Gazette,* **IV**, 124; first printer of Missouri, **IV**, 346

Charlesfort, abandonment of, **IV**, 315; burned by the Spanish, **V**, 126

Charleston, S. C., planted by the English, **II**, 116; city directory appears in, **II**, 148; earthquake, **II**, 181; Huguenot Church, **III**, 57; in Queen Anne's War, **IV**, 389; siege at (1779), **IV**, 477; during Southern campaigns (1780–81), **V**, 129

Charleston and Hamburg Railroad, and internal improvements, **III**, 138; financing and construction of, **IV**, 406

Charleston *Mercury,* southern newspaper, **V**, 123

Charleston *News and Courier,* and Tillmanism, **V**, 269

Charlestown (Mass.) Dock, **II**, 156

Charlotte, Camp, established, **II**, 177

Charlotte, Fort, **I**, 353; **II**, 3

Charlton, E. P., and Company, Woolworth combines with, **II**, 279

Charter Colonies, and governors, **I**, 418; and British colonial policy, **I**, 421

Charter Oak, Connecticut's charter of 1662 hidden in, **II**, 22

Charter of Liberties, adopted by York's proprietary, **V**, 508

Charter of Privileges, as the established government of Pennsylvania, **IV**, 242

Charters, and privilege in colonial governments, **IV**, 350

Chartres, Fort de, census of 1723, **I**, 267; problem of British occupation of, **II**, 90; commanded by D'Artaguette, **II**, 110; founding of, **II**, 346; **III**, 67; Laclede at, **III**, 361; **V**, 11

Chase, E. B., and abolitionist literature, **I**, 3

Chase, Salmon P., and Appeal to the Independent Democrats, **I**, 89; agitates for an improved banking system, **I**, 157; and campaign of 1860, **I**, 285; and financing of the Civil War, **I**, 384; and motto, "In God We Trust," **III**, 81; and judicial review, **III**, 183; and the Kansas-Nebraska Act, **III**, 197; and legal tender cases, **III**, 262; leader of the Liberty party, **III**, 272; and the Matilda Lawrence case, **III**, 359; and Mississippi v. Johnson, **III**, 425; elected as governor of Ohio, **IV**, 161; and the Ohio State Antislavery Society, **IV**, 165; and the Pomeroy Circular, **IV**, 305; and test oath cases, **V**, 250

Chase, Samuel, and the Alexandria Conference, **I**, 47; and the Alien and Sedition Acts, **I**, 49; on mission to Montreal, **I**, 297; signer of the Declaration of Independence, **II**, 124; impeachment of, **III**, 76; seeks to win Canada to the American cause (1776), **III**, 230; and presidential exemption from subpœna, **IV**, 334

Chase, William Merritt, painter, **I**, 123

Chassanis, Peter, and New York land speculation, **IV**, 116

Chateau Thierry, and the Aisne Defensive, **I**,

38; American Expeditionary Forces at, **I**, 59; and the battle of Belleau Wood, **I**, 175; American Army at, **V**, 492

Chattanooga, battle of, **II**, 82; Army of Tennessee at, **V**, 242; Terry's Texas Rangers at, **V**, 249

Chaudière River, and Arnold's attack on Quebec, **I**, 120

Chauncey, Isaac, and Great Lakes naval campaign of 1812, **II**, 416; and capture of Fort George, **IV**, 130; at Oswego, **IV**, 191; and operations at Sackett's Harbor, **V**, 2; and capture of York (Toronto), **V**, 507

Chautauqua Movement, and adult education, **I**, 14; develops from camp meeting, **I**, 280; and Sunday Schools, **V**, 204

Chauvin, Louis, and Spanish-Missouri Fur Company, **V**, 141

Check Currency, overexpansion of, as cause of inflation, **III**, 121

Checkoff, and the United Mine Workers, **V**, 346

Checks and Balances, in first state constitution of New York, **II**, 73; by executive and Congress, **II**, 233; and the Federal Government, **II**, 257; and political theories, **IV**, 300; and separation of powers, **IV**, 327; and tyranny, **V**, 337

Cheese, and rotation of crops, **II**, 154

Cheever, Ezekiel, author of *Latin Accidence*, **V**, 40; early teacher, **V**, 43

Cheeves, Langdon, president of Second Bank of the United States, **I**, 155

Chemical Foundation, **I**, 50

Chemical Society of Philadelphia, **III**, 117

Chemical Warfare, and army supply, **I**, 119; and poison gas, **I**, 136; gas in, **I**, 350; and laws of war, **V**, 398

Chemistry, in manufacturing, **III**, 338

Chemung Canal, and locks, **III**, 292

Cheney, E. P., wheat farm, **I**, 208

Chequamegon Bay, Jesuit mission at, **III**, 174; **V**, 205

Cherokee Advocate, edited by William Potter Ross, **IV**, 127

Cherokee Country, visited by DeSoto, **II**, 141

Cherokee Indians, and Congress of Augusta (1763), **I**, 138; claim region traversed by Avery's Trace, **I**, 142; and the title Beloved Woman, **I**, 176; and Carter's Valley settlement, **I**, 320; overwhelmed by Chickasaws, **I**, 360; defeated by Creeks, **II**, 86; road opened through territory of, **II**, 98; lose land on the Cumberland River, **II**, 98; and the Dawes Commission, **II**, 113; Delaware incorporate with, **II**, 131; and Donelson's Line, **II**, 160; and the treaty of Dumplin Creek, **II**, 176; one of the Five Civilized Tribes, **II**, 279; and the Florida War, **II**, 291; and the Galphin claim, **II**, 368; in Georgia, **II**, 379; and the Great Trading and War Path,

II, 420; and treaty of Hard Labor, **III**, 9; and Holston treaty, **III**, 39; and settlement of Holston Valley, **III**, 39; and treaty of Hopewell, **III**, 45; in the Revolution, **III**, 88; compose Indian brigade, **III**, 94; and Indian Factory of Virginia, **III**, 97; during the Civil War, **III**, 98; land cessions of, **III**, 99 f.; removal of, **III**, 107; and intermarried citizens, **III**, 135; and treaty of Lochaber, **III**, 290; and battle of Long Island Flats, **III**, 299; besiege Fort Loudon, **III**, 304; and the Melungeons, **III**, 371; as Mound Builders, **IV**, 35; and treaty of New Echota, **IV**, 97; and treaty of Nogales, **IV**, 136; conquered by North Carolina troops, **IV**, 144; removed to Oklahoma, **IV**, 168; and Panton, Leslie & Co., **IV**, 211; and Fort Prince George, **IV**, 342; and prospectors, **IV**, 364; and treaty at Saluda, **V**, 19; and the Shawnee, **V**, 65; and treaty of Fort Stanwix (1768), **V**, 159; and the Sycamore Shoals treaty, **V**, 215; in Tennessee, **V**, 242; on the Tennessee River, **V**, 244; and the Trail of Tears, **V**, 303; and the Transylvania Company, **V**, 309; and Tryon's line, **V**, 328; occupy Turkey Town, **V**, 331; and the Virginia Indian Company, **V**, 379; and Virginia v. Transylvania Company, **V**, 380; and Great Warriors Path, **V**, 408; and Watauga settlement, **V**, 421; and Worcester v. Georgia, **V**, 484; and the Yamasee War, **V**, 501

Cherokee Nation v. Georgia, and states' rights, **V**, 176

Cherokee Phœnix, **I**, 352

Cherokee Strip, and Oklahoma Openings, **IV**, 169

Cherokee Trail, and the Overland Trail, **IV**, 193

Cherrington, Ernest H., and prohibition, **IV**, 357

Cherronesus, Jefferson's proposed state, **III**, 173

Cherry Creek, and Auraria, **I**, 139; gold discovery at, **I**, 426; **II**, 138; **IV**, 270

Cherry Hill Penitentiary, **IV**, 247

Cherry Valley Massacre, **III**, 88

Chesapeake, The, engages with the *Shannon*, **II**, 161; and the Embargo, **II**, 207; and battle of Lake Erie, **II**, 224; frigate, **II**, 349; fired upon by the *Leopard*, **V**, 404

Chesapeake and Delaware Canal, and coal, **I**, 81; and internal improvements, **III**, 137

Chesapeake and Ohio Canal, and aqueducts, **I**, 93; and internal improvements, **III**, 137; and Potomac Company, **IV**, 324; subsidy granted to, **V**, 194

Chesapeake and Ohio Railroad, acquires the Blue Ridge Tunnel, **I**, 205; buys James River and Kanawha Canal, **III**, 166

Chesapeake Bay, opened to inland navigation, **I**, 46; and the Alexandria Conference, **I**, 47

Chesapeake Capes, Battle of, **II**, 345; **V**, 509

Chesecocks Patent, **III**, 56

Chester, George F., and the Standard Oil Company, **V**, 156

Chester's Gap, **IV**, 221

Chetwynd, William, member of the Principio Company, **IV**, 343

Chevalier, Albert, and coster songs, **V**, 120

Cheyenne, Wyo., as a cow town, **I**, 326; **II**, 79

Cheyenne Indians, in the battle of Adobe Walls, **I**, 13; and Algonquin family, **I**, 48; Arapaho ally themselves with, **I**, 94; Fort Bascom a protection against, **I**, 165; attack at Beecher Island, **I**, 173; barter at Bent's Fort, **I**, 179; and Fort Connor, **II**, 24; and Dull Knife's campaign, **II**, 174; and the Fetterman massacre, **II**, 268; capture the Germaine girls, **II**, 382; sign treaty with Indian Commission, **III**, 95; and the Indian Country, **III**, 97; placed on reservations, **III**, 108; and the Kidder massacre, **III**, 208; and the Kiowas, **III**, 213; and Fort Laramie, **III**, 245; and treaty of Fort Laramie (1851), **III**, 245; Hancock's expedition against, **III**, 246; and Fort McKinney, **III**, 366; and Medicine Creek Council, **III**, 370; and Oklahoma Openings, **IV**, 169; and Pawnee Rock, **IV**, 229; on the Great Plains, **IV**, 281; and the Platte Bridge fight, **IV**, 286; and prospectors, **IV**, 364; and the Red River Indian War, **IV**, 431; attacked at Sand Creek, **V**, 27; and scouting on the plains, **V**, 46; and Fort Sedgwick, **V**, 55; and Sioux wars, **V**, 86; attack South Platte Route, **V**, 128; and Sumner's expedition, **V**, 202; and Camp Supply, **V**, 205; and Fort Wallace, **V**, 394; and fight on War Bonnet Creek, **V**, 400; and Sheridan's operations on Washita, **V**, 420

Cheyenne River Reservation, **V**, 127

Cheyney, John K., and sponge fisheries, **V**, 148

Chicago, and the Beaubien Land Claim, **I**, 172; exposition at (1933–34), **I**, 335; and the treaty of Greenville (1795), **II**, 115; city directory appears in, **II**, 148; and the fur trade, **II**, 360; and Illinois' northeastern boundary, **III**, 68; and the Illinois Central Railroad, **III**, 70; treaty of (1821), and Indian land cessions, **III**, 100; as livestock center, **III**, 286; and meat packing, **IV**, 199; and domestic trade, **V**, 292; and World's Columbian Exposition, **V**, 495

Chicago, Congress authorizes construction of, **II**, 283; one of the vessels of the White Squadron, **V**, 460

Chicago, Burlington and Quincy Railroad, Hill obtains control of, **II**, 419; and the Michigan Central, **III**, 393; and Montana, **IV**, 16; and Northern Securities case, **IV**, 148; reaches the Mississippi, **IV**, 407; installs streamlined trains, **V**, 188

Chicago, Milwaukee and St. Paul Railroad, electric locomotives built for, **II**, 199; and Menominee iron range, **III**, 374; and Montana, **IV**, 16; reaches the Mississippi, **IV**, 407; electrification of, **IV**, 410; installs oil-burning, streamlined steam locomotives, **V**, 188

Chicago and Alton Railroad, **IV**, 407

Chicago and North Western Railroad, and iron mining, **III**, 374; reaches the Mississippi, **IV**, 407

Chicago and Rock Island Railroad, **III**, 138; **IV**, 407

Chicago Associated Press, **I**, 131

Chicago Board of Trade, **I**, 437; **II**, 232; **IV**, 278

Chicago Crime Commission, **II**, 89

Chicago *Daily Times,* as political organ, **IV**, 129

Chicago *Evening Post,* and airplane races, **I**, 36

Chicago Fire, **I**, 356; **IV**, 38

Chicago-Illinois Route, **II**, 320

Chicago Mail Order House, **III**, 325

Chicago Portage, Illinois Fur Brigade goes through, **III**, 70; and Jolliet and Marquette, **III**, 180, 231

Chicago Sanitary District, and the Lakes-to-Gulf Deep Waterway, **III**, 231

Chicago *Times,* **II**, 58; **V**, 216

Chicago *Tribune* Building, **I**, 101; **V**, 88

Chicago Union Stockyards, **V**, 184

Chicago Zouaves, **III**, 400

Chickamauga, Army of Tennessee victorious at, **V**, 242

Chickamauga Dam, **V**, 245

Chickamauga Indians, and the Cherokee wars, **I**, 353

Chickasaw Bluff, discovered by DeSoto's expedition, **II**, 142; site of Memphis, **III**, 372; Fort San Fernando built at, **V**, 140

Chickasaw Bluffs, Sherman defeated at, **V**, 367

Chickasaw-Choctaw Trail, **III**, 104

Chickasaw Indians, in the battle of Ackia, **I**, 8; and Congress of Augusta, **I**, 138; and the opening of the Black Belt to settlement, **I**, 193; and village of Chicaca, **I**, 355; in Colbert's gang, **I**, 412; and D'Artaguette's defeat, **II**, 110; and the Dawes Commission, **II**, 113; one of the Five Civilized Tribes, **II**, 279; and treaty of Hopewell, **III**, 45; land cessions of, **III**, 100; removal of, **III**, 107; attack Fort Jefferson, **III**, 170; and Memphis, **III**, 372; and the Natchez Indians, **IV**, 57; and treaty of Natchez, **IV**, 57; grant right of way in Natchez Trace, **IV**, 57; and treaty of Nogales, **IV**, 136; removed to Oklahoma, **IV**, 168; and Panton, Leslie & Co., **IV**, 211; and treaty of Pontotoc, **IV**, 306; and scalping, **V**, 37; and the Shawnee, **V**, 65; relations with the Spanish, **V**, 140; in Tennessee, **V**, 242; expeditions against, **V**, 280

Chief Joseph, surrenders at Bear Paw Mountains, **I**, 171; and the battle of the Big Hole, **I**, 183;

and Clearwater River battle, **I**, 397; and Indian oratory, **III**, 103; and the Nez Percé War, **IV**, 129

Chief of Naval Operations, **I**, 12; **II**, 283

Chief of Staff, **I**, 115; **V**, 402

Chihuahua Trail, and Albuquerque, **I**, 46

Child, Robert, and Congregationalists, **I**, 277; and the right of petition, **IV**, 256

Child Labor, and the American Legion, **I**, 63; and the commerce clause, **I**, 434; and Fair Labor Standards Act, **II**, 239; and Hammer v. Dagenhart, **III**, 7; and implied powers, **III**, 80; and factories, **III**, 219; legislation, **III**, 222; demand for restriction of, **III**, 224; and Society for Prevention of Cruelty to Children, **V**, 113; and the sweatshop, **V**, 213; attempts to regulate hours of, **V**, 387

Child Labor Amendment, American Bar Association opposes, **I**, 162

Child Labor Cases, and Bailey v. Drexel Furniture Company, **I**, 146; and reserved powers of states, **IV**, 458; and five-to-four decisions, **V**, 207

Child Welfare, sponsored by American Legion, **I**, 62; and charity organization movement, **I**, 342; and juvenile courts, **III**, 192

Children, Dependent, and social legislation, **V**, 108

Children's Aid Society, **IV**, 260

Children's Bureau, division of the Department of Labor, **III**, 221

Children's Fund of Michigan, **II**, 314

Children's Magazine, first American periodical for juveniles, **I**, 363

Childs, Francis, starts the *Daily Advertiser*, **IV**, 125

Chiles, Joseph B., and wagon trains, **V**, 389

Chiles-Walker Party, **I**, 270

Chillicothe, and the Division Act of 1800, **II**, 155; capital of Ohio, **IV**, 160

Chilton, Mary, and Plymouth Rock, **IV**, 290

Chimney Rock, **II**, 75

China, trade with, **I**, 128, 147; relations with, **I**, 165; and Boxer Rebellion, **I**, 231; and indemnities, **III**, 84; American intervention in, **III**, 145; Kearny's mission to, **III**, 201; and the Open-door policy, **IV**, 176; and the Reed Treaty, **IV**, 434; treaties with, **V**, 317, 318

China Trade, and the Pacific Fur Company, **IV**, 195; and the Pacific Ocean, **IV**, 196

Chinese, and California gold rush, **I**, 272; students and Boxer indemnity, **III**, 84; and mobs and riots, **IV**, 3; race riots, **IV**, 394; smuggling, **V**, 103; race riots, **V**, 415

Chinese Exclusion Acts, forced by labor, **I**, 274; and the Morey letter, **IV**, 23; and U. S. v. Wong Kim Ark, **V**, 350; and the Yellow Peril, **V**, 505

Chinese Immigration, and the Greenback party, **II**, 424

Chinese Indemnity, and the Peking Congress, **IV**, 239

Chinook Jargon, **I**, 223; **V**, 415

Chippewa, battle at, **IV**, 130; **V**, 405

Chippewa Indians, as part of Algonquin family, **I**, 48; and Butte des Morts Council, **I**, 263; defeat Sioux in battle of Crow Wing, **II**, 92; Duluth makes friends with, **II**, 175; and Fort Harmar treaty, **III**, 10; and Hull treaty, **III**, 58; land cessions of, **III**, 100; removal of, **III**, 107; and battle of Kaposia, **III**, 199; and treaty of La Pointe, **III**, 245; and Leech Lake Indian Council, **III**, 260; and Leech Lake uprising, **III**, 260; and treaties of Fort McIntosh, **III**, 366; and *Mide-wiwin*, **III**, 395; and battle of Mille Lacs, **III**, 404; in Minnesota, **III**, 410; and Great Indian Council at Niagara, **IV**, 130; and treaty at Prairie du Chien, **IV**, 328; and the Red River cart traffic, **IV**, 431; and battle of Rum River, **IV**, 506; and establishment of Fort Saginaw, **V**, 5; and Saginaw treaty, **V**, 5; and treaty of Prairie du Chien, **V**, 5; and Butte des Morts treaty, **V**, 5; in battle of St. Croix Falls, **V**, 7; and treaty of St. Marys, **V**, 14; and battle of Sandy Lake, **V**, 27; at Sault Ste. Marie, **V**, 34; and the Sioux, **V**, 84, 85; and treaty of Spring Wells, **V**, 150; depend upon wild rice for their food supply, **V**, 464

Chirac v. Chirac, and naturalization, **IV**, 67

Chisholm, C. P. and J. A., and the automatic pea podder, **I**, 304

Chisholm, Jesse, establishes Chisholm Trail, **II**, 236

Chisholm Trail, and growth of cow towns, **II**, 79; and Texas, **V**, 255; Wichita on the, **V**, 461

Chisholm v. Georgia, and the Eleventh Amendment, **II**, 202; and states' rights, **II**, 379; and the problem of sovereignty, **V**, 173

Chisum, John, and the Lincoln County War, **III**, 278

Chiswell's Mine, and treaty of Hard Labor, **III**, 9; and Indian Factory of Virginia, **III**, 97; and lead production, **III**, 254; and Tryon's line, **V**, 328

Chittenden, Thomas, and the Green Mountain Boys, **II**, 422; first governor of Vermont, **V**, 362

Chivington, J. M., and the Sand Creek massacre, **V**, 26

Choate, Rufus, and oratory, **IV**, 180

Choctaw Bluff, Spanish engage with Indians at, **II**, 142

Choctaw Indians, and treaty of 1801, **I**, 9; and the battle of Amite, **I**, 68; and Congress of Augusta (1763), **I**, 138; and the opening of the Black Belt to settlement, **I**, 193; Canadian

River northern boundary of, **I**, 302; and the Chickasaws, **I**, 359; at Fort Confederation, **II**, 13; and treaty of Dancing Rabbit Creek, **II**, 108; and the Dawes Commission, **II**, 113; and treaty of Doak's Stand, **II**, 156; one of the Five Civilized Tribes, **II**, 279; and "Honored Men," **III**, 44; and treaty of Hopewell, **III**, 45; land cessions of, **III**, 100; removal of, **III**, 107; attack Fort Jefferson, **III**, 170; Jesuit missions among, **III**, 175; and Kaapa, **III**, 193; as Mound Builders, **IV**, 35; allies of the French against Natchez Indians, **IV**, 57; and treaty of Natchez, **IV**, 57; grant right of way on Natchez Trace, **IV**, 57; and treaty of Nogales, **IV**, 136; removed to Oklahoma, **IV**, 168; and Panton, Leslie & Co., **IV**, 211; and St. Stephens, **V**, 15; and scalping, **V**, 37; relations with the Spanish, **V**, 140; in the Tombigbee Valley, **V**, 280

Cholera, epidemic of, **II**, 221; and hygiene, **III**, 64; and the Missouri Pacific Railroad, **III**, 430; on the Oregon Trail, **IV**, 186; attacks Fort Riley, **IV**, 484

Chouart, Médard, discovers western end of Lake Superior, **V**, 205

Chouteau, A. P., and the fur trade, **I**, 370; partner in St. Louis Missouri Fur Company, **V**, 12; arrest of fur brigade of, **V**, 30

Chouteau, Auguste, and the fur trade, **I**, 370; and the St. Louis trade, **III**, 111; and St. Louis, **V**, 11

Chouteau, François G., establishes trading post, **I**, 370; builds post at Randolph Bluffs, **III**, 196

Chouteau, P., Jr. and Company, and the fur trade, **II**, 363

Chouteau, Pierre, and the fur trade, **I**, 370; and the St. Louis trade, **III**, 111; ascends the Missouri, **III**, 430; partner in St. Louis Missouri Fur Company, **V**, 12

Chouteau's Post, on the Columbia River, **I**, 430

Chouteau's Trading Posts, **V**, 302

Chrisman, Jesse, on *Hit or Miss*, **III**, 35

Christensen, Parley Parker, nominated for President by Farmer-Labor party of 1920, **II**, 251

Christian, William, and treaty of Long Island of Holston, **III**, 299; and battle of Point Pleasant, **IV**, 291

Christian Advocate and Journal, and Oregon missions, **IV**, 184

Christian Alliance, **IV**, 65

Christian Baptist, magazine published by Alexander Campbell, **II**, 149

Christian Cynosure, **I**, 82

Christian History, first religious periodical in America, **IV**, 445

Christian Science, **IV**, 443, 447

Christian Socialism, and Swedenborgianism, **V**, 213

Christians, unite with the Disciples, **II**, 149

Christina, Fort, **IV**, 113, 242

Christopher Columbus, whaleback, **V**, 452

Christy, David, author of *Cotton Is King*, **III**, 209

Christy Minstrels, **III**, 412; **V**, 120

Chrysler's Field, and Wilkinson's expedition against Montreal, **IV**, 18

Church, Benjamin, in King Philip's War, **III**, 211; in Queen Anne's War, **IV**, 389; traps King Philip, **IV**, 478

Church, Frederick Edwin, landscape painter, **I**, 123

Church, John B., fights duel at Weehawken, **V**, 433

Church and State, separation of, **I**, 161; **IV**, 477, 478

Church Covenants, and the compact theory, **I**, 441; and political theories, **IV**, 300

Church Membership, **IV**, 442

Church of the Transfiguration, **III**, 285

Church Peace Union, **IV**, 235

Churches, and the Bible, **I**, 181; and lotteries, **II**, 369; **III**, 303; and philanthropy and benevolence, **IV**, 260; attitude of, to slavery, **V**, 96

Churchill, Fort, and the Pony Express, **IV**, 307

Churchill, Thomas J., surrenders Arkansas Post, **I**, 106

Churchill, Winston, and fiction, **II**, 270

Churubusco Convent, San Patricio Corps captured at, **II**, 141

Cíbola, Coronado's expedition to, **I**, 104; **II**, 61

Cilley, Jonathan, duels with William Graves, **II**, 174

Cimarron, Kans., and county seat wars, **II**, 74

Cimarron Crossing, and the Arkansas River route, **I**, 107

Cimarron Cutoff, **V**, 30

Cincinnati, city directory appears in, **II**, 148; as packing center, **III**, 286; as Losantiville, **III**, 390; and meat packing, **IV**, 199; and Fort Washington, **V**, 414

Cincinnati, Society of the, as veterans' organization, **V**, 365

Cincinnati, The, gunboat, **II**, 180

Cincinnati and Louisville Mail Line, **V**, 179

Cincinnati *Enquirer*, supports Copperheads, **II**, 58; and the Ohio Idea, **IV**, 163; uses straw poll, **V**, 21

Cincinnati Red Stockings, and baseball, **I**, 166

Circuit Court of Appeals, creation of, **I**, 162

Circuit Courts, and the judiciary, **III**, 185; provided by Judiciary Act of 1789, **III**, 188; and Judiciary Act of 1801, **III**, 189; and the Supreme Court, **V**, 206

Circuit Rider, brings religion to the fron .r family, **II**, 243; and the Methodists, **III**, 380

Circular Letter, Massachusetts, **III**, 358

Circus, I, 70

Cities, growth of, I, 27; and Jeffersonian Democracy, III, 171; growth of, III, 337; as political subdivisions, IV, 299; and regional planning, IV, 438; and organized sports, V, 148; and suburban growth, V, 196

Citizens Industrial Association, IV, 63

Citizens' Military Training Camps, and army peace-time work, I, 111; formation of, I, 114; and Officers' Reserve Corps, IV, 158; and preparedness, IV, 331

Citizenship, and the Fourteenth Amendment, II, 41; dual, II, 171; and impressment of seamen, III, 81; Indian, III, 95; and the Koszta case, III, 217; and Minor v. Happersett, III, 412; and naturalization, IV, 67; and Puerto Rico, IV, 380; and U. S. v. Wong Kim Ark, V, 349; required for voting, V, 383; of married women, V, 479

Citrus Industry, of Florida, II, 287; and food, II, 295; of Texas, V, 255; and domestic trade, V, 292

City Council, and municipal government, IV, 41

City Government, III, 289

City Manager, type of municipal charters, I, 347; and city council, II, 71; and local government, III, 289; and municipal government, IV, 42; and municipal reform, IV, 43; and political patronage, IV, 225

City Planning, and housing, III, 54

Civil Aeronautics Act, I, 36

Civil Aeronautics Authority, I, 12, 37, 38, 433

Civil Liberty, and arbitrary arrest, I, 121

Civil Rights, and the alien, I, 50; and the Radical Republicans, IV, 395; and U. S. v. Clark, V, 348; in wartime, V, 399

Civil Rights Act of 1866, one of the Force Acts, II, 300; sanctioned by the Fourteenth Amendment, II, 317; and the Negro, IV, 83; and Reconstruction, IV, 425; and Strauder v. West Virginia, V, 187

Civil Rights Act of 1875, declared unconstitutional, III, 177

Civil Service, and the American Legion, I, 62; in campaign of 1872, I, 286; and municipal charters, I, 347; and diplomatic secretaries, II, 306; and the merit system, III, 377; and the Pendleton Act, IV, 241; and political assessments, IV, 295; and rotation in office, IV, 503; and reform of the spoils system, V, 148

Civil War, and the United States Army, I, 113; and army contracts, I, 115; and hospitalization, I, 116; blockade in, I, 201; border states in, I, 219; and social change, I, 341; and public debt, II, 117; financing of, II, 128; demobilization after, II, 134; desertion in, II, 141; draft in, II, 163; enlistment in, II, 217; exchange of prisoners in, II, 231; United States fleet in, II, 283; Indian in, III, 97; and Indian policy, III, 106; and inflation, III, 121; and military roads, III, 402; and mobilization, IV, 2; Navy in, IV, 78; Negroes in, IV, 84; and peace movements, IV, 234; contracts and profiteering, IV, 355; and protection, IV, 365; influence of railroads in, IV, 409; and religion, IV, 442, 443; and the importance of rivers, IV, 492; and sea power, V, 48; and shipbuilding, V, 72; and ocean shipping, V, 74; and suspension of specie payments, V, 144; and state constitutions, V, 167; torpedoes in, V, 284; trade in cotton during, V, 300; and Trade with the Enemy Acts, V, 300; and army uniforms, V, 340; cost of, V, 409; loss of life in, V, 410

Civil Works Administration, created, IV, 96; as a relief measure, IV, 440

Civilian Conservation Corps, and adult education, I, 14; established, IV, 96; and Officers' Reserve Corps, IV, 158; and reforestation, IV, 435; as relief measure, IV, 440

Claflin Equalitarians, protagonists of free love, II, 332

Claiborne, Ferdinand L., destroys Weatherford's Town, II, 86; attacks and burns Econochaca, II, 184; in Natchez campaign of 1813, IV, 57

Claiborne, William, in Maryland, III, 349. See also Kent Island

Claiborne, William C. C., and the Louisiana Purchase, III, 308; and battle of New Orleans (1815), IV, 110; and martial law in New Orleans, IV, 110; as governor of territory of Orleans, IV, 189; and annexation of West Florida, V, 436

Claim Associations, and pre-emption, IV, 331; and public land sales, IV, 372

Claim Jumpers, I, 219; IV, 330

Claims, Court of, and repudiation of public debts, IV, 456

Claims Conventions of 1853, and mixed commissions, III, 432

Clamorgan, Jacques, and Spanish-Missouri Fur Company, V, 141

Clapboards, I, 249; V, 294

Clapp, Moses E., prominent in Minnesota politics, III, 411

Clark, Abraham, signer of the Declaration of Independence, II, 124

Clark, Bennett C., and American Legion, I, 62; and railroad retirement laws, IV, 404

Clark, Billy J., forms temperance society, V, 240

Clark, Champ, and campaign of 1912, I, 290

Clark, Charles E., and the Oregon, IV, 183

Clark, Daniel, and the Gaines case, II, 366; exposes the Spanish conspiracy, V, 140

Clark, Edward, governor of Texas, V, 254

Clark, Fort, built, IV, 252

Clark, Fort, Catlin stays at, **I**, 324

Clark, Fort, Treaty of (1808), and Indian land cessions, **III**, 100

Clark, Francis E., founds first Christian Endeavor Society, **I**, 370

Clark, George Rogers, takes Kaskaskia and Vincennes, **I**, 145; and Big Knives, **I**, 184; and British campaign of 1780, **I**, 240; and the Cherokee wars, **I**, 353; and galley boats, **II**, 367; and epithet "hair buyer," **III**, 3; and Harrodsburg, **III**, 14; in Illinois, **III**, 67; and Illinois County, **III**, 70; and Northwest Campaign, **III**, 88; at Vincennes, **III**, 112; begins Fort Jefferson, **III**, 170; captures Kaskaskia, **III**, 199; represents Harrodstown settlers before Virginia assembly, **III**, 204; and Kentucky County, **III**, 206; and occupation of Fort Sackville, **III**, 216; and Lochry's defeat, **III**, 291; destroys Loramie's store, **III**, 301; lands at Fort Massac, **III**, 354; and "men of the western waters," **III**, 373; his military road, **III**, 402; on the Mississippi River, **III**, 424; orders building of Fort Nelson, **IV**, 86; and the Northwest Campaign, **IV**, 162; and the battle of Piqua, **IV**, 277; and Pollock's aid to the Revolution, **IV**, 304; and the Northwest Campaign, **V**, 141; at Vincennes, **V**, 369; and the Northwest Campaign, **V**, 373; and Virginia v. Transylvania Company, **V**, 380; and the *Willing*, **V**, 468

Clark, George W., and abolitionist literature, **I**, 3

Clark, Isaac, in War of 1812, **III**, 230

Clark, J. V. H., and epic of Hiawatha, **III**, 29

Clark, John, and Georgia politics, **V**, 325

Clark, John B., and action at Glasgow, Mo., **II**, 391

Clark, W. P., and the surrender of Little Wolf's band, **II**, 175

Clark, William, becomes ex-officio Superintendent of Indian Affairs, **III**, 91; and Lewis and Clark expedition, **III**, 266; and Oregon missions, **IV**, 183; and the establishment of Fort Osage, **IV**, 189; builds Fort Shelby, **IV**, 328; and treaty of Prairie du Chien, **IV**, 329; partner in St. Louis Missouri Fur Company, **V**, 12; and Sioux treaties, **V**, 86; and the War of 1812 in the West, **V**, 406

Clark, William A., and Anaconda Copper, **I**, 71; art collection of, **I**, 124; copper millionaire, **II**, 312; feud with Marcus Daly, **IV**, 16

Clark Pass, **IV**, 222

Clark v. Tousey, **I**, 89

Clarke, Edward Y., and the Ku Klux Klan, **III**, 218

Clarke, Elijah, in battle of Kettle Creek, **III**, 208

Clarke, John, colonial agent, **I**, 415; a founder of Newport, R. I., **IV**, 121; secures a royal charter for Rhode Island, **IV**, 478

Clarke, Jonas, and Revere's ride, **IV**, 463

Clarke, William Newton, and religious thought and writings, **IV**, 447; **V**, 261

Clarke-McNary Act, and reforestation, **IV**, 434

Class Struggle, and Industrial Workers of the World, **III**, 119; and sabotage, **V**, 2; as symbol in Sacco and Vanzetti case, **V**, 2; and the socialist movement, **V**, 110; and syndicalism, **V**, 215

Clatsop, Fort, Columbia River post, **I**, 430; Lewis and Clark winter at, **III**, 266

Clay, C. C., and Confederate activities in Canada, **I**, 298; and the peace movement of 1864, **IV**, 233

Clay, Cassius M., and abolition movement, **I**, 2; and the Madison County antislavery war, **II**, 322

Clay, Henry, and the American System, **I**, 65; makes home at Ashland, **I**, 205; and campaign of 1812, **I**, 281; and campaign of 1824, **I**, 282; nominated for Presidency, **I**, 283, 284; and Committee of Thirteen, **I**, 436; and Compromise of 1850, **I**, 442; sponsors the Compromise Tariff of 1833, **I**, 443; and Corrupt Bargain charges, **II**, 63; introduces Herefords, **II**, 78; and the Democratic party, **II**, 136; duels with John Randolph, **II**, 174; and Force Acts, **II**, 299; and treaty of Ghent, **II**, 387; and Hispanic American wars of independence, **III**, 32; uses expression, "I had rather be right than be President," **III**, 65; and internal improvements, **III**, 137; and the Land Distribution Bill, **III**, 234; and recognition of Latin-American Republics, **III**, 250; and Masonry, **III**, 352; imports mules, **IV**, 40; and the National Republican party, **IV**, 62; and oratory, **IV**, 180; pleads for formation of an American System, **IV**, 203; and right of petition, **IV**, 256; and protection, **IV**, 365; and the Raleigh Letter, **IV**, 412; and the Rice-Campbell debates, **IV**, 480; and origin of term "Salt River," **V**, 19; and distribution of surplus revenue, **V**, 209; and the General Survey Act of 1824, **V**, 209; as leader of the War Hawks, **V**, 403; and the War of 1812, **V**, 406; and the Whig party, **V**, 455; and inter-American system, **V**, 487

Clay-Eaters, **II**, 83

Claypoole, David C., publishes the *Pennsylvania Packet and Daily Advertiser*, **IV**, 125

Clayton, J. M., as Secretary of State, **V**, 162

Clayton, John, pioneer of American pharmacology, **II**, 171

Clayton, Powell, ambassador, **I**, 54

Clayton Act, and antitrust laws, **I**, 87; and arrest, **I**, 121; and boycotting, **I**, 232; extends principle of regulation, **I**, 260; and collective bargaining, **I**, 412; passage of, **I**, 433; and the Federal Trade Commission, **II**, 264; and the

injunction, **III**, 124; and interlocking directorates, **III**, 135; and interstate commerce, **III**, 144; and jury trial, **III**, 191; and *laissez-faire*, **III**, 229; and money power, **IV**, 9; and Norris-LaGuardia Anti-Injunction Law, **IV**, 143; and restraint of trade, **IV**, 460; and trusts, **V**, 327

Clayton-Bulwer Treaty, and Anglo-American relations, **I**, 76; and the Dallas Clarendon Convention, **II**, 107; modified by the Hay-Pauncefote treaties, **III**, 19; and the Mosquito Question, **IV**, 30; and Nicaraguan Canal Project, **IV**, 132; and the Panama Canal, **IV**, 204; and the Squier treaty, **V**, 152; and Tigre Island, **V**, 269; and treaties with foreign nations, **V**, 317

Clearwater River, Nez Percé Indians at, **IV**, 129

Cleaveland, Moses, and laying out of Cleveland, **I**, 397; one of the purchasers of the Western Reserve, **V**, 445

Cleburne, P. R., and battle of Missionary Ridge, **III**, 416; and battle of Ringgold, **IV**, 485

Cleeve, George, and Lygonia, **III**, 317; driven out of Saco Bay, **V**, 3

Clemens, Samuel L., adopts and makes famous the name "Mark Twain," **III**, 344. *See also* Mark Twain

Clements, William L., and Americana, **I**, 212; library of, **III**, 273

Clendenin, Charles, and Charleston, W. Va., **I**, 344

Clephane, J. O., promotes an experiment in multiplying typewriting, **III**, 281

Clermont, The, building of, **II**, 355; tested on the Hudson, **III**, 55; and river navigation, **IV**, 489; voyage of, **V**, 179; and steamboat transportation, **V**, 307

Cleveland, Grover, and the British Guiana-Venezuelan boundary dispute, **I**, 76; and the appointing power, **I**, 91; elected President, **I**, 287; defeated for the Presidency (1888), **I**, 288; elected (1892), **I**, 288; censure of, **I**, 332; and the Debs case, **II**, 116; and the Gorman-Wilson Tariff, **II**, 401; and Hawaii, **III**, 18; and the Misiones award, **III**, 415; and *modus vivendi*, **IV**, 4; and the Monroe Doctrine, **IV**, 14; and the Mugwumps, **IV**, 39; and Olney-Pauncefote treaty, **IV**, 172; and panic of 1893, **IV**, 209; insists on two bathrooms for the White House, **IV**, 289; and the Presidency, **IV**, 333; and the Pullman strike, **IV**, 381; and Sackville-West incident, **V**, 3; and the Schomburgk Line, **V**, 39; and the Spanish-American War, **V**, 136; recommends a reduction of the tariff, **V**, 222; and the Venezuelan boundary controversy, **V**, 360; whispering campaigns against, **V**, 458

Cleveland and Mahoning Railroad, **IV**, 245

Cleveland Association for Criminal Justice, **II**, 88

Cleveland Democrats, **I**, 287

Cleveland Foundation, **II**, 314

Cleveland Railway Company, uses motor buses, **IV**, 32

Cliff Dwellings, in Arizona, **I**, 104; and Mesa Verde, **III**, 379; and national monuments, **IV**, 18

Climate, and rainfall, **IV**, 411

Clinch, Gen., and battles at Withlacoochee River (1835–36), **V**, 476

Clinton, DeWitt, and Bucktails, **I**, 247; nominated for Presidency, **I**, 282; and the Democratic party, **II**, 136; and the Erie Canal, **II**, 225; and "High-minded Men," **III**, 30; and internal improvements, **III**, 139; opposed by the Martling Men, **III**, 348; opposed by the Quids, **IV**, 390; fights duel at Weehawken, **V**, 433

Clinton, Fort, **II**, 28; **V**, 438

Clinton, George, defeated for Vice-Presidency (1792), **I**, 281; elected (1804, 1808), **I**, 281; as governor of the colony of New York, **IV**, 115; elected as first governor of New York, **IV**, 116; and the Trespass Act, **V**, 322

Clinton, Henry, and André's capture, **I**, 73; and Burgoyne's invasion, **I**, 255; and the Highlands, **III**, 31; and West Point, **V**, 438; and Yorktown campaign, **V**, 509

Clinton, James, in the battle of Elmira, **II**, 204; and Sullivan campaign, **V**, 201

Clipper Ships, **I**, 151; **II**, 292; **III**, 375

Closed Shop, and labor unions, **III**, 225; opposed by National Association of Manufacturers, **IV**, 58; and railroad brotherhoods, **IV**, 400; and restraint of trade, **IV**, 460; and strikes, **V**, 190

Closson, W. B., and wood engraving, **V**, 483

Closure, adopted by the Senate, **II**, 272

Clouds, Battle of the, **III**, 300

Clough, Samuel, almanac of, **IV**, 99

Clymer, George, signer of the Constitution, **II**, 39, 124

Clymer, George, and the printing press, **IV**, 346

Coal, **I**, 79, 192, 199; **V**, 439

Coal Mining, and the checkoff, **I**, 349; importance of, **III**, 407; in Pennsylvania, **IV**, 243; and Federal taxing power, **V**, 232

Coal Zoning Plan, and Railroad Administration, **IV**, 400

Coale, Edward, and night-blindness as symptom of scurvy, **V**, 47

Coast and Geodetic Survey, **I**, 35; **III**, 63, 341

Coast Defense, **I**, 127; **II**, 310

Coast Guard, **III**, 276; **V**, 314

Coasting Trade, and Gibbons v. Ogden, **II**, 388; and Merchant Marine, **III**, 375; and Navigation Act of 1817, **IV**, 73; and ocean shipping, **V**, 73; and the Tonnage Act (1789), **V**, 280

Cobb, Fort, garrisoned by Sheridan, **V**, 420

Cobb, George W., Sr., and the open-top can, **I,** 304

Cobb, Howell, and the Confederate States, **II,** 9; and battle of South Mountain, **V,** 128

Cobblestones, earliest paving done with, **IV,** 228

Cochetope Pass, **IV,** 222

Cochise, Apache chief, **I,** 88

Cocke, John, attacks Creek band, **II,** 86

Cocke, P. St. G., at Bull Run, **I,** 251

Cockfighting, **I,** 69

Cockrell, Vard, and action at Lone Jack, **III,** 297

Coco Solo, fleet air bases at, **II,** 284

Cod Fishing, at Cape Cod, **I,** 306; off coast of Labrador, **III,** 225; and salt, **V,** 18

Coddington, William, a founder of Newport, R. I., **IV,** 121

Code Napoléon, and common law, **I,** 439

Code Noir, **V,** 89

Codes of Fair Competition, and the Blue Eagle Emblem, **I,** 204; and National Recovery Administration, **IV,** 61; encouraged by the National Industrial Recovery Act, **V,** 327

Cody, William F., and the Wild West Show, **I,** 377; as hunter, **III,** 60; as scout, **V,** 46; kills Yellow Hand in War Bonnet Creek fight, **V,** 400; and the Wild West Show, **V,** 464

Coe, G. A., and theological writings, **V,** 261

Coeducation, **I,** 6

Coercion Acts (1774), **I,** 8; **II,** 124; **V,** 198

Cœur d'Alène Indians, and Jesuit missions, **III,** 175

Cœur d'Alene Mission of the Sacred Heart, founded, **III,** 66

Cœur d'Alene Riots, **III,** 66, 347; **V,** 443

Coffee, and foreign trade, **V,** 295

Coffee, Holland, maintains trading posts, **V,** 408

Coffee, John, attacks Red Sticks at Horseshoe Bend, **II,** 87; and treaty of Pontotoc, **IV,** 306; and battle of Tallasahatchee, **V,** 217

Coffee, John F., and action at Lone Jack, **III,** 297

Coffin, Charles A., first president of General Electric Company, **II,** 376

Coffin, Jared, and the New York and Genesee Company, **IV,** 117

Coggeshall, John, president of Rhode Island's first assembly, **IV,** 478

Cohens v. Virginia, and Judiciary Act of 1789, **III,** 189

Coinage, private, of beaver money, **I,** 172; and the Crime of 1873, **II,** 89; and the silver dollar, **II,** 157; and the American Eagle, **II,** 181; and the Federal expropriation of gold, **II,** 393; and the Federal mint, **III,** 413; and our money system, **IV,** 7; and the Spanish dollar, **V,** 140; subsidiary, and token money, **V,** 276

Coinage Act of 1792, establishes system of bimetallism, **I,** 188

Coinage Act of 1853, passage of, **I,** 188

Coinage Ratio, and money, **IV,** 7

Coins, fractional, **I,** 188; and first use of the cent in America, **I,** 333; as currency, **II,** 99; *Fugio,* **II,** 354; Pine Tree Shilling, **IV,** 273; as token money, **V,** 276

Coin's Financial School, keynote of 1896 campaign, **II,** 333; and pamphleteering, **IV,** 202

Coit, Henry Leber, and certified milk, **III,** 64

Coit, Stanton, and social settlements, **V,** 109

Coke, for blast furnaces, **I,** 199

Coke, Richard, governor of Texas, **V,** 255

Coke, Thomas, and the Methodists, **III,** 380; and religious periodicals, **IV,** 445

Colbert's Ferry, Gaines' Trace begins at, **II,** 366

Cold Harbor, and campaign against Richmond, **IV,** 481

Cold Storage, and refrigeration, **IV,** 437

Colden, Cadwallader, writes first treatise on the flora, **II,** 371; and the Stamp Act riot in New York City, **V,** 155

Colden, Cadwallader and Jane, botanists, **I,** 225

Cole, Charles H., arrest of, **III,** 178

Cole, Thomas, landscape painter, **I,** 123

Cole, Timothy, wood engraver, **V,** 483

Coleman, Robert, and the Hopewell Iron Works, **III,** 45

Coleman, William, editor of the *Evening Post,* **IV,** 123

Coleman, William T., and borax, **I,** 218

Coleman v. Tennessee, **V,** 398

Colfax, Schuyler, elected Vice-President, **I,** 286; and the Crédit Mobilier, **II,** 85

Colgate and Company, and soap making, **V,** 106

Colgate v. Harvey, **IV,** 351

Collective Bargaining, and the American Federation of Labor, **I,** 60; recognized under Watson-Parker Act of 1926, **I,** 95; and the detective agency, **II,** 142; and freedom, **II,** 336; and labor parties, **III,** 223; and National Labor Relations Act, **IV,** 60; and National Recovery Administration, **IV,** 62; and government printing, **IV,** 344; and railroad brotherhoods, **IV,** 400; and strikes, **V,** 190; and the War Labor Board, **V,** 404

Collector v. Day, and reciprocal immunity from taxation, **V,** 229, 232

College of New Jersey, founding of, and the Presbyterians, **IV,** 332; now Princeton University, **IV,** 343

Colleges, invaded by the doctrine of Deism, **II,** 130; and education, **II,** 185; and lotteries, **III,** 303; municipal, **IV,** 43; and philanthropy, **IV,** 260; and revivals, **IV,** 464; in the Old South, **V,** 122; and vacations, **V,** 354; and education of women, **V,** 480

Collegiate School of New York, **V,** 41

Colles, Christopher, sets up experimental steam engine, **III**, 117; experiments with steam power, **V**, 177

Collier's Magazine, and muckraking, **IV**, 38

Collins, Caspar, and the Platte Bridge fight, **IV**, 286

Collins, Isaac, founder of the *New-Jersey Gazette,* **IV**, 127

Collins, Joel, train robber, **IV**, 159

Collins and Jones, barnstormers, **I**, 164

Collins Line, and mail contracts, **III**, 376

Collis' Independent Company of Pennsylvania Zouaves d'Afrique, **V**, 514

Collyer, Robert, starts as blacksmith, **I**, 197

Colman, Benjamin, pioneer of epidemiology, **II**, 221

Colombia, treaty with (1846), **I**, 183; and the Panama revolution, **IV**, 206; treaties with, **V**, 317, 318

Colombia Blockade Treaty (1824), **I**, 201

Colonial Agents, and colonial revenue, **V**, 155

Colonial Assemblies, and appointing power, **I**, 90; and the crown, **I**, 206; and governors, **I**, 419; and the judiciary, **I**, 419; and growth of democracy, **II**, 135; and investigating committees, **III**, 149; and judicial review, **III**, 182; and the English Parliament, **IV**, 218; and the right of petition, **IV**, 256; and privilege in governments, **IV**, 350; and proprietary provinces, **IV**, 362; and Provincial Congresses, **IV**, 368; as first representative government in America, **IV**, 452; and the American Revolution, **IV**, 466; and royal colonies, **IV**, 504; and Rules of the House, **IV**, 506; and the slave trade, **V**, 91; and taxation, **V**, 155; as unicameral legislatures, **V**, 340

Colonial Charters, and appeals to the crown, **I**, 89; and Lords of Trade and Plantation, **III**, 302; and state constitutions, **V**, 166; and state governments, **V**, 169

Colonial Councils, and royal colonies, **IV**, 504; and unicameral legislatures, **V**, 340

Colonial Governors, **II**, 406; **IV**, 504

Colonial Industries, **III**, 119

Colonial Judiciary, and royal colonies, **IV**, 504

Colonial Manufacture, and mercantilism, **III**, 374

Colonial Policy, and Board of Trade and Plantations, **I**, 206; influenced by Bristol merchants, **I**, 239; and Massachusetts Bay Company, **III**, 357; and mercantilism, **III**, 374; and Navigation Acts, **IV**, 73; and the English Parliament, **IV**, 218; and the American Revolution, **IV**, 464

Colonial Vehicles, **V**, 358

Colonial Wars, and the militia, **III**, 404; and the westward movement, **V**, 450

Colonization, and the Council for New England, **II**, 71

Colorado, and Jefferson Territory, **III**, 170; organized, and admitted, **V**, 249

Colorado Coal Strikes, and martial law, **III**, 347

Colorado Doctrine, and irrigation, **III**, 160

Colorado Fuel and Iron Company, **I**, 427

Colorado River, John W. Powell's explorations of the, **IV**, 326

Colorado River Aqueduct and Hoover Dam, **I**, 225

Colored Farmers' Alliance and Co-operative Union, **II**, 252

Colored Methodist Episcopal Church, **IV**, 83

Colquhoun, Patrick, and New York land speculation, **IV**, 116

Colt, Samuel, and interchangeable parts, **III**, 133; and rifles, **IV**, 483; explodes torpedoes by electricity, **V**, 284

Colt Revolvers, and Civil War contracts, **I**, 391

Colter, John, trapper, **II**, 235; trapping expeditions from Manuel's Fort, **III**, 335; and discovery of South Pass, **V**, 128; passes through Yellowstone Park region, **V**, 496

Colton, Walter, co-founder of the *Californian,* **IV**, 126

Columbia, S. C., burned, **I**, 317

Columbia, The, in Canton fur trade, **I**, 305; visits Hawaii, **III**, 17

Columbia Broadcasting System, **IV**, 397

Columbia College, **II**, 185; **III**, 369

Columbia Fur Company, unites with American Fur Company, **I**, 61; and Missouri River fur trade, **III**, 431; and Fort Pierre, **IV**, 268; and the Red River of the North, **IV**, 431

Columbia Railroad, **IV**, 243

Columbia River, first American fur post abandoned on, **I**, 46; and the establishment of Astoria, **I**, 133; Cook fails to discover, **II**, 55; Dalles of the, **II**, 107; discovered by Robert Gray, **II**, 235; discovery of, and the Oregon Question, **IV**, 184; and the Oregon Trail, **IV**, 186; in American diplomacy, **IV**, 492; and Vancouver's explorations, **V**, 357; discovery of, **V**, 415; Lewis and Clark arrive at mouth of, **V**, 446

Columbia Steel Company, **V**, 348

Columbian, founded by J. W. Wiley and T. F. McElroy, **IV**, 127

Columbian Agricultural Society, **I**, 26

Columbian Centinel, **II**, 223; **V**, 298

Columbus, Christopher, and discovery of America, **I**, 56; draws maps of his discoveries, **III**, 339; lands at Watling's Island, **V**, 425

Columbus, Fort, erected on Governors Island, **II**, 406

Columbus, Ky., fortified by the Confederates, **III**, 419

Columbus, N. Mex., Villa attacks, **III**, 388; **V**, 368

Columbus, The, purchased by the Continental Navy, **V,** 471

Columbus, The, ship-of-the-line, **V,** 75

Columbus *Crisis,* supports Copperheads, **II,** 58

Columbus *Dispatch,* uses straw poll, **V,** 21

Colve, Anthony, Dutch governor of New York City, **IV,** 118

Colville, Fort, Columbia River settlement, **I,** 430

Comanche Indians, in the battle of Adobe Walls, **I,** 13; besiege Fort Atkinson, **I,** 134; Fort Bascom a protection against, **I,** 165; and Buffalo Hunters' War, **I,** 248; and Catlin's paintings, **I,** 324; Chouteau carries on trade with, **I,** 370; and the Dodge-Leavenworth expedition, **II,** 157; Bourgmont leads expedition to the, **II,** 345; and Fort Griffin, **II,** 426; and the Indian Country, **III,** 97; placed on reservations, **III,** 108; and the Kiowa, **III,** 213; and Fort Mason, **III,** 350; and Medicine Creek Council, **III,** 370; and the horse, **IV,** 49; New Mexico exposed to attacks of, **IV,** 107; in Oklahoma, **IV,** 168; and Oklahoma openings, **IV,** 169; attack Parker's Fort, **IV,** 217; raid Pecos, **IV,** 238; on the Great Plains, **IV,** 281; and the Red River Indian War, **IV,** 431; and the San Patricio Trail massacre, **IV,** 486; and Rubí's tour, **IV,** 505; raid Santa Fé, **V,** 29; hold agency headquarters at Fort Sill, **V,** 79; kill Jedediah Strong Smith, **V,** 102; occupy the Staked Plains, **V,** 154; and Camp Supply, **V,** 205; and Sheridan's operations on Washita, **V,** 420; and Fort Zarah, **V,** 513

Combine, The, **I,** 23, 29; **IV,** 419; **V,** 266

Comet, The, launched by Daniel French, **V,** 179

Comic Strips, in newspapers, **IV,** 126; and yellow journalism, **V,** 505

Comité International Technique d'Experts Juridique Aériens, **I,** 35

Command and General Staff School, **I,** 118

Commander in Chief, insignia of, **I,** 114; and the Constitution, **II,** 36

Commerce, Department of, and airways, **I,** 38; and customs houses, **II,** 101

Commerce Clause, in Brown v. Maryland, **I,** 244; in Cooley case, **II,** 56; and the Lottery case, **III,** 304; and railroad mediation acts, **IV,** 402

Commerce Committee, of the Continental Congress, **IV,** 475; sanctions the Willing expedition, **V,** 469

Commerce Power, and the Mann Act, **III,** 333

Commercial Arbitration, and chambers of commerce, **I,** 338

Commercial Pacific Cable Company, **II,** 427; **IV,** 194

Commercial Treaties. *See* Treaties, Commercial

Commission for Relief in Belgium, **I,** 174; **V,** 487

Commission Internationale de Navigation Aérienne, **I,** 35

Commission Plan of City Government, **I,** 347; **II,** 71; **III,** 123, 289; **IV,** 42

Committee for Industrial Organization. *See* Congress of Industrial Organizations

Committee of National Defense, **V,** 488

Committee of the Whole, reduced by the Reed rules, **IV,** 433

Committee of Thirteen (1850), **I,** 442; **IV,** 173

Committee of Thirteen (1860), **II,** 90

Committee of Thirty-three (1860), **II,** 90

Committee on Committees, **I,** 328; **II,** 18

Committee on Militarism in Education, **IV,** 235; **V,** 395

Committee on Public Information, **V,** 492, 494

Committee on Recent Social Trends (1933), **V,** 430

Committee on Rules, **II,** 19; **V,** 142

Committee on the Conduct of the War, inaugurated to investigate Ball's Bluff, **I,** 150; and Civil War propaganda, **I,** 385; and the Radical Republicans, **IV,** 395

Committee on Ways and Means, **I,** 93

Committees, and the American Revolution, **IV,** 467

Committees of Correspondence, and Associations, **I,** 131; built up by Samuel Adams, **III,** 356; and colony of New York, **IV,** 115; and the Pembroke Resolves, **IV,** 240; and colonial postal service, **IV,** 321; as channel of propaganda, **IV,** 358; and Provincial Congresses, **IV,** 368; and the American Revolution, **IV,** 467, 474

Committees of Public Safety, World War, **V,** 492

Committees of Safety, and Provincial Congresses, **IV,** 368; and Revere's ride, **IV,** 463; as revolutionary agencies, **IV,** 474

Commodities as Money, **II,** 99

Commodities Exchange, Inc., **II,** 232

Commodity Credit Corporation, **II,** 246

Commodity Exchange Act, **II,** 407; **IV,** 279

Commodity Prices, regulated by colonial assemblies, **I,** 260; decline of, during depression of 1920, **II,** 140; and managed currency, **III,** 330

Common Law, idea of, **I,** 184; and the Constitution, **II,** 40; and employers' liability, **II,** 212; and entail of estate, **II,** 218; and freedom of speech, **II,** 336; and jury trial, **III,** 190; and restatement of law, **III,** 251; and libel, **III,** 268; and the lockout, **III,** 291; and reserved powers of the people, **IV,** 458; and restraint of trade, **IV,** 460; and rights of Englishmen, **IV,** 484; and Swift v. Tyson, **V,** 214; and unreasonable searches and seizures, **V,** 351; and wire-tapping cases, **V,** 472; and the woman movement, **V,** 477; and workmen's accident compensation, **V,** 485

Common School Almanac, **I,** 52

Common Sense, and confiscation of property, **II,**

15; and pamphleteering, **IV,** 202; and philosophical writing, **IV,** 263; and political writing, **IV,** 302; and a republican form of government, **IV,** 453; and the American Revolution, **IV,** 468; as a political tract, **V,** 291

Commons, John R., and the Wisconsin Idea, **V,** 474

Commonweal of Christ, marches to Washington, **II,** 82

Commonwealth Fund, and foreign exchange students, **V,** 192; and World War relief, **V,** 488

Commonwealth v. Hunt, and closed shop, **I,** 403

Communications Act of 1934, established the Federal Communications Commission, **II,** 256; and wire-tapping, **V,** 472

Communist Party, and antisyndicalist laws, **I,** 87; in campaigns of 1932 and 1936, **I,** 292; and class struggle, **I,** 395; Industrial Workers of the World lose members to, **III,** 119; and labor parties, **III,** 223; and labor unions, **III,** 225; as a political party, **IV,** 297; formed, **V,** 110; and the Socialist party, **V,** 111; investigated for subversive activities, **V,** 197; as third party, **V,** 262

Communists, and unlawful assembly, **I,** 130; and organized labor, **III,** 219; and "reds," **IV,** 433; and Russian recognition, **IV,** 511

Communities, Amana, **I,** 53; Bethel, **I,** 180; Bishop Hill, **I,** 191; Brook Farm, **I,** 242; Ephrata, **II,** 220; Harmony Society, **III,** 11; Hopedale, **III,** 45; Labadists, **III,** 218; Oneida, **IV,** 174; American Sect of Shakers, **V,** 63; and distribution of wealth, **V,** 429; Zoar Society, **V,** 514

Community Chests, **IV,** 227

Community of True Inspiration, **I,** 53

Compact Theory, and the British Constitution, **II,** 29; premise of Fort Hill letter, **II,** 310; and John Locke, **III,** 291; as a political theory, **IV,** 300; and ordinance of secession, **V,** 50; and right of secession, **V,** 50

Compagnie de l'Occident, and the Mississippi Bubble, **III,** 421

Companionate Marriage, and sex relations, **V,** 62

Company of Royal Adventurers to Africa, **I,** 19

Company of the Indies, **II,** 3; **III,** 305

Competition, and the Addyston Pipe Co. case, **I,** 10; and Sherman Antitrust Law, **V,** 70

Compo Point, Tryon lands troops at, **II,** 108

Compressed Air Drills, first use of, **III,** 45

Compromise of 1850, and admittance of California, **I,** 273; in campaign of 1852, **I,** 284; and Fugitive Slave Act, **II,** 354; and the Georgia Platform, **II,** 381; and the Kansas-Nebraska Act, **III,** 197; and popular sovereignty, **III,** 428; and repeal of the Missouri Compromise, **III,** 429; and the Nashville Convention, **IV,** 55; halts

secession, **V,** 51; and slavery, **V,** 96; and the Southwest, **V,** 133; and the Texas cession, **V,** 255

Compromise Tariff, composed by Henry Clay, **II,** 299; passed, **IV,** 154; and South Carolina, **V,** 125; and the Whig party, **V,** 455

Comptroller General of the United States, **I,** 12

Comptroller of the Currency, **II,** 262; **V,** 314

Comstock, Anthony, and suppression of birth-control propaganda, **I,** 191

Comstock, Billy, celebrated scout, **V,** 46

Comstock, William A., declares bank moratorium in Michigan, **I,** 159; **V,** 144

Comstock Lode, and bonanza kings, **I,** 208; discovered by Allen and Hosea Grosh, **II,** 236; and lode mining, **III,** 293; discovery of, **IV,** 93; and Ralston Ring, **IV,** 414; and silver mining, **V,** 81; and the Sutro tunnel, **V,** 212

Conant, Roger, and fishing rights at Cape Ann, **I,** 306; and the Dorchester Company, **II,** 162

Conrad, A. F., nurseryman, **IV,** 154

Conrad and Pyle, nurserymen, **IV,** 154

Concanen, Luke, one of the first Dominican bishops in America, **II,** 159

Concessions, and intervention, **III,** 146

Concessions and Agreement, and colonial assemblies, **I,** 416; forms basic law for East Jersey, **II,** 182; granted, **II,** 356; drawn up, **IV,** 104; publication of, **IV,** 120; governs West Jersey, **V,** 438

Conciliation, Industrial, and arbitration, **I,** 95; and railroad brotherhoods, **IV,** 400. *See also* Mediation, Industrial

Conciliation Service, division of the Department of Labor, **III,** 221

Concord, Minutemen at, **III,** 414; and Revere's ride, **IV,** 463

Concord Coach, and overland travel, **IV,** 193; and transportation, **V,** 309

Concurrent Resolution, and the Fourteenth Amendment, **IV,** 425

Condé, Fort, named Fort Charlotte, **I,** 345

Condon, John F., and the Lindbergh kidnapping case, **III,** 280

Conestoga Horse, **III,** 47

Conestoga Massacre, and the Paxton Boys, **IV,** 229

Conestoga Wagon, and the covered wagon, **II,** 77; freight carried in, **II,** 340; on the Lancaster Pike, **III,** 233; in Pennsylvania, **IV,** 243; and the prairie schooner, **IV,** 329; and road improvement, **IV,** 494; and travel, **V,** 306; and colonial vehicles, **V,** 358; and the Allegheny wagoners, **V,** 390

Coney, John, silversmith, **V,** 82

Confederacy, arming of the, **I,** 110; conscription in the, **I,** 110; financing of, **II,** 11; inflation in, **III,** 121; and Union sentiment, **V,** 343

Confederate Agents, and the *Alabama,* **I,** 40; and

the *Bermuda* admiralty case, **I**, 179; and Civil War diplomacy, **I**, 391; and blockade, **II**, 9

Confederate Almanac and Register, **I**, 52

Confederate Constitution, forbids foreign slave trade, **V**, 92; and "We the People," **V**, 428

Confederate Debt, and cotton money, **II**, 70

Confederate Expatriates, in Brazil, **I**, 235; in Mexico, **I**, 314; **III**, 387

Confederate Money, **IV**, 213

Confederate Paper Currency, **I**, 205

Confederate Postal Service, **IV**, 321

Confederate Prisons, **I**, 175; **III**, 268

Confederate Privateers, and ocean shipping, **V**, 74

Confederate Raiders, **IV**, 78, 353, 511

Confederate Seal, **V**, 49

Confederate States of America, and blockade, **I**, 201; recognition of the belligerency of, **I**, 176; and blockade, **III**, 228; and Montgomery convention, **IV**, 17; and blockade, **IV**, 351, 353; and right of rebellion, **IV**, 421

Confederation, incurs heavy debts, **II**, 118; and representative government, **IV**, 252

Confederation, Fort, built, **V**, 140

Confirmation, Senatorial, **II**, 19

Confiscation, and the alien, **I**, 50; and the loyalists, **III**, 313; of proprietary provinces, **IV**, 363

Confiscation Acts, **I**, 68, 388; **II**, 47, 205; **IV**, 395

Conformity Act of 1872, and the judiciary, **III**, 187

Conger, Samuel, as a prospector, **IV**, 364

Congregationalists, and Brownists, **I**, 244; and Calvinism, **I**, 277; church established by law, **I**, 371; and colleges, **I**, 413; and the Church Covenant, **II**, 76; as dissenters, **II**, 151; and evangelism, **II**, 230; and the Great Awakening, **II**, 413; and Plan of Union, **III**, 27; and the meetinghouse, **III**, 371; form the American Missionary Association, **III**, 416; and the Home Missionary Society, **III**, 417; in New England, **IV**, 97; develop from the New England Way, **IV**, 100; and New Haven Colony, **IV**, 103; split in, **IV**, 106; in New Plymouth, **IV**, 112; and the Plan of Union, **IV**, 283; and Presbyterians, **IV**, 332; and the Revolution, **IV**, 443; and revivals, **IV**, 464; church founded in Salem, **V**, 16; and the Saybrook Platform, **V**, 37; and Separatists, **V**, 58; become antislavery in sentiment, **V**, 97; and Sunday Schools, **V**, 204; and the Synod of Dort, **V**, 215; form the Andover Theological Seminary, **V**, 261; in the Western Reserve, **V**, 446; and the Westminster Confession, **V**, 448; and the Yale Band, **V**, 500

Congress, The, a frigate, **II**, 349

Congress, The, destroyed by the *Merrimack (Virginia),* **III**, 378

Congress, The United States, and the Connecticut Compromise, **I**, 443; and the Constitution, **II**, 30; creation of, **II**, 51; and the executive, **II**, 233; powers granted to, **II**, 257; and postal power, **IV**, 319; and separation of powers, **IV**, 327; and the Presidency, **IV**, 333; and representation, **IV**, 451; and power to declare war, **V**, 396. *See also* House of Representatives; Senate

Congress of Industrial Organizations, and American Federation of Labor, **I**, 60; and American Labor party, **I**, 62; and closed shop, **I**, 403; and communism, **I**, 440; v. Hague, **III**, 2; Industrial Workers of the World lose members to, **III**, 119; rise of, **III**, 220, 224; and propaganda, **IV**, 358; and sit-down strikes, **V**, 191; and subversive activity, **V**, 197; and industrial unions, **V**, 344; and the United Mine Workers, **V**, 346

Congressional Committees, and organization of political parties, **IV**, 297

Congressional Globe, **II**, 21; **III**, 182

Congressional Investigations, **II**, 19, 27, 129; **IV**, 395

Congressional Record, and closure, **I**, 403; and *Journal of Congress,* **III**, 182; and leave to print, **III**, 258

Congressional Union, and woman suffrage, **V**, 478

Conkling, Roscoe, killed in blizzard of 1888, **I**, 200; and campaigns of 1880 and 1884, **I**, 287; and Garfield-Blaine controversy, **II**, 372; and the Stalwarts, **V**, 154

Conn, Herbert William, studies bacteriology of milk, **III**, 64

Connecticut, founded, **III**, 357; extends authority over New Haven Colony, **IV**, 104; River Towns of, **IV**, 489; Blue Laws of, **V**, 203; and the Susquehanna settlers, **V**, 210; and the Yankee-Pennamite wars, **V**, 502; receives part of York's proprietary, **V**, 508

Connecticut, Charter of 1662, granted, **II**, 21; and the Western Reserve, **V**, 445; and settlement of Wyoming Valley, **V**, 497

Connecticut, Fundamental Orders of, and colonial assemblies, **I**, 416; adopted, **II**, 21, 23; as a permanent form of government, **II**, 356; and the River Towns, **IV**, 490; and state constitutions, **V**, 166

Connecticut, Old Patent of, **II**, 21, 22, 24; **IV**, 490; **V**, 36

Connecticut Compromise, and the Constitution, **I**, 443; creates Congress, **II**, 51; and state sovereignty, **V**, 173

Connecticut Land Company, and Cleveland, **I**, 397; and the Firelands, **II**, 276; and Salt Springs Tract, **V**, 19; buys part of the Western Reserve, **V**, 444, 445

Connecticut Line, mutiny of, **IV**, 50

Connecticut-New York boundary controversy, **I**, 226

Connecticut Path, or Bay Path, I, 169

Connecticut River, and the Bay Path, I, 169

Connecticut's Western Lands, and the Susque-hannah Company, V, 211; and Decree of Trenton (1782), V, 322; and public domain, V, 444; and settlement of Wyoming Valley, V, 497

Connelly, Marc, playwright, I, 166

Conner, David, and blockade of Mexican Gulf ports, III, 383, 386, 387

Connolly, John, and Dunmore's War, II, 177; at Hannastown, III, 8; and Falls of the Ohio, IV, 162; and the Pennsylvania-Virginia boundary dispute, IV, 249; takes possession of Fort Pitt, IV, 279

Connolly, John, one of the first Dominican bishops in America, II, 159

Connolly, R. B., and the Tweed Ring, IV, 485; V, 333

Connolly v. Union Sewer Pipe Company, and equal protection of law, II, 222

Connor, Fort, and Powder River campaign, IV, 326

Connor, P. E., defeats Indians at Bear River, I, 171; and Powder River campaign, IV, 326

Conolly, Horace, and the story of Evangeline, II, 230

Conoy Indians, I, 48

Conquistadores, expedition of the, II, 61; and cowboys, II, 80; and the Penitent Brothers, IV, 242

Conrad, Robert T., dramatist, II, 166

Conscience Whigs, and the Free Soil party, I, 333; as a political party, IV, 296; and the Whig party, V, 456; or Woolly-Heads, V, 484

Conscientious Objectors, and amnesty after World War, I, 69; and the Union Army, I, 112; in the World War, II, 164; and peace movements, IV, 235; the Virginia exiles as, V, 378; and the World War, V, 492

Conscription, in the Union Army, I, 112; during the Civil War, I, 387; in the Confederacy, II, 4; and the Confederate Congress, II, 6; in the Confederacy, II, 11; and the draft, II, 163; and draft riots, II, 164; and mobilization, IV, 2; attacked during the Civil War, V, 176; and volunteers, V, 382

Conscription Act of 1863, legalizes substitutes, V, 196

Conservation Districts, as political subdivisions, IV, 299

Conservation Movement, and the Audubon societies, I, 137; and the Ballinger-Pinchot Controversy, I, 149; and monopoly, IV, 12; and water power, V, 423; and inland waterways, V, 425

Considerant, Prosper Victor, and Colony of Reunion, IV, 462

Consolidated Virginia Silver Mine, I, 208

Conspiracy Doctrine, as applied to labor movements, I, 439; and the injunction, III, 123; and the Philadelphia cordwainers' case, IV, 259; and restraint of trade, IV, 460; and strikes, V, 189

Constable, William, and the Castorland Company, I, 322; and the Macomb purchase, III, 321

Constellation, The, William Rush designs figurehead for, II, 272; frigate, II, 349

Constellation-Insurgente Engagement, IV, 73

Constellation-Vengeance Engagement, IV, 73

Constitution, Fort, and the Highlands, III, 31; original name for Fort Lee, III, 260; and West Point, V, 438

Constitution, The, and the Barbary Wars, I, 162; figureheads of, II, 272; frigate, II, 349; escapes from Broke's squadron, III, 58; midshipmen taken on board, IV, 69; and warships, V, 411

Constitution, The British, and the Declaration of Independence, II, 120; and the Declaration of Rights, II, 124; and Parliament, IV, 218; and political theories, IV, 300; and the American Revolution, IV, 466; and James Otis, IV, 484

Constitution of the United States, and Anglo-American relations, I, 74; and apportionment, I, 91; and the Bill of Rights, I, 185; and citizenship, I, 378; and civil liberties, I, 381; and the Confederation, II, 14; regulatory powers derived from, II, 17; and Congress, II, 18; framing of, II, 47; and the Convention of 1787, II, 50; gives Congress exclusive legislative powers over the District of Columbia, II, 153; due process clauses of, II, 172; and enumerated powers, II, 220; and Federal expenditures, II, 234; and extra sessions, II, 237; and extradition, II, 237; and the Federal Government, II, 260; and Federal-state relations, II, 263; ratification of, and The Federalist, II, 264; and the franchise, II, 323; and general welfare clause, II, 376; implied powers of the, III, 79; and imposts, III, 80; and Indian policy, III, 105; and interstate compacts, III, 144; and judicial review, III, 183; and the judiciary, III, 185; and jury trial, III, 191; and liberal construction, III, 268; and majority rule, III, 328; and the militia, III, 403; and personal liberty laws, IV, 254; and police power, IV, 294; and political theories, IV, 301; and privileges and immunities of citizens, IV, 351; and cruel and unusual punishments, IV, 382; and reserved powers of states, IV, 457 f.; and the right of revolution, IV, 472; and the slave trade, V, 92; drafting of, V, 167; and relations between the states, V, 174; and states' rights, V, 175; and taxation, V, 225; and third-term doctrine, V, 263; defines treason, V, 313; and treaty-making power of the President, V, 315; and the name United States

of America, V, 347; Virginia in part tries to defeat the, V, 373; and voters, V, 383; and war, V, 399; and war powers of the President, V, 407; and Washington, D. C., V, 412; opening words of, V, 428

Constitutional Courant, founded by William Goddard, IV, 127

Constitutional Union Party, I, 285; V, 262

Consular Service, II, 306; V, 163

Contarini, Giovanni, map of, III, 340

Contempt, in Anderson v. Dunn, I, 73

Continental Army. *See* Revolutionary Army

Continental Association, IV, 138

Continental Congress, and the Albany Plan, I, 45; and army contracts, I, 114; and the Articles of Confederation, I, 125; enacts Articles of War, I, 127; and Associations, I, 132; inhabitants of Bermuda send delegates to, I, 180; and bills of credit, I, 187; and Boston Committee of Correspondence, I, 222; and Boston Resolutions, I, 224; and campaign of 1788, I, 280; and American invasion of Canada (1775–76), I, 297; attempts to win Canada to American cause, I, 297; convenes at Carpenters' Hall, I, 318; and the Commercial Committee, I, 434; and Committees of Safety, I, 437; and the ratification of the Constitution, II, 28; and the Convention of 1787, II, 49; issues fiat money, II, 99; enacts the New York Statute of 1784 regarding customs duties, II, 102; incurs heavy debts, II, 118; and the Declaration of Independence, II, 120; first meeting of, II, 124; and the Indian factory system, II, 238; and origin of foreign service, II, 305; and freedom of the press, II, 337; and the Highlands, III, 31; and *Journal of Congress*, III, 182; and Massachusetts Provincial Congress, III, 359; and the Minutemen, III, 414; and the "Olive Branch Petition," IV, 172; and paper money, IV, 212; and Provincial Congresses, IV, 368; and representative government, IV, 452; and the American Revolution, IV, 467; and Revolutionary committees, IV, 474; and the seal of the United States, V, 49; and slavery, V, 94; and state constitutions, V, 166; and state government, V, 169; endorses the Suffolk Resolves, V, 198; and taxation, V, 225; and Thanksgiving Day, V, 259

Continental Divide, Ashley crosses the, I, 128; and the Astor Overlanders, I, 133

Continuous Voyage, and admiralty law, I, 13; and blockade, I, 201; and freedom of the seas during the Civil War, I, 390; and the Confederate blockade, II, 9; and the *Dolphin* admiralty case, II, 158; and the *Essex* case, II, 228; and international law, III, 141; and Declaration of London, III, 296; and neutrality, IV, 89; and the *Peterhoff* admiralty case, IV, 255; in Napo-

leonic wars, IV, 506; in the *Springbok* admiralty case, V, 150; in the World War, V, 490

Contraband, and armed neutrality, I, 108; and belligerents, I, 176; and freedom of the seas during the Civil War, I, 391; and the doctrine of continuous voyage, II, 142; and foreign policy, II, 303; and freedom of the seas, II, 338; and international law, III, 141; defined in treaty with Colombia, III, 249; and Declaration of London, III, 296; and neutral rights, IV, 88, 89; in Proclamation of Neutrality, IV, 91; in Neutrality Act of 1939, IV, 91; and Declaration of Paris (1856), IV, 215; and the *Peterhoff* admiralty case, IV, 255; and the Plan of 1776, IV, 283; and prize courts, IV, 352; and retaliation in international law, IV, 461; and visit and search, V, 381; mail treated as, V, 489

Contract, Obligation of, and arrest, I, 121; and the Constitution, II, 35; in Fletcher v. Peck, II, 284; and Gelpcke v. Dubuque, II, 374; and legal tender, III, 261; freedom of, and minimum-wage laws, III, 408 f.; and Minnesota Moratorium case, III, 412; impairment of, and moratoriums, IV, 22; obligation of, and Old Court-New Court struggle, IV, 170; freedom of, and restraint of trade, IV, 460; obligation of, and Sturges v. Crowninshield, V, 192; and West Coast Hotel Co. v. Parrish, V, 436; and Wolff Packing Co. case, V, 476

Contract Clause, and the Dartmouth College case, II, 111; and Yazoo land fraud, III, 239

Contrast, The, a play written by Royall Tyler, II, 165

Contreras, Battle of, and Scott-Pillow quarrel, V, 46

Contributory Negligence Doctrine, II, 212

Convention for the Pacific Settlement of International Disputes, I, 97

Convention of 1787, preceded by Alexandria Conference, I, 47; adopts amendment clause of Constitution, I, 55; preceded by Annapolis Convention, I, 78; compromises of the, I, 182, 443; and the Confederation, II, 14; and Congress, II, 18; and the Connecticut Compromise, II, 23; and the ratification of the Constitution, II, 28; and the Continental Congress, II, 47; and dual government, II, 172; and the executive and Congress, II, 233; and export taxes, II, 236; and the Federal Government, II, 257; and Federal-state relations, II, 263; and judicial review, III, 182; and legal tender, III, 261; and the Pinckney plan, IV, 272; and political theories, IV, 301; and separation of powers, IV, 327; and the Presidency, IV, 333; and the Presidential title, IV, 334; and state sovereignty, V, 173; and treason, V, 313

Convention of 1800, and alien landholding, I, 49;

and the Consular Convention, **II**, 44; negotiation of, **II**, 148; terminates Franco-American Alliance, **II**, 327 f.; and Franco-American misunderstanding, **II**, 327 f.; and the French decrees, **II**, 344; and French spoliation claims, **II**, 347; and treaties with foreign nations, **V**, 316; and the XYZ Affair, **V**, 499

Convention of 1818, and Anglo-American relations, **I**, 75; and annexation of territory, **I**, 79; and the Bayard-Chamberlain Treaty, **I**, 169; and fisheries question, **I**, 407; confirms part of Dakota Territory to United States, **II**, 106; and the fisheries dispute, **II**, 277; and Halifax fisheries award, **III**, 6; and joint occupation, **III**, 179; and Lake of the Woods boundary problem, **III**, 231; and Louisiana boundaries, **III**, 309; and the mackerel fisheries, **III**, 321; and the Northwest Angle, **IV**, 149; and settlement of the Northwest boundary controversy, **IV**, 150; and Oregon, **IV**, 182; and the Oregon Question, **IV**, 184; and Oregon Treaty, **IV**, 187; and treaties with foreign nations, **V**, 316; and western boundaries, **V**, 441

Convention of Inter-American Conciliation (1929), **II**, 2

Convention Relating to the Regulation of Air Navigation (1919), **I**, 35

Convention to Co-ordinate Existing Treaties (1936), **II**, 2

Conventions, Party Nominating, in campaign of 1832, **I**, 283; and campaign pledges, **I**, 292; and presidential campaigns, **I**, 295; succeed the congressional caucus, **I**, 328; and party machines, **III**, 319; and representative government, **IV**, 137; and the notification speech, **IV**, 153; and party government, **IV**, 220; and party platforms, **IV**, 285; and direct primary, **IV**, 341

Convict Labor, and the Auburn Prison system, **I**, 137; and chain gangs, **I**, 336; and the commerce clause, **I**, 434

Convicts, as indentured servants, **III**, 85

Convoys, and the Danish spoliation of American commerce, **II**, 109; adopted in World War, **IV**, 78; **V**, 493

Conway Cabal, War and Ordnance Board becomes involved in, **V**, 399; and Washington at Whitemarsh, **V**, 461

Conwell, R. H., lecturer, **III**, 260

Cook, George Cram, and the Provincetown Players, **IV**, 368

Cook, James, explores the Northwest coast, **IV**, 182; and the Oregon Question, **IV**, 184; sojourns at Nootka, **V**, 415

Cook, John, as hunter, **III**, 60

Cooke, F. J., and lecturing, **III**, 260

Cooke, James W., commands the *Albemarle*, **I**, 46

Cooke, Jay, and Company, and capitalism, **I**, 310;
during the Civil War, **I**, 388; and investment banking, **III**, 150; as financial agent of Northern Pacific Railroad, **IV**, 148; failure of, and panic of 1873, **IV**, 209; and railroads, **IV**, 408

Cooke, John Esten, and calomel, **I**, 276

Cooke, Philip St. George, commands the Mormon Battalion, **IV**, 24; and wagon trains, **V**, 389

Cooke, R. T., and fiction, **II**, 270

Cooley, T. M., writes third version of song "Dixie," **II**, 156

Cooley, Thomas M., and the Kalamazoo case, **III**, 193

Cooley v. Port Wardens, and the license cases, **III**, 275

Cooley's, book auctions, **I**, 211

Coolidge, Calvin, makes his summer home at Custer State Park, **I**, 195; vetoes bonus, **I**, 210; and Boston Police Strike, **I**, 224; elected Vice-President, **I**, 291; elected President, **I**, 291; vetoes the McNary-Haugen bill, **II**, 249; and Flag Day observance, **II**, 280; attends Havana Conference, **III**, 17; and the Sixth Pan-American Conference, **IV**, 203; and the Philippine Islands, **IV**, 263; and presidential absences from American soil, **IV**, 335; and the Republican party, **IV**, 454; and Tacna-Arica controversy, **V**, 216; and public building program for Washington, D. C., **V**, 413

Coolidge, W. D., develops ductile tungsten, **II**, 198; **III**, 232

Cooper, Dexter P., and Passamaquoddy, **IV**, 221

Cooper, James B., first superintendent of the Naval Home, **IV**, 70

Cooper, James Fenimore, and book publishing, **I**, 213; and bookshops, **I**, 214; and children's books, **I**, 363; author of *Leatherstocking Tales*, **II**, 270; romanticizes the Otsego lands, **IV**, 191; and the Perry-Elliott controversy, **IV**, 253

Cooper, Myles, as president of Columbia College, **I**, 429; forced to flee from New York, **IV**, 120

Cooper, Peter, nominated by Greenback party, **II**, 424; builds "Tom Thumb" locomotive, **III**, 292; and the Protective War Claims Association, **IV**, 366; builds "Tom Thumb" locomotive, **V**, 279, 308

Cooper, Robin, shoots Edward Carmack, **I**, 129

Cooper, Samuel, becomes a general of the Confederate army, **I**, 110

Cooper, Thomas, and the Alien and Sedition Acts, **I**, 49; repudiates doctrine of natural rights, **IV**, 66; and philosophical thought and writings, **IV**, 263; and presidential exemption from subpœna, **IV**, 334; defends slavery, **IV**, 363; and proslavery literature, **IV**, 364

Cooper, William, and Burlington Company, **I**, 256; and the Otsego lands, **IV**, 191

Cooper, William, pioneer of epidemiology, **II**, 221

Cooper Institute, **I**, 250

Cooper Union, **III**, 114

Co-operative Buying, and consumer protection, **II**, 44

Co-operatives, and the agrarian movement, **I**, 22; farmers', **I**, 26; and the Farm Bureau, **II**, 245; and the Granger movement, **II**, 411; tobacco, **V**, 275

Co-operatives, Producers', and Knights of Labor, **III**, 215

Co-ordinator of Transportation, **III**, 144; **IV**, 401

Copley, John Singleton, painter, **I**, 123; **III**, 408

Coppage, O. B., and Adair v. U. S., **I**, 9

Coppage v. Kansas, and the yellow-dog contract, **V**, 504

Copper, Anaconda, **I**, 71; Calumet and Hecla Mine, **I**, 276; mines, **III**, 407; in Montana, **IV**, 16; and St. Marys Falls Ship Canal, **V**, 14; search for, and Lake Superior, **V**, 205; and foreign trade, **V**, 295

Copper Country, development of, **III**, 245

Copperheads, in Charleston riot, **I**, 345; name given those opposed to Civil War, **II**, 137; and Knights of the Golden Circle, **III**, 215; Nast satirizes in cartoons, **IV**, 55; and the Northwest Conspiracy, **IV**, 150; discredited, **IV**, 161; and Order of American Knights, **IV**, 180; and Sons of Liberty (Civil War), **V**, 120; and Vallandigham incident, **V**, 355

Copson, John, opens a public insurance office, **III**, 128; co-founder of the *American Weekly Mercury*, **IV**, 127

Copyright, and the Constitution, **II**, 33

Copyright Laws, and bookselling, **I**, 213

Corbett, Boston, and shooting of John Wilkes Booth, **III**, 279

Corbett, "Gentleman" Jim, prize fighter, **IV**, 352

Corbett, William, publisher of *Porcupine's Gazette*, **IV**, 314

Corbin, Abel Rathbone, and Black Friday (1869), **I**, 194

Corcoran, W. W., and the Gardiner award, **II**, 371

Corcoran Art Gallery, **I**, 124; **IV**, 48

Corduroy Roads, **IV**, 494; **V**, 306

Corey, Giles, pressed to death, **IV**, 337; **V**, 476

Corfield v. Coryell, **V**, 174

"Corlear," governor of New York called, **IV**, 173

Corliss, George H., improves the steam engine, **V**, 178

Corn, and agricultural adaptation to the plains, **I**, 23; governmental control of, **I**, 33; and crop failures, **II**, 91; and rotation of crops, **II**, 154; as food, **II**, 294

Corn Belt, **II**, 78

Corn Borer, **II**, 91

Corn Dance, **II**, 422

Cornbury, Lord, in the colony of New York, **IV**, 114; and land speculation in New York, **IV**, 115

Cornell, Sarah, murder of, **V**, 323

Cornplanter, and Indian oratory, **III**, 103

Cornstalk, Chief, and treaty of Camp Charlotte, **I**, 345; leads Shawnee Indians in Dunmore's War, **II**, 177; murder of, **III**, 88; in battle of Point Pleasant, **IV**, 291; murdered at Fort Randolph, **IV**, 415

Cornwall, County of, **IV**, 240; **V**, 508

Cornwallis, Lord, in the Revolutionary War, **IV**, 477; and Yorktown campaign, **V**, 509

Coromante Negroes, **IV**, 86

Coronado, Francisco Vásquez de, and exploration of the West, **I**, 57; crosses Arizona en route to Cíbola, **I**, 104; and Cíbola, **I**, 375; and exploration of the Colorado River, **I**, 427; *conquistadore*, **II**, 25; and Gran Quivira, **II**, 407; and Grand Canyon of the Colorado, **II**, 408; in Kansas, **III**, 194; and missions of the Southwest, **III**, 418; in New Mexico, **IV**, 106; in Oklahoma, **IV**, 168; and Pecos, **IV**, 238; and the Great Plains, **IV**, 281; visits the Pueblo Indians, **IV**, 379; and the Rocky Mountains, **IV**, 498; crosses Staked Plains, **V**, 154; at Taos, **V**, 219; and Texas, **V**, 252; in Utah, **V**, 353; captures the Zuñi towns, **V**, 515

Coronado, Kans., and the county-seat war, **II**, 74

Coroner, as county officer, **III**, 288

Corporate Consolidations, and restraint of trade, **IV**, 460

Corporation Law, in Bank of the United States v. Planters' Bank of Georgia, **I**, 155

Corporation Securities Company, **II**, 196

Corporation Tax, **II**, 163; **III**, 84; **V**, 226

Corporations, and absentee ownership, **I**, 4; regulation of, **I**, 82; public control of, **I**, 260; and capitalism, **I**, 309; Bureau of, **I**, 432; and credit, **II**, 84; and the Dartmouth College case, **II**, 111; government, **II**, 402; and government regulation, **II**, 405

Corrupt Practices Acts, and campaign expenditures, **I**, 293; and election laws, **II**, 191; and Newberry v. U. S., **IV**, 121; and publicity laws, **IV**, 378; and the Vare case, **V**, 358

Corruption, and granting of franchises, **II**, 325

Corruption in Politics, and the Hatch Act, **III**, 16

Cortereal, Miguel, and Dighton Rock, **II**, 146; visits Rhode Island, **IV**, 477

Cortland, Stephen, and Iroquois treaty (1684), **III**, 160

Corwin, Thomas, and Civil War diplomacy, **I**, 391; leads Ohio Whigs in opposing the Mexican War, **IV**, 160; and oratory, **IV**, 180

Corydon, Ind., dead city, **II**, 114; capital of Indiana territory located at, **V**, 370

Coryell, John R., inventor of character of "Nick Carter," **II**, 147

Cosa, Juan de la, compiles map of the world, **III**, 340

Cosby, William, as governor of the colony of New York, **IV**, 115; and the Zenger trial, **V**, 513

Cosmopolitan Magazine, and muckrakers, **IV**, 38

Cost-Plus Contracts, **I**, 115; **V**, 492

Costa Rica, and Bryan-Chamorro Treaty, **I**, 245

Costilla Estates, **V**, 28

Cotton, and agriculture, **I**, 27; governmental control of, **I**, 33; in Alabama, **I**, 39; and the balance of trade, **I**, 147; Bankhead Act, **I**, 156; produced in Black Belt region, **I**, 193; and boll weevil, **I**, 207; trade in, during the Civil War, **I**, 390; and Civil War diplomacy, **I**, 392; and the Confederate blockade, **II**, 8; and Confederate financing, **II**, 9; in the Confederacy, **II**, 11, 13; and crop failures, **II**, 91; grown by Indians, **III**, 87; in Louisiana, **III**, 306; and the plantation system of the South, **IV**, 284; and proslavery, **IV**, 363; and changes in rural life, **IV**, 509; exported from Savannah, **V**, 35; and the slave trade, **V**, 92; and slavery, **V**, 94; and soil exhaustion, **V**, 116; and civilization of the Old South, **V**, 122; and the Southwest, **V**, 133; and textiles, **V**, 258; and domestic trade, **V**, 293; and foreign trade, **V**, 295

Cotton, John, and the Antinomian Controversy, **I**, 82; code of, and the Bible Commonwealth, **I**, 181; author of *Spiritual Milk for Boston Babes,* **I**, 363; and Massachusetts Body of Liberties, **III**, 358; prepares *Moses His Judicials,* **IV**, 30; and the New England Way, **IV**, 100; and philosophical thought and writings, **IV**, 263; political writings of, **IV**, 302; and the importance of sermons, **V**, 59; and theocracy in New England, **V**, 260

Cotton, John, Jr., and the Praying Indians, **IV**, 330

Cotton Agents, in the Confederacy, **II**, 5

Cotton Belt, and the panic of 1857, **IV**, 209

Cotton Bureau, organized by the Confederacy, **V**, 300

Cotton Futures Act, and exchanges, **II**, 232

Cotton Gin, and abolition movement, **I**, 2; invention of, **II**, 67, 248; **III**, 148; and the linen industry, **III**, 281; invention of, **III**, 320; and the plantation system of the South, **IV**, 284; invention of, revives slavery, **V**, 94

Cotton Mills, and manufacturing, **III**, 336; New Hampshire, **IV**, 102

Cotton Picker, invention of, **II**, 248; and unemployment, **III**, 321

Cotton Stabilization Corporation, **II**, 246

Cotton Whigs, **II**, 25; **IV**, 296; **V**, 456

"Cotton-eyed Joe," fiddle tune, **II**, 270

Cottontail, increases in spite of settlement, **V**, 463

Couch, W. L., and "boomers," **I**, 215; Oklahoma squatter, **IV**, 169

Coudray, Tronson du, commissioned in the Revolutionary Army, **IV**, 473

Coughlin, Charles E., organizes the National Union for Social Justice, **IV**, 63

Coulson Packet Company, owner of the *Far West,* **II**, 244

Coulter, Ernest K., and the Big Brother movement, **I**, 183

Coulter Shoals Dam, **V**, 245

Council, City, and city government, **III**, 289

Council Bluffs, and Independence, Mo., **III**, 85

Council for New England, and British colonial policy, **I**, 421; and the Dorchester Company, **II**, 161; grants patent to the Pilgrims, **II**, 356; and the Laconia grant, **III**, 226; and Long Island, **III**, 298; and Lygonia, **III**, 316; and Maine, **III**, 326; grants Mariana to John Mason, **III**, 343; and the Mason title, **III**, 351; and Massachusetts Bay Company, **III**, 357; and the Mayflower Compact, **III**, 362; and Monhegan Island, **IV**, 9; and the New England Company, **IV**, 99; and Gorges' grant, **IV**, 101; issues patent to Pilgrims, **IV**, 112; and the Pilgrims, **IV**, 271; and the Plymouth Company, **IV**, 290; and River Towns of Connecticut, **IV**, 490; and settlement of Saco Bay, **V**, 3; as a trading company, **V**, 301; and the Trelawney plantation, **V**, 320; and York's proprietary, **V**, 507

Council Grove, as assembling place for wagon trains, **II**, 77

Council of National Defense, and the World War, **V**, 492

Council of State Governments, **V**, 175

Councils of Censors, and judicial review, **III**, 182

Councils of Revision, and judicial review, **III**, 182

Counterfeiting, and the Constitution, **II**, 33; accelerated by industrial revolution, **II**, 88; and the Secret Service, **V**, 53

Country Gentleman, farm periodical, **II**, 248

County, as a political subdivision, **IV**, 299

County Fair, **I**, 32

County Government, **III**, 288

Coureurs de bois, at Cahokia, **I**, 267; and French exploration, **II**, 345; and the fur trade, **II**, 360; explorers of the Mississippi Valley, **III**, 425

Court of Claims, **I**, 12

Court of Customs and Patents Appeal, **I**, 12

Courts-Martial, in Grafton v. U. S., **II**, 407; and military law, **III**, 401; and the Milligan case, **III**, 405

Courts of Indian Offenses, **V**, 324

"Coushatta Massacre," and the White League, **V**, 459

Couture, Jean, commands Arkansas Post, **I**, 106; and the fur trade, **II**, 362

Couzens, James, founds Children's Fund of Michigan, **II**, 314

Covenant of Grace, **I**, 83

Covenant of the League of Nations, United States takes part in formation of, **I**, 97; and neutrality, **IV**, 90; and sanctions, **V**, 26

Covenant of Works, **I**, 83

Covenanters, anti-Catholic organization, **IV**, 66

Covered Wagons, on Oregon Trail, **I**, 312; emigrants travel by, **IV**, 183; on Oregon Trail, **IV**, 186; and overland freighting, **IV**, 192; and the westward movement, **V**, 451

Coverly, Nathaniel, publisher of chapbooks, **I**, 341

Covode, John, member of the Committee on the Conduct of the War, **I**, 436

Cow, The, and dairy industry, **II**, 103; and the westward movement, **V**, 451

Cow Country, and influence on agriculture, **I**, 33; and open range cattle period, **IV**, 177

Cow Custom, and open range cattle period, **IV**, 177

Cow Horse, **III**, 46

Cow Towns, Abilene, **I**, 2; and the cattle industry, **I**, 327; Ogallala, **IV**, 159; and open range cattle period, **IV**, 177

Cowan, John, and the Helena mining camp, **III**, 24

Cowan, Robert, book collection, **I**, 212

Cowboy Songs, and rodeos, **IV**, 499; and stampedes, **V**, 156

Cowboys, and cattle drives, **I**, 326; and cow towns, **II**, 79; and longhorns, **III**, 300; and sheep wars, **V**, 67; Spanish origin of, **V**, 138; as trail drivers, **V**, 302; and the Wild West Show, **V**, 464

Cowdery, Oliver, and the *Book of Mormon*, **IV**, 26

Coweset Indians, and the Narragansetts, **IV**, 53

Cowpens, Battle of, **IV**, 477; **V**, 129

Cowperthwait and Sons, and installment buying, **III**, 126

Cox, Jacob D., and Soldiers and Sailors Conventions, **V**, 117

Cox, James M., nominated for Presidency, **I**, 291

Cox, Jesse, and Social Democratic party, **V**, 107

Cox, Zachariah, and the Muscle Shoals speculation, **IV**, 47

Coxe, Daniel, and Carolana, **I**, 316; his plan of colonial union, **I**, 420

Coxe, Tench, and pamphleteering, **IV**, 202

Coxey's Army, and the panic of 1893, **IV**, 209; and right of petition, **IV**, 256

Coyle v. Smith, and enabling acts, **II**, 213

Coyote, survives in spite of settlement, **V**, 463; specie of the wolf, **V**, 476

Crab Orchard, road built from, **II**, 96

Crabb, Henry A., filibustering activities of, **II**, 274

Craig, Andrew, and Burlington Company, **I**, 256; and the Otsego lands, **IV**, 191

Craig, Charles Franklin, and medicine, **III**, 370

Craig, Fort, and Sibley's operations on the Rio Grande, **IV**, 485; attacked, **V**, 356

Craig, Lewis, and group migration, **III**, 397

Craig v. Missouri, **I**, 238

Craighead, Thomas B., heresy trial of, **III**, 27

Craigie, Andrew, and the Holland patent, **III**, 38; trustee of the Scioto Company, **V**, 44

Craigie, William, edits *A Dictionary of American English*, **II**, 146

Cram, Ralph Adams, revolutionizes ecclesiastical architecture, **I**, 101

Cramer, Stuart W., devises an automatic humidity control, **I**, 34

Cramer, Zadok, launches *The Navigator*, **IV**, 74

Cranch, Richard, and Company, and the Spermaceti trust, **V**, 145

Crandall, J. B., and the Pioneer Stage Line, **IV**, 274

Crandall v. Nevada, **V**, 174

Crane, Charles R., and the Root mission to Russia, **IV**, 501

Crane, Stephen, and fiction, **II**, 270

Crater, Battle of the, **IV**, 256, 481

Crater Lake National Park, **IV**, 218

Crawford, Fort, building of, **II**, 320; built at Prairie du Chien, **IV**, 328; and treaty of Prairie du Chien, **IV**, 329; established, **V**, 337; and American regime in Wisconsin, **V**, 473

Crawford, John, and insects as cause of disease, **IV**, 30

Crawford, Thomas, and the Capitol dome, **I**, 311

Crawford, William, builds Fort Henry, **III**, 26

Crawford, William H., and A. B. Plot, **I**, 1; and campaign of 1816, **I**, 282; and the Democratic party, **II**, 136; and the *Washington Gazette*, **IV**, 128; and the congressional caucus, **IV**, 137; and the Yazoo fraud, **V**, 503

Crawford County Plan, and direct primary, **IV**, 341

Crawford's Defeat, **III**, 88, 408; and battle of the Olentangy, **IV**, 172

Crazy Horse, killed at Fort Robinson, **IV**, 497; Sioux chief, **V**, 85; and Sioux wars, **V**, 87; attacks at Slim Buttes, **V**, 98

Crazy Woman Creek, Cheyenne villages destroyed at, **I**, 355

Cream Separator, **II**, 105

Creccencio, develops school in water colors, **III**, 93

Crédit Mobilier, political scandal, **IV**, 298; and profiteering, **IV**, 355; and railroads, **IV**, 408; and the Union Pacific, **V**, 343

Creditor Nation, United States as a, **I**, 147; **II**, 119

Cree Indians, **I**, 48

Creek Country, visited by DeSoto, **II**, 141

Creek Indians, and Congress of Augusta, **I**, 138; and the battle of Auttose, **I**, 141; cession of, opens portion of Black Belt for settlement, **I**, 193; and Bowles expeditions, **I**, 230; and battle of Burnt Corn, **I**, 257; and the Chickamauga, **I**, 359; Chickasaw war against, **I**, 360; in Crazy Snake rebellion, **II**, 83; meet at Cusseta, **II**, 101; and the Dawes Commission, **II**, 113; and the establishment of Fort Deposit, **II**, 139; and the battle of Econochaca, **II**, 184; in battles of Emucfau Village and Enotachapco Creek, **II**, 213; one of the Five Civilized Tribes, **II**, 279; and Forbes purchase, **II**, 299; and the Galphin Claim, **II**, 368; in Georgia, **II**, 379; and Wayne's operations in Georgia, **II**, 381; and the Great Trading and War Path, **II**, 420; at Hickory Ground, **III**, 29; and Hillabee towns, **III**, 32; attacked at Horseshoe Bend, **III**, 50; in the Revolution, **III**, 89; compose Indian brigade, **III**, 94; land cessions of, **III**, 100; removal of, **III**, 107; held in servitude, **III**, 108; and treaties of Indian Springs, **III**, 108; and War of Jenkins' Ear, **III**, 173; and the McGillivray incident, **III**, 365; and massacre at Fort Mims, **III**, 405; as mound builders, **IV**, 35; Natchez campaign of 1813 against, **IV**, 57; and treaty of Nogales, **IV**, 136; removed to Oklahoma, **IV**, 168; and Panton, Leslie & Co., **IV**, 211; at Congress of Pensacola (1765), **IV**, 250; and scalping, **V**, 37; and the Seminoles, **V**, 57; relations with the Spanish, **V**, 140; and battle of Talladega, **V**, 217; and battle at Tallasahatchee, **V**, 217; at Tookabatchee, **V**, 281; and secret treaties, **V**, 316; occupy Turkey Town, **V**, 331; and the War of 1812, **V**, 406; and treaty at Fort Wilkinson, **V**, 466; and the Yamasee War, **V**, 501

Creek Wars, backwoodsmen in, **I**, 145; Fort Jackson during, **V**, 286. *See also* Jackson, Fort, Treaty of

Creel, George, Chairman of Committee on Public Information, **I**, 436; **V**, 494

Creole Affair, **I**, 68

Cresap, Michael, and Logan's speech, **III**, 294

Cresap, Thomas, settles at Old Town, **IV**, 325

Crèvecœur, Fort, **II**, 346; **III**, 67, 246; **IV**, 252

Crile, George, and surgery, **III**, 370

Crime, and slums, **V**, 99

"Crime against Kansas," **I**, 244; **III**, 198

Crime of '73, and the demonetization of silver, **I**, 189; and the Bland-Allison Act, **I**, 198; and bullion, **I**, 252; and money system, **IV**, 8

Criminal Syndicalism, **I**, 86; **II**, 88; **IV**, 433; **V**, 55

Criminals, **II**, 370

Cripple Creek, Colo., a boom town, **I**, 215; gold camp at, **I**, 426; gold discovered at, **II**, 396; and prospectors, **IV**, 364

Cripple Creek Strike of 1894, **V**, 443

Crisis, and pamphleteering, **IV**, 202; political tract by Thomas Paine, **V**, 291

Crittenden, George B., and the encounter at Mill Springs, **III**, 404

Crittenden, John J., and formation of Constitutional Union party, **II**, 44; pardons Calvin Fairbanks, **V**, 431

Crittenden, T. L., and battle of Murfreesboro, **IV**, 46

Crittenden Compromise, and Peace Convention of 1861, **I**, 219; considered by Committee of Thirteen and Committee of Thirty-three, **I**, 436; Congress rejects, **I**, 442; and secession of Southern states, **V**, 52

Croatan Indians, and the Melungeons, **III**, 371

Croatoan, and Raleigh's Lost Colony, **IV**, 413

Crocker, M. M., and battle of Raymond, **IV**, 418

Crockett, David, and the Alamo, **I**, 42; as a "bar hunter," **I**, 171; and cattle drives, **I**, 325; and tall tales, **II**, 270; bear and deer hunter, **III**, 60; and American slang, **V**, 88; and tall stories, **V**, 186; perishes in the Alamo assault, **V**, 257

Croghan, George, makes headquarters at Aughwick, **I**, 138; and Baynton, Wharton and Morgan, **I**, 170; and Burlington Company, **I**, 256; and treaty of Fort de Chartres, **I**, 348; and the treaty of Easton (1758), **II**, 183; attempts to reach Illinois, **III**, 69; fur trader, **III**, 111; and land speculation, **III**, 239; and Indian negotiations at Logstown, **III**, 295; purchases the Otsego lands, **IV**, 191; gains friendship of the Miami Indians, **IV**, 266; and Sideling Hill, **V**, 77; and western land schemes, **V**, 443

Croghan, George, and the defense of Fort Stephenson (1813), **V**, 181

Croker, Richard, and the Lexow Committee, **III**, 267

Crol, Sebastian, in New Amsterdam, **IV**, 108

Croly, Herbert, political writings of, **IV**, 302

Croly, Jane Cunningham, leader of the Sorosis Club, **V**, 477 f.; as woman journalist, **V**, 481

Crompton, William, and the loom, **II**, 67; **III**, 301

Cronin, Philip P., assassination of, **V**, 323

Crook, George, and Geronimo's campaigns, **II**, 385; recommends the establishment of Fort McKinney, **III**, 366; and Sioux wars, **V**, 87; and battle of Slim Buttes, **V**, 98

Crooks, Ramsay, and the American Fur Company, **I**, 61; fur trader, **III**, 111; in command of American Fur Company, **V**, 133

Crop Diversification, encouraged by Illinois Central Railroad, **III**, 70

Crop Failures, and climate, **I**, 398

Crop Rotation, as remedy for soil exhaustion, **V,** 116

Crops, and rainfall, **IV,** 411

Cropsey, Jasper, landscape painter, **I,** 123

Croquet, **I,** 70

Cross, Edward E., editor of the *Weekly Arizonian,* **IV,** 126

Cross Keys, battle at, **III,** 165

"Cross of Gold" Speech, **I,** 288; **II,** 333

Croswell, Edwin, editor of the *Albany Argus,* **IV,** 128

Croswell Trial, **III,** 268

Crothers, Rachel, dramatist, **II,** 166

Crothers, Samuel, and abolitionist literature, **I,** 3

Croton Aqueduct, **I,** 93; **V,** 424

Crow, Chief, arrest of, **II,** 175

Crow Indians, inform Jedediah Smith of location of South Pass, **I,** 128; and the Cheyennes, **I,** 355; on Green River, **II,** 423; and Manuel's Fort, **III,** 335; in Montana, **IV,** 16; and scouting on the plains, **V,** 46

Crowder's Mission in Cuba, **I,** 314; **II,** 94, 95

Crowe, Pat, kidnaps son of E. A. Cudahy, **III,** 208

Crown Domains, and distribution of wealth, **V,** 429

Crown Point, and the battle of Bloody Pond, **I,** 203; and the building of Fort Edward, **II,** 189; in French and Indian War, **III,** 229; and battle of Lake George (1755), **III,** 230; in the Revolutionary War, **III,** 230; French occupy (1731), **IV,** 115; capture of (1759), **V,** 362

Crowninshield, George, and yacht racing in America, **V,** 499

Crozat, Antoine, granted privilege of exploiting Louisiana, **III,** 305; and the Mississippi Bubble, **III,** 421; and territory of Orleans, **IV,** 188; lead mining grant of, **V,** 9

Cruisers. *See* Warships

Crusader, famous thoroughbred horse, **V,** 265

Cruse, Thomas, develops the Drum Lummon mine, **III,** 24

Cuba, and Caribbean policy, **I,** 313; and expansion, **II,** 233; and Guantanamo Bay, **II,** 427; intervention in, **III,** 146; and Lopez filibustering expedition, **III,** 301; and the Gulf of Mexico, **III,** 389; status of, in Neely v. Henkel, **IV,** 81; and the Ostend Manifesto, **IV,** 190; returned by England to Spain by treaty of Paris (1763), **IV,** 216; Spain relinquishes all authority over, by treaty of Paris (1898), **IV,** 216; and the Platt Amendment, **IV,** 285; and Spanish-American relations, **V,** 135; and the Spanish-American War, **V,** 136; and the Teller Resolution, **V,** 240; Isle of Pines Treaty with, **V,** 318

Cudahy, E. A., kidnapping of son of, **III,** 208

Cudahy, John, and meat packing, **IV,** 199

Cullom Committee, report of the, **III,** 144; and railroad rate wars, **IV,** 404

Culpeper, Lord, and the Fairfax proprietary, **II,** 240

Cultivator, farm periodical, **II,** 248

Cumberland, Army of the, and battle of Chickamauga, **I,** 359; and battle of Murfreesboro, **IV,** 46; evolves from the Army of the Ohio, **IV,** 162; reinforced by Army of the Tennessee, **V,** 242

Cumberland, Fort, and Braddock's Expedition, **I,** 233; and Forbes Expedition, **II,** 299

Cumberland, The, destroyed by the *Merrimack* (*Virginia*), **III,** 378

Cumberland Gap, and the Alleghenies, **I,** 51; a buffalo trail, **I,** 248; and Crab Orchard, **II,** 82; Boone makes known, **II,** 235; and the Great Trading and War Path, **II,** 420; Thomas Walker crosses through, **III,** 204; and the Miami Trail, **III,** 390; and mountain passes, **IV,** 221; Powell's Valley leads to, **IV,** 326; and Wilderness Road, **IV,** 494; Scioto Trail runs to, **V,** 45; and transportation and travel, **V,** 307; and Great Warriors Path, **V,** 408; Wilderness Road runs through, **V,** 465

Cumberland Presbyterians, adopt circuit riding, **I,** 376; and the Great Revival, **II,** 419; formed, **IV,** 332

Cumberland River, as inland waterway, **V,** 424

Cumberland Road, and influence on agriculture, **I,** 33; developed from Braddock's Road, **I,** 233; first national enterprise, **III,** 137; often called National Road, **IV,** 63; and road development, **IV,** 494; and shifts in trade routes and centers, **V,** 300; route of Allegheny wagoners, **V,** 390; and growth of Wheeling, W. Va., **V,** 455

Cumberland Settlements, and Avery's Trace, **I,** 142; Chickamauga troublesome to, **I,** 359; and the Chickasaw treaty, **I,** 361; and Nashville, **IV,** 54; and rivers, **IV,** 491; and the Old Southwest, **V,** 132; and Tennessee, **V,** 243; and the Transylvania Company, **V,** 310; and Turkey Town, **V,** 331; and the Wataugans, **V,** 421

Cumberland Valley Railroad, installs sleeping-car service, **IV,** 381

Cuming, Alexander, and the Cherokee Indians, **I,** 352

Cuming, Thomas B., acting governor of Nebraska, **IV,** 80

Cumming, Alfred, governor of Utah, **V,** 354

Cummins, A. B., leads revolt against the Payne-Aldrich Tariff Bill, **IV,** 356

Cumulative Vote Plan, **II,** 193; **IV,** 451

Cunningham, and book auctions, **I,** 211

Cunningham, Ann Pamela, founder of Mount Vernon Ladies' Association, **IV,** 36

Cunningham Syndicate, and the Ballinger-Pinchot controversy, **I,** 149

Curb Market, development of, **IV,** 118

Currency, and the silver dollar, **II,** 157; continental, **II,** 269; stabilization of, and the World Economic Conference, **V,** 486

Curricle, for travel, **V,** 306

Currie, William, and epidemics, **II,** 221

Currier and Ives Prints, **I,** 124

Currituck Sound, **I,** 46

Curry, J. L. M., and the Peabody fund, **IV,** 230

Curtis, B. R., in Cooley case, **II,** 55

Curtis, Charles, elected Vice-President, **I,** 291

Curtis, Charles G., and the steam turbine, **II,** 198; **V,** 178

Curtis, Cyrus H. K., buys the *Saturday Evening Post,* **V,** 33

Curtis, George W., and oratory, **IV,** 180

Curtis, I. W., and Pearl Harbor naval base, **IV,** 237

Curtis, S. R., and the battle of Pea Ridge, **IV,** 230; and Price in Missouri, **IV,** 339; and the battle of Westport, Mo., **V,** 449; builds Fort Zarah, **V,** 513

Curtis Institute of Music, **II,** 315

Curtis Publishing Company, and marketing research, **III,** 345

Curtiss, Glenn H., sets new world's record for flying (1910), **I,** 36; and aviation, **I,** 142; builds motor used in first government dirigible, **II,** 148

Cushing, Caleb, negotiates first treaty with China (1844), **I,** 78; and land speculation, **III,** 240; and Oregon Memorial of 1838, **IV,** 183

Cushing, Harvey, and cerebral surgery, **III,** 370

Cushing, William B., sinks the *Albemarle,* **I,** 46

Cushman, Charlotte, famous actress, **V,** 260

Cushman, Robert, and the Pilgrims, **IV,** 271

Cushnoc's Trading Post, **V,** 440

Custer, George A., builds Fort Abraham Lincoln, **I,** 4; in Black Hills, **I,** 195; and the Cheyenne Indians, **I,** 355; makes headquarters at Fort Hays, **III,** 20; and Little Big Horn battle, **III,** 284; **V,** 87; and Soldiers and Sailors Conventions, **V,** 117; begins Washita campaign, **V,** 205; and engagement at Tom's Brook, **V,** 280; and battle at Trevilian Station, **V,** 323; destroys the Cheyenne camp of Black Kettle, **V,** 420

Custis, G. W. Parke, and the Arlington National Shrine, **I,** 107; and U. S. v. Lee, **V,** 349

Customs, and colonial governors, **I,** 419; and the Constitution, **II,** 33; as internal revenue, **III,** 139; colonial, **IV,** 504; and tariff, **V,** 221; and taxation, **V,** 226

Customs Receivership, and America's relations with Dominican Republic, **II,** 159

Customs Service, under control of the Treasury Department, **V,** 314

Cutler, Manasseh, climbs and names Mt. Washington, **IV,** 36; represents Ohio Company of Associates, **IV,** 163; and the Scioto Company, **V,** 44

Cutter, Charles Ammi, and the American Library Association, **III,** 272

Cutting, Bronson M., and airplane disasters, **I,** 36

Cutting, James A., and photography, **IV,** 265

Cuyahoga, The, capture of, **II,** 144

Cuyuna Range, and iron mining, **III,** 157

Cyclone, at Galveston, **II,** 368

Cyclorama, **IV,** 211

Cypress Gardens, **I,** 344

Czolgosz, Leon, as an anarchist, **I,** 72; shoots William McKinley, **I,** 129

D

D. G. Kerr, The, Great Lakes steamship, **II,** 417

Dablon, Charles, begins mission of St. Ignace, **V,** 9

Dade, Francis L., killed by Seminoles, **V,** 57

Daggett, Ezra, pioneer of American canning, **I,** 304

Daguerreotypes, and photography, **IV,** 265

Dagworthy, George, and Forbes expedition, **II,** 299

Daily Advertiser, started by Francis Childs, **IV,** 125

Daily Graphic, pioneer picture paper, **V,** 216

Daily Mirror, **V,** 216

Daily News Building, built by Raymond Hood, **I,** 101

Daily Telegraph, founded by Hiram Brundage, **IV,** 128

Dairy Industry, **II,** 77, 154

Daisy Bradford No. 3, oil discovery, **II,** 182

Dakota Indians, expeditions of Sibley and Sully against, **II,** 106; picture writing of, **IV,** 267; and the Red River cart traffic, **IV,** 431

Dakotah Democrat, founded by Samuel J. Albright, **IV,** 127

Dale, Sam, and battle of Burnt Corn, **I,** 257

Dale, Thomas, allows private ownership of property in Jamestown, **V,** 372

Dallas, A. J., and the tariff, **V,** 221

Dallas, G. M., elected Vice-President, **I,** 284

D'Allion, Joseph de la Roche, and the oil industry, **IV,** 166

Dalton Gang, robbers, **I,** 152; **V,** 303

Daly, Augustin, playwright, **II,** 166

Daly, Marcus, and Anaconda Copper, **I,** 71; feud with W. A. Clark, **IV,** 16

Dalzel, James, slain in the battle of Bloody Run, **I,** 203; in Pontiac's War, **IV,** 306

Dame Schools, and coeducation, **I,** 408; and early

schoolteachers, V, 42; and education of women, V, 480

"Damn the Torpedoes," IV, 1

Damrosch, Leopold, and introduction of Wagnerian opera to America, IV, 48

Damrosch, Walter, produces his first opera composition, IV, 178

Dams and Locks, III, 292

Dana, Charles A., and Brook Farm, I, 243; as newspaper editor, IV, 123; and "On to Richmond," IV, 173; and the Socialist movement, V, 110

Dana, Francis, as minister to Russia, I, 108

Danbury Burned (1777), IV, 483

Danbury Hatters' Case, I, 232; III, 220, 293

Dancing, I, 69

Dancing Rabbit Creek, Treaty of, and the Choctaw land cession, I, 369; and Vicksburg, V, 367

Dandridge, alias for Bassett Town, V, 415

Danforth, Samuel, compiles the New-England Almanack for 1686, IV, 99

Danforth, Thomas, and Maine under Massachusetts, II, 401

Daniel, John W., and the Readjuster movement, IV, 419

Daniels, Josephus, and naval oil reserves, IV, 71

Danish-American Relations, I, 179

Danish West Indies. See Virgin Islands

D'Anville, Duc, and King George's War, III, 210

D'Anville, Guillaume, and topographic mapping, V, 282

Dare, Eleanor White, gives birth to first English child born in America, IV, 413

Dare, Virginia, and the Dare stone, II, 109; first English child born in America, IV, 413

"Dark Horse" Candidates, in campaigns of 1844 and 1852, I, 284

Darnall, Henry, as a proprietary agent, IV, 361

Darragh, Lydia, as a spy, V, 145; and Whitemarsh, V, 461

Darrow, Clarence, defense attorney in the McNamara case, III, 367; and oratory, IV, 180; and Scopes trial, V, 45

D'Artaguette's Defeat, I, 360

Dartmouth College, founded, II, 185; and the Great Awakening, II, 413; founded, IV, 102

Dartmouth College Case, and denominational colleges, I, 414; and the contract clause, II, 48; and denominational colleges, II, 186; and the Judiciary Act of 1789, III, 189

Darwinian Theory, and Scopes trial, V, 45; and theological writings, V, 261

Dating, Old Style and New Style, I, 268

Daugherty, H. M., and railway shopmen's strike of 1922, IV, 410

Daughters of the American Revolution, and state flags, II, 281

Daughters of the Confederacy, and Stone Mountain sculptures, I, 220

D'Aulnay, Charles, in the Penobscot region, II, 346; and Port Royal, IV, 315

Dauphine Island, Fort Gaines erected on, II, 366; seat of colonial government removed from Fort Maurepas to, III, 360

Davenport, Charles Benedict, and vital statistics, V, 382

Davenport, Homer, and political cartoons, I, 320

Davenport, John, and Connecticut, II, 21; and New Haven colony, IV, 103; manuscript writings of, and the "Phantom Ship," IV, 257; political writings of, IV, 302; and regicides in New England, IV, 438; enters into the New Haven church covenant, V, 60

Davenport, Thomas, tries to operate miniature electric railway, II, 199; and electric railways, IV, 410

David Harum, written by E. N. Westcott, I, 180

"Davids," in the Civil War, V, 193

Davids, James (John Dixwell), IV, 438

Davidson, Fort, and battle of Pilot Knob, IV, 272

Davidson, J. W., and the Red River Indian War, IV, 431

Davie, William Richardson, delegate to Convention of 1787, II, 50; diplomatic mission of, II, 148

Davies, E. T., co-founder of the Santa Fé Republican, IV, 127

Davies, Samuel, evangelist, II, 230; and American hymns, III, 65; and revivals, IV, 464

Davies v. McKeeby, IV, 214

Davis, Cushman K., Republican leader in Minnesota, III, 411

Davis, D. W., and refrigerator cars, IV, 437

Davis, David, and the Greenback party, II, 424

Davis, Dwight F., tennis player, V, 245

Davis, E. J., elected governor of Texas, V, 255

Davis, George, and flight of Confederate Cabinet, II, 5

Davis, H. G., nominated for Vice-Presidency, I, 289

Davis, Henry Winter, a Radical Republican, IV, 395; and Lincoln's plan of Reconstruction, IV, 427; and Wade Bill, V, 386

Davis, J. P., and wood engraving, V, 483

Davis, Jack, train robber, V, 303

Davis, James, founder of the North-Carolina Gazette, IV, 127; first printer of North Carolina, IV, 346

Davis, James, Secretary of Labor, III, 221

Davis, "Jeff," and the agrarian movement, I, 22

Davis, Jefferson, and the Confederate army, I, 109; studies at Transylvania College, I, 205; and western railroads, I, 312; and Chattanooga campaign, I, 348; and surrender of the Con-

federate armies, **I**, 385; and conscription in the Confederacy, **II**, 4; and flight of the Confederate Cabinet, **II**, 5; Confederate president, **II**, 9; and the cotton kingdom, **II**, 70; places Lee in command, **II**, 240; and Hampton Roads conference, **III**, 7; and Hood's Tennessee campaign, **III**, 44; and the Kansas-Nebraska Act, **III**, 197; and invasion of Maryland, **III**, 349; confined in Fortress Monroe, **IV**, 13; selected President by Montgomery Convention, **IV**, 17; and the peace movement of 1864, **IV**, 233; and invasion of Pennsylvania, **IV**, 244; political writings of, **IV**, 302; and railroad surveys, **IV**, 405; and evacuation of Richmond, **IV**, 482; and slavery, **V**, 96; indictment of, **V**, 313; and the White House of the Confederacy, **V**, 459; assists in building of Fort Winnebago, **V**, 471

Davis, Jefferson C., in the battle of Blackwater, **I**, 198; quarrels with Nelson, **IV**, 86

Davis, John, voyages to Davis Strait, **IV**, 150

Davis, John W., nominated for Presidency, **I**, 291

Davis, Mrs. Jefferson, and the White House of the Confederacy, **V**, 459

Davis, Norman, and peace conferences, **IV**, 233

Davis, Ozora Stearns, hymn writer, **III**, 65

Davis, Sylvanus, surrenders at Fort Loyal, **III**, 311

Davis, William, wins Dole Race, **I**, 36

Davis Cup Tennis Matches, **V**, 245

Davison, Nicholas, and the Pemaquid proprietors, **IV**, 240

Davy, Humphry, and the science of agriculture, **I**, 30; suggests nitrous oxide for surgery, **I**, 71; demonstrates arc light, **II**, 195

Dawes, Charles G., elected Vice-President, **I**, 291; and closure, **I**, 403

Dawes, William, warns of battle of Lexington, **III**, 267; and Revere's ride, **IV**, 463

Dawes Act of 1887, and Americanization, **I**, 68; revised by Burke Act, **I**, 256; and Indian land policy, **III**, 90; and Indian citizenship, **III**, 95; and Indian policy, **III**, 106

Dawes Commission, and the Five Civilized Tribes, **II**, 279; and Indian policy, **III**, 106; and Oklahoma, **IV**, 168

Dawes Plan, and Lausanne Agreement, **III**, 251; and the Paris Agreement, **IV**, 217; and the Reparation Commission, **IV**, 450

Dawson Pacts, and our relations with Nicaragua, **IV**, 131

Day, Benjamin, and the cheap press, **III**, 353

Day, John, unofficial explorer, **II**, 235

Day, Mahlon, publisher of chapbooks, **I**, 341

Day (or Daye), Stephen, and the almanac, **I**, 51; prints the Bay Psalm Book, **I**, 169; printer, **I**, 213, 277; and printing in America, **IV**, 344; first printer of Massachusetts, **IV**, 346

Day, William R., and the treaty of Paris (1898), **IV**, 217

Daylight Saving Time, and legislative riders, **IV**, 482

Days of Real Sport, comic strip, **I**, 431

Dayton, and the city manager plan, **I**, 380; **III**, 289

Dayton, Jonathan, signer of the Constitution, **II**, 39; and the Miami Purchase, **III**, 390; and Miranda's intrigues, **III**, 414

Dayton, William, and Civil War diplomacy, **I**, 391

Dayton-Goose Creek Railway v. U. S., **IV**, 421

Daytona Beach, speed tests made at, **I**, 139

Dead Buffalo Lake, Sibley defeats Indians at, **II**, 106

Dead Rabbits, battle Bowery Boys, **IV**, 3

Deadwood, S. Dak., mint at, **I**, 129

"Deadwood Dick," created by Edward L. Wheeler, **II**, 147

Deadwood Gulch, gold discovery in, **I**, 195

Deaf and Dumb, and philanthropy and benevolence, **IV**, 260

Deane, Silas, first to establish diplomatic contact with France, **II**, 322; and Franco-American Alliance, **II**, 326; member of the Illinois and Wabash Company, **III**, 69; and profiteering, **IV**, 355; and diplomacy of the Revolution, **IV**, 470; and profiteering, **IV**, 475

Dearborn, Fort, and the Beaubien Land Claim, **I**, 172; and Chicago, **I**, 356; massacre at, **III**, 68; and transportation, **IV**, 316

Dearborn, Henry, in first battle of Freeman's Farm, **II**, 339; and Hull court-martial, **III**, 57

Death Valley, and borax, **I**, 218; crossed by Manly's train, **II**, 236; origin of name, **II**, 313; and the Great Basin, **II**, 414; and thirst, **V**, 263

DeBarras, and the battle of Virginia Capes, **V**, 376

Debates, in Congress, **II**, 19; Lincoln-Douglas, **III**, 278; Webster-Hayne, **V**, 431

DeBow, James D. B., and proslavery literature, **IV**, 364; and civilization of the Old South, **V**, 122

Debs, Eugene V., and the American Railway Union, **I**, 65; Socialist candidate for President, **I**, 290; nominated for Presidency, **I**, 291; and alliance between populism and urban labor, **IV**, 313; and the Pullman strike, **IV**, 381; and the "reds," **IV**, 433; and Social Democratic party, **V**, 107, 110; and the Socialist party, **V**, 111

Debt, Imprisonment for, **I**, 121; **III**, 224; **V**, 484

Debt, Public, funding of Revolutionary, **I**, 132; and location of the national capital, **I**, 307; and the Constitution, **II**, 33; and public credit, **II**, 84; increase of, **II**, 128, 137; and the Phelps-

Gorham purchase, **IV,** 258; and the Public Credit Act, **IV,** 369; and public faith, **IV,** 371; repudiation of, **IV,** 455

Debt Funding Commission, **V,** 401

Debts, International, and the Drago Doctrine, **II,** 165

Decatur, Stephen, and Bank of North America, **I,** 154; and the Barbary Wars, **I,** 162; mortally wounded in duel with Barron, **I,** 198; and the Blue Lights, **I,** 204; duels with Barron, **II,** 174; captures the *Intrepid,* **III,** 147; and "Our Country, Right or Wrong," **IV,** 191; burns the *Philadelphia,* **IV,** 259; and the *President,* **IV,** 334; and tribute, **V,** 325; and the *United States,* **V,** 347

Decatur Baptist College, oldest existing junior college in the United States, **III,** 190

DeChaumont, James LeRoy, and New York land speculation, **IV,** 116

Decimal System, and money, **IV,** 7

Declaration of Independence, and antislavery agitation, **I,** 84; billeting objected to in, **I,** 187; and civil liberties, **I,** 381; and common law, **I,** 439; and colonial judiciary, **I,** 420; and the compact theory, **I,** 441; adoption of the, **II,** 46; and doctrine of equality, **II,** 223; and the Fourth of July, **II,** 318; and Jeffersonian Democracy, **III,** 171; and the Liberty Bell, **III,** 271; and Loyalists, **III,** 312; and natural rights, **IV,** 66; and the Parson's Cause, **IV,** 219; and personal liberty, **IV,** 254; and right of petition, **IV,** 256; and political theories, **IV,** 300; and right of rebellion, **IV,** 421; and the American Revolution, **IV,** 468; and Rodney's ride, **IV,** 500; condemns slave trade, **V,** 91; and antislavery movements, **V,** 97; and state constitutions, **V,** 166; drafted in the Indian Queen Tavern, **V,** 224; and the name United States of America, **V,** 347

Declaration of London, and blockades, **I,** 201

Declaration of Paris, and freedom of the seas during the Civil War, **I,** 390

Declaration of Rights (1774), adopted by Continental Congress, **II,** 46; and mercantilism, **III,** 375; and separation of powers, **IV,** 327; and the American Revolution, **IV,** 467

Deer, as Indian food, **III,** 87; destruction of, by settlement, **V,** 462

Deer Skins, Indians trade in, **III,** 109

Deere, John, and the saw-steel plow, **II,** 247; experiments on a steel plow, **IV,** 287

Deerfield Massacre, **III,** 95; **IV,** 389

Deering Harvester Company, **III,** 140

Deeter, Jasper, founder of the Hedgerow Theater, **III,** 286

Defiance, Fort, in the Wayne campaign, **V,** 427

Definitive Treaty of Peace, Signed at Paris, Sept. 3, 1783, and alien landholding, **I,** 49; as it affected aliens, **I,** 50; and international arbitration, **I,** 96; and armed neutrality, **I,** 108; violated by the states, **I,** 126; and the Border Forts, **I,** 218; and state boundaries, **I,** 226; and British debts, **I,** 240; and citizenship, **I,** 378; and Clark's Northwest campaign, **I,** 395; and fishing privileges, **I,** 407; and the Confederation, **II,** 14; releases prisoners of war, **II,** 49; and Convention of 1818, **II,** 52; and Lake Erie, **II,** 224; and the fisheries dispute, **II,** 277; and Florida, **II,** 288; and Florida boundary, **II,** 290; and the Great Lakes, **II,** 416; and Indian barrier state, **III,** 93; and Jay-Gardoqui negotiations, **III,** 168; and Jay's treaty, **III,** 169; and the Labrador fisheries, **III,** 225; and the Lake of the Woods boundary problem, **III,** 231; and claims on part of West Florida, **III,** 420; and free navigation of the Mississippi River, **III,** 422; and the Mississippi River, **III,** 424; and the Mississippi Valley, **III,** 425; and Mitchell's map, **III,** 431; and the northeast boundary, **IV,** 147; and the Northwest Angle, **IV,** 149; and the northwest boundary controversy, **IV,** 149; and peace of Paris, **IV,** 216; and the Red Line Map, **IV,** 429; and the American Revolution, **IV,** 470; and Rouse's Point boundary controversy, **IV,** 503; and the St. Croix River, **V,** 7; and Fort St. Joseph, **V,** 10; and secret treaties, **V,** 316; and treaties with foreign nations, **V,** 316; and the Trespass Act, **V,** 322; and West Florida boundary, **V,** 436

DeFonte, Bartholomew, and fake explorations, **IV,** 195

DeForest, Lee, produces the audion tube, **II,** 199; and the radio, **IV,** 397; and wireless telegraphy, **V,** 472

DeFuca, Juan, and fake exploration of the Pacific coast, **IV,** 195

D'Eglise, Jacques, in Missouri, **III,** 431

DeGrasse, Admiral, in the Revolutionary War, **IV,** 477; and the battle of Virginia Capes, **V,** 376; and Yorktown campaign, **V,** 509

Deism, and freethinking, **II,** 340; and philosophical thought and writings, **IV,** 263; and American religion, **IV,** 442; and theological writings, **V,** 261

DeKalb, Johann, at Camden, **I,** 277; **IV,** 473; in the Southern campaigns (1780–81), **V,** 129

DeKoven, Reginald, composer of light opera, **IV,** 178

DeLancey, Etienne, and Fraunces Tavern, **IV,** 118

DeLancey, James, and the colony of New York, **IV,** 115

Delancey, Oliver, and the Mischianza, **III,** 415

DeLancey, Stephen, and the Minisink patent, **III,** 410

DeLancey, William, appointed chief justice of New York, **I**, 419

Delaney, W. W., song sheets of, **V**, 120

Delanoy, Peter, mayor of New York City, **IV**, 118

DeLaval, patents the centrifugal separator, **II**, 104

Delaware, separates from Pennsylvania, **IV**, 242; as a proprietary province, **IV**, 362; and York's proprietary, **V**, 508

Delaware, Fort, prison camp at, **IV**, 347

Delaware, The, ship-of-the-line, **V**, 75

Delaware and Hudson Canal, **I**, 80, 93; **IV**, 406; **V**, 186

Delaware and Raritan Canal, **I**, 81; **IV**, 105

Delaware Bridge Commission, **V**, 175

Delaware Circle, and York's proprietary, **V**, 508

Delaware Companies, Susquehannah Company merges with, **V**, 211

Delaware Gazette, published by Jacob A. Killen, **IV**, 126

Delaware Indians, and the Algonquin family, **I**, 48; on the Allegheny River, **I**, 51; and Bouquet's Expedition, **I**, 229; and Bradstreet's Expedition, **I**, 234; capture and burn Col. Crawford, **II**, 83; in Croghan's expedition to Illinois, **II**, 90; and Dunmore's War, **II**, 177; and the treaty of Easton (1758), **II**, 183; dispossession of, **II**, 276; and establishment of the Friendly Association, **II**, 348; and treaty of Greenville, **II**, 425; and Fort Harmar treaty, **III**, 10; in the Revolution, **III**, 88; land cessions of, **III**, 100; removal of, **III**, 107; save Fort Laurens, **III**, 251; at Logstown, **III**, 295; and treaty of Logstown, **III**, 295; and treaties of Fort McIntosh, **III**, 366; and Penn's Creek massacre, **IV**, 242; and treaty at Pittsburgh (1775), **IV**, 280; and establishment of Schoenbrunn, **V**, 38; as guides, **V**, 46; and treaty of Shackamaxon, **V**, 62; migrate to the Ohio Valley, **V**, 65; and treaty of Spring Wells, **V**, 150; and Upper Sandusky, **V**, 352; sign treaty of Fort Wayne, **V**, 370; and the Walking Purchase, **V**, 392; and treaty of Fort Wayne, **V**, 426

Delaware River, controversy as to ownership of lands bordering, **II**, 130; and New Haven Colony, **IV**, 103; and colony of New Sweden, **IV**, 113

Delawarr, Lord, governor of Jamestown, **III**, 167

Delegation of Powers, and Congress, **II**, 17; and the New Deal, **IV**, 96; and quasi-judicial agencies, **IV**, 387; and Virginia-Kentucky Resolutions, **V**, 376

DeLeon, Alonso, *conquistadore,* **II**, 25; searches for LaSalle's colony, **III**, 247; explores Texas, **V**, 252

DeLeon, Daniel, and the Socialist Labor party, **V**, 110

DeLeon, Edwin, and Civil War diplomacy, **I**, 392; and political Young Americanism, **V**, 510

DeLesseps, Ferdinand, and the Panama Canal, **IV**, 204

DeLévis, Chevalier, and fall of Montreal, **IV**, 17; on the Richelieu River, **IV**, 481

Delisle, Guillaume, and mapping, **IV**, 175; **V**, 282

Delmonico's Restaurant, **II**, 55

DeLong, G. W., and polar cruise of the *Jeannette,* **IV**, 292

DeLuna, Tristán, expedition of, **II**, 289

Demarcation Line, and "No Peace Beyond the Line," **IV**, 135

Democracy, growth of, and social change, **I**, 340; and the franchise, **II**, 322 ff.; and the frontier, **II**, 350 ff.; and the Great Awakening, **II**, 413; and mass production, **III**, 353; and political theories, **IV**, 301; in the West, **V**, 435

Democratic Clubs, and the Republican party (Jeffersonian), **IV**, 453

Democratic Donkey, invented by Nast, **IV**, 56

Democratic Party, in Alabama, **I**, 39; in campaigns of 1836 and 1840, **I**, 283; in campaigns of 1844, 1848, 1852, 1856, 1860, **I**, 284; in campaigns of 1860 and 1864, **I**, 285; in campaigns of 1868, 1872, 1876, **I**, 286; in campaigns of 1876, 1880, 1884, 1888, **I**, 287; in campaigns of 1888, 1892, 1896, **I**, 288; in campaigns of 1896, 1900, 1904, **I**, 289; in campaigns of 1908, 1912, 1916, 1920, **I**, 290; in campaigns of 1920, 1924, 1928, **I**, 291; in campaigns of 1932 and 1936, **I**, 292; controlled by the cotton kingdom, **II**, 70; and free silver, **II**, 333; and free trade, **II**, 334; and the nominating convention, **IV**, 137; as a political party, **IV**, 296; and the Populists, **IV**, 314; and religion, **IV**, 443; evolution of, **IV**, 454; in the Solid South, **V**, 118; and states' rights, **V**, 176; and two-thirds rule, **V**, 336; follows the unit rule, **V**, 344; opposed by the Whigs, **V**, 455

Democratic Republicans, take name of Democrats, **IV**, 62; as a political party, **IV**, 296. *See also* Republican Party, Jeffersonian

Democratic Societies. *See* Jacobin Clubs

Demologos, steam warship, **II**, 284; **V**, 411

Demonetization. *See* Silver

DeMontmagny, Charles Huault, and "Onontio," **IV**, 175

DeMonts, Sieur (Pierre de Guast), and Acadia, **I**, 6; and Port Royal, **IV**, 315; and the St. Croix settlement, **V**, 7

Demopolis, colony started at, **V**, 280

Dempsey, Jack, prize fighter, **IV**, 353

Denby, Edwin, and naval oil reserves, **IV**, 71

Denman, Matthias, and Cincinnati, **I**, 375

Denmark, cedes the Virgin Islands, **V**, 317

Dennett, Tyler, and political writings, **IV**, 303

Denonville Expedition, at Fort Frontenac, **II**, 349

Denver, Auraria consolidated with, **I**, 139; a boom town, **I**, 215; and outfitting of caravans, **I**, 313

Denver and Rio Grande Railroad, competes with Atchison, Topeka and Santa Fé Railroad, **I**, 134; pioneer narrow-gauge road, **I**, 426

Denver Mint, gold depository at, **II**, 395

Denver Pacific Railroad, and the Kansas Pacific, **III**, 198

Department Stores, and chain stores, **I**, 336; and the distribution of merchandise, **II**, 152; and price maintenance, **IV**, 339; and trade areas, **V**, 297

DePere Mission, **II**, 422

DePeyster, Abraham, and battle of King's Mountain, **III**, 212

D'Epineuil's Zouaves, **V**, 514

Deposit, Right of, revoked by acting intendant of Louisiana, **III**, 308; and free navigation of the Mississippi, **III**, 423, 424; and the Pinckney treaty, **IV**, 273; **V**, 134

Deposit Act of 1836, **II**, 151

Deposit Insurance, made permanent, **I**, 157

Depot of Charts and Instruments, **IV**, 70

Depressions, an issue in campaign of 1932, **I**, 292; and the Federal deficit, **II**, 128; and the technocracy movement, **V**, 236

Deputies, and unicameral legislatures, **V**, 340

Derby, G. H., and scientific exploration of the Colorado River, **I**, 427

Derby, George Horatio, and *Phœnixiana*, **IV**, 264

Derby Canal, engineering feature of Newlands Reclamation Project, **IV**, 121

Derna Expedition, and the Barbary Wars, **I**, 162

DeRussy, Fort, taken in the Red River campaign, **IV**, 430

DesBarres, J. F. W., and Atlantic coast survey, **III**, 340

Deseret, Busy Bees of, **I**, 263

Deseret News, newspaper, **IV**, 127

Desert Land Act of 1877, and irrigation, **III**, 161; and the public domain, **IV**, 370; and reclamation, **IV**, 423

Desertion, in the Union Army, **I**, 112; during the Civil War, **I**, 388; in the Confederacy, **II**, 4, 11; in the Revolutionary Army, **IV**, 472

DesGroseilliers, western explorations of, **III**, 56

DeSmet, Pierre-Jean, and the Cœur d'Alene mission, **I**, 409; Indian missionary, **II**, 107; makes known much of the Northwest, **II**, 236; apostle to the Flathead Indians, **II**, 282; missionary work of, **III**, 175; founds mission among the Indians, **IV**, 16; and Oregon missions, **IV**, 184; and Sublette's Cut-off, **V**, 192

Des Moines Plan, and the initiative, **III**, 123

DeSoto, Hernando, visits Alabama coast, **I**, 39; and the battle of Alabamo, **I**, 41; explores America, **I**, 57; first white man to visit Arkansas, **I**, 105; and battle of Cabusto, **I**, 266; and battle at Chicaca, **I**, 355; encounters the Choctaw Indians, **I**, 368; *conquistadore*, **II**, 25; and Mississippi River flood, **II**, 286; and Louisiana, **III**, 304; and battle of Mauvilla, **III**, 360; and Memphis, **III**, 372; first to explore territory of Mississippi, **III**, 420; accredited with discovering the Mississippi, **III**, 423; takes over Narváez's patent, **IV**, 54; discovers the Mississippi River, **V**, 242; and Texas, **V**, 252

D'Estaing, Admiral, in the Revolutionary War, **IV**, 477; and Sullivan in Rhode Island, **IV**, 479; and siege of Savannah, **V**, 36

Destination, Enemy. *See* Continuous Voyage

Destroyers. *See* Warships

Destroying Angels, guerrilla band, **II**, 428

Detective Agencies, and industrial espionage, **II**, 228

Detroit, Bird starts his invasion of Kentucky from, **I**, 191; and Clark's Northwest campaign, **I**, 395; Senecas close source of supply for, **II**, 145; city directory appears in, **II**, 148; and the fur trade, **II**, 360; founding of, **II**, 416; surrender of, and court-martial of Hull, **III**, 57; Great Council at (1761), **IV**, 305; surrender of (1812), **V**, 405

Detroit, Fort, Pontiac's siege of, **I**, 203; and the battle of Blue Licks, **I**, 204; and attack on Boonesborough, **I**, 216; evacuation of by British, **I**, 218; and the Ecorse River Council, **II**, 184; and Fox-French wars, **II**, 319; Clark's proposed expedition against, **III**, 291; in Pontiac's War, **IV**, 306

Detroit Community Trust, **II**, 314

Detroit Gazette, founded by Sheldon and Reed, **IV**, 124, 127

Devaluation, and free silver, **II**, 333; and the Gold Reserve Act of 1934, **II**, 397; and mortgages, **IV**, 29; and repudiation of public debt, **IV**, 455; and the Thomas Amendment, **V**, 264

Devereux, John H., and the "Spirit of '76" painting, **V**, 146

Devil's Highway, **I**, 278

DeViomenil, Baron, and Yorktown campaign, **V**, 509

Devoe Manufacturing Company, **V**, 156

DeVries, David P., and Zwaanendael colony, **II**, 132; **V**, 515

Dew, Thomas R., defends slavery, **IV**, 363, 364; **V**, 123

Dewey, George, made an admiral, **I**, 12; and battle of Manila Bay, **III**, 332; **V**, 136 f.

Dewey, Melvil, and the American Library Association, **III**, 272; starts traveling libraries, **III**, 273

Dewey, Thomas E., and rackets, **IV,** 395

DeWitt, Green, and colonization of Texas, **V,** 251

"DeWitt Clinton," locomotive, **III,** 292

Dey, Anthony, and Associates of New Jersey Company, **IV,** 105

Dharma Mandal, Hindu cult, **IV,** 187

Diamond, "Legs," racketeer, **IV,** 395

Diamond Match Company, **III,** 359

Dick Act (1903), and the militia, **III,** 403; and the National Guard, **IV,** 59

Dickinson, Charles, duels with Andrew Jackson, **II,** 174

Dickinson, John, and the Annapolis Convention, **I,** 78; and Articles of Confederation, **I,** 125; signer of the Constitution, **II,** 39; delegate to Convention of 1787, **II,** 50; author of Farmer's Letters, **II,** 253; writes "Song of Liberty," **III,** 271; and pamphleteering, **IV,** 202; and the Plan of 1776, **IV,** 282; and "Song of Liberty," **V,** 350

Dickinson, Jonathan and the Presbyterians, **IV,** 332

Dickman, Joseph T., commander of American Third Army of Occupation (1918–19), **I,** 116

Dickson, Robert, fur trader, **III,** 111

Dictionaries, Webster's, **V,** 432

Dictionary of American English, edited by Sir William Craigie, **II,** 146

Dictionary of Books Relating to America, compiled by Joseph Sabin, **I,** 212, 214

Dictionary of Early Modern English, edited by Charles C. Fries, **II,** 146

Dictionary of Middle English, edited by Thomas A. Knott, **II,** 146

Dies, Martin, and subversive activities, **V,** 197

Diesel Engine, and streamlined trains, **V,** 188

Dieskau, Baron, and battle of Lake George, **III,** 230

Die-ups, accompany drouths, **II,** 170

Digestion, and St. Martin's stomach, **V,** 14

Dighton Rock, and Runic inscriptions, **IV,** 507

Dill, Daniel H., at Fort Rice, **IV,** 479 f.

Dillinger, John, gangster, **I,** 153

Dilworth, Thomas, author of *New Guide to the English Tongue,* **V,** 40

Dime Novels, **I,** 214, 363

Dingee, Charles, nurseryman, **IV,** 154

Dingley Tariff, and DeLima v. Bidwell, **II,** 133; and the Kasson treaties, **III,** 200; and reciprocity, **IV,** 423; a high point in rate, **V,** 222

Dinwiddie, Robert, and Great Meadows, **II,** 418; and Washington's mission to Fort LeBœuf, **III,** 259; and the Ohio Valley, **IV,** 165

Diorama, **IV,** 211

Diphtheria, **II,** 150, 221

Diplomatic Service. *See* Foreign Service

Direct Primary. *See* Primary, Direct

Dirigibles, and natural gas, **II,** 373; helium used in, **III,** 24

Disabled American Veterans of the World War, **V,** 365

Disabled Veterans. *See* Veterans, Disabled

Disasters: Chicago fire, **I,** 357; the *Eastland,* **II,** 183; Galveston storm, **II,** 368; hurricanes, **III,** 62; Iroquois Theater fire, **III,** 160; Johnstown flood, **III,** 178; *Lady Elgin,* **III,** 226; Last Island, **III,** 247; Ohio flood (1913), **IV,** 161; San Francisco earthquake and fire, **V,** 24; *General Slocum,* **V,** 98; tornadoes and cyclones, **V,** 284; Triangle fire, **V,** 324; Wall Street explosion, **V,** 393

Disciples of Christ, and the Cane Ridge revival, **I,** 304; and frontier preaching, **II,** 353; founded by Alexander Campbell, **IV,** 480; and the Baptists, **V,** 446

Discovery, famous thoroughbred horse, **V,** 265

Discovery, The, and founding of Jamestown, **III,** 166; **V,** 372

Diseases, Occupational, **IV,** 157

Disfranchisement, of citizens of District of Columbia, **II,** 153

Dismal Swamp Canal, subsidy granted to, **III,** 137; **V,** 194

Distilleries, and whiskey, **V,** 457

Distillers and Cattle Feeders Trust, **V,** 326

District Courts, and the judiciary, **III,** 185; provided by Judiciary Act of 1789, **III,** 188; and the Judiciary Act of 1801, **III,** 189

District Judges, and the Supreme Court, **V,** 206

District of Columbia, slave trade forbidden in, **V,** 93

District School, and education, **II,** 186; and centralization of education, **II,** 188

Disturnell, John, map publisher, **V,** 283

Disturnell's Map, and treaty of Guadalupe Hidalgo, **II,** 427; **III,** 382

Diversification, Agricultural, **I,** 28

Divine Providence, and the Puritans, **II,** 253

Division of Purchase, Storage and Traffic, **I,** 119

Division of Territories and Island Possessions, **III,** 135

Divorce, and the family, **II,** 242

Dix, Dorothy A., and treatment of insane, **III,** 125

Dixie Highway, and the Wilderness Road, **V,** 465

Dixon, Archibald M., proposes repeal of Missouri Compromise, **V,** 96

Dixon, Billy, scout, **V,** 46

Dixon, Jeremiah, and Mason and Dixon line, **III,** 350

Dixon, Jeremy, enters into New Haven church covenant, **V,** 60

Dixon, Robert, and the War of 1812 in the West, **V,** 406

Dixwell, John, regicide in New England, **IV,** 438

Doak, William, Secretary of Labor under Hoover, **III,** 221

Doak's Stand, Treaty of, and Canadian River as boundary, **I,** 302; and Indian land cessions, **III,** 100; and Vicksburg, **V,** 367

Doan's Store, Dodge City Trail crosses at, **II,** 156

Dobbs, Arthur, and Regulators of North Carolina, **IV,** 439; and the Yadkin River settlements, **V,** 499

Dock, George, and malaria, **III,** 329

Dockstader, Lew, minstrel show of, **III,** 413; **V,** 120

Doctor's Fees, **V,** 15

Dodds, H. W., and our relations with Nicaragua, **IV,** 131

Dodge, Augustus C., senator from Iowa, **III,** 152; and Kansas-Nebraska Act, **III,** 197

Dodge, David Low, organizes a peace society, **IV,** 233

Dodge, Grenville M., and the Union Pacific Railroad, **V,** 343

Dodge, Henry, and United States rangers, **IV,** 416; settles in Wisconsin, **V,** 473; and battle of Wisconsin Heights, **V,** 474

Dodge, Mary Mapes, edits *St. Nicholas* magazine, **I,** 363

Dodge City, and the Arkansas River route, **I,** 107; becomes famous because of trail-driver patronage, **I,** 326; cow town, **II,** 79

Dodge City Trail, and Texas, **V,** 255

"Dogie" Songs, **II,** 79

Doheny, E. L., and the Elk Hills oil scandal, **II,** 203; drills first successful Mexican oil well, **III,** 383; and the Pearl Harbor naval base, **IV,** 237

Dolbear, Amos E., and the telephone cases, **V,** 239

Dold, Jacob, and meat packing, **IV,** 199

Dole Race, **I,** 35, 36

Dollar, Silver. *See* Silver Dollar

Dollar Diplomacy, and Latin-American investments, **III,** 248

Dolliver, J. P., leads revolt against the Payne-Aldrich Tariff Bill, **IV,** 356

Dolores, built on Rio Grande, **IV,** 486

Dolphin, The, Congress authorizes construction of, **II,** 283; one of the vessels of the White Squadron, **V,** 460

Domestic Relations, Courts of, **I,** 342

Domínguez, Francisco, and topographic mapping, **V,** 283

Domínguez Explorations, and Texas, **V,** 252

Dominican Missions in California, **I,** 273

Dominican Republic, and the Alta Vela Claim, **I,** 52; and Caribbean policy, **I,** 313; and expansion, **II,** 234; marines in, **III,** 343; and *modus vivendi,* **IV,** 4; and treaties with foreign nations, **V,** 317

Dominicans, and the Holy Name Society, **III,** 40

Dominion of New England. *See* New England, Dominion of

Don Luis, heads the Pima revolt, **IV,** 272

Donation Land Law, and McLoughlin's land claim, **III,** 367; and the Willamette Valley settlements, **V,** 467

Donelson, A. J., member of the "kitchen cabinet," **III,** 213

Donelson, Fort, Grant's attack on, **I,** 54; the *Carondelet* fights at, **I,** 317; capture of, **I,** 389; as fortification, **II,** 311; capture of, **III,** 419; Mississippi Squadron helps capture, **III,** 425

Donelson, John, surveys line crossing near Big Moccasin Gap, **I,** 184; follows the Cumberland River, **II,** 97; and the Cumberland settlements, **II,** 98; negotiates treaty of Lochaber, **III,** 290; and founding of Nashville, **IV,** 54

Donelson's Line, and Holston Valley settlements, **III,** 39; running of, **III,** 290

Dongan, Thomas, and Iroquois treaty (1684), **III,** 160

Donham v. West Nelson Manufacturing Co., **III,** 409

Doniphan, A. W., at Brazito, **I,** 235; saves the lives of the Smiths, **IV,** 26; concludes treaty with Navaho Indians, **IV,** 68; and battle of Sacramento, **V,** 3

Donnelly, Ignatius, leader of agrarian opposition in Minnesota, **III,** 411

Donner Party, **I,** 270

Donner Pass, **IV,** 221

Donop, Count, Hessian commander, **II,** 131; and Fort Mercer engagements, **III,** 375

"Don't Give Up the Ship," Lawrence's dying words, **I,** 354; **II,** 224

Doolin, Bill, robber, **I,** 152

Doolittle, Isaac, and the printing press, **IV,** 346

Dooly, John, in battle of Kettle Creek, **III,** 208

Dorchester, Mass., founding of, **II,** 419; and the *Mary and John,* **III,** 348; and group migration, **IV,** 489

Dorchester Company, establishes fishing station at Cape Ann, **I,** 306; succeeded by New England Company, **IV,** 99; and Salem, **V,** 16; and colonial stock companies, **V,** 182; as trading company, **V,** 301

Dorlandt, Lambert, and Philipse's patent, **IV,** 263

Dorr Rebellion, **III,** 132, 347

Dorsey, Owen, and the development of the reaper, **IV,** 419

Dos Passos, John, and fiction, **II,** 270

Doshisha University, **V,** 191

Double Jeopardy Clause, and U. S. v. Lanza, **V,** 349

Doubleday, Abner, and baseball, **I,** 165

Doughty, John, builds Fort Harmar, **III**, 10

Doughty, Thomas, landscape painter, **I**, 123

Douglas, David, and gardening, **II**, 371

Douglas, Frederick, and abolitionist literature, **I**, 3

Douglas, James, and Big Bone Lick, **I**, 183

Douglas, Stephen A., nominated for President, **I**, 285; and Compromise of 1850, **I**, 442; and "Fifty-four forty," **II**, 271; and the Freeport doctrine, **II**, 340; and internal improvements, **III**, 139; and the Kansas-Nebraska Act, **III**, 197; and the Kansas struggle, **III**, 199; and Lincoln debates, **III**, 278; the "Little Giant," **III**, 285; champions repeal of Missouri Compromise, **III**, 429; and the *Chicago Daily Times,* **IV**, 129; and oratory, **IV**, 180; and popular sovereignty, **IV**, 309; and slavery, **V**, 96; and the Union Democrats, **V**, 342; as leading War Democrat, **V**, 402

Douglass, A. E., develops tree-ring dating, **V**, 320

Douglass, Frederick, and Harpers Ferry raid, **III**, 12; reform lecturer, **III**, 260

Douglass, William, and epidemics, **II**, 221

Dousman, H. L., trader at Prairie du Chien, **IV**, 328

Dove, The, brings first colonists to Maryland, **I**, 105, 423; **III**, 348

Dow, Lorenzo, frontier preacher, **IV**, 442

Dow, Neal, and prohibition in Maine, **III**, 327; **V**, 241

Dow v. Johnson, **V**, 398

Dowd, A. T., credited with discovering Calavaris grove, **V**, 58

Dowie, John Alexander, founder of Zion, **V**, 513

Dowling, Dick, at Sabine Pass, **V**, 254

Downer, Samuel, and kerosene oil, **III**, 207

Downes v. Bidwell, **III**, 127; **V**, 229

Downfall of Babylon, anti-Catholic paper, **IV**, 65

Downing, Andrew Jackson, and gardening, **II**, 371

Downing, Emanuel, and industrial research, **III**, 116

Doyle, Thomas, and Fort Massac, **III**, 354

Doyle, William M. S., and silhouettes, **V**, 78

Draft, and the Union army, **I**, 111; and conscription, **II**, 26; and enlistment in the Union army, **II**, 217; and the Fishing Creek Confederacy, **II**, 278; and volunteers, **V**, 382; and the World War, **V**, 491. *See also* Selective Service Act of 1917; *and* Conscription

Draft Riots, during the Civil War, **I**, 387; in Holmes County, **III**, 39; and Negro enlistments, **IV**, 84

Dragging Canoe, and the Chickamauga Indians, **I**, 359; Cherokee chief, **II**, 110; and the battle of Long Island Flats, **III**, 299

Drago Doctrine, and nonintervention, **IV**, 139; and Pan-American conferences, **IV**, 202

Drainage, encouraged by the Illinois Central Railroad, **III**, 70; and reclamation, **IV**, 423

Drainage Districts, as political subdivisions, **IV**, 299

Drake, Daniel, and hospital movement, **III**, 51; founder of the Medical College of Ohio, **III**, 369

Drake, E. L., and kerosene oil, **III**, 207; and early oil exchanges, **IV**, 165; and the oil industry, **IV**, 166; and wildcat oil drilling, **V**, 464

Drake, Francis, and discovery of America, **I**, 57; and Oregon, **IV**, 182, 184; as pirate, **IV**, 278; and Raleigh's first colony, **IV**, 413

Drake, Joseph Rodman, and bookshops, **I**, 214

Drake, Samuel, and barnstorming, **I**, 164

Drake, Samuel G., and book collecting, **I**, 212

Dramatic Line, and sailing packets, **IV**, 198

Draper, George, and the loom, **III**, 301

Drawbacks of Duties, **II**, 102

Drawbaugh, Daniel, and the telephone cases, **V**, 239

Drayton, John Grimke, creates the Magnolia Gardens, **I**, 344

Dreadnoughts, and warships, **V**, 412

Dred, and abolitionist literature, **I**, 3

Dred Scott Case, and campaign of 1860, **I**, 285; and citizenship, **I**, 378; and the Democratic party, **II**, 137; and the due process clause, **II**, 172; overruled by Fourteenth Amendment, **II**, 317; and the Freeport doctrine, **II**, 340; and judicial review, **III**, 183; and Lincoln-Douglas debates, **III**, 279; and popular sovereignty, **IV**, 309; and slavery, **V**, 96; and the Supreme Court, **V**, 207

Dreiser, Theodore, and fiction, **II**, 270

Dress, laws concerning, **V**, 203

Dresser, Paul, popular song writer, **V**, 120

Drew, Daniel, and Erie Railroad, **II**, 226

Drew, Edward B., and war with Korea, **III**, 216

Drew, Gov., and home rule, **III**, 41

Drewry's Bluff, Army of the James checked at, **III**, 166

Drexel, Anthony J., and great fortunes, **II**, 311

Drexel Institute, **III**, 114

Driggs, Frederick E., and land speculation, **III**, 240

Drinker, Elizabeth Sandwith, and tuberculosis, **V**, 328

Drinking Places, and the distribution of merchandise, **II**, 152

Drips, Andrew, and Missouri Fur Company, **V**, 13

Drouillard, George, interpreter of Lewis and Clark expedition, **III**, 266

Drouths, and agricultural adaptation to the plains, **I**, 22; and climate, **I**, 398; and crop fail-

ures, **II**, 91; and the Federal Emergency Relief Administration, **II**, 257; and rainfall, **IV**, 411

Drowne, Shem, and the Pemaquid proprietors, **IV**, 240

Drug Stores, and the distribution of merchandise, **II**, 152

Drum Lummon Mine, **III**, 24

Drunkenness, and liquor laws, **III**, 282

Dry Farming, and agricultural adaptation to the plains, **I**, 22; in Colorado, **I**, 426; and the Dust Bowl, **II**, 178; on the Staked Plains, **V**, 154

Dry Goods, and domestic trade, **V**, 292

Dual Citizenship, **I**, 378

Duane, James, and the Trespass Act, **V**, 322

Duane, W. J., and removal of deposits, **IV**, 448

Duane, William, and campaign of 1808, **I**, 281

Dubreuil, Louis, and Spanish-Missouri Fur Company, **V**, 141

Dubuisson, and foreign volunteers in the Revolutionary Army, **IV**, 473

Dubuque, Julien, and lead mining, **II**, 367

DuBuque Visitor, **IV**, 126

Ducking, as a colonial punishment, **IV**, 382

Duclot, Louis, publisher of *Moniteur de la Louisiane,* **IV**, 126

Dudley, B. W., medical teacher, **III**, 369

Dudley, Edward B., and "It's a damn long time between drinks," **IV**, 145

Dudley, Joseph, and treaty of Casco (1703), **I**, 321; and royal colony of Massachusetts, **III**, 355; and Dominion of New England, **IV**, 98

Dudley, Robert, maps by, **III**, 340

Dudley, Thomas, a founder of Cambridge, **I**, 277

Dudley, William, and siege of Fort Meigs, **III**, 371

Due Process Clause, and Barron v. Baltimore, **I**, 165; and the Bill of Rights, **I**, 186; and public control of business, **I**, 260; and the Constitution, **II**, 40; broadening of, **II**, 49; and the Fourteenth Amendment, **II**, 317; and farmers' moratorium, **II**, 330; and the Granger cases, **II**, 409; and Grosjean v. American Press Company, **II**, 426; in Hurtado v. California, **III**, 62; and the possessions of the United States, **III**, 127; and legal tender, **III**, 261; and minimum-wage laws, **III**, 408; and Minnesota Moratorium case, **III**, 412; and Mugler v. Kansas, **IV**, 39; in Munn v. Illinois, **IV**, 46; and Nebbia v. New York, **IV**, 80; and the Negro, **IV**, 82; and Oregon parochial school case, **IV**, 184; and police power, **IV**, 294; and private property, **IV**, 360; and Railroad Retirement Board v. Alton Railroad Company, **IV**, 404; and Slaughter House cases, **V**, 89; and social legislation, **V**, 107; and Truax v. Corrigan, **V**, 325; and U. S. v. Cruikshank, **V**, 348; and Virginian Railway Company v. System Federation No. 40, **V**, 380;

and West Coast Hotel Company v. Parrish, **V**, 436; and zoning ordinances, **V**, 514

Duelling, on Bloody Island, **I**, 202; Burr-Hamilton, **I**, 257; at Weehawken, **V**, 433

Duelling Oaks, at New Orleans, **II**, 174

Duer, William, and land speculation, **III**, 239; and the Ohio Company of Associates, **IV**, 163; and the Scioto Company, **V**, 44

Duff, Mary, barnstormer, **I**, 164

Dugdale, Richard L., and the Jukes, **III**, 189

Dug-outs, **I**, 47

Duke, James B., and machine-made cigarettes, **V**, 274

Duke, Washington, and great fortunes, **II**, 312

Duke Endowment, **II**, 314

Duke's Laws, and colonial assemblies, **I**, 416; and York's proprietary, **V**, 507

Dulany, Daniel, and taxation without representation, **V**, 230

DuLhut. *See* Duluth

Dull Knife Campaign, and the Cheyenne Indians, **I**, 355; and Fort Larned, **III**, 246

Dull Knife's Cheyenne Village, destroyed, **V**, 87

Duluth, Daniel Graysolon, Sieur, *coureur de bois,* **II**, 75; and Denonville's invasion of the Iroquois, **II**, 137; on Fox-Wisconsin waterway, **II**, 320; explores southwest, **II**, 344; rescues Hennepin, **III**, 26; and Minnesota, **III**, 410; and New France, **IV**, 101; on Lake Superior, **V**, 205; and topographic mapping, **V**, 282

Dum-Dum Bullet, used in war, **I**, 136

Dummer, Fort, built by the English, **V**, 361

Dummer, Jeremiah, first known American-born artist, **I**, 122; silversmith, **V**, 82

Dummer, Shubael, killed, **V**, 507

Dummer, William, and private schools, **V**, 41

Dummer's War, **IV**, 142

Dumont Minstrels, popularize songs, **V**, 120

Dun, R. G., and Company, **III**, 374

Dunbar, Col., and Braddock's expedition, **I**, 233

Dunbar, Daniel, and the Waldo patent, **V**, 391

Dunbar, William, and western exploration, **V**, 442

Dunbar's Line, **V**, 129

Duncan, Alexander, and origin of term "Salt River," **V**, 19

Duncan, G. B., and the Oise-Aisne operation, **IV**, 167

Duncan, James, and the Root mission to Russia, **IV**, 501

Duncan, Matthew, begins the *Illinois Herald,* **IV**, 124, 126; first printer of Illinois, **IV**, 345

Duncan, Robert Kennedy, starts industrial fellowship system, **III**, 117

Duncan, Silas, and the Falkland Islands controversy, **II**, 240

Dunkards, and communities, **I**, 440; as conscien-

tious objectors, **II,** 25; immigration of, **II,** 383; as political exiles, **IV,** 295; oppose slavery, **V,** 97

Dunlap, John, publishes the *Pennsylvania Packet and Daily Advertiser,* **IV,** 125

Dunlap, William, dramatist, **II,** 165

Dunlap's *Trip to Niagara,* and panoramas, **IV,** 211

Dunmore, Lord, and Connolly's Plot, **II,** 24; and the battle at the Great Bridge, **II,** 414; at Gwynn's Island, **II,** 430; and McDonald's expedition, **III,** 364; occupies Norfolk, **IV,** 142; takes refuge on the *Fowey,* **V,** 373

Dunmore's War, and the Baker Cabin massacre, **I,** 146; ended by treaty of Camp Charlotte, **I,** 345; precipitated by Logan, **II,** 87; Delaware Indians remain neutral during, **II,** 131; and Logan's speech, **III,** 294; and Indian treaty at Pittsburgh, **IV,** 280; Pluggy's band joins Shawnee in, **IV,** 288; and battle of Point Pleasant, **IV,** 291; and the colony of Virginia, **V,** 373

Duplex Printing Press Company Case, **I,** 232; **III,** 124

Duponceau, Pierre Étienne, serves in the Revolutionary Army, **IV,** 474

DuPont, Eleuthère Irénée, and great fortunes, **II,** 312; begins manufacture of gunpowder, **II,** 130; **IV,** 325

DuPont, Fort, **II,** 131

DuPont, Lamont, and blasting powder, **IV,** 326

DuPont, S. F., and the Navy in the Civil War, **I,** 389; uses monitors in attack on Charleston, **IV,** 10; attacks Fort Sumter, **V,** 203

DuPont Company, and patents, **IV,** 223; found guilty of violating Sherman Act, **IV,** 326

DuPont de Nemours, Samuel, founds the DuPont Company, **II,** 177

Duportail, Louis Lebegue, commissioned in the Revolutionary Army, **IV,** 473; and Valley Forge, **V,** 355

Duquesne, Fort, Indians from, maintained at Aughwick, **I,** 138; and Braddock's expedition, **I,** 233, 234; Forbes expedition against, **II,** 298; constructed by French, **II,** 342, 346; and battle of Grant's Hill, **II,** 411; built, **II,** 418; and battle of the Monongahela, **IV,** 11; and Forks of the Ohio, **IV,** 162; captured, **IV,** 163, 165; and Braddock's defeat, **IV,** 243; and Fort Pitt, **IV,** 279; erected, **V,** 65; capture of, and the westward movement, **V,** 450

Duquesne, Marquis, plans Marin's expedition, **III,** 343

Durand, Asher B., landscape painter, **I,** 123

Durand, Peter, introduces the tin can, **I,** 304

Durant, George, and the Albemarle settlements, **I,** 46; arrest of, **II,** 95

Durant, T. C., and Crédit Mobilier, **II,** 84; and the Union Pacific Railroad, **V,** 343

Durant, William C., organizes General Motors Company, **II,** 376

Durantaye, and Denonville's invasion of the Iroquois, **II,** 137

Durell, E. H., issues the Midnight Order, **III,** 395

Durfee, Amos, and the *Caroline* affair, **I,** 317; murder of, **III,** 366

Durfee and Peck, trading firm, **IV,** 238

Durham, Bishopric of, and palatine jurisdictions, **IV,** 200, 362

Durkee, John, and the Susquehanna settlers, **V,** 210; and the Yankee-Pennamite wars, **V,** 502

Durocher, Laurent, and Spanish-Missouri Fur Company, **V,** 141

Duryea, Charles, and the automobile, **I,** 140

Duryea, Frank, and the automobile, **I,** 140

Dust, and the Soil Erosion Act, **V,** 115

Dust Bowl, and climate, **I,** 398; and drouths, **II,** 170

Dust Storms, and crop failures, **II,** 91; devastate the Great Plains, **IV,** 282; and rainfall, **IV,** 411

Dustin, Hannah, and massacre at Haverhill, Mass., **III,** 117

Dustin Murders, **V,** 86

Dutch, capture New Sweden, **II,** 130; in New Netherland, **IV,** 107 ff.; and Pennsylvania, **IV,** 242

Dutch Flat Mining Camp, **I,** 171

Dutch Reformed Church, and Calvinism, **I,** 277; and the *Coetus-Conferentie* controversy, **I,** 408; and home missionary societies, **III,** 417; and foreign missions, **III,** 417; or the Reformed Church in America, **IV,** 436; and Rutgers University, **IV,** 512; establishes a theological seminary, **V,** 261

"Dutch Schultz" (Arthur Flegenheimer), racketeer, **IV,** 395

Dutch War of 1653, Rhode Island in the, **IV,** 479

Dutch West India Company, and settlement of Albany, **I,** 44; and the fur trade, **II,** 361; and Hudson River, **III,** 55; and Manhattan Island, **III,** 331; and founding of New Amsterdam, **IV,** 93; has jurisdiction of Fort Casimir, **IV,** 95; organized, **IV,** 107; and patroons, **IV,** 225; and the Petition and Remonstrance of New Netherland, **IV,** 257; as a trading company, **V,** 301; and Zwaanendael Colony, **V,** 515

Dutcher, William, and the establishment of bird sanctuaries, **I,** 190

Duties, and the custom houses, **II,** 101; ad valorem and specific, **V,** 221

DuTisne, Claude Charles, expedition of, **II,** 345; explores Missouri, **III,** 426, 430

Duveneck, Frank, painter, **I,** 123

Duyckinck, Evert, artist, **I,** 122

Dwight, Jeremiah, and land speculation, **III,** 240

Dwight, John S., and Brook Farm, **I,** 243

Dwight, Lewis, endorses the Auburn prison system, **IV,** 348

Dwight, Theodore, one of the Hartford Wits, **III,** 14

Dwight, Timothy, and the Second Awakening, **I,** 143; and freethinking, **II,** 340; one of the Hartford Wits, **III,** 14; and American hymns, **III,** 65; and religious thought and writings, **IV,** 446; and revivals, **IV,** 464; and theological writings, **V,** 261

Dyeing, as household art, **III,** 53

Dyer, Alexander B., and Civil War munitions, **I,** 393

Dyer, Eliphalet, shareholder in the Susquehannah Company, **V,** 211

Dyer, William, and Dutch War of 1653, **IV,** 479

Dylks, Joseph C., the Leatherwood God, **III,** 258

Dysentery, appears in Jamestown, **III,** 167

E

Eads, James B., and steel bridges, **I,** 238; builds the *Carondelet,* **I,** 317

Eakins, Thomas, painter, **I,** 123

Eames, Wilberforce, book collections, **I,** 213

Earhart, Amelia, fatal flight of, **I,** 35

Earl, Ralph, painter, **I,** 123

Earle, Parker, and refrigerator cars, **IV,** 437

Early, J. A., at Bull Run, **I,** 251; and battle of Chancellorsville, **I,** 340; attacked at Fisher's Hill, **II,** 277; and battle of Gettysburg, **II,** 386; and the battle of the Monocacy, **IV,** 11; and the Shenandoah campaign, **V,** 68; and Sheridan's ride, **V,** 69; and battle of Winchester, **V,** 470

Earning Power, and consumer purchasing, **II,** 45

Earp, Wyatt, cow town marshal, **II,** 79; gunman of Tombstone, **V,** 280

Earthquakes, and the Coast and Geodetic Survey, **I,** 405

East Florida, and the Adams-Onís treaty, **I,** 9; Jackson raids, **I,** 98; development of, **II,** 287; establishment of, **II,** 290; St. Augustine as government seat of, **V,** 6; under Spain, **V,** 139

East Florida Gazette, **IV,** 126

East India Company, and Associations, **I,** 132; and Boston Tea Party, **I,** 224; and duty on tea, **V,** 232

East India Marine Society, **IV,** 47

East Jersey, a division of New Jersey, **IV,** 104; Perth Amboy as capital of, **IV,** 255; as a proprietary province, **IV,** 362; Carteret receives, **V,** 438

East Texas Oil Field, **V,** 255

Eastabrook, Arthur H., and the Jukes, **III,** 189

Eastburn, Robert, story of, as Indian captive, **III,** 95

Eastern Star, Order of the, **V,** 482

Eastern State Hospital, **III,** 50

Eastman, George, benefactions and gifts of, **I,** 177; patents the Kodak, **IV,** 265

Eastman, Joseph B., as Railroad Co-ordinator, **IV,** 401

Easton, Council at, **II,** 299

Eating Places, and the distribution of merchandise, **II,** 152

Eaton, Amos, and college training for women, **V,** 480

Eaton, Dorman B., and the Pendleton Act, **IV,** 241

Eaton, John H., member of the "Kitchen Cabinet," **III,** 213; and the establishing of the *United States Telegraph,* **IV,** 128

Eaton, Theophilus, and Connecticut, **II,** 21; and New Haven Colony, **IV,** 103; and the "Phantom Ship," **IV,** 257; enters into New Haven church covenant, **V,** 60

Eaton, William, organizes expedition against Derna, **II,** 140

Eaton's Fort, and battle of Long Island Flats, **III,** 299

Ebbetts, fur trader, **IV,** 29

Ebenezer, home of the Inspirationists, **I,** 53

Ebenezer, Salzburgers settle at, **V,** 20

Ebo Negroes, imported as slaves, **IV,** 86

Echo, produced by the Hartford Wits, **III,** 15

Eckerlein Brothers, and the Monongahela River, **IV,** 11

Eclectic Series of School Readers, **III,** 365

Eclipse, The, and steamboat racing, **V,** 178

Econochaca (Holy Ground), Claiborne destroys Creek stronghold at, **IV,** 57

Economy Act, emergency legislation, **II,** 210

Eddy, George S., and book collecting, **I,** 212

Eddy, Mary Baker, founder of Christian Science, **I,** 370; and religious thought and writings, **IV,** 447

Eddy, Thomas, Quaker philanthropist, **IV,** 260

Eddy, W. A., develops kite photography, **I,** 35

Eden, William, and Peace Commission of 1778, **IV,** 231

Edenton, holds "Ladies' Tea Party," **V,** 234

Edge Act of 1919, and investment trusts, **III,** 150

Edge Hill, battle of, fought at Whitemarsh, **V,** 461

Edgefield Policy, **III,** 422

Edison, Thomas, and the incandescent lamp, **II,** 195; inventions of, **III,** 148; and the incandescent lamp, **III,** 232; and motion pictures, **IV,** 31; patents the phonograph and incandescent lamp, **IV,** 223; patents the phonograph, **IV,** 264; and electric railways, **IV,** 410; and the telephone, **V,** 239; and voting machines, **V,** 384; and telephonic devices, **V,** 441

Edison Electric Illuminating Company, **III,** 277

Edison Electric Light Company, **II,** 197

Edison General Electric Company, **II,** 375

Edmonds, Emma, Civil War spy, **V,** 146

Edouart, August, and silhouettes, V, 78

Education, and charity schools, I, 342; coeducational, I, 408; and colleges, I, 413; and growth of democracy, II, 136; Federal aid for, II, 255; and high school, III, 30; Indian, III, 86; Office of, set up, III, 135; and Jeffersonian Democracy, III, 172; and the junior college movement, III, 190; land grants for, III, 236; and the Latin Schools, III, 250; and manners, III, 334; and the Moravians, IV, 22; and municipal ownership, IV, 42; and the Ordinance of 1787, IV, 181; and the Peabody fund, IV, 230; and the public domain, IV, 370; and public land sales, IV, 372; military, IV, 457; and the district school, V, 39; and early schoolbooks, V, 40; and distribution of surplus revenue, V, 209. *See also* Schools; Land Grants for Education

Edward, Fort, scouting party from, attacks Canadians and Indians, I, 203; and the McCrea murder, III, 364

Edward Augustus, Fort, maintained by Gorrell, II, 422; and Sauk Prairie, V, 34; built at Green Bay, V, 473

Edwards, Charles, and the English colony on the Rio Grande, IV, 486

Edwards, Haden, and Fredonian revolt, II, 331

Edwards, Jonathan, and evangelism, II, 230; and the Great Awakening, II, 413; and the New Lights, IV, 106; and philosophical thought and writings, IV, 263; works for Indians, IV, 330; and religious thought and writings, IV, 446; and revivals, IV, 463; and theological writings, V, 261

Edwards, Ninian, and A. B. Plot, I, 1

Edwardsville, Treaties of, and Indian land cessions, III, 100

Eel River Indians, land cessions of, III, 100; sign treaty of Fort Wayne, V, 370, 426

Effie Afton Case, IV, 497

Effigy Mounds, IV, 34

Egan, Chief, in the Bannock War, I, 161

Egan, Michael, becomes first Bishop of Philadelphia, II, 326

Eggleston, Edward, edits *The Little Corporal*, I, 363; author of *Hoosier Schoolmaster*, II, 270

Egypt, treaties with, V, 318

Ehrenberg, Herman, explores Gadsden Purchase, II, 236

Eielson, Elling, and formation of first Norwegian Church in America, IV, 152

Eight-Hour Day, and Adamson Act, I, 10; and the bituminous coal industry, I, 192; and Haymarket riot, III, 20; and the United Mine Workers, V, 346. *See also* Wages and Hours of Labor

Eighteenth Amendment, and Anti-Saloon League, I, 84; gives new impetus to banditry, I, 152; and smuggling, I, 217; and campaign of 1928, I, 291; text of, II, 43; and liquor laws, III, 283; and prohibition, IV, 356; and territorial waters, V, 248; repeal of, V, 334; and the Volstead Act, V, 382

El Brazito, Doniphan defeats Mexicans at, II, 161

El Crepúsculo de la Libertad, IV, 127

El Paso, occupied by Doniphan, II, 161

El Salvador, and Bryan-Chamorro Treaty, I, 245

Elbridge, Giles, at Pemaquid, IV, 239, 240

Elderkin, Jedediah, shareholder in the Susquehannah Company, V, 211

Election Laws, and the assistance clause, I, 131

Elections, and the Constitution, II, 32

Electoral College, as method of choosing the President, II, 51; and growth of democracy, II, 135; and election of the President, II, 192, 193; and the Jefferson-Burr election dispute, III, 170; and the Vice-Presidency, V, 366

Electoral Commission, I, 286

Electoral Count Act, Congress passes, II, 192; provisions of, II, 195

Electors, and the Constitution, II, 31; and voters, V, 383

Electric Bond and Share Company et al v. Securities and Exchange Commission, IV, 378

Electric Light and Power, and government regulation, II, 406; and municipal ownership, IV, 43; and public ownership, IV, 375; and "yardstick," V, 503

Electric Lighting, III, 277

Electric Vehicle Company, and Selden patent, I, 140; V, 56

Electric Welding, patented by Elihu Thomson, IV, 223

Electrical Equipment, and Westinghouse Company, V, 448

Electrical Industry, and manufacturing, III, 337

Electrical Inventions, and the industrial revolution, III, 118

Electricity, and machines, III, 320; and water power, V, 422; and decline of whaling, V, 453

Electrolytic Processes, III, 338

Elevated Railways, and urban transportation, V, 305

Elevators, in apartment houses, I, 88; and skyscrapers, V, 87

Elevators, Grain, influence on agriculture, I, 34; and milling, II, 292; and the Granger movement, II, 410; and wheat, V, 453

Eleventh Amendment, and Chisholm v. Georgia, I, 368; text of, II, 40; delays Indiana Company case, III, 113; foreign creditors prevented from seeking redress by, IV, 457

Elfsborg, Fort, evacuation of, IV, 55

Elgin-Marcy Reciprocity Treaty, and Canadian-American relations, I, 300; and Halifax fisheries award, III, 6

Eliot, Jared, agricultural writer, **I**, 32

Eliot, John, translates Bible into Algonquian language, **I**, 182; **III**, 94; attempts to Christianize the Indians, **III**, 103; "Apostle to the Indians," **IV**, 330; and printing of Indian Bible, **IV**, 345; establishes the Roxbury Latin School, **V**, 41; attacks slavery, **V**, 94

Elizabeth Sprague Coolidge Foundation, **III**, 274

Elizabethan Poor Law, **IV**, 260

Elk Hills Oil Reserve, **IV**, 71, 298

Elkins Act, and Court of Commerce, **I**, 432; and the commerce clause, **I**, 433; strengthened by Hepburn Act, **III**, 27; passed, **III**, 143; and rebates, **IV**, 420; and Standard Oil Company of Indiana, **V**, 157

Elks, secret society, **V**, 53

Ellender, Sen., filibuster of, **II**, 272

Ellery, William, signer of the Declaration of Independence, **II**, 123

Ellet, Charles, and suspension bridges, **I**, 238; and flood control, **II**, 285; and naval battle before Memphis, **III**, 372

Ellicott, Andrew, surveys Dunbar's Line, **II**, 176; and Georgia's southern boundary, **II**, 382; begins southern boundary survey, **IV**, 137; **V**, 129; and survey of Washington, D. C., **V**, 412 f.

Ellicott, Joseph, surveys Buffalo, **I**, 247; and Holland Land Company, **III**, 38

Elliot, Jonathan, editor and publisher of the *Washington Gazette*, **IV**, 128

Elliott, Ezekiel Brown, and vital statistics, **V**, 382

Elliott, J. D., in battle of Lake Erie, **II**, 224; and Great Lakes naval campaign of 1812, **II**, 416; and Perry controversy, **IV**, 253

Elliott, John L., and social settlements, **V**, 109

Elliott, R. S., begins experimental work in dry farming, **II**, 171

Elliott, Robert, and carpetbaggers, **I**, 318

Elliott, Stephen, commanding officer during Fort Sumter siege, **V**, 204

Ellis, Albert G., co-founder of the *Green-Bay Intelligencer*, **IV**, 128; first printer of Wisconsin, **IV**, 346

Ellis, Edward S., writer of outdoor adventure stories, **II**, 147

Ellis, John M., and the Illinois Band, **III**, 69

Ellsworth, Kans., cow town, **II**, 79

Ellsworth, Lincoln, and Amundsen Polar expedition, **I**, 69; **IV**, 293

Ellsworth, Oliver, and the Connecticut Compromise, **II**, 51; diplomatic mission of, **II**, 148; Princeton alumnus, **IV**, 343

Ellsworth's Zouaves, **V**, 515

Ellwanger and Barry, nurserymen, **IV**, 154

Elm Grove, as starting point of caravan traffic, **I**, 312

Elmira College, and education of women, **V**, 480

Elmira Prison, and atrocity stories, **I**, 136; Civil War camp, **IV**, 347

Elmira Reformatory, **IV**, 348, 436

Ely, Richard T., author of *Principles of Economics*, **I**, 180

Emancipation, urged by abolitionists, **I**, 3; Frémont and Hunter proclamations, **II**, 15; and fugitive slave acts, **II**, 355; gradual, **IV**, 82; compensated, advocated by Burritt, **IV**, 234; and the race problem, **IV**, 393

Emancipation Proclamation, and property confiscation, **II**, 16; and the Negro, **IV**, 83; issued by Lincoln, **IV**, 335

Embalmed Beef, and meat inspection laws, **III**, 367; and Pure Food and Drug Acts, **IV**, 383

Embargo Act (1807), and the agrarian movement, **I**, 20; destroys Alexandria's tobacco trade, **I**, 47; and Amelia Island affair, **I**, 54; and Anglo-American relations, **I**, 74; opposed by the Essex Junto, **II**, 229; as factor leading to War of 1812, **II**, 307; and French decrees, **II**, 344; **IV**, 52; and neutrality, **IV**, 88; and Nonintercourse Act, **IV**, 138; and the Rose intrigue, **IV**, 502; and demand for fine-wool sheep, **V**, 67; and states' rights, **V**, 176; and foreign trade, **V**, 294; and Trade with the Enemy Acts, **V**, 300; and Virginia, **V**, 373; and the War of 1812, **V**, 404

Embree, Elihu, editor of the *Emancipator*, **II**, 206

Embury, Philip, and the Methodists, **III**, 380

Emergency, and the New Deal, **IV**, 95

Emergency Banking Act of 1933, passage of, **I**, 159; **V**, 144

Emergency Farm Credits Act, **III**, 180

Emergency Farm Mortgage Act, **III**, 180

Emergency Fleet Corporation, incorporated by Federal Government, **II**, 403; builds Hog Island Shipyard, **III**, 36; and merchant marine, **III**, 376; created, **V**, 492

Emergency Legislation, and the Agricultural Adjustment Administration, **I**, 24; and Civil Works Administration, **I**, 393; and nationalist sentiment, **IV**, 64

Emergency Railroad Transportation Act, **IV**, 401, 421

Emergency Shipping Act of 1917, **III**, 376

Emergency Tariff of 1921, **V**, 222

Emerson, Luther Orlando, sets "We are coming, Father Abra'am, etc.," to music, **V**, 428

Emerson, Ralph Waldo, and Concord Group, **II**, 2; transcendentalist, **II**, 340; and oratory, **IV**, 180; and philosophical thought and writings, **IV**, 263; and "shot heard round the world," **V**, 76; and Swedenborgianism, **V**, 213; and theological writings, **V**, 261; and transcendentalism, **V**, 304, 345; and "Young America," **V**, 510

Emery, H. C., as chairman of the Tariff Board, **V**, 223

Emigrant Aid Societies, and the Kansas struggle, III, 198; and Sons of the South, V, 121

Eminent Domain, and the Constitution, II, 40; and the contract clause, II, 48; and land titles, III, 243; and property, IV, 360; and public utilities, IV, 375

Emistesigo, attempts to relieve the British at Savannah, III, 89

Emmet, Thomas Addis, argues Gibbons v. Ogden case, II, 388

Emmett, Daniel D., composes "Dixie," II, 156; and minstrel shows, III, 412

Emory, W. H., establishes Fort Cobb, I, 406; and the Southern Railroad route, V, 131

Empire Lode Mine, II, 396

Empire State Building, I, 101

Empire Transportation Company, V, 156

Employers' Liability, and labor legislation, III, 222; and social legislation, V, 107; and five-to-four decisions, V, 207; and workmen's accident compensation, V, 485

Empresarios, and the English colony on the Rio Grande, IV, 486; and colonization of Texas, V, 251

Empress of China, and China trade, I, 365; and American ginseng, II, 390

Enabling Acts, II, 97; V, 172

Enderbury Island, under United States jurisdiction, IV, 195

Endicott, John, governor for the New England Company, II, 162; and Merry Mount, III, 378; appointed governor of Naumkeag, IV, 99; and nurseries, IV, 154; founder of Salem, V, 16

Enemy Aliens, and impressment, III, 81

Enfield Rifle, used in Civil War, I, 392

Engineering, and scientific schools, V, 44

Engineering Schools, and education, II, 187

Engineers, The Corps of, and army supply, I, 119; survey for the Baltimore and Ohio Railroad, I, 150; and flood control, II, 285; make lake surveys, III, 63; and the Keweenaw Waterway, III, 208; and river and harbor improvements, IV, 487; and enlargement of St. Marys Falls Ship Canal, V, 14

Engineers' Co-operative National Bank, IV, 400

Engines, and domestic trade, V, 292

England, John, member of the Principio Company, IV, 343

English Bill, and the Kansas struggle, III, 199; and the Lecompton Constitution, III, 259

English Institute at Santiago de Chile, III, 248

English South Sea Company, I, 19

Englishmen, Rights of. *See* Rights of Englishmen

Engraving and Printing, Bureau of, V, 314

Enlistment, in Confederate army, I, 110; and bounties, I, 228; and In re Grimley, V, 348

Enochs, Enoch, and rivermen of the Ohio, IV, 490

Enos, Roger, and Arnold's attack on Quebec, I, 120

Enrollment Act of 1863, I, 112, 228

Entail, and Jeffersonian Democracy, III, 172; and primogeniture, IV, 342; abolition of, IV, 351; abolished by Virginia, V, 373

Entangling Alliances, and associated power, I, 131; and foreign policy, II, 303

Enterprise, The, and steamboat racing, V, 178

Enumerated Commodities, and colonial commerce, I, 418; and the Navigation Acts, IV, 73

Enumerated Powers, and the Bill of Rights, I, 186; and the Constitution, II, 40; and the Federal Government, II, 257; and reserved powers of states, IV, 457; and strict construction, V, 189; and tyranny, V, 337

Envoy Extraordinary, and foreign service, V, 163

Epervier-Peacock Engagement, IV, 236

Ephrata Community, I, 162, 440

Epidemics, cholera, I, 369; and sanitation, V, 28; and city water supply, V, 424; yellow fever, V, 504

Episcopacy. *See* Protestant Episcopal Church

Episcopal Corporation, founded by William Smith, III, 129

Equal Protection Clause, and Minnesota Moratorium case, III, 412; and police power, IV, 294; and U. S. v. Cruikshank, V, 348; and U. S. v. Harris, V, 348; and Williams v. Mississippi, V, 467

Equality Citizenship Act (1934), V, 479

Equalization Fee, and the McNary-Haugen bill, III, 367

Equipoise, famous thoroughbred horse, V, 265

Equitable Life Insurance Building, uses elevators, V, 87

Equitable Life Insurance Company, III, 132

Equity Co-operative Exchange, IV, 139

Erdman Act, and industrial arbitration, I, 95; and railroad mediation, IV, 402

Eric-Jansonist Colony, V, 214

Ericsson, John, designer of the *Monitor,* IV, 10

Ericsson, Leif, and the discovery of America, I, 56; and discovery of Vinland, IV, 143; and Runic inscriptions, IV, 508

Erie, Fort, occupation of, II, 379; IV, 130; and transportation, IV, 316; battle at, V, 405

Erie, Lake, Battle of, and Fort Detroit, II, 143; and "Don't give up the ship," II, 161; and flagship *Lawrence,* III, 253; and the Perry-Elliott controversy, IV, 253; and Pittsburgh, IV, 280; and battle of the Thames, V, 258; and control of waterways, V, 406; Perry's famous words after, V, 428

Erie Canal, as influence on agriculture, I, 33; and aqueducts, I, 93; and boom towns, I, 215;

and Buffalo, **I**, 247; and Canadian annexation movement, **I**, 302; building of, **I**, 302; and government ownership, **II**, 404; and the Hudson River, **III**, 55; and inland lock navigation, **III**, 124; as internal improvement, **III**, 136; and Michigan, **III**, 391; and the Mohawk Valley, **IV**, 5; effect on New England, **IV**, 97; building of, **IV**, 117; and the New York Barge Canal, **IV**, 117; and the New York Central Railroad, **IV**, 117; and railroad rate wars, **IV**, 403; and railroads, **IV**, 407; showboats on, **V**, 76; and state debts, **V**, 168; and domestic trade, **V**, 291; and shifts in trade routes and centers, **V**, 299; and transportation and travel, **V**, 307; and Wall Street, **V**, 393; as inland waterway, **V**, 425; and the Western Reserve, **V**, 445; and the westward movement, **V**, 451

"Erie Canal," occupational ballad, **I**, 148

Erie Indians, or the Cat Nation, **I**, 322; raided by Iroquois with guns, **III**, 92; and the Iroquois league, **III**, 159; and the Senecas, **V**, 58

Erie Railroad, and railroad rate wars, **IV**, 403

Erie Railroad v. Tompkins, **V**, 214

Erle, Walter, and the Dorchester Company, **II**, 162

Erosion, and soil, **II**, 91; and dust, **II**, 178; and forests, **II**, 308; and reforestation, **IV**, 435; and soil, **V**, 115

Erskine, Robert, topographer, **II**, 216

Ervien v. U. S., and enabling acts, **II**, 214

Escalante, Silvestre Vélez de, explores the Colorado River, **I**, 427; traverses the Spanish Trail, **V**, 142; and topographic mapping, **V**, 283

Escalante-Dominguez Expedition, and Old Spanish Trail, **I**, 274; enters Utah, **V**, 353

Escalator Clause, of London Naval Treaty of 1930, **III**, 297; and naval competition, **IV**, 70

Esch-Cummins Act. *See* Transportation Act of 1920

Esopus War, **III**, 213; **IV**, 109

Espejo, Antonio de, in New Mexico, **IV**, 107; in Texas, **V**, 252

Espionage Act (1917), and freedom of speech, **II**, 337; and Schenk v. U. S., **V**, 38; and sedition, **V**, 55; creates new crimes, **V**, 399; and the World War, **V**, 492

Espuela Land and Cattle Company, **IV**, 177

"Essayons," motto of the Corps of Engineers, **II**, 217

Essex Case (1805), and the doctrine of continuous voyage, **II**, 142; and Rule of the War of 1756, **IV**, 506

Essex Junto, and the Hartford Convention, **III**, 14; and the Rose intrigue, **IV**, 502; and secession, **V**, 51

Estate Taxes, **III**, 139; **V**, 226

Estebanico (or Estevan), accompanies Cabeza de Vaca on journey, **IV**, 54; discovers the Zuñi Indians, **V**, 515

Euclid v. Ambler Realty Company, **V**, 514

Eustis, William, and the United States Military Academy, **III**, 398

Eutaw Springs, engagement at, **V**, 129

Evacuation Day, as a holiday in New York City, **IV**, 118

Evangelical Seminary in Mexico City, **III**, 248

Evangeline, **I**, 6

Evangelism, and home missionary societies, **III**, 416

Evangelists, of the Second Awakening, **I**, 143

Evans, A. W., and operations on the Washita, **V**, 420

Evans, Charles, *American Bibliography*, **III**, 35

Evans, George Henry, and the homestead movement, **III**, 42; and immigrant labor, **III**, 72; and political Young Americanism, **V**, 510

Evans, Henry, and tin can manufacture, **V**, 271

Evans, Lewis, map of, **V**, 282; his map shows Great Warriors Path, **V**, 408

Evans, N. G., at Bull Run, **I**, 251

Evans, Oliver, and the automobile, **I**, 139; and the steam engine, **II**, 214; invents flour mill, **III**, 148; and machines, **III**, 320; and mass production, **III**, 353; and patents, **IV**, 223; and railroads, **IV**, 406; and sawmills, **V**, 36; and steam power, **V**, 177

Evans, Robley D., commands fleet in cruise round the world, **I**, 168

Evaporation, and refrigeration, **IV**, 436

Evarts, Jeremiah, and the temperance movement, **V**, 240

Eveleth, Jonathan G., and the Pennsylvania Rock Oil Company, **IV**, 166

Evening Graphic, a tabloid, **V**, 216

Evening Post, edited by William Coleman, **IV**, 123

Everett, Edward, nominated for Vice-Presidency, **I**, 285; Constitutional Union party candidate, **II**, 44; and land speculation, **III**, 240; and oratory, **IV**, 180

Everitt, J. A., organizes the American Society of Equity, **V**, 275

Everybody's Magazine, and muckrakers, **IV**, 38

Evolution, and philosophical thought and writings, **IV**, 264; and religion, **IV**, 442

Ewell, R. S., at Bull Run, **I**, 251; and battle of Cedar Mountain, **I**, 330; repulses attack at Cross Keys, **II**, 91; and battle of Gettysburg, **II**, 386; and invasion of Pennsylvania, **IV**, 244; and battles at Sailor's Creek, **V**, 5; and battle of Spotsylvania Courthouse, **V**, 150; and the Army of Northern Virginia, **V**, 371; and battles of the Wilderness, **V**, 465; and battle of Winchester, **V**, 470

Ewing, Thomas, Jr., at Pilot Knob, **IV**, 272; and Soldiers and Sailors Conventions, **V**, 117

Excess Profits Taxes, **I**, 115; **III**, 84; **V**, 226

Exchange, Bills of, and the triangular trade, **V**, 296

Exchange v. McFaddon, **V**, 43

Excise Taxes, and whiskey, **I**, 20; and the Constitution, **II**, 33; as internal revenue, **III**, 139; and the public revenue, **IV**, 462; and taxation, **V**, 225 ff.; as indirect taxes, **V**, 230

Executive, and separation of powers, **IV**, 327

Executive Agent, as an unofficial observer, **V**, 351

Executive Agreements, and secret diplomacy, **II**, 147; and the Senate, **V**, 315; and treaties, **V**, 319; and veto power of the Senate, **V**, 366

Exhibition of the Industry of All Nations, **III**, 337

Expansion, and foreign policy, **II**, 304

Expatriation, right of, **I**, 50; and foreign policy, **II**, 303

Expenditures, Federal, and the Constitution, **II**, 34

Exploration Company, **I**, 71

Explosives, DuPont manufactures, **II**, 177

Export-Debenture Plan, and farm relief, **II**, 250

Export-Import Banks, and dollar diplomacy, **II**, 158

Export Taxes, and the Constitution, **II**, 35

Exports. *See* Trade, Foreign

Expositions, and art collections, **I**, 124; and postage stamps, **IV**, 318

Express Companies: Adams Express Company, **I**, 9; American Express Company, **I**, 60; carry mail, **IV**, 318, 320; Wells, Fargo and Company, **V**, 433; and the World War, **V**, 492

Exterminator, famous thoroughbred horse, **V**, 265

Extra Sessions, and the Constitution, **II**, 36

Extradition, and the Constitution, **II**, 37; and relations between the states, **V**, 174

Extraterritoriality, and the Consular Convention (1782–89), **II**, 44; introduced by Cushing's Treaty, **II**, 101; and Far Eastern policy, **II**, 243; and the Madrid Conference, **III**, 322; and the Peking Tariff Conference, **IV**, 239; and the Reed Treaty (1858), **IV**, 434; and treaties with foreign nations, **V**, 318

Ezra Church, battle of, **I**, 135

F

F–4, sinking of the, **V**, 194

Factor, John, kidnapping of, **III**, 209

Factories, and manufacturing, **III**, 336

Factory System, rise of, and leisure, **III**, 264

Factory System, The Indian, **I**, 61, 117; **III**, 322

Fair, James G., bonanza king, **I**, 208, 444; and great fortunes, **II**, 312

Fair Labor Standards Act of 1938, **I**, 362; **III**, 221, 222, 409; **IV**, 96; **V**, 387

Fair Oaks, battle of, and the Peninsular campaign, **IV**, 241

Fair Trade Laws, and advertising, **I**, 18; and price maintenance, **IV**, 340

Fair Valuation, and railroad rate law, **IV**, 402; and rate base, **IV**, 416; and Smyth v. Ames, **V**, 105; and Wisconsin Railroad Commission case, **V**, 474

Fairbank, Calvin, and Webster trials, **V**, 431

Fairbanks, C. W., elected Vice-President, **I**, 289

Fairfax Resolves, signed in Alexandria, **I**, 47

Fairweather, Bill, discovers Alder Gulch, **II**, 236

Falckner, Daniel, one of the first Lutheran ministers, **III**, 316

Falk Foundation, **II**, 314

Falkland Islands, and the Monroe Doctrine, **IV**, 13

Fall, Albert B., and the Elk Hills oil scandal, **II**, 203; convicted of bribery, **IV**, 71; and Teapot Dome oil scandal, **V**, 235

Fall Line, and the Piedmont region, **IV**, 268

Fallam, Robert, journalizes the Batts expedition, **I**, 168

Fallen Timbers, victory for Wayne, **II**, 128; and treaty of Greenville, **II**, 425; battle of, **V**, 427

Falls, and water power, **V**, 422

Falmouth, Maine, dead city, **II**, 114

Falmouth Gazette, published by Titcomb and Wait, **IV**, 126

Family Compact, and treaty of Fontainebleau, **II**, 294; and the Nootka Sound Controversy, **IV**, 142; Spain renews, **V**, 139

Family Limitation, written by Margaret Sanger, **I**, 191

Famous Players Film Company, **IV**, 32

Faneuil, Peter, and the triangular trade, **V**, 297

Faneuil Hall, built from proceeds of a lottery, **III**, 303

Fannin, James W., Jr., and massacre at Goliad, **II**, 400; and the Matamoras expedition, **III**, 359; and the Texas revolution, **V**, 257

Fanning, Edmund, and the Regulators of North Carolina, **IV**, 440

Fanning Mill, and threshing machine, **V**, 266

Fansteel Metallurgical Corporation, sit-down strike, **V**, 191

Far East, trade with, **I**, 128; and the Open-Door Policy, **IV**, 176; and Spanish-American War, **V**, 137

Far Eastern Policy, and neutrality, **IV**, 89

Far West, and Little Big Horn battle, **III**, 284

Fargo, William G., and the American Express Company, **I**, 60; contractor of the Southern Overland Mail, **V**, 130; one of the founders of Wells, Fargo and Company, **V**, 433

Farley, James A., cancels air mail contracts, **I**, 35

Farm and Farming. *See also* Agriculture

Farm Banks, **I**, 157

Farm Bloc, formation and activities of, **I**, 202; **II**, 245; and farm relief, **II**, 249

Farm Bureau, established, **I**, 26

Farm Bureau Federation, and propaganda, **IV**, 358

Farm Credit Administration, created, **I**, 157; absorbs the Federal Farm Board, **II**, 257; and government corporations, **II**, 403; a New Deal agency, **IV**, 96

Farm Credit Agencies, **I**, 32

Farm Journal, and consumer protection, **II**, 44

Farm Machinery, and agricultural adaptation to the plains, **I**, 22; the combine, **I**, 430; manufacture of, **II**, 125; encouraged by Illinois Central Railroad, **III**, 70; and interchangeable parts, **III**, 133; competitive warfare among manufacturers of, **III**, 140; advance made in production of, **III**, 320; and manufacturing, **III**, 337; the plow, **IV**, 287; the reaper, **IV**, 419; the tractor, **V**, 290; and the urban drift, **V**, 352

Farm Papers, **I**, 18, 27

Farm Prices, and the Capper-Volstead Act, **I**, 311

Farm Products, and domestic trade, **V**, 293

Farm Relief, government control of, **I**, 32; and Hoosac Mills case, **III**, 44

Farm Surpluses, and the Agricultural Adjustment Administration, **I**, 24

Farm Tenancy, and absentee ownership, **I**, 4; and the agrarian movement, **I**, 21; in North Carolina, **IV**, 145. *See also* Tenancy System

Farmer, Joseph, member of the Principio Company, **IV**, 343

Farmer-Labor Party, in Minnesota, **I**, 21; and campaign of 1920, **I**, 291; in campaign of 1932, **I**, 292; make-up of, **III**, 223; and the LaFollette party, **III**, 227; in Minnesota, **III**, 411; and the Nonpartisan League, **IV**, 140; as a political party, **IV**, 297; as a third party, **V**, 262

Farmers, as a privileged group, **IV**, 350

Farmers' Alliance, and agrarian movement, **I**, 21; and formation of citizens' alliances, **I**, 378; promotes co-operatives, **II**, 57; and co-operative elevator building, **II**, 202; and farm relief, **II**, 249; and the Populist party, **IV**, 313

Farmer's Almanac, **IV**, 99

Farmers' Declaration of Independence, **II**, 410

Farmers' Institutes, **I**, 25

Farmers' Nonpartisan League, and the agrarian movement, **I**, 21

Farmers' Union, an agrarian movement, **I**, 22; promotes co-operatives, **II**, 57; and farm relief, **II**, 249

Farnsworth, C. S., and the Ypres-Lys operation, **V**, 511

Farragut, David Glasgow, made an admiral, **I**, 12; and the Navy in the Civil War, **I**, 389 f.; in the battle of Mobile Bay, **II**, 108; and the *Hartford,* **III**, 14; and the opening of the Mississippi, **III**, 419; in battle of Mobile Bay, **IV**, 1; aided by mortar bombardment, **IV**, 28; establishes Mare Island Navy Yard, **IV**, 79; and capture of New Orleans, **IV**, 110; and siege of Port Hudson, **IV**, 315; and the *Tennessee,* **V**, 243; at Vicksburg, **V**, 367

Farringtons, The, train robbers, **V**, 303

Faulkner, C. J., imprisonment of, **I**, 122

Faulkner, William, and fiction, **II**, 270

Fauntleroy, Fort, **III**, 317

Fauntleroy, Thomas T., and Fort Riley, **IV**, 484

Fay, Jonas, and the Green Mountain Boys, **II**, 422

Fayetteville, battle at. *See* Prairie Grove, battle at

Federal Aid Road Act (1916). *See* Rural Post Roads Act

Federal Bureau of Investigation, and bandits, **I**, 153; and gangsters, **II**, 370; and the Department of Justice, **III**, 192; and kidnapping, **III**, 209; and law enforcement, **III**, 253; and the police, **IV**, 294

Federal Communications Commission, as administrative agency, **I**, 11; created, **I**, 260; gains authority over telegraph, telephone and cable, **III**, 143; and interstate commerce laws, **III**, 144; and radio broadcasting, **IV**, 398

Federal Council of Churches of Christ in America, **I**, 373; **II**, 230; **III**, 287; **IV**, 443; **V**, 488

Federal Credit Unions, **II**, 246

Federal Crop Insurance Corporation, **IV**, 308

Federal Deposit Insurance Corporation, **I**, 157, 158, 444; **III**, 134

Federal Emergency Relief Administration, **I**, 393; **IV**, 96, 440; **V**, 511

Federal Employment Stabilization Board, **I**, 432

Federal Farm Board, and the agrarian movement, **I**, 22; and the Farm Bureau, **II**, 245; created, **II**, 246, 250; and tobacco co-operatives, **V**, 276

Federal Farm Loan Act of 1916, and banking, **I**, 157; and chartering of joint-stock land banks, **III**, 179

Federal Farm Loan System, **I**, 22; **II**, 245

Federal Farm Mortgage Corporation, **II**, 118, 245

Federal Intermediate Credit Banks, creation of, **II**, 245

Federal Land Banks, **II**, 245

Federal Power Commission, **I**, 260; **II**, 27, 196; **III**, 144; **IV**, 377

Federal Radio Commission, **III**, 144; **IV**, 397

Federal Reserve Act, and acceptances, **I**, 7; passage of, **I**, 157; and branch banking, **I**, 158; and foreign investments, **III**, 150

Federal Reserve Bank Notes, introduction of, **II**, 100; and the Pittman Act, **IV**, 280

Federal Reserve Banks, created, **I**, 157; and Farm Credit Agencies, **II**, 245; and the Federal Deposit Insurance Corporation, **II**, 256; rate of interest, **III**, 134; and open market operations, **IV**, 177; as fiscal agents for the government, **V**, 196

Federal Reserve Board, as administrative agency, **I**, 11; and banking acts, **I**, 158; and Comptroller of the Currency, **I**, 444; and foreign banking, **II**, 185; and Federal expropriation of gold, **II**, 394; and managed currency, **III**, 330; and the panic of 1929, **IV**, 210; and the Thomas Amendment, **V**, 264

Federal Reserve Notes, replace bank notes, **I**, 154; introduction of, **II**, 100; and money system, **IV**, 8; as paper money, **IV**, 213

Federal Reserve System, and bank deposits, **I**, 153; and branch banking, **I**, 158; and national banks, **I**, 160; government obligations of, **II**, 128; and bills of exchange, **II**, 231; and the McFadden Banking Act, **III**, 364; and money system, **IV**, 8; and the Reconstruction Finance Corporation, **IV**, 428

Federal Safety Appliance Act, **I**, 8

Federal Security Administration, Office of Education transferred to, **II**, 188

Federal-State Relations, and the Chicago Sanitary District, **I**, 358

Federal Steel Company, **V**, 348

Federal Surplus Commodities Corporation, **IV**, 308

Federal Theater Project, **IV**, 441

Federal Trade Commission, as administrative agency, **I**, 11; and the advertising agency, **I**, 19; created, **I**, 87; and the Beef Trust cases, **I**, 173; created, **I**, 260, 396, 433; and consumer protection, **II**, 44; and government regulation, **II**, 406; and Humphrey's Executor v. U. S., **III**, 59; and interstate commerce, **III**, 144; and the judiciary, **III**, 186; and patent medicine, **IV**, 222; and prevention of manipulation in the grain markets, **IV**, 279; and regulation of public utilities, **IV**, 377; and Pure Food and Drug Acts, **IV**, 383; and trade practices, **V**, 299; and trusts, **V**, 327; and the Webb Export Act, **V**, 431

Federalist, The, Hamilton's contribution to, **I**, 185; and judicial review, **III**, 183; and the judiciary, **III**, 185; and jury trial, **III**, 191; and rights of the minority, **III**, 412; and pamphleteering, **IV**, 202; and political writings, **IV**, 302; and propaganda, **IV**, 358; Madison writes on distribution of wealth, **V**, 429; and "the wise, and good and rich," **V**, 475

Federalist Party, and the agrarian movement, **I**, 20; and the Alien and Sedition Acts, **I**, 48; and campaigns of 1788 and 1792, **I**, 280; and campaigns of 1796–1812, **I**, 281; discredited by Hartford Convention, **I**, 282; and the congressional caucus, **I**, 327; and the caucus, **I**, 328; and the Democratic party, **II**, 136; and the Essex Junto, **II**, 228; and Franco-American relations, **II**, 328; and the Hartford Convention, **III**, 14; and Jay's Treaty, **III**, 169; and the Jefferson-Burr election dispute, **III**, 170; and the Judiciary Act of 1801, **III**, 189; founded by Hamilton, **III**, 301; and Marbury v. Madison, **III**, 341; and the Mazzei Letter, **III**, 362; called Monarchists, **IV**, 7; and the Nationalist viewpoint, **IV**, 64; and the *Gazette of the United States,* **IV**, 128; and party government, **IV**, 220; as a political party, **IV**, 296; and the Republican party (Jeffersonian), **IV**, 453; and the Rose intrigue, **IV**, 502; and secession, **V**, 51; and appointments to office, **V**, 147; and states' rights, **V**, 176; and Tammany Hall, **V**, 218; and the "Terrapin War," **V**, 246; and the Washington Benevolent Society, **V**, 417; and the Whiskey Insurrection, **V**, 457; and "the wise, and good and rich," **V**, 475

Federation of Organized Trades and Labor Unions, **I**, 60

Fee, John G., and abolition movement, **I**, 2; and the Madison County antislavery war, **III**, 322

Fee Simple, **III**, 243

Feke, Robert, portraitist, **I**, 123; **IV**, 478

Fell, Jesse, and anthracite, **I**, 79

Fellow-Servant Doctrine, **II**, 212

Fellows, John, and surrender at Saratoga, **V**, 32

Fellowship, The, and the Dorchester Company, **II**, 162

Fellowship for Reconciliation, peace movement, **IV**, 235; **V**, 395

Fels (Joseph) Fund, aids single tax plan, **V**, 83

Female Seminaries, and education of women, **V**, 480

Fencing, and herd law v. free grass, **III**, 27; helps end sheep wars, **V**, 67

Fencing Wars, and barbed wire, **I**, 163; on public lands, **IV**, 373

Fenians, in Campo Bello fiasco, **I**, 296; and Canadian-American relations, **I**, 300

Fenno, John, editor of the *Gazette of the United States,* **IV**, 128

Fenwick, Edward D., and the Dominicans, **II**, 159

Fenwick, George, patentee of Saybrook, **V**, 36

Fenwick, John, gains Berkeley's western portion of New Jersey, **IV**, 104; chief proprietor of Salem, N. J., **IV**, 105; and West Jersey, **V**, 437

Ferdinand, Fort, built at Chickasaw Bluffs, **I**, 359

Ferguson, Patrick, and battle of King's Mountain, **III**, 212

Ferguson, Robert, establishes the *Knoxville Gazette,* IV, 124, 127; first printer of Tennessee, IV, 346

Ferrar, John, and the Virginia Company of London, V, 377

Ferrar, Nicholas, and the Virginia Company of London, V, 377

Ferree, Fort, erected at Upper Sandusky, V, 352

Ferries, and travel, V, 306

Ferris, A. C., and kerosene oil, III, 207

Ferris Wheel, at World's Columbian Exposition, III, 396; V, 495

Ferry, Steam, established between Hoboken and New York, IV, 105

Fertilizers, and the chemical industry, I, 351; early ignorance of proper use of, II, 247; and guano, II, 427; nitrates as, IV, 135; and soil exhaustion, V, 116; developed by Tennessee Valley Authority, V, 245

Fessenden, R. A., and wireless telegraphy, V, 472

Fessenden, T. G., author of the *New England Farmer,* II, 248

Fetterman, Fort, battle of, I, 94

Fetterman, William J., and the Cheyenne Indians, I, 355; killed, V, 86

Fetterman Massacre, occurs in Big Horn Mountains, I, 184; and Fort Phil Kearny, III, 201; and Red Cloud War, IV, 429

Feudalism, and crown lands, II, 92; and entail of estate, II, 218; and primogeniture, IV, 342; and property, IV, 359

Feuds, and crime, II, 88; Hatfield-McCoy, III, 16; Martin-Tolliver, III, 348

Few, William, signer of the Constitution, II, 39

Fiat Money, II, 99

Fiduciary Coins, V, 276

Field, Cyrus W., and the laying of the Atlantic cable, I, 135

Field, Darby, explores Mt. Washington, IV, 36

Field, David Dudley, and codification of judicial procedure, III, 188; and codification of international law, IV, 235

Field, Kate, as woman journalist, V, 481

Field, Marshall, rise of, II, 312

Field, Robert, miniature painter, III, 408

Field, S. J., and equal protection of law, II, 222; in Juilliard v. Greenman, III, 189; and the Neagle case, IV, 79

Field, Stephen D., and electric railways, IV, 410

Field Museum of Natural History, IV, 47

Fields, Al G., minstrel show of, III, 413

Fields, James T., and bookshops, I, 214

Fields, Jeremiah, and the Regulators of North Carolina, IV, 440

Fierer, Charles, publishes the *Times, and Patowmack Packet,* IV, 126; first printer in District of Columbia, IV, 345

Fifteen Gallon Law (1838), V, 241

Fifteenth Amendment, text, II, 42; nullification of the, II, 151; and Force Acts, II, 300; and the franchise, II, 323; and the Grandfather Clause, II, 409; and Guinn and Beal v. U. S., II, 428; and the Negro, IV, 82 f.; and Negro suffrage, IV, 85; and Reconstruction, IV, 426; and race toleration, V, 277; and U. S. v. Harris, V, 349; and U. S. v. Reese, V, 349; and the right to vote, V, 383; as a war amendment, V, 398

Fifth Amendment, and Adair v. U. S., I, 9; text, II, 40; due process clause of, II, 172; and minimum-wage laws, III, 409; and the wire-tapping cases, V, 472

"Fifty-four Forty or Fight," and joint occupation, III, 179; and the Oregon Question, IV, 185; V, 415

Filhiol, Don Juan, establishes Fort Miro, III, 414

Filibuster, in Congress, II, 19

Filibustering, in Latin America, III, 250; and Lopez expedition, III, 301; and visit and search, V, 381

Filling Stations, and the distribution of merchandise, II, 152

Fillmore, Millard, and the American (Know-Nothing) party, I, 64; first bathtub installed for, I, 167; candidate of American party, I, 284

Filson, John, interviews Daniel Boone, I, 216; and Cincinnati, I, 375

Filson's Map, and Great Warriors Path, V, 408

Finance Department of the Army, I, 119

Financier of the Finances, Robert Morris as, II, 178

Financing of the Revolution, IV, 467

Fincastle, Fort, built by William Crawford, III, 26; built at Wheeling, W. Va., V, 455

Fincastle County, creation of, I, 139; III, 204; and Kentucky County, III, 206

Findley, John, brings Daniel Boone to Kentucky, III, 204

Fine, Jean G., and social settlements, V, 109

Finé, Oronce, maps of, III, 340

Fingerprinting File, II, 370

Fink, Mike, hero of a cycle of bargemen legends, I, 164; riverman, IV, 490; and tall stories, V, 186

Finley, Hugh, and post roads, IV, 318

Finley, John, and suspension bridges, I, 238

Finnegan, Joseph, and battle of Olustee, IV, 172

Finney, Charles G., evangelist, II, 230; and religious thought and writings, IV, 446; pre-Civil War revivalist, IV, 464; influences development of Arminianism, V, 446

"Fip," monetary term, I, 411

Fire Insurance, III, 129

Fire Zouave Regiment, V, 514

Firelands, and Connecticut's western lands, II, 24; and the Western Reserve, V, 444, 445

Fires: Baltimore fire, **I**, 151; Chicago fire, **I**, 356; Detroit fire, **II**, 145; in New York City, **IV**, 119; prairie, **IV**, 329; Triangle fire, **V**, 324

Firestone, Harvey S., establishes rubber plantations, **IV**, 505

Fish, and domestic trade, **V**, 292; and foreign trade, **V**, 294; in the triangular trade, **V**, 296

Fish, Hamilton, and the Alabama Claims, **I**, 40; president of the Society of the Cincinnati, **I**, 376; and the Monroe Doctrine, **IV**, 14; and the Protective War Claims Association, **IV**, 366; as Secretary of State, **V**, 162; and the *Virginius* affair, **V**, 380; and the Treaty of Washington (1871), **V**, 416

Fish, Job, commands the *Walk-in-the-Water*, **V**, 392

Fisher, Carl G., and the Lincoln Highway, **III**, 279

Fisher, Fort, taken during Civil War, **I**, 390

Fisher, Irving, outlines plan for stabilizing the dollar, **III**, 329

Fisher, Mary, and the Quakers, **IV**, 386

Fisher, Warren, Jr., and the Mulligan letters, **IV**, 40

Fisheries, cod, **I**, 406; and colonial commerce, **I**, 417; Bureau of, **I**, 432; and Definitive Treaty of Peace, **II**, 129; in the colonies, **III**, 119; mackerel, **III**, 321; started by Hugh Peter, **V**, 16; salmon, **V**, 17; seal, **V**, 49; and territorial waters, **V**, 248; and the War of 1812, **V**, 406

Fisheries Dispute, and Anglo-American relations, **I**, 77; arbitration of, **I**, 96, 169; and Canadian-American relations, **I**, 300; and Convention of 1818, **II**, 52; and Halifax award, **III**, 6; and *Modus vivendi*, **IV**, 4; settled by the Treaty of Washington (1871), **V**, 416

Fishing Bounties, **I**, 407

"Fishing Expeditions," and investigating committees, **III**, 149

Fishing Industry, and refrigeration, **IV**, 437

Fishing Rights, and state boundary disputes, **I**, 227

Fishing Stages, **V**, 154

Fisk, C. B., prohibition candidate, **I**, 288

Fisk, James, and Black Friday (1869), **I**, 194; and Erie Railroad, **II**, 226; and railroads, **IV**, 408

Fisk University, founded by the American Missionary Association, **III**, 416

Fiske, Bradley A., urges creation of office of Chief of Naval Operations, **IV**, 71

Fiske, John, and evolution, **II**, 231; literary lecturer, **III**, 260; and philosophical thought and writings, **IV**, 264

Fitch, Clyde, playwright, **II**, 166

Fitch, Jabez, and epidemics, **II**, 221

Fitch, James, and the doctrine of Divine Providences, **II**, 154

Fitch, John, and the steamboat, **II**, 214, 355; **III**, 148; **IV**, 223; **V**, 177, 179, 307

Fitch, John, makes map of Northwest, **V**, 283

Fitch, S. S., writes first complete dental text in English, **II**, 138

Fitch, Thomas, and the Susquehannah Company, **V**, 211

Fithian's Silk Growers Almanac, **I**, 52

Fitz, Reginald Heber, and medicine and surgery, **III**, 369

Fitzhugh, Benjamin, and the development of the reaper, **IV**, 419

Fitzhugh, George, political writings of, **IV**, 302; and proslavery literature, **IV**, 364; and the soundness of slavery, **V**, 123

Fitzpatrick, Thomas, mountain man, **I**, 128; guides expeditions, **II**, 236; mountain man, **II**, 362; and Kearny's march to California, **III**, 201; and treaty of Fort Laramie (1851), **III**, 245; mountain man, **IV**, 37; makes effective discovery of South Pass, **V**, 128; and Ashley's expeditions, **V**, 310; and western exploration, **V**, 442

FitzSimons, Thos., signer of the Constitution, **II**, 39

Five Civilized Tribes, lose lands in Oklahoma, **I**, 215; and the Dawes Commission, **II**, 113; and education, **III**, 86; and slavery, **III**, 88; oil lands of, **III**, 103; and Indian policy, **III**, 106; removal of, **III**, 107; and Indian Territory, **III**, 109; and intermarried citizens, **III**, 135; in Oklahoma, **IV**, 168; and Oklahoma squatters, **IV**, 169; and proposed state of Sequoyah, **V**, 58; and Council of Fort Smith, **V**, 101

Five Forks, Pickett routed at, **IV**, 256; and Sheridan-Warren controversy, **V**, 69

Five Points, and slums, **V**, 99

Five-Power Naval Treaty, **V**, 414

"Five Twenties," and Jay Cooke and Company, **II**, 54; and Greenback movement, **II**, 423; and the Ohio Idea, **IV**, 163

Five Villages, as wintering place of Lewis and Clark expedition, **II**, 106; Fort Mandan built at, **III**, 330

Fixico, Hotulka, in Crazy Snake rebellion, **II**, 83

Flagellation, and the Penitent Brothers, **IV**, 242

Flagg, Josiah, first native-born professional dentist, **II**, 138; and use of gutta-percha fillings in teeth, **II**, 138

Flagler, Henry M., opens south Florida to railroad transportation, **II**, 287; and Standard Oil Company, **V**, 156

Flandrau, C. E., and defense of New Ulm, **IV**, 114

Flares, famous thoroughbred horse, **V**, 265

Flatboats, and anthracite, **I**, 80; another name for arks, **I**, 107; and bargemen, **I**, 164; used in Lewis and Clark expedition, **III**, 266; introduc-

tion of, **III**, 423; on the Mississippi, **III**, 424; for river navigation, **IV**, 489; and rivermen of the Ohio, **IV**, 490; on rivers, **IV**, 491; as store boats, **V**, 186; and domestic trade, **V**, 291; in transportation, **V**, 306; and the westward movement, **V**, 451

Flathead Indians, on Green River, **II**, 423; and Jesuit missions, **III**, 175; in Montana, **IV**, 16; and Oregon missions, **IV**, 183; and Fort Owen, **IV**, 193

Flax, and the linen industry, **III**, 281; and textiles, **V**, 258

Fleet, cruise of the, round the world, **I**, 168; and national defense, **II**, 127; and Pearl Harbor naval base, **IV**, 237

Fleet Corporation, **II**, 209

Fleet Marine Force, **III**, 343

Fleet Naval Reserve, **IV**, 72

Fleming, J. A., and utilization of electricity, **II**, 199

Fleming, John, printer of the *Spectator*, **IV**, 127; first printer of Oregon, **IV**, 346

Fleming, Klas, promoter of New Sweden Company, **IV**, 113

Fleming, William, and battle of Point Pleasant, **IV**, 291

Fleming v. Page, **V**, 398

Fletcher, Benjamin, as governor of New York, **IV**, 114; and land speculation in New York, **IV**, 115

Fletcher v. Peck, and the contract clause, **II**, 48; and judicial review, **III**, 189; and the Yazoo fraud, **V**, 503

Flint, Austin, and medicine, **III**, 369; and tuberculosis, **V**, 328

Flint, Royal, trustee of the Scioto Company, **V**, 44

Flint Hills, **I**, 205

Floating Battery, designed by John Stevens, **I**, 109

Floating Dock, built at Hoboken, N. J., **II**, 156

Flood, James C., bonanza king, **I**, 208, 444

Flood Control, and right of eminent domain, **II**, 211; and the Corps of Engineers, **II**, 217; and the Federal Power Commission, **II**, 261; and the levee system, **III**, 265; of the Mississippi, **III**, 423, 424; and river and harbor improvements, **IV**, 487; on Tennessee River, **V**, 244; and Tennessee Valley Authority, **V**, 245; and inland waterways, **V**, 425

Floods, at Cairo, **I**, 267; and climate, **I**, 398; reduced by forests, **II**, 308; Johnstown Flood, **III**, 178; on the Mississippi River, **III**, 424; in Ohio, **IV**, 161; and the Soil Erosion Act, **V**, 115; and weather forecasts, **V**, 430

Floor Leader, elected by party caucus, **I**, 328; and Congress, **II**, 18; and the Steering Committee, **V**, 181; and Ways and Means Committee, **V**, 427

Florida, and the Blount conspiracy, **I**, 203; and the Definitive Treaty of Peace, **II**, 129; and DeSoto's expedition, **II**, 141; and expansion, **II**, 234; and the Gulf of Mexico, **III**, 389; ceded by Spain to Britain, **IV**, 216; and the public domain, **IV**, 370; and repudiation of state debts, **IV**, 456 f.; organized, and admitted, **V**, 249; and the War Hawks, **V**, 403; and the War of 1812, **V**, 405; as a territory, **V**, 436

Florida, British, and Mississippi, **III**, 420; and Spanish military supplies from New Orleans, **V**, 141; Willing expedition attacks, **V**, 469

Florida, East, **II**, 181

Florida, Spanish, and the Mississippi Valley, **III**, 425

Florida, The, and Alabama claims, **I**, 40; in the Civil War, **I**, 390; and Confederate navy, **II**, 8; and prizes, **IV**, 353; captured by the *Wachusett,* **V**, 386

Florida, West, **V**, 436

Florida Purchase, and land titles, **III**, 243

Florida War, **II**, 103

Flour, and domestic trade, **V**, 292

Flour Mills, and hard wheat, **I**, 23; invented by Oliver Evans, **III**, 148; and the Twin Cities, **V**, 335

Flower, George, establishes the English settlement, **II**, 217

Flower Gap, **IV**, 221

Floyd, Fort, **V**, 202, 341

Floyd, John, builds Fort Nelson, **IV**, 86

Floyd, John, and the battle of Auttose, **I**, 141; **II**, 86

Floyd, John, and campaign of 1832, **I**, 283; and the Oregon Question, **IV**, 185

Floyd, John B., and battles at Carnifex Ferry, **I**, 316

Floyd, "Pretty Boy," gangster, **I**, 153

Floyd, William, signer of the Declaration of Independence, **II**, 124

"Floyd Collins," ballad, **II**, 293

Fluctuation of Money Value, **IV**, 8

Flying Cloud, clipper ship, **I**, 307, 402

Flying Fish, clipper ship, **I**, 307, 402

Fogel Grip, brings settlers to New Sweden, **IV**, 113

Folger, Henry Clay, collector of Shakespeare, **I**, 212; book collections of, **III**, 273

Folklore, and mountain people, **IV**, 37; and tall stories, **V**, 186

Folksongs, **I**, 148; **IV**, 51

Fonck, René, and airplane disasters, **I**, 35

Fontainebleau, Treaty of, and Louisiana, **III**, 305, 308, 310, 424, 426; **IV**, 188, 216; **V**, 12; and Texas, **V**, 252

Fontenelle, Lucien, and Missouri Fur Company, **V**, 13

Food, Spanish influence on, **V**, 139

Food Administration, and the Lever Act, **III**, 265; helps in distributing relief, **IV**, 76; World War, **V**, 492

Food Industries, trade magazine, **V**, 298

Food Preservation, and the tin can, **V**, 271

Fool's Gold, **III**, 406

Foot-and-Mouth Disease, **I**, 29

Football, and amusements, **I**, 70; and athletic rallies, **IV**, 414; as organized sport, **V**, 149

Foote, Andrew H., and the attack on the Barrier Forts, **I**, 165; and the Navy in the Civil War, **I**, 389; and capture of Island Number Ten, **III**, 161; and veterans' temperance pledge, **IV**, 70

Foote, Henry S., and Committee of Thirteen (1850), **I**, 436; and Compromise of 1850, **I**, 442

Foote, Samuel A., and the Webster-Hayne debate, **V**, 431

Foraker, J. B., and Brownsville affair, **I**, 245

Foraker Act, and Puerto Rico, **IV**, 380

Forbes, John Murray, and the Michigan Central Railroad, **III**, 393

Forbes, Robert Bennett, and yacht racing in America, **V**, 499

Forbes, William H., and the Bell Telephone Company, **I**, 66

Forbes and Company, successor to Panton, Leslie and Company, **IV**, 211

Forbes Expedition, and Fort Raystown, **I**, 173; and Fort Duquesne abandoned, **II**, 178, 343; and battle of Grant's Hill, **II**, 411; and Fort Ligonier, **III**, 277; and Fort Loudon, **III**, 304; and battle of the Loyalhanna, **III**, 312; and Fort Duquesne captured, **IV**, 162, 243; and Fort Pitt, **IV**, 279

Forbes Road, and the Alleghenies, **I**, 51; and Fort Bedford, **I**, 173; and Cumberland Road, **II**, 97; and mountain passes, **IV**, 221; and Raystown Path, **IV**, 418; route of Allegheny wagoners, **V**, 390; and the westward movement, **V**, 450

Force, Peter, book collection, **I**, 213; founder of the *National Journal,* **II**, 403; **IV**, 128

Force Act of 1833, **I**, 443; **III**, 165; **IV**, 154

Force Acts, Reconstruction, **I**, 382; **III**, 217; **IV**, 426; **V**, 349

Ford, Henry, and the automobile, **I**, 140; and Orphan Annie comic strip, **I**, 431; and great fortunes, **II**, 313; and mass production, **III**, 353; and Newberry v. U. S., **IV**, 121; and the Peace Ship, **IV**, 235; and the tractor, **IV**, 419; and the Selden patent, **V**, 56; and subsistence homesteads, **V**, 195

Ford, Thomas, and the Illinois and Michigan Canal, **III**, 69; and the Mormon War, **IV**, 25; and the murder of Joseph Smith, Jr., **IV**, 449

Ford (Jacob) Mansion, **IV**, 28

Ford Motor Company, builds Eagle boats, **II**, 181; establishes rubber plantations, **IV**, 505

Fordham, manor, **III**, 55

Fordney-McCumber Tariff Act, **III**, 249; **V**, 222, 223, 224

Ford's Theatre, Lincoln assassinated at, **III**, 279

Foreign Affairs, Committee for, **IV**, 475

Foreign Affairs, Department of, **V**, 161

Foreign and Domestic Commerce, Bureau of, **I**, 432

Foreign Corporations, and Bank of Augusta v. Earle, **I**, 154

Foreign Evangelical Society, **IV**, 65

Foreign Exchange Students, **V**, 191

Foreign Investments, **III**, 150

Foreign Loans, **II**, 118

Foreign Missions, and the Second Awakening, **I**, 143; and philanthropy, **IV**, 260

Foreign Policy, an issue in campaign of 1916, **I**, 290; and international law, **III**, 141; and most-favored-nation principle, **IV**, 31

Foreign Service, **II**, 208, 220, 306; **III**, 377; **IV**, 211; **V**, 163

Foreign Service, American Veterans of, **V**, 365

Foreign Trade. *See* Trade, Foreign

Foreign Wars, Veterans of, **V**, 365

"Foreman James Monroe," occupational ballad, **I**, 148

Forest Fires, and Federal aid, **II**, 255; and weather forecasts, **V**, 430; and the Weeks Act, **V**, 433

Forest Service, and fire control, **II**, 308; begins program of reforestation, **IV**, 434

Forestry, Bureau of, **II**, 27

Forests, National, and our land policy, **III**, 238

Forges, and early iron industries, **III**, 156

Forgotten Man, and the unprivileged group, **IV**, 350

Forrest, Edwin, and the Astor Place riot, **I**, 133; actor, **II**, 166; **V**, 260

Forrest, N. B., raids Holly Springs, **III**, 38; and the Meridian campaign, **III**, 377; and Fort Pillow massacre, **IV**, 272; and battle at Tupelo, **V**, 330

Forsyth, Benjamin, and capture of York (Toronto), **V**, 507

Forsyth, George A., attacked at Beecher Island, **I**, 173

Forsyth, J. W., and battle of Wounded Knee, **V**, 495

Forsythe, Thomas, as hunter, **III**, 60

Fort Wayne, and the fur trade, **II**, 360; and transportation, **IV**, 316

Fort Wayne Electric Works, **II**, 376

Fort Worth, Texas, cow country center, **II**, 79

Forting, **II**, 177

Forts, extend westward, **I**, 117

Fortune, makes public opinion surveys, **V**, 21

Forty-Eighters, and German immigration, **II**, 383; as political exiles, **IV**, 295

Forty Fort, and the Wyoming massacre, V, 497

Forty-Mile Desert, and the Great Basin, II, 414

Forum, III, 323

Forward, Jewish paper, II, 303

Fosdick, Harry Emerson, hymn writer, III, 65; pulpit orator, IV, 180

Fossils, from Big Bone Lick, I, 183

Foster, Emory S., and action at Lone Jack, III, 297

Foster, J. G., commands Army of the Ohio, IV, 162

Foster, John, and wood engraving, V, 482

Foster, Murphy J., governor of Louisiana, III, 307

Foster, Stephen Collins, and music, IV, 48; composes "My Old Kentucky Home," IV, 51; composes "Oh! Susanna," IV, 159; and popular songs, V, 119; and "Swanee River," V, 212; sets "We are coming, Father Abra'am, etc." to music, V, 428

Foundations, endowed by Andrew Carnegie, I, 315; endowed by John D. Rockefeller, II, 375; and grants-in-aid, II, 412; and the Peabody fund, IV, 230; Rockefeller Foundation, IV, 497; Russell Sage Foundation, IV, 510; Smithsonian Institution, V, 102

Fountain of Youth, II, 25; IV, 305

Four-Mile Strip, Senecas cede, IV, 130

Four-Minute Men, and patriotic rallies, IV, 414; as World War propaganda agency, V, 494

Four-Power Treaty, signed by United States, IV, 232; and treaties with foreign nations, V, 318; and Washington Conference on Limitation of Armaments, V, 417

Four Year Act of 1820, and the spoils system, V, 147

Fourdrinier Machine, for making paper, IV, 212

Fourierism, and Alphadelphia Association, I, 52; and communities, I, 441; advocates free love, II, 332; and colony of Reunion, IV, 462; and the socialist movement, V, 110; and Swedenborgianism, V, 213; and distribution of wealth, V, 429

Fourteen Points, and the armistice of 1918, I, 108; and freedom of the seas, II, 338; and indemnities, III, 84; and the League of Nations, III, 255; and open covenants, IV, 175; as presidential message, IV, 336; and treaty of Versailles, V, 364; and the Peace Conference (1919), V, 490, 492; and World War propaganda, V, 494

Fourteenth Amendment, and amnesty, I, 69; and centralization, I, 334; and citizenship, I, 379; and the Civil Rights Act, I, 381; and protection of civil rights, I, 382; text, II, 41 f.; and Coppage v. Kansas, II, 57; due process clause of, II, 172; and equal protection of law, II, 222; and doctrine of equality, II, 223; and Force

Acts, II, 300; and freedom of speech and of the press, II, 337; and the Granger cases, II, 409; and Hague v. C. I. O., III, 3; formulated by the Joint Committee on Reconstruction, III, 179; and Lochner v. New York, III, 291; and McCardle case, III, 363; and minimum-wage laws, III, 409; and Minnesota Moratorium case, III, 412; and Minor v. Happersett, III, 412; and rights of the minority, III, 412; and the Negro, IV, 82 f.; and Oregon parochial school case, IV, 184; and pardon and amnesty, IV, 214; and peonage, IV, 252; and police power, IV, 294; and privileges and immunities of citizens, IV, 351; and Reconstruction, IV, 425; and repudiation of the Confederate war debts, IV, 456; and Slaughter House cases, V, 89; and Strauder v. West Virginia, V, 187; and race toleration, V, 277; and U. S. v. Harris, V, 348; and the right to vote, V, 383; as war amendment, V, 398; and West Coast Hotel Co. v. Parrish, V, 436; and Williams v. Mississippi, V, 467; and Wolff Packing Company case, V, 476

Fourth Amendment, text, II, 40; prohibits unreasonable searches and seizures, V, 351; and the wire-tapping cases, V, 472

Fourth of July, celebration of, I, 163

Fourth Offenders, and the Baumes Law, I, 169

Fowle, Daniel, founder of the *New-Hampshire Gazette,* IV, 127; first printer of New Hampshire, IV, 346

Fowle and Draper, publishers of chapbooks, I, 341

Fowler, Jacob, and the fur trade, II, 362; traverses the Taos Trail, V, 220

Fox, George, and the Quakers, IV, 386

Fox, George H., makes an elevator, II, 201

Fox, Gustavus V., and the Navy in the Civil War, I, 389; IV, 75

Fox, J. W., Jr., works of, I, 180

Fox, Livingston Company, organize the Union Fur Company, IV, 29

Fox Hunting, I, 69

Fox Indians, and Algonquin family, I, 48; Fort Armstrong located near village of, I, 109; in the battle of Bad Axe, I, 145; and Fort Beauharnois, I, 172; and the Black Hawk purchase and war, I, 194; and treaty of Fort de Chartres, I, 348; defeated by the Chippewa, I, 367; make war with French, II, 143; and Galena-Dubuque mining district, II, 367; and the half-breed tract, III, 5; and land cessions, III, 100; removal of, III, 107; Jesuit mission founded among, III, 174; and Neutral Ground, IV, 87; and Oklahoma Openings, IV, 169; party to treaty of Prairie du Chien, IV, 329; in battle of St. Croix Falls, V, 7; and British attack on St. Louis (1780), V, 11; Sauks unite with, V, 33;

depend upon wild rice for their food supply, V, 464; and Wisconsin, V, 473

Fox Sisters, and Rochester Rappings, IV, 497; and spiritualism, V, 147

Fox-Wisconsin Waterway, and Duluth's explorations, II, 175; discovery of, II, 344; and Green Bay, II, 422; and Jolliet and Marquette, III, 180; and portages, IV, 316; and Prairie du Chien, IV, 328; and Fort Winnebago, V, 471; opened by Jolliet and Marquette, V, 473

Foxardo Case, II, 240

Foxe, Luke, explores Fox Channel, IV, 151

"Foxy Grandpa," comic character, I, 431

Fractional Currency, established, II, 99; and money system, IV, 8; as paper money, IV, 213; and the Resumption Act (1875), IV, 461; and shin plasters, V, 72

Fraeb, Henry, and Ashley's expedition, V, 310

Fram, The, used in polar expedition, IV, 293

France, Naval War with, IV, 72; American Joint Commission to, IV, 470; V, 316, 318

Franchise, The, and political campaigns, I, 295; depending on church membership, I, 372; and growth of democracy, II, 135; in Rhode Island, II, 162; and election laws, II, 191; and elections, II, 192; the right of, II, 322; and freeholders, II, 338; and immigrants, III, 73; and the Indian, III, 95; and labor parties, III, 223; and the legislature, III, 263; and the literacy test, III, 283; and Minor v. Happersett, III, 412; in Mississippi, III, 420; and the Negro, IV, 85; and the poll tax, IV, 303; property qualifications for, IV, 361; and the Republican party (Jeffersonian), IV, 453; and political rings, IV, 485; and state constitutions, V, 167

Franchises, and Public Utilities, II, 49, 196; IV, 12, 375, 377

Francis, Edward, and medicine, III, 370

Francis, Peter, and cruise of the *Saginaw's* gig, V, 5

Francis, Philip, and letters of Junius, III, 190

Franciscans, and the discovery of America, I, 57; destroyed in Apalache massacre, I, 88; work among Hopi Indians, I, 104; and the Beltrán-Espejo expedition, I, 177; in California, I, 273, 275; and the Capuchins, I, 311; and Escalante-Domínguez expedition, II, 227; in Spanish Florida, II, 288; in Florida, II, 289; in Georgia, II, 380; attempt to Christianize the Indians, III, 103; in the Southwest, III, 418; convert the Pueblo Indians, IV, 379; found San Antonio missions, V, 23; and topographic mapping, V, 283

Franco-American Alliance of 1778, and Consular Convention, II, 44; and the Definitive Treaty of Peace, II, 129; and Franco-American misunderstanding of 1798–1800, II, 327; annulled, II, 328; and neutral rights, IV, 87; and Peace Commission of 1778, IV, 231; and the American Revolution, IV, 469; and diplomacy of the Revolution, IV, 470; and financing of the Revolution, IV, 471; and the Revolutionary Army at Valley Forge, IV, 476; and secret treaties, V, 316; and treaties with foreign nations, V, 316; and the army at Valley Forge, V, 356; and the XYZ affair, V, 499

Franco-American Misunderstanding, and Trade with the Enemy Acts, V, 300

Franco-American Relations, and the *Little Sarah* incident, III, 285

Frank, Leo, murder trials of, V, 323

"Frank Merriwell," character created by William Gilbert Patten (Burt L. Standish), II, 147

"Frank Reade," stories of, II, 147

Frankford, Pa., arsenal at, I, 122

Frankfort Land Company, and Germantown, II, 385

"Frankie," narrative song, I, 148

Franking, and postage stamps, IV, 318

Franklin, Benjamin, and early advertisements, I, 16; and the Albany Plan, I, 45; and antislavery societies, I, 58; founds the American Philosophical Society, I, 64; forms the Associators, I, 132; depositor and stockholder of the Bank of North America, I, 154; writes his *Autobiography,* I, 189; *Bonhomme Richard* named for, I, 208; as book collector, I, 212; as a printer, I, 213; on missions to Montreal, I, 297; and political cartoons, I, 320; as colonial agent, I, 415; publishes the *Pennsylvania Gazette,* I, 420; signer of the Constitution, II, 39; and the Consular Convention (1782–89), II, 44; delegate to Convention of 1787, II, 49; and daylight saving, II, 113; and the drafting of the Declaration of Independence, II, 120; signer of the Declaration of Independence, II, 124; and the Definitive Treaty of Peace (1783), II, 129; selects motto, *E Pluribus Unum,* II, 180; and Pennsylvania College, II, 185; early experimenter in electricity, II, 195; and the Indian factory system, II, 238; author of *Poor Richard's Almanac,* II, 252; experiments with the *Philadelphische Zeitung,* II, 302; philanthropies of, II, 314; appointed to joint diplomatic commission, II, 322, 326; invents stove, III, 23; and the Hutchinson letters, III, 62; points out need for hospital for mental cases, III, 125; seeks to win Canada to the American cause (1776), III, 230; and land speculation, III, 239; and the American Philosophical Society, III, 256; and libraries, III, 272; favors lotteries, III, 303; and magazine publishing, III, 323; and Masonry, III, 351; and medicine, III, 369; and the Navigation Acts, IV, 74; and the Paxton Boys, IV,

229; founder of the University of Pennsylvania, **IV**, 244; buys the *Pennsylvania Gazette*, **IV**, 246; co-founder of Pennsylvania Hospital, **IV**, 247; and philosophical thought and writings, **IV**, 263; and the Plan of 1776, **IV**, 282; bathtub of, **IV**, 289; author of *Poor Richard's Almanac*, **IV**, 307; and colonial postal service, **IV**, 321; proposes rattlesnake as national emblem, **IV**, 417; and the Red Line map, **IV**, 430; and diplomacy of the Revolution, **IV**, 470; and financing the Revolution, **IV**, 471; owner and publisher of the *Pennsylvania Gazette*, **V**, 33; colonial agent, and the Stamp Act, **V**, 155; and the foreign service, **V**, 163; as type founder, **V**, 336; and western land schemes, **V**, 443; and woodcuts, **V**, 482

Franklin, Fort, replaces Fort Venango, **V**, 359

Franklin, James, Jr., establishes the *Newport Mercury*, **IV**, 122; founder of the *Rhode-Island Gazette*, **IV**, 127; first printer of Rhode Island, **IV**, 346

Franklin, John, and search for a Northwest Passage, **IV**, 151; and polar expeditions, **IV**, 292

Franklin, John, and the Susquehannah Company, **V**, 211

Franklin, Mo., and caravan travel, **I**, 312; and the Santa Fé Trail, **V**, 30

Franklin, State of, backwoodsmen organize, **I**, 145; and Dumplin Creek treaty, **II**, 176; the fourteenth colony, **II**, 318; and the Muscle Shoals speculation, **IV**, 47; grows out of Watauga, **V**, 132; organized, **V**, 243

Franklin, Tenn., Hood assaults Schofield's army at, **III**, 44; Army of Tennessee (C.) defeated at, **V**, 242

Franklin, The, ship-of-the-line, **V**, 75

Franklin, William, and Burlington Company, **I**, 256; governor of New Jersey, **IV**, 104; and the Pulteney purchase, **IV**, 381; and western land schemes, **V**, 443

Franklin, William B., and battle of Antietam, **I**, 81; and the Mud March, **IV**, 39; and battle of South Mountain, **V**, 128; and battle at White Oak Swamp, **V**, 460

Franklin Academy, established, **III**, 420

Franklin and Armfield, slave trading company, **V**, 92

Franklin and Hall, publish Evans' map, **II**, 230

Franklin Cent, **II**, 354

Franklin Institute for the Promotion of Mechanic Arts, **III**, 114

Franks, David, and Company, in competition with Baynton, Wharton and Morgan, **I**, 170; and the fur trade, **II**, 361

Frankstown Path, **I**, 51

Franquelin, Jean Baptiste Louis, and topographic mapping, **V**, 282

Franquelin's Map (1682), and the Ohio River, **IV**, 164

Fraser, Alexander, attempts to reach Illinois, **III**, 69

Fraser, Charles, miniature painter, **I**, 123; **III**, 408

Fraser, Simon, and the search for the western sea, **V**, 446

Fraternal Organizations. *See* Secret Societies

Fraunces Tavern, Washington bids farewell to his officers at, **IV**, 118; headquarters of Sons of the Revolution, **V**, 121

Frayser's Farm (or Glendale), battle of, and the Peninsular campaign, **IV**, 241; assaults at, **V**, 60

Frazee, John, sculptor, **I**, 123

Frazer, John, establishes post at Venango, **V**, 359

Frazier, Lynn J., and the Nonpartisan League, **IV**, 140

Freckles, written by Gene Stratton Porter, **I**, 180

Frederica, Spanish prepare to attack, **I**, 203

Frederick, Md., Lee concentrates at, **I**, 81; and invasion of Maryland, **III**, 349

Free Banking System, **I**, 153, 156; **V**, 164

Free Grass, and barbed wire, **I**, 163

Free Land, disappearance of, and social change, **I**, 341; and Jeffersonian Democracy, **III**, 171; and the panic of 1857, **IV**, 209

Free Negroes, and the American Colonization Society, **I**, 59; and Confederate conscription, **II**, 4; and fugitive slave acts, **II**, 355; and Kansas Free-State party, **III**, 196; kidnapping of, **III**, 209; and the Lecompton constitution, **III**, 259; and Liberia, **III**, 270; and manumission, **III**, 339; and Missouri, **III**, 426; and the Missouri Compromise, **III**, 428; and the churches, **IV**, 83; in War of 1812, **IV**, 84; in Civil War, **IV**, 84; in Ohio, **IV**, 160; and the race problem, **IV**, 393; and civilization of the Old South, **V**, 122; and the Topeka constitution, **V**, 281

Free Range, and Dodge City, **II**, 156

Free Ships, Free Goods, and Convention of 1800, **II**, 52; and Franco-American relations, **II**, 327; doctrine of, **IV**, 89; and the Plan of 1776, **IV**, 282

Free Silver, and the Bland-Allison Act, **I**, 198; and campaign of 1896, **I**, 288; and the Crime of 1873, **II**, 89; and the Cross of Gold speech, **II**, 92; and the Democratic party, **II**, 137; and money system, **IV**, 8; and the Populist party, **IV**, 313

Free Soil Party, and the antislavery movement, **I**, 86; and Appeal of the Independent Democrats, **I**, 89; Barnburners unite with, **I**, 164; attacks Ohio Black Laws, **I**, 196; in campaigns of 1848, 1852, **I**, 284; and Compromise of 1850, **I**, 442; Conscience Whigs join, **II**, 25; and homestead movement, **III**, 42; Liberty party merges with, **III**, 272; aided by New Eng-

land Emigrant Aid Company, **IV,** 99; and the Ohio State Antislavery Society, **IV,** 165; as a political party, **IV,** 296; and nonextension of slavery, **IV,** 454; as a third party, **V,** 262

Free-State Hotel, and sack of Lawrence, **III,** 253

Free State Newspaper, and the sack of Lawrence, **III,** 253

Free-State Party. *See* Kansas Free-State Party

Free Trappers, of the Rocky Mountains, **II,** 362

Freeboldsen, Freebold, and tall stories, **V,** 186

Freebooters, **I,** 246

Freedmen, and the Emancipation Proclamation, **II,** 206; and Force Acts, **II,** 300; and the Ku-Klux Klan, **III,** 217; in Mississippi, **III,** 420; and Radical rule in the South, **IV,** 395; and the churches, **IV,** 427

Freedmen's Bureau, and carpetbaggers, **I,** 318; and the Negro, **IV,** 83; and Negro education, **IV,** 84; and Reconstruction, **IV,** 425; and the churches, **IV,** 427; and the Regulators, **IV,** 439; and religion, **IV,** 443

Freedom of Speech, and the Bill of Rights, **I,** 185; and the Constitution, **II,** 39; as a colonial privilege, **IV,** 350; and sedition acts, **V,** 55; and war, **V,** 399

Freedom of the Press, and the Bill of Rights, **I,** 185; and the Constitution, **II,** 39; achieves victory in Croswell libel suit, **II,** 92; and Grosjean v. American Press Company, **II,** 426; and the Zenger case, **III,** 268; and pamphleteering, **IV,** 202; and sedition acts, **V,** 55; and war, **V,** 399; and the Zenger case, **V,** 513

Freedom of the Seas, and Anglo-American relations, **I,** 75; and armed neutrality, **I,** 108; and the armistice of 1918, **I,** 108; and the Civil War, **I,** 390; and foreign policy, **II,** 303; and the Fourteen Points, **II,** 317; Wilson attempts to include in Versailles Treaty, **II,** 332; issue at Geneva Conference, **II,** 377; and immunity of private property, **III,** 76; and neutral rights, **IV,** 87; and neutrality, **IV,** 89; United States prefers war to peace in order to defend, **IV,** 230; and the Plan of 1776, **IV,** 282; and the *Trent* affair, **V,** 321

Freedom of Will, by Jonathan Edwards, **IV,** 263

Freeholder, and Jeffersonian Democracy, **III,** 172; and property, **IV,** 360; and the quitrent, **IV,** 390

Freeman, M. E. W., and fiction, **II,** 270

Freeman, Samuel H., and Company, **I,** 212

Freeman, Thomas, builds Fort Adams, **I,** 9; begins survey of the Southern boundary, **V,** 129; and western exploration, **V,** 442

Freeman's Farm, Battles of, **I,** 255; **IV,** 476

Freeman's Journal, merges with the *Centinel of the North-Western Territory,* **I,** 333; absorbed by the *Scioto Gazette,* **V,** 44

Freeman's Oath, first job known to have been printed in America, **IV,** 344

Freemen, elect assistants, **I,** 131; and borough government, **I,** 221; and colonial charters, **I,** 417; and governors, **I,** 418; and the Fundamental Orders of Connecticut, **II,** 23; of the General Court, **II,** 375; and town government, **III,** 288; and the franchise in Massachusetts Bay, **III,** 356; and proprietary provinces, **IV,** 362; and unicameral legislatures, **V,** 340

Freeport Doctrine, and Lincoln-Douglas debates, **III,** 279; and popular sovereignty, **IV,** 309

Freer, Charles L., art collection of, **I,** 124

Freer Gallery, added as branch of Smithsonian Institution, **V,** 102

Freight Rates, and U. S. v. Trans-Missouri Freight Association, **V,** 349

Frelinghuysen, Theodore, and campaign of 1844, **I,** 284

Frémont, John Charles, and the Bear Flag Revolt, **I,** 170; attack on Belmont, **I,** 176; and Cahuenga capitulation, **I,** 267; and conquest of California, **I,** 271; nominated for Presidency, **I,** 284; and Civil War contracts, **I,** 391; attacks at Cross Keys, **II,** 91; issues emancipation proclamation, **II,** 205; and campaign slogan of 1856, **II,** 333; in the Great Basin, **II,** 414; and Great Salt Lake, **II,** 419; and Hawk's Peak episode, **III,** 18; and Jessie Scouts, **III,** 174; secures control of the Kansas Pacific Railroad, **III,** 198; quarrels with Kearny, **III,** 201; at Lassen's trading post, **III,** 247; and the Mexican War, **III,** 386; given soubriquet of "The Pathfinder," **IV,** 224; and battle of Port Republic, **IV,** 315; and Price in Missouri, **IV,** 339; and the Radical Republicans, **IV,** 395; as first Republican candidate for President, **IV,** 454; Californians surrender to, **V,** 24; traverses Smoky Hill Trail, **V,** 103; and the Stockton-Kearny quarrel, **V,** 184; and topographic mapping, **V,** 283; and Fort Uintah, **V,** 337; and the Army of Virginia, **V,** 374; and western exploration, **V,** 442; explores Wyoming, **V,** 496

Frémont Pass, **IV,** 221

French, as political exiles, **IV,** 295

French, Daniel, launches the *Comet,* **V,** 179

French, Daniel Chester, sculptor, **I,** 124; and Minute-man statue, **V,** 76

French, William, killed in the Westminster massacre, **V,** 448

French Alliance. *See* Franco-American Alliance of 1778

French and Indian War, and billeting, **I,** 187; and Bloody Pond, **I,** 203; Crown Point in, **II,** 93; Lake Erie in, **II,** 224; and the Mississippi Valley, **III,** 425; brought to an end by the Treaty of Paris (1763), **IV,** 216; and Pennsyl-

vania, **IV**, 243; and the American Revolution, **IV**, 465; and the importance of rivers, **IV**, 492; and the Stamp Act, **V**, 154; halts westward expansion, **V**, 450

French Camp, **I**, 275

French-Eversole Feud, **II**, 269

French Exiles, at Champ d'Asile, **I**, 338

French Spoliation Claims, and the Convention of 1800, **II**, 52; and Franco-American Alliance, **II**, 328; and mixed commissions, **III**, 431; and American claims on Naples, **IV**, 52

French's New Sensation, showboat, **V**, 76

Freneau, Philip, editor of the *National Gazette,* **IV**, 59, 123, 128

Frick, Henry C., attempted assassination of, **I**, 72; art collection of, **I**, 124; and great fortunes, **II**, 312; and Swiss origin, **V**, 215; and the United States Steel Corporation, **V**, 348

Friendly Society for the Mutual Insuring of Houses against Fire, **III**, 128

Friends Asylum of the Philadelphia Quakers, **III**, 125

Friends of Peace, an antiwar organization, **V**, 395

Fries, Amos A., and chemical warfare, **I**, 350

Fries, Charles C., edits *A Dictionary of Early Modern English,* **II**, 146

Fries, John, and treason trials, **V**, 313

Fries (Hot Water) Rebellion, **II**, 349

Frieseke, Frederick C., painter, **I**, 123

Frigates, **I**, 51; **V**, 411

Frobisher, Martin, and Northwest Passage, **IV**, 150

"Front Porch" Campaign, **I**, 289, 296

Front Royal, Jackson's attacks at, **III**, 165

Frontenac, Count, and Duluth's explorations, **II**, 175; as governor of New France, **III**, 246

Frontenac, Fort, and Bradstreet's Expedition, **I**, 233; fall of, **II**, 343; founded by Count Frontenac, **III**, 246; built by Raudin, **IV**, 175

Frontenac, The, built by LaSalle (1678), **I**, 301

Frontenac, The, first steam-driven craft on the Great Lakes (1816), **I**, 301

Frontier, and the agrarian movement, **I**, 21; Army on the, **I**, 116; army posts help westward extension of, **I**, 117; and the back country, **I**, 145; and barter, **I**, 165; and social change, **I**, 340; and national defense, **II**, 126; and the growth of democracy, **II**, 135; disappearance of, and farm tenancy, **II**, 250; and fencing laws, **II**, 266; and fiction, **II**, 270; lawlessness of the, **III**, 252; and home missionary societies, **III**, 416 f.; and the pioneers, **IV**, 274; religion on the, **IV**, 441, 444; and the West, **V**, 434

Frontier Days, Cheyenne's annual exhibition, **IV**, 499

Frontier Scout, newspaper, **IV**, 127

Fruit Fly, menace to crops, **II**, 91

Fruit-Growing Industry, and the Southwest, **V**, 133

Fruitlands, and transcendentalism, **V**, 304

Fruits of Philosophy, written by Charles Knowlton, **I**, 191

Fry, Capt., and the *Virginius* affair, **V**, 380

Fry, Joshua, and Great Meadows, **II**, 418; and topographic mapping, **V**, 282

Fry, W. H., composer of the opera *Leonora,* **IV**, 178

Frye, Chaplain, and Lovewell's fight, **III**, 310

Frye, W. P., and the Wheeler Compromise (1876), **V**, 454

Fuel Administration, **III**, 265; **V**, 492

Fugill, Thomas, enters into New Haven Church Covenant, **V**, 60

Fugio Cent, **I**, 333

Fugitive Slave Act of 1793, and Jones v. Van Zandt, **III**, 181; and personal liberty laws, **IV**, 254; and Prigg v. Commonwealth of Pennsylvania, **IV**, 341

Fugitive Slave Act of 1850, and Ableman v. Booth, **I**, 2; and abolitionist literature, **I**, 3; and Burns case, **I**, 257; and Champaign County rescue cases, **I**, 338; and the Committee of Thirteen, **I**, 436; and Compromise of 1850, **I**, 443; and Negroes as contraband, **II**, 47; and Hamlet case, **III**, 6; and higher-law doctrine, **III**, 31; and Negro stealing, **IV**, 85; and personal liberty laws, **IV**, 255; and *Uncle Tom's Cabin,* **V**, 337

Fugitive Slave Acts, and kidnapping of Free Negroes, **III**, 209

Fugitive Slaves, and the "Address of the Southern Delegates," **I**, 10; and Oberlin-Wellington rescue case, **IV**, 155; and the *Pearl* case, **IV**, 237; and the Underground Railroad, **V**, 338

"Full Dinner Pail," **I**, 289

Full Faith and Credit, and relations between the states, **V**, 174

Fuller, George, painter, **I**, 123

Fuller, Margaret, and transcendentalism, **V**, 304

Fuller and Lord, iron works, **I**, 216

Fullinwider, S. P., perfects the mine, **IV**, 148

Fulton, Robert, as painter, **I**, 123; and the *Demologos,* **II**, 137; and steam navigation, **II**, 214; and Erie Canal, **II**, 226; builds the *Demologos,* **II**, 284; and steamboat monopoly rights, **II**, 388; and the steamboat, **III**, 148; designs and builds the *Nautilus,* **IV**, 68; and river navigation, **IV**, 489; and the steamboat, **V**, 177; and steamboat monopolies, **V**, 178; and steamboats, **V**, 179; and the *Nautilus,* **V**, 194; and torpedoes, **V**, 284; and launching of the *Clermont,* **V**, 307

Fulton-Livingston Patents, and building of the *New Orleans,* **IV**, 110; and the *Phœnix,* **IV**, 264; and river steamboats, **V**, 179

Functional Representation, **IV**, 452

Fundamental Constitutions of Carolina, and colonial assemblies, I, 416; and manors, III, 334

Fundamental Orders of Connecticut. *See* Connecticut, Fundamental Orders of

Fundamentalists, and religion, IV, 443; and theological writings, V, 261

Funk, Isaac K., prepares *A Standard Dictionary*, II, 146

Funston, Frederick, and martial law, III, 347; describes the water cure, V, 421

Fur Trade, and Alaska, I, 42; and American Fur Company, I, 61; and Ashley's expeditions, I, 128; and establishment of Astoria, I, 133; mountain, I, 178; and *bourgeois*, I, 229; at Fort Bridger, I, 237; in California, I, 273; and the canoe, I, 305; and meaning of *Chantier*, I, 341; and the Chouteau family, I, 369; in Colorado, I, 426; and exploration of the Colorado River, I, 427; and the *coureurs de bois*, II, 75; at Fort Crawford, II, 83; of the Pacific Northwest, II, 107; at Albany, II, 179; and Indian factory system, II, 239; and French and Indian War, II, 342; actuates French exploration in the West, II, 344; on Green River, II, 423; Fort Hall and the, III, 6; and Hudson's Bay Company, III, 56; and the Indian, III, 87; and the Indian in the Revolution, III, 88; and liquor, III, 91; and Indian traders, III, 109 f.; as colonial industry, III, 119; and the Iroquois Beaver Land Deed, III, 159; and Fort Kiowa, III, 213; and the Laconia grant, III, 226; use of liquor in, III, 281; and Lisa and Company, III, 283; and *mangeurs de lard*, III, 331; and Manuel's Fort, III, 335; and Merry Mount, III, 378; and Michigan, III, 391; in Missouri, III, 426, 427; on the Missouri, III, 430 f.; and the Mohawk Valley, IV, 5; opened on upper Missouri, IV, 16; at Fort Mortimer, IV, 29; and Mountain Men, IV, 36; monopolized by Johan Printz, IV, 113; at Ogdensburg, IV, 159; on the Ohio River, IV, 164; at Fort Okanagan, IV, 167; and Lake Ontario, IV, 175; and Oregon, IV, 182; and Fort Ouiatenon, IV, 191; and mountain passes, IV, 221; and Pembina, IV, 240; and Prairie du Chien, IV, 328; and the Red River cart traffic, IV, 430; on the Red River of the North, IV, 431; of the Rocky Mountains, IV, 498; St. Louis as center of, V, 11; on Scioto Trail, V, 45; and Indian migration, V, 65; of the Great Lakes, V, 133; of the Upper Mississippi, V, 133; on Lake Superior, V, 205; and topographic mapping, V, 282; for export, V, 292; and foreign trade, V, 294; and trappers' rendezvous, V, 310; on the Upper Mississippi and Missouri Rivers, V, 311; and Fort Union, N. Dak., V, 341; *voyageurs* in the, V, 385; and evacuation of border forts, V,

440; and western exploration, V, 442; and western merchants, V, 444; and destruction of wild life, V, 462; in Wisconsin, V, 473; wolf skins as item of, V, 477; and the Yellowstone River expedition, V, 506

Furniture, artistic value of, I, 124; and chair making, I, 337; as a household art, III, 53

Furniture Manufacturing, in North Carolina, IV, 145

Future Trading Act of 1921, IV, 279

G

Gabriel, The, Bering's ship, I, 42

Gabriel's Slave Insurrection, V, 90

Gadsden, Christopher, and the Rattlesnake Flag, IV, 417

Gadsden, James, and treaty of Payne's Landing, IV, 229

Gadsden Purchase, made, I, 79; and Arizona, I, 104; and Lower California, III, 311; and Mesilla, III, 379; and the Mexican boundary, III, 382; and the public domain, IV, 370; and territorial claims of the United States, V, 247; and treaties with foreign nations, V, 317

Gag Rule, and right of petition, IV, 256, 257

Gage, Thomas, and Connolly's plot, II, 24; and the Quartering Act, IV, 387; and the Townshend Acts, V, 289

Gaine, Hugh, founder of the *New-York Gazette*, IV, 127

Gaines, E. P., and battles at Withlacoochee Creek, V, 476

Gaines, Fort, as coast defense, I, 405

Gaines, Fort, early name for Fort Ripley, IV, 487

Gaines' Mill, battle of, and the Peninsular campaign, IV, 241; and Seven Days' Battles, V, 60

Gale, William A., and hide and tallow trade, III, 29

Galena and Chicago Union Railroad, I, 356, 357

Galena Lead Mining District, III, 254

Gales, Joseph, and A. B. Plot, I, 1; and the *National Intelligencer*, IV, 60, 128; chosen as government printer, IV, 344

Gall, Chief, and the Sioux Council, V, 85

Gallant Fox, famous thoroughbred horse, V, 265

Gallatin, Albert, and the abolition movement, I, 3; and Americanization, I, 67; signs Convention of 1818, II, 52; aids and counsels Jefferson, II, 208; and treaty of Ghent, II, 387; compiles Indian linguistic tables and distribution map, III, 87; Swiss immigrant, V, 215; and the War of 1812, V, 406

Gallatin's Report on Roads, Canals, Harbors and Rivers, III, 137; V, 209

Gallaudet, Thomas Hopkins, heads school for deaf and dumb, II, 115

Galleys, for river navigation, IV, 489

Gallipolis, settlement of, II, 346; V, 44

Galloway, G. N., relates secession of Jones County, III, 181

Galtier, Lucian, builds log chapel at St. Paul, V, 334

Galveston, and commission government, I, 434

Galveston Hurricane, III, 62

Galveston Island, French exiles withdraw to, I, 338

Galvez, Bernardo, captures British posts in West Florida, III, 305; captures Fort Panmure, IV, 210; captures Pensacola, IV, 250; and capture of British posts, V, 139; and Spanish military supplies from New Orleans, V, 141; receives the Willing expedition, V, 469

Gálvez, José de, and Spanish occupation of California, I, 275

Gamblers, and rivermen of the Ohio, IV, 490

Gangsters, and prohibition, IV, 357

Gansevoort, Peter, and battle of Oriskany, IV, 188

Gant, Capt., and trapping, V, 311

Gantt, Henry L., and industrial management, III, 115

Gaps, or mountain passes, I, 51; IV, 221

Garages, and the distribution of merchandise, II, 152

Garbage Removal, and sanitation, V, 29; and street cleaning, V, 188

Garcés, Francisco, and Cajon Pass, I, 267; explores the Colorado River, I, 427; and missions of the Southwest, III, 418; visits the Mohave Indians, IV, 4; traverses the Spanish Trail, V, 142

Garcia, Manuel, launches operatic season in New York, IV, 48

Garden, Alexander, botanist, I, 225

Gardiner, Lion, and settlement of Saybrook, Conn., V, 36

Gardiner Award, I, 63

Gardiner Lyceum, for industrial education, III, 114

Gardner, Abbie, ransomed after Spirit Lake massacre, V, 146

Gardner, Alexander, and photography, IV, 265

Gardner, Frank, surrenders Port Hudson, IV, 315

Gardner, Rowland, and Spirit Lake massacre, V, 146

Gardner's Hole, III, 37

Gardoqui, Diego de, and Jay negotiations, III, 168; and the Spanish conspiracy, V, 139

Garfield, Harry A., fuel administrator, V, 492

Garfield, James A., shot by Charles Guiteau, I, 129; elected President, I, 287; and the Crédit Mobilier, II, 85; and the DeGolyer case, II, 130; and the Morey letter, IV, 23; assassination of, and political patronage, IV, 224; and the Presidency, IV, 333; nominated for the Presidency, IV, 454

Garland, Alexander H., in Mississippi v. Johnson, III, 425

Garland, Augustus H., governor of Arkansas, I, 105

Garland, Hamlin, and fiction, II, 270

Garland Case, IV, 214; V, 250

Garner, J. N., elected Vice-President, I, 292

Garnett, R. S., and battle of Rich Mountain, IV, 481

Garrard, T. T., at Camp Wild-Cat, I, 280

Garretson, J. E., and dentistry, II, 138

Garrett, Mary, and college training for women, V, 477

Garrie, John, invents the cold-air machine, IV, 437

Garrison, L. M., and the World War, V, 491

Garrison, William Lloyd, and abolition movement, I, 3; and Genius of Universal Emancipation, II, 377; editor of the Liberator, III, 270; and formation of the New England Non-Resistance Society, IV, 234; speeches of, IV, 302; and the abolition movement, IV, 363; and attitude of churches toward slavery, V, 97

Garrison School, for army training, I, 118

Garry, Fort, and the Red River cart traffic, IV, 430

Gary, Elbert H., and American Iron and Steel Institute, I, 62; art collection of, I, 125; and the United States Steel Corporation, V, 348

Gary, Ind., and martial law, III, 347

Gary, T. A., pioneer nurseryman, IV, 154

Gas, Natural, in heating, III, 24; for lighting, III, 276; in Louisiana, III, 306; municipal ownership of, IV, 375; in West Virginia, V, 439

Gas in Warfare. See Chemical Warfare

Gas Ring, and municipal reform, IV, 43; and political scandals, IV, 298

Gasoline Tax, V, 227

Gaspee Affair, I, 408; IV, 478; V, 289

Gates, Horatio, and Burgoyne's Invasion, I, 255; at Camden, I, 277; and the Conway Cabal, II, 54; and Freeman's Farm battles, II, 339; in the Revolutionary War, IV, 476 f.; and Rumsey's steamboat, IV, 507; and surrender at Saratoga, V, 32; in the southern campaigns (1780–81), V, 129; as president of War and Ordnance Board, V, 399

Gates, John W., and barbed wire, I, 163; and great fortunes, II, 312

Gates, Thomas, accompanies Somers on voyage to Virginia, V, 119; and the Virginia Company of London, V, 376

Gates, William, Jr., and match-making machinery, III, 359

Gatling Machine Guns, I, 393; III, 319

Gatty, Harold, encircles the globe, I, 143

Gauntlet, Running the, V, 285

Gayoso de Lemos, Manuel, and treaty of Natchez, IV, 57

Gazette of the United States, official voice of the Federalist party, II, 403; as organ of Alexander Hamilton, IV, 128; and "Pacificus" and "Helvidius," IV, 197

Geary, J. W., and border war, I, 220; and the Kansas struggle, III, 198; and battle of Wauhatchie, V, 425

Gebelein, George C., silversmith, V, 82

Geddes, Henry, in naval war with France, IV, 73

Geddes, James, builder of Erie Canal, II, 226

Gee, Joshua, member of the Principio Company, IV, 343

General Accounting Office established, I, 247

General Act for Suppression of the Slave Trade (1890), V, 317

General Advertiser, original name for the *Aurora,* I, 139

General Assembly's Board of Missions, III, 417

General Court, and the assistants, I, 131; and colonial assemblies, I, 416; and colonial land grants, III, 235; and town government, III, 288; and franchise in Massachusetts Bay, III, 356; of the Massachusetts Bay Company, III, 357; and Massachusetts Circular Letter, III, 358; and Massachusetts Provincial Congress, III, 359; laws made by, IV, 112; and the River Towns of Connecticut, IV, 490; divides into two houses, V, 134; and town government, V, 287; and town meetings, V, 287; and training day in New England, V, 304; and United Colonies of New England, V, 345

General Education Board, endowed by John D. Rockefeller, II, 314; and medical professorships, III, 369

General Electric Company, II, 197; V, 448

General Electric Research Laboratory, III, 232

General Federation of Women's Clubs, V, 482

General Grant National Park, IV, 218

General Land Office, and Department of the Interior, III, 90, 134; and weather observations, V, 430

General Magazine, published by Benjamin Franklin, III, 323

General Managers' Association, and the Pullman strike, IV, 381

General Motors Acceptance Corporation, III, 127

General Motors Company, founded, I, 140; sit-down strike at, V, 191

General Motors Institute, III, 115

General Order No. 38, and Vallandigham incident, V, 355

General Orders No. 100, and prisoners of war, IV, 348; and laws of war, V, 397

General Slocum Disaster, II, 149. *See also Slocum, General*

General Staff. *See* Army, General Staff

General Store, V, 185, 297

General Taylor's Rough and Ready Almanac, I, 52

General Welfare Clause, and Federal taxing power, V, 231

Genesee Farmer, farm periodical, II, 248

Genêt, and Franco-American relations, II, 327; arrives in Philadelphia, III, 166; and the *Little Sarah,* III, 285; plans to attack Louisiana, III, 308

Geneva Arbitration (1871), I, 76

Geneva Conventions, United States participates in, V, 398

Geneva Drug Convention of 1925, IV, 179

Genius of Universal Emancipation, I, 3; II, 206

Gentleman's Agreement, and Japanese exclusion, III, 168; V, 505

Gentlemen's Agreements, and monopoly, IV, 12

Geographer, provided for by the Ordinance of 1785, III, 237

Geological Society of America, III, 257

Geological Survey, and air photography, I, 35; inaugurated, V, 283; and water power conservation, V, 423

George, Fort (Maine), and the Pejepscot purchase, IV, 239

George, Fort (Niagara River), and the evacuation of Fort Erie, II, 223; capture of, IV, 130

George, Fort (Virginia), and Fortress Monroe, IV, 12

George, Fort, Astoria renamed, I, 133

George, Fort, at the mouth of the Cheyenne River, IV, 29

George, Henry, and anti-poverty societies, I, 83; political writings of, IV, 302; author of *Progress and Poverty,* IV, 356; and the single tax plan, V, 83

George, Milton, founder of National Farmers' Alliance, II, 251

George-Deen Act (1936), and agricultural education, I, 25

George Peabody College for Teachers, IV, 230

"George Smith's Bank," I, 160

George Washington Bridge, III, 55; IV, 119

George Washington Episode, and the Barbary Wars, I, 162

Georgia, invaded by Spanish, I, 202; and the Cherokee Indians, I, 352; and the Creeks, II, 86; and Creek lands, II, 101; the debatable land, II, 116; and repudiation of state debts, IV, 457; and states' rights, V, 176; western land claims of, V, 444; Worcester v., V, 484; Yamasee war facilitates establishment of, V, 501

Georgia Compact, and boundary delimitation, II, 380; and Indian policy, III, 106; and treaty

at Fort Wilkinson, V, 466; and the Yazoo fraud, V, 503

Georgia Gazette, published by James Johnston, IV, 126; first newspaper in Savannah, V, 35

Georgia Platform, and the Union Rights party, V, 343

Georgia Trustees, and the Moravians, IV, 22

Georgia v. Stanton, III, 363

Georgiana Company, and land grants, III, 235; and land speculation, III, 239; and group migration, III, 396

Gerard, Conrad, member of the Illinois and Wabash Company, III, 69

Gerhard, William Wood, and medicine, III, 369; and tuberculosis, V, 328

Germaine Girl Captives, and Wagon Train charge, V, 388

German-American Bund, and subversive activities, V, 197

German Baptist Brethren, II, 176

German Coast, after failure of Law's venture, I, 106

German Flats, settlement of, V, 450

German Immigration, and Dutch Fork, II, 178; and Germantown, Pa., II, 385; as a part of immigration in general, III, 74; and the Lutherans, III, 316; to Missouri, III, 427; to Pennsylvania, IV, 242, 246; to St. Louis, V, 12; to Wisconsin, V, 473

German Mercenaries, in the battle of Bennington, I, 178; and prisoners of war, IV, 348

German Reformed Church, and Calvinism, I, 277; and Pietism, IV, 269; and theological seminaries, V, 261

Germans, and colonial society, I, 424; and group migration, III, 396; in North Carolina, IV, 144; as political exiles, IV, 295; and the westward movement, V, 450; settle along the Yadkin River, V, 499

Germantown, Pa., settled, IV, 242; Washington attacks at, IV, 476

Germany, treaty with, ending World War, I, 179; and the partitioning of Samoa, V, 317; treaties with, V, 318

Geronimo, Apache chief, I, 88; captured, IV, 107

Gerrard, Thomas, and court leet, II, 75

Gerry, Elbridge, elected Vice-President, I, 282; and social change, I, 340; delegate to Convention of 1787, II, 50; signer of the Declaration of Independence, II, 123; diplomatic mission of, II, 148, 327; and gerrymandering, II, 386; and pamphleteering, IV, 202; and the Society for the Prevention of Cruelty to Children, V, 112; and the XYZ affair, V, 498

Gerrymander, and representation, I, 92; and Congress, II, 18; and apportionment of congressional districts, II, 153

Gertrude Clarke Whittall Foundation, III, 274

Gessner, Abram, and kerosene oil, III, 207

Getty, G. W., establishes Fort Bascom, I, 165

Gettysburg, Battle of, I, 127; IV, 244, 267

Gettysburg Address, II, 404

Ghent, Treaty of, and Anglo-American relations, I, 75; Astoria returned to United States by, I, 133; and Canadian-American relations, I, 300; and fishing privileges, I, 407; and Convention of 1818, II, 52; bearing of Lake Champlain campaign on, III, 230; and battle of New Orleans, IV, 110; and Northeast boundary, IV, 147; negotiations for peace, IV, 150; and Rouse's Point boundary controversy, IV, 503; condemns slave trade, V, 104; and treaty of Spring Wells, V, 150; and treaties with foreign nations, V, 316; and War of 1812, V, 406

Ghost Dance, as an Indian ceremony, III, 97; and the Messiah War, III, 379; and battle of Wounded Knee, V, 495

Ghost Towns, II, 114; IV, 479

Gibbon, John, attacks Chief Joseph's camp, I, 183; and the Nez Percé war, IV, 129; and Sioux wars, V, 87

Gibbon Pass, IV, 222

Gibbons, Ambrose, and Mariana, III, 343

Gibbons, James Sloan, author of the poem "We are coming, Father Abra'am, etc.," V, 428

Gibbons v. Ogden, supplemented by Brown v. Maryland, I, 244; and the Commerce Clause, I, 433; and steamboat monopolies, II, 356; and the Judiciary Act of 1789, III, 189; and the license cases, III, 275; and steamboat monopolies, V, 178

Gibbs, James, invents a sewing machine, III, 148; V, 61

Gibson, Alexander, and Fort Recovery, IV, 428

Gibson, Fort, Dodge-Leavenworth expedition starts from, II, 156; founded by Matthew Arbuckle, IV, 168; treaty of, and removal of the Seminoles, V, 57

Gibson, John, and Logan's speech, III, 294

Gibson-Linn Episode, V, 141

Giddings, Joshua R., and abolitionist literature, I, 3; attacks slavery, I, 86; and the Ohio State Antislavery Society, IV, 165; and the *Pearl* case, IV, 237

Gift of God, sent out by the Plymouth Company, IV, 290; and the Popham Colony, IV, 308

Gift Taxes, as internal revenue, III, 139

Gihon, Albert Leary, pioneer of naval hygiene, III, 64

Gila Route, and mountain passes, IV, 221

Gilbert, Cass, builds the Woolworth Building, I, 101; introduces the "super-skyscraper," V, 88; designs new capitol building of West Virginia, V, 439

Gilbert, Humphrey, and his colonial venture in Newfoundland, I, 15; and Raleigh's patent, IV, 413

Gilbert, Mathew, enters into New Haven church covenant, V, 60

Gilbert, Raleigh, and the Popham Colony, IV, 308

Gilbertsville Dam, V, 245

Gilbreth, Frank B., pioneer in industrial management, III, 116

Gillem, A. C., and battles of Tule Lake, V, 329

Gillespie, Archibald, and battle of San Pascual, V, 26

Gillette, William, playwright, II, 166

Gilliland, Will, and capture of Ticonderoga (1775), V, 267

Gillmore, Q. A., captures Fort Pulaski, IV, 380; and attack on Wagner Battery, V, 388

Gilman, George Francis, starts the Great Atlantic and Pacific Tea Company, II, 412

Gilman, Nicholas, signer of the Constitution, II, 39

Gilman Country Day School, V, 41

Gilmer, T. W., killed by explosion on the *Princeton*, IV, 343

Gilmore, J. R., and the peace movement of 1864, IV, 233

Gilmore's Concert Garden, III, 322

Gilpin, Thomas, and paper-making machinery, IV, 212

Gilpin, William, and Sangre de Cristo grant, V, 28

Ginn, Edward, endows the World Peace Foundation, IV, 235

Ginseng, in China trade, I, 365

Girard, Stephen, philanthropy of, IV, 260

Girard College, established, IV, 260

Girl of the Limberlost, written by Gene Stratton Porter, I, 180

Girty, Simon, at Bryan's Station, I, 246; and attack on Fort Recovery, IV, 428

Gist, Christopher, visits Big Bone Lick, I, 183; his plantation on Braddock's Road, I, 233; sent to explore land along Ohio River, II, 342; enters Kentucky, III, 204; and Washington's mission to Fort LeBœuf, III, 259; at Logstown, III, 295; in the Monongahela River region, IV, 12; mentions Murdering Town, IV, 46; and the Ohio Company of Virginia, IV, 163; and Pickawillany, IV, 266; as early surveyor, V, 210

"Give Me Liberty or Give Me Death," IV, 482

Glacier National Park, IV, 218

Gladden, Washington, and religious thought and writings, IV, 447; and the Social Gospel, V, 107; and theological writings, V, 261

Gladwin, Henry, gives Dalzel permission to attack Pontiac's camp, I, 203; and the siege of Fort Detroit, II, 143; in Pontiac's War, IV, 306

Glanton, John, and Fort Yuma, V, 512

Glasgow, E. A. G., and fiction, II, 270

Glaspell, Susan, and the Provincetown Players, IV, 368

Glass, artistic value of, I, 124; for windows, I, 249; industry, of Pittsburgh, IV, 280

Glass, Hugh, mountain man, I, 128; his fight with a grizzly bear, I, 171

Glasscock, W. E., and martial law, III, 347

Glassford, P. D., and Bonus Army, I, 211

Glavis, L. R., and the Ballinger-Pinchot controversy, I, 149

Gleaves, Albert, as Chief of Convoy Operations, II, 53; commands the Transport Force in the World War, V, 493

Glen, James, builds Fort Prince George, IV, 342; makes treaty with Cherokees at Saluda, V, 19

Glendale, Battle of. See Frayser's Farm, Battle of

Glenn, Hugh, and the Fowler expedition, II, 319; arrives in Santa Fé, V, 30

Glennon, James H., and Root mission to Russia, IV, 501

Glidden, Carlos, and the typewriter, V, 336

Glidden, J. F., sells first piece of barbed wire, I, 163

Glidden Tours, I, 58

Globe, supersedes the *United States Telegraph,* II, 403; as political organ, IV, 128

Glorietta, battle at, IV, 107, 485

Glorious Fourth, origin of term, II, 318

Glover, Goodwife, executed for witchcraft, V, 475

Glover, Jose, and printing in America, IV, 344

Gnadenhutten, massacre at, III, 408

"Go Down, Moses," song, II, 293

Goats, IV, 4

Goddard, William, founder of the *Constitutional Courant,* IV, 127; and colonial postal service, IV, 321; and the printing press, IV, 346; establishes the *Providence Gazette,* IV, 368

Godey's Lady's Book, III, 323

Godfrey, Edward, and province of Maine, II, 401

Godfrey, Thomas, author of the play, *Prince of Parthia,* II, 165

Godin, Antoine, and battle of Pierre's Hole, IV, 269

Godkin, E. L., as newspaper editor, IV, 123

Godyn, Samuel, patroonship of, IV, 226; and Zwaanendael Colony, V, 515

Goebel, Arthur, wins Dole Race, I, 36

Goebel, William, assassination of, I, 129; V, 323

Goelet, Ogden, book collection, I, 213

Goethals, George W., and the Panama Canal, II, 217; IV, 205

Goff, John W., and the Lexow Committee, III, 268

Goffe, William, regicide in New England, IV, 438

Gogebic Range, and iron mining, III, 157

Gold, attempt to corner (1869), **I**, 194; discovery of, in Black Hills, **I**, 195; discovery of, in California, and the "rush," **I**, 272; and the Cripple Creek mining boom, **II**, 89; and the founding of Denver, **II**, 138; flight of, during depression of 1920, **II**, 140; devaluation of, **II**, 145; discovery of, in Idaho, **III**, 66; discovery of, in the Klondike, **III**, 214; discovery of, in California, **III**, 407; discovery of, in Montana, **IV**, 16; discovery of, and the Rocky Mountains, **IV**, 498; and the Southwest, **V**, 133; and specie payments, **V**, 144; Federal expropriation of, **V**, 144; **V**, 152

Gold Certificates, and the Gold Reserve Act of 1934, **II**, 397; as paper money, **IV**, 213

Gold Clause Cases, and the public faith, **IV**, 371; and repudiation of public debt, **IV**, 455

Gold Democratic Party, formed, **I**, 398

Gold Mining, in California, **I**, 272; at Cheyenne, Wyo., **I**, 355; at Helena, **III**, 24; and water power, **V**, 422

Gold Reserve Act of 1934, **I**, 252; **II**, 145, 394, 395, 398; **IV**, 8, 213; **V**, 79, 144, 152

Gold Standard, and the bimetallic system, **I**, 188; suspended during World War, **I**, 252; and campaigns of 1892 and 1896, **I**, 288; in campaign of 1904, **I**, 289; and the Cleveland Democrats, **I**, 398; and the crime of 1873, **II**, 89; attacked by Bryan, **II**, 91; abrogation of, 1933 and 1934, **II**, 100; established, **II**, 332, 393; and money system, **IV**, 7; and the panic of 1893, **IV**, 209; and Sherman Act of 1890, **V**, 70; and specie payments, **V**, 143; suspension of, and the Tripartite Agreement, **V**, 325; and the World Economic Conference, **V**, 486

Goldberger, Joseph, conquest of pellagra, **III**, 370

Golden Age, published by Alexander S. Gould, **IV**, 126

Golden Argosy, 19th century magazine, **I**, 363

Golden Gate, The, salvaging of, **V**, 19

Golden Hill, Battle of, **IV**, 115, 294

Golden Hind, The, Drake courses the Pacific in, **II**, 165

Golden Spike, driven into the first transcontinental railroad, **IV**, 358

Goldman, Emma, and anarchists, **I**, 72; influences assassination of McKinley, **I**, 129

Goldsborough, L. M., commander of North Atlantic Squadron, **IV**, 10

Golf, **I**, 71

Goliad Massacre, **IV**, 447; **V**, 257

Gómez, Vicente, and the Panoche Grande claim, **IV**, 210

Gompers, Samuel, and Buck Stove and Range case, **I**, 246; and the McNamara case, **III**, 367

Gondra, Manuel, at Pan-American conference, **IV**, 203

Gondra Convention, **IV**, 232; **V**, 31

Gone with the Wind, written by Margaret Mitchell, **I**, 180

Gonzales, in Texas revolution, **II**, 145; **V**, 257

Gooch, D. W., member of the Committee on the Conduct of the War, **I**, 436

Good Hope, Fort, **III**, 52

Good Neighbor Policy, and Caribbean policy, **I**, 314; and Latin-American relations, **III**, 249; and peace conferences, **IV**, 232

Good Roads Movement, and state aid, **V**, 163

Goodhue, Bertram, revolutionizes ecclesiastical architecture, **I**, 101

Goodhue, James M., founder of the *Minnesota Pioneer,* **IV**, 127; first printer of Minnesota, **IV**, 346

Goodman and Goodwife, **II**, 135

Goodnight, Charles, and sheep wars, **V**, 67

Goodnight Loving Trail, and cattle drives, **I**, 326; and Texas, **V**, 255

Goodrich, Charles A., author of *History of the United States,* **V**, 40

Goodrich, Chauncey A., edits an edition of Webster's dictionary, **V**, 433

Goodrich, Samuel G., and bookshops, **I**, 214; under pen name of "Peter Parley," **IV**, 255; and early schoolbooks, **V**, 40

Goodspeed, The, and founding of Jamestown, **III**, 166; **V**, 372

Goodwin, ————, publisher of the *Frontier Scout,* **IV**, 127; first printer of North Dakota, **IV**, 346

Goodwin, Hannibal, and photography, **IV**, 265

Goodwin, W. A. R., and the restoration of Williamsburg, **V**, 468

Goodyear, Amasa, and hardware, **III**, 9

Goodyear, Charles, and rubber, **IV**, 504

Goodyear, Moses, and the Trelawney plantation, **V**, 320

Goodyear Grant, and settlement of Saco Bay, **V**, 3

Goodyear Rubber Patents, **IV**, 223

Gookin, Daniel, and the Praying Indians, **IV**, 330; and regicides in New England, **IV**, 438

Gordillo, Francisco, and the discovery of America, **I**, 57

Gordon, Anna A., president of the W. C. T. U., **V**, 479

Gordon, George A., and religious thought, **IV**, 446

Gordon, James F. and John H., and the development of the reaper, **IV**, 419

Gordon, John B., and Appomattox, **I**, 91; and battles at Sailor's Creek, **V**, 5; assaults Fort Stedman, **V**, 180

Gore, Obadiah, and anthracite, **I**, 79

Gorgas, W. C., and malaria, **III**, 329; and eradication of yellow fever, **III**, 369; **IV**, 205; **V**, 505

Gorgeana Settlement, **I**, 20

Gorges, Ferdinando, and the first municipal corporation in America, **I**, 20; and Bristol trade, **I**, 239; and the Council for New England, **II**, 71; and feudalism, **II**, 269; and Isles of Shoals, **III**, 162; and the Laconia grant, **III**, 226; and Lygonia, **III**, 317; and Maine, **III**, 326; and the Mason title, **III**, 351; president of Council for New England, **III**, 357; granted much of what is Maine and New Hampshire, **IV**, 101; leader in the Plymouth Company, **IV**, 290; receives royal charter for Maine, **IV**, 362

Gorges, Thomas, deputy governor of province of Maine, **II**, 401

Gorges Patent, purchase of, **III**, 327

Gorham, Marquis L., and the development of the reaper, **IV**, 419

Gorham, Nathaniel, signer of the Constitution, **II**, 39; and Phelps purchase, **IV**, 257

Gorman-Wilson Tariff Bill, and the Cleveland Democrats, **I**, 398; as factor in the Spanish-American War, **II**, 307; introduces income tax, **III**, 83; and Pollock v. Farmers Loan and Trust Company, **IV**, 303; and reciprocity, **IV**, 423; ends reciprocity agreement with South America, **V**, 124; enacted, **V**, 222

Gorrell, James, and Green Bay, **II**, 422

Gorton, Samuel, and founding of Warwick, **IV**, 477; purchases Shawomet from the Indians, **V**, 65

Gosnold, Bartholomew, and discovery of America, **I**, 57; names Cape Cod, **I**, 306, 406; and founding of Jamestown, **III**, 166; death of, **III**, 167; visits the Maine coast, **III**, 203, 326; and bringing of oats to America, **IV**, 155; leader in the Jamestown settlement, **V**, 372

Gospel, Society for the Propagation of the. *See* Society for Propagation of the Gospel

Gough, John B., temperance lecturer, **III**, 260; **V**, 241

Gould, Alexander S., publishes *Golden Age*, **IV**, 126

Gould, James, and the Litchfield Law School, **III**, 283

Gould, Jay, and Black Friday, **I**, 194; and the Denver and Rio Grande Railway, **II**, 139; and Erie Railroad, **II**, 226; rise of, **II**, 311; and the Kansas Pacific Railroad, **III**, 198; and the Missouri, Kansas and Texas Railway, **III**, 428; purchases the Missouri Pacific Railroad, **III**, 430; and the railroad strikes of 1886, **IV**, 405; and railroads, **IV**, 408; acquires the Texas and Pacific Railway Company, **V**, 255; obtains control of Atlantic and Pacific Telegraph Company, **V**, 447

Gouvion, commissioned in the Revolutionary Army, **IV**, 473

Government Printing, and newspapers as political organs, **IV**, 128

Government Printing Office, **II**, 17; **III**, 182; **IV**, 344

Government Regulation, of business, **I**, 260; and due process, **II**, 173; of manufacturing, **III**, 338

Governor, of the General Court, **II**, 375; and the Presidency, **IV**, 333; proclamations of the, **IV**, 354; and state constitutions, **V**, 167; and state government, **V**, 169; colonial, and unicameral legislatures, **V**, 340

Governors' Conference, **V**, 175

Governors Island, fort built on, **IV**, 107; as prison camp, **IV**, 347

Gowans, William, bookseller, **I**, 214

Gowen, Franklin B., and the "Molly Maguires," **IV**, 6

Grace, Robert, and the Franklin stove, **II**, 329

Grady, Henry W., and the New South, **IV**, 112; and oratory, **IV**, 180

Graf Zeppelin, **I**, 439

Graffenried, Christopher de, founder of first Swiss colony in America, **V**, 215

Graft, and granting of franchises, **II**, 325

Graham, Isaac, deportation of, **I**, 170

Graham, Sylvester, lecturer, **III**, 260

Graham-Tewksbury Feud, **V**, 67

Grain, and foreign trade, **V**, 295

Grain Corporation, and the Lever Act, **III**, 265

Grain Futures Act, and prevention of manipulation in the grain markets, **IV**, 279

Grain Market, and the "Pit," **IV**, 278

Grain Stabilization Corporation, **II**, 246

Grain Standards Act, and exchanges, **II**, 232

Grammar, teaching of, **V**, 40

Grand Army of the Republic, and Decoration Day, **II**, 125; and soldier vote, **V**, 117; as veterans' organization, **V**, 365

Grand Canyon National Park, **IV**, 218

Grand Canyon of the Colorado, **I**, 104, 427; **II**, 61; **IV**, 106

Grand Coulee Dam, and government ownership, **II**, 404; and the Bureau of Standards, **V**, 157; and water power, **V**, 423

Grand Ecore, and Natchitoches, **IV**, 58; in the Red River campaign, **IV**, 430

Grand Ohio Company, formation of, **I**, 170; and Indiana Company, **III**, 113; and the Vandalia Colony, **V**, 357

Grand Portage, and Hudson's Bay Company, **III**, 56; and liquor in the fur trade, **III**, 282; as western headquarters of the North West Company, **III**, 410; **IV**, 147; explored by Vérendrye, **V**, 205

Grand Teton National Park, **IV**, 218

Grand Trunk Railroad, and railroad rate wars, **IV**, 403

Grande Ronde Valley, and the Oregon Trail, **IV**, 186

Grandfather Clause, and disfranchisement of the Negro, **II**, 151, 271, 324; in Guinn and Beal v. U. S., **II**, 428; and Negro suffrage, **IV**, 85; **V**, 199

Grange, The, and rural free delivery, **IV**, 508

Granger, Francis, and the Silver Grays, **V**, 80

Granger, Gordon, and soldiers and sailors conventions, **V**, 117

Granger Cases: Munn v. Illinois, **IV**, 46; and railroad rate wars, **IV**, 404

Granger Laws, passed, **I**, 34; and railroad rate law, **IV**, 402

Granger Movement, as part of the agrarian movement, **I**, 21; and agricultural societies, **I**, 26; and anti-monopoly parties, **I**, 82; and consumer co-operatives, **II**, 56; and Farmers' Co-operatives, **II**, 56; and farm periodicals, **II**, 249; and farm relief, **II**, 249; and demand for free silver, **II**, 333; and mail-order houses, **III**, 325; and Patrons of Husbandry, **IV**, 225; and propaganda, **IV**, 358; and railroads, **IV**, 408; and tobacco co-operatives, **V**, 275; in the West, **V**, 435. *See also* Patrons of Husbandry

Granite State, The, ship-of-the-line, **V**, 75

Grant, Charles, occupies Fort Loudon, **III**, 304

Grant, Heber J., president of Mormon church, **IV**, 27

Grant, U. S., at Appomattox, **I**, 91; and the battle of Belmont, **I**, 176; and the gold corner, **I**, 194; attacks the Bloody Angle, **I**, 202; elected President, **I**, 286; and battle of Champion's Hill, **I**, 339; and Chattanooga campaign, **I**, 348; at Cold Harbor, **I**, 412; and proposed annexation of Dominican Republic, **II**, 158; and the capture of Fort Donelson, **II**, 160; and exchange of prisoners, **II**, 232; and "Fight it out on this line if it takes all summer," **II**, 272; and capture of Fort Henry, **III**, 26; withdraws from Holly Springs, **III**, 38; and restoration of home rule in the South, **III**, 41; and insignia of rank in United States Army, **III**, 126; recommends the item veto, **III**, 164; in battle of Jackson, Miss., **III**, 164; and legal tender cases, **III**, 262; and the phrase "Let us have peace," **III**, 264; and Army of the Mississippi, **III**, 419; and the Monroe Doctrine, **IV**, 14; and battle of North Anna, **IV**, 144; and the panic of 1873, **IV**, 209; and siege of Petersburg, **IV**, 255; and battle at Port Gibson, **IV**, 315; and the Presidency, **IV**, 333; nominated for the Presidency, **IV**, 454; and campaign against Richmond, **IV**, 481; and battle of Shiloh, **V**, 71; and battle of Spotsylvania Courthouse, **V**, 150; and the Supreme Court Packing Bills, **V**, 208; and Army of the Tennessee, **V**, 242; and third-term doctrine, **V**, 263; nicknamed "Unconditional Surrender," **V**, 337; campaigns against Vicksburg, **V**, 367;

and the Whiskey Ring, **V**, 458; and battles of the Wilderness, **V**, 464

Grant's Hill, Battle of, **II**, 299; **III**, 277

Grants-in-aid, and centralization, **I**, 334; promoted for schools, **V**, 41; and the Smith-Hughes Act, **V**, 102; and the Smith-Lever Act, **V**, 102; provided by Social Security Act, **V**, 108

Granville Grant, **I**, 317; **IV**, 362

Grapefruit, and the citrus industry, **I**, 379

Grapes, for wine making, **V**, 471

Grass, John, and the Sioux Council, **V**, 85

Grasshoppers, brought by drouth, **II**, 91; and tall stories, **V**, 186

Grattan, J. L., killed by Sioux, **V**, 86

Grattan Massacre, **I**, 127; **III**, 245

Gratz, Barnard, and the Illinois and Wabash Company, **III**, 69

Gratz, Barnard and Michael, Jewish merchants, **III**, 176

Grave Creek Mound, **IV**, 34

Graves, Thomas, founder of Charlestown, Mass., **I**, 345

Graves, William, duels with Jonathan Cilley, **II**, 174

Graves, William S., commands American Expeditionary Forces in Siberia, **V**, 77

Graves, Z. C., and college training for women, **V**, 480

Graves v. New York *ex rel* O'Keefe, **V**, 228

Gray, Asa, builds the *Adventure,* **I**, 15

Gray, Asa, and gardening, **II**, 371

Gray, Elisha, and the Postal Telegraph Company, **IV**, 322; and the telephone, **V**, 239; and the Western Electric Company, **V**, 441

Gray, Robert, and the China trade, **I**, 365; and the Columbia River, **I**, 430; **II**, 235; visits Hawaii, **III**, 17; discovers the Columbia River, **IV**, 182; and the Oregon Question, **IV**, 184; sees Puget Sound, **IV**, 380; and territorial claims of the United States, **V**, 246; discoverer of the Columbia River, **V**, 357, 415

Grayson, William S., and land speculation, **III**, 240

Grazing, Division of, created, **III**, 135

Grazing Homestead Act (1916), and the public domain, **IV**, 371

Great American Desert, Dust Bowl called, **II**, 178; Great Plains known as, **IV**, 282; and western explorations, **V**, 442; and the westward movement, **V**, 452

Great Atlantic and Pacific Tea Company, as chain store, **I**, 336

Great Awakening, and the Baptists, **I**, 161; and the Congregationalists, **II**, 16; and the Edwardian theology, **II**, 189; and evangelism, **II**, 230; and the New Lights, **IV**, 106; and philosophical thought and writings, **IV**, 263; and the praying

Indians, **IV**, 330; and American religion, **IV**, 442; and religious liberty, **IV**, 445; and religious periodicals, **IV**, 445; and revivals, **IV**, 463

Great Basin, crossed by Bonneville Expedition, **I**, 209; and Utah, **V**, 353

Great Britain, treaties with, **V**, 316 f.

Great Eastern, begins laying cable, **I**, 135

Great Lakes, Agreement for Disarmament on the, **I**, 75; navigation on, **I**, 301; and canal building, **I**, 302; located on French map, **II**, 344; French adventurers on, **II**, 346; and river and harbor improvements, **IV**, 488; and topographic mapping, **V**, 282; and domestic trade, **V**, 292; and the search for the western sea, **V**, 446

Great Massacre of 1622, Jamestown a place of refuge during, **III**, 167; and plans for Christian education of Indians, **IV**, 330; and the Jamestown settlement, **V**, 372; and the Virginia Company of London, **V**, 378

Great Meadows, on Braddock's Road, **I**, 233; Washington defeated at, **II**, 177, 342. *See also* Necessity, Fort

Great Migration, and Cambridge Agreement, **I**, 277; and founding of Dorchester, Mass., **II**, 161; and the *Mary and John*, **III**, 348; and Massachusetts Bay Company, **III**, 357

Great Nine Partners Patent, **III**, 56

Great Northern Railroad, and Fisk's overland trails, **II**, 278; and Minnesota, **III**, 411; and Montana, **IV**, 16; controlled by Northern Securities Company, **IV**, 148; and rail transportation, **V**, 309; completed, **V**, 415

Great Plains, as central portion of cow country, **II**, 78; drouths on, **II**, 170; dry farming on, **II**, 171; and French exploration, **II**, 345; and Indian removal, **III**, 107; and the westward movement, **V**, 452

Great Republic, The, famous Cape Horn ship, **I**, 307

Great Revival, reduces freethinkers, **II**, 340; and American religion, **IV**, 442; in the Western Reserve, **V**, 446

Great Salt Lake, Bridger discovers, **I**, 128; **II**, 235; and Utah, **V**, 353

Great Salt Lake Valley, and Escalante-Domínguez expedition, **II**, 227; and Stansbury exploration, **V**, 158

Great Seal, on presidential flag, **II**, 280

Great Separation, and the Quakers, **IV**, 386

Great Sioux Reservation, embraces the Black Hills, **I**, 195; and the Sioux Council, **V**, 85; created by treaty of Laramie (1868), **V**, 127

Great Smoky Mountains National Park, **IV**, 218

Great Spirit, and Ecorse River Council, **II**, 184; and Manitou, **III**, 332

Great Swamp Fight, Narragansetts destroyed in, **III**, 210; **IV**, 53

Great Trading Path, and Choctaw Trail, **I**, 369; joined by Great Warriors Path, **III**, 104

Great Train Robbery, first American story picture, **IV**, 31

Great Village of the Illinois, **III**, 199

Great Warriors Path. *See* Warriors Path, Great

Great Western, The, construction of, marks new era in ocean transportation, **III**, 118

Great Western Railroad, and internal improvements, **III**, 138

Greathouse, Daniel, leader in Yellow Creek massacre, **II**, 87

Greek Slave, sculpture of, **I**, 123

Greeley, Horace, nominated for Presidency, **I**, 286; and dead cities, **II**, 114; and the Emigrant Aid Movement, **II**, 211; and the Exhibition of the Industry of All Nations, **II**, 233; and expression "Go west, young man, go west," **II**, 392; and the homestead movement, **III**, 42; and Kansas Free-State party, **III**, 197; and land grants for education, **III**, 236; and the Liberal Republican party, **III**, 269; as newspaper editor, **IV**, 123; and the peace movement of 1864, **IV**, 233; and peace movements, **IV**, 234; and printer's devil, **IV**, 344; and the Socialist movement, **V**, 110; and the stagecoach, **V**, 308; and the Union Colony, **V**, 342

Greely, A. W., and polar expeditions, **IV**, 293

Green, Bartholomew, printer of the *Boston News-Letter,* **I**, 223; **IV**, 127

Green, Duff, and the *United States Telegraph,* **II**, 392; **IV**, 128; journalist, **V**, 123

Green, H. L., Company, prepares to open stores in Great Britain, **II**, 279

Green, John C., and the Michigan Central Railroad, **III**, 393

Green, Paul, dramatist, **II**, 166; and the "Little Theater" movement, **III**, 286

Green, Roger, and the Albemarle Settlements, **I**, 46

Green, Samuel, publishes the *New-England Almanack for 1686,* **IV**, 99; printer of Eliot's Indian Bible, **IV**, 345

Green, Timothy, II, publishes the *New London Summary,* **IV**, 126

Green, Timothy, IV, co-founder of the *Vermont Gazette,* **IV**, 127; first printer of Vermont, **IV**, 346

Green Bay, and legend concerning Fox-Wisconsin Waterway, **II**, 320; and the fur trade, **II**, 360; first American post at, **III**, 54; settlement of, **V**, 473. *See also* LaBaye

Green-Bay Intelligencer, founded by A. G. Ellis and J. V. Suydam, **IV**, 128

Green Corn Dance, **II**, 86; **III**, 97

Green Mountain Boys, and the Beech Seal, **I**, 173; take Crown Point, **II**, 93; and Onion

River Land Company, **IV**, 174; as partisan band, **IV**, 219; and capture of Ticonderoga, **V**, 267; and the New Hampshire Grants, **V**, 362

Green River, Ashley reaches, **I**, 128

Green Spring, battle of, **III**, 51

Greenback Movement, and agrarian aims, **I**, 21; and the Bland-Allison Act, **I**, 198; and hard money, **III**, 9; and mortgages, **IV**, 29; as a political party, **IV**, 297; and Socialist Labor party, **V**, 110; and soft currency, **V**, 113; as a third party, **V**, 262

Greenbacks, and the bimetallic system, **I**, 189; an issue in campaigns of 1868 and 1876, **I**, 286; authorized by Legal Tender Act of 1862, **I**, 384; depreciation of, during Civil War, **I**, 388; as currency, **II**, 99; and the Federal deficit, **II**, 128; as fiat money, **II**, 269; and Five-twenties, **II**, 280; depreciation of, **II**, 394; and the gold exchange, **II**, 395; and inflation, **III**, 121; as legal tender, **III**, 261; and legal tender acts, **III**, 261; and money system, **IV**, 7; and the Ohio Idea, **IV**, 163; as paper money, **IV**, 213; and repudiation of public debt, **IV**, 455; and the Resumption Act (1875), **IV**, 461; prolong suspension of specie payments, **V**, 144; and Treasury notes, **V**, 314

Greene, Christopher, and Fort Mercer engagements, **III**, 375

Greene, Nathanael, and the court-martial of André, **I**, 73; works in father's foundry, **I**, 197; replaces Gates, **I**, 278; and Cherokee wars, **I**, 353; and the battle of Eutaw Springs, **II**, 229; and battle of Germantown, **II**, 385; and battle of Guilford Court House, **II**, 428; and battle of Hobkirk's Hill, **III**, 36; besieges Ninety-Six, **IV**, 134; in the Revolutionary War, **IV**, 477; hero of the 1781 campaign, **IV**, 478; and Sullivan in Rhode Island, **IV**, 479; in the Southern campaigns (1780–81), **V**, 129; in battle of Springfield, N. J., **V**, 151; and the trench, **V**, 321; and Washington's eight months army, **V**, 419

Greene, S. D., assumes command of the *Monitor*, **IV**, 10

Greenhow, Rose O'Neal, Confederate spy, **V**, 146

Greenleaf, James, and organization of North American Land Company, **IV**, 144

Greenough, Horatio, sculptor, **I**, 123

Greenville, Treaty of, and Brownstown treaty, **I**, 245; and Chicago, **I**, 356; and Fort Dearborn, **II**, 115; and Indian land cessions, **III**, 100; obnoxious to the Indians, **III**, 105; and Indiana, **III**, 112; and Loramie's store, **III**, 301; signed by Little Turtle, **III**, 390; and settlement of Miami Purchase, **III**, 390; and opening up of Ohio, **IV**, 151; and Fort Recovery, **IV**, 428; and Sandusky, **V**, 27; and the Shawnee, **V**, 65; and

crusade of Tecumseh, **V**, 237; ends the Wayne campaign, **V**, 427

Greenway, Robert, master of the *Welcome*, **V**, 433

Greenwood, Caleb, and wagon trains, **V**, 389

Greenwood, Isaac, early science lecturer, **III**, 260

Greenwood, John, invents foot-drill and platesprings for dentists, **II**, 138

Greenwood's Cut-off, **V**, 192

Greer County Dispute, and state boundaries, **I**, 227; caused by a "gore," **II**, 401; and Marcy's exploring expeditions, **III**, 342; settled, **IV**, 168; and Oklahoma squatters, **IV**, 169; and U. S. v. Texas, **V**, 349

Gregg, D. McM., and battle at Yellow Tavern, **V**, 506

Gregg, John, and battle of Raymond, **IV**, 418

Gregory, J. H., finds gold in Colorado, **I**, 426

Gregory, McLeod and Company, added to North West Company, **IV**, 147

Gregory, Samuel, admits women to medical lectures, **V**, 480

Gregory Gold Mine, **II**, 396

Grenville, James, and Board of Trade, **I**, 207

Grenville, Richard, and Raleigh's first colony, **IV**, 413

Gresham's Law, and the bimetallic system, **I**, 188

Greve Trophy Race, **I**, 37

Grey Beard, and the Wagon Train charge, **V**, 388

Greysolon, Charles de, builds trading posts on Lake Superior, **V**, 205

Gridley, C. V., and the order "Fire when you are ready," **II**, 275

Grier, R. C., in Hepburn v. Griswold, **III**, 262

Grierson, B. H., and battle at Tupelo, **V**, 330

Griffin, Fort, and outfitting of caravans, **I**, 313

Griffin, G. G., compiler of *Writings on American History*, **III**, 35

Griffith, David W., motion picture director, **IV**, 32

Griffon, The, built by LaSalle, **I**, 301; launched on Lake Erie, **II**, 224; and LaSalle's explorations, **III**, 246; vanishes near Michilimackinac, **III**, 394

Grigsby-Ide Company, **I**, 270

Grimes, J. W., and impeachment trial of Andrew Johnson, **III**, 77; wages campaign for governor of Iowa, **III**, 153

Grimké, Sarah and Angelina, work for women's rights, **II**, 265; and the woman movement, **V**, 477

Grimley, In re, and U. S. v. Clark, **V**, 348

Grinnell, George Bird, forms the Audubon Society, **I**, 137

Grinnell, Henry, finances DeHaven's exploring expedition, **II**, 130

Grinnell College, founded by Congregationalists, **II**, 17

Griswold, Fort, attack on, **IV**, 106

Griswold, George, and the Michigan Central Railroad, **III**, 393

Grocery Stores, and the distribution of merchandise, **II**, 152

Gros Ventres Indians, and battle of Pierre's Hole, **IV**, 269

Groseilliers, Medart Chouart, Sieur de, on Chequamegon Bay, **I**, 351; *coureur de bois,* **II**, 75; fur trader, **III**, 110; and Minnesota, **III**, 410; and the Mississippi Valley, **III**, 425; and Radisson's Relation, **IV**, 398

Grosh, Allen and Hosea, discover the Comstock Lode, **II**, 236

Grosscup, P. S., and the Pullman strike, **IV**, 381

Grosvenor, Mason, organizer of the Illinois Band, **III**, 69

Grover, Sharp, scout, **V**, 46

Grover, W. O., patents a sewing machine, **V**, 61

Grow, Galusha A., introduces homestead bill, **III**, 42

Grubb, Peter, and the Hopewell Iron Works, **III**, 45

Grundy, Felix, as a leader of the War Hawks, **V**, 403

Guadalajara Explorations, and Texas, **V**, 252

Guadalupe Hidalgo, Treaty of, and Mixed Claims Commissions, **I**, 63; and annexation of territory, **I**, 79; and international arbitration, **I**, 96; and state boundaries, **I**, 226; and Disturnell's Map, **II**, 154; and the Gardiner award, **II**, 371; and Lower California, **III**, 311; and the Mexican boundary, **III**, 382; ends the Mexican War, **III**, 387; makes New Mexico part of the United States, **IV**, 107; and peace conferences, **IV**, 231; and the Rio Grande, **IV**, 486; and territorial claims of the United States, **V**, 247; includes secret article, **V**, 316; and treaties with foreign nations, **V**, 317; and the Trist mission, **V**, 325. *See also* Mexican Cession

Guam, and acquisition of territory, **I**, 79; ceded to the United States, **III**, 78; as an insular possession, **III**, 128; ceded to the United States, **IV**, 216; **V**, 136, 137; and territorial claims of the United States, **V**, 247; and the Yap mandate, **V**, 502

Guano, as fertilizer, **II**, 268

Guaranty Securities Corporation, **III**, 127

Guardians of Liberty, **IV**, 66

Guerrière, The, flagship of Decatur's cruise to Algiers, **II**, 119

Guerrillas, in the Civil War, **I**, 387; cowboys and skinners as, **II**, 81; Jessie Scouts as, **III**, 174; and the Mississippi Squadron, **III**, 425; and partisan bands, **IV**, 219

Guffey Coal Acts, and Carter v. Carter Coal Company, **I**, 319; and labor, **I**, 404; and the New

Deal, **IV**, 96; and the United Mine Workers, **V**, 346

Guggenheim, Meyer, copper millionaire, **II**, 312; builds smelter, **V**, 101

Guggenheim (Florence) Foundation, **II**, 314

Guggenheim (John Simon) Memorial Foundation, **II**, 314

Guilford Court House, Battle of (1780), **V**, 129

Guinan, Texas, and night clubs, **IV**, 133

Guinn and Beal v. U. S., and the grandfather clause, **II**, 409

Guiteau, Charles J., shoots James A. Garfield, **I**, 129; **II**, 372

Gunboats, Eads, **II**, 180; of United States fleet, **II**, 282; for river navigation, **IV**, 489; as warships, **V**, 411

Gunnison, J. W., and government railroad surveys, **IV**, 405

Gunpowder, and munitions, **IV**, 44

Gunpowder Trade Association, **IV**, 326

Guntersville Dam, **V**, 245

Gutch, Robert, and Kennebec settlements, **III**, 204

Guthrie, Okla., a boom town, **I**, 215

Gwin, William McK., and the Pacific Republic movement, **IV**, 197; and the Pony Express, **IV**, 306

Gwinnett, Button, signer of the Declaration of Independence, **II**, 124

Gyles, John, as Indian captive, **III**, 95

H

Habeas Corpus, and arbitrary arrest, **I**, 121; Supreme Court upholds its right to issue, **I**, 208; and civil liberties, **I**, 381; suspended (1861), **I**, 386; in the Confederacy, **II**, 4; and the Confederate Congress, **II**, 6, 12; and the Constitution, **II**, 34; and the Ku-Klux Act, **III**, 217; McCardle denied benefit of, **III**, 363; writ of, and the Merryman case, **III**, 379; Lincoln orders suspension of, **IV**, 335; states' rights faction opposes suspension of, **V**, 176; in wartime, **V**, 399

Hadfield, George, and the Capitol at Washington, **I**, 311

Haggin, James B., and Anaconda Copper, **I**, 71

Hague Court of Arbitration, creation of, **I**, 96; and settlement of the fisheries dispute, **II**, 277; and international law, **III**, 141; creation of, **IV**, 232; and Pious Fund controversy, **IV**, 275; and the Root treaties, **IV**, 501; and blockade of Venezuela, **V**, 359. *See also* Permanent Court of International Justice

Hague Opium Convention of 1912, **IV**, 179

Hague Peace Conferences, and international arbitration, **I**, 96; and the General Orders No.

100, **I**, 385; and international conciliation, **II**, 2; and capture of private property, **III**, 76; and international law, **III**, 141; and intervention, **III**, 146; and isolation, **III**, 163; and Ladd's peace plan, **III**, 226; and neutrality, **IV**, 89; and nonintervention, **IV**, 139; and Pan-American Conferences, **IV**, 202; and partisan bands, **IV**, 220; and Permanent Court of Arbitration, **IV**, 232; and prisoners of war, **IV**, 348; and prize courts, **IV**, 352; and treaties with foreign nations, **V**, 318; and laws of war, **V**, 398

Haish, Jacob, and the barbed wire patent case, **I**, 163

Haiti, military occupation of, **I**, 314; marines in, **III**, 343; and treaties with foreign nations, **V**, 317

Haldimand, Fort, **I**, 218

Haldimand Negotiations, **III**, 230; **V**, 363

Hale, Edward Everett, and the Emigrant Aid movement, **II**, 211; attends librarians conference, **III**, 272

Hale, J. P., nominated for Presidency, **I**, 284; Free Soil party supports, **II**, 334; nominated by the Liberty party, **III**, 272

Hale, Nathan, spy of the Revolution, **V**, 145

Hale, Sarah Josepha, made literary editor of *Godey's Lady's Book*, **II**, 392

Half Moon, The, **I**, 44

Halfbreeds, and the Stalwarts, **V**, 154

Halford, William, and cruise of the *Saginaw's* gig, **V**, 5

Halfway Covenant, **II**, 16; **IV**, 442

Haliburton, Thomas Chandler, "Sam Slick," **V**, 20

Halifax, Earl of, and Board of Trade and Plantations, **I**, 206

Halifax Mixed Commission, **I**, 76

Hall, A. O., and the Tweed Ring, **IV**, 485; **V**, 333

Hall, Charles F., polar expedition of, **IV**, 293

Hall, Charles Martin, and aluminum, **I**, 53

Hall, David, as partner in *Pennsylvania Gazette*, **IV**, 246

Hall, Edward W., murder of, **V**, 323

Hall, Edwin O., first printer of Idaho, **IV**, 345

Hall, Fort, and the Great Basin, **II**, 414; established, **III**, 66; and the Oregon Trail, **IV**, 186; and stagecoach lines of the greater southwest, **V**, 153

Hall, John, patents the breech-loading carbine, **IV**, 483

Hall, Joseph, establishes the *Pittsburgh Gazette*, **IV**, 124, 281

Hall, Lyman, signer of the Declaration of Independence, **II**, 124

Hall, Mrs. E. W., trial of, **V**, 323

Hall, Prince, and Negro Masonry, **III**, 352

Hall, William, and the *Pennsylvania Gazette*, **IV**, 246

Hall, William, Jr., and the *Pennsylvania Gazette*, **IV**, 246

Hallam, William, and the theater, **V**, 259

Halleck, Fitz-Greene, and bookshops, **I**, 214

Halleck, Henry W., and the Corps of Engineers, **II**, 216; and Army of the Mississippi, **III**, 419; appointed to command land forces of the United States, **IV**, 241; and the Red River Campaign, **IV**, 430

Haller, Granville O., and the Yakima Indian wars, **V**, 500

Hallet, Stephen, and the Capitol at Washington, **I**, 311

Hallett, Samuel, secures control of Kansas Pacific Railroad, **III**, 198

Halsted, William Stewart, and medicine and surgery, **III**, 369

Hambletonian Stake, **III**, 49

Hamburg Riot, and the Red Shirts, **IV**, 432

Hamilton, A. J., and the Ab-Initio Movement, **I**, 2; governor of Texas, **V**, 254

Hamilton, Alexander, and the Annapolis Convention, **I**, 78; and assumption and funding of Revolutionary debt, **I**, 132; depositor and stockholder of the Bank of North America, **I**, 154; financial program of, **I**, 156; comments on the Bill of Rights in *The Federalist*, **I**, 185; financial report of, **I**, 188; duels with Burr, **I**, 257; and the location of the National Capital, **I**, 307; second president of the Society of the Cincinnati, **I**, 376; and the American coinage system, **I**, 410; and ratification of the Constitution, **II**, 29; signer of the Constitution, **II**, 39; delegate to Convention of 1787, **II**, 50; and the Croswell Libel suit, **II**, 92; and assumption of public debt, **II**, 117; and exchange of prisoners, **II**, 231; and *The Federalist*, **II**, 264; and the Federalist party, **II**, 264; and Genêt's mission, **II**, 377; and the *Gazette of the United States*, **II**, 403; and Jay's treaty, **III**, 169; supports cause of judicial review, **III**, 183; and jury trial, **III**, 191; and the Croswell trial, **III**, 268; and liberal construction, **III**, 268; papers of, purchased for the government, **III**, 274; advocates loose construction, **III**, 301; Report on Manufactures, **III**, 339; and the United States Military Academy, **III**, 398; and Miranda's intrigues, **III**, 414; and our money system, **IV**, 7; attacked by *National Gazette*, **IV**, 59; and Associates of the Jersey Company, **IV**, 105; and *Gazette of the United States*, **IV**, 128; defends the Neutrality Proclamation of 1793, **IV**, 197; and political theories, **IV**, 301; and the Presidency, **IV**, 333; and the Public Credit Act, **IV**, 369; and the public domain, **IV**, 370; and public faith, **IV**, 371; and the Revolutionary debt, **IV**, 471; and secession, **V**, 51; and silver legislation,

V, 80; inaugurates a national sinking fund, V, 84; and state sovereignty, V, 173; and duty on tea, V, 232; on the coinage system, V, 276; appointed as first Secretary of the Treasury, V, 314; denounces treatment of the loyalists, V, 322; founds the Society for Establishing Useful Manufactures, V, 353; and the Whiskey Insurrection, V, 457; whispering campaigns against, V, 458; and Yorktown campaign, V, 509

Hamilton, Alice, and industrial hygiene, III, 64

Hamilton, Andrew, and colonial postal service, IV, 321

Hamilton, Andrew, lawyer in Zenger case, II, 337; and Independence Hall, III, 85; and the Zenger trial, V, 513

Hamilton, C. S., and battle of Iuka, III, 164

Hamilton, Charles A., and the Marais des Cygnes massacre, III, 341

Hamilton, Charles K., and airplane racing, I, 36

Hamilton, Fort, founded, III, 390

Hamilton, George E., and Iowa Corn Song, III, 153

Hamilton, Henry, and Clark's Northwest campaign, I, 395; and the epithet "hair buyer," III, 3

Hamilton, James, Fort Hill letter addressed to, II, 310

Hamilton, John Randolph, constructs a floating battery, II, 284

Hamilton, Morgan, and Ab-Initio Movement, I, 2

Hamilton, Philip, fights duel at Weehawken, V, 433

Hamilton-Burr Duel, II, 174; V, 433

Hamilton's Battery, guards military stores at West Point and Fort Pitt, I, 113

Hamilton's Plan (1699), for frontier defense, I, 420

Hamlin, Hannibal, elected Vice-President, I, 285

Hamline, L. L., editor of The Ladies' Repository, III, 226

Hamm, W., Jr., kidnapping of, III, 209

Hammer v. Dagenhart, and Stare decisis, V, 161

Hammerstein, Oscar, and the opera, IV, 178

Hammond, James H., and King Cotton, III, 209; and "It's a damned long time between drinks," IV, 145; political writings of, IV, 302; defends slavery, IV, 363; and proslavery literature, IV, 364; and the soundness of slavery, V, 123; and state bank of South Carolina, V, 126

Hammond, W. A., bans calomel, I, 276

Hammond, W. S., Democratic governor of Minnesota, III, 411

Hampstead Academy, established, III, 420

Hampton, Wade (1751–1835), and battle of Chateaugay, I, 348; in War of 1812, III, 230

Hampton, Wade (1818–1902), at Bull Run, I, 251; and the burning of Columbia, I, 429; and the Red Shirts, IV, 432; and Tillmanism, V, 269; and battle at Trevilian Station, V, 323

Hampton Institute, III, 416

Hampton Roads Conference (1865), IV, 233

Hampton v. United States, V, 224

Hamtranck, J. F., and Fort Knox, III, 216; begins building Fort Steuben, V, 181; names Fort Wayne, V, 426

Hanbury, John, and western land schemes, V, 443

Hancock, Chief, and the Tuscarora War, V, 332

Hancock, John, and Boston Massacre, I, 223; signer of the Declaration of Independence, II, 121; and the Essex Junto, II, 228; and Revere's ride, IV, 463; and the bonding provision of the sugar acts, V, 200

Hancock, Thomas, frontier merchant, II, 352

Hancock, Winfield Scott, nominated for Presidency, I, 287; at Fort Larned, III, 246; and the railroad strike of 1877, IV, 404; and battle of Spotsylvania Courthouse, V, 150

Hand, Edward, and Fort Pitt, IV, 280; and the Squaw Campaign, V, 151; and the Sullivan-Clinton campaign, V, 202

Handbook of Composition, written by Edwin C. Woolley, I, 180

Handel and Haydn Society of Boston, IV, 48

Hangars, I, 37

Hanging, as a colonial punishment, IV, 382

Hanging Rock, battle of, fought in the Waxhaws, V, 426

Hanks, John, and the term "Rail Splitter," IV, 399

Hanna, L. B., and the Nonpartisan League, IV, 140

Hanna, Marcus A., and campaign of 1896, I, 288; and Ohio's conservatism, IV, 161

Hannibal and St. Joseph Railroad, completed, V, 10

Hans Brinker, by Mary Mapes Dodge, I, 363

Hanson, Elizabeth, captured by the Indians, III, 95

Hanson, John, chosen President under Articles of Confederation, II, 330

Hanway, Casper, tried for treason, I, 371

Hapgood, A. S., and canning, I, 304

"Happy Hooligan," comic character, I, 431

Harbor Improvements, and the Corps of Engineers, II, 217

Harbors, Gallatin's Report on, II, 367

Hard Labor, Treaty of, and Indian land cessions, III, 99; and treaty of Lochaber, III, 290; and new Indian boundary line, IV, 354; and treaty of Fort Stanwix (1768), V, 159

Hard Money Theory, I, 81

Hard Roads. See Roads

Hard-Shell Baptists, I, 161

Hardee, W. J., and battle of Missionary Ridge, **III**, 416; and battles on Peachtree Creek, **IV**, 236; and siege of Savannah (1864), **V**, 36; and Army of Tennessee, **V**, 242

Harding, Chester, painter, **I**, 123

Harding, Chester, and action at Glasgow, **II**, 391

Harding, Warren G., vetoes bonus, **I**, 210; elected President, **I**, 291; calls National Agricultural Conference, **II**, 249; and the League of Nations, **III**, 255; and naval oil reserves, **IV**, 71; and normalcy, **IV**, 142; and presidential absences from American soil, **IV**, 335; and the Republican party, **IV**, 454; whispering campaigns against, **V**, 458

"Hards," appearance of term, **III**, 60

Hardware, and domestic trade, **V**, 292

Hardy, R. W. H., explores the lower Colorado River, **I**, 427

Hare System, of proportional representation, **IV**, 361

Hargis-Callahan-Cockrill Feud, **II**, 269

Hargous, P. A., and the Gadsden Purchase, **II**, 365

Harkness, Edward S., makes gift to Yale University, **V**, 501

Harkness, Stephen V., original stockholder of Standard Oil Company, **V**, 156

Harkness Memorial, architecture of, **I**, 101

Harlem, annexed to New York City, **IV**, 118

Harley (Henry) and Company, lay pipelines, **IV**, 276

Harmar, Josiah, at Fort Washington (Ohio), **V**, 414

Harmar's Expedition, and the militia, **III**, 403; against Wabash towns, **V**, 386; and the Wayne campaign, **V**, 427

Harmony Community, **I**, 440; **III**, 397

Harness Racing, **III**, 49

Harney, Ben, and appearance of jazz, **V**, 120

Harney, W. S., and battle of Ash Hollow, **I**, 127; appointed to Indian commission, **III**, 95; attacks Sioux camp near Ash Hollow, **V**, 86

Harney Massacre, **III**, 245

Harpe, Bernard de la, expedition of, **II**, 345

Harpe Brothers, bandits, **I**, 152, 329

Harper, Chancellor, defends slavery, **IV**, 363

Harper, John L., and Osborn v. United States Bank, **IV**, 189

Harper, Robert Goodloe, and "Millions for defense, etc.," **III**, 405

Harper, William, and proslavery literature, **IV**, 364; **V**, 123

Harper, William R., and higher criticism, **III**, 31; and the junior college movement, **III**, 190; and religious education, **IV**, 444

Harper and Brothers, publishers, **I**, 213

Harper's *Bible*, woodcuts in, **V**, 482

Harpers Ferry, and battle of Antietam, **I**, 81; and the Baltimore and Ohio Railroad, **I**, 151; Jackson detached to capture, **III**, 350

Harpers Ferry Raid, the Coppocs participate in, **II**, 58; Sharps rifles used in, **V**, 64; and slave insurrections, **V**, 90

Harper's Magazine, and advertising, **III**, 323; and wood engraving, **V**, 482

Harper's Weekly, political cartoons appear in, **I**, 320; **IV**, 55

Harper's Young People, 19th century magazine, **I**, 363

Harpur, Robert, and Rouse's Point boundary controversy, **IV**, 503

Harrigan, Edward, playwright, **II**, 166

Harrigan and Hart, popular song writers, **V**, 120

Harriman, Edward H., and great fortunes, **II**, 312; and the Northern Pacific Railroad, **IV**, 148; and the Northern Securities case, **IV**, 148; and railroads, **IV**, 408; and the Union Pacific Railroad, **V**, 343

Harris, B. G., and the Copperheads, **II**, 58

Harris, Benjamin, first American newspaper editor, **IV**, 123; publisher of *Publick Occurrences,* **IV**, 127, 379

Harris, Carlyle, and the murder of Helen Potts, **II**, 88

Harris, Chapin A., and dentistry, **II**, 138

Harris, Eli, printer of the *Texas Republican,* **IV**, 127

Harris, Joel Chandler, author of Uncle Remus books, **I**, 363; and Negro folklore, **II**, 270

Harris, Paul, and rotary clubs, **IV**, 502

Harris, W. T., and philosophical thought and writings, **IV**, 264

Harris and Habersham, first commercial house in Savannah, **V**, 35

Harrisburg Memorial (1827), and the tariff, **V**, 222

Harrison, Benjamin (1726?–1791), signer of the Declaration of Independence, **II**, 124; saved by Jouett's ride, **III**, 182; alumnus of William and Mary College, **V**, 467

Harrison, Benjamin (1833–1901), nominated for Presidency, **I**, 287; defeated for Presidency (1892), **I**, 288; brings Marine Band to Easter egg rolling scene, **II**, 183; and Neagle case, **IV**, 79; nominated for the Presidency, **IV**, 454

Harrison, Carter H., and the Haymarket riot, **III**, 20

Harrison, Fort, advance base in battle of Tippecanoe, **V**, 272

Harrison, Fort, Grant captures, **IV**, 256

Harrison, Francis Burton, administers the Philippine Islands, **IV**, 262

Harrison, W. H., nominated for Presidency, **I**, 283; elected, **I**, 283; occupies Detroit (1813), **II**,

143; and the Division Act of 1800, II, 155; wins battle of the Thames, II, 224; inauguration of, III, 82; becomes ex-officio superintendent of Indian Affairs, III, 91; appointed governor of Indiana Territory, III, 112; and Fort Meigs, III, 371; and battle of Mississinewa, III, 419; destroys Prophet's Town, IV, 361; negotiates treaty of Spring Wells, V, 150; and crusade of Tecumseh, V, 237; and battle of the Thames, V, 258; and battle of Tippecanoe, V, 272; and "Tippecanoe and Tyler Too!", V, 273; erects Fort Ferree at Upper Sandusky, V, 352; arrives at Vincennes, V, 370; and treaty of Vincennes, V, 370; suffers severe losses at Tippecanoe, V, 405; victorious in battle of the Thames, V, 405; negotiates treaties at Fort Wayne, V, 426; concludes treaty of Fort Wayne, V, 426; Perry's message to, after battle of Lake Erie, V, 428; and the Whig party, V, 455

Harrison Almanacs, I, 52

Harrison Land Act (1800), and public land sales, IV, 372; and the Relief Act of 1821, IV, 441

Harrison Narcotic Law, IV, 53, 179

Harrison's Landing, and the Peninsular campaign, IV, 241; McClellan fortifies his army at, V, 60

Harrod, James, hunter, III, 60; locates and begins building Harrodstown, III, 204; as early surveyor, V, 210

Harrodsburg, first permanent settlement in Kentucky, I, 205

Hart, Albert Bushnell, accepts Galloway's story of Jones County secession, III, 181

Hart, C. W., and development of the reaper, IV, 419

Hart, Capt., and the Navy in the World War, V, 493

Hart, David, and the Transylvania Company, V, 309

Hart, John, signer of the Declaration of Independence, II, 124

Hart, Nathaniel, and the Transylvania Company, V, 309

Hart, Thomas, and the Transylvania Company, V, 309

Harte, Bret, and fiction, II, 270

Hartford, George H., and the Great Atlantic and Pacific Tea Company, II, 413

Hartford, The, Farragut's flagship, II, 108; in battle of Mobile Bay, IV, 1; wooden screw sloop, V, 99

Hartford, Treaty of (1650), III, 299; IV, 109

Hartford, Treaty of (1786), and Boston Ten Townships, I, 224; and the State of New York, IV, 116; and the Phelps-Gorham purchase, IV, 257

Hartford Convention, effect on campaign of

1816, I, 282; and the Essex Junto, II, 229; and the Federalist party, II, 265; and nullification, IV, 153; and secession, V, 51; and the War of 1812, V, 406

Hartford Insurance Company, III, 129

Hartford Wits, I, 213

Harvard College, founded, I, 277; and Congregationalists, II, 16; founded, II, 185; and football, II, 298; and the origin of the public library movement, III, 272; New England medical education begins at, III, 369; and the printing press, IV, 344; and the Unitarians, V, 345

Harvard Divinity School, V, 261

Harvard Medical School, III, 51

Harvester, first patented by McCormick, IV, 223

Harvester, The, written by Gene Stratton Porter, I, 180

Harvesting Machinery, invention of, II, 247

Harvey, George, antagonistic to the League of Nations, III, 255

Harvey, John, pays Calvert a visit, III, 349

Harvey, W. H. ("Coin"), author of *Coin's Financial School,* I, 412

Harwood, H. J., and match-making machinery, III, 359

Hasinai Tribes, called Tejas by the Spanish, V, 238

Hassam, Childe, painter, I, 123

Hasse, A. R., indexes of, III, 34

Hassler, Ferdinand Rudolph, and the Coast and Geodetic Survey, I, 404; advocates erection of two observatories, IV, 156

Hasting's Cutoff, and the Great Basin, II, 414

Hastings-Semple Company, I, 270

Hat Act of 1732, and colonial manufacture, I, 172, 418; and British colonial policy, I, 422; and restriction of colonial manufactures, III, 335

Hatch Act of 1887, and agricultural experiment stations, I, 25, 31

Hatch Act of 1939, and relief, IV, 441

Hatfield and McCoy Feuds, II, 88, 269

Hathorne, Col., and the Minisink Indian raid, III, 410

Hauptmann, Bruno, and the Lindbergh kidnapping case, III, 280; V, 323

Havana, Pan-American conference at (1928), V, 203

Havemeyer, Henry O., and great fortunes, II, 312

Haverhill, French and Indian raids on, IV, 389

Haverly's Minstrel Show, III, 413

Haviland, William, drives French from Lake Champlain, III, 230; IV, 18

Hawaii, annexed, I, 79; opening of relations with, I, 128; annexed by the United States, III, 78; an incorporated territory, III, 127; as an insular possession, III, 128; and "manifest destiny,"

III, 332; missionary activity in, III, 415; annexation of, and our influence in the Pacific, IV, 196; as cane area, V, 200; and territorial claims of the United States, V, 247; organized as a territory, V, 249; treaties with, V, 317; and the United States as a world power, V, 486
Hawaii National Park, IV, 218
Hawaii v. Mankichi, III, 127
Hawdon, Michael, purchases the Kakiate patent, III, 193
Hawes-Cooper Act, and prison industries, IV, 347
Hawes-Cutting Act, passed over Hoover's veto, V, 336
Hawkeye State, and steamboat racing, V, 178
Hawkins' Zouaves, V, 514
Hawks, Frank, flies across the continent, I, 142
Hawks Peak Episode, and the Bear Flag Revolt, I, 170
Hawley, Thomas, and Oblong Patent, IV, 156
Hawley-Smoot Tariff, I, 301; V, 222, 223, 224
Hawthorne, Alice (Septimus Winner), V, 119
Hawthorne, Nathaniel, at Brook Farm, I, 243; and children's books, I, 363; and Concord Group, II, 2; and the story of Evangeline, II, 230; author of *The Scarlet Letter*, II, 270; and "Peter Parley," IV, 255; and the Socialist movement, V, 110
Hay, and rotation of crops, II, 154
Hay, John, and Anglophobia, I, 78; and the Open-Door Policy, I, 128; co-author of *Abraham Lincoln: A History*, I, 190; and Boxer Rebellion, I, 231; and the Open-Door Policy, I, 364; and the Far Eastern Policy, II, 243; and isolation, III, 163; and the Open-Door Policy in Manchuria and Manchoukuo, III, 330; and the Olney-Pauncefote treaty, IV, 172; and the Open-Door Policy, IV, 176; and the Panama revolution, IV, 207; and the peace movement of 1864, IV, 233; and the Perdicaris affair, IV, 253; and blockade of Venezuela, V, 359; and the United States as a world power, V, 486
Hay—Bunau-Varilla Treaty, and the Panama revolution, IV, 207
Hay-Corea, protocol, IV, 132
Hay-Herran Treaty, and Colombia Canal controversy, I, 415; and the Panama Canal, IV, 204; and the Panama revolution, IV, 206
Hay-Pauncefote Treaty, and Anglo-American relations, I, 77; supersedes the Clayton-Bulwer arrangement, I, 396; and the Monroe Doctrine, IV, 14; and Nicaraguan Canal project, IV, 132; and the Panama Canal, IV, 204; and the Panama Tolls question, IV, 207; V, 279; and treaties with foreign nations, V, 317
Hayden, F. V., railroad survey of, V, 283
Hayden, Horace H., and dentistry, II, 138

Hayden, Lewis, and the Webster-Fairbank trials, V, 431
Hayden Foundation, II, 315
Hayes, I. I., polar expedition of, IV, 293
Hayes, Lucy Webb, called "First Lady of the Land," II, 276
Hayes, Max S., nominated by Farmer-Labor party of 1920, II, 251
Hayes, Rutherford B., and the appointing power, I, 91; and the election of 1876, I, 286; elected President, I, 287; and Garfield-Blaine-Conkling controversy, II, 372; and restoration of home rule in the South, III, 41; inauguration of, III, 82; and the phonograph, IV, 264; and the Presidency, IV, 333; and the railroad strike of 1877, IV, 404; nominated for the Presidency, IV, 454; and the Wormley conference, V, 495
Hayne, Paul Hamilton, poet, V, 123
Hayne, Robert Y., and Webster debate, V, 431
Haynes, Elwood, and the automobile, I, 140
Hays, Jack, and the Texas Rangers, V, 256
Hays, Kans., cow town, II, 79
Hays, Seth, establishes settlement at Council Grove, II, 72
Hays, Upton, and action at Lone Jack, III, 297
Haywood, "Big Bill," and Cœur d'Alene riots, I, 409
Hazard, powder producing agency, IV, 326
Hazard, Thomas, blacksmith philosopher, I, 197
Hazen, W. B., reoccupies Fort Cobb, I, 406; captures Fort McAllister, III, 363
Hazlett, R. H., cattleman, I, 206
Heald, Nathan, commandant of Fort Dearborn, II, 115
Health, Public, and the dairy industry, II, 104; and hookworm, III, 44; and hygiene, III, 63; and quarantine, IV, 387; and the Rockefeller Foundation, IV, 497; and sanitation, V, 28; and the Treasury Department, V, 314
Hearst, George, and Anaconda Copper, I, 71; and great fortunes, II, 312
Hearst, Mrs. Phoebe, co-founder of the National Congress of Mothers, IV, 215
Hearst, William Randolph, and Anglophobia, I, 78; offers prize for flight across the United States, I, 142; and comic strips, I, 431; and great fortunes, II, 312; as newspaper editor, IV, 123; and syndicating colored comics, IV, 123; and rise of tabloids, V, 216; and yellow journalism, V, 505
Hearst Services, and news reporting, IV, 123
Hearst's *Comic Weekly*, I, 431
Heart Disease, II, 150
Heath Grant, I, 316; IV, 144; V, 125
Heceta, Bruno, and the Columbia River, I, 430; and Oregon, IV, 182; lands on Washington soil, V, 415

Hecker, Isaac T., founder of the Paulists, **IV,** 226
Heckewelder, John, and Schoenbrunn, **V,** 38
Hedgerow Theater, founded, **III,** 286
Hedges, Isaac, promotes sorghum making, **V,** 121
Hedspeth's Cutoff. *See* Hudspeth's Cutoff
Heenan, John C., prize fighter, **IV,** 352
Heikes, W. F., founds a nursery in Alabama, **IV,** 154
Heintzelman, S. P., and Fort Yuma, **V,** 512
Heinz, Henry John, and food packing, **II,** 297
Heiss, John P., editor of the *Washington Union,* **II,** 404
Helderberg War, **I,** 83
Helena, Mont., mint at, **I,** 129; a boom town, **I,** 215; earthquake, **II,** 181; gold found at, **IV,** 16
Helium, in natural gas, **II,** 373
"Hell among the Yearlings," fiddle tune, **II,** 270
Helm, Leonard, appointed as civil and military commandant of Vincennes, **V,** 369
Helper's *Impending Crisis,* **I,** 3, 85; **IV,** 302
Hemingway, Ernest, and fiction, **II,** 270
Hemp, and textiles, **V,** 258
Hempstead, Thomas, and Missouri Fur Company, **V,** 13
Henderson, Alexander, and the Alexandria Conference, **I,** 47
Henderson, J. B., and the Thirteenth Amendment, **V,** 264
Henderson, Richard, makes settlement at Boonesborough, **II,** 96; and the Cumberland settlements, **II,** 98; in Kentucky, **III,** 204, 235; and land speculation, **III,** 239; and the Regulators of North Carolina, **IV,** 439; organizes the Transylvania Company, **V,** 132; and the Sycamore Shoals treaty, **V,** 215; buys land in Tennessee, **V,** 243; and the Transylvania Company, **V,** 309; and Virginia v. Transylvania Company, **V,** 380
Henderson, Robert, and the Klondike rush, **III,** 214
Hendricks, Thomas A., nominated for Vice-President, **I,** 286
Hendrik, Mohawk chieftain, killed in battle of Lake George, **III,** 231
Heney, Francis J., exposes Oregon land frauds, **IV,** 183
Henkels, Stan V., and book auctions, **I,** 212
Hennepin, Louis, ascends the Mississippi, **II,** 344; and the Great Lakes, **II,** 416; sails in the *Griffon,* **II,** 426; explores the Upper Mississippi, **III,** 246; and Minnesota, **III,** 410; and New France, **IV,** 101; and Niagara Falls, **IV,** 131; names St. Anthony Falls, **V,** 6; cartographic records of, **V,** 282
Hennessey, David C., assassination of, **III,** 323
Henri, Robert, painter, **I,** 123
Henry, Alexander, first English trader to reach
La Pointe, **I,** 351; fur trader, **III,** 110; occupies Pembina, **IV,** 240; and the Red River cart, **IV,** 430; searches for the western sea, **V,** 446
Henry, Andrew, commands Ashley's first expedition, **I,** 128; first to trap west of Rockies, **II,** 235; partner in St. Louis Missouri Fur Company, **V,** 12; and topographic mapping, **V,** 283; and Ashley's expeditions, **V,** 310; enters Wyoming, **V,** 496
Henry, Charles L., builds first interurban electric railway, **III,** 145
Henry, Fort (Va.), Batts-Fallam expedition sent out from, **I,** 168; erected, **IV,** 81
Henry, Fort (Wheeling), and Forman's massacre, **II,** 310; later name for Fort Fincastle, **V,** 455
Henry, Fort (Tennessee River), the *Carondelet* fights at, **I,** 317; taken during Civil War, **I,** 389; as fortification, **II,** 311; capture of, **III,** 419; captured by Mississippi Squadron, **III,** 425
Henry, Fort (Idaho), established, **III,** 66
Henry, J. D., and battle of Wisconsin Heights, **V,** 474
Henry, Joseph, invents the telegraph, **III,** 148; and Princeton University, **IV,** 343; as secretary of the Smithsonian Institution, **V,** 102; inaugurates the first published weather forecasts, **V,** 430
Henry, Patrick, and Camden-Yorke Opinion, **I,** 278; attacked in "Decius" letters, **II,** 120; and "Give me liberty or give me death" oration, **II,** 390; saved by Jouett's ride, **III,** 182; and liberalism, **III,** 269; and oratory, **IV,** 179; and the Parson's cause, **IV,** 219; and Pollock's aid to the Revolution, **IV,** 304; and the American Revolution, **IV,** 465 f.; utters his famous "Give me liberty or give me death," **IV,** 482; Stamp Act speech of, **V,** 313; approves the Virginia Resolves (1769), **V,** 379
Henry Clay Almanac, **I,** 52
Henry Frank, The, carries record load, **V,** 180
Henrys, The, rifle makers, **IV,** 483
Henson, Matthew, and Peary's polar expeditions, **IV,** 237, 293
Hepburn Act of 1906, and the Delaware, Lackawanna and Western Railroad, **II,** 131; passed, **III,** 143; and railroad rate law, **IV,** 402; and rebates, **IV,** 420; and the warehouse system, **V,** 408
Hepburn v. Griswold, and Juilliard v. Greenman, **III,** 189; legal tender case, **III,** 262; and unconstitutionality of the legal tender acts, **IV,** 455; and the Supreme Court Packing Bills, **V,** 208
Herald of Freedom, Atchison proslavery men destroy office of the, **I,** 133; and sack of Lawrence, **III,** 253

Herbert, Victor, composer of light opera, **IV,** 178

Herefords, introduction of, **II,** 78

Herkimer, Nicholas, and Burgoyne's Invasion, **I,** 255; and battle of Oriskany, **IV,** 188

Herne, James A., playwright, **II,** 166

"Heroes of America," and peace movements in the Confederacy, **II,** 4; and Union sentiment in the South, **V,** 344

Heroin, and opium trade, **IV,** 179

Herold, David E., and Lincoln's assassination, **III,** 279

Herrera Map, **III,** 340

Herreshoff, Nathanael, American naval architect, **V,** 499

Herrick, Myron T., and Lindbergh's reception in Paris, **III,** 280

Herrmann, Augustine, and the Labadists, **III,** 218; surveys of, **V,** 282

Herron, F. J., and battle at Prairie Grove, **IV,** 329

Hertel, François, and attack on Salmon Falls, **V,** 17

Hesse, Emmanuel, and British attack on St. Louis (1780), **V,** 11

Hesselius, Gustavus, artist, **I,** 122

Hessians, in battle of Cooch's Bridge, **II,** 54; and Washington's crossing of the Delaware, **II,** 131; and German mercenaries, **II,** 384; and Fort Mercer engagements, **III,** 375; in the American Revolution, **IV,** 468; and battle of Trenton, **V,** 322

Hester Case, and Perth Amboy, **IV,** 255

Hetch-Hetchy Valley, **I,** 93

Heth, Henry, and battle of Gettysburg, **II,** 386; and Pickett's charge, **IV,** 267

Hewes, Joseph, signer of the Declaration of Independence, **II,** 124

Hewitt, Abram S., and Cooper Union, **II,** 56; and industrial research, **III,** 338

Hewitt, H. S., organizes ambulance companies, **I,** 54

Hexing, and folklore, **II,** 293

Heye Foundation, **IV,** 48

Heyes, Pieter, and Zwaanendael Colony, **V,** 515

Heyl, Henry R., and photography, **IV,** 265

Heyward, Thomas, Jr., signer of the Declaration of Independence, **II,** 124

Heywood, Joseph, killed in Northfield Bank robbery, **IV,** 149

Hezeta, Bruno. *See* Heceta, Bruno

Hiawatha, helps organize Iroquois League, **III,** 159

Hibbins, Anne, hanged for witchcraft, **V,** 475

Hickok, "Wild Bill," cow town marshal, **II,** 79; at Fort Hays, **III,** 20

Hickory Ground, Indians set up their own government at, **II,** 83

Hicks, Edward, artist, **I,** 123

Hicksites, and Quakerism, **IV,** 386

Hidatsa Indians, and the Cheyennes, **I,** 355; and the Five Villages, **II,** 280; and the Mandans, **III,** 331

Hide and Tallow Trade, and "California bank notes," **I,** 271; in California, **I,** 273, 275; on Santa Catalina Island, **I,** 322

Hide (buffalo) Hunters, **I,** 248

Hides, and *contrabandistas,* **II,** 48; and drogher trade, **II,** 170; and foreign trade, **V,** 295

Higgins, Frank W., and insurance investigation, **III,** 132

Higginson, Francis, minister of Salem, **V,** 16

High Backbone, Sioux chief, **II,** 268

High Schools, and academies, **I,** 5; and coeducation, **I,** 408; and general education, **II,** 187; and the Kalamazoo case, **III,** 193; and teachers colleges, **V,** 234; and education of women, **V,** 480

Higher Criticism, applies scientific inquiry to Bible, **II,** 340; and heresy trials, **III,** 28; and religion, **IV,** 442

Highlands, The, and Burgoyne's Invasion, **I,** 255; operations at, **IV,** 476

Highway Robbery, **I,** 152

Highways. *See* Roads.

Hi-Jackers, **I,** 152

Hildreth, S. P., and petroleum, **IV,** 166

Hill, A. P., and battle of Antietam, **I,** 81; at Bristoe Station, **I,** 239; and battle of Frayser's Farm, **II,** 330; in battle of Gettysburg, **II,** 386; and invasion of Maryland, **III,** 350; and battle of Mechanicsville, **III,** 368; and invasion of Pennsylvania, **IV,** 244; and battle of Spotsylvania Courthouse, **V,** 150; and the Army of Northern Virginia, **V,** 371; and battles of the Wilderness, **V,** 465

Hill, Benjamin, and the Confederate Congress, **II,** 6

Hill, D. H., and Lee's Lost Order, **III,** 303; and battle of South Mountain, **V,** 128

Hill, David B., calls "Snap Convention," **V,** 106

Hill, Isaac, helps carry New Hampshire for Jackson, **IV,** 102

Hill, J. J., and the Great Northern Railroad Company, **II,** 419; **III,** 411; and the Northern Pacific Railroad, **IV,** 148; and the Northern Securities case, **IV,** 148; and railroads, **IV,** 408

Hill, Nathaniel P., and smelters, **V,** 100

Hill, Samuel Eugene, founds the Gideon Society, **II,** 389

Hill and M'Gunnegle, hold contract for Jefferson Barracks, **IV,** 322

Hillman, Sidney, and American Labor party, **I,** 62

Hillsborough, Viscount, and Board of Trade, **I,** 207

Hilton, Edward, founder of Dover, N. H., **IV**, 101

Hindman, T. C., and battle at Prairie Grove, **IV**, 329; joins Shelby's Mexican expedition, **V**, 68

Hines, T. H., and the Northwest conspiracy, **IV**, 150

Hines, W. D., and Railroad Administration, **IV**, 400, 408

Hise Treaty, and the Squier treaty, **V**, 152

Hispanic Society of America, **IV**, 48

Historical Records Survey, **I**, 103

History of the Life and Voyages of Christopher Columbus, written by Washington Irving, **I**, 189

Hitchcock, E. A., and the Florida War, **II**, 291

Hitchcock, P. W., introduces the Timber Culture Bill, **V**, 320

Hitchman Coal v. Mitchell, and the yellow-dog contract, **V**, 504

Hite, Joist, and the Shenandoah Valley, **V**, 69

Hoar, George Frisbie, anti-imperialist, **I**, 82; and the Wheeler Compromise (1876), **V**, 454

Hoar, Rockwood, and the Treaty of Washington (1871), **V**, 416

Hoarding, and banking crisis of 1933, **I**, 158

Hoban, James, architect, **I**, 100; and the White House, **V**, 459

Hobart, J. H., and the Oxford movement, **IV**, 194

Hobbs Fight, in Vermont, **V**, 361

Hobkirk's Hill, engagement at, **V**, 129

Hobson, Richmond Pearson, and sinking of the *Merrimac,* **III**, 378; **V**, 137

Hoch, Edward W., and prohibition in Kansas, **III**, 195

Hoch Deutsch Americanische, **I**, 52

Hockaday and Liggett's Stage Line, **IV**, 510

Hockey, **I**, 71

Hodge, Charles, and religious thought, **IV**, 446

Hodges, G. H., proposes plan to modernize Kansas government, **III**, 195

Hoe, Richard, invents rotary press, **III**, 148

Hoe, Robert, book collection, **I**, 213

Hoe (R.) and Company, buys patent for hand press, **IV**, 346

Hoffman, John T., and the Tweed Ring, **V**, 333

Hoffman, W. H., and prison camps, **IV**, 347

"Hog Eye," fiddle tune, **II**, 270

Hog Island Shipyard, building of, **II**, 209

Hogg, James, and the Transylvania Company, **V**, 309

Hogs, Indiana produces, **III**, 112

Hoisting Machinery, introduction of, **III**, 118

Holabird and Roche, architects of the Tacoma Building, **I**, 101; **V**, 88

Holabird and Root, builders of Chicago Board of Trade, **I**, 101

Holbrook, Josiah, lecturer, **III**, 260; and the lyceum movement, **III**, 316

Holcombe, J. P., and Confederate activities in Canada, **I**, 298; and the peace movement of 1864, **IV**, 233

"Hold the Fort," popular song, **I**, 51

Holden, Oliver, hymn writer, **III**, 65

Holden, W. W., impeached, **III**, 41; and Union sentiment in the South, **V**, 344

Holden v. Hardy, **III**, 291; **V**, 387

Holding Companies, and antitrust laws, **I**, 87; and the Clayton Act, **I**, 396; and electrical industry, **II**, 196; and monopoly, **IV**, 12; regulation of, **IV**, 96; and regulation of public utilities, **IV**, 377; and the Sherman Antitrust Law, **V**, 70; and trusts, **V**, 326

Hole-in-the-Wall Gang, train robbers, **I**, 152

Holladay, Ben, and Butterfield Overland Dispatch, **I**, 263; purchases holdings of Central Overland, California and Pikes Peak Express, **I**, 334; and Overland Mail, **IV**, 193; takes over interests of Russell, Majors and Waddell, **IV**, 510; **V**, 152

Holland, George, and the "Little Church Around the Corner," **III**, 285

Holland, John, constructs submarines, **V**, 194

Holland, Samuel, and Atlantic coast survey, **III**, 340

Holland Land Company, and Big Tree treaty, **I**, 184; and Indian land cessions, **III**, 100; and land speculation, **III**, 239; and leasehold, **III**, 257; and land speculation, **IV**, 116

Hollandaer, Peter, first governor of New Sweden, **IV**, 113

Holley, Myron, leader of the Liberty party, **III**, 272

Holliday, Cyrus, charters Atchison and Topeka Railway, **I**, 133

Holly Springs, burning of Union supply depot at, **V**, 367

Holmes, Hodgen, patents a cotton gin, **II**, 69

Holmes, John Haynes, hymn writer, **III**, 65

Holmes, O. W., in Schenk v. U. S., **V**, 38; and war powers, **V**, 399; and the wire-tapping cases, **V**, 472

Holmes, Oliver Wendell, writes "Old Ironsides," **II**, 29; and use of drugs, **II**, 171; and American hymns, **III**, 65; and medicine, **III**, 369

Holmes, T. H., and battle of Frayser's Farm, **II**, 330; and battle at Helena, **III**, 24

Holmes, William, establishes post at present Windsor, **II**, 21; and House of Hope, **III**, 52; and Plymouth Trading Post, **IV**, 291

Holmes County Rebellion, **IV**, 161

Holston River, and the westward movement, **V**, 450

Holston Settlements, Cherokees attack, **I**, 353; and the Wataugans, **V**, 421

Holston Treaty (1791), opens Cumberland Road

through Cherokee country, II, 98; and Indian land cessions, III, 100

Holy Experiment, and the Quakers, IV, 386

Holy Ground, Battle at. *See* Econochaca

Holy Name Society, founded and advanced by the Dominicans, II, 160

Homan, Sheppard, and American mortality, V, 382

Homan's *Banker's Magazine*, V, 298

Home Building and Loan Association v. Blaisdell et al., III, 411

Home Insurance Building, built by William LeBaron Jenney, I, 101; architecture of, V, 87

Home Loan Bank Act, and Building and Loan Associations, I, 249

Home Loan Bank System, government corporation, II, 403

Home Missions, and the Second Awakening, I, 143; Baptists organize, I, 161

Home Owner's Loan Corporation, II, 118, 262; IV, 96

Home Rule, in the South, IV, 83; restored in North Carolina, IV, 145; and Reconstruction, IV, 426; restoration of, in the South, V, 495

Home Rule, and municipal charters, I, 347; and local government, III, 289; and municipal government, IV, 42

Homer, Winslow, painter, I, 123

Homespun Textiles, V, 258

Homestake Gold Mine, I, 195; II, 312, 396

Homestead Act, and foreign trade, I, 147; and enlistments, I, 228; and campaign of 1860, I, 285; increases caravan traffic, I, 313; and the Civil War, I, 388; and Desert Land Act, II, 141; and free land, II, 331; and immigration, III, 75; and land policy, III, 238; and land speculation, III, 240; and the Oklahoma Openings, IV, 169; and open range cattle period, IV, 177; and Oregon land frauds, IV, 183; and the public domain, IV, 370; and public land sales, IV, 372; and sheep wars, V, 67

Homestead Strike, I, 288; V, 180

Homewood, architecture of, I, 99

Honan, Daniel, purchases the Kakiate patent, III, 193

Honduras, intervention in, III, 146

Hone, Philip, and summer resorts, IV, 460

Hood, J. B., in the battle of Allatoona Pass, I, 50; forced out of Atlanta, I, 134; relieves Johnston in Atlanta campaign, I, 135; and the battle of Ezra Church, II, 238; attacks at Franklin, II, 329; and battle of Nashville, IV, 54; and battles on Peachtree Creek, IV, 236; and Sherman's march to the sea, V, 71; and engagement at Spring Hill, V, 150; replaces J. E. Johnston, V, 242

Hood, John B., co-founder of the *Mobile Centinel*, IV, 124, 126

Hood, Raymond, builds the *Daily News* building, I, 101

Hooker, Joseph, at Antietam, I, 81; and battle of Chancellorsville, I, 339; captures Lookout Mountain, I, 348; receives Burnside's command, II, 331; and battle on Lookout Mountain, III, 300; and battle of Missionary Ridge, III, 416; and the Mud March, IV, 39; and invasion of Pennsylvania, IV, 244; and battle of Ringgold, IV, 485; and battle of Wauhatchie, V, 425

Hooker, Thomas, at Cambridge, I, 277; and the Compact Theory, I, 441; manuscript writings of, and the "Phantom Ship," IV, 257; political writings of, IV, 302

Hookworm Disease, disappearing, II, 150; new species of, found, III, 370; and the Rockefeller Foundation, IV, 497

Hooper, John L., and the advertising agency, I, 18

Hooper, William, signer of the Declaration of Independence, II, 124

Hoosac Tunnel, V, 329

Hoosier Schoolmaster, written by Edward Eggleston, II, 270

Hoover, Herbert, and administrative reorganization, I, 12; and Belgian relief, I, 175; vetoes bonus, I, 210; elected President, I, 291; defeated for Presidency, I, 292; and Colorado River projects, I, 428; and the Department of Commerce, I, 432; and congressional regulation, II, 17; and farm relief, II, 250; and food administration, II, 296; supports Lily-White group, III, 277; and London Naval Treaty of 1930, III, 296; proposes moratorium, IV, 21; and philanthropy and benevolence, IV, 261; and the Philippine Islands, IV, 263; and pump-priming, IV, 382; and relief, IV, 440; and the Republican party, IV, 454; and the World Economic Conference, V, 486; and World War relief, V, 487; as Food Administrator, V, 492

Hoover, Mrs. Herbert, introduces Maypole, II, 183

Hoover (Boulder) Dam, and the Federal Power Commission, II, 261

Hoover Moratorium, Germany ceases paying reparations by the, I, 147; and Lausanne Agreement, III, 251

Hopedale Community, I, 440

Hopewell, Treaty of (1785), follows Holston treaty, III, 39; and Indian land cessions, III, 100

Hopewell Culture, IV, 34

Hopi (or Moqui) Indians, discovered by detachment of Coronado's expedition, I, 104; pray for rain, II, 170; missions among, III, 418; discovery of, IV, 106; and the snake dance, V, 105

Hopkins, Esek, and the Rattlesnake Flag, **IV**, 417; appointed commander in chief of the Continental Navy, **IV**, 471, 478

Hopkins, Harry L., Federal Emergency Relief administrator, **II**, 257

Hopkins, Lemuel, one of the Hartford Wits, **III**, 15

Hopkins, Samuel, and religious thought and writings, **IV**, 446; and antislavery among Congregationalists, **V**, 97; and theological writings, **V**, 261

Hopkins, Stephen, signer of the Declaration of Independence, **II**, 123; and pamphleteering, **IV**, 202

Hopkins Grammar School of New Haven, **V**, 41

Hopkinson, Francis, signer of the Declaration of Independence, **II**, 124; first native American composer on record, **IV**, 48

Hopkinson, Joseph, writes "Hail Columbia," **III**, 3; and McCulloch v. Maryland, **III**, 364

Hornaday, W. T., and buffalo, **I**, 248

Hornbooks, used in Dame schools, **II**, 108; as early schoolbooks, **V**, 40

Hornby, John, and New York land speculation, **IV**, 116

Horse, the Blackfeet acquire the, **I**, 197; cowhorse, **I**, 242; Spanish, herding and handling of, **II**, 80; and the Indian, **III**, 92; Spanish, **IV**, 49; thoroughbred, **V**, 264

Horse-Drawn Vehicles, **I**, 318

Horse Racing, as an amusement, **I**, 69; at county fairs, **II**, 74; and gambling, **II**, 369; and rodeos, **IV**, 499; and organized sports, **V**, 148

Horseless Age, first automotive trade journal, **I**, 140

Horseshoe Bend, Battle of, **II**, 86, 87, 184, 213

Horseshoes, **I**, 70

Horsley, David and William, in Hollywood, **III**, 38

Horstman and Sons, introduce the Jacquard loom, **III**, 166

Hortalez et Cie, Beaumarchais' fictitious commercial company, **II**, 326; established to aid the Americans in the Revolution, **IV**, 475

Horticultural Register, farm periodical, **II**, 248

Horticultural Societies, **II**, 371

Horton, A. E., founder of present metropolis of San Diego, **V**, 23

Hosack, David, gives Elgin Botanical Garden to New York, **II**, 371

Hosmer, Frederick Lucian, hymn writer, **III**, 65

Hosmer, William, political writings of, **IV**, 302

Hospitalization, Army, **I**, 115

Hospitals: Mayo Foundation, **III**, 362; Pennsylvania Hospital, **IV**, 247

Hot Oil Case, and executive orders, **II**, 233; and special powers granted to the President, **IV**, 335

Hot Water Rebellion. *See* Fries Rebellion

Hotels, bathtub in, **I**, 167; and taverns, **V**, 224; and domestic trade, **V**, 293

Hotze, Henry, and Civil War diplomacy, **I**, 392

Houdini, Harry, and spiritualism, **V**, 147

Houghton, Douglas, and Lake Superior copper, **II**, 57

Houghton Farm, **I**, 25

Hours of Labor. *See* Wages and Hours of Labor

House, E. M., diplomatic mission of, **II**, 148; and the Fourteen Points, **II**, 317; and the Inquiry, **III**, 124; and the League of Nations, **III**, 255; and the World War Peace Conference, **V**, 489; and the World War, **V**, 491

House, Royal E., patents the automatic printing telegraph, **V**, 238

"House Divided," and the Lincoln-Douglas debates, **III**, 278

House of Hope, established by the Dutch, **II**, 21; and the fur trade, **II**, 361; established by the Dutch, **IV**, 291; capture of (1653), **IV**, 479

House of Representatives, and constitutional apportionment, **I**, 92; and appropriation bills, **I**, 93; creation of, **II**, 30 f.; Speaker of, **V**, 142

House of Seven Gables, architecture of, **I**, 99

House Raisings, **I**, 70

Household Utensils, artistic value of, **I**, 124

Houses, architecture of early, **I**, 99

Housing Administration, **II**, 260; **III**, 135; **IV**, 96, 378

Houston, E. and W. T. R. Co. v. U. S., **V**, 77

Houston, Samuel, and the Alamo, **I**, 41; removes archives to Houston, **I**, 102; and the Mier expedition, **III**, 396; and "Remember the Alamo," **IV**, 447; and battle of San Jacinto, **V**, 25; and secession of southern states, **V**, 51; as president of the Republic of Texas, **V**, 253; tries to prevent the secession of Texas, **V**, 254; and the Texas navy, **V**, 256; and the Texas revolution, **V**, 257; and Torreys' Trading Post, **V**, 285

Houston and Texas Central Railroad, **III**, 428

Hovey, Oliver P., co-founder of the *Santa Fé Republican,* **IV**, 127

Howard, Bronson, playwright, **II**, 166

Howard, Charles H., and the Salt war, **V**, 19

Howard, Fort, building of, **II**, 320, 422; and American regime in Wisconsin, **V**, 473

Howard, O. O., in the Bannock War, **I**, 161; and battle of Chancellorsville, **I**, 340; attacks at Clearwater River, **I**, 397; commissioner for Freedmen's Bureau, **II**, 336; and Lapwai Indian Council, **III**, 245; and the Nez Percé War, **IV**, 129; and Sherman's march to the sea, **V**, 71; replaces McPherson, **V**, 242; and battle of Wauhatchie, **V**, 425

Howard, Sidney, playwright, **II**, 166

Howard of Effingham, Lord, and Iroquois treaty (1684), **III**, 160

Howe, E. W., author of *A Story of a Country Town,* II, 270

Howe, Elias, invents a sewing machine, III, 148; IV, 223; V, 61

Howe, Hezekiah, printer, I, 214

Howe, Julia Ward, writes "Battle Hymn of the Republic," I, 168; reform lecturer, III, 260; and women's clubs, V, 477; and woman suffrage, V, 478

Howe, Robert, and the Florida Rangers, II, 291; and mutiny of New Jersey regiments, IV, 50; and mutiny of Pennsylvania troops, IV, 248

Howe, Samuel Gridley, and philanthropy and benevolence, IV, 260

Howe, Sir William, and Burgoyne's Invasion, I, 255; and the Mischianza, III, 415; and prisoners of war, IV, 348

Howell, David, and Trevett v. Weeden, V, 323

Howell, Edward, and Southampton, L. I., V, 128

Howells, W. D., author of *The Rise of Silas Lapham,* II, 270

Howland, Andrew M., establishes Land of Shalam, V, 63

Howland Island, annexed by the United States, IV, 195

Hoyt, George W., and the Red Legs, IV, 429

Hubard, Master, boy silhouettist, V, 78

Hubbard, Elbert, and message to Garcia, II, 370

Hubbard, Gardiner G., finances Bell's telephone experiments, I, 66

Hubbard, Gurdon, trail-marker, II, 235; and Illinois Fur Brigade, III, 71

Hubbard, Moses G., and the development of the reaper, IV, 419

Hubbardton, Battle of, I, 255; II, 422; III, 230; V, 362

Hudson, Edward, and dentistry, II, 138

Hudson, Henry, at Albany, I, 44; discovers Delaware Bay, II, 132; and the *Half Moon,* III, 5; visits Manhattan Island, III, 331; discovers Hudson Bay, IV, 150; sets out for the North Pole, IV, 292

Hudson and Manhattan Railroad, V, 329

Hudson and Manhattan Tubes, V, 198

Hudson Motor Car Company, I, 140

Hudson River Chain, III, 31; V, 438

Hudson River Railroad, III, 55; IV, 117

Hudson Tunnels, and interstate compacts, III, 144

Hudson's Bay Company, and Alaska, I, 42; and Anglo-American relations, I, 75; and Arrowsmith's Map, I, 122; and Ashley's expeditions, I, 128; at Fort Boisé, I, 207; post in Oregon, I, 269; in California, I, 275; and the Five Villages, II, 280; and the fur trade, II, 362, 363; and the Great Valley, II, 421; buys Fort Hall, III, 6; and liquor for the Indian, III, 91, 282; and

the North West Company, IV, 146; sends out expeditions to search for Northwest Passage, IV, 151; and Fort Okanagan, IV, 167; and Oregon missions, IV, 184; and the Oregon treaty, IV, 187; and Pembina, IV, 240; and the Pemmican War, IV, 241; founding of, IV, 399; and the Red River of the North, IV, 431; and San Francisco Bay, V, 23; and seizure of San Juan, V, 25; and Snake River, V, 106; takes over Spokane House, V, 148; and the steel trap, V, 180; and topographic mapping, V, 283; and frontier trading posts, V, 302; and trappers' rendezvous, V, 310; and treaty of Utrecht, V, 354; western headquarters at Fort Vancouver, V, 357; in the Northwest, V, 415; and the Whitman massacre, V, 461; and Wilkes exploring expedition, V, 466; and the Willamette Valley settlements, V, 466; and the Yukon, V, 512

Hudspeth's Cutoff, and the Great Basin, II, 414; V, 192

Hue and Cry, I, 121

Hueco Tanks, as watering place, V, 421

Hughes, Charles E., and Progressives, I, 250; nominated for Presidency, I, 290; as counsel of joint committee on insurance investigation, III, 132; and the League of Nations, III, 255; summarizes Milligan case, III, 347; and money power investigation, IV, 9; and the Monroe Doctrine, IV, 15; and the Open-Door Policy, IV, 176; at Sixth Pan-American Conference, IV, 203; and quasi-judicial agencies, IV, 388; and the Reparation Commission, IV, 450; and commercial treaties, V, 315

Hughes, David E., patents the printing telegraph, V, 238

Hughes, Howard R., flies from Los Angeles to Newark, I, 142

Hughes, Robert Ball, wax modeler, V, 426

Hugoton, Kans., and county-seat wars, II, 74

Huguenin, T. A., commanding officer during Fort Sumter siege, V, 204

Huguenots, in Charleston, S. C., I, 343; and colonial society, I, 424; patentees of New Paltz, II, 180; in Florida, II, 288; as refugees, II, 347; as political exiles, IV, 295

Huidekoper, F. L., and preparedness, IV, 331

Hulbert, E. J., discovers Calumet and Hecla Mine, I, 276

Hull, Cordell, and tariff reduction, II, 335; heads American delegation at Lima Conference, III, 278; and Mexican relations, III, 385; at Seventh Pan-American Conference, IV, 203; attends Buenos Aires Peace Conference, IV, 231; and reciprocal trade agreements, IV, 422, 423; and the tariff, V, 223; and the World Economic Conference, V, 486

Hull, Edward, and Dutch War of 1653, IV, 479

Hull, George, and the Cardiff giant, **I,** 313

Hull, Isaac, and the *Constitution-Java* engagement, **II,** 30; appointed to Board of Navy Commissioners, **IV,** 75

Hull, John, silversmith, **V,** 82

Hull, William, and Brownstown and Detroit treaties, **I,** 244; and invasion of Canada, **I,** 245; **II,** 143; and the surrender of Detroit, **II,** 144; cuts Hull's Trail, **III,** 58; surrenders at Detroit, **V,** 405

Hull-Rust-Mahoning-Susquehanna Pit, **III,** 379

Human Sacrifice, engaged in by Natchez Indians, **IV,** 57

Humanitarianism, and the abolition movement, **I,** 2; and slavery, **I,** 84, 85; and imprisonment for debt, **II,** 117; and transcendentalism, **II,** 340; and the Great Awakening, **II,** 413; and juvenile courts, **III,** 192; and home missionary societies, **III,** 416; and pauperism, **IV,** 228; and philanthropy and benevolence, **IV,** 260; and the Republican party (Jeffersonian), **IV,** 453; and slavery, **V,** 94, 123

Humboldt, Alexander von, surveys and maps the Pacific coast, **III,** 341

Humboldt Trail, and the Great Basin, **II,** 414

Hume, George W., and canning, **I,** 304

Humiliation, Days of, **II,** 253

Humor, Dry, **II,** 170

Humphrey, W. E., and Humphrey's Executor v. U. S., **I,** 91; removed from office by the President, **IV,** 448

Humphreys, A. A., and battles at Sailor's Creek, **V,** 5

Humphreys, David, one of the Hartford Wits, **III,** 14

Humphreys, Joshua, designs the *Constitution,* **II,** 29; designs the *United States,* **V,** 347

Humphry, John, and the Providence Island Company, **IV,** 367

Hundred and One Ranch Wild West Show, **V,** 464

Hungarians, in New Buda, **IV,** 94; as political exiles, **IV,** 295

Hungary, treaties with, **V,** 318

Hunkers, as a political party, **IV,** 296

Hunley, H. L., designs hand-operated submarine, **III,** 51

Hunnewell, Kans., cow town, **II,** 79

Hunt, Alfred E., and aluminum, **I,** 53

Hunt, George W. P., first state governor of Arizona, **I,** 104

Hunt, Isaac, author of the tract, *A Humble Attempt at Scurrility,* **V,** 291

Hunt, Richard M., architect, **I,** 101

Hunt, Robert, leader in the Jamestown settlement, **V,** 372

Hunt, Theodore, forms the Missouri Fur Company, **V,** 13

Hunt, William E., on secret mission to Santo Domingo, **V,** 32

Hunt, Wilson Price, at Astoria, **I,** 46; leads the Astor Overlanders, **I,** 133; crosses Big Horn Mountains, **I,** 184; and the Astorians, **II,** 235; visits the Green River Valley, **II,** 423; partner in the Pacific Fur Company, **IV,** 195

Hunter, C. G., captures Alvarado against orders, **III,** 383

Hunter, David, issues emancipation proclamation, **II,** 205; enlists Negroes in the Civil War, **IV,** 84; and the Shenandoah campaign, **V,** 68; and battle at Trevilian Station, **V,** 323

Hunter, George, aids in Dunbar's Expedition, **II,** 176; and western exploration, **V,** 442

Hunter, R. M. T., and the Confederate Congress, **II,** 6; and Hampton Roads Conference, **III,** 7

Hunter, Robert, as governor of colony of New York, **IV,** 115; and land speculation in New York, **IV,** 115

Hunter, William, and colonial postal service, **IV,** 321

"Hunters," and the Patriot War, **IV,** 224

Hunting Grounds, and Indian migration, **V,** 65

Huntington, Collis P., and great fortunes, **II,** 312; and the Southern Pacific Railroad Company, **V,** 130; and construction race between Texas and Pacific, and Southern Pacific Railways, **V,** 255

Huntington, Henry E., art collection of, **I,** 124; and book collecting, **I,** 212; **III,** 273

Huntington, Samuel, signer of the Declaration of Independence, **II,** 123

Hunt's *Merchant's Magazine,* **V,** 298

Hurd, J. C., political writings of, **IV,** 302

Hurd, Jacob, silversmith, **V,** 82

Hurd v. Railroad Bridge Company, **IV,** 497

Hurdy-Gurdies, **III,** 43

Hurlbut, S. A., commander in chief of Grand Army of the Republic, **II,** 407

Huron, Lake, visited by Champlain, **II,** 344

Huron Indians, and Champlain, **I,** 339; raided by Iroquois with guns, **III,** 92; and the Iroquois league, **III,** 159; and Jesuit missions, **III,** 174; destroyed by the Iroquois, **III,** 391; and Great Indian Council at Niagara, **IV,** 130; attack Oneidas at Nichols Pond, **IV,** 132; and the Ottawa Indians, **IV,** 191; and Sandusky, **V,** 27; and the Senecas, **V,** 58. *See also* Wyandot Indians

Hurricanes, and climate, **I,** 398; Florida, **II,** 287

Hurst, Cecil, and the League of Nations, **III,** 255

Huse, Caleb, Confederate agent, **II,** 5

Husking Bees, **I,** 69, 174

Hussey, Obed, and the reaper, **II,** 247; **III,** 363; **IV,** 419

Hutchins, Thomas, surveys the Geographer's

Line, **II**, 377; and Seven Ranges survey, **V**, 60; first official Surveyor and Geographer of the United States, **V**, 210; and topographic mapping, **V**, 283; and Vincennes, **V**, 369; shows Great Warriors Path on his map, **V**, 408

Hutchin's Almanac, **I**, 52

Hutchinson, Anne, and the Antinomian Controversy, **I**, 82; and heresy trials, **III**, 27; banishment of, **III**, 147, 357

Hutchinson, Thomas, and the Pejepscot purchase, **IV**, 239

Hutchinson, Thomas, and Boston Tea Party, **I**, 224; royal governor of Massachusetts, **III**, 356

Hutchinson's Republican Songster for the Campaign of 1860, **I**, 294

Huterian Brethren, communities of, **I**, 440

Hyatt, Thaddeus, and match-making machinery, **III**, 359

Hyde, Edward, and Cary's rebellion, **I**, 321

Hyde, Udney, and Champaign County rescue cases, **I**, 338

Hyde Expedition, **I**, 209

Hydroelectric Power, beginning of, **II**, 197; at Elephant Butte Dam, **II**, 200; and Tennessee Valley Authority, **V**, 245; and the turbine, **V**, 330; and water power, **V**, 422

Hydrographic Office, and Bowditch's *Navigator,* **I**, 230; publications of, **IV**, 76

Hyer, Tom, prize fighter, **IV**, 352

Hygiene, and prostitution, **IV**, 365

Hylton v. U. S., **I**, 319

Hynson, Joseph, as a spy, **V**, 146

I

Iberville, Pierre le Moyne, settles Biloxi, **I**, 188; **III**, 305; erects Fort Maurepas, **III**, 360; founds Biloxi, **III**, 420; on the Mississippi River, **III**, 424; establishes Biloxi, **III**, 425; and lead mining, **V**, 8; visits the Taënsa Indians, **V**, 216

Iberville River, and Isle of Orleans, **III**, 161; and Manchac, **III**, 330; and West Florida controversy, **V**, 436

Icarian Colony, and the Socialist movement, **V**, 110

Ice. *See* Refrigeration

Ice Cream, **II**, 105

Idaho, organized, and admitted, **V**, 249

Ide, William B., and erection of the Republic of California, **I**, 171

Illegitimacy, and sex relations, **V**, 62

Illinoia, Jefferson's proposed state, **III**, 173

Illinois, military tract of, **III**, 403; organized, and admitted, **V**, 248

Illinois and Michigan Canal, as influence on agriculture, **I**, 33; and Chicago, **I**, 356; and Chicago Portage, **I**, 358; and state credit, **III**, 68;

and internal improvements, **III**, 138; completed, **III**, 231; subsidies granted to, **V**, 194

Illinois and Wabash Company, and land speculation, **III**, 239

Illinois Central Railroad, and Cairo, **I**, 267; grant to, **III**, 237; and public land, **IV**, 407

Illinois College, and Illinois Band, **III**, 70; and Yale Band, **V**, 500

Illinois Country, British plan to recapture, **I**, 240; and *coutume de Paris,* **II**, 76; problem of British occupation of, **II**, 90; and D'Artaguette's defeat, **II**, 110; and Denonville's invasion, **II**, 137; Indians driven westward to, **III**, 211

Illinois Creek, battle at. *See* Prairie Grove, battle at

Illinois Herald, begun by Matthew Duncan, **IV**, 124, 126

Illinois Indians, Croghan makes formal treaty with, **II**, 90; and the Fox, **II**, 320; raided by Iroquois with guns, **III**, 92; Jesuit mission established for, **III**, 174; and Johnson and Graham's Lessee v. McIntosh, **III**, 178; Great Village of the, founded near Starved Rock, **V**, 161

Illinois State Journal, as mouthpiece of Abraham Lincoln, **IV**, 129

Illinois State Register, as political organ, **IV**, 129

Illinois Warehouse Act, regulates grain elevators, **II**, 201

Illustrated Daily News, and tabloids, **V**, 216

I'm Alone Case, arbitration of, **I**, 96; and Canadian-American relations, **I**, 301

Imboden, J. D., at Bull Run, **I**, 251; in battle of New Market, **IV**, 106

Immaculate Conception, Mission of the, at Kaskaskia, **III**, 174, 199

Immediatist Doctrine, **I**, 85

Immigrants, return of, **II**, 211; and quarantine, **IV**, 387; and the urban drift, **V**, 352

Immigration, and alien landholding, **I**, 49; and Americanization, **I**, 67; and assimilation, **I**, 130; and foreign trade, **I**, 147; encouraged during Civil War, **I**, 388; restriction of, and democratization, **II**, 136; and Ellis Island, **II**, 203; and foreign language press, **II**, 302; French-Canadian, **II**, 343; German, **II**, 383; and internal improvements, **III**, 139; Irish, **III**, 153; Italian, **III**, 163; and labor, **III**, 219; and naturalization services, **III**, 221; and the literacy test, **III**, 283; and manufacturing, **III**, 337; and growth of New York City, **IV**, 119; Norwegian, **IV**, 152; and population, **IV**, 311; and the quota system, **IV**, 391; and race elements in America, **IV**, 392; and religion, **IV**, 442; Scotch-Irish, **V**, 45; and slums, **V**, 99; Swedish, **V**, 213; Swiss, **V**, 214; Welsh, **V**, 434; and the westward movement, **V**, 451

Immigration Act of 1907, and Japanese exclusion, III, 168

Immigration Act of 1924, and Free State quota, III, 154; and Japanese exclusion, III, 168

Immigration Laws, and Chinese, I, 367

Impeachment, of Justice Chase, I, 348; in Congress, II, 19; and the Constitution, II, 31; of Andrew Johnson, V, 246

Impending Crisis. See Helper's *Impending Crisis*

Imperial Dam, I, 50, 428

Imperialism, and campaign of 1900, I, 289; reaction against, I, 314; and foreign policy, II, 304; and treaty of Paris (1898), IV, 217

Implied Powers, and Congress, II, 17; and the Constitution, II, 34; and Indian policy, III, 105; and investigating committees, III, 149; and Juilliard v. Greenman, III, 189; and loose construction, III, 301; and McCulloch v. Maryland, III, 364; and reserved powers of states, IV, 458

Import Duties, V, 226

Imports. *See* Trade, Foreign

Impressment of Seamen, and Anglo-American relations, I, 74; in the *Baltimore* incident, I, 151; and the Embargo, II, 207; and treaty of Ghent, II, 387; and the *Leander* incident, III, 256; and the Monroe-Pinkney treaty, IV, 15; and neutrality, IV, 89; and the press gang, IV, 337; in the War of 1812, V, 404

Imprisonment for Debt, II, 53

"In God We Trust," inscription on coins, I, 412

In His Steps, written by Charles Monroe Sheldon, I, 180

Inauguration of the President, change in date of, III, 232

Incandescent Lamp, Edison credited with producing, II, 195; development of, II, 197; invention of, III, 148; and lighting, III, 277; patented by Edison, IV, 223

Income Tax Cases, and the Supreme Court, V, 207

Income Taxes, an issue in campaign of 1896, I, 288; and Collector v. Day, I, 413; and the Gorman-Wilson tariff, II, 401; and the Greenback party, II, 424; as internal revenue, III, 139; and Pollock v. Farmers Loan and Trust Co., IV, 303; and the public revenue, IV, 462; and the Secret Service, V, 53; and the Sixteenth Amendment, V, 87; upheld in Springer v. U. S., V, 150; adopted in 1894, V, 226; as direct taxes, V, 230; and the Federal taxing power, V, 231

Indentured Servants, in agriculture, I, 27; and apprenticeship, I, 92; redemptioners as, IV, 432; as teachers, V, 43; and sex relations, V, 62; slaves as, V, 91; and slavery, V, 93

Independence, Declaration, II, 120 ff.; and the Definitive Treaty of Peace (1783), II, 128

Independence, Mo., as starting point of caravan traffic, I, 312; and the central route, I, 334; as assembling place for wagon trains, II, 77; and the Santa Fé Trail, V, 30; and western merchants, V, 444; and Westport, V, 449

Independence, The, ship-of-the-line, V, 75

Independence, The, and the Texas navy, V, 256

Independence, The, first steamboat to ascend the Missouri, III, 430

Independence Gold Mine, II, 396

Independence Hall, architecture of, I, 99

Independent, Harper's Weekly consolidates with, III, 12; as a religious periodical, IV, 445

Independent Chronicle, "Decius" letters appear in, II, 120

Independent Journal, II, 264

Independents. *See* Separatists

Indian, The, treaties made with, at army posts, I, 117; and army on the frontier, I, 117; and the Articles of Confederation, I, 126; northwest confederacy of, and border forts, I, 219; as a camp follower, I, 279; education of, I, 314; and the covenant chain, II, 77; education of, II, 110; tribal relationships of, II, 113; and the gun, II, 359; and liquor, II, 359, 362; education of, III, 15; treaties with, III, 105; and miscegenation, III, 415; and the American Missionary Association, III, 416; and Moravians, IV, 22; treaties with, V, 85; and the tomahawk, V, 279; and the War Department, V, 402; and Wheeler-Howard Act, V, 454; and William and Mary College, V, 467

Indian Affairs, Commissioner of, III, 106

Indian Affairs, Office of, and education, II, 189; and Indian treaties, III, 96; removed from War Department, III, 135

Indian Barrier State, and Anglo-American relations, I, 74; and treaty of Ghent, II, 387; and Indian trade, III, 110; and Jay's treaty, III, 169; proposed, IV, 150; and the War of 1812, V, 406

Indian Bible, printing of, IV, 345

Indian Bureau, and the army on the frontier, I, 117

Indian Captivities, I, 216

Indian Commissions, and the treaty of Fort Laramie (1868), III, 246

Indian Country, Dakota Territory known as, II, 106; Sully organizes for march into, II, 106; set aside by Indian Intercourse Act, III, 98; reduced by land cessions, III, 101; and Indian removal, III, 107; Great Plains as, IV, 282; and pre-emption, IV, 330; and the Red River raft, IV, 432

Indian Factory System, II, 238; III, 105; V, 302

Indian Intercourse Act (1834), and agency system,

III, 90; undertakes to define Indian Country, III, 106; and Indian removal, III, 107

Indian Land Cessions, and Congress of Augusta (1763), I, 138; and Black Hawk Purchase, I, 194; and Camden-Yorke opinion, I, 278; and treaties of Indian Springs, III, 108; and treaty of LaPointe, III, 245; and Medicine Creek Council, III, 370; of the Miamis, III, 390; of the Osage, IV, 189; and the Great Plains, IV, 282; and treaty of Pontotoc, IV, 306; and Saginaw treaty, V, 5; of the Sioux, V, 86; and the Trail of Tears, V, 303; and treaty of Traverse des Sioux, V, 312; and treaty of Vincennes, V, 370

Indian Missions, and philanthropy, IV, 260

Indian Oratory, II, 184; III, 96, 294

Indian Paths, II, 420, 421; IV, 493

Indian Policy, and the army on the frontier, I, 117; and Burke Act, I, 256; colonial, III, 90; Quaker, IV, 385

Indian Pottery, IV, 325

Indian Queen Tavern, V, 224

Indian Removal, policy of, II, 140; and land treaties, III, 89; and Indian Country, III, 96; and Indian Intercourse Act, III, 98; and National Indian policy, III, 106; and treaty of Payne's Landing, IV, 229; and the Great Plains, IV, 282; and profiteering, IV, 355; and the Act of 1830, IV, 448; and the Trail of Tears, V, 303; and western merchants, V, 445

Indian Reservations, created in Dakota Territory, II, 106; and the Dawes General Allotment Act, II, 113; and Indian policy, III, 106; inclosure of lands on, forbidden, IV, 178

Indian Rights Association, IV, 385

Indian Stream Republic, and the gore, II, 401

Indian Territory, and Anti-Horse Thief Association, I, 81; and boomer movement, I, 215; creation of, III, 97; and Indian removal, III, 108; division of Northwest Territory, IV, 151; and Oklahoma, IV, 168; and Oklahoma squatters, IV, 169; and proposed state of Sequoyah, V, 58; and "sooners," V, 121

Indian Trade, and Congress of Augusta (1763), I, 138; and the Proclamation of 1763, IV, 354; and the West India trade, V, 437

Indian Wars, Veterans of, V, 365

Indian Wars and Campaigns, V, 410

Indiana, state bank of, V, 163; organized and admitted, V, 248

Indiana, The, and blockade of Santiago, V, 31; one of the first American battleships, V, 412

Indiana Company, organized, I, 170; and land speculation, III, 239; and "suffering traders," V, 198; and western land schemes, V, 443

Indiana Gazette, established by Elihu Stout, IV, 124, 126

Indiana Territory, creation of, II, 155

Indianapolis Auto Races, I, 139

Indianola, The, the ironclad destroyed by the Confederates, I, 168

Indies, Company of the, and the Ursulines, V, 353

Indigo, and the plantation system, I, 27; bounties for raising, I, 228; as colonial staple, V, 159; and domestic trade, V, 292; and foreign trade, V, 294

Industrial Farms, and prison reform, IV, 349

Industrial Management, and machines, III, 320; and piece work, IV, 267; introduced by Frederick W. Taylor, V, 236; and technology, V, 237

Industrial Management, business paper, V, 298

Industrial Property Convention of 1883, V, 317

Industrial Research, III, 118, 338

Industrial Revolution, and inventions, I, 218; and engineering, II, 214; and machines, III, 320

Industrial Workers of the World, and antisyndicalist laws, I, 86; and class struggle, I, 395; and organized labor, III, 219; and the Lawrence strike, III, 253; and one big union, IV, 173; introduce sabotage, V, 1; and syndicalism, V, 215; as an industrial union, V, 344; Western Federation of Miners ally with, V, 443

Industrialism, and the agrarian movement, I, 21; and distribution of wealth, V, 429

Industry, Fort, Treaty of, II, 275

Inflation, and the agrarian movement, I, 21; and the Federal deficit, II, 128; and Jeffersonian Democracy, III, 172; and "managed currency," IV, 8; and the panic of 1873, IV, 209; and the Resumption Act, IV, 461; and silver legislation, V, 80; in war, V, 397

Inflation Bill (1874), vetoed by Grant, V, 144

Influenza, epidemic of, II, 221

Ingalls, Kans., and county-seat wars, II, 74

Ingersoll, E. P., launches first automotive trade journal, I, 140

Ingersoll, Jared, nominated for Vice-Presidency, I, 282; signer of the Constitution, II, 39; and the Philadelphia cordwainers' case, IV, 259; colonial agent, and the Stamp Act, V, 155

Ingersoll, Robert G., "Plumed Knight" speech, I, 286; and free-thinking, II, 340; and lecturing, III, 260; and oratory, IV, 180

Inglefield, E. A., searches for Sir John Franklin, IV, 292

Ingles, Mary (Mrs. William), and Burning Spring, I, 256; captured by the Shawnee Indians, II, 166

Ingles, Mrs., comes to Kentucky, III, 204

Ingles, Thomas, and Draper's Meadows, II, 166

Ingraham, Prentiss, writer of outdoor adventure stories, II, 147

Ingram, David, and settlements about the Kennebec River, III, 203

Inherent Power, eminent domain as, II, 211; and reserved powers of states, IV, 458

Inheritance Taxes, as internal revenue, III, 139; IV, 462; V, 226

Initiative, adopted in Arkansas, I, 105; and municipal charters, I, 347; an experiment in democracy, II, 135; and election laws, II, 191; and the franchise, II, 323; and the legislature, III, 263; and the Oregon system, IV, 185; and state constitutions, V, 167

Injunction, and the American Railway Union, I, 65; and arrest, I, 121; in Buck Stove and Range case, I, 246; an issue in campaign of 1896, I, 288; and the Clayton Act, I, 396; and freedom for organized labor, II, 336; government by, II, 402; and the Hitchman case, III, 35; and Norris-LaGuardia Act, IV, 143; issued in the Pullman Strike, IV, 381; and the railway shopmen's strike of 1922, IV, 410; and restraint of trade, IV, 461

Inkpaduta, and Spirit Lake massacre, V, 146

Inland Waterways, and the Corps of Engineers, II, 216

Inland Waterways Commission, II, 27

Inman, Henry, painter, I, 123

Innes, Harry, and the Spanish conspiracy, V, 140

Inness, George, landscape painter, I, 123

Innocents, The, or Plummer's gang, IV, 290

Inns. See Taverns

Inquiry, Power of, and Kilbourn v. Thompson, III, 209

Inquiry, The, and the World War Peace Conference, V, 489

Insane, The, and philanthropy and benevolence, IV, 260

Insignia of Rank in Army, I, 114; V, 341

Installment Plan, I, 141; IV, 28

Institute of Mining Engineers, II, 215

Instructions to Colonial Governors, I, 419

Insular Cases, II, 133; IV, 380

Insular Possessions, and Federal taxing power, V, 231; and the Naval Treaty of Washington (1922), V, 414

Insull, Samuel, extradition of, II, 237

Insull Utility Investments, II, 196

Insurance, of bank deposits, I, 154, 157, 158; old-age, IV, 170; and railroad brotherhoods, IV, 400

Insurance Companies, and the Reconstruction Finance Corporation, IV, 428; and the stock market, V, 182. See also Unemployment Insurance

Insurance Company of North America, III, 129

Insurance Investigation, and the Tontine plan, V, 281

Insurgente-Constellation Engagement, IV, 73

Insurrection, and military aid to the civil power, III, 399

Interborough Rapid Transit Company, V, 197

Interchangeable Parts, in chair making, I, 337; in clockmaking, I, 402; and rise of agricultural machinery, II, 248; Whitney's system of, III, 148; and machines, III, 320; in manufacturing, III, 336; and mass production, III, 353; and munitions, IV, 44

Intercollegiate Football Association, II, 298

Intercollegiate Socialist Society, and youth movements, V, 511

Intercolonial Congress (1689–91), I, 420

Interlocking Directorates, and the Clayton Act, I, 396; and the Federal Trade Commission, II, 264; and monopoly, IV, 12

Internal Combustion Engine, III, 337

Internal Improvements, and the agrarian movement, I, 20; and the American system, I, 65; English investments in, I, 147; and Bonus Bill, I, 211; and Indiana state canals, III, 113; and the Maysville Veto, III, 362; and the panic of 1791, IV, 208; and the public domain, IV, 370; and the Republican party (Jeffersonian), IV, 454; and sectionalism, V, 54; and distribution of surplus revenue, V, 209; and the General Survey Act of 1824, V, 209

Internal Revenue, and drawbacks, II, 167; as source of public revenue, IV, 462; collectors of, V, 314. See also Excise Taxes

International Harvester Company, and the development of farm machinery, II, 248

International Joint Commission, creation of, I, 301; investigations of, I, 301; and Great Lakes-St. Lawrence Waterway, II, 416; set up by Boundary Waters Treaty of 1909, V, 317; and the Waterways Treaty, V, 425

International Labor Organization, rejected by the Treaty of Berlin (1921), I, 179; and joint resolutions, V, 319; established by Treaty of Versailles, V, 364

International Law, and armed neutrality, I, 108; and belligerents, I, 176; and the doctrine of continuous voyage, II, 142; and exchange of prisoners, II, 231; and intervention, III, 145; and neutrality, IV, 88; and Proclamation of Neutrality, IV, 91; and Pan-American conferences, IV, 202; codification of, IV, 235; and prize courts, IV, 352; and policy of recognition, IV, 424; retaliation in, IV, 461; and the submarine, V, 192 f.

International Mercantile Marine Company, III, 376

International Nickel Company, IV, 132

International Peace Garden, IV, 146

International Postal Convention, IV, 320

International Telephone and Telegraph Corporation, **IV**, 322

International Treaties, and state boundaries, **I**, 226

Interstate Barriers, and the Constitution, **II**, 35; and inspection acts, **III**, 126

Interstate Commerce, and the Addyston Pipe Company case, **I**, 10; and centralization, **I**, 334; and the Debs case, **II**, 116; and Federal Trade Commission, **II**, 264; and steamboat monopoly rights, **II**, 388; and the Greenback party, **II**, 424; and the license cases, **III**, 275; and Munn v. Illinois, **IV**, 46; and original-package doctrine, **IV**, 187; and Railroad Retirement Board v. Alton Railroad Company, **IV**, 404; and Schechter v. U. S., **V**, 38

Interstate Commerce Act, influence on agriculture, **I**, 34; and Big Business, **I**, 259; and railroad regulation, **I**, 310; and Court of Commerce, **I**, 432; develops out of the findings of the Cullom committee, **II**, 95; supplemented by the Elkins Act, **II**, 203

Interstate Commerce Commission, as administrative agency, **I**, 11; created, **I**, 260; and Civil Aeronautics Act, **I**, 380; and Court of Commerce, **I**, 432; and the commerce clause, **I**, 433; and congressional regulation, **II**, 17; and government regulation, **II**, 405; and Hepburn Act, **III**, 27; and the judiciary, **III**, 186; uses merit system, **III**, 377; urged to regulate all water carriers, **IV**, 64; and railroad pools, **IV**, 307; and the Pope-McGill Farm Act of 1938, **IV**, 308; as a quasi-judicial agency, **IV**, 388; and Railroad Administration, **IV**, 400; and railroad rate laws, **IV**, 402, 404; and railroads, **IV**, 408; defines rebates, **IV**, 420; and the recapture clause, **IV**, 421; and the Reconstruction Finance Corporation, **IV**, 428; and Shreveport rate case, **V**, 77; and Wisconsin Railroad Commission case, **V**, 474

Interstate Commission, on the Delaware River Basin, **IV**, 438; on the Ohio River Basin, **IV**, 438; on the Delaware River Basin (Incodel), **V**, 175; on Conflicting Taxation, **V**, 175; on the Ohio River Basin (Incohio), **V**, 175; on Crime, **V**, 175

Interstate Compacts, and the Constitution, **V**, 174; authorized by the Weeks Act, **V**, 433

Interstate Co-operation, **V**, 175

Intervention, and the Civil War, **I**, 391 f.; and the Monroe Doctrine, **IV**, 13

Intestate Estates, **I**, 89

Intolerable Acts, **I**, 408; **IV**, 467; **V**, 373

Intrepid, The, in the Barbary wars, **I**, 162; a ketch, **III**, 207

Inventions, and shoemaking industry, **I**, 218; and manufacturing, **III**, 337; the phonograph, **IV**, 264; photography, **IV**, 265; telegraph, **V**, 238; telephone, **V**, 239; television, **V**, 239; typewriter, **V**, 336; voting machine, **V**, 384; and wages and prices, **V**, 388

Investment Banking, **I**, 158

Investors, and the national income, **III**, 82

Invincible, The, and the Texas navy, **V**, 256

Iowa, organized and admitted, **V**, 249

Iowa, The, and the blockade of Santiago, **V**, 31

Iowa Indians, removal of, **III**, 107; and Oklahoma openings, **IV**, 169; party to treaty of Prairie du Chien, **IV**, 329

Iowa-Missouri Boundary Dispute, **I**, 227; **III**, 43

Iowa Territory, Dakota becomes part of (1838), **II**, 106

Iredell, James, and pamphleteering, **IV**, 202

Ireland, Archbishop, and the Faribault Plan, **II**, 244

Ireson, Floyd, tarred and feathered, **V**, 220

Irish, The, and colonial society, **I**, 424

Irish-Americans, and the Fenian movement, **II**, 267

Irish Immigration, **III**, 74

Iron, smelting of, **I**, 199; and domestic trade, **V**, 293; in the triangular trade, **V**, 296

Iron Act of 1750, and colonial commerce, **I**, 418; and British colonial policy, **I**, 422; passage of, **II**, 309; and restriction of colonial manufactures, **III**, 335

Iron and Steel Engineers' Association, and safety first movement, **V**, 4

Iron Furnaces, Spotswood's, **V**, 149

Iron Industry, in the colonies, **II**, 309; **III**, 119; and manufacturing, **III**, 338; of Pittsburgh, **IV**, 280; and the Principio Company, **IV**, 343; in Rhode Island, **IV**, 478; and domestic trade, **V**, 292; and foreign trade, **V**, 294; and Tredegar Iron Works, **V**, 319; and the United States Steel Corporation, **V**, 348

Iron Mining, bog, **I**, 207; and the Marquette Iron Range, **III**, 345; and the Menominee Iron Range, **III**, 373; and Mesabi Iron Range, **III**, 379; in the colonies, **III**, 406; in Minnesota, **III**, 411; in Pennsylvania, **IV**, 243; and construction of St. Marys Falls Ship Canal, **V**, 14

"Iron Mountain" Railroad, **III**, 345

Ironclad Oath, and Test Laws, **V**, 250

Ironclad Rams, **IV**, 414

Ironclads, in the Civil War, **I**, 390; introduced by Confederate navy, **II**, 8; first Federal fleet of, **II**, 180; in operations at Island Number Ten, **III**, 161; and the Mississippi Squadron, **III**, 425; and battle of the *Monitor* and *Merrimack*, **IV**, 10; and monitors, **IV**, 10; attack Fort Sumter, **V**, 203; as warships, **V**, 411

Irondequoit Bay, rendezvous of Denonville's men in invasion of Iroquois, **II**, 137

Irons, Martin, and railroad strikes of 1886, **IV**, 405

Iroquois Indians, and the Albany Congress, I, 45; make war on the Algonquins, I, 48; annihilate the Cat nation, I, 322; and Champlain, I, 339; Sullivan expedition against, I, 354; LaSalle erects fort as protection against, II, 87; acknowledged to be English subjects by Treaty of Utrecht, II, 93; and the Delaware Indians, II, 131; French determine to subdue, II, 137; and the Treaty of Easton (1758), II, 183; and Lake Erie, II, 223; form confederacy, II, 320; and French claims in Ohio, II, 344; and destruction of Onondaga, II, 350; on the Great Lakes, II, 415; and the Great Trading and War Path, II, 420; and "burying the hatchet," III, 16; confederacy founded by Hiawatha, III, 29; at war with the Hurons, III, 61; destroy Great Village of the Illinois, III, 69; war with the Illinois, III, 71; in the Revolution, III, 88; and the gun, III, 92; make treaty at Lancaster, III, 99; removal of, III, 107; houses of, III, 111; Jesuit missions among, III, 175; in King William's War, III, 211; raid at Lachine, III, 226; on Lake Champlain, III, 229; and LaSalle's explorations, III, 246; at Logstown, III, 295; and Treaty of Logstown, III, 295; long houses of, III, 298; destroy the Huron nation, III, 391; Mingos as, III, 408; and the Mohawk Valley, IV, 5; humbled by New France, IV, 101; and the New York and Genesee Company, IV, 117; and Great Indian Council at Niagara, IV, 130; and the Ohio Valley, IV, 165; and Great Council House at Onondaga, IV, 175; defeat the Hurons, IV, 191; and Fort Plain, IV, 281; humbled by New France, IV, 316; and scalping, V, 37; Seneca Indians as part of the confederacy, V, 58; and the Shawnee and Delaware, V, 65; and treaties of Fort Stanwix, V, 159; and "suffering traders," V, 198; and the Sullivan-Clinton campaign, V, 201; and the Susquehannah Company, V, 211; subjugate the Susquehannock, V, 211; and Treaty of Utrecht, V, 354; and Virginia v. Transylvania Company, V, 380; and the Walking Purchase, V, 392; and wampum, V, 394; and settlement of interior New York, V, 450; and the White Woman of the Genesee, V, 460; and the Wyoming massacre, V, 497. See also Six Nations

Iroquois Theater Fire, II, 276

Iroquois Trail, III, 104

Irrigation, and agricultural adaptation to the plains, I, 22; and the All American Canal, I, 50; and climate, I, 400; and the conservation movement, II, 27; and Grand Coulee Dam, II, 408; and reclamation, IV, 423; and the Rocky Mountains, IV, 498; subsidies provided for, V, 195; in Utah, V, 353; and the water law, V, 421; public lands set aside for, V, 423

Irrigation Districts, as a political subdivision, IV, 299

Irvine, William, repairs Fort Pitt, IV, 280

Irving, Pierre M., author of Life and Letters of Washington Irving, I, 190

Irving, Washington, biographical works of, I, 189; and story of Rip Van Winkle, I, 325; and "burying the hatchet," III, 16; and Rip Van Winkle, IV, 487; and Sleepy Hollow, V, 97

Isaacs, John D., and motion pictures, IV, 31

Iselin, Isaac, and great fortunes, II, 312

Island Number Ten, evacuation of, I, 317; taken during Civil War, I, 389; and Army of the Mississippi, III, 419; evacuation of, III, 419; and the Mississippi Squadron, III, 425

Isle of Orleans, bounded by Iberville River, III, 65

Isle of Pines, and the Platt Amendment, IV, 286; Treaty of 1904, V, 318

Isles of Shoals, and the Laconia grant, III, 226; Mason's title to, III, 351

Isthmian Canal, and the Biddle mission, I, 183; and Bryan-Chamorro treaty, I, 245; and the Clayton-Bulwer treaty, I, 396; influence of Mexican War on the, III, 387

Isthmian Canal Commission, and Nicaraguan Canal project, IV, 132

Italian Government, and indemnities, III, 84

Italian Race Riots, IV, 394

Italy, treaties with, V, 318

Item Veto, and legislative riders, IV, 482

Iuka, Army of the Mississippi fights at, III, 419

Ives, Brayton, book collector, I, 212

Ives, James M., and colored prints, II, 101

Ives, Joseph C., and scientific exploration of the Colorado River, I, 427; and the Grand Canyon, II, 408

Ives, L. S., conversion of, and the Oxford movement, IV, 194

Izard, Mark W., territorial governor of Nebraska, IV, 80

J

J. M. White, The, sets steamboat record, V, 178, 179

Jack, Capt., and battles of Tule Lake, V, 329

"Jack Harkaway," stories of, II, 147

Jack Rabbits, can exist without water, II, 170

Jackman, S. D., and action at Glasgow, II, 391

Jackson, Andrew, raids East Florida (1818), I, 98; and the United States Army, I, 113; leads backwoodsmen in Creek War and Battle of New Orleans, I, 145; dispute with Biddle, I, 155; prejudice against banks, I, 156; and campaign of 1824, I, 282; elected President (1828), I, 282; censured by Congress, I, 332; negotiates treaty

of Chickasaw Council House, I, 360; conducts campaign against the Creeks, II, 86; and the Democratic party, II, 136; and the formation of the Democratic Republicans, II, 136; establishes Fort Deposit, II, 139; negotiates treaty of Doak's Stand, II, 156; duels with Charles Dickinson, II, 174; defeats the Creeks, II, 184; and the battles of Emucfau Village and Enotachapco Creek, II, 213; and "Our Federal Union! It must and shall be preserved!", II, 264; invades East Florida, II, 290; and the Force Acts, II, 299; and French Spoliation claims, II, 328, 347; builds Fort Gadsden, II, 365; and government ownership, II, 404; buys Hermitage Plantation, III, 28; and the homestead movement, III, 42; attacks at Horseshoe Bend, III, 50; closes the Iberville River, III, 66; inauguration of, III, 82; and Indian removal, III, 106, 107; opposes internal improvements, III, 137; and the "kitchen cabinet," III, 213; strict constructionist, III, 269; establishes martial law in New Orleans, III, 347; and the Maysville veto, III, 362; attacks the Second Bank of the United States, IV, 9; and mutiny, IV, 50; and the National Republican party, IV, 62; and Battle of New Orleans, IV, 110; and the *United States Telegraph*, IV, 128; denounces nullification, IV, 154; called "Old Hickory," IV, 170; and "Our Federal Union! It must and shall be preserved!", IV, 191; and the panic of 1837, IV, 208; and political patronage, IV, 224; seizes Pensacola, IV, 250; makes office of Postmaster General a Cabinet position, IV, 317; Bank Veto, as presidential message, IV, 336; alarmed by the Northern attack upon slavery, IV, 363; and policy of recognition, IV, 424; and the executive power of removal, IV, 447; and the Removal Act of 1830, IV, 448; and removal of deposits, IV, 448; and alignment of National and Democratic Republicans, IV, 454; and the Rhea Letter, IV, 477; and rotation in office, IV, 503; occupies St. Marks, V, 13; leads expedition against Seminoles, V, 57; invades Florida, V, 135; and the spoils system, V, 147; and distribution of surplus revenue, V, 209; and battle of Talladega, V, 217; and battle at Tallasahatchee, V, 217; and the Tariff of Abominations, V, 223; and annexation of Texas, V, 251; and third-term doctrine, V, 263; signs treaty with the Creeks at Fort Jackson, V, 286; attacks at Villere's plantation, V, 369; born in the Waxhaws, V, 426; and the Whig party, V, 455; whispering campaigns against, V, 458; and Worcester v. Georgia, V, 484

Jackson, Charles T., and anæsthesia, I, 72

Jackson, Chevalier, and the bronchoscope, III, 370

Jackson, Claiborne F., attacked by Sigel at Carthage, I, 320; and the secession movement in Missouri, II, 3; attempts to keep Missouri neutral during the Civil War, IV, 339

Jackson, David, and caravan traffic on the Great Plains, I, 312; mountain man, II, 362; and the Rocky Mountain Fur Company, IV, 498; and Ashley's expeditions, V, 310

Jackson, Fort, erected, III, 29; later name for Fort Toulouse, V, 286

Jackson, Fort, Treaty of, Creeks lose much land by, II, 86; Creek War ended by, II, 87; and battle of Fowltown, II, 319; and Indian land cessions, III, 100

Jackson, Fred S., and prohibition in Kansas, III, 195

Jackson, George, as a prospector, IV, 364

Jackson, H. E., and Pollock v. Farmers Loan and Trust Company, IV, 303

Jackson, James, aids Wayne in Georgia, II, 381; and the Yazoo fraud, V, 503

Jackson, James, and tuberculosis, V, 328

Jackson, Mich., Republican party formally adopts its name at, IV, 454

Jackson, Richard, colonial agent, I, 415

Jackson, Thomas J. ("Stonewall"), and battle of Antietam, I, 81; at Bull Run, I, 251; at Second Bull Run, I, 251; and battle of Cedar Mountain, I, 330; fatally wounded at Chancellorsville, I, 340; and battle of Chantilly, I, 341; and the Valley Campaign, II, 91; and battle of Frayser's Farm, II, 330; and the Barbara Fritchie legend, II, 349; and battle of Front Royal, II, 349; and battle of Gaines' Mill, II, 366; and battle of Groveton, II, 426; and capture of Harpers Ferry, III, 11; in battle at Kernstown, III, 207; and Lee's Lost Order, III, 303; and invasion of Maryland, III, 349; and battle at McDowell, Va., III, 364; and battle of Mechanicsville, III, 368; and the Valley Campaign, IV, 241; and battle of Port Republic, IV, 315; and Seven Days' battles, V, 59; and the Army of Northern Virginia, V, 371; and battle at White Oak Swamp, V, 460; and battle of Winchester, V, 470

Jackson and St. Philip, Forts, and the Navy in the Civil War, I, 389; as coast defense, I, 405; and opening of the Mississippi, III, 419; bombarded, IV, 28; and capture of New Orleans, IV, 110

Jackson Mining Company, III, 345

Jacksonian Democracy, and the agrarian movement, I, 20; as a new era, II, 135; and the Democratic party, II, 137; and the Presidency, IV, 333; and religion, IV, 443; and state constitutions, V, 167; and the Whig party, V, 455

Jackson's Hole, trappers' rendezvous, II, 362; III, 37

Jacobi, Abraham, and the Forty-eighters, **II**, 313

Jacobs, H. E., and religious thought, **IV**, 447

Jacquard Loom, and carpet manufacture, **I**, 318; and textiles, **V**, 258

Jadwin Plan, of flood protection, **II**, 285

Jail Rock, **II**, 75

James, Alfred, co-founder of the *Territorial Enterprise*, **IV**, 127; first printer of Nevada, **IV**, 346

James, Edwin, climbs Pikes Peak, **III**, 300; **IV**, 269

James, Fort, seizure of (1689), **III**, 263

James, Frank, and the Northfield bank robbery, **IV**, 149

James, Henry, Senior, and Swedenborgianism, **V**, 213

James, Jesse, commemorated by folk singer, **I**, 148; bandit leader, **II**, 88; and the Northfield bank robbery, **IV**, 149

James, Thomas, arrives in Santa Fé, **V**, 30

James, William, and philosophical thought and writings, **IV**, 264; and theological writings, **V**, 261

James Baines, The, Cape Horn ship, **I**, 307

"James Bird," occupational ballad, **I**, 148

James Gang, robbers, **I**, 152; introduce bank holdups, **I**, 156; and train robberies, **V**, 303

James H. Lucas, The, and steamboat racing, **V**, 178

James River, and the Alleghenies, **I**, 51

James River and Kanawha Canal, **III**, 137

James River Company, formed with aid of state funds, **II**, 402; Washington gives his shares in, to Washington and Lee University, **V**, 416

Jamestown (or Hot Water), Battle of, **III**, 51

Jamestown, Va., blacksmith at, **I**, 197; Thomas Dale arrives in, **II**, 107; dress in, **II**, 168; and "fool's gold," **III**, 406; Negro slaves introduced into, **V**, 91; starving time at, **V**, 161; settlement of, **V**, 372

Janeway, Edward Gamaliel, and tuberculosis, **V**, 328

Janson, Eric, founder of Bishop Hill Colony, **I**, 191

Japan, and extraterritoriality, **II**, 238; Perry's expedition to, **IV**, 253; treaties with, **V**, 317, 318

Japanese, in Hawaii, **III**, 18

Japanese Exclusion Acts, and the Yellow Peril, **V**, 505

Japanese Immigration, and California land laws, **I**, 271

Jaquess, J. F., and the peace movement of 1864, **IV**, 233

Jarratt, Devereux, and the Methodists, **III**, 380

Jarvis Island, annexed by the United States, **IV**, 195

Jasper, Sergeant, killed in siege of Savannah (1779), **V**, 36

Jay, Fort, erected on Governors Island, **II**, 406

Jay, John, and antislavery societies, **I**, 58; depositor and stockholder of the Bank of North America, **I**, 154; and the Consular Convention (1782–89), **II**, 44; and the Definitive Treaty of Peace, **II**, 129; diplomatic mission to England, **II**, 147; and *The Federalist*, **II**, 264; and the Jefferson-Burr election dispute, **III**, 170; and pamphleteering, **IV**, 202; and republican form of government, **IV**, 453; as Secretary of Foreign Affairs, **V**, 161; works for repeal of laws contrary to Definitive Treaty of Peace, **V**, 322

Jay, William, and peace movements, **IV**, 233

Jay-Gardoqui Negotiations, and free navigation of the Mississippi, **III**, 422; and Pinckney's Treaty, **IV**, 272; and Spanish-American relations, **V**, 134; and western separatism, **V**, 447

Jayhawkers, or the Regulators, **IV**, 439

Jay's Treaty (1794), and alien landholding, **I**, 49; as it affected aliens, **I**, 50; and Anglo-American relations, **I**, 74; and annexation of territory, **I**, 79; and international arbitration, **I**, 96; and the balance of trade, **I**, 147; and border forts, **I**, 219; and British debts, **I**, 240; and campaign of 1796, **I**, 281; and Canadian-American relations, **I**, 300; British yield Detroit by, **II**, 143; and diplomatic missions, **II**, 148; and Lake Erie, **II**, 224; and Wayne's victory at Fallen Timbers, **II**, 241; and Federalist party, **II**, 264; and Franco-American Alliance, **II**, 327; and Franco-American Misunderstanding, **II**, 327; and Grand Portage, **II**, 409; Fort Miami yielded to the Americans by, **III**, 390; and Michigan, **III**, 391; and mixed commissions, **III**, 431; and Monroe's mission to France, **IV**, 15; and proposed Monroe-Pinkney treaty, **IV**, 15; and Niagara Carrying Place, **IV**, 130; and Fort Niagara, **IV**, 130; and the Northeast boundary, **IV**, 147, 149; and Ogdensburg, **IV**, 159; and peace conferences, **IV**, 231; and the St. Croix River, **V**, 7; and treaties with foreign nations, **V**, 316; and western unity, **V**, 435; and western boundaries, **V**, 441; and western separatism, **V**, 447; and the XYZ affair, **V**, 498

Jazz Singer, part-talking picture, **IV**, 32

Jeannette, The, polar cruise of, **IV**, 292

Jeffers, W. N., and the Paraguay expedition, **IV**, 213

Jefferson, Fort (Fla.), and national monuments, **IV**, 19

Jefferson, Fort (Ohio), and St. Clair's defeat, **V**, 7

Jefferson, Joseph, actor, **V**, 260

Jefferson, Peter, and topographic mapping, **V**, 282

Jefferson, Thomas, and architecture, **I**, 100; and the location of the National Capital, **I**, 132; and the issue of assumption, **I**, 132; depositor

and stockholder of the Bank of North America, I, 154; makes collection of some of the bones found at Big Bone Lick, I, 183; uses Virginia Declaration of Rights as a model in drawing up Declaration of Independence, I, 185; and Burr Conspiracy, I, 208; and book collecting, I, 212; and Burr Conspiracy, I, 257; and Burr Trial, I, 258; elected Vice-President (1796), I, 281; elected President (1800), I, 281; and the location of the National Capital, I, 307; and the westward movement, I, 309; warned of the dangers if agriculture gave place to industry, I, 341; and separation of church and state, I, 371; and the Coast and Geodetic Survey, I, 404; and the disposition of western lands, II, 14; and the drafting of Declaration of Independence, II, 120; signer of the Declaration of Independence, II, 124; and Deism, II, 130; and the origin of the Democratic party, II, 136; and the District of Columbia, II, 153; friend of the DuPonts, II, 177; selects motto, *E Pluribus Unum,* II, 180; and the Embargo, II, 207; and the phrase, "Entangling alliances," II, 219; designs mould board for the plow, II, 247; and gardening, II, 371; and Genêt's mission, II, 377; and gunboats, II, 429; inauguration of, III, 82; and Indian removal, III, 105, 106; and international law, III, 141; and Jay's Treaty, III, 169; saved by Jouett's ride, III, 182; Lafayette visits, III, 227; and Yazoo land fraud, III, 239; interested in scientific discoveries, III, 266; and liberal construction, III, 268; and the Croswell trial, III, 268; influence on liberal thought, III, 269; library of, becomes nucleus of the Library of Congress, III, 273; and the *Little Sarah,* III, 285; and Logan's speech, III, 294; favors lotteries, III, 303; and the Louisiana Purchase, III, 308; and the Mazzei Letter, III, 362; denounces the Mecklenburg Declaration of Independence, III, 368; and the Mediterranean Fund, III, 371; and Miranda's intrigues, III, 414; and the Mobile Act, IV, 1; and money system, IV, 7; and the Monroe-Pinkney treaty, IV, 15; and Monticello, IV, 17; sponsors *National Gazette,* IV, 59; and Natural Bridge of Virginia, IV, 66; and natural rights, IV, 66; and proclamation of neutrality, IV, 91; and the *National Gazette,* IV, 128; and Nonintercourse Acts, IV, 138; and the Ordinance of 1784, IV, 181; and philosophical thought and writings, IV, 263; and the plow, IV, 287; and political theories, IV, 300; writes of cultivating potatoes, IV, 323; encourages DuPont to produce powder, IV, 325; and the Presidency, IV, 333; refuses to be subpœnaed, IV, 334; and primogeniture, IV, 342; alarmed at northern attack upon slavery, IV, 363; and the public domain, IV, 370; and

public land sales, IV, 371; author of American recognition policy, IV, 424; and separation of church and state, IV, 445; and the Republican party, IV, 453; influences the passage of the Ordinance of 1787, IV, 454; and the right of revolution, IV, 472; interested in Mississippi Valley, V, 25; advocates the district school system, V, 39; and secession, V, 51; and Sedition Act of 1798, V, 55; attacks slavery, V, 94; and vaccination, V, 100; and the spoils system, V, 147; commissioned as first Secretary of State, V, 162; and states' rights, V, 175; and strict construction, V, 189; and surveying, V, 210; drafts Declaration of Independence in the Indian Queen Tavern, V, 224; and the Louisiana Purchase, V, 252; and third-term doctrine, V, 263; and town government, V, 287; and negotiation of treaties, V, 315; and the State of Virginia, V, 373; founder of the University of Virginia, V, 375; author of the Kentucky Resolutions, V, 375; secures the Virginia Company of London transcripts, V, 378; approves the Virginia Resolves (1769), V, 379; and warships, V, 411; and the West, V, 435; and western exploration, V, 442; and designs for the White House, V, 459; alumnus of William and Mary College, V, 467; and the XYZ affair, V, 498

Jefferson Barracks, erection of, I, 176

Jefferson-Burr Election Dispute, I, 281; II, 191, 194, 264; V, 334

Jefferson College, founded, III, 420

Jefferson Territory, organized, I, 426

Jeffersonian Democracy, influence of, II, 135; and the Democratic party, II, 136; and the Hartford Wits, III, 15; and the philosophy of inequality, III, 120; and religion, IV, 443

Jefferson's Proposed States, outlined on McMurray's map, V, 283

Jeffries, David, and the Pejepscot purchase, IV, 239

Jeffries, James J., prize fighter, IV, 353

Jeffries, John, makes first balloon crossing of the English Channel, I, 149

Jemison, Mary, called the White Woman of the Genesee, V, 460

Jencks, Joseph, Jr., establishes iron works at Pawtucket, IV, 478

Jenifer, Daniel of St. Thomas, and the Alexandria Conference, I, 47; signer of the Constitution, II, 39

Jenkins, Charles J., and the Georgia Platform, II, 381

Jenkins' Ear, War of, I, 202; II, 116

Jenkins Ferry, Price at, IV, 339; attacked by Kirby-Smith during Red River campaign, IV, 430

Jenks, Joseph, invents a scythe, II, 247

Jenness, J. C., killed in Wagon Box fight, V, 388

Jenney, Elisha, organizer of the Illinois Band, III, 69

Jenney, William LeBaron, architect of the Home Insurance Building in Chicago, I, 101; V, 87

Jennings, Abraham, becomes member of New England Council, IV, 9

Jennings, O. B., stockholder of Standard Oil Company, V, 156

Jennings, W. N., and balloon photographs, I, 35

Jennison, Charles R., and Jayhawkers, III, 168

Jernegan, William L., co-founder of the *Territorial Enterprise*, IV, 127; first printer of Nevada, IV, 346

Jerome, Chauncey, and clockmaking, I, 402

Jerome, William Travers, and the Thaw murder trial, V, 323

Jersey Prison-Ship, I, 243; IV, 347

Jerusalem Community, I, 440

Jervis, John B., and the Michigan Southern Railroad, III, 393

"Jesse James," outlaw ballad, II, 293

Jesuit Relations, and Lake Erie, II, 223; Franquelin's map published in, II, 330; and topographic mapping, V, 282

Jesuits, The, penetrate southern Arizona, I, 104; at Arkansas Post, I, 106; at Fort Beauharnois, I, 172; in California, I, 273, 275; and the Capuchins, I, 312; and Catholic parochial school system, I, 323; and Council Bluffs, II, 71; oppose the *coureurs de bois*, II, 75; in Florida, II, 289; joined by the Franciscans, II, 325; in Georgia, II, 380; on the Great Lakes, II, 415; visit Green Bay, II, 422; and Indian education, III, 86; attempt to Christianize the Indians, III, 103; at Kaskaskia, III, 199; and Maryland, III, 349; in Florida, III, 373; at Michilimackinac, III, 391, 394; expulsion of, III, 418; in Missouri, III, 426; and Fort Owen, IV, 193; and the Pima revolt, IV, 272; and the Pious Fund controversy, IV, 275; Mission of St. Ignace, V, 9; and designation Sault Ste. Marie, V, 34; on Lake Superior, V, 205; and topographic mapping, V, 282; at Tubac, V, 328

Jesup, T. S., and battle at Lundy's Lane, III, 315

Jesús, Antonio Margil de, missionary father, III, 418

Jetties, Eads, II, 180

Jewett, Charles C., and librarians conferences, III, 272

Jewett, S. O., and fiction, II, 270

Jewish Joint Distribution Committee, V, 488

Jews, as political exiles, IV, 296; in Rhode Island, IV, 477

Jig, used to obtain identical parts, III, 133

"Jiggs," comic character, I, 431

"Jim Crow," popular song introduced by T. D. Rice, III, 412

"Jim Crow" Laws, and Plessy v. Ferguson, IV, 287

Jitney, appears in 1914, IV, 33; and urban transportation, V, 305

Jocelyn, Henry, deputy governor of province of Maine, II, 401

Jockey Club of New York, V, 265

Jockey Hollow, encampment at, IV, 28

"Joe Bowers," occupational ballad, I, 148

Jogues, Isaac, on the Great Lakes, II, 415; Jesuit missionary, III, 174; and Sault Ste. Marie, V, 34; on Lake Superior, V, 205

Johansen, Frederik, polar expedition of, IV, 293

"John Brown's Body," and the writing of "Battle Hymn of the Republic," I, 168

John Carter Brown Library, I, 212

John Gilpin, The, famous Cape Horn ship, I, 307

"John Henry," narrative song, I, 148

John Martin's Book, children's magazine, I, 364

John Street Theater, V, 259

Johns Hopkins Medical School, III, 369; V, 477

Johns Hopkins University, and graduate work, I, 414

Johnson, Alexander, and organized charity periodicals, I, 342

Johnson, Allen, editor of *Dictionary of American Biography*, II, 146

Johnson, Andrew, and the appointing power, I, 91; elected Vice-President, I, 285; member of the Committee on the Conduct of the War, I, 436; introduces resolution similar to the Crittenden Resolution, II, 90; offers reward for capture of Jefferson Davis, II, 112; introduces Homestead Bill, III, 42; impeachment trial of, III, 77; and Joint Committee on Reconstruction, III, 179; impeachment trial of, III, 363; nonslaveholder, IV, 141; and pardon and amnesty, IV, 214; and the Presidency, IV, 333; and the Radical Republicans, IV, 395; and Reconstruction, IV, 424 f.; impeachment trial of, IV, 425; plan of Reconstruction, IV, 427; vetoes the Tenure-of-Office Act, IV, 448; and the Republican party, IV, 454; as senator from seceded state, V, 50; and Soldiers and Sailors Conventions, V, 117; and the Supreme Court, V, 206; and Supreme Court Packing Bills, V, 208; and "Swinging Round the Circle," V, 214; military governor of Tennessee, V, 243; vetoes the Tenure-of-Office Act, V, 246; and ratification of the Thirteenth Amendment, V, 264; as a Union Democrat, V, 342; as leading War Democrat, V, 402

Johnson, Eastman, painter, I, 123

Johnson, Edward, and battle at McDowell, Va., III, 364

Johnson, Fort, and Fort Edwards, II, 189

Johnson, George A., on the Colorado River, I, 427

Johnson, Guy, and the Indians in the Revolution, **III**, 88; Superintendent of Indian Affairs, **III**, 104

Johnson, H. V., nominated for Vice-Presidency, **I**, 285; and the Confederate Congress, **II**, 6

Johnson, Henry, commands the *Lexington*, **III**, 266

Johnson, Hiram, opposes the World Court, **V**, 485

Johnson, Horace, and the Holland patent, **III**, 38

Johnson, Hugh S., and the Blue Eagle emblem, **I**, 204; heads National Recovery Administration, **IV**, 62

Johnson, J. B., captures Dull Knife's people, **II**, 175

Johnson, Jack, prize fighter, **IV**, 353

Johnson, James, and Mangas Coloradas wars, **III**, 331

Johnson, John, lays the first tile ditch, **II**, 165

Johnson, John, passes up Lake Champlain to raid the Mohawk Valley, **III**, 230; at Fort Niagara, **IV**, 130; and battle of Oriskany, **IV**, 188

Johnson, John, commanding officer during Fort Sumter siege, **V**, 204

Johnson, John A., governor of Minnesota, **III**, 411

Johnson, Marmaduke, prints Eliot's Indian Bible, **III**, 94; **IV**, 345

Johnson, Nelson T., ambassador to China, **I**, 54

Johnson, Richard Mentor, chosen Vice-President, **I**, 283; and battle of the Thames, **V**, 259; elected Vice-President by the Senate, **V**, 366; as a leader of the War Hawks, **V**, 403

Johnson, Samuel, first president of Columbia College, **I**, 429; and philosophical thought and writings, **IV**, 263

Johnson, Samuel, author of *Taxation No Tyranny*, **V**, 229

Johnson, Samuel William, and first farm institute, **II**, 252

Johnson, Seth, and the Holland patent, **III**, 38

Johnson, Thomas, resident of Frederick, Md., **II**, 330

Johnson, W. H., and the Oise-Aisne operation, **IV**, 167

Johnson, William, and the Albany Congress, **I**, 45; and the Treaty of Fort Stanwix (1768), **I**, 170; in battle of Bloody Pond, **I**, 203; and Bouquet's Expedition, **I**, 229; commands expedition against Fort St. Frederic, **II**, 93; and the Detroit Indian Council, **II**, 143; commander of expedition against Crown Point, **II**, 189; and the Four-mile Strip, **II**, 316; and "hairdressers," **III**, 3; and Indian agencies, **III**, 90; appointed Superintendent of Indian Affairs, **III**, 104; and the Iroquois League, **III**, 159; and the Kayoderosseras patent, **III**, 200;

and kerosene oil, **III**, 207; in French and Indian War, **III**, 229; and battle of Lake George, **III**, 230; and land speculation, **III**, 239; and the Iroquois, **IV**, 5; keeps friendship of the Six Nations, **IV**, 115; captures Fort Niagara from the French, **IV**, 115, 130; calls Great Indian council at Niagara, **IV**, 130; made a baronet, **IV**, 136; and council at Fort Ontario, **IV**, 191; and the Pontiac War, **IV**, 305 f.; and Indian missions, **IV**, 330; and the Proclamation of 1763, **IV**, 354; and healing waters of Saratoga, **V**, 32; and Treaty of Fort Stanwix (1768), **V**, 159; and settlement of Wyoming Valley, **V**, 498

Johnson, William, in Gibbons v. Ogden, **II**, 388

Johnson, William S., signer of the Constitution, **II**, 39; delegate to Convention of 1787, **II**, 50; and state sovereignty, **V**, 173

Johnson Act of 1924, and assimilation, **I**, 130

Johnson-Clarendon Convention (1868), **I**, 40

Johnson's Island, attempt to free Confederate prisoners on, **I**, 170, 279; and Beall's raid, **IV**, 150; prison camp at, **IV**, 347

Johnston, Albert Sidney, becomes a general of the Confederate Army, **I**, 110; and Marcy's march, **III**, 342; and Army of the Mississippi, **III**, 419; and the Mormon expedition, **IV**, 24; and battle of Shiloh, **V**, 71; Terry's Texas Rangers join, **V**, 249; sent to suppress supposed rebellion in Utah, **V**, 354

Johnston, James, publishes the *Georgia Gazette*, **IV**, 126; first printer in Georgia, **IV**, 345; sets up first printing press in Savannah, **V**, 35

Johnston, Joseph E., and Appomattox, **I**, 91; becomes a general of the Confederate Army, **I**, 110; and the Atlanta campaign, **I**, 134; attacks at Bentonville, **I**, 178; and First Bull Run, **I**, 251; surrender of, **I**, 317, 385; and his controversy with Davis, **II**, 112; and the battle of Fair Oaks, **II**, 239; and battle of Jackson, Miss., **III**, 164; and battle of Kenesaw Mountain, **III**, 203; and battles at New Hope Church, **IV**, 104; replaced by Hood, **IV**, 236; and the Peninsular campaign, **IV**, 241; and Army of Tennessee, **V**, 242; and battle of Williamsburg, **V**, 468

Johnston, Samuel, and the development of the reaper, **IV**, 419

Johnston, W. H., and the Ypres-Lys operation, **V**, 511

Johnston, William, and the Transylvania Company, **V**, 309

Johnstone, George, and Peace Commission of 1778, **IV**, 231

Johnstown Flood, **II**, 149, 286

"Join or Die," snake cartoon, **I**, 320

Joiner, C. M. (Dad), discovers oil in East Texas, **II**, 182

Joint Commission, and the Alaskan Boundary Question, **I**, 44; and American-Mexican claims, **I**, 63

Joint Committee on Reconstruction, **II**, 17; **IV**, 425

Joint Occupation, and Convention of 1818, **II**, 52; of Oregon, **II**, 271; and Oregon Memorial of 1838, **IV**, 183; and the Oregon Question, **IV**, 184; and the Oregon Treaty, **IV**, 187; of the Northwest, **V**, 415

Joint Resolution of Congress, and naturalization, **IV**, 67; Texas annexed by, **V**, 319; and declaration of war, **V**, 396

Joint Sales Agencies, and restraint of trade, **IV**, 460

Joint-Stock Company, **I**, 16

Joint Stock Land Banks, **II**, 246

Jolliet, Louis, recognizes importance of Chicago Portage route, **I**, 358; and Lake Erie, **II**, 223; on the Fox-Wisconsin Waterway, **II**, 320; on the Mississippi River, **III**, 423; and the Mississippi Valley, **III**, 425; explores Missouri, **III**, 426; and New France, **IV**, 101; his map of 1674, and the Ohio River, **IV**, 164

Jolliet and Marquette, visit Arkansas, **I**, 105; reach mouth of the Arkansas River, **I**, 106; discover coal, **I**, 192; voyages of, **II**, 344; explore the Mississippi, **II**, 415; return to Mackinac by Illinois River and Chicago Portage, **III**, 231; first to visit site of Prairie du Chien, **IV**, 328; at Starved Rock, **V**, 161; and topographic mapping, **V**, 282; open the Fox-Wisconsin Waterway, **V**, 473. *See also* Marquette, Jacques

Joncaire, Daniel de, erects Fort Little Niagara, **IV**, 129

Joncaire, Louis Thomas de, constructs the Magazin Royal, **IV**, 129

Jones, Anson, and the Republic of Texas, **V**, 253

Jones, Catesby ap Rogers, encounters the *Monitor*, **IV**, 10

Jones, Christopher, master of the *Mayflower*, **III**, 361

Jones, D. R., at Bull Run, **I**, 251

Jones, George W., imprisonment of, **I**, 122; senator from Iowa, **III**, 152

Jones, Heman, and early pipe lines, **IV**, 276

Jones, J. S., and the Leavenworth and Pikes Peak Express, **III**, 258; **IV**, 510

Jones, Jacob, commander of the *Wasp*, **V**, 420

Jones, John Gabriel, represents the Harrodstown settlers before the Virginia assembly, **III**, 204; and Kentucky County, **III**, 206; and Virginia v. Transylvania Company, **V**, 380

Jones, John P., and great fortunes, **II**, 312

Jones, John Paul, depositor in and stockholder of Bank of North America, **I**, 154; and the Bergen prizes, **I**, 179; and the *Bonhomme Richard-Serapis* engagement, **I**, 208; and figureheads, **II**, 272; flies United States flag, **II**, 281; raids British coast, **IV**, 77; and the *Ranger-Drake* engagement, **IV**, 416; and the Navy in the Revolution, **IV**, 471

Jones, Margaret, executed for witchcraft, **V**, 475

Jones, Nancy Anne, and governor of North Carolina to governor of South Carolina, **IV**, 145

Jones, Robert, and Missouri Fur Company, **V**, 13

Jones, S. J., and the sack of Lawrence, **III**, 253

Jones, Sam, revivalist, **IV**, 464

Jones, Thomas ap Catesby, at Lake Borgne, **I**, 221; seizes Monterey, Calif., **IV**, 17; negotiates treaty with Hawaiian government, **IV**, 76

Jones, Thomas Hudson, and the tomb of the Unknown Soldier, **V**, 351

Jones, Walter, and McCulloch v. Maryland, **III**, 364

Jones, William, and regicides in New England, **IV**, 438

Jones, William, president of the Second Bank of the United States, **I**, 155

Jones, William Cary, printer of *Du Buque Visitor*, **IV**, 126; first printer of Iowa, **IV**, 345

Jones, William E., raid, **III**, 72

Jones, William Richard, and mass production, **III**, 353

Jones Act (1916), and Philippine independence, **IV**, 261, 262

Jones Act, and Puerto Rico, **IV**, 380

Jones Bill, and governmental control of agriculture, **I**, 32

Jones-Ketcham Bill, and export debenture plan, **II**, 236

Jonquiere, and Pickawillany, **IV**, 266

Jordan, Robert, awarded the Trelawney plantation, **V**, 320

Jornada del Muerto, avoided by the Arkansas River route, **I**, 107; and thirst, **V**, 263

Josh Billings' Almanac, **I**, 52

Joss-Houses, and oriental religions and cults, **IV**, 187

Josselyn, John, and fruit growing, **II**, 353; and scurvy, **V**, 47

Journal of the Times, and the Townshend Acts, **V**, 290

Journalism, in the Old South, **V**, 123; trade, **V**, 298; women in, **V**, 481

Journals of the Continental Congress, and the name United States of America, **V**, 347

Journey in the Seaboard Slave States, **I**, 85

Joutel, Henri, explorations of, **II**, 345

"Joys of Mary," song, **II**, 293

Juchereau, Charles, engages the Mascouten as hunters, **III**, 350

Judge, William Q., and theosophy, V, 262

Judges, retirement of, I, 217; III, 187; in royal colonies, IV, 504

Judges' Cave, regicides live in, IV, 438

Judicial Arbitration Court, attempt to establish, I, 97; and international law, III, 141

Judicial Interpretation, and the rule of reason, IV, 505

Judicial Review, and Convention of 1787, II, 51; and Holmes v. Walton, III, 39; and the Judiciary Act of 1789 III, 189; of colonial cases, III, 302; and Marbury v. Madison, III, 341; and the McCardle case, III, 363; and the Supreme Court, V, 207; and Trevett v. Weeden, V, 323

Judiciary, The, and the Constitution, II, 33, 37; provided for in Convention of 1787, II, 51; and courts of Domestic Relations, II, 158; and constitutional interpretation, II, 258; and separation of powers, IV, 327; and state constitutions, V, 167; and state government, V, 169; and the Virginia-Kentucky Resolutions, V, 376

Judiciary Act of 1789, and Erie Railroad Company v. Tompkins, II, 226; and judicial review, III, 183; and Marbury v. Madison, III, 341; and the Supreme Court, V, 206

Judson, Edward Z. C., writer of outdoor adventure stories, II, 147

Jueces del Campos, II, 76

Juengling, Frederick, and wood engraving, V, 483

Juilliard v. Greenman, III, 262; IV, 455

Julian, G. W., member of the Committee on the Conduct of the War, I, 436; among the leaders of the Radical Republicans, IV, 395

Jumano Indians, and the Mendoza expedition, III, 373

Jumonville, killed at Great Meadows, II, 418

Junandot, Fort, erected, V, 27

Juneau, gold found in, II, 396

Jungle, The, written by Upton Sinclair, II, 270; IV, 38

"Junto," and libraries, III, 272

Jury Trial, and the Bill of Rights, I, 186; and the Constitution, II, 37, 40; and the Milligan case, III, 405

Justice, Department of, and the F. B. I., II, 255

Justice of the Peace, and the judiciary, III, 184; and marriage, III, 345

"Justin Morgan," famous horse, III, 47

Juvenile Courts, II, 158

K

Kadiak Island, first Russian church at, IV, 511; first permanent Russian settlement in America, V, 47

Kakiate Patent, III, 56

Kalamazoo Case, and high schools, II, 187; V, 42

Kalb. See DeKalb

Kalispel Indians, and Jesuit missions, III, 175

Kalmar Nyckel, The, brings settlers to New Sweden, IV, 113

Kamiakin, leader of the Yakima Indian wars, V, 500

Kanawha, Battle of the. See Point Pleasant, The Battle of

Kanawha River, and the Alleghenies, I, 51; Donelson's Line runs to mouth of, II, 160

Kanawha Salt, V, 18

Kane, Elisha K., polar expedition of, IV, 293

Kane, John, artist, I, 123

Kanesville, Mormon town, II, 71

Kankakee River Portage, V, 10

Kansas, slavery struggle in, and abolitionist literature, I, 3; Court of Industrial Relations, I, 95; Border War in, I, 195; 219; and Blue Lodges, I, 205; and border ruffians, I, 219; Beecher's Bibles in, I, 173; and Buford Expedition, I, 249; and Emigrant Aid Movement, II, 210; and the English Compromise of 1858, II, 217; guerrilla warfare in, II, 428; and Jayhawkers, III, 168; and the New England Emigrant Aid Company, IV, 99; and popular sovereignty, IV, 309; Border War and Sharps rifle, V, 64; as a "marginal state," V, 132; organized, and admitted, V, 249; and the westward movement, V, 451; Industrial Court of, V, 476; and the Wyandotte Constitution, V, 496

Kansas City, and domestic trade, V, 293

Kansas Free-State Party, and the Kansas struggle, III, 198; and Lecompton Constitution, III, 259; and the Potawatomie massacre, IV, 323; and Topeka Movement and Constitution, V, 281; and the Wakarusa War, V, 390

Kansas Indians, visited by Bourgmont, I, 230; encountered by DeSoto's expedition, II, 142; land cessions, III, 100

Kansas-Nebraska Act, and the Appeal of the Independent Democrats, I, 89; and the Dred Scott case, II, 167; and the Indian Country, III, 97; and the Kansas struggle, III, 198; and Missouri, III, 427; and repeal of the Missouri Compromise, III, 429; and popular sovereignty, IV, 309; and the Republican party, IV, 454; and slavery, V, 96

Kansas Pacific Railway, Abilene on, I, 2; and experimental work in dry farming, II, 171; built to Fort Hays, III, 20; and the Union Pacific, IV, 408

Kansas v. Colorado, and inherent powers, III, 122

Kansas Weekly Herald, published by W. H. Adams, IV, 126

Kaposia Battle, V, 84
Karlsefni, Thorfinn, and Norsemen in America, IV, 143
Karpis, Alvin, gangster, I, 153
Kaskaskia, taken by Clark, I, 145; and Baynton, Wharton and Morgan, I, 170; census of 1723, I, 267; Charlevoix at, I, 345; garrison at Fort de Chartres withdrawn to, I, 347; and Clark's Northwest Campaign, I, 395; dead city, II, 114; and the fur trade, II, 363; Clark takes possession of, III, 67; Jesuit mission at, III, 174
Kaskaskia Indians, and the Algonquin family, I, 48; and treaty of Fort de Chartres, I, 348; begin the DesPeres Village, II, 142; of the Illinois, III, 71; land cessions of, III, 100; removal of, III, 107; and treaty of Fort Wayne, V, 370
Kasson Treaties, V, 315
Kataka Indians, and the Red River Indian War, IV, 431
Kaufman, George, playwright, II, 166
Kaulbach, John, and consumer co-operatives, II, 56
Kearney, Dennis, leads agitation for Chinese exclusion, I, 366
Kearneyites, and the Chinese riots, I, 367
Kearny, Fort, and battle of Ash Hollow, I, 127
Kearny, Fort Phil, and Bozeman Trail, I, 232; and Red Cloud War, II, 268; IV, 429; V, 86
Kearny, Lawrence, and the opening of China to American commerce, I, 78, 365
Kearny, Philip, killed in battle of Chantilly, I, 341
Kearny, Stephen W., quarrel with Frémont, I, 272; and the Gila Trail, II, 389; and Magee expedition, III, 324; and the Mexican War, III, 386; invades New Mexico, IV, 107; and battle of San Gabriel, V, 24; and battle of San Pascual, V, 26; occupies Santa Fé, V, 29; and the Southern Railroad route, V, 131; and Stockton quarrel, V, 184; and the Yellowstone River expedition, V, 506
Kearsarge, The, sinks the Alabama, I, 390
Keayne, Robert, and the "Sow Case," V, 134
Keelboatmen, I, 164; II, 282
Keelboats, supersede bateaux, I, 167; used in Lewis and Clark expedition, III, 266; on the Mississippi, III, 423, 424; on the Missouri, III, 430, 431; and pack trains, IV, 198; used in Pike's expedition, IV, 269; and Pittsburgh, IV, 280; for river navigation, IV, 489; and rivermen of the Ohio, IV, 490; and domestic trade, V, 291; in the Yellowstone River expedition, V, 506
Keil, William, establishes Bethel Community, I, 180
Keimer, Samuel, establishes the Pennsylvania Gazette, IV, 246
Keith, B. F., and vaudeville, V, 358

Keith, Myron R., and Standard Oil Company, V, 156
Kelley, B. F., and the skirmish at Philippi, IV, 261
Kelley, Lt., flies nonstop from New York to San Diego, I, 142
Kelley, Oliver H., organizes Patrons of Husbandry, I, 26; and the Granger movement, II, 410
Kellogg, A. N., and newspaper syndicates, IV, 123
Kellogg, Clara Louise, and the opera, IV, 178
Kellogg, Frank B., in Minnesota, III, 411
Kellogg, W. P., and the Midnight Order (1872), III, 395; and the New Orleans riots, IV, 111; and the Wheeler Compromise (1876), V, 454
Kellogg Pact. See Briand-Kellogg Pact
Kelly, James K., conducts a campaign in the Walla Walla Valley, V, 500
Kelly, William, and steel making, III, 156, 337
Kemper, Samuel, and the Gutiérrez-Magee expedition, II, 429
Kendall, Amos, and burning of antislavery literature, I, 85; member of the "Kitchen Cabinet," III, 213; and removal of deposits, IV, 448; journalist, V, 123
Kendall, George, and founding of Jamestown, III, 166; shot, III, 167
Kendrick, J., nurseryman, IV, 154
Kendrick, John, builds the Adventure, I, 15; and China Trade, I, 365
Kenesaw Mountain, Sherman attacks at, I, 134
Kenly, John R., defeated at Front Royal, II, 349
Kennebec and Chaudière River Route, and Arnold's attack on Quebec, I, 120
Kennebec River, and the Popham Colony, IV, 308
Kennecott, Robert, surveys the Yukon, V, 512
Kennedy, Joseph P., and fiction, II, 270; writer of the Old South, V, 123
Kennedy-Franklin Plan (1751), I, 421
Kensett, John Frederick, landscape painter, I, 123
Kensett, Thomas, Sr., pioneer of American canning, I, 304
Kensico Reservoir, and city water supply, V, 424
Kensington Stone, and Runic inscriptions, IV, 508
Kent, Gen., captures San Juan, V, 25
Kent Island, Claiborne settlement on, I, 394; III, 349
Kenton, Simon, of the Bluegrass Country, I, 205; early explorer, II, 235; hunter, III, 60
Kentucke Gazette, founded by John Bradford, IV, 124; published by John and Fielding Bradford, IV, 126
Kentucky, invasion of (1782), I, 204; Bluegrass Country, I, 205; founding of Boonesborough, I, 216; bank of, I, 238; invasion of, II, 96; the

"Dark and Bloody Ground," **II**, 110; army of, **III**, 419; invasion of, **IV**, 161; state of, organized, **V**, 132; and the Spanish conspiracy, **V**, 139

Kentucky and Virginia Resolutions. *See* Virginia and Kentucky Resolutions

Kentucky County, organized, **V**, 380

Kentucky Derby, **III**, 49

Kentucky v. Dennison, and relations between the states, **V**, 174

Kenyon, Cox and Company, failure of, and panic of 1873, **IV**, 209

Kepley, Ada, receives law degree, **V**, 481, 482

Kern, Edward, and Frémont's explorations, **II**, 414

Kern, Edward and Richard, at Taos, **V**, 220

Kern, Jerome, book collection, **I**, 213

Kern, R. H., and Inscription Rock, **III**, 126

Kerosene, used for lighting, **III**, 276

Kerr Tobacco Act, and governmental control of agriculture, **I**, 32

Kershaw, J. B., and battle of Spotsylvania Courthouse, **V**, 150

Ketch, in transportation, **V**, 306

Kettle Creek, patriots win at, **II**, 379

Key, Francis Scott, writes "Star Spangled Banner," **I**, 150; **II**, 330; **III**, 349, 365; **V**, 160

Key to Uncle Tom's Cabin, **I**, 3

Keyes, Henry, control of Atchison, Topeka and Santa Fé Railroad passes to, **I**, 134

Keystone Zouaves, **V**, 514

Kiala, Fox chief, **II**, 320

Kickapoo Indians, and Algonquin family, **I**, 48; and treaty of Fort de Chartres, **I**, 348; land cessions of, **III**, 100; removal of, **III**, 107; and the Mascouten, **III**, 350; and Oklahoma openings, **IV**, 169; and treaty of Fort Wayne (1803), **V**, 370; and treaty of Fort Wayne (1809), **V**, 426

Kidd, Meredith H., and the Dawes Commission, **II**, 113

Kidd, William, at Gardiner's Island, **II**, 372; and pirate gold, **IV**, 277

Kidnapping, carried on by organized gangs, **I**, 153; a product of the industrial age, **II**, 88; of Negroes, **II**, 332, 354; **III**, 6; for indenture, **III**, 85

Kieft, William, and the Dutch-Indian War, **II**, 179; Indian policy of, **IV**, 94; as director-general at New Amsterdam, **IV**, 108; and the Pavonia massacre, **IV**, 228; and the Petition and Remonstrance of New Netherland, **IV**, 257

Kier, Samuel M., and kerosene oil, **III**, 207; **IV**, 166

Killbuck, Delaware chieftain, and massacre at Fort Seybert, **V**, 62

Killdeer Mountain, Sully attacks Indians at, **II**, 107

Killen, Jacob A., publishes the *Delaware Gazette*, **IV**, 126

Kilpatrick, H. J., and Buckland Races, **I**, 246; and Dahlgren's raid, **II**, 103; and engagement at Hanover (Pa.), **III**, 8; and Sherman's march to the sea, **V**, 71

Kimball, Sumner I., and the Lifesaving Service, **III**, 276

Kinetoscope, patented by Coleman Sellers, **IV**, 31

King, Alfred Freeman Africanus, and mosquitoes, **IV**, 31

King, Charles, and Columbia College, **I**, 429

King, Charles P., and the automobile, **I**, 140

King, Clarence, railroad survey of, **V**, 283

King, Fort, Maj. Dade sets out to re-enforce, **II**, 103

King, H. C., and religious thought and writings, **IV**, 447; **V**, 261

King, John, editor of *DuBuque Visitor*, **IV**, 126; and first newspaper of Iowa, **IV**, 345

King, Leicester, and the Ohio State Antislavery Society, **IV**, 165

King, Rufus, and British debts, **I**, 240; and campaign of 1808, **I**, 281; defeated for Presidency, **I**, 282; signer of the Constitution, **II**, 39; delegate to Convention of 1787, **II**, 50; and Miranda's intrigues, **III**, 414; and the Northwest boundary controversy, **IV**, 149

King, Rufus, as American minister to the Papal States, **IV**, 211

King, W. R., elected Vice-President, **I**, 284

King George's War, expeditions planned to take Fort St. Frederic during, **II**, 93; and Louisburg expedition, **III**, 304

King Kullen Markets, **V**, 205

King Philip, an Algonquin leader, **I**, 48

King Philip's War, and Bull Garrison House, **I**, 250; and treaty of Casco (1678), **I**, 321; and Great Swamp Fight, **II**, 420; and Indians as slaves, **III**, 108; Narragansett Indians in, **IV**, 53; and the Praying Indians, **IV**, 330; and Providence Plantations, **IV**, 368; and regicides in New England, **IV**, 438; and Rhode Island, **IV**, 478; Saco Bay settlements abandoned during, **V**, 3; temporarily checks the westward movement, **V**, 450

King William Parish, set aside for the Huguenots, **III**, 57

King Williams School, now St. Johns College, **V**, 9

King William's War, paper currency issued during, **II**, 118; and Haverhill massacre, **III**, 17; ended by the Peace of Ryswick, **IV**, 512

Kingan, Samuel, and meat packing, **IV**, 199

King's College, medical department of, merged with Columbia College, **III**, 369

King's Ferry, connects Stony Point with Verplanck's Point, **V**, 185

"King's Mill," Battle of, **IV**, 6

King's Mountain, Battle at, I, 145; IV, 477; V, 129

King's Province, and Dominion of New England, IV, 98

King's Troops, colonies defended by, I, 112

King's Use, and Pennsylvania Quaker experiment in politics, IV, 385

Kingsbury, Jacob, builds Fort Bellefontaine, I, 176

Kingsbury Furnace, IV, 343

Kingsley, N. W., and dentistry, II, 138

Kinkaid Act (1904), and the public domain, IV, 370

Kinnersley, Ebenezer, early science lecturer, III, 260

Kinney, Henry L., filibustering activities of, II, 274

Kinney, N. C., establishes Fort C. F. Smith, V, 101

Kino, Eusebio Francisco, explores Alta California, I, 52; penetrates southern Arizona, I, 104; and Camino del Diablo, I, 278; and the Spanish horse, III, 48; missionary career of, III, 175; and missions of the Southwest, III, 418

Kinsman, D. O., and the Wisconsin Idea, V, 474

Kinzie, John, first white settler of Chicago, I, 356

Kinzie, John H., averts Indian attack on Fort Winnebago, V, 471

Kiowa Indians, in the battle of Adobe Walls, I, 13; besiege Fort Atkinson, I, 134; Fort Bascom a protection against, I, 165; Chouteau carries on trade with, I, 370; and the Dodge-Leavenworth expedition, II, 157; and Fort Griffin, II, 426; and the horse, III, 92; and the Indian Country, III, 97; and Fort Mason, III, 350; and Medicine Creek Council, III, 370; in Oklahoma, IV, 168; and Oklahoma openings, IV, 169; and the Peyote cult, IV, 257; picture writing of, IV, 267; and the Red River Indian War, IV, 431; and Santanta's wars, V, 31; agency headquarters for, at Fort Sill, V, 79; and Camp Supply, V, 205; harass McLeod's Texan-Santa Fé expedition, V, 251; and Sheridan's operations on Washita, V, 420; and Fort Zarah, V, 513

Kipp, Jacobus, and Rumbout's patent, IV, 507

Kirby, F. M., and Company, Woolworth combines with, II, 279

Kirby, Thomas E., and book auctions, I, 211

Kirby, William, organizer of the Illinois Band, III, 69

Kirby-Smith, Edmund, becomes a general in the Confederate provisional army, I, 110; surrenders to Canby, I, 385; and Confederate surrender, II, 13; and battle at Jenkins Ferry, III, 173; and invasion of Kentucky, III, 205; calls the Marshall convention, III, 346; and Morgan's raids, IV, 23; and battle of Perryville, IV, 254; and the battle at Pine Bluff, IV, 273; and the Red River Campaign, IV, 430; and battle of Richmond (Ky.), IV, 481; joins Shelby's Mexican expedition, V, 68

Kirk, Samuel, silversmith, V, 82

"Kitchen Cabinet," and party machines, III, 319

Kittanning, raid on (1756), IV, 219

Kittanning Trail, and pack trains, IV, 197

Kittson, Norman W., and fur trade post at Pembina, IV, 431

"Kitty O'Neal," fiddle tune, II, 270

Kittyhawk Island, the Wright brothers experiment at, I, 142

Kiwanis Clubs, I, 261

Klickitat Indians, and Yakima Indian wars, V, 500

Klondike, placer mines discovered in, I, 43; and prospectors, IV, 364; gold rush to, V, 512

Kneeland, Abner, and freethinking, II, 340

Knickerbocker Club of New York, and baseball, I, 165

Knickerbocker Theater, collapse of roof of, I, 201

Knickerbocker Trust Company, failure of, and panic of 1907, IV, 210

Knight, M. M., and companionate marriage, I, 441

Knight, Sarah, and toll bridges, V, 278

Knight Case, and Addyston Pipe Company case, I, 10; and restraint of trade, I, 65; and trusts, V, 326. See also U. S. v. E. C. Knight Co.

Knights, Will J., founds the Gideon Society, II, 389

Knights of Columbus, V, 53, 488

Knights of Labor, and the American Federation of Labor, I, 60; and blacklisting I, 197; and Burlington strike, I, 256; and child labor, I, 361; and miners' labor organizations, I, 404; and Industrial Brotherhood, III, 114; and labor movements, III, 219; and labor parties, III, 223; and labor unions, III, 224; and one big union, IV, 174; and the railroad strikes of 1886, IV, 405; and the United Mine Workers, V, 346

Knights of Luther, anti-Catholic organization, IV, 66

Knights of Pythias, V, 53

Knights of the Golden Circle, oppose Union program in Civil War, I, 385, 388; Copperheads form, II, 58; and the Fishing Creek Confederacy, II, 278; and Order of American Knights, IV, 180; support the Pacific Republic movement, IV, 197; and peace movements, IV, 234; as a secret society, V, 53

Knights of the Golden Horseshoe, and the Shenandoah Valley, V, 69

Knitting Machine, invention of, III, 320

Knolls Looms, III, 301

Knote v. U. S., IV, 215

Knott, Thomas A., edits *A Dictionary of Middle English,* II, 146

Know-Nothing Party. *See* American (or Know-Nothing) Party

Knowlton, Charles, author of *Fruits of Philosophy,* I, 191

Knowlton, Col., and battle of Harlem, III, 10

Knox, Fort, as site for a gold depository, II, 395

Knox, Frank, nominated for Vice-Presidency, I, 292

Knox, Henry, takes over artillery duties, I, 127; and the Bingham Purchase, I, 189; suggests Society of the Cincinnati, I, 375; and McGillivray incident, III, 365; and the United States Military Academy, III, 398; and Miranda's intrigues, III, 414; and state sovereignty, V, 173; and capture of Ticonderoga, V, 268; and Society of the Cincinnati, V, 365; purchases part of the Waldo patent, V, 391; appointed secretary of War and Ordnance Board, V, 399

Knox, S. H., and Company, Woolworth combines with, II, 279

Knox-Castrillo Loan Convention, not ratified, IV, 131

Knox College, founding of, III, 397

Knox v. Lee, legal tender case, III, 262; IV, 455; and the Supreme Court Packing Bills, V, 208

Knoxville, Terry's Texas Rangers at, V, 249

Knoxville Gazette, established by Roulstone and Ferguson, IV, 124, 127

Kodak, invention of the, IV, 265

Kodiak Island. *See* Kadiak Island

Kosciusko, Tadeusz, placed in charge of construction at West Point, III, 31; commissioned in the Revolutionary Army, IV, 473; and construction work at West Point, V, 438

Kossuth, Louis, and the Hülsemann incident, III, 58; visit of, III, 60; as political exile, IV, 295

Koster and Bial's Music Hall, IV, 31

Koszta, Martin, and Hülsemann incident, III, 58

Krag-Jorgensen Magazine Rifle, IV, 483

Kresge, S. S., founds a five-and-ten-cent store, II, 279

Kresge Foundation, II, 315

Kress, S. H., and Company, established, II, 279

Krishna, Hindu cult, IV, 187

Kruel, Gustav, and wood engraving, V, 483

Ku Klux Act, and U. S. v. Harris, V, 348

Ku Klux Klan, and crime, II, 88; keeps down Negro voting, II, 271; and Force Acts, II, 300; and intolerance, III, 147; and the Union League, III, 312; and Negro suffrage, IV, 85; and Reconstruction, IV, 426; and the Regulators, IV, 439; in Tennessee, V, 243

Ku Klux Klan (20th Century), and campaign of 1924, I, 291; and Catholicism, I, 323; and intolerance, III, 147; and nativism, IV, 66; secret society, V, 53; and whispering campaigns, V, 458

Kuhn, Adam, first to teach botany regularly, II, 371

Kuhn, Fritz, head of German-American Bund, V, 197

Kuhn, Walt, painter, I, 123

Kullyspell House, established, III, 66

L

Labaddie, Sylvestre, partner in St. Louis Missouri Fur Company, V, 12

Labadist Community, I, 440

LaBarre, LeFebvre, and treaty of LaFamine (1684), III, 226

LaBaye, and Charlevoix journey, I, 345; and the fur trade, II, 360; name for Green Bay, II, 422

LaBaye, Fort, and Fox-Wisconsin waterway, II, 320

Labor, and the Sherman Antitrust Act, I, 433; and communism, I, 440; foreign, II, 49; organized, supports Coxeyites, II, 82; immigrant, III, 72; and riots, IV, 3; and one big union, IV, 174; and the Socialist movement, V, 110; migratory, and seasonal unemployment, V, 339; and distribution of wealth, V, 429; and youth movements, V, 511

Labor, Department of, and Government Contract Board, I, 11; agency of mediation and conciliation, I, 95; conciliation service of, II, 2; Employment Service as bureau in, II, 213; Wage and Hour Division created in, II, 239; established, III, 219

Labor Colleges, attempts to establish, III, 115

Labor Legislation, and the Populist party, IV, 313

Labor Parties, and labor unions, III, 225

Labor Reform Party, and Greenback Movement, II, 423; as a third party, V, 262

Labor Unions, and the American Federation of Labor, I, 60; and Americanization, I, 67; and the Anthracite Strike, I, 80; and bituminous mining, I, 192; and blacklisting, I, 197; and boycott, I, 232; and the checkoff, I, 349; and the Clayton Act, I, 396; and closed shop, I, 403; legal recognition of, I, 439; and the Congress of Industrial Organizations, II, 20; and the Cripple Creek strikes, II, 89; in Danbury Hatters' case, II, 108; and the detective agency, II, 142; and industrial espionage, II, 227; and freedom, II, 336; and Gastonia riots, II, 374; and Herrin massacre, III, 28; and the Homestead strike, III, 43; and the immigrant, III, 72; and injunctions, III, 123; and labor, III, 218; established, III, 219; and leisure, III, 264; and the McNamara case, III, 367; and National Trades' and Workers' Association, IV, 63; and Philadelphia cordwainers' case, IV, 259; and

picketing, **IV**, 266; and Populism, **IV**, 313; and profiteering, **IV**, 355; and restraint of trade, **IV**, 460; and the scab, **V**, 37; and strikes, **V**, 190; and syndicalism, **V**, 215; and the United Mine Workers, **V**, 346; and the walking delegate, **V**, 392; and the white-collar class, **V**, 458; and the yellow-dog contract, **V**, 504

Labor's Non-Partisan League, **I**, 62

Lachaise, Gaston, sculptor, **I**, 124

Laclede (Ligueste), Pierre, establishes firm of Maxent, Laclede and Company, **III**, 360; founds St. Louis, **III**, 426; **V**, 11

Laconia, granted to Mason and Gorges, **III**, 351

Laconia Company, receives Isles of Shoals, **III**, 162; settles Strawberry Bank, **IV**, 101; **V**, 187

Ladd, E. F., introduces pure food legislation to North Dakota, **IV**, 146

Ladd, William, and the American Peace Society, **I**, 64; and peace movements, **IV**, 233 f.; founder of the oldest antiwar organization, **V**, 395

Laddie, written by Gene Stratton Porter, **I**, 180

LaDemoiselle, Miami chief, and Pickawillany, **IV**, 266

Ladies Magazine, bought by Godey, **II**, 392

"Ladies' Tea Party," held at Edenton, **V**, 234

Ladue, Joseph, lays out Dawson City, **III**, 214

LaFarge, John, painter, **I**, 123

Lafayette, Fort, as prison camp, **IV**, 347

Lafayette, Marquis de, and Arnold's raid in Virginia, **I**, 120; and Bunker Hill Monument, **I**, 254; visits America, **II**, 328; and introduction of the mule into the colonies, **IV**, 40; as foreign volunteer in the Revolutionary Army, **IV**, 473; and Sullivan in Rhode Island, **IV**, 479; and Yorktown campaign, **V**, 509

Lafayette Escadrille, American flyers join, **I**, 143

Lafitte, Jean, at Barataria, **I**, 162; at Galveston Island, **I**, 338; Gulf pirate, **II**, 368; and the Long expedition, **III**, 298; and smuggling, **V**, 103

Lafitte, Pierre, at Barataria, **I**, 162

Laflin and Rand, powder producers, **IV**, 326

LaFollette, R. M., and the progressive bloc, **I**, 202; and campaign of 1912, **I**, 290; and campaign of 1924, **I**, 291; supported by Farmer-Labor party of Minnesota, **II**, 251; and oratory, **IV**, 180; and political parties, **IV**, 297; political writings of, **IV**, 302; and the Progressive Movement, **IV**, 356; and the Taft-Roosevelt split, **V**, 217; dominates Wisconsin politics, **V**, 474; and the Wisconsin Idea, **V**, 474

LaFollette Progressives, and the agrarian movement, **I**, 21; as third party, **V**, 262

LaForest, François Daupin de, and Illinois, **III**, 67; erects Fort St. Louis, **IV**, 252; erects Fort Pimitoui, **IV**, 272

LaFramboise, Joseph, and Fort Pierre, **IV**, 268

Lahontan, Baron de, claims to have discovered the Great Salt Lake, **II**, 419; explores Missouri, **III**, 426; cartographic records of, **V**, 282

Lahontan Dam, engineering feature of Newlands Reclamation Project, **IV**, 121

Laird Rams, **I**, 40

Laissez-Faire, and antitrust laws, **I**, 87; and private banks, **I**, 160; and the Dartmouth College case, **II**, 111; and government regulation, **II**, 405

Lake, Simon, and submarines, **V**, 194

Lake Champlain, discovery of, **II**, 344; Macdonough's victory on, **II**, 387; **III**, 318; and battle of Valcour Island, **V**, 355; and Vermont, **V**, 361; in the War of 1812, **V**, 405

Lake Champlain Bridge Commission, **V**, 175

Lake Chautauqua Portage, **IV**, 316

Lake George, Battle of, **III**, 229

Lake Mills, Wis., Aztalan located near, **I**, 144

Lake Mohonk Arbitration Conferences, **IV**, 235

Lake of the Woods, and Definitive Treaty of Peace, **II**, 129; and the Northwest Angle, **IV**, 149; and the Northwest boundary controversy, **IV**, 149; and western boundaries, **V**, 441; and the search for the western sea, **V**, 446

Lake Superior Consolidated Iron Mines, **V**, 348

Lakehurst, the ZR-1 is set up at, **II**, 148

Lakes, Great. *See* Great Lakes; Ontario, Lake; Erie, Lake; Huron, Lake; Michigan, Lake; Superior, Lake

Lakes-to-Gulf Deep Waterway, **IV**, 488

LaLande, Baptiste, and Santa Fé Trail, **V**, 29; at Taos, **V**, 219

LaLande and Fynje, and Dutch loans, **II**, 178

Lamar, Charles A. L., and the *Wanderer*, **V**, 395

Lamar, Mirabeau, and Texan-Santa Fé expedition of 1841, **V**, 251; as president of the Republic of Texas, **V**, 253; and the Texas navy, **V**, 256

Lamar v. Browne, **V**, 398

"Lame-Duck" Amendment. *See* Twentieth Amendment

La Mesa, Battle of, **V**, 24

Lancashire Furnace, **IV**, 343

Lancaster, Iroquois make treaty at, **III**, 99

Lancaster Gap Mine, **IV**, 132

Lancaster Pike, and road building, **IV**, 494; and Valley Forge, **V**, 355

Land, Indian conception of ownership of, **III**, 98; and the privileged class, **IV**, 350

Land Act of 1796, and land speculation, **III**, 240; and public land sales, **IV**, 372; and French defection at Vincennes, **V**, 370

Land Act of 1820, and public land sales, **IV**, 372; and the Relief Act of 1821, **IV**, 441

Land Banks, and colonial New York loan offices, **III**, 287

Land Bounties, and Texas revolution, **V**, 253

Land-Grant Colleges, **I**, 14, 388, 414; **IV**, 457

Land Grants, for education, **II**, 186; for railroads, **III**, 70, 138; for education, **III**, 238; to railroads, **III**, 238; **IV**, 407; **V**, 309; to the Union Pacific Railroad, **V**, 342; to railroads, **V**, 429

Land Policy, and agriculture, **I**, 30

Land Riots, New Jersey, **IV**, 105

Land Speculation, and the Loyal Land Company, **III**, 311; and military tracts, **III**, 402; and Onion River Land Company, **IV**, 174; and the panics of 1791, 1837 and 1857, **IV**, 208; and public land sales, **IV**, 372; in Tennessee River region, **V**, 244; and the Virginia Military Reserve in Ohio, **V**, 379; and the West, **V**, 435; and western land schemes, **V**, 443; and western separatism, **V**, 447; and the Yazoo fraud, **V**, 503

Land System, and the township, **V**, 290

Land Titles, and the Torrens system, **V**, 285

Landais, Pierre, and the Bergen prizes, **I**, 179

Landgraves, and Fundamental Constitutions of Carolina, **I**, 316

Landis, Kenesaw M., and Standard Oil Company of Indiana, **V**, 157

Landon, Alfred M., nominated for Presidency, **I**, 292; American delegate to Lima Conference, **III**, 278

Landsteiner, Karl, awarded Nobel prize in medicine, **III**, 370

Lane, James H., suicide of, **III**, 194; and the Kansas Free-State party, **III**, 196, 198; and Quantrill's raid, **IV**, 387; and the Topeka movement, **V**, 281; and the Wakarusa War, **V**, 391

Lane, John, and the steel-faced plow, **II**, 247

Lane, Joseph, nominated for Vice-Presidency, **I**, 285

Lane, Ralph, governor of Roanoke Island Colony, **IV**, 144, 413

Lane, Samuel, and the threshing machine, **II**, 248

Lane, Sen., and the Pacific Republic movement, **IV**, 197

Lane Seminary, and the Oberlin movement, **IV**, 155

Langdon, John, and campaign of 1812, **I**, 281; signer of the Constitution, **II**, 39; and Republican (Jeffersonian) party in New Hampshire, **IV**, 102; and Fort William and Mary, **V**, 467

Langlade, Charles de, and British campaign of 1780, **I**, 240; at Pickawillany, **IV**, 266; and the Sauk Indians, **V**, 34; helps defeat Braddock, **V**, 473

Langley, Samuel P., endeavors to solve problem of power-driven gliders, **I**, 142; fails in experiment with tandem monoplane, **III**, 214; third secretary of Smithsonian Institution, **V**, 102

Langley Field, the *Roma* is assembled at, **II**, 148

Langmuir, Irving, develops high-vacuum tube, **II**, 199; and the incandescent lamp, **III**, 232

Lanier (James F. D.) House, architecture of, **I**, 100

Lanphier, Charles H., and the *Illinois State Register,* **IV**, 129

Lansing, Robert, and Declaration of London, **III**, 296; and the secret protocol, **V**, 52; and the Virgin Islands, **V**, 371; and the World War Peace Conference, **V**, 490; as Secretary of State during World War, **V**, 491

Lansing-Ishii Agreement, and relations with Manchuria, **III**, 330; cancellation of, **IV**, 134; and secret protocol, **V**, 52; abrogation of, **V**, 417

LaPerrière, Boucher de, and Minnesota, **III**, 410

La Pointe à la Chevelure, **II**, 93

La Pointe Settlement, **V**, 473

La Presentation, mission founded by François Picquet, **IV**, 159

Lapsley v. Brashears, **IV**, 170

Lapwai Mission, founded, **III**, 66

La Radiere, Lt. Col., and West Point, **V**, 438

Laramie, Fort, and the Mormon Trail, **IV**, 24; and the Oregon Trail, **IV**, 186; as frontier trading post, **V**, 302

Laramie, Fort, Treaty of (1851), Assiniboine assigned to reservation by, **I**, 130; and Bozeman Trail, **I**, 232; and Indian land cessions, **III**, 100; and Indian policy, **III**, 106; and Wyoming, **V**, 497

Laramie, Fort, Treaty of (1868), and Black Hills, **I**, 195; negotiated by Indian Commission, **III**, 96; and abandonment of Fort Phil Kearny, **III**, 201; ends Red Cloud War, **IV**, 429; and the Sioux Council, **V**, 85; and Sioux wars, **V**, 86; terminates Red Cloud War, **V**, 87; creates Great Sioux Reservation, **V**, 127

Laramie, Jacques, unofficial explorer, **II**, 235; enters Wyoming, **V**, 496

L'Archevêque, Juan de, killed in Pawnee attack on Villasur's expedition, **V**, 369

Larkin, John D., and mail-order houses, **III**, 325

Larkin, T. O., and news of California gold discovery, **I**, 272; and the Mexican War, **III**, 385

Larned, William A., tennis player, **V**, 245

La Ronde, Louis Denis, Sieur de, at Chequamegon Bay, **I**, 351

LaSalle, Robert Cavelier, Sieur de, visits Arkansas, **I**, 105; lays claim to entire Mississippi Valley for France, **I**, 106; builds the *Frontenac* and *Griffon,* **I**, 301; builds Fort Prudhomme, **I**, 359; and the building of Fort Conti, **II**, 46; encamps at Pimitéoui, **II**, 87; launches first ship on Lake Erie, **II**, 224; and Mississippi River flood, **II**, 286; and the Franciscans, **II**, 325; and French claims in Ohio, **II**, 343; explores Mississippi basin, **II**, 344; and Fort Frontenac, **II**, 349; explores the Mississippi, **II**, 415; builds the *Griffon,* **II**, 426; and Hennepin's narratives, **III**, 26; and Illinois, **III**, 67; claims Louisiana for

the king of France, **III**, 304 f.; and the Mas-couten, **III**, 350; claims Mississippi River basin for France, **III**, 420; explores the Mississippi River, **III**, 423; and the Mississippi Valley, **III**, 425; explores Missouri, **III**, 426; and New France, **IV**, 101; alleged discovery of Falls of the Ohio, **IV**, 162; and discovery of the Ohio River, **IV**, 164; and the Ohio Valley, **IV**, 165; builds post at mouth of Niagara River, **IV**, 175; claims territory of Orleans, **IV**, 188; builds Fort Crève-cœur, **IV**, 252; erects fort on site of Prud-homme Bluffs, **IV**, 369; passes Fort St. Joseph, **V**, 10; builds Fort St. Louis, **V**, 11; and St. Louis of Texas, **V**, 13; at Starved Rock, **V**, 161; visits the Taënsa Indians, **V**, 216; in Texas, **V**, 252

Las Animas Grant, **III**, 236

LaSaussaye, makes settlement at Mount Desert, **IV**, 35

Lassen Volcanic National Park, **IV**, 218

Lassen's Road, and the Great Basin, **II**, 414

Lassiter, William, and Tacna-Arica controversy, **V**, 216

Last Chance Gulch, gold discovered in, **III**, 24

Last Roundup at Dodge City, **IV**, 499

Latham, M. S., and the Pacific Republic movement, **IV**, 197

Latin America, concessions in, **II**, 1; good neighbor policy with, **II**, 400

Latin-American Republics, recognition of the, **V**, 135

Latin Grammar Schools, **I**, 5; **II**, 185; **III**, 30

La Tour, in the Penobscot region, **II**, 346; and Port Royal, **IV**, 315

Latrobe, Benjamin H., builds Bank of North America, **I**, 100; and the rebuilding of the Capitol at Washington, **I**, 311; and the White House, **V**, 459

Latter-Day Saints. *See* Mormons

Laud Commission, and British colonial policy, **I**, 421

Laudonnière, René de, in Florida, **II**, 288

Lauf v. E. G. Shimer, **IV**, 267

Laufer, Berthold, and potatoes, **IV**, 323

Laura Spelman Rockefeller Memorial, and World War relief, **V**, 488

Laurens, Henry, and the Definitive Treaty of Peace, **II**, 129; makes charges of fraud against the firm of Willing and Morris, **IV**, 475; attacks slavery, **V**, 94; and the bonding provision of the Sugar Acts, **V**, 200

Lausanne Agreement, and reparations, **IV**, 450

LaVerendrye. *See* Verendrye

Law, common, **I**, 438; French, **II**, 76; colonial, **II**, 174; Spanish, **V**, 138; state, uniform, **V**, 170; statutory, **V**, 177

Law, Hervey, and match-making machinery, **III**, 359

Law, John, sends German colonists to develop his concession on the Arkansas River, **I**, 106; organizes the Western Company, **III**, 305; and the Mississippi Bubble, **III**, 421; and territory of Orleans, **IV**, 188; and lead mining, **V**, 9

Law Schools, and education, **II**, 187; Litchfield Law School, **III**, 283; opened to women, **V**, 481

Lawrence, Amos, and the Emigrant Aid movement, **II**, 211; and land speculation, **III**, 240

Lawrence, James, and the capture of the *Chesapeake*, **I**, 354; dying words of, "Don't give up the ship," **II**, 161; and the *Hornet-Peacock* engagement, **III**, 46

Lawrence, Kans., raided (1856), **I**, 133, 220; **III**, 198; Quantrill's raid on, **IV**, 387

Lawrence, The, Perry's flagship in battle of Lake Erie, **II**, 224

Lawrence, William, at Fort Bowyer, **I**, 231

Lawrence Scientific School, **V**, 44

Lawson, Ernest, painter, **I**, 123

Lawson, Thomas W., and frenzied finance, **II**, 348; **IV**, 38

Lawton, H. W., and the Philippine insurrection, **IV**, 261; at El Caney, **V**, 25

Lazear, J. W., and yellow fever, **V**, 505

Lea, Albert M., names Iowa, **III**, 152

Lea-McCarren Civil Aeronautics Act, **I**, 380

Lead Mining, **II**, 93, 172, 367; **III**, 407, 426; **V**, 8

Leadville, Colo., a boom town, **I**, 215; silver camp at, **II**, 138; and the building of the Denver and Rio Grande Railway, **II**, 139

League Against War and Fascism, **IV**, 235

League of Nations, Article Ten of, **I**, 125; rejected by the treaty of Berlin, **I**, 179; and Briand-Kellogg Pact, **I**, 236; and the campaigns of 1920 and 1924, **I**, 291; and international conciliation, **II**, 2; and the Democratic party, **II**, 137; members obliged to register treaties, **II**, 147; and Far Eastern policy, **II**, 243; and foreign policy, **II**, 305; covenant of, **II**, 377; and Hitchcock reservations, **III**, 35; and international law, **III**, 142; and isolation, **III**, 163; and Japanese exclusion, **III**, 168; and Ladd's peace plan, **III**, 226; and Latin-American relations, **III**, 249; and the Lodge Reservations, **III**, 293; and mandates, **III**, 331; and the Monroe Doctrine, **IV**, 14; and open covenants, **IV**, 176; and World War Peace Conference, **IV**, 232; Senate rejects, **IV**, 235; and trading with the enemy, **V**, 301; and the Treaty of Versailles, **V**, 363; and white-slave traffic, **V**, 460; establishes the World Court, **V**, 485; and the United States as a world power, **V**, 487; and World War Peace Conference, **V**, 490; and the Yap mandate, **V**, 503

League of Nations Association, **IV**, 235

League of Universal Brotherhood, **IV**, 234

League of Women Voters, **I**, 382; **III**, 287; **IV**, 337

League to Enforce Peace, **IV**, 235, 331

Learned Societies, **I**, 64

Leasehold System, **I**, 83

Leather, and foreign trade, **V**, 295

"Leather Breeches," fiddle tune, **II**, 270

Leatherstocking Tales, written by J. F. Cooper, **II**, 270

Leavenworth, Fort, Staff School at, **I**, 114; Infantry and Cavalry School established at, **I**, 118; School for Army General Service, **I**, 118; established, **III**, 194; and Russell, Majors and Waddell, **IV**, 510

Leavenworth, Henry, negotiates treaty with Sioux, **II**, 244; establishes Fort Snelling, **V**, 106; and the Yellowstone River expedition, **V**, 506

Leavenworth and Pikes Peak Express, **IV**, 270, 510; **V**, 152

Leaverett, Thomas, and the Waldo patent, **V**, 391

Leavitt, George A., and book auctions, **I**, 211

Leavitt, Humphrey H., and Champaign County rescue cases, **I**, 338

LeBœuf, Fort, built by French, **II**, 177, 342, 344, 346; Gist travels to, **II**, 390; garrisoned, **III**, 343; falls in Pontiac's War, **IV**, 306

LeCaron, Joseph, and Lake Huron, **III**, 61

Lecompton Constitution, and the English Compromise of 1858, **II**, 217; and the Kansas struggle, **III**, 198; and Popular Sovereignty, **IV**, 309

LeConte, John and Joseph, scientists, **V**, 122

Lecturing, and the lyceum movement, **III**, 316

Ledyard, Isaac, answers Hamilton regarding treatment of loyalists, **V**, 322

Lee, Ann, and the Shakers, **I**, 440; **V**, 63

Lee, Arthur, appointed to joint diplomatic commission, **II**, 322; and Franco-American Alliance, **II**, 326; and the Mississippi Company of Virginia, **III**, 421; and diplomacy of the Revolution, **IV**, 470; and profiteering in the Revolution, **IV**, 475; and the old regime in Virginia, **V**, 375

Lee, Charles, and the battle of Monmouth, **IV**, 11; as prisoner of war, **IV**, 348; and Washington's eight months army, **V**, 419

Lee, Fitzhugh, and Buckland Races, **I**, 246; and battle at Trevilian Station, **V**, 323

Lee, Fort, located at Charleston, W. Va., **I**, 344

Lee, Francis Lightfoot, signer of the Declaration of Independence, **II**, 124

Lee, G. W. Custis, and Arlington National Shrine, **I**, 107; and U. S. v. Lee, **V**, 349

Lee, H. J., and Peary's polar expeditions, **IV**, 237

Lee, Henry, and the phrase "First in War, etc.," **II**, 276; and battle of the Haw River, **III**, 17; and surprise attack of Paulus Hook, **IV**, 226

Lee, Jason, makes known much of the Northwest, **II**, 236; holds first Protestant religious services at Fort Hall, **III**, 6; establishes the Oregon Mission, **IV**, 182; and Oregon Memorial, **IV**, 183; and Oregon missions, **IV**, 184; and the Willamette Valley settlements, **V**, 466

Lee, John D., and the Mountain Meadows massacre, **IV**, 36

Lee, Mrs. Robert E., and U. S. v. Lee, **V**, 349

Lee, Richard Henry, and the motion for independence (1776), **I**, 125; and the Declaration of Independence, **II**, 120, 124; saved by Jouett's ride, **III**, 182; and land speculation, **III**, 239; and pamphleteering, **IV**, 202; and resolution for independence, **IV**, 499; approves the Virginia Resolves, **V**, 379

Lee, Robert, E., and the battle of Antietam, **I**, 81; and Appomattox, **I**, 91; becomes a general of the Confederate Army, **I**, 110; and the improvement of the Mississippi River, **I**, 202; and the attack on the Bloody Angle, **I**, 202; and Bristoe campaign, **I**, 238; at Second Bull Run, **I**, 251; and battle of Cerro Gordo, **I**, 335; and battle of Chancellorsville, **I**, 339; at Cold Harbor, **I**, 412; and the Confederacy, **II**, 12; and the Corps of Engineers, **II**, 216; placed in command of Confederate Army, **II**, 240; and battle of Frayser's Farm, **II**, 330; and battle of Gaines' Mill, **II**, 366; and battle of Gettysburg, **II**, 386; and Harpers Ferry raid, **III**, 12; and the "Lost Order," **III**, 303; and battle of Malvern Hill, **III**, 329; and invasion of Maryland, **III**, 349; and battle of Mechanicsville, **III**, 367; and the Mine Run campaign, **III**, 405; and battle of North Anna, **IV**, 144; and the Peninsular campaign, **IV**, 241; and invasion of Pennsylvania, **IV**, 244; and the siege of Petersburg, **IV**, 255; and Pickett's charge, **IV**, 267; and battle at Rappahannock Station, **IV**, 416; and campaign against Richmond, **IV**, 481; and burning and evacuation of Richmond, **IV**, 482; and Seven Days' battles, **V**, 59; and battle of South Mountain, **V**, 128; blocks Grant at North Anna River, **V**, 150; placed in command of the Army of Northern Virginia, **V**, 371; becomes president of Washington College, **V**, 416; and battles of the Wilderness, **V**, 464

Lee, S. D., and the battle of Ezra Church, **II**, 238

Lee, S. P., and prize money, **IV**, 353

Lee, Stephen Louis, and Sangre de Cristo grant, **V**, 27

Lee, Thomas, and the Mississippi Company of Virginia, **III**, 421; builds Stratford Hall, **V**, 187; and the colony of Virginia, **V**, 373

Leete, William, governor of New Haven Colony, **IV**, 104; and regicides in New England, **IV**, 438

Lefevres, The, rifle makers, **IV**, 483

LeFlore, Greenwood, chief of the Choctaws, and the treaty of Dancing Rabbit Creek, **II**, 108

Legal Tender, and Bronson v. Rodes, **I**, 242; extended to all forms of United States currency (1933), **I**, 252; commodities as, **I**, 437; and the Constitution, **II**, 34; and the crime of 1873, **II**, 89; Spanish coins as, **II**, 99; greenbacks as, **II**, 424; and mortgages, **IV**, 29; and silver legislation, **V**, 80; and specie payments, **V**, 143; and token money, **V**, 276; and the trade dollar, **V**, 298

Legal Tender Act (1862), passage of, **I**, 384; and first issue of greenbacks, **IV**, 461

Legal Tender Acts, and the Supreme Court Packing Bills, **V**, 208

Legal Tender Cases, and Juilliard v. Greenman, **III**, 189; and repudiation of public debt, **IV**, 455; and the Supreme Court, **V**, 207. *See also* Knox v. Lee

Legardo, Elias, early Jewish settler, **III**, 176

Legends, Indian, **III**, 101

Legislature, and the right of petition, **IV**, 256; and state constitutions, **V**, 167; and state government, **V**, 169

Lehigh Canal, **I**, 80; **IV**, 245

Lehigh Coal and Navigation Company, **IV**, 245

Lehigh University, as a scientific school, **V**, 44

Lehigh Valley Railroad, leases the Morris Canal, **IV**, 27; built on a canal right of way, **IV**, 245

Leib, Michael, and Tammany societies, **V**, 218

Leigh, John, experiments with opium, **II**, 171

Leisler, Jacob, and the Albany Convention, **I**, 45; and King William's War, **III**, 211; rebellion of, **III**, 404; **IV**, 114, 118

Leisy v. Hardin, and the original-package doctrine, **IV**, 187 f.

Leitch, Maj., and battle of Harlem, **III**, 10

Leiter, Levi, and book collections, **I**, 213; and great fortunes, **II**, 312

Leland, W. G., and N. D. Mereness, *American Official Sources . . . of the World War*, **III**, 34

Lemans, The, rifle makers, **IV**, 483

Lemhi Pass, **IV**, 222

Lemon, George E., founder of *National Tribune*, **IV**, 63

Lemons, and the citrus industry, **I**, 379

LeMoyne, Jacques, early drawings of, **II**, 288

L'Enfant, Pierre Charles, and city planning, **I**, 380; commissioned in the Revolutionary Army, **IV**, 473; and plan for Washington, D. C., **V**, 412; and the White House, **V**, 459

Leni-Lenape, or Delaware Indians, **II**, 131

Lenox, James, book collector, **I**, 212; and the New York Public Library, **III**, 272

Leonard, Zenas, trapper, **V**, 311

Leonora, first known opera composed by an American, **IV**, 178

Leoti, Kans., and the county-seat war, **II**, 74

Lernoult, Fort, another name for Fort Pontchartrain Du Detroit, **IV**, 305

Le Rocher, or Starved Rock, **V**, 161

LeRoux, Bartholomew, silversmith, **V**, 82

Lescarbot, Marc, and topographic mapping, **V**, 282

LeSueur, Pierre Charles, and Minnesota, **III**, 410

"Let the end be legitimate . . .," in McCulloch v. Maryland, **III**, 364

Letcher, John, nonslaveholder, **IV**, 141; and the Ruffner pamphlet, **IV**, 505

Letterman, Jonathan, expands ambulance corps, **I**, 54

Letterman General Hospital, **I**, 116

Leutze, Emanuel, painter of picture "Washington Crossing the Delaware," **II**, 132

Levees, and flood control, **II**, 285; constructed in Louisiana, **III**, 306; on the Mississippi, **III**, 423; and New Orleans, **IV**, 109; and river and harbor improvements, **IV**, 488

Lever Act, and food control, **II**, 296; and Fuel Administration, **II**, 354; and the World War, **V**, 492

Leverett, John, first lay president of Harvard, **III**, 15

Levinson, S. O., and the Kellogg Pact, **IV**, 233

"Levy," monetary term, **I**, 411

Levy, Uriah, and Monticello, **IV**, 17

Lewelling, H., first nurseryman in Oregon, **IV**, 154

Lewin, John, as a proprietary agent, **IV**, 361

Lewis, Andrew, patents Burning Spring, **I**, 256; at Charleston, W. Va., **I**, 344; prepares for expedition against Shawnee towns, **II**, 177; as agent of the Greenbrier Company, **II**, 425; at Gwynn's Island, **II**, 430; and battle of Point Pleasant, **IV**, 291

Lewis, Charles, and battle of Point Pleasant, **IV**, 291

Lewis, "Commodore," and Miranda's intrigues, **III**, 414

Lewis, Dio, on temperance, **V**, 479

Lewis, E. M., and Ypres-Lys operation, **V**, 511

Lewis, Fort, established by American Fur Company, **I**, 178

Lewis, Francis, signer of the Declaration of Independence, **II**, 124

Lewis, J. O., artist present at signing of treaty of Prairie du Chien, **IV**, 329

Lewis, James Hamilton, designated as party whip, **V**, 456

Lewis, John, leading spirit of Loyal Land Company, **III**, 311; and the Shenandoah Valley, **V**, 69

Lewis, John L., and the American Labor party, **I**, 62

Lewis, Morgan, leader of the Quids, **IV**, 390

Lewis, Reuben, partner in St. Louis Missouri Fur Company, **V**, 12

Lewis, Sinclair, author of *Main Street*, **II**, 270; wins Nobel prize in literature, **IV**, 136

Lewis, Thomas, begins settlement north of Saco River, **V**, 3

Lewis, William B., member of the "Kitchen Cabinet," **III**, 213

Lewis, William H., killed in Dull Knife's campaign, **II**, 175

Lewis and Clark Expedition, and accounts of the grizzly bear, **I**, 171; and the Cheyenne Indians, **I**, 355; explores the Columbia River, **I**, 430; discovers Crow Indians, **II**, 92; winters at Five Villages, **II**, 106; reaches the Five Villages, **II**, 280; builds Fort Mandan, **III**, 330; explores the Missouri River, **III**, 430; helped by the Nez Percé Indians, **IV**, 129; reaches Oregon, **IV**, 182; and the Oregon Question, **IV**, 184; and the Oregon Trail, **IV**, 185; and mountain passes, **IV**, 222; and the Great Plains, **IV**, 282; makes a portage at Great Falls, Mont., **IV**, 317; and the Rocky Mountains, **IV**, 498; and Shehaka's visit to President Jefferson, **V**, 12; and the Sioux, **V**, 85; follows Snake River, **V**, 106; and territorial claims of the United States, **V**, 246; discovers first overland route to the Pacific, **V**, 283; strengthens America's claim to the Oregon Country, **V**, 415; and western exploration, **V**, 442; and the search for the western sea, **V**, 446

Lewis Machine Guns, **III**, 319

Lexington, Mass., minutemen at, **III**, 414; Revere arrives at, **IV**, 463

Lexington, Mo., captured by Price, **IV**, 339

Lexington, The, and the Falkland Islands controversy, **II**, 240

Lexington and Concord, and the American Revolution, **IV**, 467; battle of, **IV**, 476

Lexow Committee, **II**, 88

L'Huillier, Fort, French outpost in Minnesota, **III**, 410

Libbies, C. F., and book auctions, **I**, 211

Libby, A. A., and meat packing, **IV**, 199

Libby Prison, **I**, 136; **II**, 8

Libel, Hamilton brings about liberalizing of, **II**, 92; and the Zenger trial, **V**, 513

Liberal Republican Party, **I**, 286; **V**, 262

Liberator, The, **I**, 3, 85; **II**, 372

Liberia, and the American Colonization Society, **I**, 59; Negroes from the *Echo* returned to, **II**, 183; freedmen sent to, **II**, 204

Liberty, definition of, **IV**, 254

Liberty, The, scuttling of (1769), **IV**, 478

Liberty, The, and the Texas navy, **V**, 256

Liberty Bell, in Independence Hall, **III**, 86

Liberty Bell Gold Mine, **II**, 396; **V**, 25

Liberty Bonds, advertising as an aid in selling, **I**, 17; and public debt, **II**, 117; and gold clause cases, **II**, 394

Liberty Boys, The. *See* Sons of Liberty (Revolutionary)

Liberty Loans, and the Federal deficit, **II**, 128; Four-minute Men promote sale of, **II**, 316; and Treasury notes, **V**, 314; for World War financing, **V**, 489

Liberty Party, **I**, 284, 292; **II**, 333; **IV**, 296; **V**, 262

"Liberty Song," and "United We Stand, Divided We Fall," **V**, 350

Liberty Trees, and Sons of Liberty (Revolutionary), **V**, 120

Libraries, growth of, and adult education, **I**, 14; as history sources, **III**, 34; and municipal ownership, **IV**, 42

Library of American Biography, by Jared Sparks, **I**, 189

Library of Congress, archives available in, **I**, 103; and collections of folk songs, **I**, 149; department for the blind created at, **I**, 200; and Thomas Jefferson's library, **I**, 212; regulated by a committee of Congress, **II**, 17; and copyright, **II**, 58; as source of history, **III**, 34; and the Virginia Company of London transcripts, **V**, 378; as a national institution, **V**, 413

Licensed Automobile Manufacturers, Association of, **I**, 140

Lick Observatory, **IV**, 156

Licks. *See* Salt Licks

Lieber, Francis, and Americanization, **I**, 67; draws up General Orders No. 100, **I**, 384; and the Forty-eighters, **II**, 313; leader of the Loyal Publication Society of New York, **III**, 312; political writings of, **IV**, 302; political scientist, **V**, 122; prepares General Orders No. 100, **V**, 397

Life Insurance, **III**, 130; **V**, 281

Life Saving Service, replaced by Coast Guard, **I**, 405

Liggett, Hunter, and the Meuse-Argonne offensive, **III**, 381

Light, Edwin B., and the Silver League, **V**, 80

Lighthouses, Bureau of, **I**, 432

Lighting, by candles, **I**, 303; by electricity, **II**, 195 ff.; by oil, **IV**, 166; and the whaling industry, **V**, 452

Lignery, Marchand de, invades Wisconsin, **II**, 320

Ligonier, Bouquet occupies, **II**, 299

Liguesto. *See* Laclede

Liliuokalani, Queen, and Hawaii, **III**, 18

Lillie, Gordon W., and the Wild West show, **V**, 464

Lima, Peru, Pan-American Conference at (1938), **IV**, 203

Limitation of Naval Armaments, Treaty for the, **V**, 318

Limited Powers of President, **II,** 257

Limited Vote Plan, **II,** 193

Lincecum, Gideon, and the medicine show, **III,** 370

Lincoln, Abraham, issues proclamations suspending writ of habeas corpus, **I,** 121; assassination of, **I,** 129; courts Mary Todd, **I,** 205; and first Bull Run, **I,** 251; elected President, **I,** 285; plan of Reconstruction, **I,** 385; and the Civil War, **I,** 385 ff.; and Civil War diplomacy, **I,** 391; and the Confederate States, **II,** 10; and the Corning letter, **II,** 60; and the Crittenden Compromise, **II,** 90; Davis charged with planning assassination of, **II,** 112; and the Emancipation Proclamation, **II,** 205; and compensated emancipation, **II,** 205; and enlistment, **II,** 218; and the Freeport doctrine, **II,** 340; delivers Gettysburg address, **II,** 387; and definition of democracy, **II,** 404; authorizes suspension of writ of habeas corpus, **III,** 1; and Hampton Roads Conference, **III,** 7; and Harrison's Landing letter, **III,** 13; signs the Homestead Law, **III,** 43; and "House divided" speech, **III,** 51; his plan of Reconstruction, and impeachment trial of Andrew Johnson, **III,** 77; inauguration of, **III,** 82; and liberalism, **III,** 269; and the Merryman case, **III,** 378; and the *Monitor,* **IV,** 10; "Old Abe," **IV,** 169; and oratory, **IV,** 180; and pardon and amnesty, **IV,** 214; defines democracy in Gettysburg address, **IV,** 301; and the Pomeroy Circular, **IV,** 305; debates with Douglas, **IV,** 309; and the Presidency, **IV,** 333; and special powers granted to Presidents, **IV,** 335; and the Prize Cases, **IV,** 351; and the Radical Republicans, **IV,** 395; as the "Rail Splitter," **IV,** 399; his plan of Reconstruction, **IV,** 424, 426; nominated for the Presidency, **IV,** 454; participates in the Rock Island Bridge case, **IV,** 497; and representation of seceded states, **V,** 50; assassination of, and *"sic semper tyrannis,"* **V,** 77; and the Singleton peace plan, **V,** 83; sends fleet to relieve Fort Sumter, **V,** 203; and surveying, **V,** 210; and Thanksgiving Day, **V,** 259; and the *Trent* affair, **V,** 321; and the Vallandigham incident, **V,** 355; and the Virgin Islands, **V,** 371; pockets the Wade-Davis Bill, **V,** 386; war powers of, **V,** 407; and the poem "We are coming, Father Abra'am, etc.," **V,** 428; signs West Virginia statehood bill, **V,** 439; whispering campaigns against, **V,** 458; elected on the Wilmot Proviso platform, **V,** 469; second inaugural address of, **V,** 476

Lincoln, Benjamin, and the capture of Charleston, **I,** 343; in skirmish near Harlem River, **II,** 343; in the Revolutionary War, **IV,** 477; and siege of Savannah, **V,** 36; and Shays' Rebellion, **V,** 66; and the southern campaigns (1780–81),

V, 129; appointed secretary of War and Ordnance Board, **V,** 399; and Yorktown campaign, **V,** 509

Lincoln Highway, and Raystown Path, **IV,** 418; and roads, **IV,** 496

Lind, John, as executive agent, **II,** 232; governor of Minnesota, **III,** 411

Lindbergh, Charles A., prominent in Minnesota politics, **III,** 411; and the Nonpartisan League, **IV,** 140

Lindbergh, Charles A., flies the Atlantic, **I,** 36, 143; **II,** 328; at Sixth Pan-American Conference, **IV,** 203

Lindbergh Kidnapping Case, **III,** 208; **V,** 323

Lindenthal, Gustav, and bridges, **I,** 237, 238

Lindo, Moses, and indigo industry, **III,** 114

Lindsey, Benjamin, and companionate marriage, **I,** 441; and juvenile courts, **III,** 193

Ling, Matthew, and the Minisink patent, **III,** 410

Lining, John, and first history of yellow fever, **II,** 221

Linn, Lewis F., presents Oregon Memorial to the Senate, **IV,** 183; and the Oregon Question, **IV,** 185

Linn, William, and Gibson episode, **II,** 389

Linnean Society, **IV,** 47

Linotype, invented by Mergenthaler, **III,** 148; first used by New York *Tribune,* **IV,** 126

Linsey-Woolsey, and household arts, **III,** 53

Linton, W. J., and wood engraving, **V,** 483

Lions Club, **I,** 261

Lippard, George, literary lecturer, **III,** 260

Lippmann, Walter, and political writings, **IV,** 303

Liquor, consumption of, **II,** 169; and the Indian, **III,** 91, 109; and local option, **III,** 290; and the McConnelsville Ordinance, **III,** 363; smuggling of, **V,** 103; and the Volstead Act, **V,** 382. *See also* Rum; Whiskey

Lisa, Fort, **III,** 431; **IV,** 80; **V,** 13, 302

Lisa, Manuel, on Big Horn River and Oregon Trail, **II,** 235; and the fur trade, **II,** 362, 363; builds Manuel's Fort, **III,** 335; father of navigation on the Missouri, **III,** 430; opens fur trade on upper Missouri, **IV,** 16; partner in St. Louis Missouri Fur Company, **V,** 12; forms the Missouri Fur Company, **V,** 13; and the War of 1812, **V,** 406

Litchfield, Edwin, and the Michigan Southern Railroad, **III,** 393

Litchfield Law School, **III,** 252

Literacy Tests, as voting restriction, **II,** 271; in Mississippi, **III,** 421; and the suffrage, **V,** 199; and the Negro vote, **V,** 383

Literary Digest, straw polls of, **I,** 217; **V,** 21

Littell, Isaac W., commands the Cantonment Division, **I,** 296

Little, George, captain of the *Boston,* **I,** 222

Little, Henry, killed in battle of Iuka, **III**, 164

Little America, **I**, 264

Little Big Horn, Battle of, Arapaho participate in, **I**, 94; Custer's force annihilated at, **I**, 184, 195; Indian reservations in Dakota reduced after, **II**, 106; and the *Far West*, **II**, 244; and Sioux wars, **V**, 87

Little Corporal, children's magazine, **I**, 363

Little Crow, and the Dustin murders, **II**, 178; Sioux chief, **V**, 85; and Sioux uprising in Minnesota, **V**, 86; and battle of Wood Lake, **V**, 483

"Little Egypt," at World's Columbian Exposition, **III**, 396; **V**, 495

Little Niagara, Fort, **IV**, 129

Little Pittsburg Mine, **III**, 254

Little Sarah Case, and Genêt, **II**, 377

Little Shepherd of Kingdom Come, written by J. W. Fox, Jr., **I**, 180

"Little Theater" Movement, **I**, 14; **V**, 109, 260

Little Thunder, defeated at Ash Hollow, **I**, 127

Little Turtle, Indian leader, **II**, 241; leads the Miamis against LaBalme, **III**, 218; leader of the Miamis, **III**, 390

Little Wolf, in Dull Knife's campaign, **II**, 174

Littlefield, Ephraim, witness in the Webster-Parkman murder, **V**, 432

Littleton, Martin W., and the Thaw murder trial, **V**, 323

Live Stock Credit Corporations, **II**, 246

Livermore, Mary A., lecturer, **III**, 260

Livestock, early phases of, **I**, 22; and dairy industry, **I**, 28; breeding improved, **I**, 32; in New England, **I**, 33; on the Bluestem Pastures, **I**, 205

Livingston, Fargo and Company, **I**, 60

Livingston, John, and the New York and Genesee Company, **IV**, 117

Livingston, John H., and the *Coetus-Conferentie* controversy, **I**, 409

Livingston, Manor of, **III**, 55

Livingston, Phil., signer of the Declaration of Independence, **II**, 124

Livingston, Robert, his plan of colonial union, **I**, 420; and Dongan's charters, **II**, 160

Livingston, Robert R., and the drafting of the Declaration of Independence, **II**, 120; and Franco-American relations, **II**, 328; and "Fulton's folly," **II**, 355; and steamboat monopoly rights, **II**, 388; administers the oath at Washington's inauguration, **III**, 82; and the steamboat, **III**, 148; and the Louisiana Purchase, **III**, 308; first Secretary of Foreign Affairs, **V**, 161; works for repeal of all laws contrary to the Definitive Treaty of Peace, **V**, 323

Livingston, William, signer of the Constitution, **II**, 39

Llewellyn Iron Works, bombing of, **III**, 367

Lloyd, Henry D., and Populism, **IV**, 313

Lloyd, Thomas, and the Keith controversy, **III**, 202

Lo Lo Pass, **IV**, 222

Lobbyists, and the DeGolyer case, **II**, 130; and pressure groups, **IV**, 337; and propaganda, **IV**, 358

Local Government, in counties, **II**, 74; in cities, **IV**, 41; and state constitutions, **V**, 167; in towns, **V**, 286 f.; township as unit of, **V**, 290

Local Option, and Anti-Saloon League, **I**, 84; and liquor laws, **III**, 282; and the Mulct Law, **IV**, 39; and prohibition, **IV**, 357

Locarno Treaties, and Briand-Kellogg Pact, **I**, 236

Lochaber, Treaty of (1768), establishes line crossing near Big Moccasin Gap, **I**, 184; and Donelson's Line, **II**, 160; **III**, 39; and Indian land cessions, **III**, 99; T. Walker participates in negotiating, **III**, 311; and Proclamation of 1763, **IV**, 354; and first treaty of Fort Stanwix, **V**, 159

Lochner v. New York, **V**, 387

Lockard, Ray W., and Iowa Corn Song, **III**, 153

Locke, John, and antislavery, **I**, 84; and Fundamental Constitutions of Carolina, **I**, 316; and the compact theory, **I**, 441; and the British constitution, **II**, 29; and natural rights concept, **IV**, 66; and personal liberty, **IV**, 254; political theories of, **IV**, 300; and the right of rebellion, **IV**, 420; and the right of revolution, **IV**, 472; and Fundamental Constitutions of Carolina, **V**, 125

Locke, Richard A., and the moon hoax, **IV**, 19

Locke, Sylvanus D., and the development of the reaper, **IV**, 419

Lockouts, and industrial arbitration, **I**, 95; opposed by National Association of Manufacturers, **IV**, 58; and the War Labor Board, **V**, 404

Locks, and mill streams, **III**, 404; and water power, **V**, 422

Lockwood, Belva A., and Equal Rights party, **II**, 222

Lockwood, J. B., polar expedition of, **IV**, 293

Loco-Focos, as a political party, **IV**, 296

Locomotive Engineers, Brotherhood of, **IV**, 400

Locomotive Firemen and Enginemen, Brotherhood of, **III**, 225; **IV**, 400

Locomotives, and railroads, **IV**, 406; "Stourbridge Lion," **V**, 186; "Tom Thumb," **V**, 279

Lode Mining, and mineral patent laws, **III**, 406; and law of the mining camp, **III**, 409

Lodge, Henry Cabot, and the Alaska Boundary Tribunal, **I**, 44; as floor leader, **II**, 287; and the League to Enforce Peace, **III**, 255

Lodge Corollary of the Monroe Doctrine, **III**, 323

Loftus, Arthur, attempts ascent of the Mississippi, III, 68

Loftus Heights, I, 9

Log Cabin, as first house, I, 249; and the frontier family, II, 243; and the pioneers, IV, 275

Log Cabin Song Book, I, 294

Log College, established, IV, 86; and revivals, IV, 464

Logan, Mingo chief, goes on the warpath, I, 146; and the murder of his family, II, 87; and his "speech," II, 87; and Indian oratory, III, 103

Logan, Benjamin, and the battle of Piqua, IV, 277

Logan, Daniel Boone, and ending of Martin-Tolliver feud, III, 348

Logan, James, and book collecting, I, 212; as a proprietary agent, IV, 361; and the founding of Schuylkill Fishing Company, V, 43

Logan, John A., and the origin of Decoration Day, II, 125; commander in chief of the Grand Army of the Republic, II, 407; among the leaders of the Radical Republicans, IV, 395; and battle of Raymond, IV, 418; temporarily replaces McPherson, V, 242

Logan, Martha Daniel, and gardening, II, 371

Logan County Camp Meeting, I, 280

Logan's Fort, II, 82

Logrolling, and propaganda, IV, 359

Logstown, and Washington's mission to Fort LeBœuf, III, 259; treaty of, IV, 163; develops Indian trade, IV, 165; treaty of, IV, 266; and Raystown Path, IV, 418

Loisel, Regis, post of, on the Missouri River, III, 431

Lok, Michael, and fake explorations of the Pacific Coast, IV, 195

Lomax, John A., collects cowboy songs, V, 120

Lomax, L. L., and engagement at Tom's Brook, V, 280; and battle at Yellow Tavern, V, 506

London, Declaration of (1909), defines contraband, II, 48; and neutrality, IV, 89; and prize courts, IV, 352; and the World War, V, 490

London, Jack, author of *Call of the Wild,* I, 180

London and Bristol Company, as trading company, V, 301

London Associates, and New York land speculation, IV, 116

London Naval Treaty of 1930, and national defense, II, 127; and the "escalator" clause, II, 227; and naval competition, II, 280; IV, 70; and parity, IV, 217; and peace conferences, IV, 233; and the submarine, V, 193; and Naval Treaty of Washington (1922), V, 414

London Naval Treaty of 1936, and the "escalator" clause, II, 227; and naval competition, IV, 70

Loneliness, and the pioneers, IV, 275

Lonergan, Philip J. and Thomas, establish Ogallala, IV, 158

Long, Alexander, and the Copperheads, II, 57

Long, Crawford W., first uses sulphuric ether, I, 71; pioneer in anæsthesia, V, 123

Long, Huey P., and the agrarian movement, I, 22; shot by C. A. Weiss, I, 129; and the filibuster, II, 272; and Grosjean v. American Press Company, II, 426; governor of Louisiana, III, 306; and corn pone, IV, 322

Long, James, leads filibustering expedition into Texas, III, 382; IV, 486

Long, John, fur trader, III, 111

Long, John Luther, playwright, II, 166

Long, Pierse, and Fort William and Mary, V, 467

Long, Stephen H., and the Great American Desert, II, 140; and the James expedition, III, 166; in Minnesota, III, 411; and the Great Plains, IV, 282; follows the Platte River Trail, IV, 286; and the Rocky Mountains, IV, 498; establishes Fort Smith (Ark.), V, 101; and the *Western Engineer,* V, 442; and western exploration, V, 442; expedition of, V, 506

Long Beach, N. J., as a summer resort, IV, 460

Long Drive, and the livestock industry, III, 286

Long Hunters, pass through Cumberland Gap, II, 96; follow the Cumberland River, II, 97; referred to as "men of the western waters," III, 373

Long Island, and York's proprietary, V, 508

Long Island, Battle of (1776), IV, 476

Long Island of Holston, Treaty of (1777), III, 88

Long Island Oil Company, V, 156

Long Knives, I, 184

Longeuil, Charles Lemoyne de, earliest known white man to visit Big Bone Lick, I, 183

Longfellow, Henry W., author of "Evangeline," II, 230; and "Hiawatha," III, 29

Longhorns, and cattle drives, I, 326; and the cattle tick, I, 327; and cowboy songs, II, 79; herding and handling of, II, 80; and stampedes, V, 155

Longstreet, Augustus Baldwin, writer, V, 123

Longstreet, James, and battle of Antietam, I, 81; repulses Tyler's attack at Blackburn's Ford, I, 197; at Bull Run, I, 251; and battle of Chickamauga, I, 359; and battle of Frayser's Farm, II, 330; and battle of Gettysburg, II, 386; and siege of Knoxville, III, 216; and battle on Lookout Mountain, III, 300; and battle of Mechanicsville, III, 368; and invasion of Pennsylvania, IV, 244; and battle of South Mountain, V, 128; and operations at Suffolk, V, 198; and battles of the Wilderness, V, 465

Longueuil, and Pickawillany, IV, 266

Longworth, Nicholas, and wine production, V, 471

Longworth, Nicholas, as floor leader, II, 287

Looking Backward, by Edward Bellamy, **IV**, 302

Lookout, Fort, Treaty of, **V**, 86

Lookout Mountain, capture of, **I**, 348

Loom, Crompton, **II**, 91; Jacquard, **III**, 166; for wire weaving, **III**, 320

Loose Construction, Federalists advocate, **II**, 264

López, Francisco de, and missions of the Southwest, **III**, 418; and the Rodríguez-Chamuscado expedition, **IV**, 500

López, Narciso, and the Atarés massacre, **I**, 133; filibustering activities of, **II**, 94, 273

López, Nicholás, and the Mendoza expedition, **III**, 373; explorations of, in Texas, **V**, 252

López de Cárdenas, García, discovers the Grand Canyon, **II**, 408

Lord, John, literary lecturer, **III**, 260

"Lords and Gentlemen," and the Old Patent of Connecticut, **IV**, 490

Lords of Trade and Plantations, replaced by the Board of Trade and Plantations, **I**, 206; and British colonial policy, **I**, 422; and the Council for Foreign Plantations, **II**, 71; and the Massachusetts Bay Company, **III**, 358; and treaty of Fort Stanwix (1768), **V**, 159

Lords Proprietors, and charter colonies, **I**, 346; and colonial charters, **I**, 417

Lorimer, George Horace, as editor of the *Saturday Evening Post,* **V**, 33

Lorimer, William, and political corruption, **II**, 64; and political scandals, **IV**, 298

Lorimier, Louis, at Cape Girardeau, **I**, 307

Lorimier, Pierre Louis, founder of Loramie's store, **III**, 301

Los Adaes, as capital of Spanish Texas, **V**, 252

Los Angeles, The, name given the airship ZR-3, **II**, 149

Los Angeles *Star,* advocates the Pacific Republic movement, **IV**, 197

Los Angeles *Times,* bombing of the, **III**, 367

Losantiville, original name of Cincinnati, **I**, 375; settlement of, **III**, 390

"Lost Order," finding of the, **III**, 349

Lotbinière, Marquis de, begins Fort Ticonderoga, **V**, 268

Lotteries, to finance Avery's Trace, **I**, 142; to raise public funds, **II**, 118; and gambling, **II**, 369; used to finance building of Genesee Road, **II**, 376; Georgia land, **II**, 381; in Louisiana, **III**, 307; to finance the Revolution, **IV**, 471

Loudoun, Fort (on the Tennessee River), Cherokees at, **I**, 352; captured and destroyed, **V**, 19; built by the English, **V**, 242

Loudoun, Lord, in French and Indian War, **III**, 229

Louis, Joe, prize fighter, **IV**, 353

Louisa Land Company, **V**, 215

Louisburg, restored to France, **I**, 38; and D'Anville's expedition, **II**, 109; fall of, **II**, 343; **III**,

210; colonial militia at, **III**, 404; and Port Royal, **IV**, 315

Louisiana, banking system of, **I**, 156; and the Blount Conspiracy, **I**, 203; civil code of, **I**, 407; and the *Coutume de Paris,* **II**, 76; Anthony Crozat given monopoly over, **II**, 93; and expansion, **II**, 234; ceded to Spain, **II**, 294; name given the entire Mississippi Valley by LaSalle, **III**, 247; and the levee system, **III**, 265; Revolution of 1768, **III**, 372; and the Mississippi Bubble, **III**, 421; LaSalle takes possession of, **III**, 423; District of, and Missouri, **III**, 426; territory of, and Missouri, **III**, 426; and Northwest boundary controversy, **IV**, 150; ceded to Spain by France, **IV**, 216; and repudiation of state debts, **IV**, 457; Railway Commission and Shreveport rate case, **V**, 77; Specie Reserve System of, **V**, 164; and sugar cane, **V**, 200; and sugar mill inventions, **V**, 201; and territorial claims of the United States, **V**, 246; territory of, renamed Missouri Territory, **V**, 249; organized, and admitted, **V**, 249; French in, **V**, 252

Louisiana Lottery, **II**, 369; **III**, 303

Louisiana Purchase, and the treaty of Amiens, **I**, 68; and territorial expansion, **I**, 79; region of Arkansas becomes American territory through the, **I**, 105; United States claims title to Baton Rouge by, **I**, 167; and Colorado, **I**, 426; and Convention of 1818, **II**, 52; greater part of Dakota Territory included in, **II**, 106; and the right of deposit, **II**, 140; exploration of, **II**, 176; and United States claims, **II**, 289; and Franco-American relations, **II**, 328; and Freeman's expedition, **II**, 339; and French spoliation claims, **II**, 347; and the fur trade, **II**, 363; and Iberville River, **III**, 66; and Jefferson's removal policy, **III**, 106; and Isle of Orleans, **III**, 162; and land titles, **III**, 243; affords Jefferson a pretext for sending an expedition to explore the western country, **III**, 266; and liberal construction, **III**, 269; made possible by Napoleon's need for money, **III**, 305; and the Mexican boundary, **III**, 382; Minnesota as part of, **III**, 411; and free navigation on the Mississippi, **III**, 423; and the Mississippi River, **III**, 424; gives the Mississippi Valley to the United States, **III**, 425; and Missouri, **III**, 426; and the Missouri Compromise, **III**, 428; and Pike's expedition, **IV**, 269; and Pike's southwestern expedition, **IV**, 270; and the Great Plains, **IV**, 282; and the public domain, **IV**, 369; and the Rio Grande, **IV**, 486; and the Rocky Mountains, **IV**, 498; and St. Louis, **V**, 12; and treaty of San Ildefonso, **V**, 25; antagonizes the Federalists, **V**, 51; and Spanish-American relations, **V**, 134; and the organization of territories, **V**, 249; and annexation of Texas, **V**, 251; and Texas, **V**, 252;

and inland waterways, V, 425; and the West, V, 435; and annexation of West Florida, V, 436; and West Florida controversy, V, 436

Louisville, The, gunboat, II, 180

Louisville and Nashville Railroad, II, 96; IV, 407

Louisville and Portland Canal, subsidy granted to, III, 137; V, 194

Louisville *Journal,* V, 123

Louisville Medical Institute, III, 369

Loup Indians, III, 325

Louther, Fort, and Carlisle, Pa., I, 314

Louvigny, Sieur de, undertakes punitive expedition, II, 319

Love, Alfred, and the Universal Peace Union, IV, 235

Lovelace, Francis, and the capture of New York (1673), IV, 114; and land speculation in New York, IV, 115; as governor of New York, IV, 118

Lovell, Mansfield, and capture of New Orleans (1862), IV, 110; and fortification of Vicksburg, V, 367

Lovell, Solomon, and the Penobscot expedition, IV, 249

Loving, Oliver, and Goodnight Loving Trail, II, 400

Low, Frederick F., and war with Korea, III, 216

Low, Juliette, founder of the Girl Scouts, II, 390

Low, Seth, president of Columbia College, I, 429

Lowden, Frank O., and state administrative reorganization, II, 406

Lowe, Ralph P., becomes first Republican governor of Iowa, III, 153

Lowe, Thaddeus S. C., balloonist, I, 149

Lowell, A. Lawrence, and the League to Enforce Peace, III, 255

Lowell, James Russell, and antislavery literature, I, 85; author of the *Biglow Papers,* I, 184; and American hymns, III, 65; and "Peter Parley," IV, 255

Lowell Institute, and the lyceum movement, III, 316

Lowell Observatory, IV, 157

Lower Brule Reservation, V, 127

Lower California, colonized, I, 275

Lower Counties of Delaware, II, 130

Lower Lakes, II, 416. *See also* Upper, and Lower, Lakes

Lowrie Gang, and lawlessness, III, 252

Lowry, Robert, recognizes need for new industries in Mississippi, III, 421

Loyal, Fort, surrender of, III, 211

Loyal Associated Refugees, I, 131

Loyal Land Company, and Kentucky, III, 204; and land speculation, III, 239

Loyal Leagues. *See* Union (Loyal) Leagues

Loyal Publication Society, and Civil War propaganda, I, 388

Loyalhanna, attacks upon, II, 299

Loyalists (or Tories), and Anglo-American relations, I, 74; Associated, I, 131; in battle of Bennington, I, 178; and British campaign of 1777, I, 239; and British debts, I, 240; and Burgoyne's invasion, I, 255; in Butler's Rangers, I, 263; migration of, I, 298; and Canadian-American relations, I, 299; and unpopularity of the Anglican church, I, 371; apprehended by Committees of Safety, I, 437; and confiscation of property, II, 15; strong measures recommended against, II, 90; at Hanging Rock, III, 7; and Jay's treaty, III, 169; in battle of King's Mountain, III, 212; and the Minutemen, III, 413; forced to flee from New York, IV, 120; and Newport, IV, 122; in battle of Oriskany, IV, 188; and pamphleteering, IV, 202; in Pennsylvania, IV, 243; and Revolutionary Committees, IV, 474; aided by *Rivington's Gazette,* IV, 493; tarred and feathered, V, 220; harsh treatment of, V, 322; United Empire, V, 346; and distribution of wealth, V, 429; and the Wyoming Massacre, V, 497

Lubbock, Tom S., and Terry's Texas Rangers, V, 249

Lucas, Charles, duels with Thomas H. Benton, II, 174

Lucas, Eliza, and indigo culture, III, 114

Lucas, Robert, governor of Iowa, III, 152

Lucban, Vicente, and the Philippine insurrection, IV, 262

Luce, Mrs., and Spirit Lake massacre, V, 146

Luce, Stephen B., and establishment of Naval War College, IV, 72

Ludlow, Israel, and Cincinnati, I, 375; and settlement of the Miami Purchase, III, 390

Ludlow, Noah M., and barnstorming, I, 164

Ludlow, Roger, and Connecticut Code of Laws, II, 21; drafts Fundamental Orders of Connecticut, II, 23; and settlements in Connecticut Valley, III, 396; leads migration to the River Towns, IV, 490; and beginning of the westward movement, V, 450

Ludlow Massacre, I, 427

Ludlow Resolution, and war-declaring powers, V, 397

Ludlow's Code, and bachelor houses, I, 144

Ludwick, Christopher, philanthropy of, IV, 260

Luks, George, painter, I, 123

Lumber, and rivers, IV, 491; and domestic trade, V, 292; and foreign trade, V, 295; in the triangular trade, V, 296

Lumber Mills, V, 36

Lumber Products, of colonial industries, III, 119

Lumbering, and forests, II, 308 f.; as industry of the Rockies, IV, 499

Luna, Antonio, and the Philippine insurrection, **IV,** 262

Luna, Tristan de, and first settlement at Pensacola, **IV,** 249

Lundy, Benjamin, and abolition, **I,** 3; establishes *Genius of Universal Emancipation,* **II,** 377; contributes to *The Philanthropist,* **IV,** 260

Lundy's Lane, Battle of, **II,** 223; **IV,** 130; **V,** 340, 405

Lupton, Fort, synonymous with Fort Lancaster, **III,** 232

Lusitania, The, sinking of, **I,** 94; **V,** 491

Lutherans, immigration of, **II,** 383; and foreign missions, **III,** 417; and Pietism, **IV,** 269; open a theological seminary, **V,** 261

Luttrell, John, and the Transylvania Company, **V,** 309

Lyceum Movement, and adult education, **I,** 14; and the Army School System, **I,** 118; and lecturing, **III,** 260

Lydius, John, and the Susquehannah Company, **V,** 211

Lyford, John, and the Dorchester Company, **II,** 162

Lygonia, **II,** 401; **III,** 204

Lykins, Johnston, editor of *Siwinowe Kesibwi,* **IV,** 126

Lyman, Phineas, builds Fort Edward, **II,** 189; and Georgiana, **II,** 381; shareholder in the Susquehannah Company, **V,** 211

Lyman's Toy Theater, **III,** 286

Lynch, Thomas, Jr., signer of the Declaration of Independence, **II,** 124

Lynch Law, and Chiswell's mines, **I,** 368; and lawlessness, **III,** 252; and mobs and riots, **IV,** 3; and race riots, **IV,** 394

Lynd, R. S. and H. M., and adult education, **I,** 14

Lyon, Fort, Fort Wise renamed, **I,** 179

Lyon, Mary, and college training for women, **V,** 477, 480

Lyon, Matthew, establishes a paper mill, **IV,** 212

Lyon, Nathaniel, at Boonville, **I,** 216; and Camp Jackson affair, **I,** 279; and the battle of Carthage, **I,** 320; and the battle of Dug Springs, **II,** 174; captures Camp Jackson, **IV,** 339; and battle of Wilson's Creek, **V,** 470

Lyons and Iowa Central Railroad, **I,** 269

M

Macadam Roads. *See* Roads

MacCallum, William George, and malaria, **III,** 329

Macdonough, Thomas, victory on Lake Champlain, **II,** 387; **III,** 230; **IV,** 287; **V,** 406

MacDowell, Edward, American composer, **IV,** 48

MacDowell, Joseph, and battle of King's Mountain, **III,** 212

Macfadden, Bernarr, and rise of tabloids, **V,** 216

Machault, Fort, established, **II,** 346; **V,** 359

Machin, Thomas, and the Hudson River Chain, **III,** 55

Machine, Party, and Albany Regency, **I,** 46; and campaign of 1800, **I,** 281; and political corruption, **II,** 65; and growth of democracy, **II,** 135; and political patronage, **IV,** 225; and political rings, **IV,** 485; and the spoils system, **V,** 147; and the ward leader, **V,** 407

Machine Gun, Gatling's, **II,** 374; Maxim's, **III,** 361; as a munition, **IV,** 45

Machinery, and industrial revolution, **III,** 117 f.; and interchangeable parts, **III,** 133; and labor, **III,** 219, 225; and domestic trade, **V,** 292

Mack, Alexander, and the Dunkards, **II,** 176

Mack Brothers, build first motor bus, **IV,** 32

Mackay, Alexander, partner in the Pacific Fur Company, **IV,** 195

Mackay, James, leads third expedition of Spanish-Missouri Fur Company, **V,** 141

Mackay, John W., bonanza king, **I,** 208; cofounder of Commercial Cable Company, **I,** 434; and the Big Bonanza, **I,** 444; and great fortunes, **II,** 312; elected president of the Postal Telegraph Company, **IV,** 322

MacKaye, Percy, dramatist, **II,** 166

MacKenzie, A. S., and mutiny on the *Somers,* **V,** 119

MacKenzie, Alexander, reaches the Pacific (1793), **V,** 446

MacKenzie, Donald, partner in the Pacific Fur Company, **IV,** 195; builds Fort Nez Percé, **V,** 393

MacKenzie, Kenneth, establishes a distillery at Fort Union, **III,** 282; builds Fort Union, N. Dak., **V,** 341

Mackenzie, Ranald S., and the Red River Indian War, **IV,** 431; destroys Dull Knife's Cheyenne village, **V,** 87

Mackenzie College at São Paulo, **III,** 248

Mackinac, headquarters of American Fur Company, **I,** 61; Charlevoix arrives at, **I,** 345; fall of fort at, **II,** 144; Jesuit mission at, **III,** 174; attacked in Pontiac's War, **IV,** 306; Mission of St. Ignace at, **V,** 9. *See also* Michilimackinac

Mackinaw Boats, name given to Missouri bateaux, **I,** 167; and the Missouri River fur trade, **III,** 431

MacMonnies, Frederick, sculptor, **I,** 124

Macomb, Alexander, in War of 1812, **III,** 230; and battle of Plattsburg, **IV,** 287

Macomb Purchase, and the Castorland Company, **I,** 322

Macon, The, name given to the airship ZRS-5, **II,** 149

Macon's Bill No. 2 (1810), **II**, 344; **IV**, 138

Macpherson's Directory for the City and Suburbs of Philadelphia, **II**, 148

Macready, Lt., flies nonstop from New York to San Diego, **I**, 142

Macune, C. W., and the Farmers' Alliance, **II**, 252

Mad House, Williamsburg, Va., first insane asylum, **III**, 50

Madawaska, Maine, **I**, 6, 121

Maddox, Thomas H., and the Sandbar Duel, **V**, 27

Madison, Dolly, serves ice cream at White House, **II**, 105; said to have introduced Easter egg rolling on Capitol grounds, **II**, 183

Madison, Fort, first American fort in Iowa, **III**, 152

Madison, James, and the Annapolis Convention, **I**, 78; and battle of Bladensburg, **I**, 198; and blockades, **I**, 201; vetoes Bonus Bill, **I**, 211; elected President, **I**, 281; signer of the Constitution, **II**, 39; delegate to Convention of 1787, **II**, 50; and *The Federalist,* **II**, 264; inauguration of, **III**, 82; vetoes Bonus Bill (1816), **III**, 137; and Jay's Treaty, **III**, 169; and Marbury case, **III**, 183; papers of, purchased for the government, **III**, 274; and Marbury case, **III**, 341; and Miranda's intrigues, **III**, 414; as "Helvidius," **IV**, 197; subscribes to principle of separation of powers, **IV**, 327; Princeton alumnus, **IV**, 343; and the Protestant Episcopal Church, **IV**, 366; and separation of church and state, **IV**, 445; and the Republican party (Jeffersonian), **IV**, 453; and right of secession, **V**, 50; and the problem of sovereignty, **V**, 173; and states' rights, **V**, 175; and the tariff, **V**, 221; and day of thanksgiving, **V**, 259; on governing body of University of Virginia, **V**, 375; author of Virginia Resolutions, **V**, 375; and declaration of war, **V**, 396; and the War of 1812, **V**, 405; and distribution of wealth, **V**, 429; and annexation of West Florida, **V**, 436

Madisonian, becomes organ of President Tyler, **II**, 403

Madockawando, leads the attack on York, Maine, **V**, 507

Madrid, Treaty of (1670), and effective occupation, **II**, 189; recognizes British occupation of Florida, **II**, 290; and "No peace beyond the line," **IV**, 136

Maffitt, John N., runs blockade with the *Florida,* **II**, 289

Mafia, Italian secret society, **I**, 194

Magazin Royal, construction of, **IV**, 129

Magazine of Business, **V**, 298

Magdalen Society, **II**, 314

Magee, A. W., and the Gutiérrez expedition, **II**, 429

Magistrates, assistants become, **I**, 131

Magna Carta, and civil liberties, **I**, 381; and the British constitution, **II**, 29; and due process clauses, **II**, 172

Magnetic Telegraph Company, **V**, 238

Magnolia Gardens, **I**, 344; **II**, 371

Magoffin, Beriah, and secessionist movement in Kentucky, **II**, 3; issues neutrality proclamation for Kentucky, **III**, 206

Magoon, Charles E., becomes provisional governor of Cuba, **II**, 95

Magruder, J. B., and recapture of Galveston, **II**, 368; attacks at Savage Station, **V**, 35; joins Shelby's Mexican expedition, **V**, 68

Mahan, A. T., and the Perry-Elliott controversy, **IV**, 253; and sea power, **V**, 47; and laws of war, **V**, 398

Mahican Indians, **I**, 48; **II**, 227

Mahone, William, and the Readjuster Movement, **IV**, 418; **V**, 374

Maidstone, The, attack on (1765), **IV**, 478

Mail Contract Act of 1928, and ocean shipping, **V**, 74

Mail-Order Houses, and the distribution of merchandise, **II**, 152; and price maintenance, **IV**, 340; and rural free delivery, **IV**, 508

Mail Subsidies, **III**, 376, 377; **V**, 72

Mails, Obstruction of, and the Debs case, **II**, 116

Main Street, written by Sinclair Lewis, **II**, 270

Maine, "As goes Maine," **I**, 127; granted to Gorges, **II**, 72; under Massachusetts, **II**, 401; granted to Mason and Gorges, **III**, 351; added to Massachusetts, **III**, 355; admitted as free state, **III**, 428; as a proprietary province, **IV**, 362; demands prohibition, **V**, 241

Maine, The, Congress authorizes construction of, **II**, 283; destruction of, **IV**, 447; raising of, **V**, 20; sinking of, **V**, 135, 136; and yellow journalism, **V**, 505

Maine Baptist Missionary Association, **III**, 416

Maize, and archæology, **I**, 98; chief Indian crop, **III**, 87

Majority Rule, as pillar of democracy, **IV**, 301

Majors, Alexander, forms partnership with William H. Russell, **IV**, 510; and stagecoach lines, **V**, 152

Makemie, Francis, father of American Presbyterianism, **IV**, 332

Malaeska; the Indian Wife of the White Hunter, first dime novel, **II**, 146

Malaria, and Ayllon's expedition, **I**, 144; in the Black Swamp, **I**, 196; and calomel, **I**, 276; disappearing, **II**, 150; appears in Jamestown, **III**, 167; and yellow fever, **V**, 504

Malbone, Edward Green, miniature painter, **I**, 123; **III**, 408

Malden, Fort, **I**, 245

Maldonado, Lorenzo Ferrer, and fake explorations of the Pacific coast, **IV**, 195

Malecite Indians, **I**, 48

Mallet Brothers, and Colorado region, **I**, 426; journeys of, **II**, 345; and Santa Fé Trail, **V**, 29

Mallory, Stephen R., and flight of Confederate Cabinet, **II**, 5; secretary of Confederate navy, **II**, 7

Malone, Dumas, editor of the *Dictionary of American Biography*, **II**, 146

Malvern Hill, battle of, **IV**, 241; **V**, 60

Mammoth Oil Company, and Teapot Dome oil scandal, **V**, 235

Man o'War, famous thoroughbred horse, **V**, 265

Managed Currency, **IV**, 8

Manassas, The, Confederate privateer ram, **III**, 158

Manchac, and the fur trade, **II**, 363

Manchac, Fort, captured by Spaniards, **V**, 139

Manchurian Crisis, **I**, 77

Mandan Indians, and bull boats, **I**, 250; and Catlin's paintings, **I**, 324; and the Five Villages, **II**, 280; Lewis and Clark reach towns of, **III**, 266; use steel traps, **V**, 180

Mandates, Yap, **V**, 502

Mandeville, Lambert, and Juchereau's tannery, **III**, 182

Mandingo Negroes, imported as slaves, **IV**, 86

Maneuvers, and United States Army, **I**, 111

Mangeurs de Lard, **V**, 385

Mangum, W. P., in campaign of 1836, **I**, 283

Manhattan Company, private bank, **I**, 160; undertakes New York City's first public water supply, **IV**, 119; **V**, 423

Manhattan Island, divided into bouweries, **I**, 230; settlement moved to, **IV**, 108

Manhattan Savings Institution, robbery of, **I**, 156

Manifest Destiny, and Cuba, **II**, 94; and Hawaii, **III**, 18; and Mexican relations, **III**, 384, 387; and the Pacific Ocean, **IV**, 196; and Spanish-American relations, **V**, 135; and the West, **V**, 435; and "Young America," **V**, 509

Manila Bay, Battle of, **II**, 275; **V**, 136 f.

Manitou, and God of Michilimackinac, **III**, 391

Manly, Basil, educational reformer, **V**, 122

Manly, William L., crosses Death Valley, **II**, 236

Manly-Hunt Party of Emigrants, attack on, **II**, 116

Mann, A. Dudley, and Civil War Diplomacy, **I**, 392

Mann, Horace, and abolitionist literature, **I**, 3; and educational reform, **V**, 39; advocates consolidation of schools, **V**, 41

Mann-Elkins Act of 1910, passed, **III**, 143

Mann White Slave Act, **I**, 433; **IV**, 365; **V**, 460

Manner, Marion M., printer of the *Montana Post,* **IV**, 127

Manning, James, president of Brown University, **I**, 244

Manning, John, and capture of New York (1673), **IV**, 114

Manors, and colonial land grants, **III**, 235

Mansfield, Arabella M., admitted to the bar, **V**, 478, 482

Mansfield, J. K. F., at Antietam, **I**, 81

Manson, M. D., and battle of Richmond (Ky.), **IV**, 481

Manual, Fort, abandoned, **III**, 283; established, **V**, 13

Manufactures, Gallatin's Report on, **II**, 367; and domestic trade, **V**, 293; and foreign trade, **V**, 295

Manufacturing, and prices of grain, **I**, 27; and mass production, **III**, 354; and the urban drift, **V**, 352

Manumission, **I**, 59

Manure, as fertilizer, **II**, 268

Map of the United States of Mexico, by H. S. Tanner, **II**, 154

Maple Syrup, in New England, **IV**, 98

Maps, Arrowsmith's, **I**, 122; Disturnell's, **II**, 154; Evans', **II**, 230; Franquelin's, **II**, 329; Geological Survey, **II**, 378; compiled and drafted by United States General Land Office, **III**, 237; Mitchell's, **III**, 431; Red Line, **IV**, 429; Topographic, **V**, 282

Marais des Cygnes Massacre, **I**, 220

Marbury v. Madison, and judicial review, **III**, 183; and the Midnight Judges, **III**, 395; and the Supreme Court, **V**, 207

March, C. P., and the Belknap scandal, **I**, 175

March, John, in Queen Anne's War, **IV**, 389

Marcos de Niza, reconnaissance of, **IV**, 106; discovers the Zuñi Indians, **V**, 515

Marcy, Randolph B., conducts caravan travel, **I**, 312; and the Mormon expedition, **IV**, 24

Marcy, W. L., proposes purchase of Alaska, **I**, 43; criticizes Foote for action in attack on Barrier Forts, **I**, 165; and the *Black Warrior* affair, **I**, 196; and Hülsemann incident, **III**, 58; and the Ostend Manifesto, **IV**, 190; declines to accede to Declaration of Paris, **IV**, 215; and political patronage, **IV**, 224; and the spoils system, **V**, 147

Mardi Gras, in New Orleans, **IV**, 109

Mare Clausum, and the Aleutian Islands, **I**, 47; and Bering Sea seal fisheries, **V**, 50

Mare Island Navy Yard, **IV**, 79

Mare Liberum, **III**, 342

Mares, José, and Texan-Santa Fé expeditions, **V**, 251

Marest, Gabriel, and the founding of Kaskaskia, **III**, 199

Mariana, granted to John Mason, **III**, 351

Marias Pass, missed by Stevens' exploring parties, **V**, 182

Marietta, and Fort Harmar, III, 10; and land speculation, III, 240; first legal American settlement in Northwest Territory, IV, 151; settlement begun at, by Ohio Company of Associates, IV, 163

Marihuana Tax Act, IV, 53

Marin, John, painter, I, 123

Marin, Joseph, aids in making peace to end Fox-French War, II, 320

Marin, Pierre Paul, and Fort Presque Isle, IV, 337; at Venango, V, 359

Marine, Department of, IV, 475

Marine Corps, at Army War College, I, 119; occupies Santo Domingo City, II, 159; United States Naval Academy graduates commissioned in, IV, 69; Reserves, IV, 72; affairs of, handled by Navy Department, IV, 75; and our relations with Nicaragua, IV, 131; in the World War, V, 493

Marine Hospital Service, III, 22

Marine Insurance, III, 129

Marion, Fort, Apaches interned at, I, 88. See also San Marco, Fort

Marion, Francis, and partisan bands, IV, 219; in the Southern campaigns (1780–81), V, 129

Maritime Commission, III, 377; V, 75

Mark Twain, author of Tom Sawyer, I, 180; and publishing, I, 214; and children's books, I, 363; and fiction, II, 270; and the gilded age, II, 390; as humorous lecturer, III, 260; and American slang, V, 88

Markham, A. H., polar expedition of, IV, 293

Markle Foundation, II, 314

Marlatt, Earl, hymn writer, III, 65

Marmaduke, John S., at battle of Boonville, I, 216; and battle at Prairie Grove, IV, 329

Marque and Reprisal, and the Constitution, II, 33; and privateering, IV, 349

Marquette, Jacques, and the Alton petroglyphs, I, 53; at Chequamegon Bay, I, 351; first white man of record to sojourn on site of Chicago, I, 356; on the Fox-Wisconsin Waterway, II, 320; establishes missions among the Indians, III, 174; expedition with Jolliet, III, 180; stops at Memphis, III, 372; labors at Michilimackinac, III, 394; on the Mississippi River, III, 423; and the Mississippi Valley, III, 425; explores Missouri, III, 426; conducts Mission of St. Ignace, V, 9; considered founder and first chronicler of Sault Ste. Marie, V, 34

Marquette Range, and iron ore, III, 157

Marriage, and divorce, II, 155; and polygamy, IV, 304

Married Women's Property Rights, II, 266; IV, 360

Marschalk, Andrew, first printer of Mississippi, IV, 346

Marsh, Charles W. and William W., and the development of the reaper, IV, 419

Marsh, Grant, commander of the Far West, II, 244

Marsh, Henry, and wood engraving, V, 483

Marshall, Charles H., operates the Black Ball Line, I, 192

Marshall, Humphry, botanist, I, 225

Marshall, James W., discovers gold, I, 272; II, 313, 393

Marshall, John, and the Alien and Sedition Acts, I, 49; and the Antelope slave case, I, 79; and Bank of United States v. Planters' Bank of Georgia, I, 155; author of Life of Washington, I, 189; and Burr Conspiracy trial, I, 208; and Brown v. Maryland, I, 244; and Burr trial, I, 258; and the commerce clause, I, 433; and the contract clause, II, 48; and Craig v. Missouri, II, 83; diplomatic mission of, II, 148; and the Fairfax proprietary, II, 240; and the Federalist party, II, 264; and "First in war, etc.," II, 276; and Fletcher v. Peck, II, 284; makes special mission to France, II, 327; and Gibbons v. Ogden, II, 388; and doctrine of implied powers, III, 79; and Marbury v. Madison, III, 183; and Yazoo land fraud, III, 239; and liberal construction, III, 269; and Marbury v. Madison, III, 341; and McCulloch v. Maryland, III, 364; and "Millions for defense, etc.," III, 405; and Ogden v. Saunders, IV, 159; and Osborn v. United States Bank, IV, 189; ridicules equalitarian doctrine, V, 123; and Gibbons v. Ogden, V, 178; and taxation, V, 225; and reciprocal immunity from taxation, V, 228; and treason trials, V, 313; and negotiation of treaties, V, 315; and the Virginia-Kentucky Resolutions, V, 376; and Worcester v. Georgia, V, 484; and the XYZ affair, V, 498

Marshall, R. C., Jr., commands the Cantonment Division, I, 296

Marshall, S. S., and the Wheeler Compromise (1876), V, 454

Martelaer's Rock, fortified, III, 31

Marten, destruction of, by settlement, V, 462

Martial Law, and the Constitution, II, 38; and Force Acts, II, 300; and military aid to the civil power, III, 399; and military law, III, 401

Martiau, Nicholas, and the Huguenots in America, III, 57; patents land along York River, V, 508

Martin, Abraham, and Plains of Abraham, I, 4

Martin, Homer D., landscape painter, I, 123

Martin, Jacob L., and diplomatic service to Papal States, IV, 211

Martin, John, and founding of Jamestown, III, 166; V, 372

Martin, Joseph, and the Cherokee wars, I, 353; builds first cabin in Powell's Valley, IV, 326

Martin, Luther, delegate to Convention of 1787, **II**, 50; and McCulloch v. Maryland, **III**, 364; and pamphleteering, **IV**, 202

Martín Explorations, and Texas, **V**, 252

Martin-Tolliver Feud, **II**, 269

Martin v. Hunter's Lessee, and the Fairfax proprietary, **II**, 240; and the Judiciary Act of 1789, **III**, 189

Martinas, Maria, Indian potter, **III**, 93

Martínez, Pedro, slain by the Indians, **III**, 174

Martin's Restaurant, **II**, 55

Martin's Station, overwhelmed by Bird, **I**, 191

Martling Men, and Tammany Hall, **V**, 218

Marxism, and distribution of wealth, **V**, 429

Mary and John, The, sent out by the Plymouth Company, **IV**, 290; and the Popham Colony, **IV**, 308

Mary and John, The, carries vanguard of the Great Migration, **II**, 161

Mary Ann, The, American merchantman seized by Algiers, **I**, 162

Maryland, *Ark* and *Dove* bring first colonists to, **I**, 105; and the Claiborne settlement, **I**, 394; feudalism in, **II**, 269; University of, first Southern medical school at, **III**, 369; as a proprietary province, **IV**, 362; refuses to ratify the Articles of Confederation until surrender of land claims, **V**, 444

Maryland Charter of 1632, and the Mason and Dixon Line, **III**, 350

Maryland Gazette, published by William Parks, **IV**, 126

Mascoutin Indians, and Algonquin family, **I**, 48; village of, **II**, 320; in Iowa, **III**, 152

Mason, A. T., killed in duel with J. M. McCarty, **I**, 198

Mason, George, and the Alexandria Conference, **I**, 47; and the Virginia Declaration of Rights, **I**, 185, 187; delegate to Convention of 1787, **II**, 50; and pamphleteering, **IV**, 202; recommends motto *"sic semper tyrannis"* for Virginia, **V**, 77; drafts the Virginia Declaration of Rights, **V**, 373, 378

Mason, James M., and Confederate diplomacy, **I**, 392; and recognition of the Confederacy, **II**, 5; and the *Trent* affair, **V**, 321

Mason, John, and Isles of Shoals, **III**, 162; and the Laconia grant, **III**, 226; and Maine, **III**, 326; granted Mariana, **III**, 343; granted land in Maine and New Hampshire, **IV**, 101; his heirs and Randolph's commission, **IV**, 415; and Strawberry Bank, **V**, 187

Mason, John, and the Mohegan case, **IV**, 5; and the Pequot War, **IV**, 252

Mason, John Tufton, sells his New Hampshire lands, **III**, 351

Mason, John Y., and the Ostend Manifesto, **IV**, 190

Mason, Lowell, musical pioneer, **IV**, 48; and "My Country, 'Tis of Thee," **IV**, 50

Mason, R. B., and California gold, **I**, 272

Mason, Samuel, at Cave-in-Rock, **I**, 329; highwayman, **III**, 12

Mason, William, improves the loom, **III**, 301

Mason, William S., collection of Franklin, **I**, 212

Mason and Dixon Line, and Delaware, **II**, 130; and Delaware Circle, **II**, 132; and the origin of "Dixie," **II**, 155; and Pennsylvania-Maryland boundary dispute, **IV**, 247; and the Pennsylvania-Virginia boundary dispute, **IV**, 249

Masons, and Anti-Masonic movements, **I**, 82; and the Illuminati of New England, **III**, 72; and the Morgan trials, **IV**, 23; first in America, **V**, 53

Mass Impression, and propaganda, **IV**, 359; and public opinion, **IV**, 374

Mass Production, and capital, **I**, 308; and engineering, **II**, 215; made possible, **III**, 118; and interchangeable parts, **III**, 133, 148; and machines, **III**, 320; and manufacturing, **III**, 337; destroys local industries in New England, **IV**, 98

Massachusetts, colony of, **I**, 16; apprenticeship in Bay Colony, **I**, 92; Bay Company and the *Arbella,* **I**, 94; assistants in Bay Company, **I**, 131; and the Bay Path, **I**, 169; Colony of, as Bible Commonwealth, **I**, 181; Bill of Rights, **I**, 187; ironworks in, **I**, 199; Boston made capital of, **I**, 222; Committee of Safety of, **I**, 222; Provincial Congress of, **I**, 222; claims to New York lands, **I**, 224; boundary controversy with Rhode Island, **I**, 226; boundary controversy with New Hampshire, **I**, 226; Brownists in Bay Colony, **I**, 244; Cambridge Agreement and Bay Colony, **I**, 277; and cod fishing, **I**, 406; and the River Towns of Connecticut, **II**, 23; Turnpike Act of 1805, **II**, 63; patent of, and the Council for New England, **II**, 72; land bank of (1740), **II**, 100; Dorchester planted, **II**, 161; reared on foundations laid by Dorchester Company, **II**, 162; and Gorges' province of Maine, **II**, 401; and the Great Migration, **II**, 418; and Lygonia, **III**, 317; and Maine, **III**, 327; and Mariana, **III**, 343; and Merry Mount, **III**, 378; Bay Company as successor to New England Company, **IV**, 99; and New York land speculation, **IV**, 116; and the Pequot War, **IV**, 252; and the Phelps-Gorham purchase, **IV**, 257; Bay Company and Puritanism, **IV**, 384; Bay Company and the Quakers, **IV**, 386; Bay Colony and *quo warranto,* **IV**, 391; Bay Colony and Randolph's commission, **IV**, 415; and roads, **IV**, 493 f.; Bay Colony as a theocracy, **V**, 260; Bay Company as a trading company, **V**, 301; western land claims of, **V**, 444

Massachusetts, Fort (Mass.), attacked, **V**, 361

Massachusetts, Fort, established, **I**, 426; and Marcy's march, **III**, 342; and the Mormon expedition, **IV**, 24

Massachusetts, The, and the blockade of Santiago, **V**, 31; one of the first American battleships, **V**, 412

Massachusetts Centinel, and political cartoons, **I**, 320

Massachusetts Circular Letter, demand that it be rescinded, **I**, 207; and Liberty poles, **III**, 272; and "ninety-two and forty-five," **IV**, 135; and the American Revolution, **IV**, 466

Massachusetts General Hospital, **III**, 51

Massachusetts Government Act, **I**, 408; **III**, 147; **V**, 288

Massachusetts Historical Society, **III**, 33

Massachusetts Humane Society, and lifesaving service, **III**, 275

Massachusetts Indians, **I**, 48

Massachusetts Institute of Technology, **V**, 44

Massachusetts Missionary Society, **III**, 416

Massacre Island, first name of Dauphine Island, **II**, 112

Massasoit, Algonquin leader, **I**, 48

Massé, Ennemond, Jesuit missionary, **III**, 174

Masses, barred from the mails, **IV**, 433

Massey, John E., and the Readjuster Movement, **IV**, 418

Massey, Lt. Col., and battle of LaBelle Famille, **III**, 218

Massie, Nathaniel, member of the Chillicothe Junto, **I**, 364; and military tracts, **III**, 402; founder of first settlement in the Virginia Military Reserve district, **V**, 379

Matador Company, **IV**, 177

Matanuska Colonization Project, **I**, 43

Match Industry, **II**, 145

Match-making Machinery, **III**, 320

Matches, made at Wheeling, W. Va., **V**, 455

Matchless Mine, **III**, 254

Maternal Health Leagues, **I**, 191

Maternal Welfare, and social legislation, **V**, 108

Mather, Cotton, author of *Life of His Excellency Sir William Phips*, **I**, 189; as book collector, **I**, 212; as botanist, **I**, 225; author of *A Perfect Recovery*, **II**, 150; pioneer of epidemiology, **II**, 221; and fast days, **II**, 254; and introduction of inoculation, **V**, 100; and witchcraft, **V**, 475

Mather, Increase, as book collector, **I**, 212; and doctrine of Divine Providences, **II**, 154; pioneer of epidemiology, **II**, 221; and the regicides in New England, **IV**, 438; defends inoculation, **V**, 100

Mather, Richard, portrait of, cut by John Foster, **V**, 482

Mathew, Theobald, and the temperance movement, **V**, 241

Mathews, George, and attempted seizure of East Florida, **II**, 181

Mathews, John, and soda fountains, **V**, 113

Mathews, Shailer, and religious thought and writings, **IV**, 447; and the social gospel, **V**, 107; and theological writings, **V**, 261

Matilda Ziegler Magazine for the Blind, **I**, 200

Mattson, Henry, painter, **I**, 123

Maugham, Russell L., and aviation, **I**, 142

Maumee-Miami Portage, **IV**, 316

Maumee-Wabash Portage, **IV**, 316

Maurepas, Lake, and Isle of Orleans, **III**, 161

Maury, James, and the Parson's Cause, **IV**, 219

Maury, Matthew Fontaine, and Confederates in Mexico, **I**, 314; purchases the *Georgia*, **II**, 380; hydrographic work of, **III**, 63; oceanographer, **V**, 123

Mauvila, Spanish engage with the Indians at, **II**, 141

Mavericks, laws passed defining, **II**, 79; and open range cattle period, **IV**, 177

Maxent, Gilbert Antoine de St., and Spanish-Indian relations, **V**, 140

Maxent, Laclede and Company, and the fur trade, **II**, 363

Maxim, Hudson, and preparedness, **IV**, 331

Maxim Machine Guns, **III**, 319

Maximilian, and French in Mexico, **III**, 388

Maximilian of Wied, and Montana, **IV**, 16

Maxwell, George Troup, and malaria, **III**, 329

Maxwell, William, attacks at Cooch's Bridge, **II**, 54; and Sullivan-Clinton campaign, **V**, 202

Maxwell, William, publishes the *Centinel of the North-Western Territory*, **I**, 333; **IV**, 124, 127; first printer of Ohio, **IV**, 346

Maxwell Bros., nurserymen, **IV**, 154

Maxwell Land Grant, **III**, 236

Maxwell Ranch, Arkansas River route passes, **I**, 107

May, Cornelius Jacobsen, visits Delaware Bay, **II**, 132; builds Fort Nassau, **IV**, 55

May, Henry, imprisonment of, **I**, 122

May, Jan C., polar expedition of, **IV**, 292

May, Samuel J., and abolition, **I**, 3

May Day, Coxey's Army arrives on, **II**, 82; at Merry Mount, **III**, 378

Mayflower, The, tonnage of, **I**, 423; brings emigrants to New Plymouth, **IV**, 111; and the Pilgrims, **IV**, 270

Mayflower, The, carries Marietta settlers, **II**, 367

Mayflower Compact, and the Compact Theory, **I**, 441; and growth of democracy, **II**, 135; and fundamental constitutions, **II**, 356; Pilgrims draw up, **IV**, 112, 271; and state constitutions, **V**, 166

Mayhew, Thomas, granted Martha's Vineyard, **III**, 347

Mayhew, Thomas, Jr., converts the Indians, **IV,** 330

Maynard Rifle, **IV,** 483

Mayo Brothers, and surgery, **III,** 370

Mayor, and city government, **III,** 289

Mayor-Council, type of municipal charter, **I,** 347

Maysville Turnpike Bill, Jackson vetoes, **II,** 404; **III,** 138; **IV,** 495

McAdoo, William G., and the Hudson Tubes, **III,** 56; and Railroad Administration, **IV,** 400; and railroads, **IV,** 408; and World War transportation system, **V,** 492

McAllister, Fort, captured, **V,** 36

McAllister, Ward, and the "Four hundred," **II,** 316

McArthur, Arthur, and the Philippine insurrection, **IV,** 261

McArthur, Duncan, and military tracts, **III,** 402

McCall, G. A., and battle of Mechanicsville, **III,** 368

McCall, John, first printer of Michigan, **IV,** 346

McCardle Case, and Reconstruction, **IV,** 425

McCarthy, Charles, political writings of, **IV,** 302 f.; and the Wisconsin Idea, **V,** 474

McCarthy, Harry, and the "Bonnie Blue Flag," **I,** 209

McCarty, J. M., kills A. T. Mason in duel, **I,** 198

McCausland, John, and burning of Chambersburg, **I,** 338

McClary, John, and surrender of St. Stephens, Ala., **V,** 15

McClary's Path, **V,** 265

McClellan, George B., and battle of Antietam, **I,** 81; and the battle of Ball's Bluff, **I,** 150; nominated for Presidency, **I,** 285; and the skirmish at Corrick's Ford, **II,** 63; and the Corps of Engineers, **II,** 216; and enlistment in the Union Army, **II,** 217; and the battle of Fair Oaks, **II,** 239; and battle of Frayser's Farm, **II,** 330; loses command of Army of the Potomac, **II,** 330; and battle of Gaines' Mill, **II,** 366; and Harrison's Landing letter, **III,** 13; and Lee's Lost Order, **III,** 303; and battle of Malvern Hill, **III,** 329; and invasion of Maryland, **III,** 349; and battle of Mechanicsville, **III,** 367; and the Peninsular campaign, **IV,** 241; placed in command of Army of the Potomac, **IV,** 324; and the Radical Republicans, **IV,** 395; and battle of Rich Mountain, **IV,** 481; and Seven Days' battles, **V,** 59; and battle of South Mountain, **V,** 128; and Stevens' railroad survey, **V,** 182; and Stuart's ride, **V,** 191; and battle at White Oak Swamp, **V,** 460; and battle of Williamsburg, **V,** 468

McClernand, John A., forces surrender of Arkansas Post, **I,** 106; and Army of the Mississippi, **III,** 419; and battle at Port Gibson, **IV,** 314; and Soldiers and Sailors Conventions, **V,** 117

McClure, George, and the Niagara campaigns, **IV,** 130

McClure, R. J. L. M., and Northwest Passage, **IV,** 151

McClure, S. S., and popular magazines, **III,** 323

McClure's Magazine, and muckrakers, **IV,** 38

McConnell, Felix G., introduces Homestead Bill, **III,** 42

McCook, A. McD., and battle of Murfreesboro, **IV,** 46

McCormick, Cyrus H., and the Root mission to Russia, **IV,** 501

McCormick, Cyrus Hall, and the reaper, **II,** 247; and great fortunes, **II,** 312; and installment selling, **III,** 126; Harvesting Machine Company, **III,** 140; invents the reaper, **III,** 148, 320; patents the harvester, **IV,** 223; and the invention of the reaper, **IV,** 419

McCormick, Vance, as chairman of the War Trade Board, **V,** 407

McCosh, James, and Princeton University, **IV,** 343

McCoy, F. R., member of Lytton Commission of Inquiry, **III,** 256

McCoy, Isaac, and Westport, Mo., **V,** 449

McCoy, John, lays out Westport, Mo., **III,** 196; **V,** 449

McCoy, Joseph G., establishes Abilene, **I,** 2; opens cattle market at Abilene, **I,** 326

McCoy, Tim, attempts to revive the Wild West show, **V,** 464

McCoy-Hatfield Feud, **III,** 16

McCreary, Joseph, patents the air washer, **I,** 34

McCrory, J. G., opens five-and-ten-cent store, **II,** 279

McCulloch, Ben., and battle of Wilson's Creek, **V,** 470

McCulloch, Hugh, as first Comptroller under National Banking System, **V,** 164

McCulloch v. Maryland, and doctrine of implied powers, **III,** 79; and the Judiciary Act of 1789, **III,** 189; and liberal construction, **III,** 269; and Osborn v. United States Bank, **IV,** 189; and reciprocal immunity from taxation, **V,** 228

McCulloh, Henry, and the Yadkin River settlements, **V,** 499

McCunn, John H., and the Tweed Ring, **V,** 333

McDonald, Angus, raids Wapatomica towns, **II,** 177

McDonald, Finan, on the Columbia River, **I,** 430

McDonald Observatory, **IV,** 157

McDonnell, Miles, and the Pemmican War, **IV,** 241

McDonough, James W., and the telephone, **V,** 239

McDougal, Duncan, Astoria established under, **I,** 133; partner in the Pacific Fur Company, **IV,** 195

McDougall, Alexander, and battle of White Plains, V, 460

McDougall, Alexander, first to construct whale-backs, V, 452

McDougall, Walt, and political cartoons, I, 320

McDowell, Battle of, III, 165

McDowell, Ephraim, and medicine, III, 369; contribution to surgery, V, 123

McDowell, Irvin, and the battle of Blackburn's Ford, I, 197; and first Bull Run, I, 250; and Jackson's Valley Campaign, III, 165; and campaigns against Richmond (1864–65), IV, 481; and the Army of Virginia, V, 374

McDowell, Mary, and social settlements, V, 109

McDowell, William Adair, and tuberculosis, V, 328

McDowell's College, as prison camp, IV, 347

McElroy, Thornton F., co-founder of the Columbian, IV, 127; first printer of Washington, IV, 346

McEnery, John, and the New Orleans riots, IV, 111

McFadden-Pepper Act, and branch banking, I, 158

McGarrahan, William, and the Panoche Grande claim, IV, 210

McGary's Fort, settlement at, III, 204

McGillivray, Alexander, and Bowles, I, 230; proposes ceding Creek lands to Georgia, II, 101; and Panton, Leslie and Company, IV, 211; and Spanish-Indian relations, V, 140. See also New York, Treaty of

McGivney, Michael, and the Knights of Columbus, III, 214

McGlachlin, Edward F., Jr., assumes command of American Forces in Germany (1919), I, 116

McGoffin, Beriah, and the Madison County anti-slavery war, III, 322

McGrain v. Daugherty, II, 46

McGraw, John, and land speculation, III, 240

McGready, James, evangelist, I, 143; and the Great Revival, II, 419

McGregor, Gregor, and the Amelia Island affair, I, 54

McGuffey's Readers, I, 180; IV, 171; V, 40

McGuire, Peter J., and Labor Day, III, 221

McHenry, Fort, bombardment of, I, 150; defense of, I, 405; as prison camp, IV, 347; sea fencibles defend, V, 47; and the "Star-Spangled Banner," V, 160

McHenry, Fort, formerly Fort Nogales, V, 367

McHenry, James, signer of the Constitution, II, 39

McIntire, Rufus, and the Aroostook War, I, 121

McIntire, Samuel, wood-carver, I, 123

McIntosh, Fort, treaty of, III, 10

McIntosh, James, and the battle of Dug Springs, II, 174

McIntosh, Lachlan, duels with Gwinnett, II, 429; erects Fort Laurens, III, 251

McIntosh, William, murdered by Creek Indians, II, 86

McIntosh, William, and Johnson and Graham's Lessee, III, 178

McIntyre Garrison, and log cabins, III, 294

McKay, Donald, builds the Flying Cloud, II, 292

McKay, Fort, Fort Shelby becomes, IV, 328

McKay Machine, in shoe manufacturing, V, 75

McKean, Fort, as part of Fort Abraham Lincoln, I, 4

McKean, Thomas, signer of the Declaration of Independence, II, 124; votes for Lee's resolution for independence, IV, 500

McKee, Alexander, and Lochry's defeat, III, 291; and Maumee Indian Convention, III, 360

McKendree, William, evangelist of the Awakening, I, 143

McKenna, Charles H., and the Holy Name Society, III, 40

McKenney, T. L., and Butte des Morts Council, I, 263; editor of the Washington Republican, IV, 128

McKenzie. See also MacKenzie

McKenzie, William Lyon, and the Caroline affair, I, 317

McKim, C. F., and Washington, D. C., V, 413

McKim, Mead and White, architectural firm, I, 101; design Madison Square Garden, III, 322; architects of the White House, V, 459

McKinley, William, shot by Leon Czolgosz, I, 129; nominated for the Presidency, I, 288; elected President, I, 289; and Olney-Pauncefote treaty, IV, 172; assassinated, IV, 203; and the Presidency, IV, 333; nominated for the Presidency, IV, 454; and the Spanish-American War, V, 136

McKinley-Adkins Bill, and export debenture plan, II, 236

McKinley Tariff, and campaign of 1892, I, 288; and Field v. Clark, II, 270; and the Gorman-Wilson Tariff, II, 401; and Latin America, III, 249; and the "Pop-Gun Bills," IV, 308; reciprocity provision of the, IV, 422; and commerce with South America, V, 123; and campaign pledges, V, 222; places duty on imported tin plate, V, 272

McKinnon, Archibald S., and the Dawes Commission, II, 113

McLane, Louis, and the Pioneer Stage Line, IV, 274

McLaughlin, James, and the Sioux Council, V, 85

McLaughlin, Patrick, and silver mining, V, 81

McLean, John, nominated for Presidency, I, 283

McLean, Wilmer, and the surrender at Appomattox, I, 91

McLeod, Alexander, arrest of, **I,** 317; and the Webster-Ashburton Treaty, **V,** 431

McLeod, Hugh, and Texan-Santa Fé expedition, **V,** 251

McLeod v. U. S., **V,** 398

McLoughlin, John, and Hudson's Bay Company, **III,** 56; as chief factor at Fort Vancouver, **V,** 357; in the Northwest, **V,** 415

McMahon, William, attacked at Fort Recovery, **IV,** 428

McMahon-Clyman Company, **I,** 270

McManes, James, and the Philadelphia Gas Ring, **IV,** 259

McManigal, Ortie, and the McNamara case, **III,** 367

McMath, Margaret, kidnapping of, **III,** 209

McMath-Hulbert Observatory, **IV,** 157

McMillan Plan, for Washington, D. C., **V,** 413

McMurray's Map, **V,** 283

McNary, Charles L., as floor leader, **II,** 287

McNary Act, or Norris Farm Export Act, **IV,** 143

McNary-Haugen Bill, and export debenture plan, **II,** 236; and the Farm Bureau, **II,** 245; vetoed by Calvin Coolidge, **II,** 249

McNutt, Paul V., appointed resident commissioner of the Philippines, **IV,** 263

McParlan, James, and the "Molly Maguires," **IV,** 7

McPherson, J. B., and battles on Peachtree Creek, **IV,** 236; and battle at Port Gibson, **IV,** 315; and battle of Raymond, **IV,** 418; and battle of Shiloh, **V,** 71; killed in battle at Atlanta, **V,** 242

McQueen, Peter, and battle of Burnt Corn, **I,** 257

McRae, Alexander, and battle of Valverde, **V,** 356

McRae, C. J., Confederate agent, **II,** 5

McRae, Milton Alexander, and the United Press, **V,** 346

McReynolds, J. C., in West Coast Hotel Company v. Parrish, **V,** 436; and the wire-tapping cases, **V,** 472

McSween, Alexander A., and the Lincoln County War, **III,** 278

Meade, George G., and Bristoe campaign, **I,** 238; and the Corps of Engineers, **II,** 216; and battle of Gettysburg, **II,** 386; attacks at Kelly's Ford, **III,** 202; and the Mine Run campaign, **III,** 405; and invasion of Pennsylvania, **IV,** 244; and battle at Rappahannock Station, **IV,** 416

Meade, Richard W., in Samoa, **V,** 20

Mears, John O., and the Gardiner award, **II,** 371

Meat, and refrigeration, **IV,** 437

Meat Inspection Act of 1906, **III,** 126; **IV,** 294, 383; **V,** 29

Meat Packing, by Armour and Company, **I,** 109

Mechanic's Lien Law, and the Working Man's party, **V,** 484

Mechanics' Union of Trade Associations, **III,** 224

Mechanicsville, Battle of, and the Peninsular campaign, **IV,** 241; **V,** 59

Mediæval Academy of America, **III,** 257

Mediation, Industrial, and arbitration, **I,** 95; and conciliation, **II,** 2; and railroad brotherhoods, **IV,** 400; railroad acts, **IV,** 402; and the War Labor Board, **V,** 404. *See also* Conciliation, Industrial

Medical College of Ohio, founded by Daniel Drake, **III,** 369

Medical Department, and army supply, **I,** 119

Medical Schools, and education, **II,** 187; founded in Old South, **V,** 122; opened to women, **V,** 480

Medicine Creek Treaty (1854), **V,** 181

Medicine Lodge Treaty of 1867, Arapaho attend, **I,** 94; and Santanta, **V,** 31

Medill, Joseph, as newspaper editor, **IV,** 123

Medora, Dakota, cow town, **II,** 79

Meeker, Jotham, printer of *Siwinowe Kesibwi,* **IV,** 126; takes press to Kansas, **IV,** 345

Meeker, Nathan C., organizes the Union Colony, **V,** 342

Meek's Cut-Off, **V,** 192

Meigs, Fort, established by W. H. Harrison, **V,** 258

Meigs, John R., and Burnt District, **I,** 257

Meigs, Josiah, first to take weather observations, **V,** 430

Meigs, Montgomery C., and Fort Pickens, **IV,** 266

Meigs, R. J., attacks at Sag Harbor, **V,** 4

Melgares Expedition, uses Raton Pass, **IV,** 417

Melish, John, map of 1818, **III,** 382; map publisher, **V,** 283

Mellier Process, of paper making, **IV,** 212

Mellon, Andrew W., art collection of, **I,** 124

Mellon, Thomas, and great fortunes, **II,** 312

Mellon Collection, **V,** 413

Mellon Educational and Charitable Trust, **II,** 315

Mellon Institute of Industrial Research, **III,** 117

Memminger, C. G., and Confederate financing, **II,** 9; nonslaveholder, **IV,** 141; and state bank of South Carolina, **V,** 126

Memphis, settled, **I,** 359; and opening of the Mississippi, **III,** 419; naval victory at, **III,** 425

Menace, no-Popery newspaper, **IV,** 66

Menard, Pierre, and Manuel Lisa and Company, **III,** 283; partner in St. Louis Missouri Fur Company, **V,** 12

Ménard, René, Jesuit missionary, **I,** 351; **III,** 174; on Lake Superior, **V,** 205

Mendenhall, T. C., chairman of United States Board on Geographic Names, **II,** 378

Mendota, Treaty of (1851), **V,** 86

Mendoza, Antonio de, **I,** 57

Menendez de Avilés, Pedro, in Georgia, **II,** 116; attacks Ribaut, **II,** 288; makes first permanent

settlement in Spanish Florida, **II,** 288; settles St. Augustine, **II,** 289; **V,** 6

Menke Brothers, noted river showmen, **V,** 77

Mennonites, Amish, **I,** 68; as conscientious objectors, **II,** 25; immigration of, **II,** 383; and group migration, **III,** 397; and pacifism, **IV,** 197; as political exiles, **IV,** 295; oppose slavery, **V,** 97; and the westward movement, **V,** 450; and Turkey red wheat, **V,** 454

Menominee Indians, and Butte des Morts Council, **I,** 263; and Great Indian Council at Niagara, **IV,** 130; and British attack on St. Louis (1780), **V,** 11; depend upon wild rice for their food supply, **V,** 464

Menominee Range, and iron mining, **III,** 157

Mental Cases, care of, **III,** 125

Mental Healers, and New Thought movement, **IV,** 113

Menzies, William, book collector, **I,** 212

Mercantilism, and the balance of trade, **I,** 146; and government regulation, **II,** 405; as pre-Revolutionary imperial idea, **III,** 78; and *laissez-faire,* **III,** 228; and royal disallowance, **IV,** 504; and tobacco, **V,** 274; and York's proprietary, **V,** 507

Mercator, Gerard, and mapping, **III,** 340

Mercer, Fort, the *Augusta* attacks fleet defending, **I,** 138

Mercer, Hugh, and Forbes expedition, **II,** 298; and battle of Princeton, **IV,** 342

Merchant Fleet Corporation, **II,** 209; **V,** 75

Merchant Marine, and Civil War, **I,** 76; and the balance of trade, **I,** 147; and Civil War diplomacy, **I,** 392; acts of 1920 and 1928, **III,** 376; Naval Reserve, **IV,** 72; and shipbuilding, **V,** 72; and ocean shipping, **V,** 73; mail subsidies granted to, **V,** 195; and the Tonnage Act (1789), **V,** 280; act of 1920, and trusts, **V,** 327

Merchants Exchange of St. Louis, **I,** 437

Meredith, Hugh, buys the *Pennsylvania Gazette,* **IV,** 246

Mergenthaler, Ottmar, invents the linotype, **III,** 148, 281; **IV,** 126

Merino Sheep, in New England, **IV,** 98; in New Hampshire, **IV,** 102; introduction of, **V,** 66; and textiles, **V,** 258; and wool growing, **V,** 483

Merit System, consular service placed under, **II,** 306; and political patronage, **IV,** 224

Meritorious Services Citation Certificate, **IV,** 384

Merriam, George and Charles, and Webster's Dictionary, **V,** 433

Merrill, Joshua, and kerosene oil, **III,** 207

Merrimack (Virginia), The, and abandonment of the Norfolk Navy Yard, **I,** 389; Confederate ironclad, **I,** 390; and the Confederate navy, **II,** 8; and ironclad warships, **III,** 158; engages the *Monitor,* **IV,** 10; and the Peninsular campaign,

IV, 241; first Confederate ram, **IV,** 414; sinking of, **V,** 137. *See also Monitor*

Merritt, Ezekial, and the Bear Flag Revolt, **I,** 171

Merritt, Wesley, and Meeker massacre, **III,** 371; and the Philippine insurrection, **IV,** 261; and battle of Manila Bay, **V,** 136; and the Thornburgh fight, **V,** 264; and engagement at Tom's Brook, **V,** 280; and fight on War Bonnet Creek, **V,** 400

Merritt Brothers, and Mesabi Iron Range, **III,** 379

Merry Mount, and liquor in the fur trade, **III,** 281; and May Day, **III,** 361

Merryman, *ex parte,* and arbitrary arrests, **I,** 122; and writ of habeas corpus, **III,** 1

Merry's Museum for Boys and Girls, **I,** 363

Mesa Verde National Park, **IV,** 218

Mesa Verde Ruins, and Escalante-Domínguez expedition, **II,** 227

Mesabi Range, and iron mining, **III,** 157

Messenger, English thoroughbred horse, **III,** 47

Messiah War, Sioux take refuge in Badlands after, **I,** 146; last Sioux uprising, **V,** 87

Metallurgy, and machines, **III,** 320

Methodist Book Concern, established, **I,** 214

Methodists, Negro, **I,** 19; and circuit riders, **I,** 376; and colleges, **I,** 413; as dissenters, **II,** 151; and the Epworth League, **II,** 221; and evangelism, **II,** 230; and frontier preaching, **II,** 353; and the Great Revival, **II,** 419; and Indian missions, **III,** 103; and home missionary societies, **III,** 417; and foreign missions, **III,** 417; and mountain people, **IV,** 37; and Oregon missions, **IV,** 184; and Pietism, **IV,** 269; and Reconstruction, **IV,** 428; and the American religion, **IV,** 442; General Conference prays for President Johnson's conviction, **IV,** 443; and revivals, **IV,** 464; pass antislavery legislation, **V,** 97; and Sunday Schools, **V,** 204; and theological seminaries, **V,** 261; and the Church of the United Brethren, **V,** 345; in the Western Reserve, **V,** 446

Metropolitan Areas, and local government, **III,** 290; and regional planning, **IV,** 438

Metropolitan Museum of Art, **I,** 124; **IV,** 48

Metropolitan Opera, **IV,** 178

Metropotamia, Jefferson's proposed state, **III,** 173

Metz, Christian, leader of the Inspirationists, **I,** 53

Meuse-Argonne Offensive, American Expeditionary Forces in the, **I,** 59

Mexican Cession, and the Alabama Platform, **I,** 41; and land titles, **III,** 243; and the Missouri Compromise, **III,** 428; and the Great Plains, **IV,** 282; and the public domain, **IV,** 370; and early government railroad surveys, **IV,** 405; and

secession, V, 51; and the organization of territories, V, 249

Mexican Land Grants, I, 274; V, 27

Mexican War, and the United States Army, I, 113; and the *Biglow Papers*, I, 184; blockade in, I, 201; financing of, II, 128; demobilization after, II, 134; enlistment in, II, 217; and Manifest Destiny, III, 332; and the Mexican boundary, III, 382; capture of Mexico City, III, 386; and mobilization, IV, 2; Navy in, IV, 77; and the Rio Grande, IV, 486; and annexation of Texas, V, 96; and Trade with the Enemy Acts, V, 300; and army uniforms, V, 340; National Association of Veterans of the, V, 365; cost of, V, 409; loss of life in, V, 410; and the Wilmot Proviso, V, 469

Mexico, French in, II, 328; claims against, II, 365; and mixed commissions, III, 432; treaties with, V, 317

Mexico City, Pan-American Conference at (1902), IV, 202

Mey, Cornelis Jacobsen. *See* May

Meyer, Balthasar, and the Wisconsin Idea, V, 474

Meyer v. Nebraska, III, 412

Mezes, Sidney E., and the Inquiry, III, 124; V, 489

Miami, Fort, founding of, II, 346; built by La-Salle, III, 246; falls in Pontiac War, IV, 306; in the Wayne campaign, V, 427

Miami, The, galley boat on Ohio River, II, 367

Miami, The, put to flight by the *Albemarle*, I, 46

Miami Canal, IV, 160, 165

Miami Conservancy District, and flood control, II, 285; creation of, II, 286

Miami Indians, and Algonquin family, I, 48; and treaty of Fort de Chartres, I, 348; and treaty of Greenville, II, 425; in the Revolution, III, 88; land cessions of, III, 100; removal of, III, 107; in Iowa, III, 152; and LaBalme's expedition, III, 218; and treaty of Logstown, III, 295; and battle of Mississinewa, III, 419; found Pickawillany, IV, 266; and treaty of Spring Wells, V, 150; and treaty of Fort Wayne, V, 370, 426

Miami Purchase, and Fort Washington (Ohio), V, 414

Miamisburg Mound, IV, 34

Miantonomo, Narragansett chief, killed, IV, 53; aids in the Pequot War, IV, 252

Michaelius, Jonas, first ordained minister to New Netherland, IV, 94

Michaux, François André, introduces tea growing in the South, V, 233

Michigamea Indians, I, 48; III, 71

Michigan, territory of, II, 106; and Ordinance of 1787, II, 353; boundary dispute with Ohio, III, 392; and repudiation of state debts, IV, 456; organized, and admitted, V, 248

Michigan, Lake, discovered by Nicolet, II, 344

Michigan, The, first iron ship in United States Navy, III, 157

Michigan, The, dreadnought, II, 167; V, 412

Michigan, University of, receives William L. Clements' library, III, 273

Michigan Central Railroad, and internal improvements, III, 138; and the New York Central, IV, 118; and the Railroad Conspiracy, IV, 401; and tunnels, V, 329

Michigan Essay, published at Detroit, IV, 124; started by James M. Miller, IV, 127

Michigan Southern Railroad, III, 138; IV, 118

Michigania, Jefferson's proposed state, III, 173

Michilimackinac, evacuation of by British, I, 218; and British campaign of 1780, I, 241; and the Fox-Wisconsin Waterway, II, 320; reoccupied, II, 346; and the fur trade, II, 360; and liquor in the fur trade, III, 282; God of, III, 391; fur trade center on Lake Michigan, III, 392; and water routes, IV, 316. *See also* Mackinac

Michilimackinac Company, and American Fur Company, I, 61; bought out by the Southwest Fur Company, V, 133

Micmac Indians, I, 48

Midcontinent Oil Region, IV, 167

Middle Passage, V, 90, 91

Middlesex Canal, completed without public aid, III, 136; and oxen, IV, 194

Middleton, Arthur, signer of the Declaration of Independence, II, 124

Middleton, "Doc," Nebraska outlaw leader, IV, 159

Middleton Place, colonial garden at, I, 344; II, 371

Middletown, and adult education, I, 14

Midnight Judges, and Marbury v. Madison, III, 183; and the Judiciary Act of 1801, III, 189

Midvale Steel Company, Taylor experiments at, III, 115; and munitions, IV, 45

Midway Islands, United States occupies, IV, 195

Midway Plaisance, of the World's Columbian Exposition, V, 495

Mifflin, Thomas, and the Definitive Treaty of Peace, II, 14; signer of the Constitution, II, 39

Migration, Group, IV, 489; V, 214

Migratory Birds Act, III, 431

Milan Decree. *See* Napoleon's Decrees

Milbank Memorial Fund, establishment of, II, 314

Miles, James, endeavors to popularize the idea of codification of international law, IV, 234

Miles, Nelson A., defeats the Nez Percé at Bear Paw Mountains, I, 171; orders return of Germaine girls, II, 382; and Geronimo's campaigns, II, 386; and the Messiah War, III, 380; forces the surrender of Chief Joseph, IV, 129;

and the Red River Indian War, **IV**, 431; and
Sioux wars, **V**, 87; occupies Puerto Rico, **V**, 137;
and water holes, **V**, 421
Miles City, Mont., cow town, **II**, 79
Military Academy, United States, and the Corps
of Engineers, **II**, 216; established at West Point,
V, 438
Military Aid to the Civil Power, **III**, 347
Military Bounties, **I**, 228
Military Service, uses merit system, **III**, 377
Military Tracts, and land bounties, **III**, 234; in
New York, **IV**, 117; Virginia, **V**, 379
Military Tribunals, and the Milligan case, **III**,
405
Military Warrants, and the Miami Purchase, **III**,
390
Militia, in the Union army, **I**, 111; in the colo-
nies, **I**, 112; call for (1861), **I**, 386; and the Con-
stitution, **II**, 34, 39; and desertion, **II**, 141; dogs
as auxiliaries to, **II**, 157; colonial, and enlistment, **II**, 217; and Martin v. Mott, **III**, 348;
and mobilization, **IV**, 2; and muster day, **IV**, 50;
and National Guard, **IV**, 59; colonial, and
parades, **IV**, 213; and the Revolutionary Army,
IV, 472; colonial, and training day in New England, **V**, 304; and volunteers, **V**, 382
Milk, and the dairy industry, **II**, 104; condensed,
II, 105; bottles for, **II**, 105; condensed, **II**, 297;
bottles for, **III**, 64; and hygiene, **III**, 64
Mill Machinery, patents for, **IV**, 223
Millennial Harbinger, magazine published by
Alexander Campbell, **II**, 149
Miller, Adam, settles in present Page County, **V**,
69
Miller, Alfred J., illustrations of the mountain
man, **V**, 312
Miller, David Hunter, and the League of Na-
tions, **III**, 255
Miller, Elizabeth Smith, introduces the bloomer
dress, **I**, 203
Miller, Emily H., edits *The Little Corporal,* **I**,
363
Miller, George M., and wax portraits, **V**, 426
Miller, James, and battle at Maguaga, **III**, 325
Miller, James M., starts the *Michigan Essay,* **IV**,
127
Miller, Lewis, and Chautauqua movement, **I**, 348
Miller, Lewis F., and the development of the
reaper, **IV**, 419
Miller, Phineas, finances invention of the cotton
gin, **II**, 69
Miller, S. F., and Slaughter House cases, **V**, 89
Miller, Samuel, co-founder of the *Mobile Cen-
tinel,* **IV**, 124, 126
Miller, William, and the Adventists, **I**, 15
Miller Brothers, and the Wild West show, **V**, 464
Miller-Tydings Act (1937), **V**, 327

Miller v. Wilson, **V**, 387
Millerism, and the American religion, **IV**, 442;
and Seventh-day Adventists, **V**, 60; in the West-
ern Reserve, **V**, 446
Miller's Run Gap, **IV**, 221
Milligan Case, and trial by military commissions,
I, 122; and powers of President as commander
in chief, **I**, 431; death sentence imposed, **II**, 58;
and martial law, **III**, 347; and the McCardle
case, **III**, 363; and the Radical Republicans, **IV**,
395; and treason trials, **V**, 313; and war powers
of the government, **V**, 399
Milling, **II**, 291
Millington, John, author of *Elements of Civil
Engineering,* **II**, 215
Millionaires, **II**, 311
Mills, B. Fay, revivalist, **IV**, 464
Mills, Capt., and battle of Slim Buttes, **V**, 98
Mills, Eleanor, murder of, **V**, 323
Mills, Robert, architect, **I**, 100
Mills, William M., and the Midcontinent Oil
Region, **III**, 394
Milroy, R. H., defeated by Jackson, **III**, 165
Milwaukee Harvester Company, **III**, 140
Milwaukee Leader, barred from the mails, **IV**, 433
Mims, Fort, massacre at, starts Creek War, **II**, 86
Mina Expedition, backed by the Mexican Asso-
ciation, **III**, 382
Minabozho, cult of, **III**, 395
Mind That Found Itself, by C. W. Beers, **III**, 64
Mine-Layers, and the Navy in the World War,
V, 493
Mine Run Campaign, **III**, 202
Mineral Patent Law, rejects fifths mining tax, **II**,
271; and lode mining, **III**, 293; and law of the
mining camp, **III**, 409
Mineral Springs, **V**, 151
Miners, limitation of working hours for, **V**, 387
Miners' National Association, **I**, 404
Mines, antisubmarine measure, **IV**, 78; Northern
Mine Barrage, **IV**, 148; known as torpedoes
during the Civil War, **V**, 193
Mines, Bureau of, **I**, 432; **III**, 135
Mines, Output of, and domestic trade, **V**, 293
Mingo Bottom, Crawford sets out from, **II**, 83;
and Pluggy's band, **IV**, 288
Mingo Indians, murdered at Baker's cabin, **I**,
146; in the Revolution, **III**, 88; and treaty at
Pittsburgh (1775), **IV**, 280; and Pluggy's band,
IV, 288
Minguez, Juan, killed in the Pawnee attack on
Villasur's expedition, **V**, 369
Minimum Wage Board, **I**, 10
Minimum Wage Laws, **III**, 222, 229
Minimum Wages, and due process, **II**, 173; and
the Supreme Court, **V**, 207; movement for, **V**,
387; and West Coast Hotel Co. v. Parrish, **V**, 436

Mining, coal, I, 79 f., 192; copper, II, 57; gold, II, 396; iron, III, 157; lead, III, 254; silver, V, 81; Spanish origin of, V, 138; stocks, V, 183

Mining Law, II, 396

Minister Plenipotentiary, and foreign service, V, 163

Minnesota, organized, and admitted, V, 248

Minnesota Massacre, effects creation of Indian reservations in Dakota, II, 106

Minnesota Moratorium Law, II, 49; IV, 22, 29

Minnesota Pioneer, founded by James M. Goodhue, IV, 127

Minnesota Territory, Dakota becomes part of (1849), II, 106

Minor, Benjamin Blake, as editor of the *Southern Literary Messenger,* V, 130

Minor, Stephen, and survey of the Southern boundary, V, 129

Minority, Rights of, I, 269; III, 172; V, 124

Minot, George Richards, awarded Nobel prize in medicine, III, 370

Minot, Stephen, and the Pejepscot purchase, IV, 239

Minstrel Shows, I, 70

Mint, Director of the, transferred to the Treasury Department, V, 314

Mints, assaying done at, I, 129; and coinage, I, 410; colonial, I, 411; and the crime of 1873, II, 89; and gold mining, II, 396; and money, IV, 7

Minuit, Peter, establishes Fort Christina, I, 371; buys Manhattan Island, III, 331; appointed director-general at New Amsterdam, IV, 108; promoter of New Sweden Company, IV, 113; and Pennsylvania, IV, 242

Minutemen, at Lexington and Concord, III, 267; in the Revolution, IV, 2

Miranda, Guadalupe, and the Maxwell land grant, III, 361

Miranda's Intrigue, and the Levy, III, 265

Miró, Estevan, and Spanish-Indian relations, V, .140

Miró, Fort, American settlement discovered at, II, 176

Misbranding, practice reduced by Federal Trade Commission, II, 264; and Pure Food and Drug Acts, IV, 383

Miscegenation, and sex relations, V, 62

Missasaga Indians, I, 48

Missionary Ridge, in Chattanooga campaign, I, 348

Mississippi, and repudiation of state debts, IV, 456; organized, and admitted, V, 248; and West Florida, V, 436

Mississippi, Army of, reorganized as Army of Tennessee (C.), V, 241

Mississippi Bubble, III, 305

Mississippi Company, and land grants, III, 235; and land speculation, III, 239; and western land schemes, V, 443

Mississippi Gazette, pioneer newspaper in the Mississippi Territory, IV, 124; founded by Benjamin M. Stokes, IV, 127

Mississippi Plan, and the franchise, II, 324; and restoration of home rule in the South, III, 41; and Reconstruction, IV, 426; and the franchise, V, 199

Mississippi River, free navigation of, I, 33; bridge over, I, 357; free navigation of, II, 139; discovered by DeSoto expedition, II, 142; floods of, II, 286; navigation of, and Jay-Gardoqui negotiations, III, 168; discovery of, by Marquette and Jolliet, III, 180; levee system of, III, 265; free navigation of, III, 424; IV, 216, 273; and water routes, IV, 316; and river and harbor improvements, IV, 488; in American diplomacy, IV, 492; free navigation of, V, 134, 139, 406; as inland waterway, V, 424; free navigation of, V, 447

Mississippi Squadron, in the Civil War, I, 390; Eads gunboats as nucleus of, II, 180; in naval battle before Memphis, III, 372

Mississippi Stock, and first use of land scrip, III, 238

Mississippi Territory, and the Yazoo-Chattahoochee Line, V, 503

Mississippi v. Johnson, III, 363

Mississippi Valley, influenced by Cumberland Road, II, 97; French adventurers in, II, 346; claimed by LaSalle for the King of France, III, 247; and rivers, IV, 491; and domestic trade, V, 292

Mississippi-Yazoo Delta, opened for settlement, V, 367

Missouri, and the Platte purchase, IV, 286; state bank of, V, 164; organized, and admitted, V, 249

Missouri, Kansas and Texas Railway, and the state of Texas, V, 254

Missouri, University of, encourages junior colleges, III, 190

Missouri Compromise, and abolition movement, I, 2; and the Crittenden plan, II, 90; and the Democratic party, II, 137; and the Dred Scott case, II, 167; and judicial review, III, 183; repeal of the, III, 197; and state of Missouri, III, 426; and the Nashville Convention, IV, 55; and popular sovereignty, IV, 309; and proslavery literature, IV, 364; and slavery, V, 95; repeal of, V, 96; and the Tallmadge Amendment, V, 218; and the Wilmot Proviso, V, 469

Missouri Fur Company, and the fur trade, II, 362; and the Leavenworth expedition, III, 259; establishes fort at Three Forks of the Missouri, III, 428; and Missouri River fur trade, III, 430; and the Oregon Trail, IV, 185; and trappers' rendezvous, V, 310

Missouri Gazette, founded by Joseph Charless, **IV**, 124, 127

Missouri Pacific Railroad, **II**, 139; **III**, 428; **IV**, 407; **V**, 255

Missouri Republican, advertises for trappers and traders, **V**, 310

Missouri River Region, and domestic trade, **V**, 293

Missouri Territory, **II**, 106; **V**, 249

Missouri v. Lewis, equal protection of law in, **II**, 222

Missouri Valley, Bourgmont's explorations of, **I**, 229

Missouri Zouaves, **V**, 515

Mitchel, Colin, and Forbes Purchase, **II**, 299

Mitchell, H. G., dismissed because of heresy, **III**, 28

Mitchell, J. C., commanding officer during Fort Sumter siege, **V**, 204

Mitchell, John, and anthracite strike of 1902, **I**, 80; and Buck Stove and Range case, **I**, 246; and the United Mine Workers, **V**, 346

Mitchell, John, botanist, **I**, 225; and calomel, **I**, 276; and epidemics, **II**, 221

Mitchell, John Kearsley, and malaria, **III**, 328

Mitchell, Langdon, dramatist, **II**, 166

Mitchell, Margaret, author of *Gone with the Wind,* **I**, 180

Mitchell, S. W., and fiction, **II**, 270

Mitchell, Samuel Augustus, map publisher, **V**, 283

Mitchell, W. M., and abolitionist literature, **I**, 3

Mitchell Astronomical Observatory, **V**, 430

Mitchell-Hazzen Line, **I**, 226

Mitchell's Map, and the Northwest boundary controversy, **IV**, 149; and the Red Line Map, **IV**, 430; and the St. Croix River, **V**, 7; and topographic mapping, **V**, 282

Mix, Elijah, and the Rip Raps contract scandal, **IV**, 486

Mixed Claims Commission, adjudicates claims arising from *Arabic* case, **I**, 94; and international arbitration, **I**, 96; and settlement of War Claims Act, **V**, 400

Mobile, Spanish base at (1813), **I**, 39; Fort Condé at, **II**, 3; founding of, **II**, 346; and the fur trade, **II**, 362; and the Gulf of Mexico, **III**, 389; and Spanish-American relations, **V**, 135; captured by Spaniards, **V**, 139; treaty of 1784, and Spanish-Indian relations, **V**, 140; as a frontier post, **V**, 302

Mobile Act, and West Florida controversy, **V**, 436

Mobile *Advertiser,* southern newspaper, **V**, 123

Mobile Bay, in the Civil War, **I**, 390; battle of, **II**, 108; attack on, **V**, 193; and capture of the *Tennessee,* **V**, 244

Mobile Centinel, founded by Miller and Hood, **IV**, 124, 126

Mobilization of Industry, **IV**, 182

Moccasin Gap, **IV**, 221

Moderator, elected at town meeting, **V**, 288

Modern Chivalry, written by H. H. Brackenridge, **II**, 270

Modern Language Association of America, **III**, 257

Modjeski, Ralph, and bridges, **I**, 237

Modoc Indians, and battles of Tule Lake, **V**, 329

Modus Vivendi, entered into by the Dominican government, **II**, 159

Mohair Industry, in Texas, **V**, 255

Mohammedans, **IV**, 27

Mohawk and Hudson Railroad, **IV**, 117, 406

Mohawk Indians, and the Esopus War, **II**, 227; one of the Five Nations, **II**, 279; and the Iroquois League, **III**, 159; and the Kayoderosseras patent, **III**, 200; enter New York by way of Lake Champlain, **III**, 229

Mohegan Indians, and Algonquin family, **I**, 48; as refugees from King Philip's War, **III**, 211; at war with Narragansetts, **IV**, 53; and the Pequot War, **IV**, 252

Mojave Indians, and scouting on the plains, **V**, 46

Molasses, and the Triangular Trade, **I**, 417; as an enumerated commodity, **II**, 219; and mercantilism, **III**, 374; and the rum trade, **IV**, 506; and colonial staples, **V**, 160; and foreign trade, **V**, 294; in the Triangular Trade, **V**, 296; in the West India trade, **V**, 437

Molasses Act (1733), and colonial agents, **I**, 415; and colonial commerce, **I**, 418; and the English Parliament, **IV**, 218; and colonial smuggling, **V**, 104; enactment of, **V**, 199; and foreign trade, **V**, 294; and the Triangular Trade, **V**, 297; and the West India trade, **V**, 437

Molestation, freedom from, as colonial privilege, **IV**, 350

Moley, Raymond, and "Brain Trust," **I**, 234

Molino del Rey, Battle of (1847), **III**, 386

Moll, Herman, produces first postroad map of North America, **V**, 282

Molly Maguires, and lawlessness, **III**, 253

Molton, Robert, builds the *Blessing of the Bay,* **I**, 199

Moluntha, Shawnee chief, **I**, 216

Monadnock Block, architecture of, **V**, 87

Monarch Mine, **III**, 24

Money, bills of credit as, **I**, 187; and the bimetallic system, **I**, 188; Continental, **II**, 13; and the Constitution, **II**, 33; purchasing power of, **II**, 45; and the silver dollar, **II**, 157; purchasing power of, **IV**, 8; and the National Monetary Commission, **IV**, 61; tobacco as, **V**, 275

Money Order System, **IV**, 320

Money Power, and the Pujo committee, **IV**, 380

Monhegan Island, fishing colony, **I**, 406; settlement of, **III**, 203; trading post at, **III**, 326

Monis, Judah, first instructor in Hebrew at Harvard, **III**, 176

Moniteur de la Louisiane, published by Louis Duclot, **IV**, 126

Monitor, The, battle with the *Merrimack,* **I**, 390; and blockade of the Confederacy, **II**, 8; revolving turret of, **II**, 284; and ironclad warships, **III**, 158. *See also Merrimack*

Monks Mound, **I**, 267; **IV**, 34

Monmouth Court House, engagement at, **IV**, 476

Monmouth Purchase, **IV**, 104

Monocacy, Wallace defeated at, **V**, 68

Monopolies, and antitrust laws, **I**, 87; and campaign of 1900, **I**, 289; and the Clayton Act, **I**, 396; and the Federal Trade Commission, **II**, 264; and free trade, **II**, 334; and government regulation, **II**, 405; curbed by Sherman Antitrust Act, **III**, 144; and Payne-Aldrich tariff, **IV**, 229; and public ownership, **IV**, 375; and rebates, **IV**, 420; and the Sherman Antitrust Law, **V**, 70

Monro, Lt. Col., and the surrender of Fort William Henry, **III**, 229; **V**, 467

Monroe, Fort, modern name for Fort Miro, **III**, 414

Monroe, Fortress, school of artillery instruction begun at, **I**, 118; Jefferson Davis imprisoned at, **I**, 385; **II**, 112

Monroe, James, depositor and stockholder of the Bank of North America, **I**, 154; at battle of Bladensburg, **I**, 198; and campaign of 1808, **I**, 281; elected President, **I**, 282; mission to France, **II**, 327, 328, 344; and disarmament on Great Lakes, **II**, 415; inauguration of, **III**, 82; and Indian removal, **III**, 107; and internal improvements, **III**, 137; and recognition of Latin-American Republics, **III**, 250; and the Louisiana Purchase, **III**, 308; and the Northwest boundary controversy, **IV**, 150; and the Rhea Letter, **IV**, 477; dispatched to France, **V**, 25; and *Tertium Quids,* **V**, 249; on governing board of University of Virginia, **V**, 375; alumnus of William and Mary College, **V**, 467

Monroe Doctrine, and Anglo-American relations, **I**, 76; and Civil War diplomacy, **I**, 392; and the Clayton-Bulwer Treaty, **I**, 396; and the Falkland Islands controversy, **II**, 241; and foreign policy, **II**, 303; and the Caribbean, **III**, 79; and international law, **III**, 141; and Latin-American relations, **III**, 249; and the Lodge Reservations, **III**, 293; and Lower California, **III**, 311; and the Magdalena Bay Resolution, **III**, 324; and the French in Mexico, **III**, 388; and convention of Miramar, **III**, 414; and neutrality, **IV**, 89; Olney corollary of, **IV**, 172; and peace conferences, **IV**, 232; reaffirmed by Polk, **IV**, 303; as presidential message, **IV**, 336; Roosevelt cor-

ollary to the, **IV**, 501; and sea power, **V**, 49; and Spanish-American relations, **V**, 135; and the Squier treaty, **V**, 152; and blockade of Venezuela, **V**, 359; and the Venezuela boundary controversy, **V**, 360; and the Virgin Islands, **V**, 371; and World War Peace Conference, **V**, 490

Montagnais Indians, **I**, 48

Montana, organized, and admitted, **V**, 249

Montana Post, edited by John Buchanan, **IV**, 127

Montana Territory, cut off from Dakota Territory (1864), **II**, 106

Montauk Indians, **I**, 48

Montcalm, Marquis de, defeated by Wolfe, **II**, 343; and Oswego, **IV**, 190; and the capture of Quebec (1759), **IV**, 388; and operations at Ticonderoga (1758–59), **V**, 268; and massacre at Fort William Henry, **V**, 467

Monterey, and the Mexican War, **III**, 386

Monterey Mission and *Presidio* Founded, **I**, 275

Montevideo, Pan-American Conference at (1933), **IV**, 203

Montgomery, Fort (N. Y.), strengthened, **II**, 28

Montgomery, Fort, on site of "Fort Blunder," **IV**, 503

Montgomery, J. E., and naval battle before Memphis, **III**, 372

Montgomery, James, author of "Decius" letters, **II**, 120

Montgomery, James, uses Sharps rifles, **V**, 64

Montgomery, John B., establishes American rule in San Francisco Bay, **V**, 23

Montgomery, John J., and airplane disasters, **I**, 35

Montgomery, Richard, and the march on Quebec (1775), **I**, 120; and invasion of Canada (1775–76), **I**, 297; and capture of Montreal (1775), **IV**, 18; captures forts on Richelieu River, **IV**, 481

Montgomery, Robert, and Margravate of Azilia, **I**, 144

Montgomery Convention, organizes the Confederacy, **II**, 5; and the Confederate Constitution, **II**, 6; and the Confederacy, **II**, 9

Monthly Catalog of United States Public Documents, **II**, 405

Monticello, architecture of, **I**, 100; **III**, 171; Lafayette visits, **III**, 227

Montreal, capture of (1775), **I**, 297; surrender of (1760), **II**, 343; capture of (1775), **III**, 230; fall of (1760), **III**, 230; campaign against (1813), **V**, 405

Montresor, John, erects Fort Erie, **II**, 223

Monts, Sieur de, and Maine, **III**, 326

Mooar, J. Wright, as hunter, **III**, 60

Moody, Dwight L., evangelist, **II**, 230; **IV**, 442, 464

Moody, W. H., and immunity bath, **III**, 76

Moody, William Vaughn, dramatist, **II**, 166

Moon, James, nurseryman, **IV**, 154

Moonshiners, and bootleggers, **I**, 217; and the Secret Service, **V**, 53

Moore, Capt., and Kearny's march to California, **III**, 201

Moore, E. W., captures Tobasco, **V**, 256

Moore, H. T., and the *Jürgen Lorentzen* prize case, **III**, 190

Moore, Henry, and the Kayoderosseras patent, **III**, 200; and Rouse's Point boundary controversy, **IV**, 503

Moore, Henry J., suggests building International Peace Garden, **III**, 142

Moore, Hiram, and the development of the reaper, **IV**, 419

Moore, J. H., and the Diamond Match Company, **II**, 145

Moore, James, and the Apalache massacre, **I**, 88; and the battle of Ayubale, **I**, 144; and Georgia missions, **II**, 380; attacks Fort Marion, **III**, 344; ravages Tallahassee region, **V**, 126

Moore, James, and the Tuscarora War, **V**, 332

Moore, John Bassett, and the World Court, **V**, 485

Moore, N. H., Woolworth combines with, **II**, 279

Moore, W. H., and the Diamond Match Company, **II**, 145

Moor's Indian Charity School, and the growth of Dartmouth College, **II**, 110

Moose, secret society, **V**, 53

Moqui Indians. *See* Hopi Indians

Mora Grant, **III**, 236

Moraga, Jose Joaquin, and the Anza expedition, **I**, 87

Morals, and early American advertisements, **I**, 16; and the Blue Laws, **I**, 204; and courts of domestic relations, **II**, 158; and free love, **II**, 332

Moratoriums, bank, **I**, 157, 159; for farmers, **II**, 251, 330; bank, **II**, 394; Minnesota, **III**, 411; and mortgages, **IV**, 28; and Old Court-New Court struggle, **IV**, 170; Hoover's, **IV**, 450; and stay and valuation acts, **V**, 177; Hoover's, **V**, 401

Moravian Indians, and Gnadenhutten, **II**, 392

Moravians, plant town of Betharaba, **I**, 180; influence the Delaware Indians to keep peace, **II**, 177; immigration of, **II**, 383; attempt to Christianize the Indians, **III**, 103; and foreign missions, **III**, 417; and Pietism, **IV**, 269; and Schoenbrunn mission, **V**, 38; and distribution of wealth, **V**, 429; plant the Wachovia colony, **V**, 499

Morehead, C. S., imprisonment of, **I**, 122; joins Shelby's Mexican expedition, **V**, 68

Morehead, J. M., and "It's a damned long time between drinks," **IV**, 145

Morehead Case, and minimum wages, **III**, 409; **V**, 387

Morehead v. New York, and *stare decisis*, **V**, 161

Morey Letter, and the Chinese riots, **I**, 367

Morgan, A. E., removed from office by the President, **IV**, 448

Morgan, Charles, as a spy, **V**, 145

Morgan, Charles, and coastwise steamship lines, **I**, 406

Morgan, Daniel, in battle of Cowpens, **II**, 81; in first battle of Freeman's Farm, **II**, 339; in the Southern campaigns (1780–81), **V**, 129

Morgan, Fort, in the Civil War, **I**, 390; as coast defense, **I**, 405; and battle of Mobile Bay, **IV**, 1

Morgan, Fred O., et al. v. U. S., **IV**, 388

Morgan, George, of the firm of Baynton, Wharton and Morgan, **I**, 170; and galley boats, **II**, 367; leader in founding New Madrid, Mo., **IV**, 106; and Indian treaty at Pittsburgh, **IV**, 280

Morgan, George W., fortifies Cumberland Gap, **II**, 96

Morgan, Helen, and night clubs, **IV**, 133

Morgan, Henry, sacks and destroys Panama City, **IV**, 206

Morgan, John, elected medical professor of Philadelphia College, **III**, 369; and medicine, **III**, 369; early member of Pennsylvania Hospital staff, **IV**, 247

Morgan, John, at Buffington Island, **I**, 249

Morgan, J. Pierpont, art collection of, **I**, 124; as book collector, **I**, 212; backs Edison Electric Light Company, **II**, 197; rise of, **II**, 311; library of, **III**, 273; and the Northern Securities case, **IV**, 148; and the Pujo Committee, **IV**, 380; and the United States Steel Corporation, **V**, 348; and the World War, **V**, 490

Morgan, J. P., and Company, private bankers, **I**, 160; and the panic of 1907, **IV**, 210

Morgan, Jonathan, and match-making machinery, **III**, 359

Morgan, Junius S., rise of, **II**, 311

Morgan, Kemp, and tall stories, **V**, 186

Morgan, Morgan, makes first white settlement in West Virginia, **V**, 439

Morgan, Thomas Hunt, awarded Nobel prize in medicine, **III**, 370

Morgan, William, and the anti-Masonic trials, **I**, 82; kidnapping and alleged slaying of, **III**, 352

Morgan, Willoughby, and the Magee-Kearny expedition, **III**, 324

Morgan's Raid, **II**, 58; **IV**, 161

Morgenthau, Henry, and Near East Relief, **V**, 488

Mormon, The Book of, and Reorganized Latter Day Saints, **IV**, 450

Mormon Battalion, captures Tucson, **I**, 104; and the Gila Trail, **II**, 389; and wagon trains, **V**, 389

Mormon Expedition, and overland freighting, **IV**, 192; and Russell, Majors and Waddell, **IV**, 510; and Utah, **V**, 354

Mormon Tabernacle, **V**, 19, 215

Mormon Trail, and road building, **IV**, 495

Mormons, take over Fort Bridger, **I**, 237; and beet sugar, **I**, 174; and caravan traffic, **I**, 312; as a community, **I**, 440; at Council Bluffs, **II**, 71; and Danite order, **II**, 109; form State of Deseret, **II**, 140; and the polygynous system, **II**, 242; found Far West, Mo., **II**, 244; charged with Gunnison massacre, **II**, 429; and Haun's Mill massacre, **III**, 17; found Lemhi Mission, **III**, 66; and irrigation, **III**, 160; and marriage, **III**, 346; and group migration, **III**, 397; in Missouri, **III**, 427; at Nauvoo, **IV**, 68; in Nevada, **IV**, 93; on the Great Plains, **IV**, 282; and polygamy, **IV**, 304; and the American religion, **IV**, 442; and religious thought and writings, **IV**, 447; and Reorganized Latter Day Saints, **IV**, 449; found Salt Lake City, **V**, 19; and Stansbury exploration, **V**, 158; and the Strangite Kingdom, **V**, 187; as first permanent settlers in Utah, **V**, 353; in the Western Reserve, **V**, 446; move to Utah, **V**, 451

Morocco, and the Algeciras Conference, **I**, 48; and the Barbary Wars, **I**, 162; treaties with, **V**, 316

Morrill Act (1862), and agricultural education, **I**, 25, 414; and Federal aid for education, **II**, 255; aids agricultural schools, **II**, 296; and land grants for education, **III**, 236; and land scrip, **III**, 239; and the militia, **III**, 403; and Reserve Officers' Training Corps, **IV**, 457; gives rise to state colleges of mechanic arts, **V**, 44

Morrill Tariff (1861), precipitates secession, **II**, 307

Morris, Charles, at Hampden, **III**, 7

Morris, G. P., and the motto "United We Stand, Divided We Fall," **V**, 350

Morris, Gouverneur, and social change, **I**, 340; and coinage names, **I**, 411; signer of the Constitution, **II**, 39; delegate to Convention of 1787, **II**, 50; and the Erie Canal, **II**, 225; as an executive agent, **II**, 232; and land speculation, **III**, 239; and our money system, **IV**, 7; and Monroe's mission to France, **IV**, 15; and New York land speculation, **IV**, 116; subscribes to principle of separation of powers, **IV**, 327

Morris, John A., and the Louisiana lottery, **III**, 307

Morris, Lewis, and the Zenger trial, **V**, 513

Morris, Lewis, signer of the Declaration of Independence, **II**, 124

Morris, Nelson, and the packing industry, **V**, 184

Morris, Richard, and the Trespass Act, **V**, 322

Morris, Robert, organizes the Bank of North America, **I**, 154, 156; and Big Tree treaty, **I**, 184; chief figure of the Commercial Committee, **I**, 434; signer of the Constitution, **II**, 39; delegate to Convention of 1787, **II**, 50; signer of the Declaration of Independence, **II**, 124; and Dutch loans, **II**, 178; and American ginseng, **II**, 390; member of the Illinois and Wabash Company, **III**, 69; and land speculation, **III**, 239; and the Federal mint, **III**, 413; and money system, **IV**, 7; and New York land speculation, **IV**, 116; and organization of North American Land Company, **IV**, 144; and the Phelps-Gorham purchase, **IV**, 258; and the Pine Barren speculation, **IV**, 273; and the Plan of 1776, **IV**, 282; and the Pulteney purchase, **IV**, 381; appointed Superintendent of Finance (1781), **IV**, 471; made Agent of Marine in charge of naval affairs, **IV**, 471; and profiteering in the Revolution, **IV**, 475

Morris Canal, **I**, 80, 93, 216; **IV**, 105

Morris Packing Company, and the Beef Trust cases, **I**, 173

Morrisania, manor, **III**, 55

Morrison, Frank, and Buck Stove and Range case, **I**, 246

Morrison, William, and Manuel Lisa and Company, **III**, 283; partner in St. Louis Missouri Fur Company, **V**, 12

Morrissey, *In re,* and the Articles of War, **I**, 126

Morrissey, John, establishes gambling house at Saratoga Springs, **II**, 369

Morrissey, John, prize fighter, **IV**, 352

Morristown, N. J., Washington's headquarters at, **II**, 131; and Jockey Hollow, **III**, 177; mutiny of Pennsylvania troops at, **IV**, 248; Washington at, **IV**, 342

Morristown Encampment, and Fort Nonsense, **IV**, 141

Morro Castle, The, and admiralty law, **I**, 13

Morrow, Dwight W., and the Mexican oil controversy, **III**, 384; and Mexican relations, **III**, 385

Morse, Jedediah, and the Illuminati of New England, **III**, 71; author of a *Geography*, **V**, 40; and the temperance movement, **V**, 240

Morse, Samuel F. B., as painter, **I**, 123; and the daguerreotype, **II**, 103; and the telegraph, **III**, 148; **IV**, 223; **V**, 238

Mortgage Companies, and the Reconstruction Finance Corporation, **IV**, 428

Mortgages, and the Minnesota Moratorium case, **III**, 411; and moratoriums, **IV**, 21

Morton, Camp, as prison camp, **IV**, 347

Morton, George, and *Mourt's Relation*, **IV**, 38

Morton, J. Sterling, and the origin of Arbor Day, **I**, 98; **V**, 319

Morton, John, signer of Declaration of Independence, **II**, 124

Morton, Levi P., nominated for Vice-Presidency, I, 287

Morton, Nathaniel, author of *New England's Memorial,* II, 150

Morton, Thomas, and liquor in the fur trade, III, 281; and Merry Mount, III, 378

Morton, Thomas, publisher of the *Nebraska Palladium,* IV, 127

Morton, W. T. G., and painless extraction, I, 71

Morton, William, polar expedition of, IV, 293

Mosby's Rangers, as partisan band, IV, 219

Mosca Pass, IV, 221

Moses, G. H., opposes the World Court, V, 485

Moses His Judicials, and New Haven Colony, IV, 103

Mosher, Hugh, and the "Spirit of '76" painting, V, 146

Mosley, C. C., wins air trophy (1920), I, 36

Mosquito, and yellow fever, V, 505

Mosquito Coast, and the Squier treaty, V, 152

Most, John J., and anarchists, I, 72

Most-Favored-Nation Principle, and Convention of 1800, II, 52; and Cushing's Treaty, II, 101; and Kearny's mission to China, III, 201; incorporated in treaty with Colombia, III, 249; and the Open-Door Policy, IV, 176; and reciprocal trade agreements, IV, 422; in commercial treaties, V, 315; included in treaties of commerce, V, 318

Motard, Joseph, and Spanish-Missouri Fur Company, V, 141

Mother Earth, anarchist magazine, I, 72

Mother Lode Mine, III, 293

Motion Pictures, as an amusement, I, 71; and political campaigns, I, 295; and growth of democracy, II, 135; and Hollywood, III, 38; and leisure, III, 264; influence of, on manners, III, 334; as agency of mass impression, III, 352; and photography, IV, 265; and propaganda, IV, 359; and public opinion, IV, 375; and the Southwest, V, 133; and the theater, V, 260

Moton, Robert Russa, and Tuskegee Institute, V, 332

Motor Bus, and urban transportation, V, 305; and transportation and travel, V, 309

Motor Carrier Act of 1935, passed, III, 143

Motor Truck, as influence on agriculture, I, 34; freight carried by, II, 341; and railroads, IV, 408; and transportation and travel, V, 309

Mott, John R., and the Root mission to Russia, IV, 501

Mott, Lucretia, and women's rights convention at Seneca Falls, II, 265; V, 58; and the woman movement, V, 477

Moulthorpe, Reuben, and wax portraits, V, 426

Moulton, Jeremiah, and the Norridgewock fight, IV, 142

Moultrie, Fort, as coast defense, I, 405; fires on the *Star of the West,* V, 160; and Fort Sumter, V, 203

Moultrie, William, and defense of Charleston Harbor, I, 344

Mound Builders, and Adena prehistoric culture, I, 10; in the American Bottom, I, 59; and Fort Ancient, I, 72; Arkansas Indians as, I, 106; at Cahokia, I, 267; and the Great Serpent Mound, II, 420; and the Hopewell culture, III, 45; art of, III, 93; and Indian burial, III, 94; and maize, III, 328; and the Miamisburg Mound, III, 391; in the Ozarks, IV, 194

Mound City, The, gunboat, II, 180

Mount, William Sidney, painter, I, 123

Mount Desert, sack of, III, 326

Mount McKinley National Park, IV, 218

Mount Palomar Observatory, IV, 157

Mount Pleasant, Fort, construction of, II, 96

Mount Rainier National Park, IV, 218

Mount Rushmore Memorial, I, 195, 220

Mount Savage Rolling Mill, IV, 410

Mount Wilson Observatory, IV, 156

Mountain Men, and Ashley's expedition, I, 128; and Bowie knife, I, 230; in Colorado, I, 426; and the coyote, II, 82; in fur-trading ventures, II, 235, 362; hold fairs in Green River Valley, II, 423; of the Rockies, IV, 498; and trail marking, V, 308; and trappers' rendezvous, V, 310; and trapping, V, 311; join the Willamette Valley settlements, V, 466

Mountain People, and civilization of the Old South, V, 122

Mourner's Bench, and the protracted meeting, IV, 367

Moyer, Charles H., and Cœur d'Alene riots, I, 409; and the murder of Gov. Steunenberg, III, 21

Mrs. O'Leary's Cow, I, 357

Muckrakers, and fiction, II, 270; and political scandals, IV, 298

Mud Fort, original name of Fort Mifflin, III, 396

Muddy Pass, IV, 222

Mudge, I. G., *Guide to Reference Books,* III, 34

Mugwumps, and campaign of 1884, I, 287

Mühlenberg, Henry Melchior, and Lutherans, III, 316; and Pietism, IV, 269

Muir, C. H., and the Oise-Aisne operation, IV, 167

Muir, James, and cruise of the *Saginaw's* gig, V, 5

Mulattoes, and miscegenation, III, 415; and the race problem, IV, 394

Mule, and Santa Fé trade, V, 30; Spanish origin of, V, 138; for wagon trains, V, 390

Mulford, Elisha, political writings of, IV, 302

Mulford, John, and natural rights concept, IV, 66

Mullan, John, and Montana gold seekers, **IV,** 16

Mulligan, J. A., and siege of Lexington, Mo., **III,** 266

Mullins, E. Y., and theological writings, **V,** 261

Multilateral Treaties, **V,** 318

Munfordville, attack on, **III,** 205

Munger, Theodore T., and religious thought, **IV,** 446; and theological writings, **V,** 261

Municipal Bankruptcy Act of 1934, **I,** 159

Municipal Courts, and the judiciary, **III,** 188

Municipal Government, and apportionment, **I,** 92; and the borough, **I,** 221; and city manager plan, **I,** 380; and commission form of government, **I,** 434; and home rule, **III,** 40; and the recall, **IV,** 421

Munitions, Civil War, **I,** 392; in Confederacy, **II,** 10; and the Revolutionary Army, **IV,** 473

Munn v. Illinois, and public control of business, **I,** 260; and grain elevator legislation, **II,** 202; and the Granger Cases, **II,** 409, 411; and price fixing, **IV,** 338; and businesses clothed with a public interest, **IV,** 371; upholds the Granger laws, **IV,** 402

Munro, George P., and dime novels, **II,** 147

Munson, Edward Lyman, and military hygiene, **III,** 64

Münsterberg, Hugo, and spiritualism, **V,** 147

Murchison Letter, and Anglophobia, **I,** 78; and Sackville-West Incident, **V,** 2

Murder Act (1774), **I,** 8

Murdock, Victor, leads revolt against the Payne-Aldrich Tariff Bill, **IV,** 356

Murfree, Mary N., and fiction, **II,** 270

Murfreesboro (Stone River), Army of Tennessee fights at, **V,** 242; Terry's Texas Rangers at, **V,** 249

Murphy, Charles F., and party machines, **III,** 319

Murphy, Frank, appointed resident commissioner of the Philippines, **IV,** 263

Murphy, Henry C., book collector, **I,** 212

Murphy, Isaac, governor of Arkansas, **I,** 105

Murphy, John Benjamin, and abdominal surgery, **III,** 370

Murphy, L. G., and the Lincoln County War, **III,** 278

Murphy, William Parry, awarded Nobel prize in medicine, **III,** 370

Murphy Wagons, and the prairie schooner, **IV,** 329

Murrah, Pendleton, joins Shelby's Mexican expedition, **V,** 68

Murray, James, and capture of Montreal (1760), **IV,** 18

Murray, John, and the Universalists, **V,** 350

Murray, Lindley, author of a *Grammar,* **V,** 40

Murray, William, and the Illinois and Wabash Company, **III,** 69

Murray, William Vans, diplomatic mission of, **II,** 148

Murrell, John A., bandit, **I,** 152; **III,** 252

Muscat, treaties with, **V,** 317

Muscle Shoals, and State of Franklin, **II,** 329; nitrogen plant at, **IV,** 326; and the Spanish conspiracy, **V,** 139; land speculation, **V,** 244; and water power, **V,** 423

Museum of Comparative Zoology, **IV,** 47

Music Pass, **IV,** 221

Musical Fund Society of Philadelphia, **IV,** 48

Musick, Edwin C., and airplane disasters, **I,** 36; and the *China Clipper,* **I,** 365

Muskets, as munitions, **IV,** 44

Muskingum, crossing-place on the, **II,** 421

Muskingum Valley, Delaware Indians in, **II,** 131

Muskogee-speaking Tribes, houses of, **III,** 111

Musquakie, native name of Fox Indians, **II,** 319

Musser, Mrs. Burton W., heads peace caravan, **IV,** 231

Mustang, and the bronco, **I,** 242; and the cow horse, **III,** 46; and the Spanish horse, **III,** 48; Spanish origin of, **V,** 138

Muster Day, and parades, **IV,** 213; and the militia, **V,** 382

Mutilation, as a colonial punishment, **IV,** 383

Mutiny Act of 1765, and billeting, **I,** 187

"Mutt and Jeff," comic characters, **I,** 431

Mutton, and rotation of crops, **II,** 154

Mutual Broadcasting System, **IV,** 397

Muybridge, Eadweard, and photography, **IV,** 265

My Bondage and My Freedom, by Frederick Douglass, **I,** 3

Myer, Fort, airplane disaster at, **I,** 35; flight of first government dirigible held near, **II,** 148

Myers v. U. S. (1925), **I,** 91; **III,** 59; **IV,** 448

Myra, The, whaling ship, **V,** 4

N

Naches Pass, McClellan fails to explore, **V,** 182

Nacogdoches, missions founded near, **II,** 182; and the Long expedition, **III,** 298; established as chief Spanish center in East Texas, **V,** 252

Nago Negroes, imported as slaves, **IV,** 86

Nahant, as a summer resort, **IV,** 460

Nails, **I,** 249

Naismith, James, inventor of game of basketball, **I,** 167; **V,** 149

Nampeo, famous Indian potter, **III,** 93

Nanking Incident (1927), **III,** 146

Nansen, Fridtjof, polar expedition of, **IV,** 293

Nanticoke Indians, **I,** 48

Napoleon's Decrees, and the Embargo, **II,** 207; and nonintercourse, **IV,** 138; and retaliation in international law, **IV,** 461; and the War of 1812, **V,** 404

Narcotic Drugs Import and Export Act, and opium, IV, 179

Narcotics Limitation Convention of 1931, IV, 179

Nardone et al. v. U. S., V, 472

Nares, George S., polar expedition of, IV, 293

Narragansett Bay, explored, I, 57

Narragansett Indians, and Algonquin family, I, 48; and Great Swamp Fight, II, 420; and King Philip's War, III, 210; as refugees from King Philip's War, III, 211; and the Pequot War, IV, 252; in King Philip's War, IV, 478; and Shawomet, V, 65

Narragansett Pacer, III, 47

Narragansett Planters, IV, 478

Narrow-gauge Railroads, I, 426; II, 139

Narvaez Expedition, and exploration of America, I, 57; Cabeza de Vaca with, I, 264; and the conquistadores, II, 25; and the Franciscans, II, 325

Nasby, Petroleum V., humorous lecturer, III, 260

Nashville, and the Cumberland River, II, 97; and the Cumberland settlers, II, 98; battle of, III, 44; Army of Tennessee defeated at, V, 242

Nashville Convention, and Compromise of 1850, I, 442; assembled, V, 51; and slavery, V, 96; and the Tarpley letter, V, 224

Nason, Joseph, and hot water heating, III, 23

Nason, Thomas, engraver, I, 124

Nast, Thomas, and political cartoons, I, 320; III, 12

Natchez, and British campaign of 1780, I, 240; captured by Spaniards, V, 139; as a frontier trading post, V, 302

Natchez Indians, and the fur trade, II, 362; sold into slavery, III, 108; and Louisiana, III, 305; as mound builders, IV, 35; and Fort Rosalie, IV, 502

Natchez Trace, and treaty of Fort Adams, I, 9; Murrell robs travelers along, I, 152; and Choctaw Trail, I, 369; flatboatmen return by, II, 282; and Gaines' Trace, II, 366; and Indian paths, III, 104; Mason Band operates over, III, 351

"Natchez under the Hill," fiddle tune, II, 270

Natchitoches, and the Aguayo expedition, I, 34; mission founded near, II, 182; and Los Adaes, III, 302; and the Red River raft, IV, 432; St. Denis' expedition starts from, V, 8; and boundaries of Louisiana Purchase, V, 252; as a frontier post, V, 302

Nation, uses term "party machines," III, 318

Nation, Carrie, hatchet of, III, 16; and prohibition in Kansas, III, 195

National Academy of Sciences, IV, 62

National Aeronautic Association, I, 36

National Agricultural Conference, called by Warren G. Harding, II, 249

National American Woman Suffrage Association, V, 478

National Anthem, V, 160

National Archives, I, 103; III, 33

National Army, formation of, I, 113; cantonments of, I, 296; and the draft, II, 164; raised, IV, 2

National Association for the Advancement of Colored People, III, 317

National Association of Manufacturers, maintains lobbies, III, 287; as a pressure group, IV, 337; and propaganda, IV, 358

National Association of Sales Finance Companies, III, 127

National Bank Notes, introduced, I, 154; II, 99; and the Federal Reserve System, II, 262; and increase in dollar value of gold stock, II, 394; and money system, IV, 7; as paper money, IV, 213; and specie payments, V, 143

National Banking System, and the agrarian movement, I, 21; and the Aldrich-Vreeland Law, I, 47; and deposits, I, 153; and bank failures, I, 153; creation of, I, 157; and branches, I, 158; established, I, 388; and Comptroller of the Currency, I, 444; and foreign banking, II, 185; and Federal Reserve System, II, 261; and Greenback movement, II, 423; and interest laws, III, 134; and the Louisiana system, III, 307; and the McFadden Banking Act, III, 364; and sectionalism, V, 54; and distribution of wealth, V, 429

National Bell Telephone Company, I, 66

National Bituminous Coal Commission, II, 428; III, 135

National Board of Fire Underwriters, III, 130

National Broadcasting Company, IV, 397

National Budget and Accounting Act (1921), II, 128

National Canners Association, II, 297

National Capital, location of, II, 153

National Cash Register Company, and salesmanship, V, 17

National Catholic Welfare Conference, I, 324; V, 488

National Christian Association, I, 82

National Civil Service Reform League, I, 382; IV, 359

National Cloak and Suit Company, III, 325

National Collection of Fine Arts, V, 102

National Commission on Law Observance and Enforcement, V, 461

National Committee on the Cause and Cure of War, V, 395

National Committee on Unemployment Relief, IV, 440

National Committees, and organization of political parties, IV, 297

National Conference of Commissioners on Uniform State Laws, V, 175

National Cordage Company, and panic of 1893, IV, 209

National Council for the Prevention of War, IV, 235, 359; V, 395

National Currency Act, I, 157

National Debt of the United States. *See* Debt, Public

National Defense, and merchant marine, III, 377

National Defense Acts, and armaments, II, 127; and enlistment, II, 217; and the militia, III, 404; and mobilization, IV, 2; and Army Nurse Corps, IV, 155; and Officers' Reserve Corps, IV, 158; and preparedness, IV, 331; and recruiting, IV, 428; and Reserve Officers' Training Corps, IV, 457; and volunteers, V, 382; and the War Department, V, 402

National Emergency Council, V, 162

National Era, I, 86

National Farm Loan Associations, II, 245

National Federation of Miners, I, 404

National Forest Reserves, and the public domain, IV, 371

National Forests, and the Weeks Act, V, 433

National Gallery of Art, V, 413

National Gazette, suspension of the, I, 139; edited by Philip Freneau, IV, 123; as organ of Thomas Jefferson, IV, 128

National Geographic Society, I, 209; III, 248

National Guard, and Army peace-time work, I, 111; and the United States Army, I, 112; and the Army school system, I, 118; camps of the, I, 296; and defense, II, 127; as military aid to the civil power, III, 400; and the militia, III, 403; during World War, IV, 2; V, 491

National Guard Zouaves, V, 514

National Industrial Recovery Act, and antitrust laws, I, 87; and the coal industry, I, 404; and codes of fair competition, I, 408; and the commerce clause, I, 434; and the Congress of Industrial Organizations, II, 20; as emergency legislation, II, 210; and Export-Import Banks, II, 236; and the Fair Labor Standards Act, II, 239; and "Hot Oil" case, III, 51; as an interstate commerce law, III, 144; and the Supreme Court, III, 184; and price fixing, IV, 339; and Schechter v. U. S., V, 38; and the trade association, V, 297; and trade practices, V, 299; and trusts, V, 327; and wages and hours of labor, V, 387. *See also* National Recovery Administration

National Institution for the Promotion of Science, I, 124

National Intelligencer, Jeffersonian-Republican newspaper, II, 403; as political organ, IV, 128; publicizes the Pomeroy Circular, IV, 305; and

government printing, IV, 344; office of, burned, V, 417

National Interest, and peace, IV, 230

National Journal, founded by Peter Force, II, 403; as political organ, IV, 128

National Kansas Committee, formed, III, 253

National Labor and Reform Party of 1872, III, 223

National Labor Relations Act (Wagner Act), and blacklisting, I, 197; passed, I, 261; and closed shop, I, 403; and the commerce clause, I, 434; and implied powers, III, 80; and the Supreme Court, III, 184; and lockouts, III, 291; and the New Deal, IV, 96; and picketing, IV, 267; and the yellow-dog contract, V, 504

National Labor Relations Board, as administrative agency, I, 11; and delegation of powers, II, 133; and the judiciary, III, 186; and the National Recovery Administration, IV, 62; and sit-down strikes, V, 191

National Labor Union of Baltimore, III, 224

National Linseed Oil Trust, V, 326

National Lord's Day Society, IV, 20

National Monetary Commission, created, I, 47, 157; and the Federal Reserve System, II, 261

National Munitions Control Board, V, 162

National Museum, I, 124; IV, 47

National Packing Company, I, 173

National Pan-Hellenic Association, V, 482

National Park Service, established, III, 135; and development of International Peace Garden, III, 142

National Parks, as amusement areas, I, 71; and forests, II, 309; and our land policy, III, 238; and national monuments, IV, 18; Yellowstone, V, 506; Yosemite, V, 509

National Police Academy, II, 256

National Recovery Administration, and the Blue Eagle emblem, I, 204; and codes, I, 261; and delegation of powers, II, 17; and consumer protection, II, 45; created, IV, 96; and restraint of trade, IV, 461. *See also* National Industrial Recovery Act

National Reform Association, III, 42

National Repository, monthly periodical, III, 226

National Republican Party, in campaign of 1836, I, 283; followers of Adams and Clay become known as, II, 136; and the nominating convention, IV, 137; as a political party, IV, 296

National Research Council, III, 117, 257

National Resources Board, created, IV, 61; and regional planning, IV, 438

National Road, another name for Cumberland Road, II, 97; III, 137; and Ohio National Stage Company, IV, 164; and road development, IV, 494; and transportation and travel, V, 307; Zane's Trace develops into the, V, 512

National Safety Council for Industrial Safety, **I**, 8

National Security League, and Preparedness, **IV**, 331

National Silver Party, **I**, 288

National Society of Professional Engineers, **II**, 216

National Steel Company, **V**, 348

National Student Federation of America, **V**, 511

National Trades Union Convention, **III**, 42

National Transit Company, **IV**, 166

National Tribune, and the Arrears Pension Act, **IV**, 251

National Tube Company, **V**, 348

National Union Party, as a political party, **IV**, 297

National Woman's Party, **II**, 266; **V**, 478

National Youth Administration, **II**, 257; **IV**, 441

Nationalism, Alexander Hamilton as strong believer in, **I**, 132; and state sovereignty, **V**, 173; and the Webster-Hayne debate, **V**, 431; in the West, **V**, 435; and the Whig party, **V**, 456

Native American Party, **I**, 65, 130

Natividad, Battle of, **I**, 271

Nativism, and the American (Know-Nothing) party, **I**, 64; and the American Protective Association, **I**, 64; and the American Republican party, **I**, 65; and Americanization, **I**, 67; and the Bedini riots, **I**, 173; and Bloody Monday, **I**, 203; and foreign groups, **II**, 302; and immigration, **III**, 73; and the Maria Monk controversy, **III**, 342; and mobs and riots, **IV**, 3; and the Philadelphia riots, **IV**, 259; and the Order of United Americans, **V**, 345; and the burning of the Ursuline Convent, **V**, 353; and the "Wide-awakes," **V**, 462

Natural Bridges, Utah, **IV**, 19

Natural Gas, and bituminous coal, **I**, 192; and glass, **II**, 391

Natural Gas Act of 1938, and the Federal Power Commission, **II**, 261

Natural Resources, Conservation of. *See* Conservation Movement

Natural Rights, and the British Constitution, **II**, 29; and the Declaration of Independence, **II**, 120; and doctrine of equality, **II**, 222; and freedom, **II**, 336; Locke's doctrine of, **III**, 291; and political theories, **IV**, 300; and proslavery literature, **IV**, 364; and right of revolution, **IV**, 472; and the slave trade, **V**, 91; and slavery, **V**, 94; and the South as a conscious minority, **V**, 124

Naturalization, and the First Congress, **I**, 50; and assimilation, **I**, 130; and the Constitution, **II**, 33; and dual citizenship, **II**, 171; and expatriation, **II**, 234; and the franchise, **II**, 323; and politics, **III**, 73; and impressment of seamen, **III**, 81; and international law, **III**, 141; and U. S. v. Wong Kim Ark, **V**, 350

Nautical Almanac Office, **IV**, 70

Nautilus, The, the submarine of Robert Fulton, **V**, 194

Nauvoo, Mormon settlement, **II**, 114; and the Mormon War, **IV**, 24; built by the Mormons, **IV**, 26, 449

Navajo Indians, at Bosque Redondo, **I**, 221; cattle sold to feed, **II**, 400; and the horse, **III**, 92; New Mexico exposed to attacks of, **IV**, 107; overwhelmed by Kit Carson, **IV**, 107; raid Santa Fé, **V**, 29; at Fort Sumner, **V**, 202

Naval Observatory, **IV**, 76

Naval Oil Reserves, and the Elk Hills oil scandal, **II**, 203; and Teapot Dome oil scandal, **V**, 235

Naval Power on the Great Lakes, **II**, 415

Naval Radio Station, at Tutuila Island, **V**, 333

Naval Reserves, in the World War, **V**, 493

Naval Retrenchment, **II**, 280

Naval Stores, and bounties, **I**, 228; of Cape Fear River settlements, **I**, 307; as enumerated commodities, **II**, 219; Palatines brought to make, **II**, 382; and colonial industries, **III**, 119; and mercantilism, **III**, 374; and the Navigation Acts, **IV**, 74; and colony of New York, **IV**, 115; and the Palatines, **IV**, 201; and tar, **V**, 220; and foreign trade, **V**, 294

Naval Treaties, at London, **III**, 296 f.; at Washington, **V**, 417f.

Naval War Code of 1900, and blockades, **I**, 201

Naval War with France, **I**, 151; **II**, 28

Navigation, Bureau of, **I**, 432; **IV**, 70

Navigation Act of 1817, and the coasting trade, **I**, 406

Navigation Acts, and the Board of Trade and Plantations, **I**, 206; and colonial commerce, **I**, 418; and British colonial policy, **I**, 421; and the Council for Foreign Plantations (1660), **II**, 71; as factor in war, **II**, 307; and freedom of the seas, **II**, 338; regulate logwood trade, **III**, 295; Massachusetts refuses to recognize, **III**, 357; and mercantilism, **III**, 374; and Randolph's Commission, **IV**, 415; and the American Revolution, **IV**, 465; and ocean shipping, **V**, 73; and colonial smuggling, **V**, 103; and foreign trade, **V**, 294; and York's proprietary, **V**, 507. *See also* Trade Acts

Navy Department, and national defense, **II**, 126; and Maury's charts, **III**, 360; evolution of the, **IV**, 475

Navy of the United States, and the Constitution, **II**, 33; and national defense, **II**, 126; constructs stone docks, **II**, 156; and the fleet, **II**, 282; and mine sweeping, **III**, 406; petroleum reserves of, **IV**, 237; warships of the, **V**, 411; in World War, **V**, 493

Nazareth, Pa., founded by the Moravians, **IV**, 22

NC–4, first plane to cross the Atlantic, **I**, 142, 439

Neagle, John, painter, **I**, 123

Neale, Thomas, granted monopoly of the carriage of letters (1691), **IV**, 321

Neale, Walter, and Strawberry Bank, **V**, 187

Near East Relief, **V**, 488

Near v. Minnesota, **III**, 412

Nebbia v. New York, and businesses clothed with a public interest, **IV**, 371

Nebraska, organized, and admitted, **V**, 249

Nebraska One-House Legislature, **V**, 340

Nebraska Palladium, **IV**, 127

Nebraska Territory, Dakota included in (1854), **II**, 106

Necessity, Fort, erected at Great Meadows, **II**, 418; battle of, **III**, 295

"Ned Buntline," pen name of Edward Z. C. Judson, writer of outdoor adventure stories, **II**, 147

Needham, James, visits Tennessee, **V**, 242

Needlework, development of, **I**, 124

Neesima, Joseph, foreign exchange student, **V**, 191

Neff, Mary, and massacre at Haverhill, Mass., **III**, 17

Negative Voice, claimed in the "Sow Case," **V**, 134

Negro, Fort, destroyed, **II**, 429; **V**, 57

Negro, Free. *See* Free Negroes

Negro Ballads, **I**, 148

Negro Militia, and the Red Shirts, **IV**, 432

Negro Plot of 1741, and colonial punishments, **IV**, 382

Negro Soldiers, and Brownsville affair, **I**, 245; and the Emancipation Proclamation, **II**, 206

Negro Suffrage, and the Fourteenth Amendment, **II**, 42; and disfranchisement, **II**, 151; and the Fifteenth Amendment, **II**, 271; and the Ku Klux Klan, **II**, 323; abolished, **II**, 335; and the Grandfather Clause, **II**, 409; and Reconstruction, **IV**, 426 f.; and Tillmanism, **V**, 269

Negroes, disfranchisement of, **I**, 40; Americanization of, **I**, 68; in private schools, **I**, 179; and the Black Codes, **I**, 193; and Ohio Black Laws, **I**, 196; as camp followers, **I**, 279; and the Dred Scott case, **II**, 167; and doctrine of equality, **II**, 223; as freedmen, **II**, 335; and Liberia, **III**, 270; and the Lily-White movement, **III**, 277; and lynching, **III**, 317; as Masons, **III**, 352; and miscegenation, **III**, 415; and the American Missionary Association, **III**, 416; and home missionary societies, **III**, 417; and the Black and Tan Convention, **III**, 420; disfranchisement of, **III**, 422; and riots, **IV**, 3; as indentured servants, **IV**, 82; and peonage, **IV**, 252; education of, **IV**, 260; and the plantation system of the South, **IV**, 284; and the race problem, **IV**, 393; and race riots, **IV**, 394; and Radical rule in the South, **IV**, 395; equal rights for, **IV**, 425; in Rhode Island, **IV**, 478; and Democratic party in the

Solid South, **V**, 118; and the suffrage, **V**, 199; education of, **V**, 332; and the urban drift, **V**, 352; as indentured servants, **V**, 372; disfranchisement of, **V**, 374; and the Visible Admixture Law, **V**, 381; and voodooism, **V**, 382; as voters, **V**, 383; and educational tests for voting, **V**, 384; disfranchisement of, **V**, 467

Nelson, Commander, commands sub-chasers in the World War, **V**, 493

Nelson, John, and American claims on Naples, **IV**, 52

Nelson, Knute, Republican leader in Minnesota, **III**, 411

Nelson, Samuel, and the Treaty of Washington (1871), **V**, 416

Nelson, Thomas, signer of the Declaration of Independence, **II**, 124; organizes the Greenbrier Company, **II**, 425; saved by Jouett's ride, **III**, 182

Nelson, William, and battle of Richmond (Ky.), **IV**, 481

Nemacolin's Path, and the Monongahela River, **IV**, 12; Washington (Pa.) on, **V**, 415

Nesmith, J. W., and the Yakima Indian wars, **V**, 500

Nesters, and cattle drives, **I**, 326

Netcher, George E., discovers Howland's Island, **III**, 54

Netherlands, treaties with, **V**, 316, 318

Netherlands Award, and Northeast boundary, **IV**, 147, 503

Nettleton, Asahel, *Village Hymns*, **III**, 65

Neutral Flag, and Declaration of Paris (1856), **IV**, 215

Neutral Goods, and Declaration of Paris (1856), **IV**, 215

Neutral Ground, and the Black Hawk Purchase, **I**, 194

Neutral Ground, N. Y., "cowboys and skinners" operate in, **II**, 81

Neutral Ground Agreement, and Louisiana boundaries, **III**, 309; and Natchitoches, La., **IV**, 57; and Louisiana Purchase, **V**, 252

Neutral Indians, raided by Iroquois, **III**, 92; and the Iroquois League, **III**, 159; and the Senecas, **V**, 58

Neutral Rights, and the *Essex* case, **II**, 228; and international law, **III**, 142; and Declaration of London, **III**, 296; and proclamation of neutrality, **IV**, 91; and Orders in Council, **IV**, 180; defined in the Plan of 1776, **IV**, 282; and *Polly* admiralty case, **IV**, 304; and prize courts, **IV**, 352; and retaliation in international law, **IV**, 461; and Rule of the War of 1756, **IV**, 505; and the submarine, **V**, 192; and the War of 1812, **V**, 404

Neutrality, and freedom of the seas, **II**, 338; and

international law, III, 141; and visit and search, V, 381; and the World War, V, 490

Neutrality Act of 1794, III, 141; IV, 88, 91

Neutrality Acts of 1935, 1937 and 1939, and contraband of war, II, 48; and foreign policy, II, 303; and isolation, III, 163; and the League of Nations, III, 256; and visit and search, V, 381

Neutrality Proclamation of 1793, III, 162; IV, 197

Nevada, organized, and admitted, V, 249

Neville, John, at Fort Pitt, IV, 279; and the Whiskey Insurrection, V, 457

Nevins, Allan, and political writings, IV, 303

New Albion, name for California, II, 165

New Amsterdam, settlement of, IV, 108; and New York City, IV, 118; and paving, IV, 228

New Bedford Textile School, III, 115

New Brunswick, Howe forced back to (1777), IV, 476

New Castle, taken by the English, II, 130; granted to Duke of York, II, 132; and the "turf and twig" ceremony, V, 330; and York's proprietary, V, 508

New Castle and Frenchtown Railway, II, 130

New Croton Aqueduct, V, 329

New Deal, and the Agricultural Adjustment Administration, I, 24; and the alphabetical agencies, I, 52; and "boondoggling," I, 215; and Brain Trust, I, 234; and campaign of 1932, I, 292; and the coal industry, I, 404; and public debt, II, 118; Democratic party supports, II, 137; and emergency legislation, II, 210; and Home Owners Loan Corporation, III, 40; and labor unions, III, 224; and lobbying, III, 287; and nationalist sentiment, IV, 64; and planned economy, IV, 283; and pump-priming, IV, 382; and Resettlement Administration, IV, 459; supported by the South, V, 118; and states' rights, V, 175; and subsistence homesteads, V, 195; and the Supreme Court, V, 207; and the Supreme Court Packing Bills, V, 208; and taxation, V, 227

New Echota, Treaty of, I, 352; V, 303

New England, Dominion of, and colonial assemblies, I, 416; and colonial plans of union, I, 420; Andros annexes Connecticut to, II, 22; and Lords of Trade and Plantations, III, 302; establishment of, III, 327; and Massachusetts, III, 355; and franchise in Massachusetts Bay, III, 356; and the Massachusetts Bay Company, III, 358; Rhode Island as a part of, IV, 478; and rights of Englishmen, IV, 484; and York's proprietary, V, 508

New England Anti-Slavery Society, I, 58; III, 270

New England Company, formed, II, 162

New England Council. See Council for New England

New England Council, and conferences of governors, II, 406

New England Emigrant Aid Company, I, 220; III, 196; V, 64

New England Farmer, farm periodical, II, 248

New England Minimum Wage Compact, III, 144

New England Mississippi Company, II, 381

New England Non-Resistance Society, IV, 234

New-England Primer, as a best seller, I, 180; and children's books, I, 363; Benjamin Harris, printer of, IV, 379; and religious education, IV, 444; as a schoolbook, V, 40

New England's Memorial, written by Nathaniel Morton, II, 150

New English Canaan, written by Thomas Morton, III, 378

New France, conquest of, II, 143; and Detroit, II, 144; and frontier posts, II, 346; and the fur trade, II, 359; and LaSalle's explorations, III, 246

New Freedom, by Woodrow Wilson, IV, 303; term popularized, V, 327

New Glarus Colony, V, 214

New Granada, Treaty with (1846), V, 317. See also Bidlack-Mallarino Treaty

New Hampshire, granted to Mason, III, 351

New Hampshire, The, ship-of-the-line, V, 75

New Hampshire Gazette, first newspaper in New Hampshire, IV, 102; founded by Daniel Fowle, IV, 127

New Hampshire Grants, Vermont known as, I, 173; road from Crown Point to No. 4 makes lands desirable in, II, 93; and the fourteenth colony, II, 318; and the Green Mountain Boys, II, 422; disputed by New York, III, 235; and Onion River Land Company, IV, 174; and Vermont, V, 362; and the Westminster massacre, V, 448

New Harmony Community, I, 441; II, 114; V, 110, 429

New Haven Church Covenant, V, 60

New Haven Clock Company, I, 402

New Haven Colony, as Bible Commonwealth, I, 181; and the Blue Laws, I, 204; formation of, II, 21; and settlement of Southold, L. I., III, 299; and Newark, N. J., IV, 120; and the "Phantom Ship," IV, 257; and Southold, V, 131; as a theocracy, V, 260

New Haven Railroad, IV, 409

New Helvetia, I, 275

New Hope Church, Battle of, I, 134

New Idria Quicksilver Mine, IV, 210

New Ironsides, in the Civil War, I, 390; attacked by the "David," II, 112; and ironclad warships, III, 158

New Jersey, division of, II, 182; Elizabethtown Associates in, II, 202; as a proprietary province,

IV, 362; Councils of the Proprietors of, IV, 362; York leases, V, 508

New-Jersey Gazette, founded by Isaac Collins, IV, 127

New Jersey Iron Company, I, 216

New Jersey Plan, and compromises of the Federal Constitution, I, 443

New Jersey v. Wilson, and the contract clause, II, 48

New Line, and sailing packets, IV, 198

New London Summary, published by Timothy Green, Second, IV, 126

New Madrid, Mo., Earthquake, II, 181

New Mexican Area, and domestic trade, V, 293

New Mexico, and Oñate's explorations, IV, 173; organized, and admitted, V, 249

New Netherland, blacksmith at, I, 197; and the Dutch-Indian War, II, 179; and treaty of Hartford, III, 14; and House of Hope, III, 52; and *Kermis,* III, 206; English conquer, III, 299; granted to Duke of York, IV, 104; and Nicoll's Commission, IV, 133; and Pennsylvania, IV, 242; Petition and Remonstrance of, IV, 256; colonized by the Walloons, V, 394; and treaty of Westminster, V, 448; as York's proprietary, V, 507

New Netherland Company, and the fur trade, II, 361

New Orleans, and the right of deposit, II, 139; city directory appears in, II, 148; founding of, II, 346; assay office, II, 396; and the Mafia incident, III, 323; Mardi Gras in, III, 342; and the Gulf of Mexico, III, 389; surrender of (1862), III, 419; founded, III, 424; IV, 188; and Fort St. John, V, 9; and domestic trade, V, 292; and frontier trading posts, V, 302; and Vieux Carré, V, 368

"New Orleans," song, II, 293

New Orleans, Battle of, backwoodsmen in, I, 145; and Lake Borgne engagement, I, 221; and Chalmette plantation, I, 337; British defeated at, V, 406

New Orleans, The, ship-of-the-line, V, 75

New Orleans, The, building of, II, 356; first Mississippi steamboat, III, 423; makes historic trip from Pittsburgh to New Orleans, III, 424; and river navigation, IV, 489; inaugurates steamboating on western waters, V, 178, 179

New Orleans *Bee,* southern newspaper, V, 123

New Orleans *Picayune,* southern newspaper, V, 123

New Paltz, patentees of, II, 180

New Plymouth. *See* Plymouth Colony

New River, and routes across the Alleghenies, I, 51

New Smyrna, planted by Andrew Turnbull, II, 288

New Sweden, Fort Christina as capital of, I, 371; founded, II, 130; and Pennsylvania, IV, 242; and Philadelphia, IV, 258; and Plowden's New Albion, IV, 288

New Ulm, defense of, V, 86

New York, Charter of Liberties, I, 346; dairying industry in, II, 105; land speculation in, III, 235; Long Island becomes part of, III, 299; as a proprietary province, IV, 362; western land claims of, V, 444

New York, The, and blockade and battle of Santiago, V, 31

New York, Treaty of, composes Creek hostilities, II, 86; and Indian land cessions, III, 100; repudiated by Creeks, IV, 136; and Spanish-Indian relations, V, 140

New York and Boston Illinois Land Company, III, 240, 403

New York and Erie Railroad, IV, 407

New York and Harlem Railroad, IV, 117, 406

New York Assay Office, gold depository at, II, 396

New York Barge Canal, IV, 117

New York *Call,* barred from the mails, IV, 433

New York Central Railroad, and Cornelius Vanderbilt, II, 311; Michigan Central becomes part of, III, 393; Michigan Southern consolidated with, III, 393; Mohawk and Hudson Railroad becomes a part of, IV, 4; and railroad rate wars, IV, 403; and other railroad systems, IV, 406; installs streamlined trains, V, 188; and rail transportation, V, 308

New York City, Brooklyn becomes part of, I, 243; directory appears in, II, 148; granted charter, II, 160; as New Amsterdam, IV, 94

New York Coffee and Sugar Exchange, II, 232

New York Coffee Exchange, I, 437

New York College of Physicians and Surgeons, III, 369

New York Cotton Exchange, I, 437; II, 232

New York *Daily Graphic,* and photoengraving, IV, 126

New York *Daily News,* prints comic strips, I, 431

New York *Evening Post,* and news reporting, IV, 122; prints the poem "We are coming, Father Abra'am, etc.," V, 428

New York Fire (1835), and insurance, III, 129

New York *Gazette,* advertises ice cream, II, 105; first newspaper in New York City, IV, 118; founded by William Bradford, IV, 127; continued at Newark, N. J., by Hugh Gaine, IV, 127

New York *Herald,* and airplane races, I, 36; prints news of gold discovery, II, 313; and news reporting, IV, 122; and newspaper editing, IV, 123; uses straw poll, V, 21

New York Historical Society, IV, 48

New York *Journal,* and comic strips, I, 431; pro-

Cuban propaganda in, **II**, 94; and the destruction of the *Maine,* **IV**, 447

New York *Ledger,* published by Robert Bonner, **III**, 323

New York Missionary Society, **III**, 103

New York *Morning Journal,* and yellow journalism, **V**, 505

New York *Observer,* **IV**, 125

New York Philharmonic Society, **IV**, 48

New York Produce Exchange, **I**, 437; **II**, 232

New York Public Library, **III**, 272

New York Safety-Fund System, **V**, 164

New York Society for the Prevention of Pauperism, **I**, 342

New York State Barge Canal, **II**, 226

New York Stock Exchange, **I**, 4, 310; **II**, 63, 84, 232; **V**, 393

New York *Sun,* attacks the Crédit Mobilier, **II**, 85; and the moon hoax, **IV**, 19; and origin of modern news reporting, **IV**, 122; and introduction of syndicate news, **IV**, 123; as "penny" paper, **IV**, 125

New York *Times,* and airplane races, **I**, 36; and news reporting, **IV**, 122; and "Public Be Damned," **IV**, 369

New York *Tribune,* and books as subscription inducements, **I**, 214; and term "border ruffians," **I**, 219; and censorship, **I**, 331; and the "Go West, Young Man" editorial, **II**, 392; homestead movement aided by, **III**, 42; and land grants for education, **III**, 236; operates a linotype, **III**, 281; and news reporting, **IV**, 122; uses Mergenthaler's linotype, **IV**, 126; and "On to Richmond," **IV**, 173

New York Warehouse and Securities Company, failure of, and panic of 1873, **IV**, 209

New York *Weekly Journal,* and the Zenger trial, **IV**, 115; Zenger established as printer of, **V**, 513

New York *World,* and airplane races, **I**, 36; uses editorial cartoons, **I**, 320; and funny papers, **I**, 431; pro-Cuban propaganda in, **II**, 94; and news reporting, **IV**, 122; and the destruction of the *Maine,* **IV**, 447; and yellow journalism, **V**, 505

Newark Gazette and New Jersey Advertiser, first newspaper in Newark, **IV**, 121

Newberry, J. S., and the Grand Canyon, **II**, 408

Newberry, T. H., and political scandals, **IV**, 298

Newberry Library, **I**, 212; **III**, 273

Newberry v. U. S., and campaign expenditures, **I**, 293

Newbold, Charles, patents cast-iron plow, **II**, 247

Newbrough, John B., influences establishment of Land of Shalam, **V**, 63

Newburgh Addresses, **II**, 13

Newcomb, Simon, and managed currency, **III**, 329

Newell, William A., introduces bill for aiding shipwrecked persons, **III**, 276

Newhouse Trap, **V**, 180

Newlands Act (1913), and industrial arbitration, **I**, 95; and railroad mediation, **IV**, 402

Newlands Reclamation Act (1902), **II**, 27; **III**, 161; **IV**, 423; **V**, 195

Newman, E. M., travel talks of, **III**, 260

Newman, Robert, enters into New Haven church covenant, **V**, 60

Newman, W. P., Great American Water Circus, **V**, 77

Newport, French army at, **II**, 343, 345; founding of, **IV**, 477

Newport, Christopher, and founding of Jamestown, **III**, 166; returns to Jamestown, **III**, 167; commands the *Sarah Constant,* **V**, 32; accompanies Somers on voyage to Virginia, **V**, 119; and Colony of Virginia, **V**, 372

Newport Mercury, Rhode Island's first permanent newspaper, **IV**, 122

Newspapers, and advertising, **I**, 16; and the Associated Press, **I**, 131; colonial, **I**, 420; government, **II**, 403; as history sources, **III**, 34; as agency of mass impression, **III**, 352; and pamphleteering, **IV**, 202; and printing in America, **IV**, 345; and public opinion, **IV**, 375; Sunday, **V**, 1; government subsidies to, **V**, 195; and rise of tabloids, **V**, 216; and trade journalism, **V**, 298; and yellow journalism, **V**, 505. *See also* Journalism

Newton, Kans., cow town, **II**, 79

Newtown, Battle of (1779), **V**, 202

Nez Percé, Fort, established by Donald MacKenzie and Alexander Ross, **V**, 393

Nez Percé Indians, surrounded at Bear Paw Mountains, **I**, 171; and the battle of the Big Hole, **I**, 183; on Green River, **II**, 423; and Lapwai Indian Council, **III**, 245

Nez Percés Pass, **IV**, 222

Niagara, Indians plan concerted drive on, **II**, 144; and the fur trade, **II**, 360

Niagara, Fort, evacuated by British (1796), **I**, 218; surrendered by French (1759), **I**, 234; Indian treaty signed at (1764), **II**, 316; founding of, **II**, 346; and battle of LaBelle Famille, **III**, 218; and the Colony of New York, **IV**, 115; attacked by British (1759), **IV**, 129; and Niagara Falls, **IV**, 131; surrendered by British (1796), **IV**, 175; attacked in Pontiac's War, **IV**, 306; and transportation, **IV**, 316; capture of (1813), **V**, 405. *See also* Magazin Royal

Niagara, The, in battle of Lake Erie, **II**, 224; and the Perry-Elliott controversy, **IV**, 253

Niagara, The, wooden screw sloop, **V**, 99

Niagara Campaigns, and the War of 1812, **V**, 405

Niagara Falls, as described by Hennepin, **III**, 26; water power of, **V**, 422

Niantic Indians, and the Narragansetts, **IV**, 53; and the Pequot War, **IV**, 252

Nicaragua, and Bryan-Chamorro treaty, **I**, 245; intervention in, **I**, 313; and the Dallas-Clarendon convention, **II**, 107; Hise treaty with, **III**, 32; marines in, **III**, 343; Squier treaty with, **V**, 152

Nicholas, John, probable author of "Decius" letters, **II**, 120

Nicholls, F. R. T., establishes home rule in Louisiana, **III**, 41; and the Louisiana lottery, **III**, 307

Nicholson, Francis, and French and English clashes on Lake Champlain, **III**, 229; flies from New York, **IV**, 114; takes Port Royal, **IV**, 315; in Queen Anne's War, **IV**, 389; urges creation of an Indian trading concern in Virginia, **V**, 379

Nicholson, John, and organization of North American Land Company, **IV**, 144

Nicholson, John H., founds the Gideon Society, **II**, 389

"Nick Carter," created by John R. Coryell, **II**, 147

Nickerson, Thomas, and the Atchison, Topeka and Santa Fé Railroad, **I**, 134

Nicolay, John G., co-author of *Abraham Lincoln: A History*, **I**, 190

Nicolet, Jean, discovers Lake Michigan, **II**, 344; on the Great Lakes, **II**, 415; discovers Green Bay region, **II**, 422; and the Indian and the gun, **III**, 92; and Lake Michigan, **III**, 392; and the Mississippi Valley, **III**, 425; reaches Sault Ste. Marie, **V**, 34; and topographic mapping, **V**, 282; and the discovery of Wisconsin, **V**, 473

Nicollet, Joseph N., in Minnesota, **III**, 411

Nicolls, Richard, charters New Harlem and Manhattan, **II**, 160; draws up Duke of York's Laws, **II**, 174; and the Elizabethtown Associates, **II**, 202; as governor of New York, **IV**, 118; and York's proprietary, **V**, 508

Niebuhr, Reinhold, and theological writings, **V**, 262

Night Clubs, and bootlegging, **I**, 217; and prohibition, **IV**, 357

Night Riding, and tobacco growers, **I**, 196; **V**, 276

Nimham, Algonquin leader, **I**, 48

Nine-Power Treaty, and the Far Eastern policy, **II**, 243; and international law, **III**, 142; and American policy toward Manchuria, **III**, 330; and the Open-door policy, **IV**, 176; and parity, **IV**, 217; signed by United States, **IV**, 232; and treaties with foreign nations, **V**, 318; and Washington Conference on Limitation of Armaments (1921–22), **V**, 417

Nineteenth Amendment, text, **II**, 43; and the franchise, **II**, 324; and married women's property rights, **III**, 346

Ninety-Six, Morgan sent to threaten, **II**, 81; engagement at (1781), **V**, 129

Ninety-Two and Forty-Five, and Liberty poles, **III**, 272

Ninigret, becomes sachem of the Narragansetts, **IV**, 53

Nininger, Minn., dead city, **II**, 114

Nipissing Indians, **I**, 48

Nipmuc Indians, and Algonquin family, **I**, 48; and King Philip's War, **III**, 210; as refugees from King Philip's War, **III**, 211; and the Narragansetts, **IV**, 53

Nirdlinger, Charles Frederic, and popularization of term "First Lady of the Land," **II**, 276

Nitrate Plants, on Tennessee River, **V**, 244

Nitrates, and industrial chemistry, **I**, 351; as fertilizer, **II**, 268; and the explosive industry, **IV**, 326

Niza, Marcos de, and exploration of America, **I**, 57; and missions of the Southwest, **III**, 418

No Man's Land, the proposed territory of Cimarron as, **I**, 375

Noah, Mordecai M., Jewish editor and publisher, **III**, 176

Nobel Prize, in medicine, **III**, 370

Nobile, Umberto, polar flight of, **IV**, 293

Nobility, Titles of, and the Constitution, **II**, 34

Noble's Road, and the Great Basin, **II**, 414

Nogales, Fort, built by the Spaniards at Vicksburg, Miss., **V**, 366

Nogales, Treaty of, **I**, 360; **II**, 13; **V**, 140

Noguchi, Hideyo, and medicine, **III**, 370

Nohoroco, Fort, in the Tuscarora War, **V**, 332

Nolan, D. E., directs espionage service during World War, **V**, 146

Nolan, Philip, and the West, **V**, 435

Nonconformists, **II**, 151. *See also* Dissenters

Nonconsumption, and the Continental Congress, **II**, 46

Nonexportation, and the Continental Congress, **II**, 46

Nonimportation, during the Napoleonic wars, **I**, 74; and associations, **I**, 131; followed Boston Resolutions, **I**, 224; and the Continental Congress, **II**, 46; and Committees of Inspection, **III**, 126; and Napoleon's Decrees, **IV**, 52; and the Colony of New York, **IV**, 115; and the American Revolution, **IV**, 466; and duty on tea, **V**, 232; and trade in tea, **V**, 233; and the Townshend Acts, **V**, 289

Nonintercourse Act, and the agrarian movement, **I**, 20; and Anglo-American relations, **I**, 74; as factor leading to War of 1812, **II**, 307; and French decrees, **II**, 344; and Macon's Bill No. 2, **III**, 322; and foreign trade, **V**, 294; and the War of 1812, **V**, 405

Nonintervention Policy, and the Algeciras Conference, **I**, 48; and isolation, **III**, 162

Nonpartisan League, and grain elevators, **II**, 202; and farm relief, **II**, 249; and the Farmer-Labor party of Minnesota, **II**, 251; and the LaFollette party, **III**, 227; appears in Minnesota, **III**, 411; in North Dakota, **IV**, 146

Nonrecognition, and attitude toward China, **I**, 364; and Far Eastern policy, **II**, 243; and international law, **III**, 142; and the League of Nations, **III**, 256; and Manchuria, **III**, 330; and the Nine-Power pact, **IV**, 134; and Pact of Paris, **IV**, 424

Nootka Convention, and the Oregon Question, **IV**, 184; and Vancouver's exploration, **V**, 357

Nootka Sound, building the *Adventure* on, **I**, 15

Nord Americanische Kalender, written by Francis Bailey, **II**, 254

Norfolk Navy Yard, abandoning of, during Civil War, **I**, 389; and the Confederate navy, **II**, 8; stone dock built at, **II**, 156; site used before Revolution, **IV**, 79

Normal Schools, and academies, **I**, 6; and teachers, **V**, 43, 234; and education of women, **V**, 480

Norridgewock, destroyed by the Abenaki, **I**, 1

Norridgewock Indians, **I**, 48

Norris, Frank, author of *The Octopus,* **II**, 270

Norris, George W., sponsors "lame-duck" amendment, **III**, 232; and Nebraska one-house legislature, **IV**, 81; leads revolt against the Payne-Aldrich Tariff Bill, **IV**, 356

Norris Dam, construction of, **V**, 244

Norris-LaGuardia Act, and arrest, **I**, 121; and the injunction, **III**, 124; upheld in Lauf v. E. G. Shimer, **IV**, 267; and the yellow-dog contract, **V**, 504

Norris v. Alabama, **III**, 412

Norsemen, **I**, 56

North, Frank, and the Wild West show, **V**, 464

North, Frank and Luther, as guides, **V**, 46

North, Frank Mason, hymn writer, **III**, 65

North, Simeon, and interchangeable parts, **III**, 133

North American Commercial Company, **I**, 43

North American Kerosene Gas Light Company, **III**, 207

North American Review, and dime novels, **II**, 147

North Anna River, and campaign against Richmond, **IV**, 481

North Carolina, boundary dispute with South Carolina, **I**, 226; western lands of, **II**, 329; and repudiation of state debts, **IV**, 457; western land claims of, **V**, 444

North Carolina, The, ship-of-the-line, **V**, 75

North-Carolina Gazette, founded by James Davis, **IV**, 127

North Dakota, created from Dakota Territory, **II**, 106; and the Nonpartisan League, **IV**, 140; organized, and admitted, **V**, 249

North Dakota State Historical Society, and development of International Peace Garden, **III**, 142

North East Forge, **IV**, 343

North Pacific Surveying Expedition, **III**, 63

North Pole, Peary reaches the, **IV**, 237

North Star Mine, **II**, 396; **III**, 24

North West Company, challenged by American Fur Company, **I**, 61; and Astoria, **I**, 133; post on the Columbia River, **I**, 430; and the Five Villages, **II**, 280; and the fur trade, **II**, 360, 363; and Grand Portage, **II**, 409; and Hudson's Bay Company, **III**, 56; and liquor in the Indian trade, **III**, 91; and Indian trade, **III**, 110; and Leech Lake Indian council, **III**, 260; and liquor in the fur trade, **III**, 282; and Minnesota, **III**, 410; and Fort Okanagan, **IV**, 167; and Pembina, **IV**, 240; and the Pemmican War, **IV**, 241; and the Red River of the North, **IV**, 431; and St. Marys Falls Ship Canal, **V**, 14; maintains post at Sault Ste. Marie, **V**, 34; and the Southwest Fur Company, **V**, 133; builds Spokane House, **V**, 148; removes post at Grand Portage, **V**, 205; and Fort Nez Percé, **V**, 393; and Wisconsin, **V**, 473; and Wyoming, **V**, 496

Northeast Boundary, and the Aroostook War, **I**, 120; and the Netherlands award, **IV**, 87; and the Red Line map, **IV**, 430; and the Webster-Ashburton Treaty, **V**, 431

Northern Line, and steamboat navigation, **V**, 179

Northern Neck, and the Fairfax proprietary, **II**, 240

Northern Pacific Railroad, financed by J. Cooke and Company, **II**, 54; Hill obtains control of, **II**, 419; land grant to, **III**, 237; and Minnesota, **III**, 411; and Montana, **IV**, 16; builds westward, **IV**, 408; surveys for, **IV**, 480; and rail transportation, **V**, 309

Northern Railway Route, **V**, 182

Northern Securities Company, and trust-busting, **V**, 326

Northrop, James, and the loom, **III**, 301

Northwest Angle, and "farthest north," **II**, 253; created, **III**, 231

Northwest Boundary, and Convention of 1818, **II**, 52

Northwest Boundary Dispute, and Treaty of Washington (1871), **I**, 41

Northwest Conspiracy, and Confederate activities in Canada, **I**, 298; and the Copperheads, **II**, 58; Sons of Liberty involved in, **III**, 215; **V**, 120

Northwest Ordinances. *See* Ordinances of 1784, 1785 and 1787

Northwest Passage, Amundsen leads first expedition through, **I**, 69; Ayllon searches for, **I**, 144; Rogers intent on finding, **I**, 320; Carver sets

out to find, **II**, 320; and Hudson's Bay Company, **III**, 56; and polar expeditions, **IV**, 292; and *Radisson's Relation*, **IV**, 399; and topographic mapping, **V**, 282; and search for the western sea, **V**, 446

Northwest Territory, and social change, **I**, 340; laws of, **II**, 76; and the Division Act of 1800, **II**, 155; and treaty of Greenville, **II**, 425; and Indiana, **III**, 112; and Marietta, **III**, 343; and Michigan, **III**, 391; and Ohio, **IV**, 160; and the Old Northwest, **IV**, 171; and the state-making process, **V**, 172; reduced by creation of new territories, **V**, 248; and state universities, **V**, 350; and western lands, **V**, 444

Northwestern Pike, **I**, 51

Norton, John N., proposes one-house legislature for Nebraska, **IV**, 81

Norton Brothers, can manufacturers, **II**, 297

Nortz v. U. S., **II**, 394

Norway, treaties with, **V**, 316

Norwegian Immigration, and Oleana, **IV**, 171; to Wisconsin, **V**, 474

"Not Worth a Continental," **II**, 100

Notre Dame, University of, founded, **III**, 40

Nott, Josiah Clark, and mosquitoes as cause of malaria, **IV**, 30; and proslavery literature, **IV**, 364; ethnologist, **V**, 122

Noyes, John Humphrey, and the Oneida Colony, **IV**, 174

Noyes, Oliver, and the Pejepscot purchase, **IV**, 239

Nullification, and Calhoun's *Disquisition*, **I**, 269; and Compromise Tariff of 1833, **I**, 443; develops in Cotton Kingdom, **II**, 70; favored by Essex Junto, **II**, 229; and Federal-state relations, **II**, 263; Jackson opposes, **II**, 264; and the Force Acts, **II**, 299; and Fort Hill letter, **II**, 310; and Jacksonian Democracy, **III**, 165; and Mississippi, **III**, 420; and Jackson's toast, "Our Federal Union, etc.," **IV**, 191; and Palmetto Cockades, **IV**, 201; and right of secession, **V**, 51; in South Carolina, **V**, 125; and states' rights, **V**, 175; and the tariff, **V**, 222; and the Tariff of Abominations, **V**, 224; and the Virginia and Kentucky Resolutions, **V**, 375; and the Whig party, **V**, 455

Nullifiers, as a political party, **IV**, 296

Number 4, Amherst orders road cut from Crown Point to, **II**, 93; Rogers arrives at, **V**, 8; attacked, **V**, 361

Nurseries, and reforestation, **IV**, 434

Nuthead, William, and printing in America, **IV**, 345 f.

Nuttall, Thomas, and gardening, **II**, 371; and western exploration, **V**, 442

Nyce, Benjamin, and refrigeration, **IV**, 437

Nye, Bill, humorous lecturer, **III**, 260

O

Oakley, Annie, joins the Wild West show, **V**, 464

Oakley, Thomas J., argues Gibbons v. Ogden case, **II**, 388; **V**, 178

Oats, and agricultural adaptation to the plains, **I**, 23; and cost of transportation, **I**, 33; and rotation of crops, **II**, 154

Oberlin Association, develops Arminianism, **V**, 446

Oberlin College, founding of, **II**, 17; **III**, 397

Oberlin Movement, **V**, 97

Obookiah, and missionary activity in Hawaii, **III**, 415

O'Brien, W. S., bonanza king, **I**, 208, 444

O'Brien, William, Dominican priest, **II**, 159

Obscenity Law of 1873, **I**, 191

Observer, and the Lovejoy riots, **III**, 310

Obsolescence, of machines, **III**, 320

Occaneechi Trail, **III**, 104

Occupational Diseases, and workmen's compensation, **V**, 485

Ocean-Mail Contracts, **IV**, 320

Ochsner, Albert J., and Swiss origin, **V**, 215

O'Conor, Charles, and Mississippi v. Johnson, **III**, 425

Octopus, written by Frank Norris, **II**, 270

Oddfellows, introduced in America, **V**, 53

Odell, M. F., member of the Committee on the Conduct of the War, **I**, 436

O'Donnell, James, and rural free delivery, **IV**, 508

O'Fallon, Benjamin, and the Yellowstone River expedition, **V**, 506

Officers' Reserve Corps, and army peace-time work, **I**, 111; and the Army School System, **I**, 118; and Citizens' Military Training Camps, **I**, 378; and Reserve Officers' Training Corps, **IV**, 457

Ogallala, Neb., becomes famous because of trail-driver patronage, **I**, 326; cow town, **II**, 79

Ogden, Amos, and expedition against St. Francis, **V**, 8

Ogden, Edmund A., and Fort Riley, **IV**, 484

Ogden, Samuel, founds Boonton Iron Works, **I**, 216

Ogden, Samuel, and Miranda's intrigues, **III**, 414

Ogden's Hole, **III**, 37

Ogdensburg, founding of mission near, **III**, 228

Ogilvie, James, literary lecturer, **III**, 260

Oglesby, Richard J., and the term "Rail Splitter," **IV**, 399

Oglethorpe, James Edward, founds Augusta, Ga., **I**, 138; and the battle of Bloody Marsh, **I**, 203; founds Georgia, **II**, 86; lays out Frederica, Ga., **II**, 330; and Georgia, **II**, 379; and war of Jenkins' Ear, **III**, 173; and siege of Fort Marion,

III, 344; and settlement of Savannah, V, 35; attacks slavery, V, 94

O'Hara, James, brings salt down the Allegheny, IV, 198

Ohio, Army of the, II, 96

Ohio, Falls of the, and the Wilderness Road, V, 465

Ohio, Forks of the, Fort Duquesne at, II, 177; and French forts, II, 342; and western land schemes, V, 443; and the westward movement, V, 450

Ohio, The, launched, I, 243; ship-of-the-line, V, 75

Ohio and Erie Canal, I, 397; IV, 160, 165, 245; V, 300

Ohio and Mississippi Railroad, IV, 407

Ohio Company of Associates, and the Big Bottom massacre, I, 183; and Gallipolis, II, 346; and land speculation, III, 240; and settlement of Marietta, III, 343, 397; and the Ordinance of 1787, IV, 181; and the Scioto Company, V, 44; and surveying, V, 210; and western lands, V, 444

Ohio Company of Virginia, and Braddock's Road, I, 233; and Fort Cumberland, II, 96; and Forks of the Ohio, II, 177; and French and Indian War, II, 342, 344; and Gist's travels, II, 390; and Great Meadows, II, 418; land grant to, III, 235; and land speculation, III, 239; and treaty of Logstown, III, 295; and the Monongahela River, IV, 12; and Forks of the Ohio, IV, 162; and the Pennsylvania-Virginia boundary dispute, IV, 249; utilizes the Potomac Valley, IV, 325; and early road building, IV, 494; formed, V, 373; and western land schemes, V, 443

Ohio Idea, as an issue in campaign of 1868, I, 285; and Greenback movement, II, 423

Ohio Life Insurance Company, failure of, and panic of 1857, IV, 208; and suspension of specie payments, V, 144

Ohio Mechanics Institute, III, 114

Ohio-Michigan Boundary Dispute, I, 227; IV, 164; V, 277, 351

Ohio River, floods on, II, 286; navigation of, IV, 490; as inland waterway, V, 424

Ohio Valley, influenced by Cumberland Road, II, 97; Duquesne moves to occupy, II, 177; and rivers, IV, 491

Oil, and the whaling industry, V, 452

Oil Administration, established, III, 135

Oil City, Pa., a boom town, I, 215; use of gas at, II, 372

Oil (or Petroleum) Industry, and the Bradford field, I, 233; gains in importance after Civil War, I, 383; and Drake's well, II, 165; and East Texas field, II, 182; and El Dorado field, II,

190; at Eternal Center, II, 229; and the industrial revolution, III, 118; as kerosene oil, III, 207; in Louisiana, III, 306; and manufacturing, III, 337; and Midcontinent Oil Region, III, 394; in Oklahoma, IV, 168; and the Osage Indians, IV, 189; and early pipe lines, IV, 276; and Pithole, IV, 279; and the South Improvement Company, V, 128; and the Southwest, V, 133; of Texas, V, 255; and domestic trade, V, 293; and foreign trade, V, 295; in West Virginia, V, 439; and decline of whaling, V, 453; and wildcat drilling, V, 464

Oil Lands, Indian, III, 103

Oil Scandals, II, 88. *See also* Elk Hills Oil Reserve; Teapot Dome Oil Reserve; Naval Oil Reserves

Oil Well Supply Company, V, 348

Ojibwa. *See* Chippewa Indians

Oklahoma, and the Boomer Movement, I, 215; Cherokee Strip becomes part of, I, 353; and "sooners," V, 121; opened for settlement, V, 452

Oklahoma City, a boom town, I, 215

O'Laughlin, Michael, and Lincoln's assassination, III, 280

Olcott, Henry Steel, and theosophy, V, 262

Old Abraham, Chief, and battle of Long Island Flats, III, 299

Old-Age Assistance, and internal revenue, III, 140; and relief, IV, 441; and social security, V, 108

Old-Age Pensions, and labor legislation, III, 223

Old-Age Retirement Benefits, for railroad employees, V, 109

Old-Age Revolving Pension, and the Townsend Plan, V, 288

Old-Age Security, and state laws, V, 107

"Old Blue," song, II, 293

Old Britain, Miami chief, and Pickawillany, IV, 266

"Old Cap Collier," dime novel series, II, 147

Old Chillicothe, and the battle of Piqua, IV, 277

"Old Chisholm Trail," cowboy song, II, 293

Old Corner Book Store, I, 214

Old Court-New Court Struggle, III, 205; V, 177

Old Dominion, Virginia as the, V, 372

"Old Ironsides," nickname of the *Constitution*, II, 29

"Old Ironsides," locomotive, III, 292

Old Northwest, and Harmar's expedition, III, 10; and the Miami Purchase, III, 390; and the westward movement, V, 451

Old Oklahoma, IV, 168

Old Providence Company, as a trading company, V, 301

Old School and New School Presbyterians, I, 374

"Old Sleuth," dime novel series, II, 147

Old Southwest, and the westward movement, V, 451

Old Spanish Trail. *See* Spanish Trail

Old Town, Treaty of (1818), and Indian land cessions, III, 100

Oldham, John, killed by Pequot Indians, IV, 252; and settlement of Saco Bay, V, 3

Olds, R. E., and the automobile, I, 140

Oleana, Pa., dead city, II, 114

Olive Branch Petition, and the American Revolution, IV, 468

Oliver, James, and the chilled steel plow, II, 247; IV, 287

Oliver Iron Mining Company, III, 379

Olmstead v. Rittenhouse's Executives, I, 8

Olmstead v. U. S., wire-tapping case, V, 472

Olmstead, F. L., Jr., and Washington, D. C., V, 413

Olney, Richard, and the Debs case, II, 116; and the Venezuela boundary controversy, V, 360

Olson, Culbert L., pardons Mooney, IV, 19

Olson, Floyd B., elected governor of Minnesota, II, 251; III, 411

Olustee, battle of, II, 287

Olympia, The, in battle of Manila Bay, III, 332

Omaha, famous thoroughbred horse, V, 265

Omaha, Fort, army uses dirigible at, II, 148

O'Mahoney, Joseph C., as chairman of the Temporary National Economic Committee, V, 327

O'Mahony, John, leads the Fenian movement, II, 267

Omnibus Bill, offered by the Committee of Thirteen (1850), I, 436, 442

On the Freedom of the Will, Edwards' famous dissertation, II, 189

Oñate, Juan de, crosses Arizona, I, 104; *conquistadore,* II, 25; and the Spanish horse, III, 48; and Inscription Rock, III, 126; in New Mexico, IV, 107; and the Rodríguez-Chamuscado expedition, IV, 500; at Taos, V, 219; and Texas, V, 252

One-Horse Shay, I, 319

One Hundred and One Ranch Exhibition, IV, 499

Oneida Community, and Perfectionists, I, 440; group marriage scheme of, II, 242; protagonist of free love, II, 332; and manners, III, 333; and marriage, III, 346; and Perfectionism, IV, 253; and polygamy, IV, 304; and the American religion, IV, 442; makes the Newhouse trap, V, 180

Oneida Indians, one of the Five Nations, II, 279; taken as prisoners by the French, II, 350; and the Iroquois League, III, 159; and treaty of La Famine, III, 226; and Nichols Pond, IV, 132

O'Neil, Margaret, and the Peggy Eaton affair, II, 183

O'Neill, Eugene, playwright, II, 166; and "little

theater" movement, III, 286; and the Provincetown Players, IV, 368

Onion, Stephen, member of the Principio Company, IV, 343

Onondaga, destroyed by Frontenac, II, 350

Onondaga Indians, one of the Five Nations, II, 279; and the Iroquois League, III, 159; and treaty of LaFamine, III, 226

"Onontio," governor of Canada called, IV, 173

Ontario, Fort, evacuated by the British, I, 218; erected by the British, IV, 190

Ontario, Lake, visited by Champlain, II, 344

Opechancanough, plans the Great Massacre, II, 418

Open Covenants, and the Fourteen Points, II, 317

Open Covenants Openly Arrived at, and secret diplomacy, II, 147

Open-Door Policy, and Anglo-American relations, I, 77; and trade with Asia, I, 128; and attitude toward China, I, 364; and Far Eastern policy, II, 243; and foreign policy, II, 305; and international law, III, 142; and isolation, III, 162; and Kearny's mission to China, III, 201; and Lansing-Ishii agreement, III, 244; in Manchuria and Manchoukuo, III, 330; and Nine-Power pact, IV, 134; and the Root-Takahira Agreement, IV, 502; and Washington Conference on Limitation of Armaments, V, 417; and the United States as a world power, V, 486

Open-Hearth Process, III, 156

Open-Market Operations, and banking acts, I, 157; of the Federal Reserve banks, II, 262

Open Range, and cattle business, I, 28; and barbed wire, I, 163; and the fence war, II, 266; and fencing laws, II, 266; and livestock industry, III, 286; and "nesters," IV, 86; and the Great Plains, IV, 282; and rodeos, IV, 499

Open Shop, adopted by United States Steel Company, V, 180. *See also* Closed Shop

Ophir Mine, V, 81

Opium, and the Anglo-Chinese War, I, 78; John Leigh experiments with, II, 171; conferences concerning, III, 255; trade in, IV, 52; smuggling of, V, 103

Opper, Frederick, and political cartoons, I, 320

Optlandt, Fort, erected, V, 515

Orange, Fort, settlement at, I, 44. *See also* Albany

Orange Industry, I, 379; V, 6

Orchard, Harry, kills Frank Steunenberg, I, 409; III, 21

Ord, E. O. C., and battle of Iuka, III, 164; commands Army of the Potomac, III, 166; and the McCardle case, III, 363

Ord, Pacificus, and the Panoche Grande claim, IV, 211

Order of American Knights, **II**, 58; **III**, 215; **V**, 120

Order of Friars Minor, **II**, 325

Order of Friars Preachers, **II**, 159

Order of the Star Spangled Banner, **I**, 64. *See also* American (or Know-Nothing) Party

Orders in Council, and blockades, **I**, 201; and the Embargo, **II**, 207; and Jay's Treaty, **III**, 169; British abandonment of, **IV**, 52; and nonintercourse, **IV**, 138; and the War of 1812, **V**, 404

Ordinance-Making Power, of the President, **IV**, 335

Ordinances of 1784, 1785 and 1787, that of 1784 known as the Northwest Ordinance, **II**, 14; and State of Franklin, **II**, 329; and fugitive slave acts, **II**, 355; and the Geographer's Line, **II**, 377; and the Indian agent, **III**, 91; and Indiana, **III**, 112; and Jefferson's proposed states, **III**, 172; and Jones v. Van Zandt, **III**, 181; and Land Act of 1796, **III**, 233; and land grants for education, **III**, 236; and United States General Land Office, **III**, 237; and land speculation, **III**, 240; and settlement of Marietta, **III**, 343; and the Miami Purchase, **III**, 390; and the Northwest Territory, **III**, 391; and Michigan boundary, **III**, 392; and Northwest Territory, **IV**, 151; Cutler's part in, **IV**, 163; and the Ohio-Michigan boundary dispute, **IV**, 164; and survey of public lands, **IV**, 373; and the Republican party, **IV**, 454; and survey of the Seven Ranges, **V**, 60; exclude slavery from the Old Northwest Territory, **V**, 94; and state-making process, **V**, 171; and territorial governments, **V**, 247; and territories of the United States, **V**, 248; and the Toledo War, **V**, 277; and the township system, **V**, 290; and state universities, **V**, 350; and the Upper Peninsula of Michigan, **V**, 351; and French defection at Vincennes, **V**, 370; and the West, **V**, 435; and western lands, **V**, 444

Ordnance, Naval, **IV**, 71

Ordnance Department, and army supply, **I**, 119; in charge of arsenals, **I**, 122; formed, **IV**, 44

Oregon, settlement of, **I**, 128; settlers of, and Champoeg convention, **I**, 339; migration to, and the Great American Desert, **II**, 140; and Hudson's Bay Company, **III**, 56; and joint occupation, **III**, 179; and Manifest Destiny, **III**, 332; and the Mexican boundary, **III**, 382; emigrants to, and the Great Plains, **IV**, 282; and the public domain, **IV**, 370; and territorial claims of the United States, **V**, 246; and the organization of territories, **V**, 249; organized, and admitted, **V**, 249; America gets her first claim to, **V**, 415

Oregon, The, voyage of, and the Panama Canal, **IV**, 204; and blockade and battle of Santiago, **V**, 31; one of the first American battleships, **V**, 412

Oregon-California Trail, and Independence, Mo., **III**, 85; Indians grant Federal Government rights along, **III**, 97

Oregon Missions, at the Dalles, **II**, 107; established by Jason Lee, **IV**, 182; and the Oregon Question, **IV**, 184

Oregon Question, and the Monroe Doctrine, **IV**, 13

Oregon Short Line Railroad, **IV**, 408

Oregon Steam Navigation Company, **IV**, 148

Oregon Trail, as influence on agriculture, **I**, 33; and Ashley's expedition, **I**, 128; Fort Bernard on the, **I**, 180; and Fort Boisé, **I**, 207; and Fort Bridger, **I**, 237; as part of California Trail, **I**, 274; caravan travel over, **I**, 312; and outfitting of caravans, **I**, 313; Courthouse Rock a landmark on, **II**, 75; Lisa and the Astorians on, **II**, 235; and the Great Basin, **II**, 414; and Fort Hall, **III**, 6; Independence Rock a landmark on, **III**, 86; and Fort Kearny, **III**, 200; and Fort Laramie, **III**, 245; and the Mormon Trail, **IV**, 24; and settlement of Oregon, **IV**, 182; emigrants follow, **IV**, 183; and overland companies, **IV**, 192; Overland Trail as variation of, **IV**, 193; and mountain passes, **IV**, 222; and the Pawnee Indians, **IV**, 229; and the Platte River Trail, **IV**, 286; and road building, **IV**, 495; parallels Snake River, **V**, 106; and South Pass, **V**, 128; and Sublette's cut-off, **V**, 192; wagon trains on, **V**, 389; and western exploration, **V**, 442; and the westward movement, **V**, 451; becomes great highway across Wyoming, **V**, 496

Oregon Treaty of 1846, and Anglo-American relations, **I**, 75; and annexation of territory, **I**, 79; and the Haro Channel dispute, **III**, 11; and Northwest boundary controversy, **IV**, 150; ends thirty years of rivalry, **IV**, 182; and treaties with foreign nations, **V**, 317

Oregon v. Muller, **V**, 387

O'Reiley, Peter, and silver mining, **V**, 81

O'Reilly, Alexandro, establishes Spanish authority in Louisiana, **II**, 76; **III**, 305, 372

O'Reilly, Henry, and the telegraph, **V**, 238

Oreto, The, **II**, 289

Orford Copper Company, **IV**, 132

Organized Labor. *See* Labor Unions

Organized Reserve, and National Guard, **IV**, 60; and Officers' Reserve Corps, **IV**, 158

Organized Trades and Labor Unions of the United States and Canada, **III**, 224

Oriental Immigration, and the Yellow Peril, **V**, 505

Oriskany, Battle of, and Burgoyne's Invasion, **I**, 255; St. Leger's column defeated at, **IV**, 476

Orleans, Fort, **I**, 230; **II**, 345, 363

Orleans, Isle of, **III**, 307

Orleans, Territory of, **III**, 307

O'Rourke, Matthew J., and the Tweed Ring, V, 333

"Orphan Annie," comic strip, I, 431

Orphan Asylums, and philanthropy and benevolence, IV, 260

Orpheum Vaudeville Circuit, V, 358

Orteig Prize, and airplane disasters, I, 35; won by Lindbergh, I, 36; III, 280

O'Ryan, J. F., and Ypres-Lys operation, V, 511

Osage, Fort, Bonneville expedition starts from, I, 209; first expedition of St. Louis Missouri Fur Company leaves, V, 12

Osage Hedge, planted for fences, II, 243

Osage Indians, Chouteaus trade among the, I, 370; treaty with, at Council Grove (1825), II, 72; encountered by DeSoto expedition, II, 142; and the fur trade, II, 363; land cessions of, III, 100; oil lands of, III, 103; and Indian reservations, III, 108; evangelized by Jesuits, III, 175; and Lisa and Company, III, 283; and Lovely's Purchase, III, 310; in Oklahoma, IV, 168; and Oklahoma squatters, IV, 169; as guides, V, 46

Osage Pastures, I, 205

Osawatomie, burned, I, 220

Osborn, Charles, and abolitionist literature, I, 3; establishes The Philanthropist, IV, 260

Osborn v. Bank of the United States, IV, 160

Oscar II, Ford's peace ship, II, 301

Osceola, arrest and imprisonment of, V, 57; and battles at Withlacoochee River, V, 476

O'Shaughanessy Dam, V, 424

Osler, William, author of Practice and Principles of Medicine, II, 150

Ostend Manifesto, linked with Black Warrior affair, I, 196; claims right to annex Cuba, II, 94; and Spanish-American relations, V, 135

O'Sullivan, John L., and Manifest Destiny, III, 332

Oswegatchie, Fort, construction begun on, IV, 159

Oswego, and the fur trade, II, 361; council at (1766), IV, 306; as a frontier post, V, 302

Oswego, Fort, IV, 115, 175

Otis, E. S., and the Philippine insurrection, IV, 261

Otis, Elisha G., and elevators, II, 201

Otis, Harrison Gray, and the Federalist party, II, 264; and the Hartford Convention, III, 14

Otis, James, author of Vindication of the British Colonies, I, 425; opposes writs of assistance, III, 355; and oratory, IV, 179; and pamphleteering, IV, 202; and political theories, IV, 300; and the American Revolution, IV, 465; author of Rights of the British Colonies Asserted and Proved, IV, 484; and taxation without representation, V, 229; opposes writs of assistance, V, 495

Ottawa Indians, split off from the Chippewa, I, 367; and Fort Harmar treaty, III, 10; and Hull treaty, III, 58; in the Revolution, III, 88; land cessions of, III, 100; removal of, III, 107; and treaties of Fort McIntosh, III, 366; and Great Indian Council at Niagara, IV, 130; and treaty at Pittsburgh (1775), IV, 280; and treaty of Spring Wells, V, 150; on Lake Superior, V, 205

Otterbein, Philip William, joint founder of the Church of the United Brethren, V, 345

Otto, John Conrad, and medicine, III, 369

Ouachita Post, first name for Fort Miro, III, 414

Ouiatenon, Fort, Croghan reaches, III, 69; falls in Pontiac's War, IV, 306

Ouray, Ute chief, and Meeker massacre, III, 371

Out of Gloucester, by J. B. Connolly, I, 306

Outcault, R. F., "Origin of a New Species," forerunner of colored "funny paper," I, 431

Overland California Mail Bill, IV, 495

Overland Freighting, and the Great Plains, IV, 282

Overland Mail Route, preyed on by Indians, I, 171; and development of California, I, 274; and the Pioneer Stage Line, IV, 274; and the Pony Express, IV, 306

Overland Trail, Fort Davis established on the, II, 112; becomes great continental highway, IV, 80; and South Platte Route, V, 128

Overman Act (1918), and administrative reorganization, I, 12; and the World War organization, V, 492

Overseers, and absentee ownership, I, 4; and the plantation system of the South, IV, 284

Overton, John, settles Memphis, I, 359

Owen, Robert D., experiment at New Harmony, I, 441; IV, 102; and the Socialist movement, V, 110; and the Working Man's party, V, 484

Oxen, and Oregon caravans, IV, 183; for wagon trains, V, 389

Oxenstierna, Axel, promoter of New Sweden Company, IV, 113

Oxford Group, as youth movement, V, 511

Oxford New English Dictionary on Historical Principles, II, 146

Ozark, name applied to the Arkansas River, the mountains north of it, and post near its mouth, I, 107

P

Paca, William, signer of the Declaration of Independence, II, 124

Pace, Richard, and the saving of Jamestown, II, 418

Pacific Fur Company, post at Astoria, I, 46, 133; and Indian trade, III, 110; builds Fort Okanagan, IV, 167; and Oregon, IV, 182; establishes Astoria, IV, 184

Pacific Mail Steamship Company, I, 406; III, 376

Pacific Railroad, and the agrarian movement, I, 21; explorations for, proposed, I, 104; and repeal of the Missouri Compromise, III, 429

Pacific Railway Act (1862), I, 334

Pacifism, and attitude of churches toward war, I, 374; and the Embargo, II, 207

Pacifists, form League of Universal Brotherhood, IV, 234

Pacing White Mustang, IV, 49

Pack Trains, and roads, IV, 493

Packaged Goods, and trade-marks, V, 299

Packard Motor Company, I, 140

Packenham, Edward, and battle of New Orleans, IV, 109

Packers and Stockyards Act of 1921, and Stafford v. Wallace, V, 152

Packet Boats, for river navigation, IV, 489; and rivermen of the Ohio, IV, 490

Packets, Sailing, I, 192

Packing, Meat, I, 173; and the livestock industry, III, 286; and the Packers' Agreement, IV, 198; and soap making, V, 106; and stockyards, V, 184. *See also* Meat

Packing of Foods, II, 297

Padilla, Juan de, and missions of the Southwest, III, 418

Padock, Judah, co-founder of the *Vermont Gazette*, IV, 127

Padoucas, visited by Bourgmont, I, 230

Page, David S., makes first condensed milk can, I, 304

Page, T. J., commands the *Stonewall*, V, 185

Page, T. N., and fiction, II, 270

Page, Walter Hines, as an anglomaniac, I, 78

Page, William Tyler, compiles American's Creed, I, 68

Pago Pago, ceded to the United States, V, 20

Paine, Clarence S., and the Mississippi Valley Historical Association, III, 426

Paine, Robert Treat, signer of the Declaration of Independence, II, 123

Paine, Thomas, and *Common Sense*, I, 439; and confiscation of property, II, 15; and *The Crisis*, II, 90; and Deism, II, 130; author of *Age of Reason*, II, 340; advises confiscation of loyalist property, III, 313; and natural rights, IV, 66; and pamphleteering, IV, 202; and philosophical thought and writings, IV, 263; political writings of, IV, 302; propagandistic writings of, IV, 358; and republican form of government, IV, 453; and the American Revolution, IV, 468; attacks Robert Morris as profiteer, IV, 475; as author of *Rights of Man*, IV, 484; and state constitutions, V, 166; and theological writings, V, 261; and "Times That Try Men's Souls," V, 271; and political tracts, V, 291

Paiute Indians, in the Bannock War, I, 161; attack Manly-Hunt party, II, 116; Digger Indians as one tribe of, II, 146; and origin of the Ghost Dance, II, 388; designation of, V, 105

Palatines, settle at German Flats, N. Y., II, 382; in colony of New York, IV, 115; in Pennsylvania, IV, 246; as political exiles, IV, 295; and the westward movement, V, 450

Palisades Interstate Park Commission, IV, 438; V, 175

Palladino, Eusapia, and spiritualism, V, 147

Palmer, Elihu, founds Deist societies, II, 340

Palmer, J. M., and the Gold Democrats, II, 395

Palmer, Joel, co-operates in the Stevens' Indian treaties, V, 181

Palmer, Potter, and great fortunes, II, 312

Palmer, Volney B., and the advertising agency, I, 18

Palmer, W. J., and narrow gauge railroads, I, 426; and the incorporation of the Denver and Rio Grande Railway, II, 138

Palmes, Maj., captures and executes Canonchet, III, 211

Palms, Francis, and land speculation, III, 240

Pamlico Indians, I, 48

Pamphlets, I, 86

Pan-American Airways Corporation, I, 36, 38; III, 396

Pan-American Conferences, and international law, III, 142; and policy of intervention, III, 145; and Latin-American relations, III, 250; and the Monroe Doctrine, IV, 14; and nonintervention, IV, 139; and nonrecognition, IV, 141; and peace, IV, 232; and reciprocity, IV, 422; and treaties with foreign nations, V, 318

Pan-American Convention of Commercial Aviation (1928), I, 35

Pan-American Petroleum and Transport Company, Elk Hills oil reserve leased to, II, 203; and Pearl Harbor naval base, IV, 237

Pan American Union, and the Havana Conference, III, 17; establishment of, IV, 202; and Buenos Aires Peace Conference, IV, 231; projected reform of, V, 31; and Secretary of State, V, 162

Panama, Isthmus of, and the discovery of America, I, 57

Panama, Republic of, and Hay—Bunau-Varilla treaty, III, 19

Panama Canal, and Anglo-American relations, I, 75; building of, I, 303; and Cape Horn, I, 307; and Caribbean policy, I, 313; and controversy with Colombia, I, 415; constructed by the Corps of Engineers, II, 217; and foreign policy, II, 304; and government ownership, II, 404; United States secures permission to construct, III, 19; and the Hay-Herrán treaty, III, 19; and

the Hay-Pauncefote treaties, III, 19; safe-
guarded by United States, III, 79; and the Gulf
of Mexico, III, 389; and the Monroe Doctrine,
IV, 14; and the *Oregon*, IV, 183; and the Panama
revolution, IV, 206 f.; and river and harbor improvements, IV, 487; and sea power, V, 49; and
United States commerce with South America,
V, 124; and the Squier treaty, V, 152; and Tolls
Exemption Act, V, 279; and domestic trade, V,
292; and elimination of yellow fever, V, 505.
See also Isthmian Canal

Panama Congress, and the Monroe Doctrine, IV,
13; first true Pan-American Conference, IV, 202

Panama Railroad, completed, IV, 204

Panama Revolution, and the Bidlack-Mallarino
treaty, I, 183; and the Panama Canal, IV, 204

Panama Tolls Question, I, 78; IV, 205

Panay, The, the sinking of, II, 429

Panic of 1819, and Old Court-New Court struggle,
IV, 170; and protection, IV, 365; and suspension
of specie payments, V, 143; and Stay and Valuation Acts, V, 177

Panic of 1837, and anti-bank movement, I, 81;
and foreign trade, I, 147; and bankruptcy laws,
I, 159; and business cycles, I, 262; and campaign of 1840, I, 284; and the Distribution Act
of 1836, II, 152; and Indiana state canals, III,
114; and internal improvements, III, 138; and
labor, III, 219; and labor parties, III, 223; and
Louisiana banking system, III, 307; and mercantile agencies, III, 374; and municipal ownership, IV, 42; and repudiation of state debts,
IV, 456; hastened by the Specie Circular, V, 143;
and suspension of specie payments, V, 144; and
banking, V, 164; and distribution of surplus
revenue, V, 209

Panic of 1857, and business cycles, I, 262; and
labor, III, 219; and labor parties, III, 223; and
labor unions, III, 224; and railroads, IV, 407

Panic of 1873, and the Bland-Allison Act, I, 198;
and business cycles, I, 262; and free silver, II,
333; and labor parties, III, 223; set off by the
failure of Jay Cooke, IV, 148; and railroad rate
wars, IV, 403; and Ralston's Ring, IV, 414; and
state debts, IV, 457; and Southern Pacific Railroad, V, 130; halts work on Texas and Pacific
Railroad, V, 255

Panic of 1893, and bankruptcy laws, I, 159; and
business cycles, I, 262; and Coxey's Army, II,
82; and free silver, II, 333; and Kelly's industrial army, III, 203; and the Populist party, IV,
313; and the Pullman Strike, IV, 381; and the
Sherman Act of 1890, V, 70; and suspension of
specie payments, V, 144; and the Union Pacific
Railroad, V, 343

Panic of 1907, and business cycles, I, 262; and
suspension of specie payments, V, 144

Panic of 1920, I, 262

Panic of 1929, and bankruptcy laws, I, 159; and
business cycles, I, 262; and public debt, II, 118;
and the gold standard, II, 398; and reciprocity,
IV, 423; causes defeat of Herbert Hoover, IV,
455; and suspension of specie payments, V, 144

Panics, and insurance, III, 129 f.

Panmure, Fort, later name for Fort Rosalie, IV,
502

Pantages Vaudeville Circuit, V, 358

Panton, Leslie and Company, and Bowles, I, 230;
has headquarters at Pensacola, IV, 250; remains
in St. Marks, Fla., V, 13; and Spanish-Indian
relations, V, 140

Pápago Indians, and Camino del Diablo, I, 278;
at Camp Grant, I, 279; and scouting on the
plains, V, 46

Paper, and newspapers, IV, 126; and foreign trade,
V, 295

Paper Money, and the agrarian movement, I, 20;
loan office established in Missouri for issuing,
II, 83; and national credit, II, 85; and currency,
II, 99; and colonial currency, II, 100; and
colonial debts, II, 118; and fiat money, II, 269;
and fractional currency, II, 321; and the "Know
Ye" party, III, 216; as legal tender, III, 261;
and the money system of the United States, IV,
8; colonial use of, IV, 29; and profiteering, IV,
355; emitted to finance the Revolution, IV, 470;
and "old and new tenor," V, 246; and the state
of Virginia, V, 373

Papin, Denis, experiments in steamboat building,
V, 307

Paraguay Expedition, the *Fulton* takes part in,
II, 355

Parcel Post Service, and mail-order houses, III,
325; established, IV, 320; and rural free delivery, IV, 508

Pardon, and amnesty, I, 68; II, 42

Paris, Declaration of (1856), and privateering,
III, 76, 345; and neutrality, IV, 89; and Plan of
1776, IV, 283; and privateering, IV, 350, 353

Paris, F. J., as a proprietary agent, IV, 361

Paris, Pact of (1928). *See* Briand-Kellogg Pact

Paris, Treaty of (1763), and fisheries, I, 407; Cuba
returned to Spain by, II, 93; Spain cedes
Florida by, II, 287; ends French and Indian
War, II, 343; gives permanent possession of
Penobscot River to the English, II, 346; and
Indian barrier state, III, 93; and Isle of Or-
leans, III, 162; and Louisiana, III, 305; and
Maine, III, 326; Britain gains portion of Loui-
siana by, III, 420; and free navigation of the
Mississippi River, III, 422; France loses New
World possessions by, III, 424; and Proclama-
tion of 1763, IV, 353

Paris, Treaty of (1898), and the Foraker Act, II,

298; and cession of Guam, **II**, 427; and the Philippine Islands, **IV**, 262; and the Platt Amendment, **IV**, 286; and Spanish-American relations, **V**, 136; ends Spanish-American War, **V**, 137

Paris Agreement (1925), and settlement of War Claims Act, **V**, 400

Parish, as a political subdivision, **IV**, 299

Parity, and national defense, **II**, 127

Parke, J. G., and government railroad surveys, **IV**, 405; surveys the Southern Railroad Route, **V**, 131

Parker, Alton B., nominated for Presidency, **I**, 289; and the "gold telegram," **II**, 399; repudiates free coinage of silver, **V**, 79

Parker, Cynthia Ann, captured by the Indians, **IV**, 217

Parker, Isaac, wages war against lawlessness, **III**, 252

Parker, John, and Kennebec settlements, **III**, 204

Parker, Philip S., and Hull court-martial, **III**, 57

Parker, Quanah, and mediation between Indians and whites, **IV**, 217

Parker, Theodore, and the abolition movement, **I**, 3; transcendentalist, **II**, 340; and lecture days, **III**, 259; and religious periodicals, **IV**, 445; and transcendentalism, **V**, 345

Parker Dam, **I**, 428; **V**, 423

Parker v. Davis, legal tender case, **III**, 262; **IV**, 455

Parkman, George, murder of, **II**, 88; **V**, 323, 432

Parks, National. *See* National Parks

Parks, William, publisher of the *Maryland Gazette*, **IV**, 126; founder of the *Virginia Gazette*, **IV**, 127

Parley's Magazine, **I**, 363

Parochial Schools, and Oregon, **IV**, 184

Parole System, and prison reform, **IV**, 349

Parr, C. H., and development of the reaper, **IV**, 419

Parran, Thomas, and social hygiene, **III**, 64

Parrant, Pierre, stakes a claim on the site of St. Paul, Minn., **V**, 334

Parris, Samuel, and Salem witchcraft, **V**, 475

Parris Island, settlement of, **IV**, 315

Parry, Edward, polar expedition of, **IV**, 292

Parry, W. E., and search for Northwest Passage, **IV**, 151

Parsons, Mary, indicted for witchcraft, **V**, 475

Parsons, Samuel H., agent for Ohio Company of Associates, **IV**, 163; and Salt Springs Tract, **V**, 19; and West Point, **V**, 438

Parsons and Company, nursery of, **IV**, 154

Parson's Cause, and the American Revolution, **IV**, 465; and the Two Penny Act, **V**, 335

Parton, James, biographer, **I**, 190

Party Conventions, and the Albany Regency, **I**, 46

Party Government, **II**, 53; **III**, 164

Party Machines, **III**, 318

Party System, and the Federal Government, **II**, 259

Passamaquoddy Bay, and water power, **V**, 423

Passamaquoddy Indians, **I**, 48

Pasteurization, **II**, 104

Pastorius, Francis Daniel, and founding of Germantown, **II**, 385

Pate, Capt., and the battle of Black Jack, **I**, 196

Patent Medicines, and advertising, **I**, 16; and the medicine show, **III**, 370; and quacks, **IV**, 385

Patent Office, **I**, 30, 432; **III**, 135; **V**, 162, 430

Patents, and the Constitution, **II**, 33; and monopoly, **IV**, 12

Paterson, N. J., and the Society for Establishing Useful Manufactures, **V**, 353

Paterson, William, and the New Jersey Plan, **I**, 443; signer of the Constitution, **II**, 39; delegate to Convention of 1787, **II**, 50; and political theories, **IV**, 301; Princeton alumnus, **IV**, 343; and Vanhorne's Lessee v. Dorrance, **V**, 358

"Pathfinder of the Seas," Maury called, **III**, 360

Paths, and roads, **IV**, 493; and travel, **V**, 306

Patman Bill (1932), provides for fiat money, **I**, 210

Patman Bill (proposed), and chain stores, **I**, 337

Patrick, Daniel, and the Pequot War, **IV**, 252

Patrick Henry, Fort, renamed Fort Knox, **III**, 216

Patrick's Pence, **I**, 411

Patronage, and senatorial confirmation, **II**, 15; and political scandals, **IV**, 298

Patrons of Husbandry, organized in 1867, **I**, 26; and consumer co-operatives, **II**, 56; and grain elevators, **II**, 201; and the Granger Movement, **II**, 410 f.; and Industrial Congress convention, **III**, 114; and Sovereigns of Industry, **V**, 134. *See also* Granger Movement

Patroonships, and manors, **III**, 334; provided for, **IV**, 108

Patten, William Gilbert, creates "Frank Merriwell," **II**, 147

Patterson, Daniel T., defends New Orleans (1814), **IV**, 77

Patterson, Frederick Douglass, and Tuskegee Institute, **V**, 332

Patterson, James W., and the Crédit Mobilier, **II**, 85

Patterson, John, and technique of salesmanship, **V**, 17

Patterson, Joseph M., and rise of tabloids, **V**, 216

Patterson, Malcolm, pardons Coopers in killing of Carmack, **I**, 129

Patterson, Robert, and Cincinnati, **I**, 375; and settlement of the Miami Purchase, **III**, 390

Patterson, Robert, in Shenandoah Valley (1861), **I**, 250

Patti, Adelina, opera debut of, IV, 178

Pattie, James O., and the Colorado River, I, 427; at Taos, V, 219

Pattie, Sylvester and James O., and the fur trade, II, 362

Pattison Brothers, as tinware peddlers, V, 272

Patton, James, and Holston River, III, 39

Paul, Alice, and women's rights, II, 266; and woman suffrage, V, 478; and the National Woman's party, V, 479

Paul J. Rainey Wild Life Sanctuary, I, 190

Paul Revere House, architecture of, I, 99

Paulding, John, and the capture of André, I, 73

Pauperism, and charity organization movements, I, 342; and the franchise, IV, 361

Pauw, Michel, patroonships of, IV, 226

Pavonia, Kieft attacks Indians at, II, 179

"Pawnee Bill," nickname for Gordon W. Lillie, V, 464

Pawnee Indians, and the Dodge-Leavenworth expedition, II, 157; and horses, III, 48; IV, 49; and Oklahoma Openings, IV, 169; on the Great Plains, IV, 281; as guides, V, 46; attack Villasur's expedition, V, 369

Pawnee Rock, beginning of hostile Indian country, I, 106

Pawpaw Negroes, imported as slaves, IV, 86

Pawtucket, Arkwright machinery installed in, I, 107

Paxton Boys, and the Conestoga Massacre, II, 3; and the Susquehanna settlers, V, 210; and the West, V, 435; and the Yankee-Pennamite wars, V, 502

Pay Department, and army supply, I, 119

Payne, D. L., and "boomers," I, 215; Oklahoma squatter, IV, 169

Payne, John Howard, dramatist, II, 166; writes "Home, Sweet Home," III, 40

Payne, Lewis, and Lincoln's assassination, III, 280

Payne-Aldrich Tariff, and the agrarian movement, I, 22; and the Progressive Movement, IV, 356; and reciprocity, IV, 423; and the "Standpatters," V, 158; and the Taft-Roosevelt split, V, 217; enacted, V, 222; and commercial treaties, V, 315; defended in the Winona speech, V, 472

Payne's Landing, treaty of, II, 291; V, 57

Pea Ridge (Elkhorn), Battle of, III, 98; IV, 339

Peabody, Francis G., and religious thought and writings, IV, 447; and theological writings, V, 261

Peabody, George, philanthropies of, II, 314; IV, 260

Peabody Museum, IV, 47

Peace and Constitutional Union Society, II, 4; V, 344

Peace Commission of 1778, IV, 469, 470

Peace Conference (1919). See World War: Peace Conference

Peace Conference at Buenos Aires (1936), I, 97; III, 385

Peace Convention of 1861, I, 219

Peace Dale Manufacturing Company, IV, 355

Peace Movements, and the Bible, I, 181; during the Civil War, I, 388; Holden's, III, 37; and youth organizations, V, 511

Peace Society, and Union sentiment in the South, V, 344

"Peacemaker," explodes on the Princeton, IV, 342

Peachtree Creek, Johnston transfers army to, I, 135

Peale, Charles Willson, painter, I, 123; portraits of the Signers by, III, 86; miniature paintings of, III, 408; establishes a museum, IV, 47

Peale, James, miniature painter, III, 408

Peale, Raphael, painter, I, 123

Peale, Rembrandt, painter, I, 123; establishes a museum, IV, 47

Pearce, Richard, and smelters, V, 100

Pearl, Raymond, and studies of population growth, V, 382

Pearl Harbor, fleet air bases at, II, 284; and naval oil reserves, IV, 71

Pearl River, and the Florida boundary, II, 290; as boundary of Mississippi Territory, III, 420; and annexation of West Florida, V, 436

Pearson, R. M., law school of, III, 252

Peary, Robert E., polar expeditions of, IV, 293

Pease, E. M., governor of Texas, V, 255

Peck, Fort, Dam, and the Federal Power Commission, II, 261; and water power, V, 423

Peck, Fort, Reservation, Assiniboines moved to, I, 130

Peck, John M., and Star Route frauds, V, 160

Pecos, Chamuscado expedition to, IV, 500

"Pecos Bill," and tall stories, V, 186

Pedlars, and Yankee notions, V, 502

Peerson, Cleng, and Norwegian immigration, IV, 152

"Peggy Stewart" Tea Party, V, 233

Pegram, John, and battle of Rich Mountain, IV, 481

Pegram, W. J., and the Army of Northern Virginia, V, 371

Peik v. the Chicago and North Western Railway, II, 410, 411

Peirce, C. S., and philosophical thought and writings, IV, 264

Peking Congress, and indemnities, I, 231; III, 84

Pelham, manor of, III, 55

Pelham, Henry, miniature painter, III, 408

Pelham, John, and the Army of Northern Virginia, V, 371

Pelican, The, rechristened the Golden Hind, II, 400

Pelisipia, Jefferson's proposed state, **III**, 173

Pemaquid, fishing colony, **I**, 406; dead city, **II**, 114; fort at, **III**, 204; in King William's War, **III**, 211; settlement of, **III**, 326; post established at, **IV**, 9; and York's proprietary, **V**, 508

Pemberton, Fort, and the Yazoo Pass expedition, **V**, 504

Pemberton, J. C., and the battle of Big Black River, **I**, 183; and battle of Champion's Hill, **I**, 339; replaces Earl Van Dorn, **V**, 367

Pembina, visited by S. H. Long, **III**, 300; and the Pemmican War, **IV**, 241; and the Red River cart, **IV**, 430; one of the first settlements on the Red River of the North, **IV**, 431

Pemmican, used by North West Company, **IV**, 147; in the Red River cart traffic, **IV**, 430

Pender, W. D., and battle of Gettysburg, **II**, 386; and Pickett's charge, **IV**, 267

Pendergast Machine, **III**, 319; and political scandals, **IV**, 298

Pendleton, G. H., nominated for Vice-Presidency, **I**, 285

Pendleton Act (1883), passage of, **I**, 91; and campaign contributions, **I**, 293; and civil service, **I**, 383; and the merit system, **III**, 377; and political patronage, **IV**, 224; and political assessments, **IV**, 295

Peninsula Mound, **II**, 107

Peninsular Campaign, ended by battle of Malvern Hill, **III**, 329; and the *Monitor*, **IV**, 10; and the Army of the Potomac, **IV**, 324

Penitentiaries, **I**, 47

Penn, John, signer of the Declaration of Independence, **II**, 124

Penn, Richard, and the "Olive Branch Petition," **IV**, 172

Penn, Thomas, and the Walking Purchase, **V**, 392

Penn, William, and brewing, **I**, 236; grants Charter of Privileges, **I**, 346; "Briefe and Plaine Scheam" for Union (1697), **I**, 420; and the West Jersey "Concessions," **II**, 2; in Delaware, **II**, 130; and treaty at Shackamaxon, **II**, 131; and East Jersey, **II**, 182; and the fifths mining tax, **II**, 271; and Free Society of Traders, **II**, 333; and his Frame of Government, **II**, 356; and gardening, **II**, 371; and German immigration, **II**, 383; and "Great Law" of Pennsylvania, **II**, 417; Holy Experiment of, **III**, 40; and Indian land cessions, **III**, 99; and Laws, Concessions and Agreements, **III**, 254; and Lower Counties-on-Delaware, **III**, 311; and Maryland, **III**, 349; and the Mason and Dixon line, **III**, 350; receives title to New Castle, **IV**, 95; secures division of New Jersey into East and West, **IV**, 104; purchases East Jersey, **IV**, 104; and his Laws, Concessions and Agreements, **IV**, 105; and the Palatines, **IV**, 201; secures grant of Pennsylvania, **IV**, 242; and Pennsylvania-Maryland boundary dispute, **IV**, 247; and Philadelphia, **IV**, 258; as a proprietary agent, **IV**, 361; Delaware subgranted to, **IV**, 362; and the Holy Experiment, **IV**, 385; and Quakerism, **IV**, 386; and treaty of Shackamaxon, **V**, 62; and "turf and twig" ceremony, **V**, 330; and the Walking Purchase, **V**, 392; sails on the *Welcome*, **V**, 433; presides over witchcraft trials, **V**, 475; receives part of York's possessions, **V**, 508

Penn Proprietary, and confiscation of property, **II**, 15

Pennacook Indians, **I**, 48; **III**, 211

Pennamite and Yankee Wars. *See* Yankee-Pennamite Wars

Pennell, Joseph, etcher, **I**, 124

Pennock Brothers, develop mechanical seeding, **II**, 247

Pennsylvania, and the jurisdiction of Delaware, **II**, 130; feudalism in, **II**, 269; as a proprietary colony, **IV**, 362; Quakers in, **IV**, 386; and second treaty of Fort Stanwix, **V**, 159; and the Western Reserve, **V**, 445; and settlement of Wyoming Valley, **V**, 497; and York's proprietary, **V**, 508

Pennsylvania, The, ship-of-the-line, **V**, 75

Pennsylvania, University of, and Latin America, **III**, 248; and medical schools, **III**, 369; founded in Philadelphia, **IV**, 258

Pennsylvania Academy of Fine Arts, **IV**, 47

Pennsylvania Canal System, and the Allegheny Portage Railway, **I**, 51; and anthracite, **I**, 80; and the *Hit or Miss*, **III**, 35; and internal improvements, **III**, 137; and locks, **III**, 292; and Pennsylvania Railroad, **IV**, 248; and railroads, **IV**, 406; showboats on, **V**, 76; and shifts in trade routes and centers, **V**, 300

Pennsylvania College, **II**, 185

Pennsylvania-Connecticut Boundary Dispute, **V**, 211, 322, 502

Pennsylvania Dutch, as first settlers of West Virginia, **V**, 439

Pennsylvania Evening Post and Daily Advertiser, published by Benjamin Towne, **IV**, 125

Pennsylvania Fireplace, **II**, 329; **III**, 23

Pennsylvania Fiscal Agency, **II**, 84

Pennsylvania Gazette, and political cartoons, **I**, 320; published by Franklin, **I**, 420; announces a lottery, **III**, 303; and the *Saturday Evening Post*, **V**, 33

Pennsylvania Hospital, founded, **III**, 50; and treatment of the insane, **III**, 125; and organized benevolence, **IV**, 260

Pennsylvania Institution for the Deaf and Dumb, **IV**, 260

Pennsylvania Journal, **II**, 90

Pennsylvania Packet, becomes first daily newspaper in America, **IV,** 258

Pennsylvania Packet and Daily Advertiser, published by Dunlap and Claypoole, **IV,** 125

Pennsylvania Prison System, **II,** 53; **IV,** 347, 348

Pennsylvania Property Company, **IV,** 144

Pennsylvania Railroad, buys Portage Railroad, **I,** 51; Delaware and Raritan Canal passes under dominance of, **II,** 132; and the Hudson River, **III,** 55; and the Lancaster Pike, **III,** 233; and locomotives, **III,** 292; and Pennsylvania canals, **IV,** 245; and railroad rate wars, **IV,** 403; and canals, **IV,** 407; and Standard Oil Company, **V,** 156; and rail transportation, **V,** 308; and tunnels, **V,** 329; and Westinghouse Company, **V,** 448

Pennsylvania Rock Oil Company, **IV,** 166

Pennsylvania Station, architecture of, **I,** 101

Pennsylvania Troops, Mutiny of, **II,** 14; **III,** 177; **IV,** 50

Pennsylvania Tubing and Transportation Company, **IV,** 276

Pennsylvania-Virginia Boundary Dispute, **I,** 139; **V,** 449

Penrose, Charles B., and the Buckshot War, **I,** 246

Pensacola, and British campaign of 1780, **I,** 240; Spanish at, arm the Upper Creeks, **II,** 86; founding of, **II,** 288; and the fur trade, **II,** 363; treaty of (1784), and the McGillivray incident, **III,** 365; and the Gulf of Mexico, **III,** 389; captured by Spaniards, **V,** 139; treaty of (1784), and Spanish-Indian relations, **V,** 140; and frontier trading posts, **V,** 302

Pensacola Navy Yard, **II,** 8; **IV,** 79

Pensions, for the blind, **I,** 200; military, **I,** 210; in campaign of 1888, **I,** 288; and demobilization of 1901, **II,** 134; and the Grand Army of the Republic, **II,** 407; and Hayburn's case, **III,** 20; and the *National Tribune,* **IV,** 63; and privileged groups, **IV,** 350; and soldier vote, **V,** 117; and the War Department, **V,** 402

Pensions Office, made part of Veterans Administration, **III,** 135

Pentegoet, and Castine, **I,** 321; site of St. Castin's trading house, **V,** 6

People v. North River Sugar Refining Company, **V,** 201

People's Party. *See* Populist Party

Peoria, Fort Crèvecœur located opposite southern limit of, **II,** 87

Peoria Indians, and Algonquin family, **I,** 48; of the Illinois, **III,** 71; removal of, **III,** 107; in Iowa, **III,** 152

Pepin, Lake, Fort Beauharnois erected on, **I,** 172

Pepper, George Wharton, and the Vare case, **V,** 358; opposes the World Court, **V,** 485

Pepperell, William, and the Louisburg Expedition, **III,** 304; made a baronet, **IV,** 136

Pequot Indians, and the River Towns of Connecticut, **II,** 23; and the Mohegans, **IV,** 5

Pequot War, and Indians as slaves, **III,** 108; Narragansett Indians join English in, **IV,** 53; clears northern shore of Long Island Sound of Indians, **IV,** 103; Saybrook as center of, **V,** 37

Peralta, Pedro de, in New Mexico, **IV,** 107; founder of Santa Fé, **V,** 29

Percy, George, leader in the Jamestown settlement, **V,** 372

Perdido River, and United States claims, **II,** 289; as Florida-Louisiana boundary, **II,** 290; **III,** 309; as boundary of Mississippi Territory, **III,** 420; and West Florida, **V,** 436; and West Florida controversy, **V,** 436

Perez, Juan, and Oregon, **IV,** 182; probably first white man to sight the Washington shore, **V,** 415

Perfect Recovery, written by Cotton Mather, **II,** 150

Perfectionists, and the Bishop Hill Colony, **I,** 191; communities of, **I,** 440; and the Oneida Colony, **IV,** 174

Periodicals, as agency of mass impression, **III,** 352

Perkins, Frances, Secretary of Labor under F. D. Roosevelt, **III,** 221; and the General Motors sit-down strike, **V,** 191; first woman to hold a Federal Cabinet position, **V,** 478

Perkins, Jacob, and refrigeration, **IV,** 437

Perkins, Joseph, and Missouri Fur Company, **V,** 13

Permanent Court of Arbitration. *See* Hague Court of Arbitration

Permanent Court of International Justice. *See* World Court

Perrine, Henry, victim of Indian Key massacre, **III,** 98

Perrot, Nicolas, *coureur de bois,* **II,** 75; visits the Fox Indians, **II,** 319; on the Fox-Wisconsin Waterway, **II,** 320; visits Green Bay, **II,** 422; and lead mining, **III,** 254; visits the Mascouten, **III,** 350; builds Fort St. Antoine, **V,** 6

Perry, John D., and the Kansas Pacific Railroad, **III,** 198

Perry, Matthew C., expedition to Japan, **III,** 63; and blockade of Mexican Gulf ports, **III,** 383, 387; missionaries assist, during expedition to Japan, **III,** 415; makes treaty with Japan, **IV,** 76; expedition to Japan as expression of American interest in the Pacific Ocean, **IV,** 196; and whaling, **V,** 452

Perry, Oliver Hazard, and battle of Lake Erie, **II,** 143, 161, 224; builds the *Lawrence,* **III,** 253; on mission to Venezuela, **V,** 359; and "We have

met the enemy, etc.," V, 428; fights duel at Weehawken, V, 433

Perry v. U. S., gold clause case, IV, 455

Perryville, Battle of, III, 205

Pershing, John J., and the A. E. F., I, 59; II, 134; and insignia of rank in United States Army, III, 126; at tomb of Lafayette, III, 227; and the Meuse-Argonne offensive, III, 381; punitive expedition into Mexico, III, 385, 388; and the United States Military Academy, III, 399; and operations at St. Mihiel, V, 14; and Tacna-Arica controversy, V, 216; and the World War, V, 491

Persia, treaties with, V, 317

Personal Liberty, and Adair v. U. S., I, 9

Personal Liberty Laws, and nullification, IV, 153; and Prigg v. Commonwealth of Pennsylvania, IV, 341; and states' rights, V, 176

Personnel Work, and industrial relations, III, 116

Perth Amboy, founding of, II, 182; IV, 105

Pet Banks, Government makes all deposits with, I, 156

Peter, Hugh, minister of Salem, starts fisheries, V, 16

Peter Force Collection, purchase of, III, 274

"Peter Parley," as a best seller, I, 180; travel stories by, I, 363; founds *Parley's Magazine,* I, 363; and early schoolbooks, V, 40

Peterhoff Case, and continuous voyage, II, 142

Peters, Andrew J., and the Boston police strike, I, 223

Peters, Richard, serves as secretary on War and Ordnance Board, V, 399

Peters, Samuel A., and the Connecticut Blue Laws, I, 204; V, 203

Peters, T. J., finances building of Atchison, Topeka and Santa Fé Railroad, I, 134

Peters, W. S., organizes the Texan Emigrant and Land Company, V, 250

Petersburg, battle of, II, 83; and campaign against Richmond, IV, 481; trench warfare develops at, V, 321

Petition, Right of, and the Bill of Rights, I, 185; II, 39; and lobbying, III, 287; and the abolitionists, IV, 257

Petition and Remonstrance of New Netherland, IV, 109

Petiver, James, creator of Bartholomew de Fonte, IV, 195

Petrified Forest, Ariz., IV, 19

Petroleum Industry. *See* Oil Industry

Petroleum Stocks, V, 183

Pettibone, George A., and Cœur d'Alene riots, I, 409; and the murder of Gov. Steunenberg, III, 21

Pettigrew, J. J., killed in skirmish near Falling Waters, II, 241; and battle of Gettysburg, II, 386; and Pickett's charge, IV, 267

Phagan, Mary, murder of, V, 323

Pharmacology, II, 171

Phelps, Anson G., supports the Finney revivals II, 275

Phelps, Dodge Corporation, and copper, II, 57

Phelps-Gorham Purchase, I, 247; III, 239; IV, 116, 130, 381

Phi Beta Kappa, organized, IV, 412; V, 467

Philadelphia, Germantown and Norristown Railroad, IV, 406

Philadelphia, The, and the Barbary Wars, I, 162; burning of, III, 148

Philadelphia Academy of Fine Arts, I, 124

Philadelphia Academy of Natural Sciences, IV, 237

Philadelphia and Lancaster Turnpike, IV, 243, 494

Philadelphia and Reading Railroad, failure of, and panic of 1893, IV, 209

Philadelphia College, and medical schools, III, 368

Philadelphia Contributionship for the Insurance of Houses from Loss by Fire, III, 128

Philadelphia Gas Ring, political influence of, IV, 485

Philadelphia General Hospital, III, 50

Philadelphia Library Company, I, 212

Philadelphia Mint, II, 396

Philadelphia Savings Fund Society, I, 160

Philadelphia Society for Promoting Agriculture, I, 26

Philanthropist, antislavery newspaper, I, 3; Cincinnati antiabolitionists destroy press of, I, 375

Philanthropy, I, 177

Philippine Insurrection, and the United States Army, I, 113; and the water cure, V, 421

Philippine Islands, and acquisition of territory, I, 79; and expansion, I, 128; II, 234; and Far Eastern policy, II, 244; and foreign policy, II, 304; ceded to the United States, III, 78; an unincorporated territory, III, 127; as an insular possession, III, 128; and the Jones Act, III, 181; and the Manila Galleon, III, 332; and American influence in the Pacific, IV, 196; ceded to the United States, IV, 216; V, 136, 137; and the Taft commission, V, 216; territorial claims of the United States, V, 247; and the Tydings-McDuffie Act, V, 336; and the United States as a world power, V, 486; and the Yap mandate, V, 502

Philips, John F., and Reorganized Latter Day Saints, IV, 450

Philipsborough, manor of, III, 55

Philipse's Highland Patent, III, 55

Phillips, Alonzo D., match patent issued to, III, 359

Phillips, David Graham, "The Treason of the Senate," IV, 38

Phillips, Isaac, and the *Baltimore* incident, **I**, 151

Phillips, John and Samuel, establish Andover and Exeter academies, **V**, 41

Phillips, Portugee, and Fort Phil Kearny, **III**, 201

Phillips, Wendell, and the abolition movement, **I**, 3; and antislavery literature, **I**, 85; lecturer, **III**, 260; and oratory, **IV**, 180

Phillips Andover Academy, foreign exchange students to, **V**, 191

Phillips v. Savage, **I**, 89; **III**, 146

Phipps, C. J., polar expedition of, **IV**, 292

Phips, William, captures and plunders Port Royal, **III**, 211; captures part of Maine, **III**, 326; and Maine under Massachusetts, **III**, 328; as royal governor of Massachusetts, **III**, 355; knighted, **IV**, 136; builds Fort William Henry, **IV**, 240; salvages gold, **IV**, 277; captures Port Royal, **IV**, 315; attacks Quebec, **IV**, 388; performs first large salvage job, **V**, 19

Phonograph, invented by Edison, **III**, 148; **IV**, 223

Phosphates, as fertilizer, **II**, 268; in Idaho, **III**, 66; and Tennessee Valley Authority, **V**, 245

Photo-engraving, **I**, 213; **IV**, 126

Photography, air, **I**, 35; and M. B. Brady, **I**, 234; and motion pictures, **IV**, 31; and the rayon industry, **IV**, 418; and the tintype, **V**, 272

Physick, Philip Syng, early member of Pennsylvania Hospital staff, **IV**, 247

Piankashaw Indians, and the Algonquin family, **I**, 48; and treaty of Fort de Chartres, **I**, 348; land cessions of, **III**, 100; and Johnson and Graham's Lessee v. McIntosh, **III**, 178; a division of the Miami, **III**, 390; sign treaty of Fort Wayne, **V**, 370

"Piasa," **I**, 53

Piave River, A. E. F. cross the, **I**, 60

Picatinny, N. J., arsenal at, **I**, 122

Picayune, monetary term, **I**, 411

Piccard, Auguste, and the stratosphere, **V**, 187

Pichardo, José Antonio, and Spain's title to Texas, **V**, 252

Pickaway Plains, Dunmore marches to, **II**, 177

Pickens, Andrew, in battle of Cowpens, **II**, 81; in battle of Kettle Creek, **III**, 208; and partisan bands, **IV**, 219; in the Southern campaigns (1780–81), **V**, 129

Pickens, Fort, and the Civil War, **I**, 386; and the Confederate States, **II**, 10; and Pensacola, **IV**, 250; and the *Powhatan* incident, **IV**, 327; and battle on Santa Rosa Island, **V**, 30

Pickering, Fort, built at Chickasaw Bluffs, **I**, 359

Pickering, Timothy, opposes the Embargo, **II**, 208; and the Rose intrigue, **IV**, 502; and secession, **V**, 51; and the War and Ordnance Board, **V**, 399

Picketing, and the A. F. of L., **I**, 60; and indus-

trial arbitration, **I**, 95; as part of a boycott, **I**, 232; and injunctions, **III**, 123; and labor unions, **III**, 225; and Norris-LaGuardia Anti-Injunction Law, **IV**, 143; and Truax v. Corrigan, **V**, 325

Pickett, G. E., in battle of Five Forks, **II**, 279; and Pickett's charge, **II**, 387; and siege of Petersburg, **IV**, 256

Pickett, John T., and Civil War diplomacy, **I**, 392

Pickman, Benjamin, and Louisburg, **V**, 16

Pickwick Landing Dam, **V**, 245

Picquet, François, and Fort LaGalette, **III**, 228; founder of the mission La Présentation, **IV**, 159

Pictet Artificial Ice Company, **IV**, 437

Pictographs, and Indian art, **III**, 93

Piece-of-eight, as colonial standard, **II**, 157; replaced by the Spanish dollar, **V**, 140

Piedmont, and the fall line, **II**, 241; of Virginia, **V**, 374; occupation of the, **V**, 450

Piegan Indians, trade with, **I**, 130

Pierce, E. D., discovers gold in Idaho, **III**, 66

Pierce, Franklin, elected President, **I**, 284; inauguration of, **III**, 82; and the Kansas-Nebraska Act, **III**, 197

Pierce, George F., and college training for women, **V**, 480

Pierce, John, and the *Leander* incident, **III**, 256

Pierce, Richard, printer of *Publick Occurrences,* **IV**, 127

Pierce, Sarah, school of, **V**, 43

Pierie, George W., as partner in the *Pennsylvania Gazette,* **IV**, 246

Piernas, Don Pedro, upper Louisiana surrendered to, **III**, 426

Pierpont Morgan Library, **I**, 212

Pierre, Fort, camp base of Sully expedition, **II**, 106. *See also* Tecumseh, Fort

Pierre Chouteau, Fort, built, **IV**, 268

Pierre's Hole, trappers' rendezvous, **II**, 362; and "holes of the mountains," **III**, 37; and expedition into Wyoming, **V**, 496

Pierson, Abraham, and Newark, N. J., **IV**, 120; and the beginning of Yale University, **V**, 500

Pierson, Thomas, surveys boundary line of Chester and New Castle counties, **II**, 132

Pietism, and the Dunkards, **II**, 176

Pig Iron, manufacturing of, **III**, 336

Piggly Wiggly Stores, Inc., introduce self-service, **V**, 56

Pike, Albert, writes new words to the song "Dixie," **II**, 156; and partisan bands, **IV**, 219

Pike, Nicholas, author of an *Arithmetic,* **V**, 40

Pike, Zebulon M., and Colorado, **I**, 426; and the Great American Desert, **II**, 140; and the Dust Bowl, **II**, 178; and Leech Lake Indian council,

III, 260; in Minnesota, III, 411; in New Mexico, IV, 107; and the Great Plains, IV, 282; and Prairie du Chien, IV, 328; arrives at the Falls of St. Anthony, V, 6; and Santa Fé Trail, V, 29; and Sioux treaties, V, 85; and site of Fort Snelling, V, 106; and topographic mapping, V, 283; southwestern expedition of, V, 442; and capture of York (Toronto), V, 507

Pikes Peak, James expedition climbs, III, 166, 300

Pikes Peak Gold Area, and domestic trade, V, 293

Pikes Peak Gold Rush, and the Arkansas River route, I, 107; and Colorado, I, 426; and gold mining, II, 396; and Hannibal and St. Joseph Railroad, III, 8; and launching of Leavenworth and Pikes Peak Express, III, 258; and overland freighting, IV, 192; and the Great Plains, IV, 282; and prospectors, IV, 364; and the Leavenworth and Pikes Peak Express, IV, 510; and Smoky Hill Trail, V, 103

Pilar, Gregorio del, and the Philippine insurrection, IV, 262

Pilcher, Joshua, and the Leavenworth expedition, III, 259; and Missouri Fur Company, V, 13

Pilgrims, The, and Brownists, I, 244; enter Cape Cod harbor, I, 306; and Council for New England, II, 72; dress of, II, 168; get supplies from Monhegan Island, III, 203; come to America in the *Mayflower*, III, 361; and the Mayflower Compact, III, 362; and New Plymouth Colony, IV, 111; and distribution of wealth, V, 428. *See also* Plymouth, The Virginia Company of; Plymouth Colony

Pillow, Fort, and opening of the Mississippi, III, 419; and the Mississippi Squadron, III, 425

Pillow, G. J., and the battle of Belmont, I, 176; and battle of Chapultepec, I, 342; quarrels with Scott, V, 46

Pillsbury, John S., Republican leader in Minnesota, III, 411

Pillsbury Flour Mills, IV, 355

Pilot Knob, Price at, IV, 339

Pima Indians, in Arizona, I, 104; rebellion of, and Tubac, V, 328

Pimitoui, LaSalle encamps at, II, 87; and Fort St. Louis, IV, 252; V, 11

Pin-Making Machinery, III, 320

Pinchot, Gifford, and controversy with Ballinger, I, 149; heads National Conservation Commission, II, 27; and the Vare case, V, 358; and water power conservation, V, 423

Pinckney, Charles, signer of the Constitution, II, 39; delegate to Convention of 1787, II, 50; and export taxes, II, 236

Pinckney, Charles Cotesworth, and campaign of 1808, I, 281; signer of the Constitution, II, 39; delegate to Convention of 1787, II, 50; diplo-

matic mission of, II, 148; French decline to receive, II, 327; and the Jefferson-Burr election dispute, III, 170; French government refuses to receive, IV, 15; and the XYZ affair, V, 498

Pinckney, Thomas, nominated for Vice-Presidency, I, 281; and diplomatic missions, II, 148

Pinckney's Treaty (or San Lorenzo), and the Adams-Onís Treaty, I, 9; and annexation of territory, I, 79; ends Carondelet intrigue, I, 317; and abandonment of Fort Confederation, II, 13; and the right of deposit, II, 139; and diplomatic missions, II, 148; recognizes Dunbar's Line, II, 176; and Ellicott's mission, II, 203; and the Federalist party, II, 264; and Florida boundary, II, 290; and Guion's expedition, II, 428; and American expansion in the southwest, III, 305; and Louisiana, III, 308; and West Florida, III, 420; and free navigation of the Mississippi, III, 423; opens Mississippi River to Americans, III, 424; and mixed commissions, III, 431; ends Spanish intrigue, IV, 137; and Fort Panmure, IV, 210; and Panton, Leslie and Company, IV, 211; and Spanish-American relations, V, 134; and Spanish-Indian relations, V, 140; stabilizes our relations with Spain, V, 316; and western unity, V, 435; and West Florida boundary, V, 436; and western boundaries, V, 441; and western separatism, V, 447; and the Yazoo-Chattahoochee Line, V, 503

Pine Coulie, battle of, III, 199

Pine Ridge Reservation, V, 127

Pine Tree Flag, II, 281

Pineda, Alonso de, and discovery and exploration of Texas, V, 252

Piney Woods People, II, 83

Pinkerton, Allan, and express robberies, I, 9; organizer of the United States Secret Service, V, 146

Pinkerton's Detective Agency, and industrial espionage, II, 228; and Star Route frauds, V, 160; and train robberies, V, 303

Pinkney, William, and McCulloch v. Maryland, III, 364; and Monroe-Pinkney Treaty, IV, 15; and American claims on Naples, IV, 52; and oratory, IV, 180

Piomingo, Chief, and Chickasaw-Creek War, I, 360; and the Chickasaw treaty, I, 361

Pioneers, and the Back Country, I, 145; and American slang, V, 88

Pious Fund, I, 63, 96

Pipe, Indian, III, 96

Pipelines, and the Standard Oil Company, V, 156

Piqua, Chillicothe located at, I, 364

Piracy, and admiralty courts, I, 13; at Barataria, I, 162; and buccaneers, I, 246; and the Constitution, II, 33; and crime, II, 87; and the Fajardo case, II, 240; at Galveston, II, 368; and

armed merchantmen, **III**, 377; and the Mosquito fleet, **IV**, 30; eradicated by Navy, **IV**, 77; and visit and search, **V**, 381

Pirogues, used on Cumberland River, **II**, 97; on the Mississippi, **III**, 423; and the Missouri River fur trade, **III**, 431; for river navigation, **IV**, 489

Piscataqua, and the Laconia grant, **III**, 226; Mason sends settlers to, **III**, 351

Pistole, as coinage, **II**, 163

Pit, The, and wheat, **V**, 453

Pitch, as naval store, **IV**, 72

Pithole, oil boom town, **IV**, 166

Pitiless Publicity, Woodrow Wilson proponent of, **II**, 147

Pitt, Fort, and United States Army, **I**, 112; and Fort Bedford, **I**, 173; and Bouquet Expedition, **I**, 229, 258; and John Connolly's plot, **II**, 24; Croghan starts expedition from (1765), **II**, 90; renamed Fort Dunmore, **II**, 177; protects Forks of the Ohio, **IV**, 162; Fort Duquesne rechristened, **IV**, 165, 243; and the Pennsylvania-Virginia boundary dispute, **IV**, 249; attacked in Pontiac's War, **IV**, 306

Pittman, Key, and the World Economic Conference, **V**, 486

Pittman, Philip, and topographic mapping, **V**, 283

Pittman Act (1918), and sale of silver, **I**, 252; and the silver dollar, **II**, 157; Federal Reserve bank notes issued under, **II**, 262; and silver legislation, **V**, 80

Pitts, John and Hiram, and the threshing machine, **II**, 248; **V**, 266

Pittsburgh, city directory appears in, **II**, 148; Forbes Road built to, **II**, 299; capturing and renaming of, **IV**, 162

Pittsburgh, Bessemer and Lake Erie Railroad, **V**, 348

Pittsburgh, The, gunboat, **II**, 180; in capture of Island Number Ten, **III**, 161

Pittsburgh, Treaty of, and Pluggy's band, **IV**, 288

Pittsburgh Gazette, first newspaper west of the mountains, **IV**, 124

Pittsburgh Reduction Company, **I**, 53

Pittsfield Fair, **II**, 73

Pittsylvania, and the Grand Ohio Company, **II**, 408

Placer Mining, and mineral patent laws, **III**, 406; and law of the mining camp, **III**, 409

Plains, and domestic trade, **V**, 293. *See also* Great Plains

Plan of 1776, and contraband of war, **II**, 48; and joint commission to France, **II**, 322; and neutral rights, **IV**, 87; and treaties with Prussia, **IV**, 369

Plan of Union (1801), for church unity, **I**, 373; and the Congregationalists, **II**, 17; and heresy

trials, **III**, 27; and the Presbyterians, **IV**, 332; and American religion, **IV**, 442; and religion in the Western Reserve, **V**, 446

Plankinton, John, and the rise of Armour and Company, **I**, 109

Plano Manufacturing Company, **III**, 140

Plant, H. B., opens south Florida to railroad transportation, **II**, 287

Plantation System, and agriculture, **I**, 27; in Alabama, **I**, 39; breakup of, **I**, 384; and cotton, **II**, 68, 70; and the Deep South, **II**, 125; and transition from frontier, **II**, 351; in Mississippi, **III**, 420; and the mule, **IV**, 40; and the overseer, **IV**, 193; as a business enterprise, **IV**, 509; and slavery, **V**, 93; and soil exhaustion, **V**, 116; development of, **V**, 122; and the old regime in Virginia, **V**, 375

Planters' Bank Bonds, **IV**, 456

Plastics, production of, **III**, 338

Platforms, Party, in campaign of 1832, **I**, 283; and campaign pledges, **I**, 292; and presidential campaigns, **I**, 295; and party government, **IV**, 220

Platon, Bishop, and Russian Church in America, **IV**, 511

Platt, C. T., imprisonment of, **II**, 240

Platt, Richard, treasurer of the Scioto Company, **V**, 44

Platt, Thomas C., and the Amen Corner, **I**, 55; and political corruption, **II**, 64

Platt Amendment, Cuba accepts the, **II**, 94; invoked in second intervention in Cuba, **II**, 95; and the Isle of Pines, **III**, 162

Platte Bridge Fight, **V**, 86

Platte Purchase, and Missouri, **III**, 426

Platte River, reached by Bourgmont, **I**, 229; and the Mormon Trail, **IV**, 24; and the Overland Trail, **IV**, 193; and mountain passes, **IV**, 222; and the Oregon Trail, **IV**, 495

Plattsburg, in the War of 1812, **III**, 230; **V**, 406

Play Party, rise of the, **II**, 270; and folklore, **II**, 293

Playfair, William, and the Scioto Company, **V**, 44

Playgrounds, **I**, 71

Playing-card Money, **II**, 99

Pleasant Hill, in the Red River campaign, **IV**, 430

Pleasants, John H., duels with Thomas Ritchie, **II**, 174

Pleasonton, Alfred, and battle of Antietam, **I**, 81; at Brandy Station, **I**, 235; in Missouri, **IV**, 339; and battle of Westport, Mo., **V**, 449

Plough Boy, farm periodical, **II**, 248

Plough Patent, **III**, 204. *See also* Lygonia

Plow, invention of, **II**, 125, 247

Plumb Plan, sponsored by railroad brotherhoods, **IV**, 400

Plumbe, John, and early government railroad surveys, **IV**, 405

Plummer, Henry, bandit leader, **II**, 88; **V**, 368

Plumsock Ironworks, **III**, 155

Plunkett, Sheriff, leads a posse against the Wyoming Valley settlements (1775), **V**, 502

Plymouth, The Virginia Company of, financed by "adventurers," **I**, 16; and British colonial policy, **I**, 421; and the Council for New England, **II**, 71; and Long Island, **III**, 298; and Maine, **III**, 326; and the Popham Colony, **IV**, 308

Plymouth Colony, blacksmith at, **I**, 197; trading post at Castine, **I**, 321; and fast days, **II**, 254; and the fur trade, **II**, 360; and Kennebec trading post, **III**, 204; and King Philip's War, **III**, 210; added to Massachusetts, **III**, 355; and the Mayflower Compact, **III**, 362; and May Day, **III**, 378; and Monhegan fishing plantation, **IV**, 9; trading post at Penobscot, **IV**, 249; and the Pilgrims, **IV**, 270; Puritans at, **IV**, 384; trading post, and the River Towns of Connecticut, **IV**, 490; food shortage at, **V**, 161; and colonial stock companies, **V**, 182; settlement of, **V**, 301; founding of, and Weston's settlement, **V**, 448. *See also* Pilgrims

"Po' Laz'us," narrative song, **I**, 148

Pocahontas, saves John Smith's life, **III**, 167

Pocahontas, and the wooden Indian, **V**, 483

Pocomoke River, and the Alexandria Conference, **I**, 47

Pocumtuck Indians, as refugees from King Philip's War, **III**, 211

Poe, Edgar Allan, editor of the *Southern Literary Messenger*, **V**, 130; student of University of Virginia, **V**, 375

Poinsett, Joel, and Force Acts, **II**, 299; sent to promote commercial relations with revolted Latin-American colonies, **III**, 250

Point Lookout, Md., prison camp at, **IV**, 347

Point Pleasant, battle of, **II**, 177; **V**, 421

Pointe Coupée, **I**, 7; **II**, 114

Poles, as political exiles, **IV**, 295

Police Power, and antisyndicalist laws, **I**, 87; and right of assembly, **I**, 130; supersedes due process clause, **I**, 260; of Congress, **I**, 433; and the contract clause, **II**, 48; and equal protection of law, **II**, 222; and liberty, **III**, 270; and Lochner v. New York, **III**, 291; and the Lottery Case, **III**, 304; and minimum-wage laws, **III**, 408; and rights of the minority, **III**, 412; and property, **IV**, 360; and quasi-judicial agencies, **IV**, 387; and social legislation, **V**, 107; and zoning ordinances, **V**, 514

Policy, as form of gambling, **II**, 369

Political Assessments, and patronage, **IV**, 225; and the Pendleton Act, **IV**, 241

Political Campaigns, and campaign literature, **I**, 280

Political Cartoons, **I**, 320

Political Greenhouse, produced by the Hartford Wits, **III**, 15

Political Machine. *See* Machine, Party

Political Parties, and election of the President, **II**, 191; as factors in elections, **II**, 193; and propaganda, **IV**, 358; and representative government, **IV**, 452

Political Rings, **IV**, 485

Political Theory, and *The Federalist*, **II**, 264

Political Tolerance, **V**, 278

Polk, James K., elected President, **I**, 284; as a "dark horse," **II**, 110; and Oregon controversy, **II**, 271; and treaty of Guadalupe Hidalgo, **II**, 426; and the Mexican War, **III**, 385 f.; and the Oregon Question, **IV**, 185; and the Oregon Treaty, **IV**, 187; and the Pacific Ocean, **IV**, 196; and the term "roorback," **IV**, 501; and annexation of Texas, **V**, 251; and declaration of war, **V**, 396; and the Wilmot Proviso, **V**, 469

Polk, Leonidas, defeats Grant at Belmont, **I**, 176; and the Meridian campaign, **III**, 377

Polk Doctrine, **IV**, 13; **V**, 511

Poll Tax, and the Mississippi Plan (1890 f.), **III**, 422; and exclusion from the suffrage, **V**, 199; preferred in southern states, **V**, 225; as a direct tax, **V**, 230

Pollard, Edward A., criticizes the Confederacy, **II**, 4; uses term "Lost Cause," **III**, 303

Pollard, Madeline, breach of promise suit of, **V**, 324

Pollock, Oliver, aids in the Revolution, **II**, 389; and Spanish military supplies from New Orleans, **V**, 141; and the Willing expedition, **V**, 469

Pollock v. Farmers Loan and Trust Company, **III**, 83; **IV**, 462

Polly Case, and neutral rights, **II**, 228; and Rule of the War of 1756, **IV**, 506

Polygamy, and enabling acts for Utah statehood, **II**, 213; and naturalization, **IV**, 67; and Reorganized Latter Day Saints, **IV**, 450; delays statehood for Utah, **V**, 354

Polypotamia, Jefferson's proposed state, **III**, 173

Polytechnic Institute of Brooklyn, **III**, 114

Pomutz, George, promotes settlement in New Buda, **IV**, 94

Ponce de Leon, Juan, and exploration of America, **I**, 57; as a *conquistadore*, **II**, 25; discovers Spanish Florida, **II**, 288

Pond, J. B., and "lecture kings," **III**, 260; and the lyceum movement, **III**, 316

Pond, Peter, fur trader, **III**, 111; and Minnesota, **III**, 410; searches for the western sea, **V**, 446

Ponderson, John, enters into New Haven church covenant, **V**, 60

Pontchartrain, Fort, founding of, **II**, 346

Pontchartrain, Lake, and Isle of Orleans, **III**, 161

Pontchartrain du Detroit, earliest fort built at Detroit, **II**, 142

Pontiac, as an Algonquin, **I**, 48; convenes Ecorse River Council, **II**, 184; and Council at Fort Ontario, **IV**, 191

Pontiac War, and siege of Fort Bedford, **I**, 173; and the battle of Bloody Run, **I**, 203; and Bradstreet's Expedition (1764), **I**, 234; and Croghan's expedition to Illinois, **II**, 90; Delaware Indians support, **II**, 131; and the siege of Fort Detroit, **II**, 143; influenced by Council at Detroit (1761), **II**, 144; and Devil's Hole, **II**, 145; and British attempts to reach Illinois, **III**, 68; and Indiana Company, **III**, 113; and land grants, **III**, 235; Fort Ligonier during, **III**, 277; and seizure of Fort Miami, **III**, 389; massacre at Michilimackinac, **III**, 394; and Niagara Carrying Place, **IV**, 130; and the Paxton Boys, **IV**, 229; and Pennsylvania, **IV**, 243; and the Proclamation of 1763, **IV**, 354; at Sandusky, **V**, 27; and Sideling Hill, **V**, 77; and the Stamp Act, **V**, 154; and "Suffering Traders," **V**, 198

Pony Express, and development of California, **I**, 274; launching of, **I**, 334; and Hannibal and St. Joseph Railroad, **III**, 8; and Overland Mail, **IV**, 193; uses Bridger's Pass, **IV**, 222; and the Great Plains, **IV**, 282; and postage stamps, **IV**, 318; operated by Russell, Majors and Waddell, **IV**, 510; links St. Joseph with California, **V**, 10; organized to carry mails, **V**, 308; taken over by Wells, Fargo and Company, **V**, 434

Poole, William F., and the American Library Association, **III**, 272

Pooling Agreements, and monopoly, **IV**, 12; and trusts, **V**, 326; and Westinghouse patent litigation, **V**, 448

Pools, and restraint of trade, **IV**, 460

Poor, C. H., and blockade off the Mississippi Deltas, **III**, 421

Poor, Enoch, and Sullivan-Clinton campaign, **V**, 202

Poor Laws, **IV**, 226

Poor Richard's Almanac, **I**, 52; **II**, 252

Poor Whites, "crackers" as, **II**, 83; and slavery, **IV**, 141; and the piney woods region, **IV**, 273; and civilization of the Old South, **V**, 122

Poore, Ben Perley, and government publications, **II**, 405

Popé, leads the Pueblo revolt, **IV**, 379; has headquarters at Taos, **V**, 219

Pope, Albert A., begins manufacture of bicycles, **I**, 182

Pope, Camp, Sibley marches from, **II**, 106

Pope, Jacob, and the threshing machine, **V**, 266

Pope, John, at Second Bull Run, **I**, 251; and battle of Cedar Mountain, **I**, 330; and battle of Chantilly, **I**, 341; builds Fort Hays, **III**, 20; and

"headquarters in the saddle," **III**, 21; and capture of Island Number Ten, **III**, 161; and Army of the Mississippi, **III**, 419; and the Porter case, **IV**, 317; and the Army of the Potomac, **IV**, 324; and government railroad surveys, **IV**, 405; surveys Southern Railroad Route, **V**, 131

Pope Manufacturing Company, purchases Selden patent, **V**, 56

Popham, George, and Maine, **III**, 326

Popham, John, leader in the Plymouth Company, **IV**, 290

Popham Colony, builds the *Virginia*, **I**, 199; established, **III**, 203; and Pemaquid, **IV**, 239; at Sagadahoc, **V**, 4

Poplar Forest, and Jeffersonian architecture, **III**, 171

Popple, Henry, his map of North America, **IV**, 175; **V**, 282

Popple, William, William, Jr., and Alured, **I**, 207

Popular (or Squatter) Sovereignty, and the Alabama Platform, **I**, 41; and the Freeport Doctrine, **II**, 340; and the Kansas Free-State party, **III**, 197; and the Kansas-Nebraska Act, **III**, 197; and the Kansas Struggle, **III**, 198; prevails in Compromise of 1850, **III**, 428; and the Omnibus Bill, **IV**, 173; as a political theory, **IV**, 300; advocated by Douglas and Cass, **V**, 96; and the Topeka constitution, **V**, 281

Population, and birth control, **I**, 191; and the lower house of Congress, **IV**, 451

Populist Party, and the agrarian movement, **I**, 21; in Alabama, **I**, 40; and calamity howlers, **I**, 268; in campaigns of 1892 and 1896, **I**, 288; and citizens' alliances, **I**, 378; and crop failures, **I**, 398; supports Coxeyites, **II**, 82; and farm periodicals, **II**, 249; and farm relief, **II**, 249; and farmers' alliances, **II**, 252; demands free silver, **II**, 333; and the income tax, **II**, 402; and Greenbackers, **II**, 424; and hard money, **III**, 9; and middle-of-the-road Populists, **III**, 395; as a political party, **IV**, 297; and soft currency, **V**, 113; as third party, **V**, 262; and distribution of wealth, **V**, 429

Porcher, Isaac, last pure-blooded Huguenot in America, **III**, 57

Pork, and rotation of crops, **II**, 154; and hog raising, **III**, 36

"Pork-Barrel," **I**, 93; **II**, 64

"Porkopolis," title given Cincinnati, **I**, 375; **IV**, 199

Port Hudson, and opening of the Mississippi, **III**, 419; fall of, **III**, 425

Port of New York Authority, **III**, 144; **IV**, 119, 438; **V**, 175

Port Republic, battle at, **III**, 165

Port Royal (N. S.), and D'Anville's expedition, **II**, 109; and King George's War, **III**, 210; cap-

ture and plunder of, **III**, 211; captured in Queen Anne's War, **IV**, 389; and Treaty of St. Germain-en-Laye, **V**, 9

Port Williams, discovered by Palmer, **IV**, 201

Portage Railway. *See* Allegheny Portage Railway

Portages, and search for the western sea, **V**, 446

Porter, Augustus, and Niagara Falls, **IV**, 130

Porter, David, and *Constellation-Insurgente* action, **II**, 28; and the cruise of the *Essex*, **II**, 228; and the Fajardo case, **II**, 240; names Madison's Island, **III**, 322; and the Mosquito Fleet, **IV**, 30; appointed to Board of Navy Commissioners, **IV**, 75; and whaling, **V**, 452

Porter, David D., made an admiral, **I**, 12; forces surrender of Arkansas Post, **I**, 106; and the Navy in the Civil War, **I**, 390; bombards Fort Fisher, **II**, 277; and battle at Grand Gulf, **II**, 408; and blockade off the Mississippi Deltas, **III**, 422; and Civil War naval mortars, **IV**, 28; as superintendent of United States Naval Academy, **IV**, 69; and Fort Pickens, **IV**, 266; and the *Powhatan* incident, **IV**, 327; on secret mission to Santo Domingo, **V**, 32; and Steele's Bayou expedition, **V**, 180; aids in assault on Vicksburg, **V**, 367; and the Yazoo Pass expedition, **V**, 504

Porter, Edwin S., and motion pictures, **IV**, 31

Porter, Fitz-John, and battle of Antietam, **I**, 81; at Second Bull Run, **I**, 252; in battle of Gaines' Mill, **II**, 366; and battle of Mechanicsville, **III**, 367; and the Radical Republicans, **IV**, 395; and Seven Days' battles, **V**, 59

Porter, Gene Stratton, and best sellers, **I**, 180

Porter, Horace, and Black Friday (1869), **I**, 194

Porter, John L., on the designing board of the *Virginia*, **IV**, 414

Porter, Noah, edits the unabridged edition of Webster's Dictionary, **V**, 433

Porter, Peter Buell, and Fort Erie, **II**, 223; proposes connecting the Great Lakes with the Mississippi, **III**, 231; and battle at Lundy's Lane, **III**, 315; and the Niagara campaigns, **IV**, 130; and Niagara Falls, **IV**, 130; as a leader of the War Hawks, **V**, 403

Porterfield, G. A., and the skirmish at Philippi, **IV**, 261

Portland Cement, **I**, 330

Portland Gold Mine, **II**, 396

Portland Standard, advocates the Pacific Republic movement, **IV**, 197

Portolá, Gaspár de, and California under Spain, **I**, 275; and horses, **III**, 48; founder of Monterey, **IV**, 17; founder of San Diego, **V**, 23; discovers San Francisco Bay, **V**, 23

Portrait Painting, **I**, 123

Ports of Entry, and state inspection acts, **III**, 126, 143

Portsmouth, N. H., Strawberry Bank changes name to, **V**, 188

Portsmouth, R. I., founded, **IV**, 477

Portsmouth, Treaty of, and spheres of influence, **III**, 330; and the Taft-Katsura memorandum, **V**, 217

Portsmouth Navy Yard, **IV**, 79

Portugal, treaties with, **V**, 318

Post, C. W., starts National Trades' and Workers' Association, **IV**, 63

Post, Christian Frederick, and the treaty of Easton (1758), **II**, 183; peace missions of, **II**, 299; visits Logstown, **III**, 295

Post, Wiley, encircles the globe, **I**, 143

Post Exchange, and the merchant sutler, **V**, 212

Post Office, antislavery literature removed from, **I**, 85; and the Constitution, **II**, 33; and consumer protection, **II**, 44; and government ownership, **II**, 404; and road improvement, **IV**, 494; and rural free delivery, **IV**, 508; and Rural Post Roads Act, **IV**, 510; and Southern Overland Mail, **V**, 130; and stagecoach travel, **V**, 153; and travel, **V**, 306

Post Office Department, and air mail, **I**, 34; and airplane disasters, **I**, 36; starts first experimental air-mail plane, **I**, 143; and Civil Aeronautics Act, **I**, 380; and the Louisiana lottery, **III**, 307; and Star Route frauds, **V**, 160

Post Roads, and the Constitution, **II**, 33; Congress given power to establish, **IV**, 319

Postage Stamps, as money, **II**, 321

Postal Savings System, **IV**, 320

Postal Telegraph Company, **I**, 434; **II**, 312

Postmasters, removal of, and Myers v. U. S., **IV**, 51

Poston, Charles D., explores Gadsden purchase, **II**, 236

Potato, as food, **II**, 295

Potawatomi Indians, and Algonquin family, **I**, 48; attack Fort Dearborn garrison, **I**, 356; and the Chicago treaties, **I**, 358; split off from the Chippewa, **I**, 367; and Fort Harmar treaty, **III**, 10; and Hull treaty, **III**, 58; and land cessions of, **III**, 100; removal of, **III**, 107; evangelized by Jesuits, **III**, 175; and Oklahoma Openings, **IV**, 169; and the Ottawa Indians, **IV**, 191; party to the treaty of Prairie du Chien, **IV**, 329; and treaty of Spring Wells, **V**, 150; sign treaty of Fort Wayne, **V**, 370, 426; depend upon wild rice for their food supply, **V**, 464

Potawatomie Massacre, **I**, 195, 220

Potomac, Army of the, at Antietam, **I**, 81; at Appomattox, **I**, 91; at Cold Harbor, **I**, 412; and investigations of Committee on the Conduct of the War, **I**, 436; and draft riots, **II**, 165; command of, given to Burnside, **II**, 330; and Army of the James, **III**, 166; and the Mine Run

campaign, **III**, 405; withdrawn from the Peninsula, **IV**, 241

Potomac Company, and Chesapeake and Ohio Canal, **I**, 354; formed with aid of state funds, **II**, 402

Potomac River, and the Alexandria Conference, **I**, 47; and the Alleghenies, **I**, 51

Potowmac Guardian, founded by Nathaniel Willis, **IV**, 128

Pottery, and archæology, **I**, 98; Indian, **I**, 144; gas for, **II**, 372; and Indian art, **III**, 93

Pourmont, Philemon, earliest teacher on record, **V**, 234

Powder, and the DuPont Company, **II**, 177

Powderly, Terence V., and immigrant labor, **III**, 72

Powell, J. W., and scientific exploration of the Colorado River, **I**, 427; **II**, 408; **III**, 87; survey of, **V**, 283

Powell, James, defeats Sioux in Wagon Box fight, **V**, 86, 388

Powell, L. W., and Committee of Thirteen (1860), **I**, 436

Power Machinery, and manufacturing, **III**, 336; and wages and prices, **V**, 388

"Power to tax involves the power to destroy"—in McCulloch v. Maryland, **III**, 364; **V**, 228

Powers, Caleb, three trials of, **V**, 323

Powers, Hiram, sculptor, **I**, 123

Powers, Separation of, in Massachusetts Bill of Rights, **I**, 187; and checks and balances, **I**, 349; and Congress, **II**, 19; and the Convention of 1787, **II**, 51; by executive and Congress, **II**, 233; and rights of the minority, **III**, 412; and political theories, **IV**, 300; and quasi-judicial agencies, **IV**, 387; and state government, **V**, 169; and tyranny, **V**, 337

Powhatan, Algonquin leader, **I**, 48

Powhatan Incident, and Fort Pickens, **IV**, 266

Powhatan Indians, and Algonquin family, **I**, 48

Pownall, John, and Board of Trade, **I**, 207

Pownall, Thomas, proposes erection of a fort on Penobscot River, **II**, 346; and the pre-Revolutionary imperial idea, **III**, 78

Practice and Principles of Medicine, written by William Osler, **II**, 150

Pragmatism, and philosophical thought and writings, **IV**, 264

Prairie Dogs, **II**, 170

Prairie du Chien, Fort Crawford built at, **II**, 83; Fox Indians removed to, **II**, 319; posts built at, **II**, 320; and the fur trade, **II**, 360; and liquor in the fur trade, **III**, 282; settlement of, **V**, 473

Prairie du Chien Treaty of 1825, **I**, 367; **V**, 5, 86, 473

Prairie du Chien Treaty of 1830, **III**, 100; **V**, 86

Prairie Fires, **II**, 79, 276

Prairie Land and Cattle Company, **IV**, 177

Prairie Schooner, successor to the Conestoga Wagon, **II**, 3; and covered wagon, **II**, 77; freight carried in, **II**, 340; and transportation, **V**, 308; and wagon manufacture, **V**, 388; and wagon trains, **V**, 389

Pratt, Charles, and Company, and the Standard Oil Company, **V**, 156

Pratt, R. H., establishes Carlisle Indian School, **I**, 314; **III**, 86

Pratte, Bernard, and Chouteau and Company, **I**, 369

Pratte, Chouteau and Company, **I**, 61

Preble, Edward, and the Barbary Wars, **I**, 162; and the *Constitution,* **II**, 29; and gunboats, **II**, 429; and the Barbary Wars, **IV**, 77

Pre-emption Act, passed, **I**, 28; and squatters, **I**, 394; and Clay's Land Distribution Bill, **III**, 234; and the public domain, **IV**, 370; and public land sales, **IV**, 372

Preferential Voting, **II**, 193; **IV**, 451

Prentice, George D., journalist, **V**, 123

Prentiss, B. M., and battle at Helena, **III**, 24

Prentiss, S. S., and oratory, **IV**, 180; and the Vick estate, **V**, 366

Preparedness, and national defense, **II**, 127; and National Defense Act, **IV**, 59; and the World War, **V**, 491

Presbyterians, and revivalism, **I**, 143; and Cambridge Platform, **I**, 277; and Calvinism, **I**, 277; and colleges, **I**, 413; separation of, in Tennessee and Kentucky, **II**, 97; as dissenters, **II**, 151; and evangelism, **II**, 230; and frontier preaching, **II**, 353; and the Great Awakening, **II**, 413, 419; and heresy trials, **III**, 27; and Indian missions, **III**, 103; Ministers' Fund, **III**, 129; resume work of the Lapwai mission, **III**, 245; and home missionary societies, **III**, 417; and foreign missions, **III**, 417; and mountain people, **IV**, 37; and the Plan of Union, **IV**, 283; found Princeton University, **IV**, 343; and the American religion, **IV**, 442; and the Revolution, **IV**, 443; and revivals, **IV**, 464; and the Saybrook Platform, **V**, 37; oppose slavery, **V**, 97; and the Synod of Dort, **V**, 215; form a theological seminary at Princeton, **V**, 261; in the Western Reserve, **V**, 446; and the Yale Band, **V**, 500

Prescott, Samuel, and Revere's ride, **IV**, 463

Prescott, William, at Bunker Hill, **I**, 253; and origin of "Don't fire till you see the white of their eyes," **II**, 161

President, The, appointing power of, **I**, 90; as commander in chief, **I**, 431; and the Constitution, **II**, 35; message of, and the Constitution, **II**, 36; succession to office of, and the Twentieth Amendment, **II**, 43; office of, created, **II**, 51; election of, **II**, 191; office of, **II**, 257; power of

removal, and Humphrey's Executor v. U. S., **III**, 59; inauguration of, **III**, 81; and investigating committees, **III**, 149; power of removal, **IV**, 51; and power of pardon, **IV**, 214; special powers granted to, **IV**, 351; proclamations of, **IV**, 354; power of removal, **IV**, 447; guarded by Secret Service men, **V**, 53; succession to office of, and Secretary of State, **V**, 162; and negotiation of treaties, **V**, 315; veto power of, **V**, 365; and declaration of war, **V**, 396; war powers of, **V**, 407

President, The, frigate, **II**, 349

President Adams, The, galley boat, **II**, 367

Presidential Preference Primary, and the Oregon system, **IV**, 185

Presidential Succession Act, **IV**, 332

Presidio, planted by Menendez in Georgia, **II**, 116; and *ranchos del rey,* **IV**, 415; and Rubí's tour, **IV**, 505; established at San Antonio, **V**, 22; founded at San Francisco, **V**, 23; established by Spaniards in Texas, **V**, 252

Presque Isle, fort at, **II**, 177, 342, 344, 346; **III**, 259, 343; **IV**, 306

Presque Isle-Allegheny Portage, **IV**, 316

Press, Freedom of the. *See* Freedom of the Press

Press Gangs, and impressment of seamen, **III**, 80 f.

Pressure Groups, and the American Labor party, **I**, 62; and campaign pledges, **I**, 292; and labor parties, **III**, 223; and lobbying, **III**, 287; and right of petition, **IV**, 256; and propaganda, **IV**, 359; and sampling referenda, **V**, 22; and the United Mine Workers, **V**, 346

Preston, W. B., and war with Korea, **III**, 216

Preston, William C., and the expression "I had rather be right than be President," **III**, 65

Preuss, Charles, Frémont's cartographer, **V**, 283

Prevost, George, and battle of Plattsburg, **IV**, 287

Prevost, Theodosia (Bartow), **IV**, 213

Pribilof Islands, as part of the Alaska Purchase, **I**, 43; and the Alaska Commercial Company, **I**, 44; seal fisheries of, **V**, 49

Price, Richard, quotes statistics of births and deaths in Boston, **III**, 129

Price, Sterling, and the battle of Blackwater, **I**, 198; and Doniphan's expedition, **II**, 161; and battle of Iuka, **III**, 164; and battle at Jenkins Ferry, **III**, 173; and siege of Lexington, **III**, 266; and battle of Pilot Knob, **IV**, 272; and the battle at Pine Bluff, **IV**, 273; and the battle of Westport, **V**, 449; and battle of Wilson's Creek, **V**, 470

Price, William, and the Red River Indian War, **IV**, 431

Price Discrimination, and the Federal Trade Commission, **II**, 264

Price Fixing, and the Addyston Pipe Company case, **I**, 10; and army contracts, **I**, 115; and

Guffey Coal Acts, **II**, 428; and the Lever Act (1917), **III**, 265; and economic mobilization for the World War, **V**, 489

Price Maintenance, and advertising, **I**, 18. *See also* Fair Trade Laws

Prices, of commodities, **I**, 438; in the Confederacy, **II**, 11; and cost of living, **II**, 66; and standards of living, **V**, 157

Prices Current, business paper, **V**, 298

Prideaux, John, besieges Fort Niagara, **IV**, 130; and Oswego, **IV**, 190

Priest, Josiah, and chapbooks, **I**, 341

Priestly, Joseph, and Unitarianism, **V**, 345

Prigg v. Pennsylvania, and personal liberty laws, **IV**, 255

Primary, Direct, and the agrarian movement, **I**, 21; an experiment in democracy, **II**, 135; and election laws, **II**, 191; and elections, **II**, 192; and the franchise, **II**, 323; introduction of, **IV**, 137; and the Oregon system, **IV**, 185; and party platforms, **IV**, 285; and preferential voting, **IV**, 331; in election of senators, **V**, 57

Primary Meridians, and survey of public lands, **IV**, 373

Primogeniture, and intestate estates, **III**, 146; and Jeffersonian Democracy, **III**, 172; and land titles, **III**, 243; abolition of, **IV**, 351; and property laws, **IV**, 360; abolished by Virginia, **V**, 373

Primrose and West Minstrel Show, **III**, 413; **V**, 120

Prince, Thomas, collector of books, **I**, 212; private library of, **III**, 273; editor of the first religious periodical in America, **IV**, 445

Prince, Walter F., and the Blue Laws of Connecticut, **V**, 203

Prince, William, owns first nursery devoted to ornamental stock, **IV**, 154

Prince of Parthia, play written by Thomas Godfrey, **II**, 165

Princeton, Battle of, **II**, 131; **IV**, 476

Princeton University, and pre-Revolutionary education, **II**, 185; opened at Elizabeth, **II**, 202; and football, **II**, 298; and the Great Awakening, **II**, 413; and Log College, **III**, 294; at Newark, **IV**, 121; theological seminary at, **V**, 261; adopts system of tutorial instruction, **V**, 332

Pring, Martin, visits the Maine coast, **III**, 203, 326; sails up the Piscataqua, **IV**, 101

Pringle, John and Samuel, on the Buckhannon River, **II**, 235

Print Cloth Yarn Fabrics, **V**, 258

Printing, Government. *See* Government Printing

Printing Press, and book publishing, **I**, 213; at Boston (1674), **I**, 222; first, at Cambridge, **I**, 277; secured by the Lapwai mission, **III**, 245; set up in New York City, **IV**, 118; and newspapers, **IV**, 125; set up in Savannah, **V**, 35

Printz, Johan, as governor of New Sweden, **IV**, 113

Prison Ships, and atrocities in war, **I**, 136; the *Jersey*, **III**, 174

Prisoners of War, Grant refuses to exchange, **I**, 136; in Confederate prisons, **II**, 8; and treaty of Versailles, **V**, 363

Prisons, Confederate, **I**, 73; Auburn favorite pattern for, **I**, 137; industries in, **II**, 53; Elmira, **II**, 204; Civil War, **III**, 178; Pennsylvania system of, **IV**, 247; Sugar House, **V**, 200

Private Banks, **I**, 160

Private Brands, and advertising, **I**, 18; and trademarks, **V**, 299

Privateering, and the *Antelope* case, **I**, 79; during the Revolution, **I**, 150; Baltimore clippers used in, **I**, 151; and the Lafittes, **I**, 162; in the Civil War, **I**, 387; and the Confederate navy, **II**, 8; supplements the Navy, **II**, 282; and liability of private property to capture, **III**, 76; and Latin-American revolutions, **III**, 250; abolished by Declaration of Paris, **III**, 345; and armed merchantmen, **III**, 377; and the Navy, **IV**, 77; and Portsmouth, **IV**, 102; abolished by Declaration of Paris, **IV**, 215; and piracy, **IV**, 278; and prize money, **IV**, 353; and prizes, **IV**, 353; in Queen Anne's War, **IV**, 389; and Rhode Island, **IV**, 478; in Dutch War of 1653, **IV**, 479; from Salem, **V**, 16; by the *Yankee*, **V**, 501

Privileges and Immunities, and the Constitution, **II**, 37; and Minor v. Happersett, **III**, 412; and the Missouri Compromise, **III**, 428; and police power, **IV**, 294; and interstate citizenship, **V**, 174

Privy Council, and appeals from colonial courts, **I**, 89; and the colonial agent, **I**, 415; and colonial assemblies, **I**, 417; and instructions to colonial governors, **I**, 419; and the judiciary, **I**, 419; and the Council for Foreign Plantations, **II**, 71; and the judiciary, **III**, 184; and Lords of Trade and Plantation, **III**, 302; and restrictions of colonial manufactures, **III**, 335; and the Mason and Dixon line, **III**, 350; and the English Parliament, **IV**, 218; and the Parson's Cause, **IV**, 219; and Pennsylvania-Maryland boundary dispute, **IV**, 247; and royal disallowance, **IV**, 504; and treaty of Fort Stanwix (1768), **V**, 159; and the Tobacco Contract, **V**, 275; and Virginia Company of London, **V**, 378; disallows the act creating the Virginia Indian Company, **V**, 379

Prize Courts, and letters of marque and reprisal, **III**, 345; and Rule of the War of 1756, **IV**, 505; and the submarine in international law, **V**, 192; and the *Trent* affair, **V**, 321

Prize Fighting, **I**, 70; **V**, 148

Prize Money, to finance the Revolution, **IV**, 471; and the *Yankee*, **V**, 501

Prizes, the *Amy Warwick* case, **I**, 71; the *Appam* case, **I**, 89; the *Essex* case, **II**, 228; in Naval War with France, **II**, 327; and liability of private property to capture, **III**, 76; the *Jürgen Lorentzen* case, **III**, 190; during Naval War with France, **IV**, 73

Processing Tax, **I**, 24; **V**, 227

Prochett, Matteo, and the Waldenses, **V**, 391

Proclamation of 1763, makes western country a permanent Indian preserve, **I**, 218; and British Florida, **II**, 287; and the Greenbrier Company, **II**, 425; and the Indian agent, **III**, 90; and Indian policy, **III**, 104; issued to stop land encroachments, **III**, 235; and the Loyal Land Company, **III**, 311; and the Mississippi Company of Virginia, **III**, 421; and Rouse's Point boundary controversy, **IV**, 503; and the Old Southwest, **V**, 132; and treaty of Fort Stanwix (1768), **V**, 159; and Tryon's line, **V**, 328; establishes West Florida as a British province, **V**, 436; and western land claims, **V**, 444; and the westward movement, **V**, 450

Procter, Henry, headquarters at Fort Miami, **III**, 390; and the Raisin River massacre, **IV**, 412; and defense of Fort Stephenson, **V**, 181; and battle of the Thames, **V**, 258

Procter and Gamble Company, **IV**, 355

Proctor, F. F., and vaudeville, **V**, 358

Production Credit Corporations, **II**, 245

Profile Lathe, invention of, **III**, 320

Profit Sharing, and industrial relations, **III**, 116

Profiteering, in the Civil War, **I**, 387; and the "cost-plus" system, **II**, 67; in the Revolutionary War, **IV**, 475

Progress and Poverty, by Henry George, **IV**, 302; **V**, 83

Progressive Movement, and constitutional amendments, **I**, 56; organizes a bloc, **I**, 202; and the LaFollette party, **III**, 227; and muckraking, **IV**, 39; and the National Nonpartisan League, **IV**, 139; supported by North Dakota, **IV**, 146; and "standpatters," **V**, 158

Progressive Party, called "Bull Moose" party, **I**, 250; and campaigns of 1912, 1916, **I**, 290; attempts to force nomination of LaFollette, **II**, 251; formed by Theodore Roosevelt, **IV**, 297; and the "Square Deal," **V**, 151; and the Taft-Roosevelt split, **V**, 217; as third party, **V**, 262; and third-term doctrine, **V**, 263; and the Wisconsin Idea, **V**, 474

Prohibition, and constitutional amendments, **I**, 56; and Anti-Saloon League, **I**, 84; and the Bahama Islands, **I**, 146; and bootlegging, **I**, 217; an issue in campaign of 1932, **I**, 292; and the Eighteenth Amendment, **II**, 43; and the Twenty-first Amendment, **II**, 44; and distilling, **II**, 151; and the Eighteenth Amendment, **II**,

190; in Kansas, III, 195; and liquor laws, III, 282; and local option, III, 290; in Maine, III, 327; and Mugler v. Kansas, IV, 39; repeal of, endorsed by F. D. Roosevelt, IV, 95; and night clubs, IV, 133; develops as a political party, IV, 297; and racketeers, IV, 395; and rum row, IV, 506; and the "speak-easy," V, 142; and the temperance movement, V, 241; and the Twenty-first Amendment, V, 334; and the Volstead Act, V, 382; and the Webb-Kenyon Act, V, 431; and whiskey, V, 457; and the Wickersham Commission, V, 461; and wine producing, V, 471; and the W. C. T. U., V, 479

Prohibition Party, in campaigns of 1932 and 1936, I, 292; as third party, V, 262; and distribution of wealth, V, 429

Promontory Point, and Central Pacific race with the Union Pacific, I, 334; V, 309, 343

Propaganda, Civil War, I, 388; and foreign language press, II, 303; and peace movements, IV, 234; and right of petition, IV, 256; World War, V, 490, 493

Property, confiscation of, II, 15; and distribution of wealth, V, 429

Property Rights, and the Fifth Amendment, I, 9; and the due process clause, II, 173

Property Taxes, V, 230

Prophet, The, medicine man, III, 370; and the Shawnee, V, 65; and crusade of Tecumseh, V, 237; and battle of Tippecanoe, V, 273, 427

Proportional Representation, II, 193; IV, 331, 451, 452

Proprietary Charters, I, 417

Proprietary Government in Pennsylvania, overthrown, IV, 243

Proprietary Lands, and distribution of wealth, V, 429

Proprietary Provinces, replace charter colonies, I, 346; and colonial councils, I, 418; and governors, I, 418; and British colonial policy, I, 421; feudalism in, II, 269; and manors, III, 334; and palatine jurisdictions, IV, 200; and the quitrent, IV, 390; and the Virginia Company of London, V, 377; York's, V, 507. See also Lords Proprietors

Proslavery, in the Old South, V, 123

Prostitution, and the Raines Law, IV, 411; and sex relations, V, 62; and white-slave traffic, V, 460

Protection, and the agrarian movement, I, 20; and the balance of trade, I, 147; and campaign of 1860, I, 285; and the consequences of the Civil War, I, 383; and free trade, II, 335; favored by Friends of Domestic Industry, II, 349; and Harrisburg Convention, III, 13; and manufacturing, III, 336; and the McKinley tariff, III, 366; and Morrill Tariff Act, IV, 27; and

the panic of 1857, IV, 209; and Payne-Aldrich tariff, IV, 229; as platform of the Republican party, IV, 454; and sectionalism, V, 54; and the tariff, V, 221; and distribution of wealth, V, 429; and the Webster-Hayne debate, V, 431; and wool in American tariff policies, V, 484

Protestant, no-Popery newspaper, IV, 65

Protestant Episcopal Church, and colleges, I, 413; and home missionary societies, III, 417; and foreign missions, III, 417; and the Oxford movement, IV, 194; and Sunday Schools, V, 204

Protestant Reformation Society, IV, 65

Providence, R. I., Roger Williams settles at, IV, 477

Providence Agreements, II, 356

Providence College, Dominicans teach at, II, 160

Providence Gazette, first newspaper of Providence, IV, 368

Provident Institution for Savings in Boston, earliest savings bank in United States, I, 160

Provincetown Players, III, 286

Provincial Congresses, in Massachusetts, III, 359; and the American Revolution, IV, 468; established by Revolutionary committees, IV, 474

Provoost, Samuel, and the Protestant Episcopal Church, IV, 366

Provost, Etienne, mountain man, I, 128; leads trappers, II, 236; and Ashley's expeditions, V, 310

Pruden, Theophil Mitchell, and hygiene, III, 64

Prudhomme, Fort, built at Chickasaw Bluffs, I, 359; built by LaSalle, V, 242

Prussia, Treaty with (1785), and prisoners of war, IV, 348; and treaties with other foreign nations, V, 316; and laws of war, V, 398

Public Contracts, Division of, of the Department of Labor, III, 221

Public Domain, sales of, and the American System, I, 66; and the Ballinger-Pinchot controversy, I, 149; and canals, I, 303; and the Carey Desert Land Grant Act, I, 313; and claim associations, I, 394; and Connecticut's western lands, II, 24; and conservation movement, II, 27; and the Constitution, II, 38; and the cow custom, II, 78; provision for, in Ohio, II, 97; and Donation Lands, II, 160; used for Federal aid, II, 255; and fencing laws, II, 266; and the Graduation Act, II, 407; and the Greenback party, II, 424; and Harrison Land Act, III, 13; and Homestead Movement, III, 41; administration of, III, 134; and internal improvements, III, 137; sale of, and irrigation, III, 161; and Land Act of 1820, III, 233; and Clay's Land Distribution Bill, III, 234; and land grants to railways, III, 237; and United States General Land Office, III, 237; and land policy,

III, 238; and land speculation, III, 240; and mineral patent laws, III, 406; and the cattle industry, IV, 86; and open range cattle period, IV, 177; survey of, and Ordinance of 1785, IV, 181; sales of, and pre-emption, IV, 330; and public land sales, IV, 371; and public land states, IV, 372; fencing of, IV, 373; and railroads, IV, 407; and the Relief Act of 1821, IV, 441; and school lands, V, 39; and national sinking fund, V, 84; and specie payments, V, 144; granted to railroads, V, 194; sales of, and distribution of surplus revenue, V, 209; and the Union Pacific Railroad, V, 342; and state universities, V, 350; for water power or irrigation, V, 423; of the West, V, 435; and western land cessions, V, 444

Public Faith, and Jeffersonian Democracy, III, 172

"Public Interest, Affected with a," and due process, II, 173; and Munn v. Illinois, IV, 46; in Nebbia v. N. Y., IV, 80; and property, IV, 360; and public utilities, IV, 376; and Wolff Packing Co. case, V, 476

Public Land States, and land grants for education, III, 236; and swamp lands, V, 212

Public Land Strip, I, 375

Public Lands. See Public Domain

Public Ledger (Phila.), and airplane races, I, 36

Public Opinion, and propaganda, IV, 358

Public Opinion in the South during the War, II, 4

Public Ownership, by cities, IV, 43

Public Utilities, and the agrarian movement, I, 21; and the corporation tax, II, 61; regulation of, II, 196; nationalization of, II, 251; franchises to, II, 325; and the holding company, III, 37; and municipal ownership, IV, 42; and rate base, IV, 416; and the Ruef ring, IV, 485; and Smyth v. Ames, V, 105; and the stock market, V, 183; and trusts, V, 327

Public Utility Act of 1935, and the Federal Power Commission, II, 261

Public Works Administration, and Bonneville Dam, I, 209; and Civil Works Administration, I, 393; and Grand Coulee Dam, II, 408; established, III, 135; a New Deal program, III, 144; and national planning, IV, 61; pump-priming agency, IV, 96; and Passamaquoddy, IV, 221; and pump-priming, IV, 382; and relief, IV, 441; and government subsidies to business, V, 195; and the Triborough Bridge, V, 324

Publicity Acts (1903 and 1909), as interstate commerce laws, III, 144

Publicity Laws, and political assessments, IV, 295

Publick Occurrences, first newspaper in American colonies, I, 420; and news reporting, IV, 122; issued by Benjamin Harris, IV, 123, 127

Publishers' Press, V, 346

Publishing, Book, I, 213

Publius, signature in The Federalist, II, 264

Pudding Furnaces, adaptation of, III, 155

Pueblo, Acoma, I, 8; Bonito and Chaco, I, 209; character of, III, 111; maize and bean diet of dwellers in, III, 328

Pueblo Indian Country, Cíbola comes to mean, I, 375

Pueblo Indians, and cliff dwellers, I, 398; hold corn dance, II, 422; and Spanish grants, III, 108; and Mesa Verde, III, 379; exploration of land of, IV, 106; settle at Pecos, IV, 238; and the Rodríguez-Chamuscado expedition (1581), IV, 500; and the Zuñi, V, 515

Pueblo Revolt, and the Jemez Indians, III, 173; destroys missions, III, 418; Santa Fé during, V, 29; and Taos, V, 219

Puerto Rico, acquired, I, 79; and Caribbean policy, I, 313; and DeLima v. Bidwell, II, 133; and the Foraker act, II, 298; ceded to the United States, III, 78; an unincorporated territory, III, 127; as an insular possession, III, 128; ceded to the United States, IV, 216; V, 136; occupied by Nelson A. Miles, V, 137; as cane area, V, 200; and taxation, V, 229; and territorial claims of the United States, V, 247

Puget Sound, explored by Vancouver, V, 357

Pujo Committee, and money power, IV, 9

Pulaski, Casimer, attacked at Egg Harbor, II, 189; commissioned in the Revolutionary Army, IV, 473; killed in siege of Savannah, V, 36

Pulitzer, Joseph, as newspaper editor, IV, 123; and syndicating colored comics, IV, 123; and yellow journalism, V, 505

Pullman, George M., and great fortunes, II, 312

Pullman Strike, and American Railway Union, I, 65; and the Debs case, II, 116; and use of injunction, II, 402; III, 123

Pullmans, and rail transportation, IV, 407; V, 309

Pulteney, William, and New York land speculation, IV, 116

Pump-Priming, and Federal expenditures, II, 235; and Public Works Administration, IV, 378; and government subsidies to business, V, 195

Punishment, capital, I, 308; ducking stool, II, 172; electrocution, II, 200; hanging, III, 7; lethal gas, III, 265; pillory, IV, 271; stocks, V, 183; whipping post, V, 456

Punishments, Cruel and Unusual, and the Bill of Rights, I, 186; II, 40

Purcell, James, and Santa Fé Trail, V, 29

Purcell, Joseph, and topographic mapping, V, 283

Purchas, Samuel, and Hakluyt's Voyages, III, 4

Purchase, Thomas, selects Pejepscot Falls for a settlement, III, 204; IV, 239

Purchasing Power. *See* Money, Purchasing Power of

Pure Food and Drugs Acts, **I,** 15; **II,** 44; **III,** 126, 367; **IV,** 222, 294; **V,** 29

Puritans, and amusements, **I,** 69; and use of the Bible, **I,** 181; attitude of, toward Christmas, **I,** 371; dress of, **II,** 168; and evangelism, **II,** 230; and fast days, **II,** 253; migration of, to Georgia, **II,** 380; and the Great Migration, **II,** 418 f.; and intolerance, **III,** 147; and philosophical thought and writings, **IV,** 263; and the Pilgrims, **IV,** 270; as political exiles, **IV,** 295; and the Providence Island Company, **IV,** 367; as Separatists, **V,** 58; in Maryland, and battle of the Severn, **V,** 61; and sex relations, **V,** 61

Purnell, Benjamin, founder of House of David, **III,** 52

Purnell Act (1925), and agricultural experiment stations, **I,** 25; and farm relief, **II,** 249

Puseyism, or the Oxford movement, **IV,** 194

Pushmataha, Choctaw chief, **I,** 368

Putnam, Fort, **II,** 310; **V,** 438

Putnam, Gideon, opens the Grand Union Hotel at Saratoga, **V,** 32

Putnam, Israel, as brewer, **I,** 236; at Bunker Hill, **I,** 253; and "Don't fire till you see the white of their eyes," **II,** 161; and battle of Long Island, **III,** 299; one of Rogers' Rangers, **IV,** 500; and entrenchments, **V,** 321; and Washington's eight months army, **V,** 419

Putnam, Rufus, builder of West Point fortifications, **II,** 216; and settlement of Marietta, **III,** 343; leading spirit of Ohio Company of Associates, **IV,** 162; surveyor, **V,** 210

Putnams, publishers, **I,** 213

Pyle, Howard, and children's books, **I,** 363

Pynchon, William, and the fur trade, **II,** 361

Q

Quackenbos, G. P., author of *First Lessons in Composition,* **V,** 40

Quaker Hill, Battle of (1778), **IV,** 479

Quakers, and the abolition movement, **I,** 2; and antislavery, **I,** 84; Associators revolt against pacific policy of, **I,** 132; and Cary's rebellion, **I,** 320; and the Civil War, **I,** 388; as conscientious objectors, **II,** 25; as dissenters, **II,** 151; establish the Friendly Association, **II,** 348; and Hicksites, **III,** 29; persecution of, **III,** 147; and the Keith controversy, **III,** 202; and manners, **III,** 333; hanged in New Hampshire, **IV,** 101; gain part of New Jersey, **IV,** 104; arrive in Newport, **IV,** 121; and pacifism, **IV,** 197; and peace movements, **IV,** 234; in Pennsylvania, **IV,** 242; in Philadelphia, **IV,** 258; as political exiles, **IV,** 295; and religious liberty, **IV,** 445; in Rhode Island, **IV,** 477; and American Sect of Shakers, **V,** 63; oppose slavery, **V,** 97; and New England law, **V,** 203; as Virginia exiles, **V,** 378; and West Jersey, **V,** 437

Quantrill Band, **II,** 428; **III,** 252

Quarries, output of, and domestic trade, **V,** 293

Quartering, as a colonial punishment, **IV,** 382

Quartering, and the Bill of Rights, **I,** 186; of British troops, **I,** 187

Quartering Act of 1765, **V,** 289

Quartering Act of 1774, **I,** 187, 408; **III,** 147

Quartermaster Department, and army supply, **I,** 119

Quartermaster General, duties of, **I,** 115

Quasi-Judicial Agencies, defined, **I,** 11; and delegation of powers, **II,** 133; and due process, **II,** 173; creation of, **II,** 259; and the judiciary, **III,** 186

Quebec, siege of (1775), **I,** 297; captured (1759), **II,** 343; attack on (1690), **III,** 211

Quebec Act (1774), and the western country, **I,** 218; introduces English criminal code, **II,** 76; and the Declaration of Rights, **II,** 124; one of the Intolerable Acts, **III,** 147; and the Proclamation of 1763, **IV,** 354; and the American Revolution, **IV,** 467; and Virginia, **V,** 373; and western land claims, **V,** 444

Queen Anne's War, **I,** 88

Queen Elizabeth, stars Sarah Bernhardt, **IV,** 32

Queen Esther, and the Wyoming massacre, **V,** 497

Queen's Rangers, and colonial rangers, **IV,** 416

Queensborough Bridge, opened, **IV,** 119

Queenston Heights, and bombardment of Black Rock, **I,** 196; defeat at, **IV,** 130

Quezon, Manuel, elected president of the Philippine Commonwealth, **IV,** 263

Quick Freezing, and refrigeration, **IV,** 437

Quilting Bees, **I,** 174

Quimby, P. P., and New Thought movement, **IV,** 113

Quincy, Josiah, opposes the Embargo, **II,** 208; and secession, **V,** 51; and the Boston Massacre trial, **V,** 323

Quinine, as remedy for ague, **I,** 34

Quintero, John, Confederate agent, **II,** 5

Quitman, J. A., and the battle of Chapultepec, **I,** 342; and the capture of Mexico City, **III,** 389

Quitrents, on crown lands, **II,** 92; Elizabethtown Associates refuse to pay, **II,** 202; and the Fairfax proprietary, **II,** 240; and national land system, **III,** 241; and Laws, Concessions and Agreements, **III,** 254; in North Carolina, **IV,** 144; and the Transylvania Company, **V,** 310; and settlement of the Wyoming Valley, **V,** 498

Quivira, and the Strait of Anián, **I,** 78; and Oñate's explorations, **IV,** 173

Quo Warranto, and dissolution of the Virginia Company of London, V, 378

R

R. J. Hackett, The, Great Lakes steamship, II, 417

Raccoon, survives in spite of settlement, V, 463

Race Distinction, and "Jim Crow" laws, III, 177

Race Problem, and proslavery, IV, 363

Race Riots, in California, I, 274; at Ellenton, II, 203; at Hamburg, S. C., III, 6; and mobs, IV, 3; in South Carolina, IV, 264; at Wilmington, N. C., V, 469

Race Track Betting, III, 49

Racial Toleration, V, 277

Racketeers, II, 88; IV, 357

Rackham Foundation, II, 314

Radcliffe College, V, 480

Radical Republicans, and amnesty, I, 68; and the Black Codes, I, 193; and the Bloody Shirt, I, 203; and the Civil War, I, 388; and the Committee on the Conduct of the War, I, 436; and impeachment trial of Andrew Johnson, III, 77; impose Ironclad Oath, III, 158; and Joint Committee on Reconstruction, III, 179; and the Union League, III, 312; and McCardle case, III, 363; denounce the Supreme Court after Milligan case, III, 405; opposition to, IV, 63; and pardon and amnesty, IV, 214; and the Pomeroy Circular, IV, 305; and the Porter case, IV, 317; and Reconstruction, IV, 424 ff.; and the Republican party, IV, 454; and Soldiers and Sailors Conventions, V, 117; and Tenure-of-Office Act, V, 246; and Test Oath cases, V, 250; and the Wade-Davis Bill, V, 386

Radicalism, and the American Liberty League, I, 63

Radio, and adult education, I, 14; and advertising, I, 17; as an amusement, I, 71; as campaign expense, I, 293; and political campaigns, I, 295, 296; division of the Department of Commerce, I, 432; and international communications, I, 440; and growth of democracy, II, 135; as educational channel, II, 188; as agency of mass impression, III, 352; and propaganda, IV, 359; and public opinion, IV, 375; and sinking of the Titanic, V, 273; manufactured by Westinghouse Company, V, 448; and wireless telegraphy, V, 472

Radio Commission, superseded by Federal Communications Commission, II, 256

Radio Corporation, and patents, IV, 223

Radio Retailing, trade magazine, V, 298

Radisson, Pierre-Esprit, on Chequamegon Bay, I, 351; coureur de bois, II, 75; western explorations of, III, 56; fur trader, III, 110; and Minnesota, III, 410; and the Mississippi Valley, III, 425; discovers western end of Lake Superior, V, 205

Raikes, Robert, and Sunday Schools, V, 204

Railroad Administration, and the Plumb plan, IV, 289; and railroads, IV, 408; World War, V, 492

Railroad Brotherhoods, refuse to submit to mediation, IV, 402

Railroad Building, and foreign trade, I, 147; and the Civil War, I, 388

Railroad Conductors, Brotherhood of, III, 225; IV, 400

Railroad Employees, legal work day established for, V, 387

Railroad Labor Board, and railroad mediation acts, IV, 402; and Transportation Act of 1920, V, 306

Railroad Pools, IV, 307

Railroad Rates, and Chicago, Milwaukee and St. Paul Railway Company v. Minnesota, I, 356; regulation of, II, 203; and the Granger cases, II, 409, 410; and Hepburn Act of 1906, III, 27; and the packing business, IV, 199; and price fixing, IV, 338; and rebates, IV, 420; and Wabash, St. Louis and Pacific Railroad v. Illinois, V, 385; and Wisconsin Railroad Commission case, V, 474

Railroad Strike of 1877, and martial law, III, 347; a result of the panic of 1873, IV, 209

Railroad Surveys, and the Great Plains, IV, 282

Railroads, and the agrarian movement, I, 21; as influence on agriculture, I, 33; and air conditioning, I, 34; the Atchison, Topeka and Santa Fé, I, 133; the Atlantic and Pacific, I, 135; the Baltimore and Ohio, I, 150; the Chicago, Burlington and Quincy, I, 355; Chicago, Milwaukee, St. Paul and Pacific, I, 356; the Chicago and North Western, I, 357; the Chicago and Rock Island, I, 357; and growth of cities, I, 378; and consequences of the Civil War, I, 383; and the commerce clause, I, 433; influence of, in Civil War, II, 11; the Delaware, Lackawanna and Western, II, 131; and the growth of democracy, II, 135; Federal aid for, II, 255; and freight, II, 340; and government ownership, II, 404; and government regulation, II, 405; the Hannibal and St. Joseph, III, 8; the Illinois Central, III, 70; and immigration, III, 75; and the industrial revolution, III, 118; and internal improvements, III, 138; transcontinental, and Kansas-Nebraska Acts, III, 197; the Kansas Pacific, III, 198; land grants to, III, 237; and Leavenworth and Pikes Peak Express, III, 258; the Lexington and Ohio, III, 267; and locomotives, III, 292; the Louisville and Nashville, III, 310; the Memphis and Charleston, III, 372; the

Michigan Central, **III,** 393; the Michigan Southern, **III,** 393; and the Mississippi River, **III,** 424; the Missouri, Kansas and Texas, **III,** 427; the Missouri Pacific, **III,** 430; the Mohawk and Hudson, **IV,** 4; and municipal ownership, **IV,** 43; the Nashville and Chattanooga, **IV,** 55; the New York Central, **IV,** 117; the North Carolina Railroad, **IV,** 146; the Northern Pacific, **IV,** 148; the Oregon Short Line, **IV,** 185; and the panic of 1837, **IV,** 208; the Pennsylvania, **IV,** 248; the Philadelphia and Reading, **IV,** 259; and the Plumb plan, **IV,** 289; as carriers of the mail, **IV,** 320; and the public domain, **IV,** 370; and the Pullman strike, **IV,** 381; and the recapture clause, **IV,** 421; and the Reconstruction Finance Corporation, **IV,** 428; and reforestation, **IV,** 434; and state debts, **IV,** 456; and Right of Way Law of 1852, **IV,** 484; and river navigation, **IV,** 489; influence on public roads, **IV,** 495; South Carolina Railroad, **V,** 127; the Southern Pacific, **V,** 130; and state debts, **V,** 168; and decline of steamboating, **V,** 179; and the stock market, **V,** 183; and stockyards, **V,** 184; and streamlined trains, **V,** 188; and subsidies, **V,** 194; and domestic trade, **V,** 291, 292; and Transportation Act of 1920, **V,** 305; and decline in river transportation, **V,** 308; the Union Pacific, **V,** 342; and U. S. v. Trans-Missouri Freight Association, **V,** 349; and the urban drift, **V,** 352; and Wabash and Erie Canal, **V,** 386; and wagoners, **V,** 390; the Western and Atlantic, **V,** 440; and destruction of the buffalo, **V,** 463; and the World War, **V,** 492

Rails, and railroads, **IV,** 406

Railton, George Scott, and the Salvation Army, **V,** 20

Railway, Street, **V,** 188

Railway Express Agency, **I,** 60

Railway Labor Act of 1926, and conciliation, **II,** 2; and Virginian Railway Company v. System Federation No. 40, **V,** 380

Railway Mail Service, **IV,** 320

Railway Trainmen, Brotherhood of, **IV,** 400

Railway Wage Board, and railroad mediation acts, **IV,** 402

Rain Makers, and drouths, **II,** 170

Rainfall, and Timber Culture Act, **V,** 270

Rains, Gabriel J., and the Yakima Indian wars, **V,** 500

Rains, James S., and the battle of Dug Springs, **II,** 174

Raisins, for wine making, **V,** 471

Raisuli, Riffian bandit, and the Perdicaris affair, **IV,** 253

Rale. *See* Rasles

Raleigh, Walter, and his attempt to settle Roanoke Island (1585), **I,** 15; the Lost Colony of,

and the Dare stone, **II,** 109; and Gilbert's patent, **II,** 390; failure of his colony, **IV,** 144

Raleigh Register, **III,** 368

Rall, Col., and battle of Trenton, **II,** 131; **V,** 322

Ralston, William C., and the big bonanza, **I,** 444

Ramage, Adam, begins manufacture of printing presses, **IV,** 346

Ramage, John, miniature painter, **III,** 408

Rams, the *Albemarle,* **I,** 46; at Forts Jackson and St. Philip, **IV,** 110; the *Stonewall,* **V,** 185

Ramsay, David, and pamphleteering, **IV,** 202

Ramsay, John, invents corn planter, **II,** 247

Ramsey, Alexander, negotiates treaty at Crow Wing, **II,** 92; governor of Minnesota, **III,** 411; convenes Sioux-Chippewa council, **V,** 84

Rand McNally and Company, **IV,** 355

Randall, Camp, as prison camp, **IV,** 347

Randall, Fort, Sully leaves prisoners at, **II,** 107; Harney builds, **III,** 11

Randall, J. R., author of "Maryland! My Maryland!", **III,** 349, 350

Randall, Robert R., and creation of Sailor's Snug Harbor, **V,** 5

Randall, S. J., as Speaker of the House, **V,** 142

Randolph, Edmund, and the Virginia Plan, **I,** 443; delegate to Convention of 1787, **II,** 50; saved by Jouett's ride, **III,** 182; draws up proclamation of neutrality, **IV,** 91; alumnus of William and Mary College, **V,** 467

Randolph, Edward, sent to investigate the New England colonies, **III,** 357

Randolph, Fort, Cornstalk murdered at, **II,** 61

Randolph, John, coins the term "doughfaces," **II,** 163; duels with Henry Clay, **II,** 174; opposes the Embargo, **II,** 208; and Yazoo land fraud, **III,** 239; and oratory, **IV,** 180; and the *Quids,* **IV,** 390; and soil erosion, **V,** 115; ridicules equalitarian doctrine, **V,** 123; and the Tariff of Abominations, **V,** 223; and the *Quids,* **V,** 249

Randolph, Peyton, and the old regime in Virginia, **V,** 375; alumnus of William and Mary College, **V,** 467

Range Cattle Industry, and the Cow Country, **II,** 78; and growth of cow towns, **II,** 79; and fencing of public lands, **IV,** 373; and the westward movement, **V,** 452

Ranger, The, United States flag flown on, **II,** 281

Ranger, The, and yacht racing, **V,** 499

Rangers, and partisan bands, **IV,** 219

Ranges, and survey of public lands, **IV,** 373

Rankin, Jeannette, first woman elected to Congress, **V,** 478

Rankin, John, and the abolition movement, **I,** 2, 3

Rapp, George, and Harmony Community, **I,** 440; **III,** 11, 397

Rappites, and the American religion, **IV,** 442; and distribution of wealth, **V,** 429

Rasles (or Rale), Jesuit missionary, killed in Dummer's War, **II,** 175; **IV,** 143

Ratcliffe, John, and founding of Jamestown, **III,** 166; **V,** 372

Rate Agreements, and railroad pools, **IV,** 307

Rate Base, and the commerce clause, **I,** 433; and franchises to public utilities, **II,** 325

Rate-Making Power of Legislatures, **V,** 105

Rate Regulation, and due process, **II,** 173

Raton Pass, Arkansas River route crosses, **I,** 107; and Santa Fé Trail, **V,** 30

Rattlesnake Flag, and the Pine Tree Flag, **IV,** 273

Rattletrap, The, galley boat, **II,** 367; used in the Willing expedition, **V,** 469

Rauschenbusch, Walter, and religious thought and writings, **IV,** 447; and the Social Gospel, **V,** 107

Rauschner, Johan Christian, and wax portraits, **V,** 426

Ravenel, Edmund, conchologist, **V,** 123

Ravenel, Henry W., mycologist, **V,** 123

Raw Materials, and national defense, **III,** 80; and domestic trade, **V,** 293; and foreign trade, **V,** 295

Rawle, Francis, and insurance, **III,** 128

Raymbault, Charles, on the Great Lakes, **II,** 415; Jesuit missionary, **III,** 174; and Sault Ste. Marie, **V,** 34; on Lake Superior, **V,** 205

Raymond, Fort, built, **III,** 283

Raymond, Henry J., as newspaper editor, **IV,** 123

Rayon, and industrial chemistry, **I,** 351; production of, **III,** 338; **V,** 79; and textiles, **V,** 258

Raystown, Fort, built as a frontier defense, **I,** 172

Raystown Path, and pack trains, **IV,** 197

Read, A. C., commands the NC-4, **IV,** 79

Read, Daniel, hymn writer, **III,** 65

Read, George, signer of the Constitution, **II,** 39; signer of the Declaration of Independence, **II,** 124; votes against Lee's resolution for independence, **IV,** 500

Read, T. Buchanan, writes poem about Sheridan's ride, **V,** 69

Read Family, in the Donner Party, **II,** 161

Reade, Benjamin, and Yorktown, **V,** 508

Reading, French and Indian raids on, **IV,** 389

Readjusters, in Virginia, **V,** 374

Reagan, John H., and flight of Confederate Cabinet, **II,** 5; appointed Confederate Postmaster General, **IV,** 321

Real Estate Bank, Arkansas repudiates debt of, **I,** 105

Reaper, invention of, **II,** 247; **III,** 148

Reaugh, Frank, artist, pictures the stampede, **V,** 156

Rebates, and the Elkins Act, **II,** 203; and profit-

eering, **IV,** 355; and railroad rate wars, **IV,** 403; and South Improvement Company, **V,** 128

Rebellion, Right of, **III,** 132

Recall, and the Arizona state constitution, **I,** 104; and municipal charters, **I,** 347; an experiment in democracy, **II,** 135; and election laws, **II,** 191; in elections, **II,** 192; and the franchise, **II,** 323; and the judiciary, **III,** 188; and the Oregon system, **IV,** 185

Recession of 1937, **I,** 262

Reciprocal Trade Agreements, encourage flow of trade, **I,** 147; and free trade, **II,** 335; and the Trade Agreements Act, **IV,** 422; the President authorized to negotiate, **IV,** 423; and the tariff, **V,** 223; and the Tariff Commission, **V,** 223; and tariff powers of the President, **V,** 224; and foreign trade, **V,** 296; and commercial treaties, **V,** 315; of the F. D. Roosevelt administration, **V,** 319

Reciprocity, Canadian-American, **I,** 76, 299; **II,** 202; and the Kasson treaties, **III,** 200; and Latin-American relations, **III,** 249; and the McKinley tariff, **III,** 366; and United States commerce with South America, **V,** 123; Canadian-American, **V,** 433

Reclamation, and development of California, **I,** 274; and the Carey Desert Land Grant Act, **I,** 313

Reclamation Act (1902), and the public domain, **IV,** 370

Reclamation Service, **II,** 200; **III,** 135

Recognition, of the Confederacy, **II,** 5; and international law, **III,** 141; of Russia, **IV,** 511

Recojedas, horse gatherings, **II,** 76

Recollects, The. *See* Franciscans

Reconstruction, and amnesty, **I,** 68; an issue in campaign of 1868, **I,** 285; and Civil Rights cases, **I,** 382; and the Clinton riot, **I,** 401; and the Fourteenth Amendment, **II,** 317; and Freedmen's Bureau, **II,** 336; and restoration of home rule in the South, **III,** 41; Joint Committee on, **III,** 179; and Knights of the White Camelia, **III,** 215; and the Ku-Klux Klan, **III,** 217; and Lincoln's assassination, **III,** 280; in Louisiana, **III,** 306; in Mississippi, **III,** 420; and the plantation system of the South, **IV,** 284; and profiteering, **IV,** 355; and the race problem, **IV,** 393; and Radical Republicans, **IV,** 395; and Radical rule in the South, **IV,** 395; and the Republican party, **IV,** 454; and repudiation of state debts, **IV,** 456; and the Democratic party in the Solid South, **V,** 118; in South Carolina, **V,** 126; and state constitutions, **V,** 167; and state debts, **V,** 168; and the Supreme Court Packing Bills, **V,** 208; and Test Oath cases, **V,** 250; in Texas, **V,** 254; and the Thirteenth Amendment, **V,** 264; and the Vicksburg riots, **V,** 367; in Vir-

ginia, V, 374; Lincoln's Plan of, and Wade-Davis Bill, V, 386

Reconstruction Acts, and carpetbaggers, I, 318; and Georgia v. Stanton, II, 381; formulated by the Joint Committee on Reconstruction, III, 179; and the McCardle case, III, 363; and Mississippi v. Johnson, III, 425; and Negro suffrage, IV, 85; and pardon and amnesty, IV, 215; passage of, IV, 426; and Texas, V, 254

Reconstruction Finance Corporation, and banking, I, 157; and the banking crisis of 1933, I, 159; and building and loan associations, I, 249; and the public debt, II, 118; and Export-Import Banks, II, 236; and Farm Credit Agencies, II, 246; and the Warren gold purchase plan, II, 397; as a government corporation, II, 403; and mortgages, IV, 29; and pump-priming, IV, 96, 382; and relief, IV, 440; and housing reform, V, 100; and bank holidays, V, 144; and government subsidies to business, V, 195

Records, Public, I, 103

Recovery, Fort, Indian attack on, II, 241; and treaty of Greenville, II, 425; in the Wayne campaign, V, 427

Recreation, I, 70

Recruiting, and national defense, II, 126

Rector, Henry M., governor of Arkansas, I, 105

Rector's Restaurant, II, 55

Red Bird, uprising of, III, 54; surrender of, ends the Winnebago War, V, 473

Red Cloud, leads Indians in war, III, 95; address of, III, 103; Sioux chief, V, 85

Red Cloud's War, and Bozeman Trail, I, 232; and the abandonment of Fort Connor, II, 24; and treaty of Fort Laramie (1868), III, 245; terminated, V, 87; and Wagon Box Fight, V, 388

Red Cross, and charity organization movement, I, 342; helped by naval forces, IV, 76; convention of 1864, V, 317; and World War relief, V, 487

Red Dog Mining Camp, I, 171

Red Horn, and the Piegan War, IV, 268

"Red Iron Ore," occupational ballad, I, 148

Red Jacket, and Indian oratory, III, 103

Red-Line Map, and the Northeast Boundary dispute, V, 431

Red River, and Greer County, II, 425; Marcy explores, III, 342

Red River Campaign, and the Mississippi Squadron, III, 425

Red River (of the North) Cart Traffic, III, 56; IV, 240

Red River Indian War, and Camp Supply, V, 206

Red River Raft, III, 423

Red River (of the North) Settlements, and the Twin Cities, V, 335

Red River (of the North) Valley Colony, established by Earl of Selkirk, IV, 147

Red River (of the North) Valley Wheat Farms, I, 208

Red Shirts, organized, III, 41

Red Star Line, and sailing packets, IV, 198

Red Sticks, at Callabee Creek, I, 276; name for Upper Creeks, II, 86

Redeemed Captive Returning to Zion, II, 126

Redemptioners, as indentured servants, III, 85; in Pennsylvania, IV, 242

Redpath, J. C., and the lyceum movement, III, 316

Redress of Grievances, and the American Revolution, IV, 467

Redstone Old Fort, erected, III, 295; and the Ohio Company of Virginia, IV, 163

Redwood Library, III, 272

Reed, D. E., and Company, editors and proprietors of the Nebraska Palladium, IV, 127

Reed, Ebenezer, co-founder of the Detroit Gazette, IV, 124, 127

Reed, Joseph, and mutiny of Pennsylvania troops, IV, 248

Reed, Rebecca Theresa, and the burning of the Ursuline Convent, V, 353

Reed, Thomas B., as floor leader, II, 287; as Speaker of the House, V, 142

Reed, Walter, and yellow fever, III, 369; student of University of Virginia, V, 375; and yellow fever, V, 505

Reed Rules, for the House, IV, 506

Reed Treaty of 1858, supplemented by Burlingame Treaty, I, 256; and American intervention in China, III, 145

Reeder, Andrew A., and Border Ruffians, I, 219; and Kansas Free-State party, III, 196; and the Kansas Struggle, III, 198

Reese, John, makes first permanent settlement in Nevada, IV, 93

Reeve, Tapping, establishes the Litchfield Law School, III, 283

Referendum, adopted in Arkansas, I, 105; and municipal charters, I, 347; an experiment in democracy, II, 135; and election laws, II, 191; and the franchise, II, 323; and the legislature, III, 263; and the Oregon system, IV, 185; and state constitutions, V, 167

Refineries, and Standard Oil Company, V, 156

Refinery Forges, and early iron making, III, 158

Reforestation, and the lumber industry, III, 314

Reform, an issue in campaign of 1876, I, 286; and Federal-state relations, II, 263; and religion, IV, 442; and religious periodicals, IV, 445

Reform Schools, and industrial farms, III, 115; and prisons, IV, 348

Reformed Church in America. See Dutch Reformed Church

Reformed Germans, immigration of, **II**, 383

Refrigeration, and fisheries, **I**, 407; and the dairy industry, **II**, 104; in drying fruits and vegetables, **II**, 169; and fruit growing, **II**, 354; and the livestock industry, **III**, 286; and meat packing, **IV**, 199

Refugio, Mission of, **III**, 418

Regicides, and King's Messengers, **III**, 212

Regional Agricultural Credit Corporations, **II**, 246

Regional Banks for Co-operatives, **II**, 245

Register of Debates, **II**, 21; **III**, 182

Registration, and election laws, **II**, 191; and elections, **II**, 192; and repeating, **IV**, 451

Regular Army, in Civil War, **I**, 111; of the United States, **I**, 112; on the frontier, **I**, 117; during World War, **IV**, 2; and National Guard, **IV**, 60; and Officers' Reserve Corps, **IV**, 158. *See also* Army, United States

Regular Army Reserve, creation of, **II**, 217

Regulation, Government, by administrative discretion, **I**, 11; of business, **I**, 260; by Interstate Commerce laws, **III**, 143 f.; and property, **IV**, 360; and public utilities, **IV**, 375 ff.; and quasi-judicial agencies, **IV**, 387; and Federal taxing power, **V**, 232

Regulators of North Carolina, and the battle of Alamance, **I**, 41; and Watauga settlement, **V**, 420; and the West, **V**, 435; and the westward movement, **V**, 450

Reichert, Frederick, and the Harmony Society, **III**, 11

Reid, Mayne, writer of outdoor adventure stories, **II**, 147

Reid, Whitelaw, as newspaper editor, **IV**, 123

Reiersen, J. R., and Norwegian immigration, **IV**, 152

Reihle, Antoine, and Spanish-Missouri Fur Company, **V**, 141

Reilly, H. I., builds first garbage furnace, **V**, 29

Reindeer Service, **II**, 189

Relief, and campaign resources, **I**, 294; and organized charity, **I**, 342; and Federal-state relations, **II**, 263; and the Hatch Act, **III**, 16; and migratory labor, **III**, 220; and lobbying, **III**, 287; and the New Deal, **IV**, 96; and pauperism, **IV**, 226; and state debts, **V**, 168; and taxation, **V**, 227

Relief Agencies, and political assessments, **IV**, 295

Religion, and the Great Awakening, **II**, 413

Religion, Freedom of, and the Bill of Rights, **I**, 185

Religious Groups, and colonial society, **I**, 424

Religious Liberty, and the Constitution, **II**, 39; growth of, **IV**, 442; in Rhode Island, **IV**, 477; and the Rogerenes, **IV**, 500; and tolerance, **V**, 277; and Toleration Acts, **V**, 278; established in Virginia, **V**, 373

Religious Papers, and advertising, **I**, 16, 18

Remington, E., and Sons, and the typewriter, **V**, 336

Remington, Frederick, artist, pictures the stampede, **V**, 156; "The Fight at the Water Hole," **V**, 263

Removal, Presidential Power of, **I**, 90

Remudas, and rodeos, **IV**, 499

Renault, Philippe François, and lead mining, **III**, 254, 407; commissioned director general of mining operations, **V**, 9

Reno, Fort, and Bozeman Trail, **I**, 232; Fort Connor rebuilt as, **II**, 24; and Red Cloud War, **IV**, 429

Reno, M. A., and Little Big Horn battle, **III**, 284

Renos, The, and train robberies, **I**, 152; **V**, 303

Rensselaer School, for industrial education, **III**, 114; **V**, 44

Rensselaerswyck, manor of, **III**, 55; patroonship of, **IV**, 108

Renters, Farm, **II**, 250

Renwick, James, author of *A Treatise on the Steam Engine*, **II**, 215; and the Morris Canal, **IV**, 27

Reparation Commission, and the Treaty of Vienna, **I**, 139; and Treaty of Versailles, **V**, 363

Reparations, and the armistice of 1918, **I**, 109; and the balance of trade, **I**, 147; and the Bank for International Settlements, **I**, 154; and the Treaty of Berlin (1921), **I**, 179; and the Dawes Plan, **II**, 113; and the building of the dirigible ZR-3, **II**, 149; and the Fourteen Points, **III**, 84; and the Paris Agreement (1925), **IV**, 217; and Treaty of Versailles, **V**, 363; and the Wadsworth Agreement, **V**, 386; and settlement of War Claims Act, **V**, 400; and war debts, **V**, 401; and the World War Peace Conference (1919), **V**, 490; and the Young Plan, **V**, 510

Representation, and apportionment, **I**, 92; and compromises of the Federal Constitution, **I**, 443; and the Convention of 1787, **II**, 51

Representatives, House of, intended to have dominant power, **II**, 258; and gag rules, **II**, 366; rules of the, **IV**, 506

Republic, newspaper of the Taylor administration, **II**, 404

Republic, The, and the first important SOS call, **V**, 472

Republican Elephant, popularized by Nast, **I**, 320; **IV**, 56

Republican Party, and the agrarian movement, **I**, 21; and the antislavery movement, **I**, 86; and Appeal of the Independent Democrats, **I**, 89; and the Barnburners, **I**, 164; and Progressives, **I**, 250; in campaign of 1856, **I**, 284; in cam-

paigns of 1860 and 1864, **I**, 285; in campaigns of 1868, 1872, 1876, **I**, 286; in campaigns of 1876, 1880, 1884, 1888, **I**, 287; in campaigns of 1888, 1892, 1896, **I**, 288; in campaigns of 1896, 1900, 1904, **I**, 289; in campaigns of 1908, 1912, 1916, 1920, **I**, 290; in campaigns of 1920, 1924, 1928, **I**, 291; in campaigns of 1932 and 1936, **I**, 292; and Federal financing of the Civil War, **I**, 384; and compensated emancipation, **II**, 205; successor to Free Soil party, **II**, 334; and "Half-Breeds," **III**, 5; and the Homestead Movement, **III**, 43; formed after repeal of Missouri Compromise, **III**, 430; and panic of 1857, **IV**, 208; as a political party, **IV**, 297; and popular sovereignty, **IV**, 309; and religion, **IV**, 443; and sectionalism, **V**, 55; and slavery, **V**, 96; in the South, **V**, 118; and states' rights, **V**, 176; and the Taft-Roosevelt split, **V**, 217; organized as third party, **V**, 262; and the Union party, **V**, 343; founded on the Wilmot Proviso principle, **V**, 469; birthplace of the, **V**, 474

Republican Party, Jeffersonian, and the agrarian movement, **I**, 20; and the Alien and Sedition Act, **I**, 48; and the Anti-Federalists, **I**, 81; *Aurora* as mouthpiece of, **I**, 139; and campaigns of 1796–1812, **I**, 281; and gerrymandering, **II**, 386; and the Jefferson-Burr election dispute, **III**, 170; and Marbury v. Madison, **III**, 341; and the Martling men, **III**, 348; and *National Intelligencer*, **IV**, 60; divides into two parties, **IV**, 62; advocates protection of states' rights, **IV**, 64; and the Northwest Territory, **IV**, 151; dominates political life of Ohio, **IV**, 160; and party government, **IV**, 220; as a political party, **IV**, 296; and first threat of secession, **V**, 51; and spoils system, **V**, 147; and states' rights, **V**, 176; and "the wise, and good and rich," **V**, 475

Republican-Progressive League, **V**, 217

Republicanism, and political theories, **IV**, 301

Repudiation of State Debts, in Arkansas, **I**, 105; and internal improvements, **III**, 138. *See also* State Debts

Requisitions, and financing of the Revolution, **IV**, 471

Rescuer, newspaper published during Oberlin-Wellington rescue case, **IV**, 156

Reserve Officers' Training Corps, and army peace-time work, **I**, 111; formation of, **I**, 114; and Officers' Reserve Corps, **IV**, 158

Reserved Powers, and the Bill of Rights, **I**, 186; and commerce clause, **I**, 433; and the Constitution, **II**, 40; police power as one of the, **IV**, 294

Reserves, The, and national defense, **II**, 127

Resettlement, and migratory labor, **III**, 220

Resettlement Administration, continues work of the Federal Emergency Relief Administration,

II, 257; and Department of the Interior, **III**, 135; and relief to farmers, **IV**, 441

Resolutions, Legislative, and the Constitution, **II**, 33. *See also* Joint Resolutions

Restraining Acts, **I**, 408

Restraint of Trade, and the Clayton Act, **I**, 396; combinations in, **I**, 433; and the injunction, **III**, 123; forbidden by Sherman Antitrust Act, **III**, 144

Resumption Act, and campaign of 1876, **I**, 286; and Greenbacks, **II**, 424; and the Greenback party, **II**, 424; passed, **V**, 144

Retail Business, and the distribution of merchandise, **II**, 152; and domestic trade, **V**, 293

Retaliation, and the submarine, **V**, 193

Retirement Annuities, provided, **IV**, 96

Revels, Hiram R., and carpetbaggers, **I**, 318

Revenue, The Public, and the Constitution, **II**, 32

Revenue Cutter Service, replaced by Coast Guard, **I**, 405; and lifesaving service, **III**, 276

Revere, Paul, and early American advertisements, **I**, 16; picture of Boston Massacre, **I**, 223; and political cartoons, **I**, 320; warns of attack on Concord, **III**, 267; and North Church, **IV**, 146; and the Penobscot expedition, **IV**, 249; as silversmith, **V**, 82; takes Suffolk Resolves to the Continental Congress, **V**, 198; and Fort William and Mary, **V**, 467

Revised Industrial Mobilization Plan of 1933, **V**, 489

Revision, Council of, abolished in New York, **IV**, 117

Revivals, the Second Awakening, **I**, 143; and the Bible, **I**, 181; and camp meetings, **I**, 280; Cane Ridge, **I**, 304; and the Cumberland Presbyterian Church, **II**, 97; and evangelism, **II**, 230; and fast days, **II**, 254; Finney's, **II**, 275; the Great, **II**, 419; and mourners' bench, **IV**, 37; and nativism, **IV**, 65; and the New Lights, **IV**, 106; and the Protestant Episcopal Church, **IV**, 366; and the Protracted Meeting, **IV**, 367; and the Quakers, **IV**, 386; and religion on the frontier, **IV**, 444; and religious thought, **IV**, 446; and antislavery movement, **V**, 97; and theological writings, **V**, 261

Revolution, American, and the Convention of Aranjuez, **I**, 94; Associations in, **I**, 131; funding of debt of the, **I**, 132; financing of, **I**, 156; bills of credit in, **I**, 187; and the Continental Congress, **II**, 46; financing of, **II**, 100; and public debt, **II**, 117; financing of, **II**, 118; and the signing of the Declaration of Independence, **II**, 121; and the Declaration of Rights, **II**, 124; financing of, **II**, 128; and the Definitive Treaty of Peace (1783), **II**, 128; and Detroit, **II**, 143; and fast days, **II**, 254; Navy in, **II**, 282; and the

Franco-American Alliance, **II**, 326; Indians in, **III**, 88; and inflation, **III**, 120; peace resolutions of British Parliament to end, **IV**, 236; and proprietary provinces, **IV**, 362; and Provincial Congresses, **IV**, 368; and British attack on St. Louis, **V**, 11; cost of, **V**, 409; loss of life in, **V**, 410; and distribution of wealth, **V**, 429

Revolution, Right of, justified by Locke, **III**, 291; and personal liberty, **IV**, 254; and political theories, **IV**, 300; and recognition policy, **IV**, 424

Revolutionary Army, formation of, **I**, 112; insignia of rank in, **I**, 114; and hospitalization, **I**, 116; and bonuses, **I**, 209; organized at Boston, **I**, 222; and bounties, **I**, 228; and the Society of the Cincinnati, **I**, 375; demobilization of, **II**, 133; enlistment in, **II**, 217; mobilization of, **IV**, 2; and uniforms, **V**, 340; encamps at Valley Forge, **V**, 355

Reynards, French name for Fox Indians, **II**, 319

Reynolds, Charlie, scout, **V**, 46

Reynolds, J. F., and battle of Gettysburg, **II**, 386

Reynolds, John, and the Black Hawk purchase, **I**, 194

Reynolds, Williams, and occupation of the Midway Islands, **III**, 395

Rezánof, Count, in California, **I**, 270; and Russian claims, **IV**, 511

Rhett, Alfred, in command of Fort Sumter, **V**, 203

Rhett, R. B., and Bluffton movement, **I**, 206; and public opinion in South during Civil War, **II**, 4; advocates secession, **II**, 275; journalist, **V**, 123

Rhineland High Commission, Gen. Allen works in conjunction with (1920), **I**, 116

Rhode and Lusk's Express, robbery of, **V**, 153

Rhode Island, center of Baptist religion, **I**, 161; Dorr's Rebellion in, **II**, 162; founded, **III**, 357; and Providence Plantations, **IV**, 367; Quakers in, **IV**, 386

Rhode-Island Gazette, founded by James Franklin, **IV**, 127

Ribaut, Jean, claims Florida for France, **II**, 288; and settlement of Port Royal (S. C.), **IV**, 315; attempts to establish a colony on Parris Island, **V**, 125

Rice, and the plantation type of agriculture, **I**, 27; governmental control of, **I**, 33; bounties, **I**, 228; and the Cape Fear River settlements, **I**, 307; and colonial commerce, **I**, 417; as enumerated commodity, **II**, 219; in Louisiana, **III**, 306; and the Navigation Acts, **IV**, 74; and the plantation system of the South, **IV**, 284; as colonial staple, **V**, 159; and domestic trade, **V**, 292; and foreign trade, **V**, 294; wild, **V**, 463

Rice, Fort, Sully's supplies carried to, **II**, 107; and Fisk's overland expeditions, **II**, 278

Rice, Thomas D., and minstrel shows, **III**, 412

Rice's (Dan) Floating Palace, **V**, 76

Rich, Caleb, and the Universalists, **V**, 350

Rich, Lorimer, and the Tomb of the Unknown Soldier, **V**, 351

Richards, Willard, editor and publisher of the *Deseret News*, **IV**, 127

Richardson, H. H., builds Trinity Church in Boston, **I**, 101; architect, **V**, 87

Richardson, John, and search for Northwest Passage, **IV**, 151

Richardson, Joseph, silversmith, **V**, 82

Richardson, W. A., territorial governor of Nebraska, **IV**, 80

Richardson, W. A., and the Sanborn contracts, **V**, 26

Richelieu River-Lake Champlain Route, **IV**, 316

Richmond, Mary, author of *Social Diagnosis*, **V**, 110

Richmond and Petersburg Railroad, **I**, 135

Richmond *Enquirer*, as political organ, **IV**, 128; and the Richmond Junto, **IV**, 482; Southern newspaper, **V**, 123

Richmond Junto, and the Richmond *Enquirer*, **IV**, 129

Richmond *Whig*, supports the Readjuster movement, **IV**, 418; Southern newspaper, **V**, 123

Rickard, Tex, prize fight promoter, **IV**, 353

Ricketts, Howard Taylor, and medicine, **III**, 370

Riddle, Eliza, barnstormer, **I**, 164

Riddleberger, H. H., and the Readjuster movement, **IV**, 419

Ridge, John, negotiates treaty of New Echota, **IV**, 97

Ridgefield, Conn., Tryon withdraws forces through, **II**, 108

Ridgely, Fort, and the expeditions of Sibley and Sully, **II**, 106; and Sioux uprising in Minnesota, **V**, 86

Riding Exhibitions, at Fort Myer, **IV**, 51

Rifles, as munitions, **IV**, 44; used by the Revolutionary Army, **IV**, 473

Rigby, Alexander, purchases Lygonia, **III**, 316

Rigdon, Sidney, and Reorganized Latter Day Saints, **IV**, 449

Riggs, Romulus, and military tracts, **III**, 403

Riggs, Stephen R., organizes the Hazelwood Republic, **III**, 21

Right of Search. *See* Visit and Search

Rights, Inalienable, **I**, 185

Rights of Englishmen, and civil liberties, **I**, 381; and colonial charters, **I**, 417; and the colonial judiciary, **I**, 419; and Otis' tract, **I**, 425; and the British constitution, **II**, 29; and freedom, **II**, 336; and personal liberty, **IV**, 254; and Stamp Act, **V**, 155; and Stamp Act Congress, **V**, 155; and unreasonable searches and seizures, **V**, 351

Rights of Man, by Thomas Paine, **IV**, 263

Riley, Bennett C., and the Yellowstone River expedition, V, 506

Riley, Edward, and Iowa Corn Song, III, 153

Riley, Fort, established, III, 194

Ringgold, Cadwalader, commander of North Pacific Surveying expedition, III, 63; IV, 77

Ringgold Gap, and Chattanooga campaign, I, 348

Rings, and party machines, III, 318

Rio de Janeiro, Pan-American Conference at (1906), IV, 202

Rio Grande River, in American diplomacy, IV, 492

Rio Napestle, name given to Arkansas River by the Spanish explorer Uribarri, I, 106

Riots, at Baltimore, I, 151; the Bedini, I, 173; the Cœur d'Alene, I, 409; at New Orleans, IV, 111

Rip Van Winkle, I, 325, 363

Riparian Ownership, and Kansas-Colorado water rights litigation, III, 196

Ripley, Fort, trouble with Indians near, II, 92

Ripley, George, and Brook Farm, I, 242

Ripon, Wis., and Republican party, IV, 454; V, 474

Rise of Silas Lapham, written by W. D. Howells, II, 270

Rising, Johan, surrender of Fort Casimir to, IV, 95, 113

Ritchie, Thomas, duels with John H. Pleasants, II, 174; editor of the Washington *Union,* II, 404; and the Richmond *Enquirer,* IV, 129; and the Richmond Junto, IV, 482; journalist, V, 123

Rittenhouse, David, first telescope maker, IV, 156

Rittenhouse, William, and the first paper mill, IV, 212

River Pirates, I, 152

River Queen, The, Hampton Roads conference held on, III, 7

River Towns of Connecticut, settled, II, 21; federate under the Fundamental Orders, II, 22; and the Old Patent, II, 23; and group migration, III, 396; and the Pequot War, IV, 252; and the Plymouth Trading Post, IV, 291; and Saybrook, V, 36; and the Western Reserve, V, 445; and the westward movement, V, 450

Rivers, Gallatin's Report on, II, 367

Rivers and Harbors, appropriations for, III, 137; and the War Department, V, 402

Rives, John C., journalist, V, 123

Rives, William C., and French spoliation claims, II, 347

Rivière aux Chevaux, and Buffalo, N. Y., I, 247

Rivière des Iroquois, French name for the Richelieu River, IV, 481

Road and Bridge Districts, as a political subdivision, IV, 299

Roads, and agriculture, I, 27; and the Department of Agriculture, I, 31; and the automobile, I, 140; legislation regarding, II, 260; Gallatin's Report on, II, 367; hard, III, 9; as internal improvements, III, 139; and state aid, V, 163; and state debts, V, 168; and the General Survey Act of 1824, V, 209; and taxation, V, 227; toll, V, 278; and touring, V, 286; and domestic trade, V, 291; and travel, V, 306; and turnpikes, V, 331; affect the wayside markets, V, 428; and the Weeks Act, V, 433

Roane, Spencer, and the Richmond *Enquirer,* IV, 129

Robbery, and crime, II, 88

Robbins, M., invents corn planter, II, 247

Robert E. Lee, The, steamboat race of, V, 178

Robert E. Lee Mine, III, 254

Roberts, Edmund, and treaties with foreign nations, V, 317

Roberts, O. J., and Rickert Rice Mills, Inc. v. Fontenot, IV, 482

Robertson, James, and the Cherokee wars, I, 353; follows the Cumberland River, II, 97; founds settlement at French Lick, II, 98; and Watauga settlement, II, 235; and expansion into Kentucky, III, 235; and founding of Nashville, IV, 54; and settlement of Tennessee, V, 242; and Watauga settlement, V, 421

Robidou, Antoine, builds Fort Uinta, II, 236; V, 337

Robidoux, Joseph, founder of St. Joseph, Mo., V, 10; and Spanish-Missouri Fur Company, V, 141

Robinhood, Kennebec chief, III, 204

Robinson, Charles, and the Kansas Free-State party, III, 197; and the Kansas Struggle, III, 198; and Topeka constitution, V, 281; and the Wakarusa War, V, 391

Robinson, Doane, and the Borglum colossal sculptures, I, 221

Robinson, Fort, Dull Knife's people placed in barracks at, II, 175

Robinson, John, and first jury trial in Anglo-Saxon America, III, 167

Robinson, John, and the Puritans, IV, 271

Robinson, John, organizes the Greenbrier Company, II, 424

Robinson, John, circus of, as showboat, V, 76

Robinson, Joseph T., nominated for Vice-Presidency, I, 291; as floor leader, II, 287

Robinson, Samuel, and the New Hampshire Grants, V, 362

Robinson-Patman Act, extends regulation of business, I, 260; and the Federal Trade Commission, II, 264; and the New Deal, IV, 96; and price maintenance, IV, 340; and trade practices, V, 299; and antitrust legislation, V, 327

Rochambeau, Jean Baptiste Donatien de Vimeur

Comte de, marches from Newport, **II**, 343; lands his army at Newport, **IV**, 122; in the Revolutionary War, **IV**, 477; and the battle of Virginia Capes, **V**, 376; and Yorktown campaign, **V**, 509

Rochdale Plan, and consumer co-operatives, **II**, 56; and Sovereigns of Industry, **V**, 134

Roche à Davion, first name of Loftus Heights, **III**, 294

Rochester, N. Y., a boom town, **I**, 215; city directory appears in, **II**, 148

Rochester Athenæum and Mechanics Institute, **III**, 114

Rock Island, Ill., Fort Armstrong located at foot of, **I**, 109; arsenal at, **I**, 122; atrocity stories concerning prison camp at, **I**, 136; prison camp at, **IV**, 347

Rockefeller, John D., benefactions and gifts of, **I**, 177; and great fortunes, **II**, 312; establishes the General Education Board, **II**, 375; and Mesabi Iron Range, **III**, 379; and philanthropy, **IV**, 260; utilizes South Improvement Company, **V**, 128; original stockholder of the Standard Oil Company, **V**, 156

Rockefeller, John D., Jr., and great fortunes, **II**, 312; restores buildings at William and Mary College, **V**, 467, 468

Rockefeller, William, original stockholder of Standard Oil Company, **V**, 156

Rockefeller Center, and architecture, **I**, 101

Rockefeller Foundation, endowment of, **II**, 314; and research in Latin America concerning yellow fever, **III**, 249; and American benevolence, **IV**, 260; grants foreign exchange fellowships, **V**, 191; and World War relief, **V**, 488

Rockefeller Sanitary Commission, and hookworm disease, **III**, 44

Rockhill, W. W., and the Peking Congress, **IV**, 239

Rockwell, D. S., invents corn planter, **II**, 247

Rocky Mountain Fur Company, and Ashley's expeditions, **I**, 128; and the fur trade, **II**, 362; and Green River, **II**, 423; and Leavenworth expedition, **III**, 258; and Missouri River fur trade, **III**, 431; and Snake River, **V**, 106; and trappers' rendezvous, **V**, 310; and exploration of Wyoming, **V**, 496

Rocky Mountain National Park, **IV**, 218

Rocky Mountain News, published by W. N. Byers, **IV**, 126

Rodeos, and Courts of the Plains, **II**, 76; Spanish origin of, **V**, 138; and the Wild West Shows, **V**, 464. *See also* Roundups

Rodgers, John, relieves Barron in the Barbary Wars, **I**, 162; and *Constellation-Insurgente* action, **II**, 28; appointed to Board of Navy Commissioners, **IV**, 75; and the *President,* **IV**, 334

Rodgers, John, **II**, commander of North Pacific Surveying expedition, **III**, 63; and war with Korea, **III**, 216; and the Mississippi Squadron, **III**, 425; **IV**, 77, 485

Rodgers and Burchfield, tin plate company, **V**, 272

Rodman, Hugh, and the Navy in the World War, **V**, 493

Rodney, Cæsar R., signer of the Declaration of Independence, **II**, 124; and the Philadelphia cordwainers' case, **IV**, 259

Rodríguez, Agustin, and the Beltrán-Espejo expedition, **I**, 177; and missions of the Southwest, **III**, 418; explorations of, **IV**, 106

Roebling, John A., and suspension bridges, **I**, 238; and Brooklyn Bridge, **I**, 243; builds railroad bridge over Niagara, **IV**, 131

Roebuck, A. C., and mail-order houses, **III**, 325

Rogers, Galbraith P., attempts to win Hearst's flying prize, **I**, 142

Rogers, James Gamble, architect of Harkness Memorial, **I**, 101

Rogers, Robert, and Carver's travels, **I**, 320; at Michilimackinac, **III**, 394; and the Pontiac War, **IV**, 305. *See also* Rogers' Rangers

Rogers, Thomas, locomotive builder, **IV**, 406

Rogers, Will, and humorous lecturing, **III**, 260

Rogers Act, and foreign service, **II**, 306; **V**, 163

Rogers Groups, of enlarged mantelpiece compositions, **I**, 123

Rogers' Rangers, and the Abenaki, **I**, 1; in French and Indian War, **III**, 229; conduct raid on St. Francis Indians, **III**, 229; and colonial rangers, **IV**, 416; expedition against St. Francis, **V**, 8

Rogue River Indians, land cessions of, **III**, 100

Rolette, Joseph, trader at Prairie du Chien, **IV**, 328

Rolfe, John, and tobacco cultivation, **III**, 167; **V**, 274, 372

Rolfe (John) House, architecture of, **I**, 99

Roller Skating, **I**, 70

Rolles, Dennis, founds Rollestown, **II**, 288

Rolling Mills, adaptation of, **III**, 155

Rolvaag, O. E., and fiction, **II**, 270

Roma, The, semirigid dirigible purchased by the Government, **I**, 148

Roman Nose, in the battle of Beecher Island, **I**, 173; and the Kidder massacre, **III**, 208

Romans, Bernard, explores the Tombigbee Valley region, **V**, 280; and topographic mapping, **V**, 283

Rookery, architecture of, **V**, 87

Roosevelt, Franklin D., and the more abundant life, **I**, 5; and administrative reorganization, **I**, 12; and the Agricultural Adjustment Administration Act of 1938, **I**, 24; and farm relief, **I**, 32; and the Brain Trust, **I**, 234; proclaims silver

price, **I**, 252; nominated for Vice-Presidency, **I**, 291; elected President, **I**, 292; and the "good neighbor policy," **I**, 314; and the National Recovery Administration, **II**, 17; and "economic royalists," **II**, 184; and emergency legislation, **II**, 210; urges a Federal wage and hour law, **II**, 239; and the Presidency, **II**, 259; and the "Forgotten Man," **II**, 310; calls in gold certificates, **II**, 394; proclaims nationwide banking moratorium, **II**, 394; and the Gold Reserve Act of 1934, **II**, 397; and the "good neighbor policy," **II**, 400; and conference of governors, **II**, 406; and the Hatch Act, **III**, 16; and Humphrey's Executor v. U. S., **III**, 59; advocates unemployment insurance, **III**, 131; recommends the item veto, **III**, 164; and managed currency, **III**, 330; and the National Recovery Administration, **IV**, 61; and the New Deal, **IV**, 95; and oratory, **IV**, 180; and Buenos Aires Peace Conference, **IV**, 231; and the Presidency, **IV**, 333; and presidential absences from American soil, **IV**, 335; and special powers granted to Presidents, **IV**, 335; and the presidential message, **IV**, 336; and pump-priming, **IV**, 382; and railroad retirement acts, **IV**, 404; and relief, **IV**, 440; and removal power, **IV**, 448; and repudiation of public debt, **IV**, 455; and Russian recognition, **IV**, 511; and bank moratoriums, **V**, 144; and the Supreme Court Packing Bills, **V**, 208; and Tammany Hall, **V**, 218; changes date of Thanksgiving Day, **V**, 259; whispering campaigns against, **V**, 458; and the World Economic Conference, **V**, 486; and the National Youth Administration, **V**, 511

Roosevelt, Nicholas, and the steamboat, **III**, 148; builds the *New Orleans,* **III**, 423; **IV**, 110

Roosevelt, The, used in Peary's polar expedition, **IV**, 237

Roosevelt, Theodore, and the Alaska Boundary Tribunal, **I**, 44; and the Algeciras Conference, **I**, 48; and the Ananias Club, **I**, 72; and the anthracite strike, **I**, 80; orders cruise of fleet round the world, **I**, 168; and the Bidlack-Mallarino Treaty, **I**, 183; bolts 1912 convention, **I**, 208; and Brownsville affair, **I**, 245; and "Bull Moose" party, **I**, 250; elected Vice-President (1900), **I**, 289; elected President (1904), **I**, 289; and campaigns of 1912 and 1916, **I**, 290; and the conservation movement, **II**, 27; and the Presidency, **II**, 259; and filling vacancies in consular service, **II**, 306; and first conference of governors, **II**, 406; and Hague Peace Conference, **III**, 2; and hyphenate groups, **III**, 65; and isolation, **III**, 163; and Japanese exclusion, **III**, 168; expedition to Latin America, **III**, 248; and the Lily-White movement, **III**, 277; and "lunatic fringe," **III**, 314; and party machines, **III**,

318; and "malefactors of great wealth," **III**, 329; and *modus vivendi,* **IV**, 4; and the Monroe Doctrine, **IV**, 14; and muckrakers, **IV**, 38; and New Nationalism, **IV**, 107; wins Nobel Peace Prize, **IV**, 136; and oratory, **IV**, 180; and the Panama revolution, **IV**, 207; modernizes the White House to include ten bathrooms, **IV**, 289; forms the Progressive party, **IV**, 297; and the treaty of Portsmouth, **IV**, 317; and Preparedness, **IV**, 331; and the Presidency, **IV**, 333; revitalizes the presidential message, **IV**, 336; and the Progressive movement, **IV**, 356; and Pure Food and Drug Acts, **IV**, 383; and race suicide, **IV**, 394; and the Republican party, **IV**, 454; and the Rough Riders, **IV**, 503; and Sampson-Schley controversy, **V**, 22; and the "Square Deal," **V**, 151; and the Taft-Katsura memorandum, **V**, 217; and the split with Taft, **V**, 217; and the "Tennis Cabinet," **V**, 246; and third-term doctrine, **V**, 263; and "trust-busting," **V**, 326; and trusts, **V**, 326; and blockade of Venezuela, **V**, 359; and water power conservation, **V**, 423; adopts the appellation, White House, **V**, 459; and the United States as a world power, **V**, 486

Roosevelt Corollary to the Monroe Doctrine, **I**, 313; **III**, 249; **IV**, 15, 139; **V**, 396

Root, Elihu, and the Alaska Boundary Tribunal, **I**, 44; and arbitration treaties of 1908, **I**, 97; organizes Army War College, **I**, 119; formulates the Platt Amendment, **II**, 94; and the Permanent Court of International Justice, **III**, 142; and Pan-American conferences, **IV**, 202; and Hague Peace conferences, **IV**, 232; and the Platt Amendment, **IV**, 286; and repeal of Tolls Exemption Act, **V**, 279; and the Waterways Treaty, **V**, 425; and the World Court, **V**, 485

Root, Erastus, and the Working Man's party, **V**, 484

Root, George F., popular songs of, **V**, 120

Rosalie, Fort, established by Bienville, **IV**, 56; the Natchez Indians allow French to build, **IV**, 57; renamed Fort Panmure, **IV**, 210

Rose, John, and the Alabama Claims, **I**, 41; and the Treaty of Washington (1871), **V**, 416

Rose, Wyckliffe, and the Peabody Fund, **IV**, 230

Rosebud Reservation, **V**, 127

Rosebud River, and the Cheyenne Indians, **I**, 355

Rosecrans, W. S., and Chattanooga campaign, **I**, 348; and battle of Chickamauga, **I**, 359; attacked at Corinth, **II**, 59; takes command of Army of the Cumberland, **II**, 96; and battle of Iuka, **III**, 164; and Army of the Mississippi, **III**, 419; and battle of Murfreesboro, **IV**, 46; and battle of Rich Mountain, **IV**, 481; and the Tullahoma campaign, **V**, 329

Rosenau, Milton Joseph, and preventive medicine and hygiene, **III**, 64

Rosenwald, Julius, joins Sears, Roebuck and Company, **III**, 325; philanthropy of, **IV**, 260

Rosenwald (Julius) Fund, **II**, 314

Rosier, James, describes Pemaquid, **IV**, 239

Ross, Alexander, builds Fort Nez Percé, **V**, 393

Ross, Alexander C., and campaign songs, **I**, 294

Ross, Charley, kidnapping of, **III**, 208

Ross, David, as Indian factor, **III**, 97

Ross, Edward Alsworth, first user of term "race suicide," **IV**, 394

Ross, Fort, and Alaska, **I**, 42; and Sutter's Fort, **V**, 212

Ross, George, signer of Declaration of Independence, **II**, 124

Ross, George, elected president of Illinois and Wabash Company, **III**, 69

Ross, John, attempts to treat with Indians of the Illinois, **III**, 68

Ross, John, Cherokee chief, during Civil War, **III**, 98; and Council of Fort Smith, **V**, 101

Ross, John, and search for Northwest Passage, **IV**, 151

Ross, William Potter, editor of the *Cherokee Advocate*, **IV**, 127

Rosser, T. L., and engagement at Tom's Brook, **V**, 280

Rossers, The, rifle makers, **IV**, 483

Rost, Pierre A., and Civil War diplomacy, **I**, 392

Rotarians, **I**, 261

Rotary Press, invented by Richard Hoe, **III**, 148

Rotation in Office, **I**, 91, 254; **V**, 147

Rotation of Crops, **II**, 154, 247

Roubideau Pass, **IV**, 221

Rough and Ready, Calif., dead city, **II**, 114

Rough Riders, capture San Juan, **V**, 25

Roulstone, George, establishes the *Knoxville Gazette*, **IV**, 124, 127; first printer of Tennessee, **IV**, 346

Roundups, and the cow custom, **II**, 79; and open range cattle period, **IV**, 177; and stampedes, **V**, 155. *See also* Rodeos

Rowan, A. S., and message to Garcia, **II**, 370

Rowan, John, and the writing of "My Old Kentucky Home," **IV**, 51

Rowell, George P., and the advertising agency, **I**, 18

Rowlandson, Mary, captured by the Indians, **III**, 95, 210

Roxbury Latin School, established by John Eliot, **V**, 41

Royal African Company, and the Triangular Trade, **V**, 296

Royal Colonies, and colonial councils, **I**, 418; and the judiciary, **I**, 419; and British colonial policy, **I**, 421; and the quitrent, **IV**, 390; Virginia becomes one, **V**, 372; voting in, **V**, 383

Royal Disallowance, and judicial review, **III**, 182; and the Privy Council, **IV**, 351

Royal Governors, and the Board of Trade and Plantations, **I**, 206; and Lords of Trade and Plantations, **III**, 302; and the formation of state governments, **V**, 169

Royce, Josiah, and philosophical thought and writings, **IV**, 264

Royer, R. F., and the Messiah War, **III**, 379

Rubber, and industrial chemistry, **I**, 351; and foreign trade, **V**, 295

Ruck, John, and the Pejepscot purchase, **IV**, 239

Ruddle's Station, overwhelmed by Bird, **I**, 191

Ruef, Abraham, and political rings, **IV**, 485

Ruffin, Edmund, and fertilizers, **II**, 268; creates the League of United Southerners, **III**, 256; defends slavery, **IV**, 363; and proslavery literature, **IV**, 364; favors marl as fertilizer, **V**, 116; soil chemist, **V**, 123

Ruffin, Frank G., and the Readjuster movement, **IV**, 418

Ruffin, Thomas, advocates secession, **II**, 275

Ruffin, William H., educational reformer, **V**, 122

Ruffner, Joseph, and the Kanawha salt works, **III**, 194

Rugged Individualism, and socializing tendencies, **V**, 111

Rule of Reason, adopted by the Supreme Court, **I**, 87; and the Sherman Antitrust Law, **V**, 70; and Standard Oil Co. of N. J. v. U. S., **V**, 157; and trusts, **V**, 326; and U. S. v. Trans-Missouri Freight Association, **V**, 349

Rule of the War of 1756, and armed neutrality, **I**, 108; and the doctrine of continuous voyage, **II**, 142; and the *Essex* case, **II**, 228; and Plan of 1776, **IV**, 283; and *Polly* admiralty case, **IV**, 304; and Trade with the Enemy Acts, **V**, 300

Rum, and the Triangular Trade, **I**, 417; distilling of, **II**, 151; popularity of, **II**, 169; the Indian and, **III**, 91; as colonial industry, **III**, 120; and the Molasses Act, **IV**, 6; and molasses trade, **IV**, 6; a colonial staple, **V**, 160; and colonial sugar acts, **V**, 199; and foreign trade, **V**, 294; in the Triangular Trade, **V**, 296; in the West India trade, **V**, 437

"Rum, Romanism and Rebellion," **I**, 287

Rum River, Battle of, **V**, 84

Rum Runners, and prohibition, **IV**, 357; and territorial waters, **V**, 248

Rumsey, James, and the steamboat, **IV**, 223; **V**, 177, 179, 307

Run-Off Primary, **IV**, 341

Rural Electrification Act, **II**, 196

Rural Free Delivery, **III**, 325; **IV**, 320

Rural New Yorker, farm periodical, **II**, 248

Rural Post Roads Act (or Federal Aid Road Act), **I**, 31; **II**, 255; **IV**, 496; **V**, 163

Rush, Benjamin, and antislavery societies, **I**, 58; and yellow fever, **I**, 276; signer of the Declaration of Independence, **II**, 124; and use of drugs, **II**, 171; describes influenza epidemic, **III**, 122; father of American psychiatry, **III**, 125; early member of Pennsylvania Hospital staff, **IV**, 247; philanthropy of, **IV**, 260; and philosophical thought and writings, **IV**, 263; institutes a suit against *Porcupine's Gazette*, **IV**, 314; Princeton graduate, **IV**, 343; and organization of First Day or Sunday School Society, **V**, 204; and the temperance movement, **V**, 240; and tuberculosis, **V**, 328; and yellow fever, **V**, 504

Rush, Richard, in battle of Bladensburg (1814), **I**, 198; signs Convention of 1818, **II**, 52; and Miranda's intrigues, **III**, 414

Rush, William, sculptor, **I**, 123; carves figurehead, **II**, 272

Rush-Bagot Agreement, and Canadian-American relations, **I**, 300; neutralizes Great Lakes, **II**, 224, 416

Russel, James, builds dock at Charlestown, **II**, 156

Russel, Samuel, and founding of Yale University, **V**, 500

Russell, Benjamin, and political cartoons, **I**, 320

Russell, Charles Edward, and the Root mission to Russia, **IV**, 501

Russell, Charles M., and the stampede, **V**, 156

Russell, Gilbert, at Cahaba Old Towns, **I**, 266

Russell, Green, discovers Auraria, **II**, 236

Russell, H. H., and the Anti-Saloon League, **I**, 83

Russell, John, and regicides in New England, **IV**, 438

Russell, John H., and Haiti, **III**, 4; **IV**, 76

Russell, Jonathan, and treaty of Ghent, **II**, 387; and the War of 1812, **V**, 406

Russell, Majors and Waddell, and cattle drives, **I**, 326; and Holladay Overland Stage Company, **III**, 38; have headquarters at Leavenworth, **III**, 258; and mule-skinners, **IV**, 40; and overland freighting, **IV**, 192; use oxen, **IV**, 194; and the Pony Express, **IV**, 306

Russell, Osborne, and trapping, **V**, 312

Russell, William, member of the Principio Company, **IV**, 343

Russell, William E., leader of the Cleveland Democrats, **I**, 398

Russell, William Green, prospector, **IV**, 364; surveys Smoky Hill Trail, **V**, 103

Russell, William H., and Central Overland, California and Pikes Peak Express, **I**, 334; and Leavenworth and Pikes Peak Express, **III**, 258

Russell-Cherokee Expedition, **IV**, 269 f.

Russell House, architecture of, **I**, 99

Russell Sage Foundation, endowment of, **II**, 314; and social work, **V**, 110

Russia, treaty with (1824), **II**, 52; Root mission to, **IV**, 501; treaties with, **V**, 317

Russian-American Company, and monopoly of Alaskan business, **I**, 42; and the purchase of Alaska, **I**, 43; established, **I**, 270; and seal fisheries, **V**, 49

Russian Fleets, Visit of, **I**, 43

Russians in California, **I**, 270, 275

Rust, destroys wheat crop, **II**, 91

Rust, Mrs. H. L., organizes the Wakefield National Memorial Association, **V**, 391

Rust, Samuel, press maker, **IV**, 346

Ruston, John, member of the Principio Company, **IV**, 343

Rutgers College, one of the early institutions of higher learning, **II**, 185; and football, **II**, 298; and the Great Awakening, **II**, 413

Rutledge, Edward, signer of the Declaration of Independence, **II**, 124

Rutledge, John, signer of the Constitution, **II**, 39; and republican form of government, **IV**, 453; proposes South Carolina canal, **V**, 126

Ruysch, Johann, map of, **III**, 340

Ryder, Albert Pinkham, painter, **I**, 123

Rynning, Ole, and Norwegian immigration, **IV**, 152

Ryswick, Treaty of, suppresses buccaneers, **I**, 246; and French claims in Ohio, **II**, 343; ends King William's War, **III**, 212; returns Maine to France, **III**, 326; restores Port Royal to the French, **IV**, 315

S

S-4, sinking of the, **V**, 194

S-51, sinking of the, **V**, 194

Saarinen, E., architect, **I**, 101; and skyscrapers, **V**, 88

Sabbath, laws concerning, **V**, 203; and tithingmen, **V**, 273; traveling on the, **V**, 312

Sabin, Joseph, author of *Dictionary of Books Relating to America*, **I**, 211; bookseller, **I**, 214; *Dictionary of Books Relating to America*, **III**, 35

Sabine River, and Adams-Onís Treaty, **I**, 9; as boundary of Louisiana, **III**, 309; **V**, 252

Sabotage, **I**, 86; **III**, 119

Sac Indians. *See* Sauk Indians

Sacajawea, Bird Woman of Lewis and Clark expedition, **III**, 266

Sacco-Vanzetti Case, and the "reds," **IV**, 433

Sackett's Harbor, and Great Lakes naval campaign of 1812, **II**, 416; and Wilkinson's expedition against Montreal, **IV**, 18

Sackville, Fort, built, **III**, 216

Sackville-West Incident, **I**, 288

Saco, French and Indian raids on, **IV**, 389

Sacramento, Doniphan victorious at, **II**, 161
"Saddle Old Spike," fiddle tune, **II**, 270
Safeguarding Clause, **II**, 227
Safety Fund System of New York, **I**, 156
Sagadahoc, and the Penobscot region, **II**, 346
Sage, Henry W., and land speculation, **III**, 240
Sage, Mrs. Russell, establishes the Russell Sage Foundation, **IV**, 510
Sage, Russell, rise of, **II**, 311
Saginaw, Treaty of (1819), and Indian land cessions, **III**, 100
Sailing Packets, for river navigation, **IV**, 489
Sailor's (Sayler's) Creek, Lee attacked at, **I**, 91
St. Albans Raid, **I**, 298; **IV**, 150
St. Anne, Fort, built by the French, **V**, 361
St. Anthony, Falls of, named by Hennepin, **III**, 26; and Minneapolis, **V**, 334
St. Anthony, Fort, original name of Fort Snelling, **V**, 106
St. Asaph, settlement at, **III**, 204; Logan's Fort, **III**, 294
St. Augustin, Marie Tranchepain de, Mother Superior of the Ursulines, **V**, 353
St. Augustine, founding of, **II**, 288; settled by Menéndez, **II**, 289; Oglethorpe attacks, **III**, 173; and Fort Matanzas, **III**, 359; Menéndez arrives at, **III**, 373; and New Smyrna Colony, **IV**, 112; built by the Spanish, **IV**, 315; destroyed in Queen Anne's War, **IV**, 389
St. Castin, Baron, in the Penobscot region, **II**, 346
St. Castine's Trading House, plundering of, **III**, 211
St. Charles, Fort, French outpost in Minnesota, **III**, 410
St. Clair, Arthur, and Burgoyne's Invasion, **I**, 255; changes name of Losantiville to Cincinnati, **I**, 375; opposes Division Act of 1800, **II**, 155; builds Fort Hamilton, **III**, 6; negotiates treaties of Fort Harmar, **III**, 10; builds Fort Jefferson (Ohio), **III**, 170; evacuates Ticonderoga, **III**, 230; and Marietta, **III**, 343; and the Northwest Territory, **IV**, 151; and Ohio, **IV**, 160; and battle of Princeton, **IV**, 342; at Ticonderoga, **V**, 268; names the Western Reserve, Trumbull County, **V**, 445
St. Clair's Defeat, and the militia, **III**, 403; and Fort Recovery, **IV**, 428; and expeditions against Wabash Towns, **V**, 386; and Fort Washington (Ohio), **V**, 414; and the Wayne campaign, **V**, 427
St. Clement's Manor, **II**, 75
St. Croix Island, one of the Virgin Islands, **V**, 370
St. Croix Portage Route, Duluth builds post on, **II**, 175
St. Croix River, and the Acadians, **I**, 6; and the Northeast boundary, **IV**, 147
St. Cyr, Hyacinthe, and Spanish-Missouri Fur Company, **V**, 141

St. David's Society, organized among the Welsh, **V**, 434
St. Denis (Denys), Charles Juchereau, tannery of, **III**, 182
St. Denis (Denys), Louis Juchereau de, attempts to open trade with Mexico, **II**, 345; establishes Natchitoches, La., **IV**, 57
St. Francis Indians, Rogers' Rangers raid village of, **III**, 230; **IV**, 500; **V**, 362
St. Francis River, Abenaki on, **I**, 1
St. Francis Xavier's Mission, founded by Claude Allouez, **III**, 174
St. François Xavier, Fort, building of, **II**, 422
St. Frédéric, Fort, serves as base for French raiding parties, **II**, 93; in the French and Indian War, **III**, 229; and Fort Ticonderoga, **V**, 268; erected by the French, **V**, 361
Saint-Gaudens, Augustus, sculptor, **I**, 124; and Robert G. Shaw memorial, **I**, 223; and *Diana* on Madison Square Garden, **III**, 322; and Washington, D. C., **V**, 413
St. George, Fort, and the Popham Colony, **IV**, 308
St. Germain-en-Laye, Treaty of, and Castin, **I**, 321; and Maine, **III**, 326
St. Ignace, Mission of, established by Jacques Marquette, **III**, 174, 180
St. John, John P., Prohibition candidate, **I**, 287
St. John Island, one of the Virgin Islands, **V**, 370
St. Johns, capture of (1775), **I**, 297; **III**, 230; **IV**, 481
St. Johns College, Md., founded, **III**, 349
St. Joseph, Fort, and the fur trade, **II**, 360; and Pontiac's War, **IV**, 306
St. Joseph, Mo., starting-point for Pony Express, **III**, 8; shares outfitting business with Independence, **III**, 85
St. Joseph-Kankakee Portage, **IV**, 316
St. Lawrence River, and the search for the western sea, **V**, 446
St. Lawrence Waterway Project, **II**, 416
St. Leger, Barry, and Burgoyne's Invasion, **I**, 255; and battle of Oriskany, **IV**, 188; at Fort Ontario, **IV**, 191; in the Revolutionary War, **IV**, 476; at Fort Schuyler, **V**, 159
St. Louis, Fort (Ill.), founding of, **II**, 346; **IV**, 252; and Fort Pimitoui, **IV**, 272; erected on Starved Rock, **V**, 161
St. Louis, Fort (Texas), built by LaSalle, **II**, 344
St. Louis, Mo., and British campaign of 1780, **I**, 241; French remove to, **I**, 267; Des Peres village located within present city limits of, **II**, 142; city directory appears in, **II**, 148; and the fur trade, **II**, 360, 363; treaty of (1816), and Indian land cessions, **III**, 100; treaties of (1823), and Indian land cessions, **III**, 100; Laclede locates his post at present site of, **III**, 361; founded by Laclede, **III**, 426; as center of fur

trade, III, 431; and domestic trade, V, 292; as a frontier post, V, 302

St. Louis, The, gunboat, II, 180

St. Louis and San Francisco Railroad, Atlantic and Pacific Railroad reorganized as part of, I, 135

St. Louis Missouri Fur Company, the Chouteaus become stockholders in, I, 370; and the fur trade, II, 362, 363; and Indian trade, III, 110; and Missouri River fur trade, III, 430

St. Louis Post-Dispatch, and airplane races, I, 36

St. Luke's Church, architecture of, I, 99

St. Lusson, Sieur de, winters on the Manitoulin Islands, III, 332; and New France, IV, 101; and pageant at Sault Ste. Marie, V, 34

St. Mark's Mission, founded by Claude Allouez, III, 174

Saint Martinville, and Acadians, I, 7

St. Marys, first permanent settlement in Maryland, I, 105

St. Marys Falls Ship Canal, I, 303; III, 208; V, 194

St. Marys River, and Georgia's southern boundary, II, 382

St. Marys River, as water route, IV, 316

St. Michael the Archangel, Jesuit mission, III, 174

St. Mihiel, American army at, I, 59; V, 492

St. Nicholas, monthly children's publication, I, 363

St. Paul and Pacific Railroad, III, 411

St. Stephens, treaty of Choctaw Trading House signed at, I, 369; and Gaines' Trace, II, 366

St. Thomas Island, one of the Virgin Islands, V, 370

St. Valentine's Day Massacre, I, 217

St. Vrain, Ceran, and the fur trade, II, 236, 362; land grant to, III, 236, 247; and Bent's Fort, V, 302

Ste. Genevieve, first permanent settlement in Missouri, III, 426

Salaries, and the national income, III, 82; and distribution of wealth, V, 429

Salem, Mass., and the Dorchester Company, II, 162; East Indies trade with, II, 182; witchcraft hysteria in, V, 475

Salem, N. C., founded by Moravians, IV, 22; V, 500

Sales Tax, V, 227

Salisbury Prison, and atrocity stories, I, 136

"Sally Good'in," fiddle tune, II, 270

Salmon, Daniel Elmer, and immunity from contagious diseases, III, 64

Salmon Falls, burning of, III, 211

Salmon Fisheries, and territorial waters, V, 248

Salmon Packing, II, 297

Salmonsen, Ella M., writes on vitamins and silicosis, III, 64

Salomon, William, art collection of, I, 125

Saloon, and prohibition, IV, 357; and the W. C. T. U., V, 479

Salsbury, Nate, and the Wild West show, V, 464

Salt, and the Avery mine, I, 141; at Cape Cod, I, 306; in the Confederacy, II, 11; along the Kanawha River, III, 194; in Louisiana, III, 306; as object of monopoly control, IV, 12; at St. Marks, V, 13

Salt Lake City, Utah, mint at, I, 129; and outfitting of caravans, I, 313; made capital of State of Deseret, II, 140; Mormons at, IV, 26

Salt Lake Trail, as route of thirst, V, 263

Salt Licks: Big Bone Lick, I, 183; and buffalo trails, I, 248; and the frontier family, II, 243; and the buffalo, III, 104; distribution of, III, 275; and roads, IV, 493

Salter, William, best known of the Iowa Band, III, 153

Saltonstall, Dudley, and the Penobscot expedition, IV, 249

Saltpeter, in the Confederacy, I, 393

Salute, Twenty-one Gun, V, 334

Salvation Army, and charity organization movement, I, 342; and philanthropy, IV, 260

Salzburgers, as Lutherans, III, 316; as political exiles, IV, 295

Sam Slick, peddles wooden clocks, I, 402

Samoa, tripartite government established, I, 89; and territorial expansion, I, 128; United States receives part of group, III, 78; as an insular possession, III, 128; American missions established in, III, 416; acquisition of, IV, 195; and influence in the Pacific, IV, 196; and territorial claims, V, 247; and Tutuila Island naval station, V, 333; and the United States as a world power, V, 486

Samoan Clipper, disappears on trial flight, I, 36

Samoset, an Algonquin leader, I, 48; learns to speak English, IV, 9; sells land to John Brown, IV, 239

Sampson, W. T., and battle of Santiago Bay, V, 31, 136 f.

San Antonio, missions removed to, II, 182; founded, V, 252

San Antonio-San Diego Mail and Stage Line, V, 254

San Carlo Opera Company, IV, 178

San Cayetán del Tumacácori, mission of, III, 418

San Diego Mission, founded, I, 275

San Felipe, Fort, built by the Spanish, IV, 315

San Fernando, Fort, erected on site of Memphis, III, 372; V, 140

San Francisco, *presidio* dedicated on site of (1776), I, 87; founded, I, 275; city directory appears in, II, 148

San Francisco Bay, discovered, I, 275

San Francisco *Californian,* publishes news of gold discovery, II, 313

San Francisco *Chronicle,* advocates the Pacific Republic movement, IV, 197

San Francisco Earthquake, II, 181; III, 347

San Francisco *Examiner,* comic strips in, I, 431; and yellow journalism, V, 505

San Francisco Mint, gold depository at, II, 396

San Gabriel de Guevavi, mission of, III, 418

San Ildefonso, Treaty of, Spain retrocedes Louisiana to France by, III, 305, 308, 424, 425; IV, 188

San Jacinto, Battle of, V, 257

San Jacinto, The, wooden screw sloop, V, 99

San Juan Archipelago, and Anglo-American relations, I, 75; and Haro Channel dispute, III, 11; and the Treaty of Washington (1871), V, 416

San Juan Hill, and the Rough Riders, IV, 503

San Lorenzo El Real Treaty. *See* Pinckney's Treaty

San Marcos, Fort, built by the Spaniards, IV, 316; defends St. Augustine, V, 6

San Miguel de Gualdape, name of Ayllon's settlement, I, 144

San Pasqual, Kearny attacks at, III, 201

San Patricio Corps, captured at Churubusco Convent, II, 141

San Xavier de Naxera, dead city, II, 114

San Xavier del Bac, Mission of, III, 175, 418

Sanborn, J. B., appointed to Indian Commission, III, 95

Sanchez-Merry Protocol, IV, 132

Sanctions, and trading with the enemy, V, 301; and the World War Peace Conference, V, 490

Sand Creek, Cheyenne villages destroyed at, I, 355

Sand Hillers, II, 83

Sand Hills of Nebraska, II, 178

Sandbar Duel, and Bowie knife, I, 230

Sanders, George Nicholas, and "Young America," V, 510

Sanders, Thomas, finances Bell's telephone experiments, I, 66

Sanders, Wilbur Fisk, and the Plummer gang, IV, 290

Sanderson, Robert, silversmith, V, 82

Sanderson, The, and the Triangular Trade, V, 296

Sandusky, and the fur trade, II, 360; falls in Pontiac's War, IV, 306

Sandwich Glass, I, 306

Sandy Hill Pass, IV, 221

Sandys, Edwin, and the Tobacco Contract, V, 275; and the Virginia Company of London, V, 377

Sandys, George, and the first English literature in America, V, 372

Sanger, Margaret, and the birth-control movement, I, 191

Sangre de Cristo Pass, IV, 221

Sanguinet, Charles, of Lisa and Company, III, 283; and Spanish-Missouri Fur Company, V, 141

Sanitary Commission, and the writing of "Battle Hymn of the Republic," I, 168; and Civil War atrocity stories, I, 385; supplies civilian relief during the Civil War, I, 388; and the Protective War Claims Association, IV, 366

Sanitation, and the use of bathtubs, I, 167; and the dairy industry, II, 104; and engineering, II, 215; and hygiene, III, 64; and plumbing, IV, 289; and street cleaning, V, 188

Sankey, Ira D., and revivals, IV, 464

Sanson Map, The, IV, 175; V, 282

Santa Anita Handicap, III, 49

Santa Anna, Antonio Lopez de, and the battle of Contreras, II, 49; in Mexican War, III, 386; at San Jacinto, V, 25

Santa Catalina Island, I, 322

Santa Cruz, Alonso de, map of, III, 340

Santa Elena, garrisons established, II, 288; Spanish name for Port Royal (S. C.), IV, 315

Santa Fé, trade with, harassed by Arapaho Indians, I, 94; Arkansas River as highway to, I, 106; Aubry's trading venture in, I, 136; commercial relations with, I, 172; and Fort Bernard, I, 180; and Old Spanish Trail, I, 274; and Great American Desert myth, II, 140; capture of (1846), II, 161; and the Fowler expedition, II, 319; Mallet brothers journey to, II, 345; horses plentiful in, by 1630, III, 48; and Missouri trade, III, 426; trade with, III, 426; capital of New Mexico founded at, IV, 107; and Fort Orleans, IV, 188; and the Great Plains, IV, 282; and western exploration, V, 442; and Westport, Mo., V, 449

Santa Fé Railroad. *See* Atchison, Topeka and Santa Fé Railway

Santa Fé Republican, founded by O. P. Hovey and E. T. Davies, IV, 127

Santa Fé Trail, as influence on agriculture, I, 33; and the Great Bend of the Arkansas, I, 106; and the Arkansas River Route, I, 107; Fort Atkinson located on, I, 134; mountain branch of the, I, 178; caravan traffic on, I, 312; and the Cherokee Trail, I, 353; and the Chihuahua Trail, I, 361; right of way granted by Osage Indians, II, 72; and Dodge City, II, 156; opened by William Becknell, II, 236; and Independence, Mo., III, 85; and Kansas City, Mo., III, 196; and the Mexican War, III, 386; established by William Becknell, IV, 107; pack trains on, IV, 198; Pawnee Rock as landmark on, IV, 229; and Raton Pass, IV, 417; and road build-

ing, **IV,** 495; and Taos Trail, **V,** 220; as route of thirst, **V,** 263; and wagon trains, **V,** 389; and water holes, **V,** 421

Santa Maria, Juan de, and the Rodríguez-Chamuscado expedition, **IV,** 500

Santa Rosa Island, Slemmer escapes to, **IV,** 266

Santee Indians, a division of the Sioux, **V,** 85

Santiago, Battle of, the *Oregon* in, **IV,** 183; and Sampson-Schley controversy, **V,** 22; and surrender of city, **V,** 26; and Spanish-American War, **V,** 136 f.

Santiago, Chile, Pan-American conference at (1923), **IV,** 203

Santiago College, **III,** 248

Santo Domingo, and the Alabama Claims, **I,** 41. *See also* Dominican Republic

Sappa Creek, Cheyenne villages destroyed at, **I,** 355

Sarah Constant, The, and founding of Jamestown, **III,** 166; **V,** 372

Saratoga, and Burgoyne's Invasion, **I,** 255; and Peace Commission of 1778, **IV,** 231

Saratoga, Jefferson's proposed state, **III,** 173

Saratoga Springs, **III,** 406; **IV,** 460

Sardell v. Murphy, **III,** 409

Sargeant, Charles S., and gardening, **II,** 371

Sargent, James, introduces the time lock, **I,** 156

Sargent, John Singer, painter, **I,** 123

Sargent, Winthrop, and the Northwest Territory, **IV,** 151; and French defection at Vincennes, **V,** 370

Sarpy, Gregoire, of Lisa and Company, **III,** 283; and the keelboat, **III,** 430

Sarpy, John B., Fort John named for, **III,** 177

Sarpy, Peter A., and Cabanne's Post, **I,** 264; at Bellevue, Neb., **IV,** 80

Sassacus, Chief, and the Mohegan Indians, **IV,** 5; slain by the Mohawks, **IV,** 252

Sassamon, John, murder of, **III,** 210

Satanta, and Indian oratory, **III,** 103

Saturday Club, **I,** 214

Saturday Evening Post, **I,** 17

Sauk and Fox Agency, Treaty of (1842), and Indian land cessions, **III,** 100

Sauk Indians, and the Algonquin family, **I,** 48; Fort Armstrong located near village of, **I,** 109; in the battle of Bad Axe, **I,** 145; and the Black Hawk Purchase and War, **I,** 194; and treaty of Fort de Chartres, **I,** 348; unite with Fox Indians, **II,** 319, 320; and the Half-Breed Tract, **III,** 5; and Fort Harmar treaty, **III,** 10; land cessions of, **III,** 100; removal of, **III,** 107; and Neutral Ground, **IV,** 87; and Oklahoma Indians, **IV,** 169; party to the treaty of Prairie du Chien, **IV,** 329; and British attack on St. Louis (1780), **V,** 11; depend upon wild rice for their food supply, **V,** 464

Sault Ste. Marie, commercial and strategic importance of, **II,** 116; Duluth makes friends with Indians at, **II,** 175; and the fur trade, **II,** 360; and Jesuit missions, **III,** 174; Great Lakes area formally annexed to France at, **III,** 391; post at, **V,** 205; pageant, **V,** 473

Sault Ste. Marie, Mich., Lock Canal. *See* St. Marys Falls Ship Canal

Saunders, Alvin, territorial governor of Nebraska, **IV,** 80

Saunders, Clarence, opens self-serve store, **V,** 56

Saur, Christopher. *See* Sower, Christopher

Savage, Henry W., organizes the Castle Square Opera Company, **IV,** 178

Savage, M. J., and lecturing, **III,** 260

Savage Station, Battle of, and the Peninsular campaign, **IV,** 241; **V,** 60

Savannah, British beat off D'Estaing's attack on, **II,** 345; settled (1733), **II,** 379; seized (1778), **II,** 379; assault on (1779), **II,** 379; evacuated (1782), **II,** 379; Wayne's operations at, **II,** 380; Creek Indians attempt to relieve British at, **III,** 89; occupation of (1778), **IV,** 477; Army of the Tennessee present at siege of, **V,** 242

Savings and Loan Associations, Federal, **I,** 249

Sawmills, **I,** 249; **III,** 314

Say, Thomas, and Long's explorations, **III,** 300

Saybrook, Winthrop establishes fort at, **II,** 21; settlement at, **III,** 301; and the Pequot War, **IV,** 252; Winthrop sent to build fort at, **IV,** 490; and York's proprietary, **V,** 508

Saybrook Platform, **I,** 277; **II,** 16; **IV,** 332

Saye and Sele, Lord, and designation "Lords and Gentlemen," **III,** 301

Sayle, William, and Charleston, S. C., **I,** 343

Sayler's Creek. *See* Sailor's Creek

Saylor, David O., manufactures Portland cement, **I,** 331

Scalawags, and the Black and Tan Convention, **III,** 420; and Reconstruction, **IV,** 426 f.; and Democratic party in the Solid South, **V,** 118

Scalp Bounties, and Lovewell's fight, **III,** 310

Scalp Dance, **III,** 97

Scandinavian Immigration, **III,** 316, 411

Scarlet Letter, written by Nathaniel Hawthorne, **II,** 270

Scarritt, Winthrop E., and the American Automobile Association, **I,** 58

Scarsdale, manor of, **III,** 55

Schaff, Philip, leader of Evangelical Alliance, **II,** 229; and Swiss origin, **V,** 215

Schechter v. U. S., and emergency legislation, **II,** 210; and special powers granted to Presidents, **IV,** 335

Schenck, R. C., at Bull Run, **I,** 251; and the Treaty of Washington (1871), **V,** 416

Schenectady, granted charter, **II,** 160

Schenk v. U. S., V, 399

Schetterly, H. R., and the Alphadelphia Association, I, 52

Schieffelen, Ed, discovers Tombstone, II, 236; V, 280

Schley, John Thomas, and settlement of Frederick, Md., II, 330

Schley, W. S., and Greely's arctic expedition, II, 421; controversy with W. T. Sampson, V, 22; at Santiago, V, 31

Schmucker, Samuel S., father of the Evangelical Alliance in America, II, 229; and religious thought and writings, IV, 446

Schofield, J. M., in battle of Franklin, II, 329; and Hood's Tennessee campaign, III, 44; commands Army of the Ohio, IV, 162; and engagement at Spring Hill, V, 150

Scholastic, school magazine, I, 364

Schomburgk Line, and the Venezuela boundary controversy, V, 360

School Books, McGuffey's Readers as, III, 365

School District, as a political subdivision, IV, 299

School Life, monthly magazine of the Office of Education, II, 188

School of Application for Infantry and Cavalry, established at Fort Leavenworth, I, 118

Schoolcraft, Henry R., and epic of Hiawatha, III, 29; in Minnesota, III, 411; and western exploration, V, 442

Schools, for the blind, I, 199; dame, II, 108; for the deaf, II, 114; private, and teachers, V, 234; in colony of Virginia, V, 372. See also Education

Schools, Public, and the Akron Law, I, 39; and education, II, 186; consolidation of, II, 187; and the Board of Education, II, 187; consolidation of, II, 188; and illiteracy, III, 71; land grants for, III, 236; and the lyceum movement, III, 316; and public land sales, IV, 372; and teachers colleges, V, 234; and the Weeks Act, V, 433; temperance instruction in, V, 479. See also Education

Schools, Superintendent of, as county officer, III, 288

Schooners, as warships, V, 411

Schroeder, Capt., surpasses Beachy's altitude record, I, 142

Schurz, Carl, and the Forty-eighters, II, 313; and the Liberal Republican party, III, 269

Schuyler, Arent, discovers a copper mine, III, 407

Schuyler, Fort, name given Fort Stanwix, V, 159

Schuyler, Peter, and Dongan's charters, II, 160; and colony of New York, IV, 114; in Queen Anne's War, IV, 389

Schuyler, Philip J., and Burgoyne's Invasion, I, 255; and invasion of Canada (1775–76), I, 297; and the trench, V, 321; works for repeal of all laws contrary to the Definitive Treaty of Peace,

V, 322; and Washington's eight months army, V, 419

Schuyler Copper Mines, V, 177

Schuylkill Canal, I, 80; V, 329

Schuylkill Water Works, I, 167

Schwab, Charles M., and great fortunes, II, 312

Schwenkfelders, as conscientious objectors, II, 25; as political exiles, IV, 295

Schwimmer, Rosika, and Ford's peace ship, II, 301

Science and Health with Key to the Scriptures, by Mary Baker Eddy, I, 370

Scientific Management. See Industrial Management

Scioto Company, and French grants, II, 346; and Gallipolis, II, 368; and land speculation, III, 240; and Ohio Company of Associates, IV, 163; and western lands, V, 444

Scioto Trail, and the Miami Trail, III, 390

Scopes Trial, and freethinking, II, 340; and religion, IV, 443

Scoresby, William, polar expedition of, IV, 292

Scotch-Irish, in Carlisle, Pa., I, 314; and colonial society, I, 424; immigration, III, 74; settle Irish Tract, III, 155; and group migration, III, 396; as mountain people, IV, 37; in New Hampshire, IV, 102; in North Carolina, IV, 144; and the Paxton Boys, IV, 229; in Pennsylvania, IV, 242; and potatoes, IV, 323; and the Presbyterians, IV, 332; and Quaker Indian policy, IV, 385; in the Shenandoah Valley, V, 69; and the Waldo patent, V, 391; as first settlers of West Virginia, V, 439; and the westward movement, V, 450; settle on the Yadkin River, V, 500

Scots Charitable Society of Boston, I, 342

Scott, Charles, suggests name for Fort Defiance, II, 128; leads expedition against Kickapoo Eel River villages, V, 386

Scott, Fort, established, III, 194

Scott, Hugh L., and the Root mission to Russia, IV, 501

Scott, R. P., and the automatic pea podder, I, 304

Scott, Thomas A., and censorship during Civil War, I, 331; and the Pennsylvania Railroad during the Civil War, IV, 248

Scott, Winfield, and the Aroostook War, I, 121; and the Black Hawk Purchase, I, 194; forces Indian land cession, I, 195; nominated for Presidency, I, 284; and battle of Chapultepec (1847), I, 342; and the battle of Chippewa, I, 367; and battle of Churubusco, I, 374; and the battle of Contreras, II, 49; and treaty of Guadalupe Hidalgo, II, 426; and battle at Lundy's Lane, III, 315; and blockade of Mexican Gulf ports, III, 383; and the Mexican War, III, 386; and capture of Mexico City, III, 389; and Niagara campaigns, IV, 130; called

"Old Fuss and Feathers," **IV**, 170; and the Protective War Claims Association, **IV**, 366; captured in battle of Queenston Heights, **IV**, 390; and recruiting, **IV**, 429; and the Trail of Tears, **V**, 303; and siege and capture of Vera Cruz (1847), **V**, 360; in War of 1812, **V**, 405; and destruction of York (Toronto), 1813, **V**, 507

Scotts Bluff (Nebr.), **IV**, 19

Scribner, Charles E., as engineer of Western Electric Company, **V**, 441

Scribner's Magazine, **III**, 323; **V**, 482

Scripps, Edward Wyllis, and the United Press, **V**, 346

Scripps-McRae Press Association, **V**, 346

Scripps Services, and news reporting, **IV**, 123

Scudder, Vida D., and social settlements, **V**, 109

Scudder's Museum, **I**, 164; **IV**, 47

Scull, John, establishes the *Pittsburgh Gazette,* **IV**, 124, 281

Sculpture, **I**, 123

Scurvy, at Andersonville Prison, **I**, 73; among the Pilgrims, **II**, 150; among the Forty-niners, **II**, 313; develops in St. Croix settlement, **V**, 8

Sea Adventure, The, used in Somers' voyage to Virginia, **V**, 119

Sea Otter Trade, and the Aleutian Islands, **I**, 47; Mexicans engage in, **I**, 275; a chief industry in Spanish California, **I**, 276; with Canton, **I**, 305; and Santa Catalina Island, **I**, 322; and China trade, **I**, 365; and the Pacific Fur Company, **IV**, 195

Sea Power, and retaliation in international law, **IV**, 461

Sea Witch, The, Cape Horn ship, **I**, 307

Seabiscuit, famous thoroughbred horse, **V**, 265

Seabrook, Whitemarsh R., and proslavery literature, **IV**, 364

Seabury, Samuel, and the Protestant Episcopal Church, **IV**, 366

Seal, Great, of the United States, **II**, 180; **V**, 162

Seal Fisheries, and Alaska, **I**, 43; and the Alaska Commercial Company, **I**, 44; and the Aleutian Islands, **I**, 47; and Anglo-American relations, **I**, 76; and international arbitration, **I**, 96; on Santa Catalina Island, **I**, 322; and the Pribilof Islands, **IV**, 338; and territorial waters, **V**, 248; and visit and search, **V**, 381

Seamen's Act, LaFollette, **III**, 228

Search, Right of. *See* Visit and Search; *also* Unreasonable Searches and Seizures

Search Warrant, and writs of assistance, **V**, 496

Sears, Barnas, first general agent of the Peabody Fund, **IV**, 230

Sears, Isaac, and battle of Golden Hill, **II**, 400

Sears, R. D., tennis player, **V**, 245

Sears, Richard W., and mail-order houses, **III**, 325

Sears, Roebuck and Company, **III**, 325

Seaton, W. W., and A. B. Plot, **I**, 1; and the *National Intelligencer,* **IV**, 60, 128; chosen as government printer, **IV**, 344

Seattle (Wash.) Mint, **I**, 129; Assay Office, **II**, 396

Seaver, James E., and the White Woman of the Genesee, **V**, 460

Seawanhaka Yacht Club, **V**, 499

Sebastian, Benjamin, and the Spanish conspiracy, **V**, 140

Secession, in Arkansas, **I**, 105; and the Civil War, **I**, 386; and compromise movement of 1860, **I**, 442; and Compromise of 1850, **I**, 442; and the Confederacy, **II**, 3, 4, 10; develops in cotton kingdom, **II**, 70; favored by Essex Junto, **II**, 229; and Federal-state relations, **II**, 263; proposed in Fort Hill letter, **II**, 310; and League of United Southerners, **III**, 256; Maryland opposes, **III**, 349; and Mississippi, **III**, 420; opposed by Southern highlanders, **IV**, 37; and personal liberty laws, **IV**, 254; and right of rebellion, **IV**, 421; and the right of revolution, **IV**, 472; right of, and the South as a conscious minority, **V**, 124; adopted by South Carolina, **V**, 126; and states' rights, **V**, 176; in Tennessee, **V**, 243; in Texas, **V**, 254; and Virginia-Kentucky Resolutions, **V**, 376; and the opening words of the Constitution, **V**, 428; and West Virginia, **V**, 439

Second Duryea's Zouaves, **V**, 514

Second Seminole War, Cooacoochee's band in, **II**, 54

Secret Aid Ships, bring foreign volunteers for the Revolutionary Army, **IV**, 473

Secret Committee, progenitor of the Commercial Committee, **IV**, 475

Secret Proceedings and Debates of the Federal Convention, **II**, 50

Secret Service, organization of, **I**, 122; and counterfeiting, **II**, 73; organized by Allan Pinkerton, **V**, 146; under the Treasury Department, **V**, 314

Secret Societies, and anti-Masonic movement, **I**, 82; and leisure, **III**, 264; "Molly Maguires," **IV**, 6; and philanthropy, **IV**, 260

Secret Treaties. *See* Treaties, Secret

Sectionalism, in Alabama, **I**, 39; and the antislavery movement, **I**, 85; in campaign of 1856; **I**, 284; and the Civil War, **I**, 389; and the Great Awakening, **II**, 413; and Jacksonian Democracy, **III**, 165; in Mississippi, **III**, 420; and the Piedmont region, **IV**, 268; as a concern of southern leaders, **IV**, 363; promoted by Southern Commercial Conventions, **V**, 130; in Tennessee, **V**, 243; and tidewater, **V**, 269; and distribution of wealth, **V**, 429

Securities and Exchange Commission, as an administrative agency, **I**, 11; and bankruptcy

laws, **I**, 159; and delegation of powers, **II**, 133; controls interstate holding companies, **II**, 196; and government regulation, **II**, 406; created, **IV**, 96; and regulation of public utilities, **IV**, 377; and the stock market, **V**, 183

Securities Exchange Act, supplements the Blue Sky Laws, **I**, 205; passed, **I**, 261; and stock exchanges, **II**, 232; and publicity acts, **IV**, 378; and Wall Street, **V**, 393

Sedgwick, John, and battle of Chancellorsville, **I**, 340; and the Mine Run campaign, **III**, 406; and battle of Spotsylvania Courthouse, **V**, 150

Sedgwick, Robert, and brewing, **I**, 236; captures Port Royal (1654), **IV**, 315

Sedgwick, William Thompson, and hygiene, **III**, 64

Sedition Act of 1798, terms of, **I**, 49; and freedom of speech, **II**, 337; and libel, **III**, 268; Thomas Cooper tried for violation of, **IV**, 334

Sedition Act of 1918, **II**, 228; **V**, 492

Seeing-Eye Dogs, **II**, 157

Segregation, not a violation of the Constitution, **IV**, 82

Segura, John Baptist, slain by the Indians, **III**, 174

Seizen, and "turf and twig," **V**, 330

Selden, Samuel L., and the Western Union Telegraph Company, **V**, 447

Selden Patent, and the automobile, **I**, 140; Ford Motor Company wins suit for, **II**, 301

Selective Service Act of 1917, forbids military bounties, **I**, 228; and the draft, **II**, 164; and the militia, **III**, 403; passed to raise a new National Army, **IV**, 2; and the World War, **V**, 491. *See also* Draft

Selectmen, and town meetings, **V**, 287

Self-Service Markets, **V**, 205

Selkirk's Colony, **III**, 56; **IV**, 147, 431

Sellers, Coleman, and motion pictures, **IV**, 31; and photography, **IV**, 265

Sellers, Isaiah, uses *nom de plume* "Mark Twain," **III**, 344

Sellers, William, as partner in *Pennsylvania Gazette*, **IV**, 246

Sells, William H., builds first automatic corn husker, **I**, 304

Sells-Floto Circus, **V**, 464

Seminole Indians, Jackson attacks, **I**, 98; and the Dawes Commission, **II**, 113; one of the Five Civilized Tribes, **II**, 279; border troubles with, **II**, 289; and the Florida War, **II**, 291; and Forbes purchase, **II**, 299; compose Indian brigade, **III**, 94; removal of, **III**, 107; **IV**, 168; and treaty of Payne's Landing, **IV**, 229; as guides, **V**, 46; and battles at Withlacoochee River (1835–36), **V**, 476

Seminole War, effect of, on campaign of 1840, **I**,

284; starts with battle of Fowltown, **II**, 319; and battle of Okeechobee, **IV**, 168

Semmes, Raphael, and the *Alabama*, **I**, 40; and the Confederate navy, **II**, 8; and the *Kearsarge* and *Alabama* engagement, **III**, 202; and capsizing of the *Somers*, **III**, 383; escapes through Pass à L'Outre, **III**, 422

Semple, Robert, co-founder of the *Californian*, **IV**, 126

Senate, The United States, and constitutional apportionment, **I**, 92; courtesy of, **II**, 15, 75; intended to play a secondary part, **II**, 258; courtesy of, and Garfield-Blaine-Conkling controversy, **II**, 372; and Lorimer case, **III**, 302; consent of, and the Root treaties, **IV**, 501; and negotiation of treaties, **V**, 315; veto power of the, **V**, 365; and the Vice-Presidency, **V**, 366

Senator Ross, The, galley boat, **II**, 367

Senators, Election of, and the Seventeenth Amendment, **II**, 42; an experiment in democracy, **II**, 135; and Seventeenth Amendment, **V**, 60

Seneca Falls Convention, and feminism, **II**, 265; and the Nineteenth Amendment, **IV**, 134; and the woman movement, **V**, 477; and woman suffrage, **V**, 478

Seneca Indians, cede land by the Big Tree treaty, **I**, 184; Brodhead's campaign against, **I**, 242; in Croghan's expedition to Illinois, **II**, 90; Denonville advances against, **II**, 138; and the council at Detroit (1761), **II**, 144; ambuscade at Devil's Hole, **II**, 145; one of the Five Nations, **II**, 279; and the Four Mile Strip, **II**, 316; land cessions of, **III**, 100; of the Iroquois League, **III**, 159; and treaty of LaFamine (1684), **III**, 226; and Niagara Carrying Place, **IV**, 129; treaty with (1764), **IV**, 130; and treaty at Pittsburgh (1775), **IV**, 280; and treaty of Spring Wells, **V**, 150; and Sullivan-Clinton campaign, **V**, 202; and the Tuscarora War, **V**, 332

Seneca Oil Company, **IV**, 166

Seneca Rattlesnake Root, as cure-all for epidemics, **II**, 221

Senegalese Negroes, imported as slaves, **IV**, 86

Senn, Nicholas, and bone surgery, **III**, 370

Senn v. Tile Layers Protective Union, **IV**, 267

Sennett, Mack, and the Keystone Comedies, **IV**, 32

Separation of Powers. *See* Powers, Separation of

Separatist Movement. *See* Western Separatism

Separatists (or Independents), and Brownists, **I**, 244; Congregationalists as, **II**, 16; and the Church Covenant, **II**, 76; as founders of New Plymouth Colony, **IV**, 111; and the Pilgrims, **IV**, 271; and Puritanism, **IV**, 384

Sequoia National Park, **IV**, 218

Sequoyah Alphabet, **I**, 352

Serpent Mound, **IV**, 34

Seth Thomas Clocks, **I**, 402

Seton, Mother Elizabeth, and Catholic parochial school system, **I**, 323

Settlement Houses, and Americanization, **I**, 67

Settlement of War Claims Act (1928), **I**, 50

Settlement Work. *See* Social Settlements

Seven Days' Battle, and the Peninsular campaign, **IV**, 241

Seven Ranges, survey of, **II**, 377; and Fort Harmar, **III**, 10; and Fort Steuben, **V**, 181; survey of, **V**, 210, 290

Seventeenth Amendment, and Congress, **II**, 18; text, **II**, 42; and the franchise, **II**, 323; and election of senators, **V**, 58

Seventh Day Baptists, and the founding of Ephrata, **II**, 220

Severn, Fort, transferred from the War Department, **IV**, 68

Sevier, John, leads expeditions against the Chickamauga Indians, **I**, 353; enters into treaty of Dumplin Creek, **II**, 176; and Watauga settlement, **II**, 235; and State of Franklin, **II**, 329; and battle of King's Mountain, **III**, 212; and the Muscle Shoals speculation, **IV**, 47

Sewage, and Chicago Drainage Canal, **I**, 357; and hygiene, **III**, 64; and plumbing, **IV**, 289; and sanitation, **V**, 28; and city water supply, **V**, 424

Sewall, Samuel, and witchcraft, **V**, 476

Seward, George F., and war with Korea, **III**, 216

Seward, William H., and the purchase of Alaska, **I**, 43; and campaign of 1860, **I**, 285; and Civil War diplomacy, **I**, 391; and the Confederate States, **II**, 10; and annexation of the Dominican Republic, **II**, 158; and the Emancipation Proclamation, **II**, 205; and enlistment in the Union Army, **II**, 218; and Hampton Roads conference, **III**, 7; and higher-law doctrine, **III**, 31; originates term "Irrepressible Conflict," **III**, 160; and the Kansas-Nebraska Act, **III**, 197; devotee of "manifest destiny," **III**, 332; and the Monroe Doctrine, **IV**, 14; and the Pacific Ocean, **IV**, 196; and the *Powhatan* incident, **IV**, 327; and right of revolution, **IV**, 424; and the *Trent* affair, **V**, 321; and the Virgin Islands, **V**, 371; and mutual right of search treaty, **V**, 381

Sewing Machines, and harness making, **III**, 11; and use of interchangeable parts, **III**, 133; invented, **III**, 148; and the garment and shoe industries, **III**, 320; patented by Howe, **IV**, 223

Sex Relations, and bachelor houses, **I**, 144; and morals, **IV**, 21; colonial laws regarding, **V**, 203

Seymour, Horatio, nominated for Presidency, **I**, 285; and draft riots, **II**, 164

Seymour, Richard, conducts the Popham Colony's first Protestant church service, **IV**, 308

Seymour, Truman, and battle of Olustee, **IV**, 172

Seymour, William H., and the development of the reaper, **IV**, 419

Shackamaxon, Treaty of, with Delaware Indians, **II**, 131; and land cessions, **III**, 99; and Pennsylvania, **IV**, 243; and the Quaker Indian policy, **IV**, 385

Shafter, W. R., in battles of El Caney and San Juan Hill, **V**, 136

Shaftesbury, Earl of, and Fundamental Constitutions of Carolina, **I**, 316

Shakers, communities of, **I**, 440; and marriage, **III**, 346; and religion, **IV**, 442; in the Western Reserve, **V**, 446

Shakopee, battle at, **V**, 84

Shannon, Wilson, and the Kansas struggle, **III**, 198; and the Wakarusa War, **V**, 391

Shannopin's Town, and Raystown Path, **IV**, 418

Share Cropping, rise of, **I**, 384; plantations replaced by, **II**, 68, 69; and the Deep South, **II**, 125; in Mississippi, **III**, 421; and changes in rural life, **IV**, 509

"Share the Wealth" Schemes, **IV**, 351

Sharkey, William L., in Mississippi v. Johnson, **III**, 425

Sharon, William, and the Big Bonanza, **I**, 444; and great fortunes, **II**, 312; and Ralston's Ring, **IV**, 414

Sharps Rifles, called Beecher's Bibles, **I**, 173; sent by New England Emigrant Aid Company, **IV**, 99; developed prior to the Civil War, **IV**, 483

Sharpsburg. *See* Antietam

Shasta Dam, and water power, **V**, 423

Shattuck, Lemuel, and hygiene, **III**, 63

Shaumberg, Bartholomew, constructs Fort Stoddert, **V**, 184

Shaw, Anna Howard, reform lecturer, **III**, 260; and woman suffrage, **V**, 478

Shaw, John, and western exploration, **V**, 442

Shawmut, the name, **I**, 221

Shawnee Indians, and the Algonquin family, **I**, 48; on the Allegheny River, **I**, 51; in Big Bottom massacre, **I**, 183; and Bouquet's expedition, **I**, 229; and Bradstreet's expedition, **I**, 234; and Brodhead's campaign, **I**, 242; and treaty of Camp Charlotte, **I**, 345; driven out by Chickasaws, **I**, 360; and Chillicothe, **I**, 364; Crawford sets out to attack, **II**, 83; in Croghan's expedition to Illinois, **II**, 90; destroy Draper's Meadow settlement, **II**, 166; and Dunmore's War, **II**, 177; and the treaty of Fort Finney, **II**, 275; and the Great Trading and War Path, **II**, 420; and treaty of Greenville, **II**, 425; in the Revolution, **III**, 88; land cessions of, **III**, 100; removal of, **III**, 107; and establishment of Logstown, **III**, 295; and treaty of Logstown, **III**, 295; and McDonald's expedition, **III**, 364; as Mound Builders, **IV**, 35; and Oklahoma

openings, IV, 169; and Penn's Creek massacre, IV, 242; and the battle of Piqua, IV, 277; and treaty at Pittsburgh (1775), IV, 280; and battle of Point Pleasant, IV, 291; and treaty of Spring Wells, V, 150; in Tennessee, V, 242; probable founders of Tookabatchee, V, 281; sign treaty of Fort Wayne, V, 370; and Great Warriors Path, V, 408

Shawnee Trail, and Texas, V, 255

Shawomet Indians, and the Narragansetts, IV, 53

Shays' Rebellion, I, 20; III, 132

Shedd, W. G. T., and theological writings, V, 261

Sheehan, James W., editor of the Chicago *Daily Times*, IV, 129

Sheep, I, 29; II, 80, 294; V, 483

Shelburne, Lord, and Board of Trade, I, 207

Shelby, Fort, another name for Fort Pontchartrain Du Detroit, IV, 305

Shelby, Fort, at Prairie du Chien, IV, 328; V, 473

Shelby, Isaac, and battle of King's Mountain, III, 212; as early surveyor, V, 210

Shelby, Joseph O., and action at Glasgow, II, 391; and battle of Westport, V, 449

Sheldon, Charles Monroe, author of *In His Steps*, I, 180

Sheldon, John P., co-founder of *Detroit Gazette*, IV, 124, 127

"Shenandoah," song, II, 293

Shenandoah, The, violates British neutrality laws, I, 40; Confederate commerce raider, I, 390; and Confederate navy, II, 8; and prizes, IV, 353

Shenandoah, The, name given the airship ZR-1, II, 148

Shenandoah Valley, Jackson's campaign in, III, 165; and the colony of Virginia, V, 373; settlement of, V, 450

Shepard, Charles Upham, Jr., and tea growing in the South, V, 233

Shepard, Morgan, edits *John Martin's Book*, I, 364

Shepard, Thomas, minister at Cambridge, I, 277

Shepard, William, and Shays' rebellion, V, 66

Shepherd, Samuel, publishes Hening's statutes, III, 26

Sheppard, Morris, heads Campaign Investigating Committee, I, 294; and prohibition, IV, 357

Sheridan, Philip H., and Burnt District, I, 257; in battle of Cedar Creek, I, 330; attacks at Fisher's Hill, II, 277; in battle of Five Forks, II, 279; makes headquarters at Fort Hays, III, 20; and Little Big Horn battle, III, 284; and Fort McKinney, III, 366; and battle of Murfreesboro, IV, 46; and siege of Petersburg, IV, 256; and the Red River Indian War, IV, 431; and battles at Sailor's Creek, V, 5; and the Shenandoah campaign, V, 68; establishes Fort

Sill, V, 79; and action at Todd's Tavern, V, 276; and battle at Trevilian Station, V, 323; operations on Washita, V, 420; and battle of Winchester, V, 470; and battle at Yellow Tavern, V, 506

Sheriff, as county officer, III, 288

Sherman, John, and the Bland-Allison Act, I, 198; endorses Helper's *Compendium*, III, 25; and resumption of specie payments, IV, 461; V, 144

Sherman, Mrs., and the "Sow Case," V, 134

Sherman, Roger, and Connecticut Compromise, II, 24; signer of the Constitution, II, 39; delegate to Convention of 1787, II, 50; and the drafting of the Declaration of Independence, II, 120; signer of the Declaration of Independence, II, 123

Sherman, W. T., in the battle of Allatoona Pass, I, 50; and the capture and burning of Atlanta, I, 134; at Bull Run, I, 251; and battle of Chickasaw Bluffs, I, 360; Johnston surrenders to, I, 385; and the burning of Columbia, I, 429; captures Cooacoochee, II, 54; and the battle of Ezra Church, II, 238; at Haines' Bluff, III, 3; and Hood's Tennessee campaign, III, 44; and insignia of rank in United States Army, III, 126; and battle of Jackson, Miss., III, 164; and battle of Kenesaw Mountain, III, 203; and the Meridian campaign, III, 377; and the battle of Missionary Ridge, III, 416; and battles at New Hope Church, IV, 104; and battles on Peachtree Creek, IV, 236; and Steele's Bayou expedition, V, 180; commands Army of the Tennessee, V, 242; and campaign against Vicksburg, V, 367; and the Yazoo Pass expedition, V, 504

Sherman Antitrust Act, and the Addyston Pipe Company case, I, 10; and the American Telephone and Telegraph Company, I, 66; and the American Tobacco case, I, 66; passed (1890), I, 87; and the Associated Press, I, 131; and boycotts, I, 232; and Big Business, I, 259; enacted, I, 260; and capitalism, I, 310; and the Clayton Act, I, 396; and collective bargaining, I, 412; and the commerce clause, I, 433; and Danbury Hatters' case, II, 108; and the Debs case, II, 116; and government regulation, II, 405; and International Harvester Company, III, 140; as an interstate commerce law, III, 144; and *laissez-faire*, III, 229; in Loewe v. Lawlor, III, 293; and the Northern Securities Company, IV, 148 f.; and railroad rate agreements, IV, 307; DuPont Corporation violates, IV, 326; and restraint of trade, IV, 460; and the rule of reason, IV, 505; and Standard Oil Company of New Jersey v. U. S., V, 157; and the Sugar Trust, V, 201; and American Tobacco Company's monopoly, V, 274; and trust-busting, V, 326; and

trusts, **V,** 326; and U. S. v. E. C. Knight Company, **V,** 348; and U. S. v. Trans-Missouri Freight Association, **V,** 349

Sherman Silver Purchase Act, and Brussels Monetary Conference, **I,** 245; and bullion, **I,** 252; and campaign of 1892, **I,** 288; revives coinage of silver dollar, **II,** 99; and mortgages, **IV,** 29; and panic of 1893, **IV,** 209; and paper money, **IV,** 213; and repudiation of public debt, **IV,** 455; and silver legislation, **V,** 80; and Treasury notes, **V,** 314

Sherman's March through the Carolinas, **I,** 317

Sherman's March to the Sea, **I,** 134; **II,** 380; **III,** 363; **V,** 36, 242

Sherry's Restaurant, **II,** 55

Shields, James, and battle of Cerro Gordo, **I,** 335; in battle at Kernstown, **III,** 207

Shiloh, the *Lexington* in battle of, **III,** 267; Army of the Tennessee fights at, **V,** 242

Shimonoseki Expedition, and indemnities, **III,** 84

Shinplasters, as fractional currency, **II,** 321; and the Resumption Act (1875), **IV,** 461

Ship-of-the-Line, as warship, **V,** 411

Ship Subsidy Act of 1936, and shipbuilding, **V,** 73; and ocean shipping, **V,** 74

Shipbuilding, and Cape Cod, **I,** 306; colonial industry, **III,** 119; and merchant marine, **III,** 375; at Newport, **IV,** 121

Shippen, William, and first maternity hospital, **III,** 50; elected medical professor of Philadelphia College, **III,** 369; early member of Pennsylvania Hospital staff, **IV,** 247

Shipping Act of 1916, and merchant marine, **III,** 376

Shipping Acts (1916 and 1920), and interstate commerce, **III,** 144

Shipping Board, and the Emergency Fleet Corporation, **II,** 209; incorporated by Federal Government, **II,** 403; predecessor of the Maritime Commission, **III,** 344; and merchant marine, **III,** 376; and merchant marine acts, **III,** 377

Shipping Board Merchant Fleet Corporation, **II,** 210

Shipping Industry, and the Emergency Fleet Corporation, **II,** 209

Ships, Colonial, **I,** 423

Shirley, Fort, and Kittanning campaign, **III,** 214

Shirley, William, and the Louisburg expedition, **III,** 304; attacks Fort Niagara, **IV,** 130; and Oswego, **IV,** 190

Shively, J. M., author of *Route and Distances to Oregon and California,* **IV,** 185

Shoddy, for clothing, during Civil War, **I,** 391

Shoe Manufacture, **I,** 217

Shoe-Pegging Machine, invention of, **III,** 320

Sholes, Christopher L., and the typewriter, **V,** 336

"Shoot the Buffalo," song, **II,** 293

Shooting Matches, **I,** 70

Short, Luke, noted quick-shot gunman, **IV,** 159

Short, Thomas, and printing in America, **IV,** 345

Shorter, Eli, and land speculation, **III,** 240

Shoshone Indians, and treaty of Fort Laramie (1851), **III,** 245; in Montana, **IV,** 16; and scouting on the plains, **V,** 46; designation of, **V,** 105; and Fort Washakie, **V,** 412; placed on the Wind River Reservation, **V,** 497

Shotgun Policy, **III,** 422

Shotwell, James T., and the Kellogg Pact, **IV,** 233

Shreve, Henry M., ships cargo of lead down the Mississippi, **II,** 367; and shallow draft steamboats, **III,** 202; builds the *Washington,* **III,** 423; and the Red River raft, **IV,** 432; and river navigation, **IV,** 489; and removal of snags from the Ohio and Mississippi, **V,** 105; builds the *Washington,* **V,** 179

Shreve, Lamb and Harmon, builders of the Empire State Building, **I,** 101

Shreveport Case, and railroad rate law, **IV,** 402

Shriver, Andrew K., patents steam-pressure kettle, **I,** 304

Shubrick, W. B., and the Kearny-Frémont quarrel, **III,** 201; and the Paraguay expedition, **IV,** 213

Shufeldt, R. W., negotiates first treaty between Korea and a western power, **IV,** 76

Shurt, Abraham, settles on Monhegan, **III,** 203; **IV,** 9; obtains grant at Pemaquid, **IV,** 239

Siam, treaties with, **V,** 317 f.

Sibert, William L., and chemical warfare, **I,** 350

Sibley, H. H., defeated at Glorietta Pass, **IV,** 107; operations on the Rio Grande, **IV,** 485; and battle of Valverde, **V,** 356

Sibley, Henry H., and his expeditions in the Dakotas, **II,** 106; relieves detachment at Birch Coulee, **I,** 190; first governor of Minnesota, **III,** 411; and Fort Ridgely, **IV,** 483; and Sioux uprising in Minnesota, **V,** 86; and the Stillwater Convention, **V,** 182; and battle of Wood Lake, **V,** 483

Sibley, Hiram, and the Western Union Telegraph Company, **V,** 447

Sibley, Solomon, and the Chicago treaties, **I,** 358

Sicard, Montgomery, rescue of, **V,** 5

Sickles, Daniel E., and the murder of Keys, **II,** 88; and the *Virginius* affair, **V,** 380

Siemens-Martin Method, **III,** 156

Sigel, Franz, attacks Jackson at Carthage, **I,** 320; and the Forty-eighters, **II,** 313; in battle of New Market, **IV,** 106; and the Shenandoah campaign, **V,** 68; and battle of Wilson's Creek, **V,** 470

Sign Language, and French exploration, **II,** 345

Signal Corps, and army supply, **I,** 119; and the weather service, **V,** 430

Sigsbee, Charles D., and destruction of the *Maine* (1898), III, 327

Sikhs, and oriental religions, IV, 187

"Silent Brigade," or Night Riders, IV, 133

Silk, importation of, I, 128; and textiles, V, 258; and foreign trade, V, 295

Sill, Fort, and the Belknap scandal, I, 175; Sheridan establishes himself at, V, 420

Silliman, Benjamin, and kerosene oil, III, 207; and early science lecturers, III, 260; and cyclones, V, 284

Silliman, Benjamin, subscribes first rifle during Kansas trouble, I, 173; makes first scientific investigation of petroleum, IV, 166

Silliman, Gold Selleck, and Tryon's retreat after the burning of Danbury, II, 108; and battle of Ridgefield, IV, 483

Silo, II, 60

Silver, as money, I, 188; legislation concerning, I, 189; coinage of, I, 189; subsidies to, I, 198; and the Crime of 1873, II, 89; in Montana, IV, 16; and the Pittman Act, IV, 280; and Sherman Act of 1890, V, 69; and specie payments, V, 144

Silver, Demonetization of, and Colorado, I, 426; and Greenback party, II, 424

Silver, Free. *See* Free Silver

Silver Certificates, created, II, 99; as paper money, IV, 213; and the Silver Purchase Act of 1934, V, 81; and specie payments, V, 143

Silver Dollar, and the bimetallic system, I, 189; overvalued and discontinued, I, 252; and the Bland-Allison Act, I, 198; "old and forgotten," I, 412; and the Crime of 1873, II, 89; as currency, II, 99; and free silver, II, 332; as money, IV, 7; and pieces of eight, IV, 268; and the Spanish dollar, V, 140; as token money, V, 277; as trade dollar, V, 298

Silver Grays, II, 25

Silver Lake Mine, V, 25

Silver Purchase Act of 1934, and bullion, I, 253; and the silver dollar, II, 157; establishes a hybrid money system, IV, 8; and silver legislation, V, 80

Silver Republican Party, I, 288

Silversmithing, Jeremiah Dummer proficient in, I, 122

Simcoe, J. G., orders building of Fort Miami, III, 389

Simkhovitch, Mary Kingsbury, and social settlements, V, 109

Simmons, William J., founder of the Ku Klux Klan (20th century), III, 218

Simms, W. G., and fiction, II, 270; and proslavery literature, IV, 364; poet, V, 123

Simon, Trent, Levy and Franks, organize Indiana Company, I, 170

Simonton, John W., and Key West, Fla., III, 208

Simpson, George, and Fort Vancouver, V, 357

Simpson, J. H., and Inscription Rock, III, 126

Simpson, Jeremiah, and calamity howlers, I, 268

Sims, Jack, printer of the *Weekly Arizonian*, IV, 126, 345

Sims, James Marion, and medicine, III, 369

Sims, Ruth Hanna McCormick, purchases the Trinchera Ranch, V, 28

Sims, W. S., commands the Navy in the World War, V, 493

Sinclair, H. F., and Teapot Dome oil scandal, V, 235

Sinclair, Upton, and the EPIC plan, II, 220; author of *The Jungle*, II, 270; and muckraking, IV, 38; and Pure Food and Drug Acts, IV, 383; and Meat Inspection Act of 1906, V, 29

Sinclair, W. P., and meat packing, IV, 199

Singer, Isaac M., invents a sewing machine, III, 148; V, 61

Singer Sewing Machine Company, and installment selling, III, 126

Single Tax, and *Progress and Poverty*, IV, 356; and Swedenborgianism, V, 213; and distribution of wealth, V, 429

Single Tax League, and the LaFollette party, III, 227

Siouan Family, Arkansas Indians a part of the, I, 106

Sioux Indians, in battle of Ash Hollow, I, 127; Assiniboine separate from, I, 130; and Fort Beauharnois, I, 172; attack at Beecher Island, I, 173; attack at Birch Coulee, I, 190; and the Black Hills gold discoveries, I, 195; and the Carver claim, I, 320; and Catlin's paintings, I, 324; Charlevoix converses with, I, 345; and the Cheyennes, I, 355; defeated by the Chippewa, I, 367; and Fort Connor, II, 24; defeated by Chippewa in battle of Crow Wing, II, 92; Dull Knife escapes to the, II, 175; Fort Ellis built as protection against, II, 203; and Faribault claim, II, 244; and the Fetterman massacre, II, 268; attack Fisk, II, 278; form confederacy, II, 320; outbreak of 1890–91, II, 388; Harney's expedition against, III, 11; and Hayfield fight, III, 20; capture Hennepin, III, 26; and the Hurons, III, 62; attempt to negotiate treaty with, III, 95; and the Indian Country, III, 97; land cessions of, III, 100; placed on reservations, III, 108; and battle of Kaposia, III, 199; oppose construction of Fort Phil Kearny, III, 200; and battle of Killdeer Mountain, III, 209; and the Kiowa, III, 213; and Fort Laramie, III, 245; and treaties of Fort Laramie, III, 245; and the Leavenworth expedition, III, 259; and Leech Lake Indian Council, III, 260; and Fort McKinney, III, 366; and the Messiah War, III, 379; and battle of

Mille Lacs (1745), **III**, 404; in Minnesota, **III**, 410; and Minnesota Uprising of 1862, **III**, 411; in Montana, **IV**, 16; and Neutral Ground, **IV**, 87; attack New Ulm, **IV**, 114; drive the Ottawa back into Michigan, **IV**, 191; on the Great Plains, **IV**, 281; and the Platte Bridge fight, **IV**, 286; and treaty of Prairie du Chien (1825), **IV**, 328; and prospectors, **IV**, 364; and Red Cloud War, **IV**, 429; and Fort Ridgely, **IV**, 483; and Fort Robinson, **IV**, 497; and battle of Rum River, **IV**, 506; in battle of St. Croix Falls, **V**, 7; and British attack on St. Louis (1780), **V**, 11; and battle of Sandy Lake, **V**, 27; and scouting on the plains, **V**, 46; attack Fort Sedgwick, **V**, 55; and Spirit Lake massacre, **V**, 146; and building of Fort Sully, **V**, 202; and treaty of Traverse des Sioux, **V**, 312; and Wagon Box fight, **V**, 388; in the War of 1812, **V**, 406; depend upon wild rice for their food supply, **V**, 464; and battle of Wood Lake, **V**, 483; and battle of Wounded Knee, **V**, 495

Siskyou Pass, **IV**, 222

Sisseton Reservation, **V**, 127

Sistare v. Sistare, **V**, 174

Sitting Bull, and Indian oratory, **III**, 103; and the Messiah War, **III**, 380; fails to stampede Sioux Council, **V**, 85; and Sioux wars, **V**, 87; with the Wild West show, **V**, 464

Siwinowe Kesibwi, a Shawnee newspaper, **IV**, 126

Six Nations, cede land to Indiana Company, **I**, 170; meeting of chiefs of, during Albany Congress, **II**, 77; made so through admittance of the Tuscaroras by the Five Nations, **II**, 280; and the Grand Ohio Company, **II**, 408; and Fort Harmar treaties, **III**, 10; and the Indiana Company, **III**, 113; and treaty of Lancaster (1744), **III**, 232; conciliated by New York, **IV**, 114; and the colony of New York, **IV**, 115; after the Tuscarora War, **V**, 332; and the Vandalia Colony, **V**, 357. *See also* Iroquois Indians

Six-Shooter, and the Texas Rangers, **V**, 256

Sixteen to One, advocated by Bryan in campaign of 1896, **I**, 189; and the Bland-Allison Act, **I**, 198. *See also* Bimetallism

Sixteenth Amendment, text, **II**, 42; and the income tax, **III**, 83 f.; and internal revenue, **III**, 139; and Pollock v. Farmers Loan and Trust Company, **IV**, 304; and the public revenue, **IV**, 462; and taxation, **V**, 226; and direct and indirect taxes, **V**, 230; and Federal taxing power, **V**, 231

Sixth Amendment, and jury trial, **III**, 191

Skelton, Samuel, minister of Salem, **V**, 16

Skenesborough, capture of (1777), **III**, 230

Sketch Book, and Rip Van Winkle, **IV**, 487

Skin Dressing, among Indians, **III**, 87

Skinner, Cortland, and the "Skinners," **II**, 81

Skinner, Halcyon, and carpet manufacture, **I**, 318

Skinner, John, imports guano, **II**, 427

Skinner, R. C., writes first American book on dentistry, **II**, 138

Skunk, encouraged by settlement, **V**, 463

Skyscrapers, and American architecture, **I**, 99; and elevators, **II**, 201

Slade, Joseph A., execution of, **IV**, 290

Slade, William, and abolition movement, **I**, 3

Slater, John F., philanthropy of, **II**, 314; Fund, **IV**, 230

Slater, Samuel, and the Arkwright machinery, **I**, 107; and cotton manufacture, **II**, 67; and textile machines, **III**, 148; introduces Arkwright machinery, **III**, 174; and spinning machines, **III**, 320; installs first Arkwright machinery at Pawtucket, **IV**, 229; and the cotton mill at Pawtucket, **IV**, 478

Slaughter-House Cases, and privileges and immunities of citizens, **IV**, 351

Slave Trade, and abolition movement, **I**, 2; and Royal African Company, **I**, 19; and the Amelia Island affair, **I**, 54; and American Colonization Society, **I**, 59; and the *Amistad* case, **I**, 68; and Anglo-American relations, **I**, 75; and the *Antelope* case, **I**, 79; Baltimore Clippers used in, **I**, 151; and Bristol, **I**, 239; and Triangular Trade, **I**, 417; and Committee of Thirteen (1850), **I**, 436; and compromises of the Federal Constitution, **I**, 444; and the Constitution, **II**, 34; and the Convention of 1787, **II**, 51; and cotton, **II**, 68; and the *Echo*, **II**, 183; and the *Encomium*, **II**, 214; and Treaty of Ghent, **II**, 387; *Hermosa* engaged in, **III**, 28; and the "middle passage," **III**, 395; and the Negro, **IV**, 82; and the rum trade, **IV**, 507; desirability of reopening the, **V**, 130; and visit and search, **V**, 381; the *Wanderer* in the, **V**, 395; and the Webster-Ashburton Treaty, **V**, 431; and the West India trade, **V**, 437

Slavery, and the abolition movement, **I**, 2; and abolitionist literature, **I**, 3; and agriculture, **I**, 27; Alabama supports, **I**, 39; and antislavery sentiment, **I**, 84; and antislavery literature, **I**, 85; prohibited in state bills of rights, **I**, 187; in the Black Belt, **I**, 193; Kentucky and Delaware continued until abolished by Thirteenth Amendment, **I**, 219; outlawed in California state constitution, **I**, 273; issue in the campaign of 1848, **I**, 284; an issue in campaign of 1860, **I**, 285; split of churches concerning, **I**, 374; and economic effect of emancipation on South, **I**, 384; and climate, **I**, 399; and the Committee of Thirteen (1850), **I**, 436; and Compromise of 1850, **I**, 442; opposed by Conscience Whigs, **II**, 25; and the Constitution, **II**, 38; and cotton, **II**, 67; and the Cotton Kingdom, **II**, 70; and

the Crittenden Compromise, **II**, 90; question of, divides Democratic party, **II**, 137; and the Dred Scott case, **II**, 167; and emancipation, **II**, 204; and the Emancipation Proclamation, **II**, 205; and the doctrine of equality, **II**, 223; as cause of food scarcity, **II**, 295; in the territories, **II**, 340; of Indians, **III**, 108; introduced at Jamestown, **III**, 167; and the Lincoln-Douglas debates, **III**, 279; and manners, **III**, 333; and manumission, **III**, 339; after the Mexican War, **III**, 387; in Missouri, **III**, 426; and the Missouri Compromise, **III**, 428 ff.; and the Nashville Convention, **IV**, 55; prohibited by Ordinance of 1787, **IV**, 181; and popular sovereignty, **IV**, 309; justified upon moral, religious and social grounds, **IV**, 363; southern public opinion supports, **IV**, 364; attacked by the Quakers, **IV**, 386; and the race problem, **IV**, 393; and religion, **IV**, 442; banished by the Ordinance of 1787, **IV**, 454; and changes in rural life, **IV**, 509; and threat of secession, **V**, 51; and sectionalism, **V**, 54; and civilization of the Old South, **V**, 122; and the Southern Rights Movement, **V**, 131; and the Tallmadge Amendment, **V**, 218; in Texas under the Mexican regime, **V**, 253; abolished by Thirteenth Amendment, **V**, 263; prohibited by Topeka constitution, **V**, 281; and Virginia, **V**, 374; and the old regime in Virginia, **V**, 375; and the Virginia Resolutions, **V**, 379; and distribution of wealth, **V**, 429; in the West, **V**, 435; to be abolished by the Willey Amendment, **V**, 440; and the Whig party, **V**, 456; and the Wilmot Proviso, **V**, 469

Slaves, and the Asiento, **I**, 129; and British debts, **I**, 240; and Code Noir, **I**, 407; confiscation of, **II**, 16; warned from streets by curfew bell, **II**, 98; present class distinction, **II**, 136; hounds kept to trace runaway, **II**, 157; and the plantation system of the South, **IV**, 283; smuggling of, **V**, 104; in the Triangular Trade, **V**, 296

Slaves, Fugitive. *See* Fugitive Slave Acts

Sledges, and roads, **IV**, 493

"Sleepers," or "Molly Maguires," **IV**, 6

Slemmer, Adam J., occupies Fort Pickens, **IV**, 266; and battle on Santa Rosa Island, **V**, 30

Sliddell, John, and Civil War diplomacy, **I**, 392; and recognition of the Confederacy, **II**, 5; and Laird rams, **III**, 228; and land speculation, **III**, 240; and the Mexican War, **III**, 385 f.; and the *Trent* affair, **V**, 321

Slim Buttes, Sioux defeated at, **V**, 87

Sloan, John, painter, **I**, 123

Sloat, J. D., and conquest of California, **I**, 271; and the Mexican War, **III**, 386; Monterey surrenders to, **IV**, 17

Slocum, H. W., and Sherman's march to the sea, **V**, 71

Sloo, A. G., and the Gadsden Purchase, **II**, 365

Sloops, in transportation, **V**, 306; as warships, **V**, 411

Slosson, E. E., popularizes modern science, **III**, 260

Slough, J. P., and Sibley's operations on the Rio Grande, **IV**, 485

Sloughter, Henry, commissioned governor of New York, **III**, 263; **IV**, 114

Slums, and the Bowery, **I**, 230; and charity organization movement, **I**, 342; and housing, **III**, 53; and philanthropy and benevolence, **IV**, 260

Smallpox, as a "love token," **II**, 150; epidemics of, **II**, 221; and public health, **III**, 21; prevalent on *Jersey* prison-ship, **III**, 174; during encampment at Morristown, **IV**, 28; and sanitation, **V**, 28; and introduction of vaccination, **V**, 355

Smallwood, William, and the battle of Paoli, **IV**, 211

Smart, Charles, and malaria, **III**, 328

Smibert, John, artist, **I**, 122; architect of Faneuil Hall, **II**, 243; in Rhode Island, **IV**, 478

Smiley, Albert, inaugurates the Lake Mohonk Arbitration Conferences, **IV**, 235

Smith, A. Cary, American naval architect, **V**, 499

Smith, A. J., and the Red River campaign, **IV**, 430; and battle at Tupelo, **V**, 330

Smith, Alfred E., nominated for Presidency, **I**, 291; and the Lily-White movement, **III**, 277; as Democratic candidate, arouses nativistic propaganda, **IV**, 66; and religion in politics, **IV**, 443; and Tammany Hall, **V**, 218; whispering campaigns against, **V**, 458

Smith, E. Kirby. *See* Kirby-Smith

Smith, Emma, and Reorganized Latter Day Saints, **IV**, 449

Smith, F. H., and fiction, **II**, 270

Smith, F. M., borax king, **I**, 218

Smith, Fort, and caravan traffic, **I**, 312

Smith, Fort C. F., and Bozeman Trail, **I**, 232; and Hayfield fight, **III**, 20; and Red Cloud War, **IV**, 429; **V**, 86

Smith, Frank L., and political scandals, **IV**, 298

Smith, Frederick, sets "Old Oaken Bucket" to music, **IV**, 171

Smith, G. W., succeeds Johnston at Fair Oaks, **II**, 240

Smith, George W., loses his life in the burning of Richmond Theater, **IV**, 482

Smith, Gerald B., and religious thought and writings, **IV**, 447

Smith, Gerrit, and the Emigrant Aid Movement, **II**, 211; leader of the Liberty party, **III**, 272

Smith, Hamilton L., patents the tintype, **V**, 272

Smith, Hyrum, murdered, **IV**, 25; court-martialed, **IV**, 26

Smith, Ida B. Wise, president of the W. C. T. U., **V**, 479

Smith, James, signer of the Declaration of Independence, **II**, 124

Smith, James, leader of the Black Boys, **I**, 193; at Sideling Hill, **V**, 78

Smith, James, tarred and feathered, **V**, 220

Smith, Jedediah S., and Ashley's expedition, **I**, 128; and Cajon Pass, **I**, 267; and overland immigration, **I**, 269; and caravan traffic on the Great Plains, **I**, 312; first to cross Utah-Nevada deserts, **II**, 235; mountain man, **II**, 362; and the Great Valley, **II**, 421; and the Mohave Indians, **IV**, 4; and Oregon fur trade, **IV**, 182; and the Rocky Mountain Fur Company, **IV**, 498; on the Spanish Trail, **V**, 142; discovers second overland route to the Pacific Ocean, **V**, 283; and Ashley's expeditions, **V**, 310; and water holes, **V**, 421; and western exploration, **V**, 442

Smith, John, author of *True Relation*, **I**, 189; maps Boston, **I**, 221; and capitalism, **I**, 309; fishing venture of, **I**, 406; describes Isles of Shoals, **III**, 162; and founding of Jamestown, **III**, 166; captured by Indians, **III**, 167; visits Maine, **III**, 326; maps by, **III**, 340; describes Monhegan Island, **IV**, 9; lands in New Hampshire, **IV**, 101; at Pemaquid, **IV**, 239; and the Potomac River, **IV**, 324; founds settlement near Richmond, **IV**, 482; and the Susquehannock Indians, **V**, 211; surveys of, **V**, 282; leader in the Jamestown settlement, **V**, 372

Smith, John, establishes a communal gristmill in Providence Plantations, **IV**, 367

Smith, Joseph, and Far West, Mo., **II**, 244; and *The Book of Mormon*, **IV**, 23, 25; murdered, **IV**, 25; revelations of, **IV**, 25; court-martialed, **IV**, 26; claims a visitation from John the Baptist, **IV**, 26; revelations of, **IV**, 26; frontier religious leader, **IV**, 444; killed at Carthage, **IV**, 449; and City of Zion, **V**, 19

Smith, Joseph, III, and Reorganized Latter Day Saints, **IV**, 449

Smith, Joseph F., president of Mormon Church, **IV**, 27

Smith, Melancthon, and pamphleteering, **IV**, 202

Smith, Nathan, promotes medical education, **III**, 369

Smith, Peter, and land speculation, **III**, 239

Smith, Peter, press maker, **IV**, 346

Smith, Robert, and Erskine's agreement, **II**, 227

Smith, S. S., and philosophical thought and writings, **IV**, 263

Smith, Samuel F., writes "My Country, 'Tis of Thee," **IV**, 50

Smith, Samuel H., establishes the *National Intelligencer*, **IV**, 60, 128

Smith, Sol, barnstormer, **I**, 164; and showboats, **V**, 76

Smith, Sooy, and the Meridian campaign, **III**, 377

Smith, Stephen, first sanitarian of New York, **III**, 63

Smith, T. A., supervises building of Fort Crawford, **II**, 83

Smith, Theobald, and immunity from contagious diseases, **III**, 64; and cattle fever, **III**, 370; and tuberculosis, **V**, 328

Smith, Thomas, and the Virginia Company of London, **V**, 377

Smith, W. and T., nurserymen, **IV**, 154

Smith, W. S., and Miranda's intrigues, **III**, 414

Smith, William, founds the Episcopal Corporation, **III**, 129; and the Protestant Episcopal Church, **IV**, 366

Smith, William Farrar, makes successful use of wire entanglements at Drewry's Bluff, **II**, 169

Smith, Winthrop B., and McGuffey's Readers, **III**, 365

Smith Charities, founding of, **II**, 314

Smith College, and the education of women, **V**, 480

Smith-Hughes Act (1917), and agricultural education, **I**, 25; and centralization of education, **II**, 188

Smith-Lever Act (1914), and agricultural education, **I**, 25; and the Department of Agriculture, **I**, 31; and the Farm Bureau, **II**, 244; and farmers' institutes, **II**, 253; and Four-H Clubs, **II**, 316

Smith-Lever Vocation Education Act of 1917, **II**, 255

Smithson, George, printer of the *Weekly Arizonian*, **IV**, 126; Arizona printer, **IV**, 345

Smithson, James, and founding of Smithsonian Institution, **V**, 102

Smithsonian Institution, Varden art collection transferred to, **I**, 124; records of early cable messages preserved at, **I**, 135; Catlin cartoon collection presented to, **I**, 324; and Latin America, **III**, 248; organized, **IV**, 47; and Washington, D. C., **V**, 413; begins to record weather observations, **V**, 430

Smuggler-Union Gold Mine, **II**, 396; **V**, 25

Smuggling, and the Amelia Island affair, **I**, 54; and colonial customs, **II**, 102; and the burning of the *Gaspee*, **II**, 373; and the *I'm Alone* case, **III**, 72; and the Molasses Act, **IV**, 6; and pirates, **IV**, 278; and the rum trade, **IV**, 507; and the Secret Service, **V**, 53; of slaves, **V**, 92; and colonial sugar acts, **V**, 199; and territorial waters, **V**, 248

Smyth, Alexander, and the Niagara campaigns, **V**, 405

Smyth, Newman, and religious thought, **IV**, 446

Smyth v. Ames, **IV**, 416

Snake Ceremony, survives among the Hopi Indians, **III**, 45

Snake Dance, **II**, 170; **III**, 97

Snake Indians, on Green River, **II**, 423; and horses, **III**, 48

Snake River, and the Oregon Trail, **IV**, 186

Snelling, Fort, flour mill constructed at, **I**, 118; Sully marches from, **II**, 107; and Hudson's Bay Company, **III**, 56; established, **III**, 411; founding of, and the Red River cart traffic, **IV**, 430; Sioux-Chippewa Council convenes at, **V**, 84; Indian agency at, **V**, 84; and Sioux treaties, **V**, 86; and Sioux uprising in Minnesota, **V**, 86

Snoqualimich Indians, fail to capture Fort Nisqually, **IV**, 135

Snoqualmie Pass, A. W. Tinkham makes trip through, **V**, 182

Snow, Elisha, commands the *Yankee*, **V**, 501

Snow, Lorenzo, president of Mormon Church, **IV**, 27

Snow, William Freeman, and social hygiene, **III**, 64

Snowshoes, Indians instruct colonists in use of, **III**, 88

Snowshoes, Battle on, Rogers' Rangers in, **IV**, 500

Snuff-Takers, **II**, 25

Snyder Act, and Indian citizenship, **III**, 106

Social Compact. *See* Compact Theory

Social Democratic Party, and class struggle, **I**, 395; as a political party, **IV**, 297; organized, **V**, 110, 111

Social Justice, weekly magazine of National Union for Social Justice, **IV**, 63

Social Science Research Council, **III**, 257

Social Security, and *laissez-faire*, **III**, 229

Social Security Act, and the blind, **I**, 200; and organized charity, **I**, 342; Government borrows funds accumulating under, **II**, 128; and public employment offices, **II**, 213; and Federal aid, **II**, 255; and Federal-state relations, **II**, 263; passed, **III**, 131; and internal revenue, **III**, 139; and the Supreme Court, **III**, 184; and labor legislation, **III**, 223; and the New Deal, **IV**, 96; and old age, **IV**, 169; and pauperism, **IV**, 227; and relief, **IV**, 441; and social legislation, **V**, 107 f.; and taxes, **V**, 227

Social Security Board, **III**, 377; **V**, 108

Social Settlements, and adult education, **I**, 14; and organized charity, **I**, 342; and philanthropy, **IV**, 260

Socialism, and distribution of wealth, **V**, 429

Socialist Labor Party, and class struggle, **I**, 395; as a political party, **IV**, 297; and Social Democratic party, **V**, 106; merges with Social Democrats, **V**, 111; as third party, **V**, 262

Socialist Party, and campaign of 1912, **I**, 290; in campaigns of 1920 and 1924, **I**, 291; in campaigns of 1932 and 1936, **I**, 292; and class struggle, **I**, 395; and communism, **I**, 440; endorses the LaFollette party, **III**, 227; as a political party, **IV**, 297; new party designation, **V**, 107; as third party, **V**, 262

Society for Prevention of Pauperism, **V**, 109

Society for the Prevention of Cruelty to Animals, **III**, 58

Society for the Prevention of Cruelty to Children, **III**, 58

Society for the Promotion of Engineering Education, **II**, 216

Society for the Propagation of the Gospel, **I**, 373; **III**, 103; **IV**, 358; **V**, 96

Society for the Reformation of Juvenile Offenders, **IV**, 260

Society for the Relief of Distressed Masters of Ships and their Widows, **IV**, 260

Society of Jesus. *See* Jesuits

Sod House, and the frontier family, **II**, 243; and the pioneers, **IV**, 275

Sodom, Fort, another name for Fort Atkinson, **I**, 134

"Softs," appearance of term, **III**, 60

Soil, and agriculture, **I**, 27; exhaustion of, **I**, 32; alfalfa puts nitrogen in, **I**, 48

Soil Conservation, diversification as a means of, **II**, 154; and Tennessee Valley Authority, **V**, 245

Soil Conservation and Domestic Allotment Act, **I**, 22, 24, 33; **II**, 245; **IV**, 308

Soil Erosion, **I**, 27; **III**, 135; **IV**, 238

Sokoki Indians, **I**, 48

Soldier Vote, and the bonus, **I**, 210; and pensions, **IV**, 251

Solicitor General, and the Department of Justice, **III**, 191

Solid South, and the Democratic party, **II**, 137; and Reconstruction, **IV**, 426; and sectionalism, **V**, 54

Somers, George, and the Virginia Company of London, **V**, 376

Somers, Richard, and explosion of the *Intrepid*, **III**, 148

Somers, The, mutiny on, **IV**, 50

Somervell, Gen., and the Mier expedition, **III**, 396

Sonora Democrat, supports the Pacific Republic movement, **IV**, 197

Sonora Pass, **IV**, 221

Sons of Liberty, and Associations, **I**, 131; and Boston Tea Party, **I**, 224; and battle of Golden Hill, **II**, 400; and the "Song of Liberty," **III**, 271; and Liberty poles, **III**, 272; and the colony of New York, **IV**, 115; organized, **IV**, 118; and the news of the battle of Lexington, **IV**, 120; and the nonimportation agreements, **IV**, 138; and pole raising, **IV**, 294; and colonial postal service, **IV**, 321; and Revolutionary committees,

IV, 474; in Savannah, **V,** 35; as secret society, **V,** 53; and Stamp Act Riot in New York City, **V,** 155; and Tammany Hall, **V,** 218

Sons of Liberty (Civil War), oppose Lincoln's administration, **I,** 388; Copperheads organize as, **II,** 58; and Knights of the Golden Circle, **III,** 215; and Northwest Conspiracy, **IV,** 150; name taken by Order of American Knights, **IV,** 180

Sons of the Revolution, own Fraunces Tavern, **II,** 330

Sooners, and Oklahoma squatters, **IV,** 169

Sophie Newcomb College, **V,** 480

Sorghum, **I,** 23, 174

Sorin, Father Edward, introduces Holy Cross Fathers into the United States, **III,** 40

Sorosis Club, and the woman movement, **V,** 477, 482

Soucek, Lt., sets altitude record, **I,** 142

Soule, J. L. B., first to use expression "Go West, Young Man, Go West," **II,** 392

Soulé, Pierre, and the *Black Warrior* affair, **I,** 196; and the Ostend Manifesto, **IV,** 190

Soule, S. W., and the typewriter, **V,** 336

Soumain, Simeon, silversmith, **V,** 82

South Carolina, and repudiation of state debts, **IV,** 457; Bank of the State of, **V,** 164; and states' rights, **V,** 176; western land claims of, **V,** 444

South Carolina, The, dreadnought, **II,** 167; **V,** 412

South-Carolina Gazette, founded by Thomas Whitmarsh, **IV,** 127

South Dakota, created from Dakota Territory, **II,** 106; organized, and admitted, **V,** 249

South Improvement Company, and Standard Oil Company, **V,** 156

South Mountain, and the battle of Antietam, **I,** 81; and invasion of Maryland, **III,** 350

South Pass, located by Jedediah Smith, **I,** 128; Astor overlanders cross, **I,** 133; and the Central Route, **I,** 334; Forty-niners travel on, **II,** 313; and the Great Basin, **II,** 414; and the Oregon Trail, **IV,** 185 f.; most important pass in Rocky Mountain chain, **IV,** 222; and the Platte River Trail, **IV,** 286; and the Oregon Trail, **IV,** 495; of the Rocky Mountains, **IV,** 498; and Jedediah Strong Smith, **V,** 101; wagons go through, **V,** 389; and western exploration, **V,** 442; gold discovery at, and settling of Wyoming, **V,** 496

South Sea Company, Asiento granted to, **I,** 129

Southampton, Earl of, and the Virginia Company of London, **V,** 377

Southern Boundary, survey of, **II,** 203; and Guion's expedition, **II,** 428; survey of, **IV,** 137; and Pinckney's treaty (1795), **V,** 134

Southern Commercial Conventions, and the Southern Rights movement, **V,** 131

Southern Education Fund, **II,** 315

Southern Overland Mail, inaugurated, **IV,** 193; and roads, **IV,** 496; begun, **V,** 152

Southern Pacific Railroad, connects with Atchison, Topeka and Santa Fé Railroad, **I,** 134; settlement made with, for extending Atlantic and Pacific Railroad, **I,** 135; acquires the Morgan steamship line, **I,** 406; and the Gila Trail, **II,** 389; builds west, **IV,** 408; and race with the Texas and Pacific, **V,** 255; and rail transportation, **V,** 309; and Fort Yuma, **V,** 512

Southern Railway, reaches Cumberland Gap, **II,** 96; leases North Carolina Railroad, **IV,** 146; acquires control of South Carolina Railroad, **V,** 127

Southern Rights Movement, **V,** 343

Southfield, The, sunk by the *Albemarle,* **I,** 46

Southside Railroad, **I,** 91

Southwest Fur Company, **I,** 61

Southwest Territory, organized, **V,** 132; and the state-making process, **V,** 172; organized, **V,** 243, 248; and western lands, **V,** 444

Southwestern Exhibition and Fat Stock Show, **IV,** 499

Sovereigns of Industry, and consumer co-operatives, **II,** 56; and Industrial Congress convention, **III,** 114

Sower (Saur), Christopher (1693–1758), printer of the Bible, **I,** 181, 182; publisher, **I,** 213; begins first permanent German publication, **II,** 302; printer and type founder, **II,** 385; invents primitive stove, **III,** 23; and the printing press, **IV,** 346; as type founder, **V,** 336

Sower, Christopher (1721–1784), and German type, **IV,** 346

Spaight, Richard Dobbs, signer of the Constitution, **II,** 39

Spalding, A. G., and baseball, **I,** 166

Spalding, Henry Harmon, establishes the Lapwai Mission, **III,** 245; and the American Board Mission in Oregon, **IV,** 182; and Oregon missions, **IV,** 184

Spalding, Lyman, inaugurates the national pharmacopœia, **II,** 171

Spalding, Thomas, and soil exhaustion, **V,** 116

Spalding and Rogers, operate first rail circus, **I,** 377; showboat of, **V,** 76

Spangenberg, Augustus Gottlieb, and the Moravians, **IV,** 22

Spangler, Edward, and Lincoln's assassination, **III,** 280

Spanish-American War, British attitude toward, **I,** 76; and hospitalization, **I,** 116; blockade in, **I,** 201; and Cuba, **II,** 94; financing of, **II,** 128; demobilization after, **II,** 134; desertion in, **II,** 141; and "manifest destiny," **III,** 332; mobilization for, **IV,** 2; Navy in, **IV,** 78; and American influence in the Pacific, **IV,** 196; terminated by

treaty of Paris (1898), **IV**, 216; and the Philippine Islands, **IV**, 262; and territorial claims of the United States, **V**, 247; and army uniforms, **V**, 341; cost of, **V**, 409; loss of life in, **V**, 410; and the United States as a world power, **V**, 486

Spanish-American War, Naval and Military Order of the, **V**, 365

Spanish-American War Veterans, **V**, 365

Spanish Capture Fort St. Joseph, **V**, 10

Spanish Coins, **II**, 100

Spanish Commercial Exploration Company, and the fur trade, **II**, 363; and Missouri River fur trade, **III**, 430

Spanish Conspiracy, and Kentucky, **III**, 205; and free navigation of the Mississippi, **III**, 422; and the Mississippi River, **III**, 424

Spanish Dollar, and coinage names, **I**, 411; dominance of, **II**, 99; used in colonial period, **II**, 157; and origin of the dollar mark, **II**, 158; as money, **IV**, 7; and pieces-of-eight, **IV**, 268; its influence on American life, **V**, 138

Spanish Influence in Exploration, **II**, 25

Spanish Land Grants, in California, **I**, 275

Spanish Missions, of East Texas, **II**, 182

Spanish Trail, as part of the California Trail, **I**, 274; explored, **I**, 275; Forty-niners travel on, **II**, 313; Frémont returns by way of, **II**, 342; and the Great Basin, **II**, 414; and mountain passes, **IV**, 221; and water holes, **V**, 421; and western exploration, **V**, 443

Sparks, Jared, biographical works of, **I**, 189; book collection of, **I**, 213

Sparrow-Hawk, The, shipwrecked at Cape Cod, **I**, 306

Spaulding, George H., and the development of the reaper, **IV**, 419

Spaulding, Lt., and the Westminster massacre, **V**, 448

Spaulding and Rogers. *See* Spalding and Rogers

Speakeasies, and bootlegging, **I**, 217; and the Eighteenth Amendment, **II**, 190; and prohibition, **IV**, 357

Speaker of the House of Representatives, nominated by party caucus, **I**, 328; **II**, 18; and the Constitution, **II**, 31; and the Reed rules, **IV**, 433

Special Delivery Service, **IV**, 320

Special Service Schools, establishment of, **I**, 118

Specie Circular (1836), **III**, 9; **IV**, 208; **V**, 144

Specie Payments, and the Bland-Allison Act, **I**, 198; suspension of, during Civil War, **I**, 388; suspended during panics of 1819 and 1837, **IV**, 208; suspension and resumption of, **IV**, 461. *See also* Resumption Act

Specie Redemption, and state banks, **I**, 156; and Suffolk banking system, **V**, 198

Specie Reserve Banking System of Louisiana, **III**, 306; **V**, 164

Specific Duties, **II**, 180

Spectator, newspaper, **IV**, 127

Speech, Freedom of. *See* Freedom of Speech

Speedwell, The, and the Pilgrims, **III**, 361; **IV**, 271

Spelling Bees, **I**, 174

Spelling Schools, on the frontier, **II**, 243

Spencer, Joseph, and Washington's eight months army, **V**, 419

Spencer, Midshipman, as mutineer on the *Somers,* **IV**, 50; **V**, 119

Spermaceti, provided by the whaling industry, **V**, 452

Sperry, Charles S., takes over command of fleet in cruise round the world, **I**, 168

Sperry, Richard, aids regicides in New England, **IV**, 438

Spices, and foreign trade, **V**, 294

Spiegler, Cæsar, constructs first dirigibles in America, **II**, 148

Spies, and the Articles of War, **I**, 126; and military intelligence, **III**, 400

Spies, August, and the Haymarket riot, **III**, 20

Spinning, Jenny, **III**, 173

Spinning Machine, developed by Arkwright, **I**, 107

Spinning Wheel, and household arts, **III**, 53

Spiring, Peter, promoter of New Sweden Company, **IV**, 113

"Spirit of St. Louis," Lindbergh's plane, **III**, 280

Spiritualism, and religion, **IV**, 442; and Rochester Rappings, **IV**, 497; and theosophy, **V**, 262; in the Western Reserve, **V**, 446

Spoils System, and the Albany Regency, **I**, 46; and the appointing power, **I**, 91; and political corruption, **II**, 65; produces chaos in Indian affairs, **III**, 91; and party machines, **III**, 319; and political patronage, **IV**, 224; and relief, **IV**, 441; and foreign service, **V**, 163

Spooner, Judah Padock, first printer of Vermont, **IV**, 346

Sports, rise of, **I**, 70; baseball, **I**, 165; basketball, **I**, 167; bicycling, **I**, 182; football, **II**, 298; leisure makes possible, **III**, 264; the Olympic games, **IV**, 172; prize fights, **IV**, 352; tennis, **V**, 245

Spotswood, Alexander, and Germanna, **II**, 385; establishes his furnaces in Virginia, **III**, 156; and Knights of the Golden Horseshoe, **III**, 215; and the Ohio River, **IV**, 164; and colonial postal service, **IV**, 321; and the "Golden Age" of Virginia colonial history, **V**, 372; and the Virginia Indian Company, **V**, 379

Spotsylvania Courthouse, Bloody Angle at, **I**, 202; and campaign against Richmond, **IV**, 481

Spotted Tail, Sioux chief, **V**, 85

Spottedtail Reservation, popular designation for the Rosebud Indian Reservation, **IV**, 502

Sprague, F. J., installs street railway system, **II**, 199; and electric railways, **IV**, 410

Sprague, Ralph, Richard and William, founders of Charlestown, Mass., **I**, 345

Sprague, William P., and carpet manufacture, **I**, 318

Sprague Electric Company, **II**, 376

Spreckels, Claus, sugar refiner, **I**, 174; and great fortunes, **II**, 312

Spring Hill, and Hood's Tennessee campaign, **III**, 44

Springbok Case, and the Confederate blockade, **II**, 9; and continuous voyage, **II**, 142

Springer v. U. S., upholds income taxes, **IV**, 462

Springfield, Ill., arsenal at, **I**, 122

"Springfield Mountain," ballad, **II**, 293

Springfield Rifle, **I**, 392; **IV**, 45, 483

Spunky, Fort, **V**, 285

Squalus, The, sinking of the, **V**, 194

Square Deal, organ of the National Trades' and Workers' Association, **IV**, 63

Squatter Sovereign, proslavery paper, **I**, 133

Squatter Sovereignty. *See* Popular Sovereignty

Squatters, and claim associations, **I**, 394; and claim jumping, **I**, 394; and the frontier family, **II**, 243; and military tracts, **III**, 403; and preemption, **IV**, 330; and public land sales, **IV**, 372; and early surveyors, **V**, 209; and the West, **V**, 435

Sri Mariya Ashrama, Hindu cult, **IV**, 187

Staats-Zeitung, newspaper, **II**, 303

Stabilization Fund, created, **I**, 253; and increase in dollar value of gold stock, **II**, 394; and the gold standard, **II**, 399

Stag-Hound, The, clipper ship, **I**, 402

Stage, and motion pictures, **IV**, 32

Stagecoaches, robbery of, **I**, 152; and overland mail, **IV**, 193; and the Great Plains, **IV**, 282; employed as carriers of the mail, **IV**, 320; and road improvement, **IV**, 494; and travel, **V**, 306

Stages, and urban transportation, **V**, 305

Stair's, Earl of, Plan (1721), **I**, 420

Staked Plains, wild horses on, **IV**, 49

"Stalwarts," and "Half-Breeds," **III**, 5

Stamp Act, and Associations, **I**, 131; and British colonial policy, **I**, 422; and the Declaration of Rights, **II**, 124; and the Declaratory Act, **II**, 125; and letters of Junius, **III**, 190; passage of, **IV**, 115; and the Nonimportation Agreements, **IV**, 138; and the English Parliament, **IV**, 218; and the American Revolution, **IV**, 466; and Savannah, **V**, 35; and Sons of Liberty, **V**, 120; and taxation, **V**, 225; Virginia resists the, **V**, 373

Stamp Act Congress (1765), and the Albany Plan, **I**, 45; and representative government, **IV**, 452; and the American Revolution, **IV**, 466

Stampedes, and cowboy songs, **II**, 79; and Texas Longhorns, **III**, 300; and trail drivers, **V**, 302

Stand Watie, Cherokee Indian, negotiates treaty of New Echota, **IV**, 97; and Council of Fort Smith, **V**, 101

Standard-Bred Trotter, **III**, 49

Standard Dictionary, prepared by Isaac K. Funk, **II**, 146

Standard Oil Case, and the Rule of Reason, **IV**, 505; **V**, 326

Standard Oil Company, perfects a safe kerosene stove, **III**, 207; and patents, **IV**, 223; and rebates, **IV**, 420; and the Sherman Antitrust Law, **V**, 70; as the first trust, **V**, 326

Standard Oil Company of Indiana, fined by Judge Landis, **V**, 157

Standards, Bureau of, **I**, 432

Standards of Living, and protection, **IV**, 366; and wages and prices, **V**, 387

Standing Rock Reservation, **V**, 127

Standish, Burt L., pseudonym of William Gilbert Patten, creator of "Frank Merriwell," **II**, 147

Standish, Laura, makes first sampler known to have been made in America, **V**, 21

Standish, Myles, and fishing rights at Cape Ann, **I**, 306; sent to arrest Thomas Morton, **III**, 378; attacks Penobscot, **IV**, 249; aids the Weston settlers, **V**, 448

Stanford, Leland, benefactions and gifts of, **I**, 177; and great fortunes, **II**, 312; and the completion of first transcontinental railroad at Promontory Point, **IV**, 358; and the Southern Pacific Railroad Company, **V**, 130; and rail transportation, **V**, 309

Stanley, Robert, and the Helena mining camp, **III**, 24

Stanley, William, and alternating current, **II**, 198

Stanley Electric Manufacturing Company, **II**, 376

Stansbury, Howard, makes survey of Great Salt Lake, **II**, 420

Stanton, Charles E., and "Lafayette, we are here," **III**, 227

Stanton, Edwin M., and censorship, **I**, 331; and General Orders No. 100, **I**, 384; and surrender of Confederate armies, **I**, 385; and enlistment in the Union army, **II**, 218; and exchange of prisoners, **II**, 231; and impeachment trial of Andrew Johnson, **III**, 77; and the peace movement of 1864, **IV**, 233; and Northern prison camps, **IV**, 347; and Soldiers and Sailors Conventions, **V**, 117; and Tenure-of-Office Act, **V**, 246

Stanton, Elizabeth Cady, and Seneca Falls Convention, **II**, 265; and the Nineteenth Amendment, **IV**, 134; calls Seneca Falls Convention, **V**, 58; and the woman movement, **V**, 477; and woman suffrage, **V**, 478

Stanton, Thomas, and the Pequot War, **IV**, 252

Stanwix, Fort, and Burgoyne's Invasion, **I**, 255; and battle of Oriskany, **IV**, 188

Stanwix, Fort, Treaty of (1768), and the Indiana Company, **I**, 170; and the Grand Ohio Company, **II**, 408; and Holston Valley settlements, **III**, 39; and Indian land cessions, **III**, 99; and the Indiana Company, **III**, 113; T. Walker participates in negotiating, **III**, 311; and the Mississippi Company of Virginia, **III**, 421; designates a new Indian boundary line, **IV**, 354; and "suffering traders," **V**, 198; and the Susquehannah Company, **V**, 211; and the Vandalia Colony, **V**, 357; and Virginia v. Transylvania Company, **V**, 380; and Watauga settlement, **V**, 420; and western land schemes, **V**, 443

Stanwix, Fort, Treaty of (1784), and treaties of Fort Harmar, **III**, 10; and Indian land cessions, **III**, 100; and treaties of Fort McIntosh, **III**, 365

Stanwix, John, and Fort Pitt, **IV**, 279

Star of the West, sent to reinforce Sumter, **V**, 52

Star Route Frauds, **II**, 88

"Star-Spangled Banner," written by Francis Scott Key, **I**, 150; and the flag, **II**, 281; and Fort McHenry, **III**, 365

Starbuck, E. D., and theological writings, **V**, 261

Stark, John, in battle of Bennington, **I**, 178; at Bunker Hill, **I**, 253; wins battle of Bennington, **IV**, 102; one of Rogers' Rangers, **IV**, 500

Starr Rifle, **IV**, 483

Stars and Bars, Confederate flag, **II**, 6

Stars and Stripes, first battle under, **II**, 54

Starved Rock, Tonti inspects as site for fort, **II**, 87; Tonti commander at, **II**, 345; LaSalle builds fort on, **III**, 67; Jesuit mission near, **III**, 174; Fort St. Louis built on, **V**, 11

State, Department of, administers arrests, **I**, 122; and foreign service, **II**, 307; evolution of, **IV**, 475

State Agencies, and state debts, **V**, 169

State Bank Notes, taxed out of existence, **I**, 154; Bank of the United States refuses to accept, **I**, 155; nicknames of, **II**, 101; and money, **IV**, 7; and specie payments, **V**, 143; and Veazie Bank v. Fenno, **V**, 358

State Banking, and the panic of 1857, **IV**, 208; and state debts, **IV**, 456; **V**, 168

State Banks, failure of, **I**, 153; growth of, **I**, 156; and branch banking, **I**, 158; and national banks, **I**, 159; and issuance of bank notes, **II**, 99; and the Federal Reserve System, **II**, 261; and removal of deposits, **IV**, 448

State Colleges of Mechanic Arts, **V**, 44

State Constitutions, and apportionment provisions, **I**, 92; and the Federal Constitution, **II**, 38; and the doctrine of equality, **II**, 223; and colonial governors, **II**, 406; and the right of petition, **IV**, 256; and separation of powers, **IV**, 327; and reserved powers of the people, **IV**, 458; and the American Revolution, **IV**, 468; and state debts, **V**, 168; and religious liberty, **V**, 277

State Debts, repudiation of, **I**, 39, 147; and the Barnburners, **I**, 164; assumption and funding of, **II**, 118; repudiation of, **IV**, 456; and state banking, **V**, 164

State Laws, Uniform, and relations between states, **V**, 175

State Legislatures, and representative government, **IV**, 452

State Sovereignty, in campaigns of 1848 and 1856, **I**, 284; and states' rights, **V**, 175; and Virginia-Kentucky Resolutions, **V**, 376

State Troops, raising of, **I**, 113

State Universities. *See* Universities, State

Staten Island, bought from the Indians, **IV**, 118

States, reserved powers of, **IV**, 457

States' Rights, sentiment for, in Alabama, **I**, 39; in campaign of 1856, **I**, 284; and the commerce clause, **I**, 433; and compromises of the Federal Constitution, **I**, 443; and the Confederacy, **II**, 4, 12; develop in Cotton Kingdom, **II**, 70; and the Democratic party, **II**, 136; and the Eleventh Amendment, **II**, 202; and the Federal Government, **II**, 257; rise of the doctrine, **II**, 263; and Georgia, **II**, 379; and lynching legislation, **III**, 317; and nationalist sentiment, **IV**, 64; and Jackson's toast, "Our Federal Union, etc.," **IV**, 191; and the Republican party, **IV**, 455; and the Richmond Junto, **IV**, 482; and secession of southern states, **V**, 51; and civilization of the Old South, **V**, 122; doctrine of, **V**, 173; and the Virginia-Kentucky Resolutions, **V**, 376; and the Webster-Hayne debate, **V**, 431

Statue of Liberty, gift of France, **II**, 328

Statute of Artificers, adopted in Virginia, **II**, 185

Stay Laws, and mortgages, **IV**, 28; and Old Court-New Court struggle, **IV**, 170

Steam Engine, Fitch's experiments with, **II**, 278; invented by Watt, **III**, 117; patents for, **IV**, 223

Steam Warship, *Demologos*, **II**, 137

Steam Whistles, **I**, 7

Steamboats, on western rivers, **I**, 28; as influence on agriculture, **I**, 33; and growth of cities, **I**, 378; on Erie Canal, **II**, 226; for carrying freight, **II**, 340; "Fulton's Folly," **II**, 355 f.; on Hudson River, **III**, 55; invented by John Fitch, **III**, 148; and Louisiana, **III**, 306; on the Mississippi, **III**, 423; on the Mississippi and Ohio, **III**, 424; on the Mississippi and Missouri, **III**, 427; on the Missouri, **III**, 430; and the Missouri River fur trade, **III**, 431; and monopoly, **IV**, 12; and New Orleans, **IV**, 109; patents for, **IV**, 223; and Pittsburgh, **IV**, 280; for river navigation, **IV**, 489; on rivers, **IV**, 491; Rumsey's, **IV**, 507; and rise of

St. Louis, V, 12; and domestic trade, V, 291; and transportation, V, 307; the *Virginia*, V, 374; *Walk-in-the-Water*, V, 391; on inland waterways, V, 424; the *Western Engineer*, V, 441; and the westward movement, V, 451; and growth of Wheeling, W. Va., V, 455; the *Yellowstone*, V, 506

Steamship Companies, and immigration, III, 75

Steamship Savannah, V, 36

Steamships on Great Lakes, II, 417

Stedman, Fort, assaulted by Lee, IV, 256

Stedman, John, ambushed by Senecas at Devil's Hole, II, 145

Steedman, J. B., and Soldiers and Sailors Conventions, V, 117

Steel Engraving, I, 213

Steel Industry, and the Homestead strike, III, 43; development of, III, 118

Steel Rails, manufactured, III, 337

Steel Workers Organization Committee, V, 180

Steele, Frederick, and battle at Jenkins Ferry, III, 173; and the Red River Campaign, IV, 430

Steering Committee, elected by party caucus, I, 328

Steffe, William, writes music for "John Brown's Body," I, 168

Steffens, Lincoln, "The Shame of the Cities," IV, 38; political writings of, IV, 302

Steinmetz, C. P., and alternating current, II, 198; consulting engineer of General Electric Company, II, 376

Steinway, Henry E., and the Forty-eighters, II, 313

Stephen, Adam, and battle of Germantown, II, 385

Stephens, Alexander H., and the Confederate peace movement, II, 4; and the Confederate Congress, II, 6; Confederate Vice-President, II, 9; and the Confederate States, II, 12; and Hampton Roads conference, III, 7; selected Vice-President by the Montgomery Convention, IV, 17; political writings of, IV, 302; and the South as a conscious minority, V, 124; and states' rights during Civil War, V, 176

Stephens, Ann S., and dime novels, II, 146

Stephens, Capt., and trapping, V, 311

Stephens, Olin J., architect of the *Ranger*, V, 499

Stephens, Samuel, court-martial of, V, 8

Stephenson, Benjamin F., founder of the Grand Army of the Republic, II, 407

Stephenson, Fort, attack on, V, 27

Steptoe, Edward J., suffers a defeat in the Spokane country, V, 500

Stereotype Process, I, 213

Sterling. *See* Stirling

Sternberg, G. M., works on disinfection, III, 64

Sterne, Maurice, painter, I, 123

Stetson, John B., book collection, I, 213

Stettler v. O'Hara, III, 408; V, 387

Steuart, Andrew, publisher of chapbooks, I, 341

Steunenberg, Frank, killed by Harry Orchard, I, 409; III, 21, 66

Stevens, Albert W., and the stratosphere, V, 187

Stevens, C. E., and abolitionist literature, I, 3

Stevens, Doris, and women's rights, II, 266

Stevens, Isaac I., killed in battle of Chantilly, I, 341; surveys railroad route, IV, 16; and hunting grounds of the Blackfoot confederacy, IV, 268; and government railroad surveys, IV, 405; and State of Washington, V, 415

Stevens, J. L., and Hawaii, III, 18

Stevens, John, designs a floating battery protected with iron plates, I, 109; and the steamboat, II, 214; designs ironclad, II, 284; and great inventions, III, 148; constructs experimental locomotive, III, 292; and steam navigation, IV, 105; designer of the *Phœnix*, IV, 264; and railroads, IV, 406

Stevens, John C., and yacht racing in America, V, 499

Stevens, John F., and railroad commission to Russia, IV, 501

Stevens, Lillian M. N., president of the W. C. T. U., V, 479

Stevens, Robert L., and the T-rail, III, 148; IV, 406, 410

Stevens, Thaddeus, and anti-Masonic movement, I, 82; and Buckshot War, I, 246; and the Joint Committee on Reconstruction, III, 179; among the leaders of the Radical Republicans, IV, 395; and admission of West Virginia as a state, V, 440

Stevens, Uriah, founder of Knights of Labor, III, 215

Stevens, W. H., discovers true nature of carbonate ore, III, 254

Stevens Battery, II, 284

Stevens-Murphy Party, I, 270; V, 389

Stevenson Plan, to control crude rubber supply, IV, 505

Stewardson, Thomas, and malaria, III, 329

Stewart, A. T., and the department store, II, 139

Stewart, Charles, captures the *Cyane* and *Levant*, II, 30

Stewart, Lazarus, head of the Paxton Boys, IV, 229; and the Yankee-Pennamite wars, V, 502

Stewart, William Drummond, and trappers' rendezvous, V, 311

Stewart, William M., and great fortunes, II, 312

Stiegel, "Baron," erects glass house, II, 391

Stiles, C. W., and hookworm disease, III, 44, 370

Stiles, Ezra, shareholder in the Susquehannah Company, V, 211

Still, A. T., and osteopathy, IV, 190

Stillwater (Minn.), battle of, V, 84

Stilwell, Silas M., and the English Colony on Rio Grande, IV, 486

Stimson, Henry L., and our attitude toward China, I, 364; as an executive agent, II, 232; and the League of Nations, III, 256; and non-recognition of Japan in Manchuria, III, 330; and our relations with Nicaragua, IV, 131; and the Philippine Islands, IV, 262

Stimson Nonrecognition Doctrine. See Nonrecognition

Stirling, Earl of, and Gardiner's Island, II, 372; assigned Long Island, III, 298; and York's proprietary, V, 507

Stirling, Thomas, occupies Illinois, II, 90; begins descent of the Ohio, III, 69

Stirling Iron Works, and Hudson River Chain, III, 55

Stites, Benjamin, and the Miami Purchase, III, 390

Stobnicza, Johannes de, maps by, III, 340

Stock Exchanges, and investment banking, III, 150; and panic of 1907, IV, 210; supervised by Securities and Exchange Commission, V, 55

Stock Issues, Corporate, II, 63

Stock Market, and panic of 1893, IV, 209; and the panic of 1929, IV, 210

Stockbridge Indians, serve as Minutemen in the Revolution, III, 88

Stocks, and colonial punishments, IV, 382

Stockton, Richard, signer of the Declaration of Independence, II, 124; IV, 343

Stockton, Robert F., and conquest of California, I, 271; and the Kearny-Frémont quarrel, III, 201; and the Mexican War, III, 386; and explosion on the Princeton, IV, 342; and battle of San Gabriel, V, 24

Stockyards, and the Beef Trust cases, I, 173; and the cattle industry, I, 327; regulation of, IV, 198; constructed in St. Joseph, Mo., V, 10

Stoddard, Amos, takes command in St. Louis, III, 426

Stoddard, John L., and travel lectures, III, 260

Stoddard, R. H., starts as blacksmith, I, 197

Stoddert, Benjamin, appointed first Secretary of the Navy, IV, 75

Stoddert, Fort, Claiborne ordered to, IV, 57

Stokes, Benjamin M., establishes the Mississippi Gazette, IV, 124, 127

Stone, Andrew, and Board of Trade, I, 207

Stone, Barton W., evangelist of the Awakening, I, 143; and the Disciples of Christ, II, 149

Stone, C. P., arrest of, I, 150; and the Radical Republicans, IV, 395

Stone, James C., and tobacco co-operatives, V, 276

Stone, John, killed by Pequot Indians, IV, 252

Stone, Lucy, feminist, II, 265; campaigns for women's rights, V, 477; and woman suffrage, V, 478

Stone, Thomas, and battle of the Severn, V, 61

Stone, Thomas, and the Alexandria Conference, I, 47; signer of the Declaration of Independence, II, 124

Stone Indians, I, 130

Stone Mountain, Confederate War Memorial at. See Gutzon Borglum

Stone River, Battle of. See Murfreesboro

Stoneman, George, and battle at Marion, III, 344

Stono, S. C., slave outbreak, V, 90

Stony Lake, Sibley defeats Indians at, II, 106

Stony Point, stormed by Wayne, III, 31

Store Boats, III, 52

Stores, General, and the distribution of merchandise, II, 152

Storrow, James J., and the Boston police strike, I, 223

Story, Joseph, in Martin v. Hunter's Lessee, III, 348; and Martin v. Mott, III, 348; and Prigg v. Commonwealth of Pennsylvania, IV, 341

Story, William Wetmore, sculptor, I, 123

Story of a Country Town, written by E. W. Howe, II, 270

Stoughton, Israel, and the Pequot War, IV, 252

"Stourbridge Lion," steam locomotive, IV, 406; V, 308

Stout, Elihu, establishes the Indiana Gazette, IV, 124, 126; first printer of Indiana, IV, 345

Stove Plates, I, 207

Stover, Charles B., and social settlements, V, 109

Stowe, Harriet Beecher, and abolitionist literature, I, 3; and antislavery literature, I, 85; author of Uncle Tom's Cabin, I, 180; and book publishing, I, 213; author of Uncle Tom's Cabin, II, 270; V, 337

Strang, James J., establishes Mormon community in lake region, III, 394; IV, 449

Stratton, W. S., stakes the Independence mine, II, 89

Straus, Nathan, established sterilized milk depots, III, 64; and tuberculosis, V, 328

Strauss, J. B., and bridges, I, 237

Strauss, Joseph, and mine sweeping, III, 406; and mine-laying during World War, V, 493

Straw Polls, and sampling referenda, V, 21

Strawberry Bank, settled, IV, 101

Strawbridge, Robert, circuit rider, I, 376; and the Methodists, III, 380

Strawn, Silas Hardy, and the Peking Tariff Conference, IV, 239

Streamlined Trains, IV, 408

Street, Barton and Murphy, and the Niagara Company, IV, 130

Street and Smith, publish "Frank Merriwell" series, II, 147

Street Cars, displaced by buses, **IV**, 33

Street Railways, municipal ownership of, **IV**, 375; and urban transportation, **V**, 305

Streeter, Alson J., supported by Greenback party, **II**, 424; and the Union Labor party, **V**, 342

Strickland, William, architect, **I**, 100; and railroads, **IV**, 406

Strict Construction, originally advocated by Jeffersonian Republicans, **II**, 136; and Jeffersonian Democracy, **III**, 172; and land grants to railways, **III**, 237; and states' rights, **V**, 175

Strikes, and the A. F. of L., **I**, 60; in the anthracite fields, **I**, 80; and industrial arbitration, **I**, 95; and unlawful assembly, **I**, 130; Cœur d'Alene, **I**, 409; Colorado coal strikes, **I**, 427; at Cripple Creek, **II**, 89; and Danbury Hatters' case, **II**, 108; and the detective agency, **II**, 142; and the Herrin massacre, **III**, 28; Homestead, **III**, 43; and immigrant labor, **III**, 73; favored by I. W. W., **III**, 119; and injunctions, **III**, 123; and labor unions, **III**, 225; the Lawrence strike, **III**, 253; and Norris-LaGuardia Anti-Injunction Law, **IV**, 143; and the panics of 1873 and 1893, **IV**, 209; Philadelphia cordwainers', **IV**, 259; and picketing, **IV**, 266; Pullman strike, **IV**, 381; and railroad brotherhoods, **IV**, 400; steel, **V**, 180; telegraphers', **V**, 238; and the War Labor Board, **V**, 404; and Western Federation of Miners, **V**, 443

Stringfellow, B. F., and border ruffians, **I**, 219

Stringham, S. H., and the Navy in the Civil War, **I**, 389; and capture of Hatteras Inlet, **III**, 17

Strong, A. H., and theological writings, **V**, 261

Strong, W. B., and the Atchison, Topeka and Santa Fé Railroad, **I**, 134

Strong, William, and Supreme Court packing, **V**, 208

Strother, Fort, as a base in attacks on Creek Indians, **II**, 213

Strouds, and Indian trade, **III**, 109

Strugels, The, rifle makers, **IV**, 483

Stuart, Charles E., and the Kalamazoo case, **III**, 193

Stuart, David, partner in the Pacific Fur Company, **IV**, 195

Stuart, Gilbert, painter, **I**, 123; **IV**, 478

Stuart, J. E. B., holds Ashby's Gap against Hooker, **I**, 127; at Brandy Station, **I**, 235; and Buckland Races, **I**, 246; and battle of Gettysburg, **II**, 387; and engagement at Hanover (Pa.), **III**, 8; and Harpers Ferry Raid, **III**, 12; and Mosby's Rangers, **IV**, 29; and the Peninsular campaign, **IV**, 241; and invasion of Pennsylvania, **IV**, 244; defeated at Todd's Tavern, **V**, 276; and the Army of Northern Virginia, **V**, 371; and battle at Yellow Tavern, **V**, 506

Stuart, John, Superintendent of Indian Affairs, **I**, 138; and Donelson's Line, **II**, 160; and treaty of Hard Labor, **III**, 8; and Indian agencies, **III**, 90; Superintendent of Indian Affairs, **III**, 104; and the Congress of Pensacola, **IV**, 250; and Indian treaties, **V**, 159; and topographic mapping, **V**, 283

Stuart, Robert, and the American Fur Company, **I**, 61; and the Astor Overlanders, **I**, 133; on the Oregon Trail, **IV**, 185; and South Pass, **V**, 128

Stuart's Town, destroyed by the Spanish, **V**, 126

Studebaker Brothers, as wagon makers, **V**, 388

Studebaker Motor Company, **I**, 140

Students' Army Training Corps, **IV**, 158

Stump Speakers, and presidential campaigns, **I**, 294, 295

Sturges v. Crowninshield, and the contract clause, **II**, 48

Sturgis, Samuel D., and the Nez Percé War, **IV**, 129

Sturtevant, Julian M., organizer of the Illinois Band, **III**, 69; member of the Yale Band, **V**, 500

Stuyvesant, Peter, rules New Sweden, **II**, 130; plants orchard, **II**, 353; creates New Haarlem, **III**, 10; and treaty of Hartford, **III**, 14; as director at New Amsterdam, **IV**, 94; recaptures Fort Casimir, **IV**, 95; as director-general at New Amsterdam, **IV**, 108; builds Fort Casimir, **IV**, 113; surrenders the city of New Amsterdam, **IV**, 118; and Petition and Remonstrance of New Netherland, **IV**, 256

Sub-Chasers, in the World War, **V**, 493

Sublette, Milton G., mountain man, **I**, 128; **II**, 362

Sublette, William L., and caravan traffic on the Great Plains, **I**, 312; on the Oregon Trail, **II**, 236; mountain man, **II**, 362; and Town of Kansas, **III**, 196; establishes Fort Laramie, **III**, 245; and battle of Pierre's Hole, **IV**, 269; and the Rocky Mountain Fur Company, **IV**, 498; and wagon trains, **V**, 389

Sublette and Campbell, fur traders, **IV**, 29

Sublette Brothers, and Ashley's expeditions, **V**, 310

Sublette Company, goes to California, **I**, 270

Sublette's Cutoff, and the Great Basin, **II**, 414

Submarine Cables Convention of 1884, **V**, 317

Submarines, in war, **I**, 77; sink the *Arabic*, **I**, 94; in the United States fleet, **II**, 284; designed by Holland, **III**, 38; designed by Hunley, **III**, 51; and sinking of the *Lusitania*, **III**, 315; and armed merchantmen, **III**, 377; and the *Nautilus*, **IV**, 68; constructed at Portsmouth Navy Yard, **IV**, 79; and retaliation in international law, **IV**, 462; raising of, **V**, 20; and torpedoes, **V**, 284; and warships, **V**, 412; in the World War, **V**, 491; and the Navy in the World War, **V**, 493

Subsidiary Coinage, and money system, **IV**, 7; use of nickel in, **IV**, 132

Subsidies, and merchant marine acts, III, 377

Subsistence Department, and army supply, I, 119

Subsistence Farmers, in the South, I, 27; and changes in rural life, IV, 508

Subsistence Homestead Division, established, III, 135

Substitutes, in the Civil War, I, 112, 387; II, 26

Subversive Activities, and the "reds," IV, 433

Subways, and urban transportation, V, 305; and tunnels, V, 329

Sudbury, French and Indian raids on, IV, 389

Suffolk Banking System, I, 156; V, 164

Suffrage. See Franchise, The

"Suff'ring Traders," attempt to recoup losses of, I, 170

Sugar, beet, I, 174; as food, II, 295; Great Western Company, II, 421; and Hawaii, III, 18, 70; in Louisiana, III, 306; and the plantation system of the South, IV, 284; and the slave trade, V, 92; as colonial staple, V, 160; and foreign trade, V, 294, 295; in the Triangular Trade, V, 296; in the West India trade, V, 437

Sugar Act of 1764, and cod fisheries, I, 407; and colonial commerce, I, 418; and British colonial policy, I, 422; and the power to tax, II, 125; as factor leading to the Revolution, II, 307; passed by Parliament, II, 425; repeals Molasses Act, IV, 6; and the American Revolution, IV, 465; and the rum trade, IV, 507; passage of, V, 155; and foreign trade, V, 294; and the Triangular Trade, V, 297

Sugar Equalization Board, agency of Food Administration, II, 297

Sugar Refineries Company, I, 65

Sullivan, James, and the Embargo, II, 208

Sullivan, John, and disaster at Three Rivers (1776), I, 297; in the battle of Elmira, II, 204; and battle of Germantown, II, 385; in Rhode Island, IV, 478; and Fort William and Mary, V, 467

Sullivan, John L., prize fighter, IV, 352

Sullivan, Louis, and the Functional or International style of architecture, I, 102; and skyscrapers, V, 88

Sullivan, "Yankee," prize fighter, IV, 352

Sullivan and Considine, in vaudeville, V, 358

Sullivan-Clinton Expedition, and the Cherry Valley massacre, I, 354; and the Minisink Indian raid, III, 410; and second treaty of Fort Stanwix (1784), V, 159; decided upon after the Wyoming massacre, V, 497

Sully, Alfred, and his expeditions in the Dakotas, II, 106; and battle of Killdeer Mountain, III, 209; occupies Fort Rice, IV, 479; expeditions in the Dakotas, V, 86; establishes Camp Supply, V, 205, 420

Sully, Thomas, painter, I, 122

Sulphur, in the Confederacy, I, 393

Sultana Disaster, II, 149

Sulzer, William, impeached, III, 77

Sumner, Charles, attacked by Brooks, I, 3, 244; and Civil Rights Act, I, 382; opposes annexation of Dominican Republic, II, 159; and doctrine of equality, II, 223; and Force Acts, II, 300; and the Kansas-Nebraska Act, III, 197; and the Liberal Republican party, III, 269; and oratory, IV, 180; and peace movements, IV, 234; among the leaders of the Radical Republicans, IV, 395; and the Thirteenth Amendment, V, 264

Sumner, E. V., at Antietam, I, 81; repulses Confederates at Savage Station, V, 35; establishes Fort Union, N. Mex., V, 341

Sumner, Fort, and the Goodnight Loving Trail, II, 400; the Navaho Indians come to, IV, 68

Sumner, William Graham, delivers "Forgotten Man" lecture, II, 310; on thrift, V, 267

Sumter, Fort, and the Union army, I, 111; bombardment of, I, 344; in the Civil War, I, 386; and the Confederate States, II, 10; floating battery attacks, II, 285; and the Powhatan incident, IV, 327; South Carolina commissioners demand evacuation of, V, 52; reinforced by the Star of the West, V, 160

Sumter, Thomas, and the battle of Enoree, II, 218; and battle of Fishdam Ford, II, 276; attacked at Fishing Creek, II, 278; at Hanging Rock, III, 7; and partisan bands, IV, 219; in the Southern campaigns (1780–81), V, 129

Sun Anti-Masonic Almanac, I, 52

Sun Building, V, 87

Sun Dance, widely practised by Indians, III, 97

Sun Worship, practised by the Natchez Indians, IV, 57

Sunbury and Erie Railroad, IV, 245

Sunday, the Sabbath Day, V, 1

Sunday, William A., evangelist, II, 230; IV, 464

Sunday Schools, and the Chautauqua movement, I, 348; and children's magazines, I, 363; and hymn writing, III, 65; started by the Protestant Episcopal Church, IV, 366; and religious education, IV, 444

Sunflowers, as Indian food plant, III, 87

Super Markets, Atlantic and Pacific, II, 413; as self-serve stores, V, 57; and trade areas, V, 297

Superintendents of Indian Affairs, and treaty of Hard Labor, III, 8; and Colonial Policy, III, 104; and the Proclamation of 1763, IV, 354; and treaty of Fort Stanwix (1768), V, 159

Superior, Lake, iron ore deposits, III, 157; and search for the western sea, V, 446

Supply, Army, I, 118

Supply, Camp, and the Dodge City Trail, II, 156; Sully ordered to establish, V, 420

Supreme Court, restriction on, in the Bill of

Rights, **I**, 186; upholds its power to issue writ of habeas corpus, **I**, 208; and the Constitution, **II**, 37; its place in the Federal Government, **II**, 257; and judicial review, **III**, 183 f.; packing bills, **III**, 184; and the judiciary, **III**, 185 ff.; provided by Judiciary Act of 1789, **III**, 188; and Judiciary Act of 1801, **III**, 189; packing the, and the New Deal, **IV**, 96; and Reconstruction, **IV**, 425; and reserved powers of states, **IV**, 458

Supreme Court of the Confederacy, **II**, 7

Surdna Foundation, **II**, 315

Surgeon General of the Army, and hospitalization, **I**, 115; and weather observations, **V**, 430

Surplus Revenue, Distribution of, **II**, 151; **IV**, 208

Surratt, John H., and Lincoln's assassination, **III**, 280; and diplomatic service to Papal States, **IV**, 211

Surratt, Mary E., and Lincoln's assassination, **III**, 280

Survey, Hydrographic, **III**, 63

Survey, National, and Ordinance of 1785, **IV**, 181

Survey of Public Domain, **V**, 60

Survey of the Summe of Church Discipline, by Thomas Hooker, **I**, 441

Surveyor General, established by Land Act of 1796, **III**, 233; and United States General Land Office, **III**, 237

Surveys and Maps, Board of, **II**, 378

Susquehanna and Tidewater Canal, **I**, 80

Susquehanna Indians, raided by Iroquois with guns, **III**, 92

Susquehannah Company, and Connecticut's western lands, **II**, 24; and Forty Fort, **II**, 313; and land speculation, **III**, 239; and the Paxton Boys, **IV**, 229; and Pennsylvania-Connecticut boundary dispute, **IV**, 246; and settlement of the Wyoming Valley, **V**, 210, 497; and the Yankee-Pennamite Wars, **V**, 502

Sussex Case, and the World War, **V**, 491

Sutherland, George, in West Coast Hotel Company v. Parrish, **V**, 436; and the wire-tapping cases, **V**, 472

Sutherland, J. B., patents first refrigerator car, **IV**, 437

Sutlers, and army post exchanges, **IV**, 317

Sutro, Adolph, tunnel of, **I**, 444; **V**, 329

Sutter, John A., and Alaska, **I**, 42; buys Fort Ross, **I**, 270; and the Forty-niners, **II**, 313; and the gold discovery, **II**, 393

Sutter's Fort, and the Bear Flag Revolt, **I**, 171; as frontier trading post, **V**, 302

Suydam, John V., co-founder of the *Green-Bay Intelligencer*, **IV**, 128; first printer of Wisconsin, **IV**, 346

Swaim, William, and the abolition movement, **I**, 2

Swain v. U. S., and Articles of War, **I**, 126

Swamp Angel, **I**, 344

Swamp Lands, reclamation of, **II**, 165; **IV**, 423

Swan, Timothy, hymn writer, **III**, 65

Swarthmore College, established by Hicksites, **III**, 29

Swartwout, Samuel, and Burr Conspiracy, **I**, 208; and the English Colony on Rio Grande, **IV**, 486; and "whitewash," **V**, 461

Swasey-Todd Company, **I**, 270

Sweatshops, and demand for minimum-wage laws, **V**, 387

Sweden, treaties with, **V**, 316

Swedes, and Pennsylvania, **IV**, 242

Swedish Immigration, **III**, 74

Sweeny, Peter B., and the Tweed Ring, **IV**, 485; **V**, 333

Sweeping Resolution, in Ohio, **IV**, 160

Swift, Edwin C., and great fortunes, **II**, 312

Swift, Gustavus F., and great fortunes, **II**, 312; and meat packing, **IV**, 199

Swift, John, comes to Kentucky, **III**, 204

Swift Packing Company, and the Beef Trust cases, **I**, 173; and stockyards, **V**, 184

Swift v. Tyson, **II**, 226

Swinnerton, James, and comic strips, **I**, 431

Swope, Gerard, and General Electric Company, **II**, 376

Sybrant, Jan, and Philipse's patent, **IV**, 263

Sycamore Shoals, Treaty of, land on Cumberland River taken from Cherokees by, **II**, 98; signing of, **II**, 110; and Indian land cessions, **III**, 99

Sylph, The, races with the *Wave*, **V**, 499

Sylvania, Jefferson's proposed state, **III**, 173

Symmes, John Cleves, and the Miami Purchase, **III**, 390

Symmes, Thomas, gives his account of Lovewell's fight, **III**, 310

Symmes Purchase, and Cincinnati, **I**, 375; and land speculation, **III**, 240

Syndicalism, and sabotage, **V**, 1

Syng, Philip, silversmith, **V**, 82

System, business paper, **V**, 298

System of Dental Surgery, first complete dental text in English, **II**, 138

T

T-Rail, of Robert Stevens, **III**, 148

Table Rock, Treaty of (1853), and Indian land cessions, **III**, 100

Tabloids, and news reporting, **IV**, 122

Tabor, H. A. W., first mayor of Leadville, **III**, 254

Taft, Lorado, sculptor, **I**, 124

Taft, William Howard, attempts to draft series of arbitration treaties, **I**, 97; and Progressive party, **I**, 250; elected President (1908), **I**, 290; defeated (1912), **I**, 290; and the conservation

movement, **II**, 27; sent by Theodore Roosevelt to aid Cuba, **II**, 95; and dollar diplomacy, **II**, 158; and civil service for diplomats, **II**, 306; president of League to Enforce Peace, **III**, 255; and naval oil reserves, **IV**, 71; and Payne-Aldrich tariff, **IV**, 229; establishes civil government in the Philippines, **IV**, 262; and the recall, **IV**, 421; and legislative riders, **IV**, 482; and the Sixteenth Amendment, **V**, 87; in Stafford v. Wallace, **V**, 152; and the Supreme Court, **V**, 206; in U. S. v. Lanza, **V**, 349; vetoes the Webb-Kenyon Act, **V**, 431; and the Winona speech, **V**, 472

Taft Agreement, and the Panama Canal, **IV**, 205

Tagliamento River, American Expeditionary Forces in battle of, **I**, 60

Tahkahokuty Mountain, battle of, **III**, 209

Tahwaccaro Indians, and Fort Belknap, **I**, 175

Talbot, John G., and cruise of the *Saginaw's* gig, **V**, 5

Talbot, Silas, and the *Constitution*, **II**, 29

Taliaferro, Lawrence, Indian agent, **III**, 91; and Indian agency at Fort Snelling, **V**, 106; on the *Virginia*, **V**, 374

Talishatchee, Jackson sacks Creek village of, **II**, 86

Tall Bull, Carr crushes the Cheyennes under, **V**, 420

Tall Stories, and the bear, **I**, 171; and dust, **II**, 178; and frontier oratory, **II**, 353; article on, **V**, 186

Talladege, Jackson crushes Creek force at, **II**, 86

Tallmadge Amendment, and "doughfaces," **II**, 163; and the Missouri Compromise, **III**, 428; introduced in the House, **V**, 95

Talmage, T. D., reform lecturer, **III**, 260

Tama Reservation, **III**, 152

Tamaroa Indians, and the Algonquin family, **I**, 48; at Cahokia, **I**, 267; come to the Des Peres village, **II**, 142; of the Illinois, **III**, 71

Tammanen, leading Indian representative at treaty of Shackamaxon, **V**, 63

Tammany Hall, grows from Burr's political machine, **I**, 281; and campaign of 1884, **I**, 287; and the Lexow Committee, **III**, 267; and Loco Foco party, **III**, 292; and the Tweed Ring, **V**, 333; and the "Wigwam," **V**, 462

Tammany Society, and the Martling men, **III**, 348; organized in Ohio, **IV**, 160; adopts title of sachem, **V**, 2

Tammany Tiger, popularized by Nast, **I**, 320; **IV**, 56

Taney, Roger B., and Ableman v. Booth, **I**, 2; questions Lincoln's control of arbitrary arrest, **I**, 122; and Bank of Augusta v. Earle, **I**, 154; and Charles River Bridge case, **I**, 343; and the commerce clause, **I**, 433; and the contract clause, **II**, 48; and the Dred Scott case, **II**, 167; and the due process clause in the Dred Scott case, **II**, 172; in Merryman case, **III**, 1; and judicial review, **III**, 183; in Luther v. Borden, **III**, 315; and the Merryman case, **III**, 379; and popular sovereignty, **IV**, 309; and removal of deposits, **IV**, 448

Tanks, use of in war, **I**, 329; and munitions, **IV**, 45

Tanner, H. S., and his *Map of the United States of Mexico,* **II**, 154; map publisher, **V**, 283

Taos, Arkansas River as highway to, **I**, 106, 107; Fonda's expedition to, **II**, 294; burned during Pueblo revolt, **IV**, 379

Taos Traders, and Fort Bernard, **I**, 180

Taos Trail, **V**, 30

Tappan, Arthur, and antislavery movement, **I**, 85; and Finney revivals, **II**, 275

Tappan, Lewis, and antislavery movement, **I**, 85; and Finney revivals, **II**, 275; starts first mercantile agency, **III**, 374

Tar, as naval store, **IV**, 72

Tar and Feathers, **I**, 133; **IV**, 474

Tarbell, Ida M., *History of the Standard Oil Company,* **IV**, 38; political writings of, **IV**, 302

Tariff, and the American System, **I**, 66; and the balance of trade, **I**, 147; of 1842, **I**, 206; an issue in campaign of 1872, **I**, 286; an issue in campaign of 1888, **I**, 287; and campaign of 1892, **I**, 288; and campaign of 1928, **I**, 291; and cotton, **II**, 68; and the Cotton Kingdom, **II**, 70; and custom houses, **II**, 101; and customs revenues, **II**, 102; and the Democratic party, **II**, 137; Dingley Act, **II**, 147; Fordney-McCumber Act, **II**, 301; and free trade, **II**, 334; Gorman-Wilson Act, **II**, 401; Hawley-Smoot Act, **III**, 18; horizontal, **III**, 46; and Jacksonian Democracy, **III**, 165; and *laissez-faire,* **III**, 228; and Clay's Land Distribution Bill, **III**, 234; and manufacturing, **III**, 336; McKinley Act, **III**, 366; Morrill Act, **IV**, 27; Payne-Aldrich Act, **IV**, 229; and the privileged class, **IV**, 350; and protection, **IV**, 365; of Abominations, **IV**, 365; and reciprocal trade agreements, **IV**, 421; as source of the public revenue, **IV**, 462; as a subsidy, **V**, 195; of Abominations, **V**, 222; and foreign trade, **V**, 295; and commercial treaties, **V**, 315; and the Underwood Act, **V**, 338; and wool industry, **V**, 484

Tariff Board, **V**, 222

Tariff Commission, exercises quasi-judicial power, **I**, 12; and flexible tariffs, **II**, 284; and reciprocal trade agreements, **IV**, 422; created, **V**, 222; and tariff powers of the President, **V**, 224; and commercial treaties, **V**, 315

Tariff Laws, and the Civil War, **I**, 388

Tarkington, Booth, and fiction, **II**, 270

Tarleton, Banastre, in battle of Cowpens, **II**, 81; and Yorktown campaign, **V**, 509

Tarleton's Quarter, becomes an expression for butchery, V, 426

Tarpley, Collin S., and the Nashville Convention, IV, 55

Tarpon Springs Exchange, and sponge fisheries, V, 148

Tattnall, Josiah, and the adage "Blood Is Thicker than Water," I, 202

Taverns, and the curfew law, II, 98; and stagecoach travel, V, 153; and inns, V, 224; effect of travel on, V, 306

Tax Appeals, Board of, I, 12

Taxation without Representation, and the Declaration of Independence, II, 120; and the Mutiny Act, IV, 50; and the American Revolution, IV, 466; and Rights of Englishmen, IV, 484

Taxes, capital gains, I, 307; capitation, I, 311; and the Constitution, II, 33; corporation, II, 61; reciprocal immunity from, II, 92; and customs, II, 102; in the colonies, II, 125; Democratic party increases, II, 137; double, II, 163; and excess profits, II, 231; export, II, 236; gasoline, II, 373; inheritance, III, 122; and McCray v. U. S., III, 363; "power to tax involves the power to destroy," III, 364; and rights of the minority, III, 412; and attempts to abolish privilege, IV, 351; and the franchise, IV, 361; sales, V, 16; direct, V, 226; direct and indirect, V, 231; reciprocal immunity from, V, 232; undistributed, V, 338; and voting, V, 383. See also Corporation Tax; Income Taxes; Inheritance Taxes

Tayacs, name for lesser chieftains in Maryland, V, 434

Taylor, Allen, and tin can manufacture, V, 271

Taylor, Bayard, popularizes the travel lecture, III, 260

Taylor, Bob, and fiddling, II, 270

Taylor, Buck, and the Wild West Show, V, 464

Taylor, Daniel, and the steel trap, V, 180

Taylor, Frederick W., father of industrial management, III, 115; and mass production, III, 353; introduces scientific management, V, 236

Taylor, George, signer of the Declaration of Independence, II, 124

Taylor, Graham, and social settlements, V, 109

Taylor, Isaac, surveys boundary line of Chester and New Castle counties, II, 132

Taylor, John, succeeds Brigham Young, IV, 27

Taylor, John, of Caroline, and philosophical thought and writings, IV, 263; political writings of, IV, 302; advocates secession, V, 51; and soil exhaustion remedy, V, 116; and civilization of Old South, V, 123; and Tertium Quids, V, 249

Taylor, Nathaniel W., and religious thought and writings, IV, 446; revivalistic preacher, IV, 464; and theological writings, V, 261

Taylor, Richard, surrenders to Canby, I, 385; succeeds Hood as commander, III, 44; and battle of Pleasant Hill, IV, 287; and the Red River campaign, IV, 430; in battle of Sabine Crossroads, V, 1; replaces Hood, V, 242

Taylor, William S., and the Goebel affair, II, 393

Taylor, Zachary, establishes Fort Brown, I, 244; at Buena Vista, I, 247; elected President, I, 284; and Compromise of 1850, I, 442; attacked at Credit Island, II, 84; erects Fort Johnson, II, 189; and the Mexican War, III, 386; and the battles of Monterey, IV, 16; and battle of Okeechobee, IV, 168; called "Old Rough and Ready," IV, 171; opposes the Omnibus bill, IV, 173; and battle of Palo Alto (1846), IV, 202; and battle of Resaca de la Palma, IV, 457

Taylor System. See Industrial Management

Tea, and trade with Asia, I, 128; and the clipper ships, I, 402; tax on, II, 182; tax on, and letters of Junius, III, 190; and burning of the Peggy Stewart, IV, 238; tax on, and the American Revolution, IV, 466

Tea Act of 1773, as factor leading to the Revolution, II, 307

Tea Inspection Act (1897), I, 15

Tea Parties, and the American Revolution, IV, 467

Tea Party, in New York, IV, 115, 118

Teachers, in district schools, V, 39

Teachers Colleges. See Normal Schools

Teaching, and women in professions, V, 481

Teapot Dome Oil Reserve, II, 64; IV, 71, 298

Tebo and Neosho Company, III, 427

Technocracy, and machines, III, 321

Technological Unemployment, V, 237, 339

Tect v. Hughes, V, 398

Tecumseh, Algonquin leader, I, 48; visit of, incites Upper Creeks, II, 86; Kickapoo Indians fight for, III, 208; and Indian conception of ownership of land, III, 233; and the battle at Maguaga, III, 325; and siege of Fort Meigs, III, 371; and the Shawnee, V, 65; and battle of the Thames, V, 259; and battle of Tippecanoe, V, 272; holds councils at Tookabatchee, V, 281; and the War of 1812, V, 405; denounces treaty of Fort Wayne, V, 426; breaks the treaty of Greenville, V, 427; Winnebago Indians as allies of, V, 471

Tecumseh, figurehead of the Delaware, II, 272

Tecumseh, Fort, early name for Fort Pierre, IV, 268; the Yellowstone reaches, V, 506

Tecumseh, The, sinking of the, II, 108; IV, 1

Tedford, W. W., starts Agricultural Wheel movement, I, 26

Tehachapi Pass, IV, 221

Tejas Indians, and the Mendoza expedition, **III**, 373

Telegraph, invention of, and the Associated Press, **I**, 131; as a new industry, **I**, 383; and international communications, **I**, 439; and growth of democracy, **II**, 135; invented by Joseph Henry, **III**, 148; patented by Morse, **IV**, 223; and the Pony Express, **IV**, 307; and railroads, **IV**, 407; and the Western Union, **V**, 447; during the World War, **V**, 492

Telegraph, Semaphore, and the Associated Press, **I**, 131

Telephone, and international communications, **I**, 439; and growth of democracy, **II**, 135; invented by Alexander Graham Bell, **III**, 148; patented by Bell, **IV**, 223; Elisha Gray invents a crude telephone, **V**, 441

Television, as agency of mass impression, **III**, 352

Teller Resolution, and first intervention in Cuba, **II**, 94; and Spanish-American relations, **V**, 136; and Spanish-American War, **V**, 136

Tellico, Treaty of (1798), and Indian land cessions, **III**, 100

Tellico, Treaty of (1805), and Southwest Point, **V**, 133

Temperance Almanac, **I**, 52

Temperance Movement, a part of the general humanitarian spirit, **I**, 2; and the Bible, **I**, 181; a result of American drinking habits, **II**, 169; and Carrie Nation's hatchet, **III**, 16; and prohibition, **IV**, 356; inaugurated by series of sermons, **V**, 59; and whiskey, **V**, 457; and the W. C. T. U., **V**, 479

Temporary National Economic Commitee, **V**, 327

Tenancy System, replaces plantation system, **II**, 68, 69; and the Deep South, **II**, 125; and land tenure, **III**, 241; and share croppers, **V**, 63; and wheat, **V**, 453. *See also* Farm Tenancy

Tenements, and apartment houses, **I**, 88; laws respecting, **III**, 53; and slums, **V**, 99

Tennent, John, pioneer of American pharmacology, **II**, 171; and epidemics, **II**, 221

Tennent, William, erects and conducts Log College, **III**, 294; **IV**, 86; and revivals, **IV**, 464

Tennessee, created from North Carolina's western lands, **IV**, 145; development of State of, **V**, 132; organized, and admitted, **V**, 248

Tennessee, Army of, designation of Army of Mississippi (C.), **III**, 419; and the Tullahoma campaign, **V**, 329

Tennessee, The, Confederate ironclad, **I**, 390; and battle of Mobile Bay, **IV**, 1

Tennessee Coal, Iron and Railroad Company, **V**, 348

Tennessee River, as inland waterway, **V**, 424

Tennessee Valley Authority, and the Federal Power Commission, **II**, 261; and flood control, **II**, 286; as a government corporation, **II**, 403; and government ownership, **II**, 404; and government regulation, **III**, 144; uses merit system, **III**, 378; set up, **IV**, 96; builds Norris Dam, **IV**, 143; and public ownership, **IV**, 375; and regional planning, **IV**, 438; and water power, **V**, 423; and "yardstick," **V**, 503. *See also* Muscle Shoals

Tennis, **I**, 70

Tenth Amendment, and governmental control of agriculture, **I**, 33; and reserved powers of states, **IV**, 457; and reserved powers of the people, **IV**, 458; and states' rights, **V**, 175

Tenure-of-Office Act, and appointing power, **I**, 91; and impeachment trial of Andrew Johnson, **III**, 77; and Myers v. U. S., **IV**, 51; and the removal power, **IV**, 448

Terminal Railroad Association Case, **V**, 326

Terrees, The, rifle makers, **IV**, 483

Territorial Enterprise, founded by Jernegan and James, **IV**, 127

Territorial Waters, and rum row, **IV**, 506

Territories, slavery in, **I**, 10, 84; and the Constitution, **II**, 38; and insular cases, **III**, 127; extracontinental, **III**, 128; and organic law, **IV**, 187; slavery in, **V**, 96; under Department of State, **V**, 162; and the state-making process, **V**, 172; taxation in, **V**, 229

Terry, A. H., and Little Big Horn battle, **III**, 284; and Sioux wars, **V**, 87

Terry, David S., duels with David Broderick, **II**, 174; killed by Neagle, **IV**, 80

Terry, Ely, and clockmaking, **I**, 402

Terry, Roderick, book collection of, **I**, 213

Terry's Texas Rangers, **V**, 254

Tesla, Nikola, and electricity, **II**, 195

Test Oath Act Case, and five-to-four decisions, **V**, 207

Teton Indians, a division of the Sioux, **V**, 85

Tevis, Lloyd, and Anaconda Copper, **I**, 71

Texas, and Anglo-American relations, **I**, 75; DeWitt's Colony in, **II**, 145; and the Mexican boundary, **III**, 382; and the Mexican Decree of 1830, **III**, 383; and the Gulf of Mexico, **III**, 389; and territorial claims of the United States, **V**, 246

Texas, Annexation of, and territorial expansion, **I**, 79; and the Mexican War, **III**, 385; and the Monroe Doctrine, **IV**, 13; and the Great Plains, **IV**, 282; and the Raleigh Letter, **IV**, 412; and the Rio Grande, **IV**, 486; and secession, **V**, 51; and slavery, **V**, 96; and the Whig party, **V**, 456

Texas, Republic of, and the Rio Grande, **IV**, 486; and the Treat mission, **V**, 314

Texas, The, Congress authorizes construction of, **II**, 283; and blockade and battle of Santiago, **V**, 31

Texas, University of, and the junior college movement, **III**, 190

Texas and Pacific Railroad, reaches Fort Worth, **II**, 310; chartered by Federal Government, **II**, 403; and the strikes of 1886, **IV**, 405; and the Southern Pacific, **V**, 130; installs streamlined train, **V**, 188

Texas Cession, and the organization of territories, **V**, 249

Texas Fever, **I**, 29

Texas Public Lands, and Texan Emigrant and Land Company, **V**, 250

Texas Railroad Commission, and Shreveport rate case, **V**, 77

Texas Rangers, carry Bowie knife, **I**, 230; use Colt six shooter, **I**, 428

Texas Republican, newspaper, **IV**, 127

Texas Revolution, and the attack on Anahuac, **I**, 72; and DeWitt's Colony, **II**, 145; first battle of, **II**, 400; and *San Felipe-Correo* affair, **V**, 23

Textile Mills, and child labor, **I**, 361

Textiles, as a household art, **III**, 53; and the industrial revolution, **III**, 117; and colonial household industry, **III**, 119; growth of, **III**, 148; and labor, **III**, 219; and machines, **III**, 320; and manufacturing, **III**, 336; in North Carolina, **IV**, 145; and patents, **IV**, 223

Thacher, Thomas, pioneer of epidemiology, **II**, 221; and medicine, **III**, 369; and origin of American medical literature, **V**, 100

Thames, Battle of the, **II**, 143, 224; **V**, 405

Thanksgiving, days of, **II**, 253; and proclamations, **IV**, 354

Thatcher, Hervey D., invents glass milk bottle, **II**, 104; **III**, 64

Thaw, Harry, and the murder of Stanford White, **II**, 88; murder trial of, **V**, 323

Thayer, Abbott H., provides funds for establishing bird sanctuaries, **I**, 190

Thayer, Eli, and the Emigrant Aid Movement, **II**, 211; incorporates the New England Emigrant Aid Company, **IV**, 99

Thayer, Sylvanus, as superintendent of the United States Military Academy, **III**, 398

Theater, as an amusement, **I**, 69; and the American drama, **II**, 166; and leisure, **III**, 264

Theocracy, and church membership suffrage, **I**, 372; and franchise in Massachusetts Bay, **III**, 356; and Massachusetts Bay Company, **III**, 357; and American religion, **IV**, 442

Theological Seminaries, in the Old South, **V**, 122; opened to women, **V**, 481

Theosophy, established in New York by Madame Blavatsky, **IV**, 187

Theus, Jeremiah, artist, **I**, 122

Third Parties, **I**, 82

Thirteenth Amendment, text, **II**, 41; and Missis-sippi, **III**, 420; and the Negro, **IV**, 82 f.; and peonage, **IV**, 252; and Reconstruction, **IV**, 425; passage of, **V**, 96; and strikes, **V**, 190; and U. S. v. Harris, **V**, 348; as war amendment, **V**, 398

Thomas, Augustus, playwright, **II**, 166

Thomas, Charles M., relieves Evans as commander of fleet in cruise round the world, **I**, 168

Thomas, F. A., and refrigerator cars, **IV**, 437

Thomas, Fort, and Newport Barracks, **IV**, 122

Thomas, G. H., and Chattanooga campaign, **I**, 348; and battle of Chickamauga, **I**, 359; succeeds Rosecrans as commander of Army of the Cumberland, **II**, 96; and Hood's Tennessee campaign, **III**, 44; and the encounter at Mill Springs, **III**, 404; and battle of Missionary Ridge, **III**, 416; and battle of Murfreesboro, **IV**, 46; and battle of Nashville, **IV**, 54

Thomas, Isaiah, and Bible printing, **I**, 182; as a publisher, **I**, 213; and chapbooks, **I**, 341; and children's books, **I**, 363

Thomas, J. B., and the Missouri Compromise, **III**, 428

Thomas, M. Carey, and college training for women, **V**, 477, 481

Thomas, Moses, and book auctions, **I**, 212

Thomas, Norman, leader of Socialist party, **V**, 110

Thomas, Robert Bailey, founder of the *Farmer's Almanac(k),* **II**, 252

Thomas, Theodore, musical pioneer, **IV**, 48

Thomas Amendment, and the bimetallic system, **I**, 189; and bullion, **I**, 252; and Federal expropriation of gold, **II**, 394; and money system, **IV**, 8; and Silver Purchase Act of 1934, **V**, 81

Thomas-Gilchrist Invention, **III**, 156

Thompson, David, explores the Columbia, **I**, 430; and Minnesota, **III**, 410; explores and maps the Columbia Valley, **V**, 415; and the search for the western sea, **V**, 446

Thompson, Dorothy, as woman journalist, **V**, 481

Thompson, Jacob, and Confederate activities in Canada, **I**, 298; and the Northwest Conspiracy, **IV**, 150; and the peace movement of 1864, **IV**, 233

Thompson, Jeremiah, credited with idea of the Black Ball Line, **I**, 192

Thompson, John, invents corn planter, **II**, 247

Thompson, John Reuben, editor of the *Southern Literary Messenger,* **V**, 130

Thompson, M. Jeff, defeated at Fredericktown, Mo., **II**, 331

Thompson, R. M., and the nickel industry, **IV**, 132

Thompson, Wiley, killed by Seminoles, **V**, 57

Thompson, William, and battle of Three Rivers, **V**, 265

Thompson, William Tappan, writer, **V**, 123

Thompson Trophy, **I**, 37

Thomson, Charles, and the American Eagle, **II**, 180; and *Journal of Congress,* **III**, 182; designs obverse side of United States seal, **V**, 49

Thomson, David, and Monhegan Island, **IV**, 9; and first settlement in New Hampshire, **IV**, 101; **V**, 187

Thomson, Elihu, shows arc lamps and dynamos, **II**, 197; patents electric welding, **IV**, 223

Thomson-Houston Company, **II**, 198, 375

Thoreau, Henry David, and the Concord Group, **II**, 2

Thorn, Jonathan, and establishment of Astoria, **I**, 133

Thornburgh, T. T., and the Meeker massacre, **III**, 371

Thorndike, E. L., and adult education, **I**, 14

Thorne, George R., and the mail-order house, **III**, 325

Thornton, Matthew, signer of the Declaration of Independence, **II**, 123; and Miranda's intrigues, **III**, 414

Thornton, The, clipper ship, **III**, 375

Thornton, William, architect, **I**, 100; and the Capitol at Washington, **I**, 311; and Fitch's steamboat experiments, **II**, 278

Thornwell, James H., and religious thought, **IV**, 446

Thorpe, George, and plan to convert and civilize the savages, **V**, 372

Thorpe, James, and the Olympic games, **IV**, 173

Three-Cornered Trade. *See* Trade, Triangular

Three Rivers, disaster at (1776), **I**, 297

Threshing, **I**, 174

Threshing Machine, and agriculture, **I**, 29; invention of, **II**, 248; and the industrial revolution, **III**, 118

Thrift Stamps, for World War financing, **V**, 489

Throckmorton, J. W., governor of Texas, **V**, 254

Thurman, Allen G., nominated for Vice-Presidency, **I**, 288

Thurston, Asa, and missionary activity in the Pacific, **III**, 415

Thwaites, Reuben G., and *Jesuit Relations,* **III**, 175

Ticonderoga, cannon from, for siege of Boston, **I**, 127; guns captured at, reach Cambridge, **I**, 222; and Burgoyne's Invasion, **I**, 255; Champlain visits, **II**, 93; captured by Ethan Allen, **II**, 414; and the Green Mountain Boys, **II**, 422; in French and Indian War, **III**, 229; in the Revolutionary War, **III**, 230; capture of (1775), **IV**, 476; battle of (1758), **IV**, 481; and Vermont, **V**, 361; seized by Ethan Allen, **V**, 363

Tidewater, and the Fall Line, **II**, 241; Region, **IV**, 268; of Virginia, **V**, 374

Tidewater Pipeline Company, and oil industry, **IV**, 166; and the Standard Oil Company, **V**, 156

Tientsin, Treaty of, and diplomacy of S. W. Williams, **III**, 415

Tierra Amarilla Grant, **III**, 236

Tiffin, Edward, member of Chillicothe Junto, **I**, 364; governor of Ohio, **IV**, 160

Tigua Indians, missions among, **III**, 418

Tikhon, Bishop, and Russian Church in America, **IV**, 511

Tilden, Samuel J., and the election of 1876, **I**, 286; and the New York Public Library, **III**, 272; and the Tweed Ring, **V**, 333

Tilden, William T., II, tennis player, **V**, 245

Tilghman, Lloyd, and capture of Fort Henry (1862), **III**, 26

Tillman, Benjamin R., and the Ananias Club, **I**, 72; and the phosphate industry, **IV**, 265

Tillman Movement, **I**, 199

Tilton, Daniel W., first printer of Montana, **IV**, 346

Tilton, James, and hut system of hospitals, **III**, 51

Tilton, Theodore, and religious periodicals, **IV**, 446; suit against H. W. Beecher, **V**, 323

Timber, and forest fires, **II**, 308; and the lumber industry, **III**, 314; and domestic trade, **V**, 292

Timber and Stone Act, and Oregon land frauds, **IV**, 183; and the public domain, **IV**, 370

Timber Conservation Board, **II**, 27

Timber Culture Act, and the Desert Land Act, **II**, 141; and the public domain, **IV**, 370; and reforestation, **IV**, 434; and tree planting, **V**, 320

Timberlake, John B., first husband of Margaret O'Neil, **II**, 183

Timby, Theodore R., and floating batteries, **II**, 284

Time Lock, introduction of, **I**, 156

Time Table Conventions, **I**, 65

Times, and Patowmack Packet, published by Charles Fierer, **IV**, 126

Times-Herald Contest, first road race of, **I**, 140

"Times that try men's souls," **II**, 90

Timrod, Henry, poet, **V**, 123

Tin, and foreign trade, **V**, 295

Tin Can, introduction of the, **I**, 304

Tin Pan Alley, beginning of, **V**, 120

Tingle, William, and Joplin lead mining district, **III**, 181

Tinkham, A. W., attempts passage through Snoqualmie Pass, **V**, 182

Tippecanoe, Battle of, and the medicine man, **III**, 370; and Prophet's Town, **IV**, 361; and the Shawnee, **V**, 65; follows the crusade of Tecumseh, **V**, 237; and the War of 1812, **V**, 405; and treaty of Fort Wayne, **V**, 427

"Tippecanoe and Tyler Too," **I**, 284, 292, 294

Tipton, John, and failure of State of Franklin, **II**, 329

Titanic, The, and admiralty law, **I**, 13; and SOS call, **V**, 472

Titcomb, Benjamin, publisher of *Falmouth Gazette*, **IV**, 126; first printer of Maine, **IV**, 346

Titcomb, Mary L., first to use book-wagon, **III**, 273

Titusville, Pa., Drake's oil well at, **II**, 165

Titusville Pipe Company, **IV**, 276

Tobacco, and plantation system, **I**, 27; governmental control of, **I**, 33; and the Bermudas, **I**, 180; and colonial commerce, **I**, 417; and crop failures, **II**, 91; as money, **II**, 99, 100; and agricultural diversification, **II**, 154; as an enumerated commodity, **II**, 219; used for ceremonials by Indians, **III**, 87; cultivated at Jamestown, **III**, 167; and mercantilism, **III**, 374; and the Navigation Acts, **IV**, 74; in North Carolina, **IV**, 145; and the plantation system of the South, **IV**, 283; and slave trade, **V**, 91; and soil exhaustion, **V**, 116; developed by Spaniards, **V**, 138; as colonial staple, **V**, 159; and domestic trade, **V**, 292; and foreign trade, **V**, 294; in the Triangular Trade, **V**, 296; John Rolfe discovers method of curing, **V**, 372; and the old regime in Virginia, **V**, 375

Tobacco Pools, and the Black Patch War, **I**, 196; and Night Riders, **IV**, 133

"Tocarryhogan," governor of Maryland called, **IV**, 173

Tod, David, governor of Ohio, **IV**, 161

Todd, Andrew, and the Spanish-Missouri Fur Company, **V**, 141

Todd, George, guerrilla band of, **II**, 428

Todd, John, heresy trial of, **III**, 27

Todd, Mary, courted by Abraham Lincoln, **I**, 205

Todd, W. J., and the Bluestem Pastures, **I**, 206

Todd, William, designs Bear Flag, **I**, 171

Token Coins, as currency, **II**, 99; and the silver dollar, **II**, 157; and money system, **IV**, 8

Tolbert, R. R., and the Phoenix riot, **IV**, 264

Toledo War, and the Ohio-Michigan boundary dispute, **IV**, 164

Toleration Act of Maryland, **III**, 349

Toll Bridges, established, **I**, 237; and Charles River Bridge case, **I**, 343; and government regulation, **II**, 405

Toll Gate Bill, **V**, 209

Tolliver, Floyd, and Martin feud, **III**, 348

Tolls (and Tollgates), on the Cumberland Gap, **II**, 96; legislation for establishing, **II**, 97; on turnpikes, **V**, 331; on the Wilderness Road, **V**, 465

Tom Sawyer, written by Mark Twain, **I**, 180

"Tom Thumb," locomotive, **III**, 292; and rail transportation, **V**, 308

Tomahawk Rights, **I**, 264

Tombecbe, Fort, and Fort Confederation, **II**, 13; established as base for expeditions against the Chickasaws, **V**, 280

Tombigbee River, Creek Indians on, **II**, 86

Tombstone, Ariz., a boom town, **I**, 215; site discovered by Ed Schieffelen, **II**, 236

Tomkins, Micah, and regicides in New England, **IV**, 438

Tompkins, D. D., elected Vice-President, **I**, 282; supports War of 1812, **IV**, 117

Tonkawa Indians, and Fort Belknap, **I**, 175; and Oklahoma openings, **IV**, 169; as guides, **V**, 46

Tonquin, The, Thorn reaches the Columbia River in, **I**, 133

Tonti, Henry de, founds Arkansas Post, **I**, 105, 106; **II**, 76; inspects Starved Rock as site for fort, **II**, 87; and Denonville's invasion of the Iroquois, **II**, 137; explorations of, **II**, 345; and Illinois, **III**, 67; erects Fort St. Louis, **IV**, 252; erects Fort Pimitoui, **IV**, 272; builds Fort St. Louis, **V**, 11; at Starved Rock, **V**, 161; visits the Taensa Indians, **V**, 216

Tontitown, dead city, **II**, 114

Too-hul-hul-suit, arrest of, **III**, 245

Toole, Joseph Kemp, governor of Montana, **IV**, 16

Toombs, Robert, and the Confederate Congress, **II**, 6; and states' rights in the Confederacy, **II**, 12; and the Cotton Kingdom, **II**, 70; and Georgia, **II**, 380; and oratory, **IV**, 180

Toonerville Folks, comic strip, **I**, 431

Top Flight, famous thoroughbred horse, **V**, 265

Topeka Constitution, and Kansas Free-State party, **III**, 197

Topeka Movement, and the Kansas struggle, **III**, 198

Topographic Mapping. *See* Maps

Topographical Engineers, United States, **II**, 212

Torbert, A. T. A., and battle at Trevilian Station, **V**, 323; and battle at Yellow Tavern, **V**, 506

Tordesillas, Treaty of, **II**, 133; **III**, 322

Tories. *See* Loyalists (or Tories)

Torkillus, Reorus, first clergyman in New Sweden, **IV**, 113

Toronto, Fort, building of, **IV**, 175

Torpedo, perfected by Confederate Navy, **II**, 8

Torpedo Boats, **II**, 112; **V**, 412

Torrens System, of registering land titles, **III**, 243

Torrey, Charles, leader of the Liberty party, **III**, 272

Torrey, John, and gardening, **II**, 371

Torrey, R. A., revivalist, **IV**, 464

Torreys' Trading Post, **V**, 302

Totem Pole, and Indian art, **III**, 93

Toulouse, Fort, and Hickory Ground, **III**, 29

Tourist Camps, and the trailer, **V**, 303

Tourists, and vacations, **V**, 355

Tousey, Frank, writer of weekly series, **II**, 147

Tower Building, introduces skeleton construction, V, 88

Towers, John T., and flight of the NC-4, IV, 79

Town, as basis of representation, I, 92

Town Government, III, 288

Town Meetings, control schools, II, 187; abolished by Massachusetts Government Act, III, 358; in New England, IV, 97; choose selectmen, V, 56

Town School, V, 39

Towne, Benjamin, begins publishing the *Pennsylvania Evening Post and Daily Advertiser*, IV, 125

Townley, A. C., launches the Nonpartisan League, IV, 140

Towns, George W., and the Union Rights party, V, 343

Townsend, Henry, purchases the Sterling Iron Works, V, 181

Townsend, Peter, proprietor of Sterling Iron Works, III, 55

Townshend, Charles, member of Board of Trade, I, 207

Townshend Acts, and Boston Resolutions, I, 224; and British colonial policy, I, 422; and the Declaration of Independence, II, 120; and Declaration of Rights, II, 124; and Dickinson's Farmer's Letters, II, 253; as factor leading to the Revolution, II, 307; and Committees of Inspection, III, 126; and the Massachusetts Circular Letter, III, 358; passed, IV, 115; and the Nonimportation Agreements, IV, 138; and the English Parliament, IV, 219; and the American Revolution, IV, 466; and taxation without representation, V, 229; and foreign trade, V, 294; protested by the Virginia Resolves, V, 379; authorize writs of assistance, V, 496

Township, and Land Act of 1796, III, 233; as unit of survey, IV, 181; as a political subdivision, IV, 299; and survey of public lands, IV, 373

Township System, and road construction, IV, 494

Townsley, James, and the Potawatomie massacre, IV, 323

Towson, Fort, founded by Matthew Arbuckle, IV, 168; and the Red River raft, IV, 432

Traces, and roads, IV, 493

Tractarian Movement, IV, 194, 366

Tractor, and agricultural adaptation to the plains, I, 23; reduces cost of production, I, 29; invention of, II, 248; and the reaper, IV, 419

Tracts, and the antislavery movement, I, 85; published by peace societies, IV, 233

Trade, Domestic, and the Federal Trade Commission, II, 264. *See also* Interstate Commerce

Trade, Foreign, and agriculture, I, 27; with Asia, I, 128; and the balance of trade, I, 147; and the

United States as a creditor nation, II, 85; and drawbacks, II, 167; with South America, V, 123

Trade, Restraint of, and the American Sugar Refining Company, I, 65; and the American Tobacco case, I, 66; and antitrust laws, I, 87

Trade, Triangular, and colonial commerce, I, 417; and molasses trade, IV, 6; and Rhode Island, IV, 478; rum in the, IV, 507; and the slave trade, V, 91; and the sugar acts, V, 199; and the West India trade, V, 437

Trade Acts, I, 13, 206; IV, 74. *See also* Navigation Acts

Trade Agreements, and antitrust laws, I, 87

Trade Agreements. *See* Reciprocal Trade Agreements

Trade and Plantations, Board of. *See* Board of Trade and Plantations

Trade Areas, and trade-marks, V, 299

Trade Associations, attempt to suppress unfair competition, V, 299; permitted by National Industrial Recovery Act, V, 327

Trade Barriers, III, 143

Trade Dollar, provided for, I, 252; forced into circulation, I, 412; and the Crime of 1873, II, 89; and silver legislation, V, 80

Trade-marks, and private brands, I, 234; and the United States Patent Office, IV, 222; and price maintenance, IV, 339

Trade Union Unity League, I, 440

Trade Unions. *See* Labor Unions

Traders Path, I, 51

Trading Companies, and charter colonies, I, 346; and chartered companies, I, 346; and colonial charters, I, 417; and the compact theory, I, 441; and the growth of corporations, II, 62; and the Council for New England, II, 71; and mercantilism, III, 374; and political theories, IV, 300; and state government, V, 169

Trading Post Number Two, V, 285

Trading-with-the-Enemy Act (1917), and confiscation, II, 16; and the banking moratorium of 1933, II, 394; and the War Trade Board, V, 407

Trail Driving, and Abilene, I, 2; cut off by barbed wire, I, 163; and cowboys, II, 80

Trail of the Lonesome Pine, written by J. W. Fox, Jr., I, 180

Trailer, as a modern covered wagon, II, 77; and tourist camps, V, 286

Trails, and roads, IV, 493; and transportation and travel, V, 307

Train-Bands, and the National Guard, IV, 59

Train Robbery, I, 152

Train Wrecks, II, 149

Training Day, and parades, IV, 213

Transcendentalism, and Brook Farm, I, 242; and freethinking, II, 340; and Fruitlands, II, 354; and philosophical thought and writings, IV,

263; and Swedenborgianism, V, 213; and the Unitarians, V, 345

Transfer Tax, V, 230

Transpacific Clippers, have Wake Island as port of call, V, 391

Transportation, and agriculture, I, 27; and the automobile, I, 140; in the "back country," I, 145; and canals, I, 302 f.; and consumer protection, II, 44; and dead cities, II, 114; and freight, II, 340; and the motor truck, IV, 33; and railroads, IV, 406 f.; and roads, IV, 493 f.; and domestic trade, V, 291; on turnpikes, V, 331; and inland waterways, V, 425

Transportation Act of 1920, and industrial arbitration, I, 95; and the commerce clause, I, 434; passed, III, 143; and interstate commerce, III, 144; and railroad pools, IV, 307; and Railroad Administration, IV, 400; and railroad mediation, IV, 402; and railroad rate law, IV, 402; and the recapture clause, IV, 421; and the Wisconsin Railroad Commission case, V, 474

Transylvania, as the fourteenth colony, II, 318

Transylvania College, establishment of, I, 205; establishes law professorship, III, 251; first western medical school at, III, 369

Transylvania Company, and Boonesborough, I, 216; Boone marks trail for, II, 96; and the Cumberland settlements, II, 98; signs Treaty of Sycamore Shoals, II, 110; and Fincastle County, II, 274; and the Henderson Land Company, III, 25; and Treaty of Sycamore Shoals, III, 99; in Kentucky, III, 204; and land grants, III, 235; and early road building, IV, 494; and the Old Southwest, V, 132; and the Treaty of Sycamore Shoals, V, 215; in Tennessee, V, 243; Virginia v. Transylvania Company, V, 380; and the Wataugans, V, 421; and the Wilderness Road, V, 465

Trappers, outfitted at Bent's Fort, I, 179; on the Gila Trail, II, 389; at St. Louis, V, 12

Trappers' Rendezvous, and Ashley's expedition, I, 128; on Wind River, I, 312; and free trappers, II, 335; and the fur trade, II, 362; on Green River, II, 423; and holes of the mountains, III, 37; at Jackson Hole, III, 164; and mountain men, IV, 37; and battle of Pierre's Hole, IV, 269

Trappers' Trail. See Cherokee Trail

Trapping, and the Rocky Mountain Fur Company, IV, 498

Trapshooters Oil Well, II, 190

Travel on Sunday, V, 1

Travelers Insurance Company, and accident insurance, III, 131

Traverse des Sioux, Treaty of (1851), and Indian land cessions, III, 100; opens Minnesota to settlement, III, 411; and Fort Ridgely, IV, 483; and Sioux land cessions, V, 86

Travis, William B., and the Alamo, I, 41; and the attack on Anahuac, I, 72; perishes in the Alamo assault, V, 257

Treason, of Benedict Arnold, I, 119; defined in Burr Conspiracy trial, I, 208; and the Conspiracies Acts, II, 28; and the Constitution, II, 37; and loyalists, III, 313

Treasure Island, exposition on, II, 399

Treasury, United States, and the Federal Deposit Insurance Corporation, II, 256; and Federal gold hoards, II, 395

Treasury Department, and Director of Budget, I, 247; and centralized purchasing, I, 335; and jurisdiction of custom houses, II, 101; evolution of the, IV, 475; and the Secret Service, V, 52

Treasury Notes, bills of credit known as, I, 187; and the Federal deficit, II, 128; as paper money, IV, 213; as legal tender, IV, 455

Treat, Robert, and Connecticut's Charter of 1662, II, 22; and settlement of Newark, N. J., IV, 120

Treat Mission, and the Texas navy, V, 256

Treaties, and the Constitution, II, 36; and collective naturalization, IV, 67; and veto power of the Senate, V, 366; and state laws, V, 408. See also Executive Agreements

Treaties, Indian. See Indian

Treatise on Human Teeth, first American book on dentistry, II, 138

Treaty-Making Power, and Missouri v. Holland, III, 431

Treaty Plan of the Continental Congress, I, 201

Tredegar Iron Works, and the Confederacy, II, 10

Tree Planting, and rain making, IV, 410; for reforestation, IV, 434

Tree-Ring Dating, and archæology, I, 98; and the cliff dwellers, I, 398; and maize, III, 328

Trefaldighet, Fort, formerly Fort Casimir, IV, 95

Trelawney Plantation, III, 317; V, 3

Trenholm, George A., and flight of Confederate Cabinet, II, 5; and Confederate financing, II, 9

Trent, William, and Great Meadows, II, 418; fur trader, III, 111; and the Indiana Company, III, 113; and the Miami Indians, IV, 266; and the Vandalia Colony, V, 357; and western land schemes, V, 443

Trent Affair, and Anglo-American relations, I, 76; and Canadian-American relations, I, 300; and freedom of the seas, I, 391; and Civil War diplomacy, I, 392; and impressment, III, 81

Trenton, Battle of, II, 131; IV, 476

Triangle Waist Factory Fire, II, 276

Triangular Trade. See Trade, Triangular

Tribune Building, V, 87

Trinchera Estates, V, 28

Tripoli, and the Barbary wars, **I**, 162; and the Derna expedition, **II**, 140; treaties with, **V**, 316

Trist, Nicholas P., executive agent, **II**, 232; negotiates treaty of Guadalupe Hidalgo, **II**, 426; seeks cession of California peninsula, **III**, 311; and the Mexican War, **III**, 386 f.; includes secret article in treaty of Guadalupe Hidalgo, **V**, 316

Tron, Charles, and the Waldenses, **V**, 391

Troop Schools, establishment of, **I**, 118

Trott, Benjamin, miniature painter, **III**, 408

Troup, George M., attempts to rid Georgia of Creek Indians, **II**, 86; and Georgia, **II**, 380

Troy and Greenfield Railroad, **III**, 45

Truax v. Corrigan, picketing found unconstitutional in, **IV**, 267

Truckee-Carson Irrigation District, operates Newlands Reclamation Project, **IV**, 121

Truckee Pass, **IV**, 221

Truckee River Route, and the Great Basin, **II**, 414

Trucks, Motor, **IV**, 33

Trudeau, Edward Livingston, and tuberculosis, **V**, 329

True Relation, written by John Smith, **I**, 189

Trueblood, Benjamin, and peace movements, **IV**, 235

Trumbull, John, painter, **I**, 123

Trumbull, Jonathan, and nickname "Brother Jonathan," **III**, 181; and the Yankee-Pennamite wars, **V**, 502

Trumbull, Lyman, and the Thirteenth Amendment, **V**, 264

Trustees' Garden, in Georgia, **II**, 371

Trusts, and the agrarian movement, **I**, 21; and American Tobacco Company, **I**, 66; and antitrust laws, **I**, 87; and capitalism, **I**, 310; and free trade, **II**, 334; and the industrial revolution, **III**, 118; and manufacturing, **III**, 337; and profiteering, **IV**, 355; and restraint of trade, **IV**, 460; and the Sherman Antitrust Law, **V**, 70; and the Standard Oil Company, **V**, 156; and the American Sugar Refining Company, **V**, 201; and U. S. v. E. C. Knight Co., **V**, 348. *See also* Monopolies

Truteau, Jean Baptiste, builds first trading post in Dakota, **II**, 106; on the Missouri, **III**, 431; leads the Spanish-Missouri Fur Company expeditions, **V**, 141

Truxtun, Thomas, commands the *Constellation*, **II**, 28; presented with gold medals, **IV**, 73

Tryon, William, and the burning of Danbury, **II**, 108; and Regulators in North Carolina, **IV**, 439; and the battle of Ridgefield, **IV**, 483; and Rouse's Point boundary controversy, **IV**, 503; and the Trespass Act, **V**, 322

Tubac, Spanish *presidio* established at, **I**, 104

Tuberculosis, **II**, 150

Tucker, Benjamin R., and anarchists, **I**, 72

Tucker, George, author of a life of Thomas Jefferson, **I**, 189

Tucker, Henry St. George, installs system of student self-government in University of Virginia, **V**, 375

Tucker, Luther, author of the *Genesee Farmer*, **II**, 248

Tucker, Richard, driven out of Saco Bay, **V**, 3

Tuckerman, Joseph, leads charity organization movement, **I**, 342

Tudor, Frederick, enters into the ice trade, **IV**, 437

Tuft, Otis, and the printing press, **IV**, 346

Tufts, Otis G., devises first closed car elevator, **II**, 201

Tugwell, R. G., and "Brain Trust," **I**, 234

Tulane University, and Latin America, **III**, 248

Tuley, Murray F., and government by injunction, **II**, 402

Tulley, John, compiles almanacs, **IV**, 99

Tunica Indians, fire upon the Loftus party, **III**, 294

Tunis, and the Barbary wars, **I**, 162; treaties with, **V**, 316

Tunnels, **I**, 93

Tunney, Gene, prize fighter, **IV**, 353

Tupper, Benjamin, leading spirit of Ohio Company of Associates, **IV**, 162

Tupper, James, and lumber rafts, **III**, 314

Turkey, treaties with, **V**, 317, 318

"Turkey in the Straw," fiddle tune, **II**, 270

Turkeys, Wild, as food, **II**, 295; abundance of, **II**, 369

Turnbull, Andrew, plants New Smyrna, **II**, 288; **IV**, 112

Turnbull, Robert J., author of states' rights pamphlet, **II**, 90

Turner, Asa, organizer of the Illinois Band, **III**, 69

Turner, Capt., in King Philip's War, **III**, 211

Turner, Frederick Jackson, author of "The Significance of the Frontier in American History," **II**, 350; and the New West, **IV**, 114; and sectionalism, **V**, 54

Turner, George, and the Alaska Boundary Tribunal, **I**, 44

Turner, James, engraves Evans' map, **II**, 230

Turner, Jonathan Baldwin, and land grants for education, **III**, 236; and the Morrill Act, **IV**, 27

Turner, Nat, slave insurrection, **V**, 90

Turner, William, barnstormer, **I**, 164

Turnpikes, Federal aid for, **II**, 255; and government regulation, **II**, 405; and the industrial revolution, **III**, 118; as internal improvements, **III**, 136; the Lancaster Pike, **III**, 232; and Right of Way Law of 1852, **IV**, 484; and tolls, **V**, 278 f.;

and transportation and travel, **V,** 307; on the Wilderness Road, **V,** 465

Turnverein, German society, **II,** 384

Turpentine, as naval store, **IV,** 72

Turtle, The, developed by David Bushnell, **V,** 194

Tuscaluza, and battle of Mauvilla, **III,** 360

Tuscarora Indians, and the Carolina proprietors, **I,** 316; admitted to Five Nations, **II,** 280; fight against the colonists, **III,** 159

T'Vault, William G., editor of the *Spectator,* **IV,** 127

Twachtman, John H., painter, **I,** 123

Tweed, William M., and corrupt rule, **II,** 64; and political rings, **IV,** 485

Tweed Ring, and crime, **II,** 88; and Nast's cartoons, **III,** 12; and party machines, **III,** 319; and municipal reform, **IV,** 43; and Nast's cartoons, **IV,** 55; and political scandals, **IV,** 298; and Tammany Hall, **V,** 218; trials of members of, **V,** 323

Twelfth Amendment, and campaign of 1800, **I,** 281; text, **II,** 41; and election of the President, **II,** 191; and separate election of President and Vice-President, **II,** 194; and the Jefferson-Burr election dispute, **III,** 170

Twentieth Amendment, and Congress, **II,** 20; text, **II,** 43; and extra sessions, **II,** 237; and filibustering, **II,** 272; and inauguration of the President, **III,** 82; and presidential succession, **IV,** 332

Twenty-first Amendment, text, **II,** 44; and the Webb-Kenyon Act, **V,** 431

Twenty Grand, famous thoroughbred horse, **V,** 265

Twenty Mule Teams, **I,** 218

Twiggs, David E., and battle of Cerro Gordo (1847), **I,** 335; begins Fort Winnebago, **V,** 471

Twiggs, John, in battle of Kettle Creek, **III,** 208

Two Bits, and coinage names, **I,** 411

Two-Party System, influence of the agrarian movement on, **I,** 20; and Jacksonian Democracy, **III,** 164; and the Jefferson-Burr election dispute, **III,** 170; and the spoils system, **V,** 147

Two Penny Act, **I,** 89; **IV,** 219

Two-Thirds Rule, abrogation of (1936), **II,** 53

Tydings-McDuffie Act, and Philippine independence, **IV,** 261, 263

Tying Agreements, and the Federal Trade Commission, **II,** 264

Tyler, Daniel, attacks at Blackburn's Ford, **I,** 197

Tyler, Elizabeth, and the Ku Klux Klan (20th century), **III,** 218

Tyler, John, and Border Slave State Convention, **I,** 219; nominated for Vice-Presidency, **I,** 283; censured by Congress, **I,** 332; and Dorr's Rebellion, **II,** 162; and the Presidency, **IV,** 333; and

annexation of Texas, **V,** 251; and "Tippecanoe and Tyler Too!" **V,** 273; and the Whig party, **V,** 456

Tyler, Royall, author of the play *The Contrast,* **II,** 165

Typesetters, and Casters, **III,** 320

Typewriter, and business, **I,** 259; invention of, **III,** 148; and productive machines, **III,** 320; and women in business, **V,** 481

Typhoid, eradication of, **II,** 150; and plumbing, **IV,** 289

Typographical Union, formation of, **III,** 224

U

Uinta, Fort, built by Antoine Robidou, **II,** 236

Ujházy, Count Ladislaus, leader of Hungarians in New Buda, **IV,** 94

Ulloa, Antonio de, first Spanish governor of Louisiana, **III,** 305; expelled from Louisiana, **III,** 310, 372

Umatilla River, and the Oregon Trail, **IV,** 186

Unalaska, founding of, **I,** 47; Ioann Veniaminov at, **IV,** 511

Unassigned Lands, of Oklahoma, **I,** 215; **IV,** 168; and Oklahoma squatters, **IV,** 169

Uncas, and the Mohegan case, **IV,** 5; leads the Mohegans in the Pequot War, **IV,** 252

Uncle Remus Books, **I,** 363

Uncle Sam's Union Almanac, **I,** 52

Uncle Tom's Cabin, as abolitionist literature, **I,** 3; and antislavery literature, **I,** 85; and the antislavery movement, **I,** 86; written by Harriet Beecher Stowe, **I,** 180; **II,** 270; stimulated by Fugitive Slave Act of 1850, **II,** 355

"Unconditional Surrender," Grant's terms at Fort Donelson, **II,** 160

Underground Railroad, and Fugitive Slave Act of 1850, **II,** 354; and Ohio, **IV,** 160; and the *Pearl* case, **IV,** 237; and Webster-Fairbank trials, **V,** 431

Underhill, John, and the Dutch-Indian War, **II,** 179; seizes House of Hope, **III,** 52; and the Pequot War, **IV,** 252; and Dutch War of 1653, **IV,** 479

Underwood, Oscar W., as floor leader, **II,** 287

Underwood, William, pioneer of American canning, **I,** 304

Underwood Tariff, and campaign of 1916, **I,** 290; reduces rates, **V,** 222

Undistributed Adjusted Net Income Tax, **V,** 227

Undistributed Profits Tax, **III,** 84

Unemployment, and labor, **III,** 220; and machines, **III,** 321; and the panic of 1893, **IV,** 209; and relief, **IV,** 440; and social legislation, **V,** 107; and Works Progress Administration, **V,** 485

Unemployment Insurance, provided in Social

Security Act, **III**, 223; **IV**, 96; and social security, **V**, 108

Unicameral Legislatures, retained by three states, **I**, 182; and the Connecticut Compromise, **II**, 23

Unicameralism, and the city council, **II**, 71

Uniform State Laws, **II**, 125

Union, Colonial, and the Albany Congress, **I**, 45

Union, Fort (N. Dak.), trading post on the Missouri, **II**, 106; Sully camps near, **II**, 107; distillery established at, **III**, 282; Mackenzie's treaty signed at, **III**, 321; important fort of the American Fur Company, **III**, 431; and the *Yellowstone*, **V**, 506

Union, Fort (N. Mex.), and battle of Glorieta, **II**, 392

Union Bank, charter of, **II**, 63; formed with aid of state funds, **II**, 402

Union Bank Bonds, repudiation of, **IV**, 456

Union Canal, and tunnels, **V**, 329

Union Fur Company, organized, **IV**, 29

Union Labels, and the American Federation of Labor, **I**, 60; and labor unions, **III**, 225; opposed by National Association of Manufacturers, **IV**, 58

Union Labor Party, and Greenback movement, **II**, 424; as a political party, **IV**, 297; as third party, **V**, 262

Union (Loyal) Leagues, and carpetbaggers, **I**, 318; and Civil War atrocity stories, **I**, 385; spread propaganda during Civil War, **I**, 388; persecute Copperheads, **II**, 58, and the Ku Klux Klan, **III**, 217; and Reconstruction, **IV**, 425

Union List of American Newspaper Files from 1821–1936, **III**, 34

Union National Convention, **I**, 285

Union Pacific Railroad, harassed by the Hole-in-the-Wall Gang, **I**, 152; and development of California, **I**, 274; race with Central Pacific, **I**, 334; and establishment of Cheyenne, Wyo., **I**, 355; and completion of North Western to Council Bluffs, **I**, 357; and Chinese immigration and labor, **I**, 366; and the Chisholm Trail, **I**, 368; eastern terminus located, **II**, 71; and Crédit Mobilier, **II**, 84; and growth of Denver, **II**, 138; chartered by the Federal Government, **II**, 403; and "Hell on Wheels," **III**, 25; and internal improvements, **III**, 138; and the Kansas Pacific, **III**, 198; control of, **IV**, 148; and Ogallala, **IV**, 159; and the Oregon Short Line, **IV**, 185; and Overland Mail, **IV**, 193; builds westward, **IV**, 282; begun, **IV**, 408; installs streamlined trains, **V**, 188; subsidies granted to, **V**, 195; and rail transportation, **V**, 309; and Fort Wallace, **V**, 394; and Fort Francis E. Warren, **V**, 408

Union Packet Line, and steamboat navigation, **V**, 179

Union Party, and Union Democrats, **V**, 342

Union (Lemke) Party, as third party, **V**, 262

Union Pass, **IV**, 222

Union Stock Yards, **III**, 286

Unit Rule, **II**, 53

Unitarians, and charity organization movement, **I**, 342; split off from Congregationalists, **II**, 16; as freethinkers, **II**, 340; and philosophical thought and writings, **IV**, 263; and the American religion, **IV**, 442; and theological writings, **V**, 261; and transcendentalism, **V**, 304

United Automobile Workers, and sit-down strikes, **V**, 191

United Colonies of New England, and colonial plans of union, **I**, 420; and fugitive slave acts, **II**, 355; and the fur trade, **II**, 361; and treaty of Hartford, **III**, 14; and the Praying Indians, **IV**, 330; and representative government, **IV**, 452; and the Warwick Commission, **V**, 412

United Confederate Veterans, **V**, 365

United Domestic Missionary Society of New York, **III**, 416

United Labor Party, as third party, **V**, 262

United Mine Workers, and the anthracite strike, **I**, 80; and the checkoff, **I**, 349; and closed shop, **I**, 403; and organized labor, **I**, 404; and Colorado coal strikes, **I**, 427; and the Hitchman case, **III**, 35; and craft unions, **V**, 344

United Press, **I**, 131

United Spanish War Veterans, **V**, 365

United States, The, W. Rush designs figurehead for, **II**, 272; frigate, **II**, 349

United States Agricultural Society, **I**, 26

United States Bank. *See* Bank of the United States

United States Express Company, **I**, 60

United States Gazette, opposed by *National Gazette*, **IV**, 59

United States Housing Authority. *See* Housing Administration

United States Iron and Tin Plate Company, **V**, 272

United States Lines, operated by the Fleet Corporation, **II**, 209

United States Mail Steamship Company, **I**, 406

United States Petroleum Company, and Pithole, **IV**, 279

United States Road, another name for Cumberland Road, **II**, 97

United States Seal, **V**, 49

United States Shipping Board, organized, **V**, 492

United States Steel Corporation, **III**, 156, 379; **V**, 180, 327

United States Telegraph, succeeded by the Washington *Globe*, **II**, 392; a Jackson campaign newspaper, **II**, 403; as political organ, **IV**, 128

U. S. v. American Tobacco Company, **IV,** 505

U. S. v. Butler, **I,** 24

U. S. v. Cruikshank, and the right of assembly, **I,** 129

U. S. v. E. C. Knight Sugar Refining Company, and *stare decisis,* **V,** 160. *See also* Knight Case

U. S. v. Fisher, and doctrine of implied powers, **III,** 79

U. S. v. Rice, **V,** 398

U. S. v. St. Louis Terminal Railway Association, **IV,** 505

U. S. v. Trans-Missouri Freight Association, **IV,** 307

United States Volunteers, **I,** 113

Universal and Critical Dictionary, published by J. E. Worcester, **II,** 146

Universal Peace Union, **IV,** 235

Universal Suffrage, and democracy, **IV,** 301

Universalists, as freethinkers, **II,** 340; and the American religion, **IV,** 442; in the Western Reserve, **V,** 446

University Extension, **I,** 14

Unknown Soldier, Tomb of the, added to Arlington Shrine, **I,** 108

Unlawful Assembly, **I,** 130

Unonius, Gustaf, and Swedish immigration, **V,** 213

Unreasonable Searches and Seizures, and the Bill of Rights, **I,** 186; and the Constitution, **II,** 40; in the wire-tapping cases, **V,** 472

Untermyer, Samuel, and the Pujo Committee, **IV,** 380

"Up in the White House," campaign song, **I,** 294

Upper Lakes, **II,** 415 f.; **IV,** 316

Upper Missouri Outfit, **I,** 430

Upper Peninsula, and Ohio-Michigan boundary dispute, **IV,** 164; and the Toledo War, **V,** 277

Upper Tract, Fort, massacre at, **V,** 62

Upshur, A. P., killed by explosion on the *Princeton,* **IV,** 343

Urban Drift, and changes in occupations, **IV,** 157

Urban Growth, and effects on amusements, **I,** 70

Urban Improvement Districts, as political subdivisions, **IV,** 299

Urbanization, and leisure, **III,** 264

Urim and Thummim, given to Joseph Smith, **IV,** 26

Urschel, Charles F., kidnapping of, **III,** 209

Usher, Hezekiah, and book publishing, **I,** 213

Usher, John, and the purchase of Maine, **II,** 401

Usher, N. L., and barnstorming, **I,** 164

Usselinx, John, attacks slavery, **V,** 94

Utah, Congress creates territory of, **II,** 140; organized, and admitted, **V,** 249

Ute Indians, and Fort Massachusetts, **III,** 354; and Meeker massacre, **III,** 371; New Mexico exposed to attacks of, **IV,** 107; and prospectors, **IV,** 364; and Uncompahgre, **V,** 337; and Fort Union, N. Mex., **V,** 341

Utility Districts, as political subdivisions, **IV,** 299

Utrecht, Treaty of (1713), and the Abenaki, **I,** 6; and the Asiento, **I,** 129; and erection of Fort St. Frederic, **II,** 93; and French claims in Ohio, **II,** 343; and Maine, **III,** 326, 328; and French recognition of British protection over Iroquois, **IV,** 5; cedes Acadia to England, **IV,** 315; concludes Queen Anne's War, **IV,** 389

V

Vaccination, and public health, **III,** 21; discovery of, **V,** 100

Vail, Alfred, brings the telegraph into use, **III,** 148; **V,** 238

Valcour Island, in the Revolutionary War, **III,** 230; **IV,** 471

Valdese, founded by the Waldenses, **V,** 391

Valerianos, Apostolos, real name of Juan de Fuca, **IV,** 195

Vallandigham, C. L., and the Birchard Letter, **I,** 190; and the Copperheads, **II,** 57; denounces General Order No. 38, **II,** 376; and New Departure policy, **IV,** 96; and the Northwest Conspiracy, **IV,** 150; arrested, **IV,** 161; and Order of American Knights, **IV,** 180; supreme commander of Sons of Liberty (Civil War), **V,** 120

Vallandigham Case, and trial by military commissions, **I,** 122; and arbitrary arrests, **I,** 387

Vallejo, Mariano, lord of the Sonoma March, **I,** 275

Valley Forge, Washington at, **IV,** 476

Valuation Act of 1913, passed, **III,** 143

Valverde, Battle of, **IV,** 485

Van Buren, Martin, and the Albany Regency, **I,** 46; Barnburners nominate for Presidency, **I,** 164; and campaign of 1812, **I,** 282; elected Vice-President, **I,** 283; elected President, **I,** 283; Free Soil candidate, **I,** 284; defeated (1840), **I,** 284; and the *Caroline* affair, **I,** 317; nominated by Free Soil party, **II,** 334; and Hull court-martial, **III,** 57; criticizes Kendall v. U. S. decision, **III,** 203; member of the "Kitchen Cabinet," **III,** 213; and the Albany Regency, **III,** 319; and the Maysville veto, **III,** 362; and the *Albany Argus,* **IV,** 128; and the Richmond Junto, **IV,** 482; and annexation of Texas, **V,** 251; and the Whig party, **V,** 455

Van Camp Packing Company, **II,** 297

Van Corlaer, Arendt, purchases Schenectady from the Indians, **V,** 38

Van Cortlandt, Stephanus, and Rumbout's patent, **IV,** 507

Van Couwenhoven, and the Petition and Remonstrance of New Netherland, **IV,** 256

Van Curler, Jacob, and House of Hope, III, 52; given first Dutch patent for land on Long Island, III, 298

Van Dam, Rip, and the Zenger trial, V, 513

Van Depoele, Charles J., and electric railways, IV, 410

Van der Donck, Adriaen, and the Petition and Remonstrance of New Netherland, IV, 256

Van Devanter, Willis, in West Coast Hotel Company v. Parrish, V, 436

Van Deventer, Christopher, and the Rip Raps contract-scandal, IV, 486

Van Dorn, Earl, attacks Corinth, II, 59; attacks at Holly Springs, III, 38; and the battle of Pea Ridge, IV, 230; Price joins, IV, 339; replaced by Pemberton, V, 367

Van Evrie, J. H., and proslavery literature, IV, 364

Van Horn, James, and the Rustler War, IV, 512

Van Lew, Elizabeth L., Grant's most valued spy, V, 146

Van Rensselaer, Kiliaen, and Albany, I, 44; patroonship of, IV, 226; and Zwaanendael Colony, V, 515

Van Rensselaer, Stephen, and the Niagara campaigns, IV, 130; and battle of Queenston Heights, IV, 390; and the Niagara campaigns, V, 405

Van Schaick, Goose, and Sullivan-Clinton campaign, V, 201

Van Staphorst and Willink, and Dutch loans, II, 178

Van Sweringen, M. J. and O. P., and Erie Railroad, II, 226

Van Syckle, Samuel, and pipe lines, IV, 276

Van Twiller, Wouter, buys Governors Island, II, 406; as director-general of New Amsterdam, IV, 108

Van Tyne, C. H., and W. G. Leland, *Guide to the Archives of the Government in Washington*, III, 34

Van Wart, Isaac, one of the captors of André, I, 73

Van Wyck, Robert A., mayor of New York City, IV, 119

Vance, Zebulon B., and Holden peace movement, III, 37; and restoration of Home Rule in the South, III, 41; and states' rights during the Civil War, V, 176

Vancouver, Fort, and the Oregon Trail, IV, 186; as John McLoughlin's post, V, 415

Vancouver, George, and mapping of west coast, III, 341; exploring expedition of, IV, 182; and the Oregon Question, IV, 184; first to explore Puget Sound, IV, 380; maps Puget Sound, V, 415

Vandalia, Ill., Cumberland Road built to, II, 97; and decline of Kaskaskia, III, 199

Vandalia Company, successor to the Grand Ohio Company, II, 409; and land grants, III, 235; and land speculation, III, 239; and the Ohio Company of Associates, IV, 163; and western land schemes, V, 443

Vanderbilt, Cornelius, and Erie Railroad, II, 226; and the Walker filibustering expedition, II, 273; rise of, II, 311; and the New York Central Railroad, IV, 117; and railroads, IV, 408

Vanderbilt, Cornelius, IV, undertakes a chain of "clean" tabloids, V, 216

Vanderbilt, Harold S., and bridge, I, 237

Vanderbilt, W. H., and "Public Be Damned," IV, 369

Vanderburg, Cornelius, silversmith, V, 82

Vanderburg, William, and Missouri Fur Company, V, 13

Vanderlyn, Pieter, artist, I, 122

Vanderspiegel, Jacobus, silversmith, V, 82

Vane, Henry, and the Antinomian Controversy, I, 83

Vanity Fair, political cartoons appear in, I, 320

Vanzetti and Sacco Case, V, 2

Vaqueros, II, 80, 81

Vardaman, James K., and the agrarian movement, I, 22

Varden, John, art collection of, I, 124

Vardill, John, as a spy, V, 146

Vare, Edwin, and corrupt rule, II, 64

Vare, W. S., and corrupt rule, II, 64; and political scandals, IV, 298

Vare Machine, III, 319

Vargas, Diego de, becomes governor of New Mexico, IV, 107

Vargas, Pedro de, leads an expedition to recover New Mexico (1692), IV, 379

Vasquez, Benito, and Spanish-Missouri Fur Company, V, 141; and Bent's Fort, V, 302

Vasquez, Louis, and Fort Bridger, I, 237

Vassar College, V, 477, 480

Vaudeville, I, 71

Vaudreuil, Marquis de, surrenders Montreal, IV, 18

Veblen, Thorstein, and technocracy movement, V, 236

Vedanta Society, Hindu cult, IV, 187

Venango, Fort, erected by French, II, 177, 342, 344, 346; III, 259; garrisoned, III, 343; falls in Pontiac's War, IV, 306

Venerable Society, II, 402

Venereal Disease, control act, III, 22; and hygiene, III, 64

Venezuela Boundary Dispute, and Anglo-American relations, I, 76; and the Monroe Doctrine, IV, 14; and Olney Corollary of Monroe Doctrine, IV, 172; and the Schomburgk Line, V, 39

Venezuelan Debt Controversy, and mixed commissions at Caracas, I, 312

Veniaminov, Ioann, and Russian Church in America, **IV**, 511

Vera Cruz, capture of (1847), **III**, 386

Vera Cruz (1914), and Mexican relations, **III**, 385

Verendrye, Pierre Gaultier de Varennes, Sieur de la, visits Hidatsa villages, **II**, 280; in Minnesota, **III**, 410; on the Missouri River, **III**, 430; discovers the Red River of the North, **IV**, 431; establishes Fort St. Charles, **V**, 6; explorations of, **V**, 205; searches for the western sea, **V**, 446

Verendrye Expedition, discovers the Big Horn Mountains, **I**, 184; journeys of, **II**, 345; on the Missouri River, **III**, 431; plants plate at Fort Pierre, **IV**, 268; and the Rocky Mountains, **IV**, 498

Vergennes, Comte de, and Franco-American Alliance, **II**, 326; and diplomacy of the Revolution, **IV**, 470

Verhulst, Willem, sails for New Netherland, **IV**, 107

Vermilion Range, and iron mining, **III**, 157

Vermont, first permanent English settlement in, **II**, 175; as the fourteenth colony, **II**, 318; white manhood suffrage in, **II**, 323; and the Green Mountain Boys, **II**, 423

Vermont, Republic of, and Haldimand negotiations, **III**, 4

Vermont, The, ship-of-the-line, **V**, 75

Vermont Gazette and Green Mountain Post-Boy, **IV**, 127

Vermont Militia, disbanding of, **II**, 133

Vernon, Mabel, and peace caravans, **IV**, 230

Vernon, Samuel, silversmith, **V**, 82

Verplanck, Gulian, and Rumbout's patent, **IV**, 507

Verrazzano, Giovanni da, explorations of, **I**, 57; and the Hudson River, **III**, 54; discovers Manhattan Island, **III**, 331; discoveries of, included on maps, **III**, 340; visits Narragansett Bay, **IV**, 53; enters the Narrows, **IV**, 54; and New France, **IV**, 100; visits Narragansett Bay, **IV**, 477; and Sandy Hook, **V**, 27

Versailles, Treaty of (1783), **IV**, 216. *See* Definitive Treaty of Peace

Versailles, Treaty of (1919), Senate refuses to ratify, **I**, 139; and the Treaty of Berlin, **I**, 179; and foreign policy, **II**, 305; Senate refuses to approve, **II**, 328; and freedom of the seas, **II**, 332; and Hitchcock reservations, **III**, 35; and indemnities, **III**, 84; United States fails to ratify, **III**, 142; and Lausanne Agreement of 1932, **III**, 251; and the League of Nations, **III**, 255; and the Lodge Reservations, **III**, 293; and mandates, **III**, 331; and Naval Armistice Commission, **IV**, 69; and the Reparation Commission, **IV**, 450; not ratified by the United States, **V**, 318; and the United States as a world power,

V, 487; and the World War Peace Conference, **V**, 490

Verville, Charles Gautier de, and the Sauk Indians, **V**, 34

Vesey, Denmark, slave insurrection, **V**, 90

Vespucius, Americus, explorations of, **I**, 56

Vestal Gap, **IV**, 221

Vested Interests, **III**, 134

Vested Rights, and the contract clause, **II**, 49

Vetch, Samuel, takes Port Royal, **IV**, 315; in Queen Anne's War, **IV**, 389

Veterans, Disabled, **I**, 62

Veterans' Administration, created, **I**, 11; Pensions Office becomes a part of, **III**, 135; and Soldiers' Homes, **V**, 118

Veterans' Bureau, established by American Legion, **I**, 62

Veterans' Lobbies, and pensions, **IV**, 251

Veterans of Foreign Wars, and soldier vote, **V**, 117

Veto, pocket, **IV**, 291; presidential, and concurrent resolutions, **IV**, 459

Veto Power, and the Constitution, **II**, 32

Vial, Pedro, and Texan-Santa Fé expeditions, **V**, 251

Vice-Presidency, and Cabinet meetings, **I**, 265; and the Constitution, **II**, 31, 35

Vick, Newitt, and settlement of Vicksburg, **V**, 367

Vicksburg, the *Arkansas* passes through Federal fleet at, **I**, 105; attack upon (1862), **I**, 106; Pemberton retreats into, **I**, 183; and battle of Chickasaw Bluffs, **I**, 360; as intrenched camp, **II**, 311; and opening of the Mississippi, **III**, 419; and the Mississippi Squadron, **III**, 425; mortar bombardment of, **IV**, 28; and Army of the Tennessee, **V**, 242; and the Yazoo Pass expedition, **V**, 503

Victorio, Apache chief, **I**, 88

Victory Loan, **III**, 271

Vienna, Treaty of (1921), ratified by Austria, **I**, 139

Vieux Carré, **IV**, 109

Vigil, Cornelio, land grant of, **III**, 247

Vigilance Committees, in Montana, **I**, 152; similar to Courts of the Plains, **II**, 76; and crime, **II**, 88; in Montana, **III**, 252; organized in San Francisco, **V**, 24

Vilas, George H., and Standard Oil Company, **V**, 156

Villa Raids, and Mexican relations, **III**, 385; and Pershing's expedition into Mexico, **III**, 388

Village, as a political subdivision, **IV**, 299

Villard, Henry, and the Forty-eighters, **II**, 313; president of Edison General Electric Company, **II**, 375; gets control of Northern Pacific Railroad, **IV**, 148

Villasur Expedition, **I**, 426; **III**, 430; **IV**, 417

Villefranche, Major, commissioned in the Revolutionary Army, IV, 473

Vincennes, taken by Clark, I, 145; and Clark's Northwest Campaign, I, 395; Croghan taken as prisoner to, II, 90; and the Division Act of 1800, II, 155; and the fur trade, II, 360; and Indiana, III, 112; and the *Willing*, V, 468

Vincennes, Sieur de, captured by the Chickasaws, II, 110; stationed on Wabash River, V, 369

Vincennes, Treaty of (1803), and Indian land cessions, III, 10c

Vincent, John H., and Chautauqua movement, I, 348; projects a uniform system of teaching, V, 204

Vindication of the British Colonies, tract by James Otis, I, 425

Vines, Richard, deputy governor of province of Maine, II, 401; begins settlement south of Saco River, V, 3; and the Trelawney plantation, V, 320

Vineyard, James R., shoots Charles Arndt, I, 129

Vinland, and Leif Ericsson, I, 56; and Cape Cod, I, 306; discovery of, IV, 143

Vinson Bill (1936), I, 63

Virgin Islands, purchased, I, 79; and expansion, II, 234; purchased by the United States, III, 79; as an insular possession, III, 128; and territorial claims of the United States, V, 247

Virgin River, and the Great Basin, II, 414

Virginia, Arnold's raid in, I, 120; and Fort Pitt, IV, 279; and plantation system, IV, 283; and western lands, V, 444

Virginia, Army of Northern, I, 81, 91; II, 240

Virginia, The, built by Popham Colony, I, 199; first ship built by Englishmen in North America, IV, 308

Virginia, The, ascends the Mississippi to Fort Snelling, III, 152

Virginia, The. *See Merrimack*

Virginia and Kentucky Resolutions, and the Alien and Sedition Acts, I, 49; and Calhoun's *Exposition,* I, 269; and the campaign of 1800, I, 281; and Federal-state relations, II, 263; and civil discord in Kentucky, III, 205; assert right of nullification, IV, 153; and party platforms, IV, 285; and right of secession, V, 51; and states' rights, V, 175 f.; and the Whig party, V, 455

Virginia Bridge Company, V, 348

Virginia Central Railroad, builds Blue Ridge Tunnel, I, 205; and battle at Trevilian Station, V, 323

Virginia City, Mont., and Alder Gulch, I, 47; and Bozeman Trail, I, 232; gold found at, IV, 16

Virginia City, Nev., a boom town, I, 215; and the Comstock Lode, I, 444

Virginia Company of London, financed by "adventurers," I, 16; and the Bermudas, I, 180; attempts to build blast furnaces, I, 199; and

British colonial policy, I, 421; and fundamental constitutions, II, 356; and Jamestown, III, 166; and lotteries, III, 303; and the Pilgrims, III, 362; IV, 111, 271; and Somers' voyage, V, 119; and colonial stock companies, V, 182; and the Tobacco Contract, V, 275; as a trading company, V, 301; and Colony of Virginia, V, 371

Virginia County of Illinois, III, 67, 70

Virginia Declaration of Rights, influence of, I, 185; adoption of, I, 187; and the *Coutume de Paris,* II, 76; drafted by George Mason, V, 373

Virginia Dynasty, dethroned, I, 282

Virginia Gazette, founded by William Parks, IV, 127

Virginia Historical Society, owns one of Céloron's lead plates, I, 330

Virginia Military Reserve in Ohio, III, 234, 238, 402; V, 444

Virginia Pass, IV, 221

Virginia Plan, and compromises of the Federal Constitution, I, 443; and dual government, II, 172

Virginia Resolves, and the American Revolution, IV, 466

Virginia University, establishes professorship of law, III, 252

Virginia v. Transylvania Company, V, 310

Virginian, The, written by Owen Wister, I, 180

Virginian's Plan of Union (1701), I, 420

Virginius Case, and Spanish-American relations, V, 135

Visit and Search, and Anglo-American relations, I, 75; and *Antelope* slave case, I, 79; right of, II, 338; and impressment of seamen, III, 80; and neutral rights, IV, 88; and the submarine in international law, V, 192

Vitamins, in food, II, 296

Vitascope, first machine for projecting pictures on a screen, IV, 31

Vittum, Harriet, and social settlements, V, 109

Vizcaíno, Sebastían, explores California, I, 270

Vizetelly, Frank H., revises Funk's dictionary, II, 146

Vladimir, Bishop, and Russian Church in America, IV, 511

Vocational Education, a part of adult education, I, 14; Board of, II, 188; and Smith-Hughes Act, V, 102

Vocational Rehabilitation, and social legislation, V, 108

Voight, Henry, builds a steam engine, II, 278

Volaperta, Giuseppi, and wax portraits, V, 426

Voliva, Wilbur Glenn, and Zion, V, 513

Vollmer, Lula, dramatist, II, 166

Volstead Act, and bootlegging, I, 217; and the Eighteenth Amendment, II, 190; and night clubs, IV, 133; and prohibition, IV, 356

Volta Bureau, to aid the deaf, **II**, 115

Volunteer Naval Reserve, **IV**, 72

Volunteers, in the Union army, **I**, 111; in Confederacy, **II**, 11; and mobilization, **IV**, 2

Von Steuben, Baron, and the Society of the Cincinnati, **I**, 375; trains Washington's lifeguard, **III**, 275; and the United States Military Academy, **III**, 398; and the Revolutionary Army, **IV**, 472, 474, 476; in the Southern campaigns, **V**, 129; and the army at Valley Forge, **V**, 356; and West Point, **V**, 438; and Yorktown campaign, **V**, 509

Voodooism, and folklore, **II**, 293

Voting, use of ballots in, **I**, 149; Negroes kept from, **II**, 150; and repeating, **IV**, 451; residence requirements for, **IV**, 459

Voting Machines, **I**, 150; **II**, 193

Voyageurs, at Cahokia, **I**, 267; and the fur trade, **II**, 360; in Indian trade, **III**, 110; and liquor in the fur trade, **III**, 282; developed by North West Company, **IV**, 147; and pemmican, **IV**, 241; at Prairie du Chien, **IV**, 328; at St. Louis, **V**, 12; and topographic mapping, **V**, 282

Vulcan, The, **I**, 73

W

W. C. T. U. *See* Woman's Christian Temperance Union

Wabash, St. Louis and Pacific Railroad v. Illinois, and state regulation, **II**, 410; and price fixing, **IV**, 338; and railroad rate laws, **IV**, 402

Wabash and Erie Canal, Indiana's first project, **III**, 113; and internal improvements, **III**, 138; and the Toledo War, **V**, 277

Wabash "Consent" Receivership (1888), **IV**, 449

Wabash Indians, and the fur trade, **II**, 363

Wabash Land Company. *See* Illinois and Wabash Company

Wabash Route, comes into use, **II**, 320

Wachovia, Betharaba planted in, **I**, 180; Moravian town, **IV**, 22; **V**, 499

Wachusett, The, forces surrender of the *Florida*, **II**, 289

Waco Indians, and Fort Belknap, **I**, 175

Waddell, Hugh, and the battle of Alamance, **I**, 41

Waddell, James, and the *Shenandoah*, **V**, 68

Wade, B. F., chairman of Committee on the Conduct of the War, **I**, 436; among the leaders of the Radical Republicans, **IV**, 395

Wade, J. F., and the Fort Apache incident, **I**, 88

Wade-Davis Bill, and the Emancipation Proclamation, **II**, 206; and Reconstruction, **IV**, 424; and Lincoln's plan of Reconstruction, **IV**, 427

Wadsworth, Decius, and forming of the Ordnance Department, **IV**, 44

Wadsworth, James S., and land speculation, **III**, 240

Wadsworth, Joseph, and Connecticut's Charter of 1662, **II**, 22

Wages, and the national income, **III**, 82; and minimum-wage legislation, **III**, 408; and salaries, **V**, 15; and standards of living, **V**, 157; and distribution of wealth, **V**, 429

Wages and Hours of Labor, an issue in the anthracite strike, **I**, 80; and industrial arbitration, **I**, 96; and the Fair Labor Standards Act, **II**, 239; and industrial relations, **III**, 116; and the labor movement, **III**, 219; Division of, in the Department of Labor, **III**, 221; in the colonial period, **III**, 222 f.; and *Laissez-faire*, **III**, 229; and Lochner v. New York, **III**, 291; and National Recovery Administration, **IV**, 62; and the War Labor Board, **V**, 404. *See also* Eight-Hour Day

Wages and Prices, and cost of living, **II**, 66

Wagner Act (1935). *See* National Labor Relations Act

Wagner Battery, taken, **I**, 344

Wagner-Peyser Act, makes United States Employment Service a bureau in the Department of Labor, **II**, 213

Wagon Box Fight, Sioux defeated in, **III**, 201; during Red Cloud War, **IV**, 429; **V**, 86

Wagons, and travel, **V**, 307

Wahpeton Reservation, **V**, 127

Waiilatpu, the Whitman mission, **V**, 394

Wait, Thomas Baker, publisher of *Falmouth Gazette*, **IV**, 126; first printer of Maine, **IV**, 346

Wakarusa War, Atchison citizens active in, **I**, 133; and the Border War, **I**, 220; and Kansas Free-State party, **III**, 197

Wake Island, annexed by the United States, **IV**, 195

Walcott, Charles Doolittle, fourth secretary of the Smithsonian Institution, **V**, 102

Wald, Lillian, founder of Henry Street Settlement, **V**, 109

Walden, Elisha. *See* Elisha Walling

Waldo, Samuel Lovett, painter, **I**, 123

Waldseemüller, Martin, globe and map of, **III**, 340

Walk-in-the-Water, first steamboat on Upper Lakes, **I**, 301; **II**, 224

Walke, Henry, commands the *Carondelet*, **I**, 317

Walker, Felix, and the term "buncombe," **I**, 253

Walker, Joseph R., and the Bonneville expedition, **I**, 209; early discoverer, **II**, 236; and Frémont's explorations, **II**, 414; and wagon trains, **V**, 389; and western exploration, **V**, 442

Walker, Robert J., recommends establishing Department of the Interior, **III**, 134; and the Kansas struggle, **III**, 198; in Mississippi v. Johnson, **III**, 425

Walker, Thomas, names Cumberland Gap, II, 96; names the Cumberland River, II, 97; enters Kentucky, III, 204; and the Loyal Land Company, III, 311; explores Powell's Valley, IV, 326; mentions Great Warriors Path, V, 408

Walker, William, filibustering activities of, II, 273; III, 311

Walker Pass, IV, 221

Walker Tariff, IV, 187; V, 222

Walking Purchase (1686 and 1737), Delaware Indians forced to give up land by, II, 131; and the Friendly Association, II, 348; and Indian land cessions, III, 99; and Quaker Indian policy, IV, 385; and Indian migration to Ohio Valley, V, 65

Wall-Blackburn Gang, stagecoach robbers, V, 153

Walla Walla, and Oregon missions, IV, 184; and the Whitman massacre, V, 461

Walla Walla, Fort, erected, V, 394

Wallace, Bigfoot, and barbed wire, I, 163; as hunter, III, 60

Wallace, H. C., and Stafford case, V, 152

Wallace, Henry A., and the Agricultural Adjustment Administration, I, 24; and governmental control of agriculture, I, 32

Wallace, John H., and registers for horses' pedigrees, III, 47

Wallace, "Lew," author of Ben Hur, I, 180; and battle of the Monocacy, IV, 11; V, 68; and battle of Shiloh, V, 71

Walling, Elisha, long hunter, III, 298

Walloons, build Fort Orange, I, 44; and the Hudson River, III, 55; in New Netherland, IV, 107

Walnut Hills, and treaty of Nogales, IV, 136

Walpole, Thomas, and forming of Grand Ohio Company, II, 408

Walpole Company, formation of, I, 170

Walsh, Thomas F., opens the Camp Bird Mine, V, 25

Walsh-Healey Act, administered by Division of Public Contracts, III, 221; and the New Deal, IV, 96

Walter, Thomas U., builds Girard College, I, 100; and the Capitol at Washington, I, 311

Waltham, Mass., first complete textile factory at, I, 223

Walther, C. F. W., organizes Missouri Synod, II, 384

Walton, George, signer of the Declaration of Independence, II, 124

Walvis, The, and Zwaanendael Colony, V, 515

Wampanoag Indians, and the Algonquin family, I, 48; and King Philip's War, III, 210, 211

Wampum, as currency, I, 437; II, 99, 100

Wampum Belt, as a ceremonial symbol, I, 321; and the covenant chain, II, 77

Wanderbird, The, probably last ship to beat round Cape Horn, I, 307

Wanderer, The, slave ship, V, 92

Wanghia, Treaty of (1844), I, 365; II, 101

Wapatomica Towns, raided, II, 177

Wappinger Indians, I, 48; III, 325

War, and capitalism, I, 310; casualties during, I, 322; attitude of churches toward, I, 373; declaration of, and the Constitution, II, 33; and insurance, III, 129; laws of, and martial law, III, 347

War, Articles of. See Articles of War

War Admiral, famous thoroughbred horse, V, 265

War and Ordnance, Board of, V, 402

"War Babies," and the stock market, V, 183

War Claims, association formed to protect (1863), IV, 366

War Claims Act. See Settlement of War Claims Act

War College, I, 114

War Dance, III, 97

War Debt, Great Britain defaults on, I, 77; and the balance of trade, I, 147; amount owed, II, 119; France defers payment of, II, 328; and the Hawley-Smoot Tariff, III, 19; and the Johnson Debt Default Act, III, 178; and the Lausanne Agreement of 1932, III, 251; and the Hoover moratorium, IV, 21; and the Reparation Commission, IV, 451; and the Thomas Amendment, V, 264

War Democrats, name given Lincoln supporters, II, 137; and the Union party, V, 343

War Department, and the Army General Staff, I, 115; supervises Garrison School, I, 118; administers arrests, I, 122; and national defense, II, 126; and Freedmen's Bureau, II, 336; and mobilization, IV, 3; develops from the Board of War, IV, 475

War Excess Profits Taxes, V, 489

War Finance Corporation, as farm credit agency, II, 246; incorporated by Federal Government, II, 403; and the Norris Farm Export Act, IV, 143

War Hawks, and Anglo-American relations, I, 74; and campaign of 1812, I, 281; and neutrality, IV, 89; proponents of War of 1812, IV, 109; V, 405; of the West, V, 435

War Industries Board, administration of, II, 17; and the Council of National Defense, II, 72; fosters trade associations, V, 299; World War economic mobilization, V, 488; and the World War, V, 492

War Labor Board, sponsors shop committees, V, 76; established, V, 492

War Labor Policies Board, V, 492

War of 1812, and Anglo-American relations, I, 74; Argus-Pelican engagement, I, 104; and the

United States Army, **I**, 113; and hospitalization, **I**, 116; as a cause of commercial growth, **I**, 147; and New England separatism, **I**, 224; first naval victory in, **II**, 30; Creek Indians in, **II**, 86; and public debt, **II**, 117; financing of, **II**, 128; demobilization after, **II**, 133; and United States fleet, **II**, 282; and treaty of Ghent, **II**, 387; and inflation, **III**, 120; and British right to free navigation of Mississippi, **III**, 423; Navy in, **IV**, 77; Negroes in, **IV**, 84; and Orders in Council, **IV**, 180; and failure of the Pacific Fur Company, **IV**, 195; and sea power, **V**, 48; and foreign trade, **V**, 294; and War Hawks, **V**, 403; cost of, **V**, 409; loss of life in, **V**, 410

War Powers of the President, and nationalist sentiment, **IV**, 64

War Profits Tax, **V**, 226

War Resisters, antiwar organization, **V**, 395

War Risk Insurance, **III**, 132

War Savings Certificates, **V**, 267, 489

War Trade Board, and Trade with the Enemy Acts, **V**, 300; and the World War, **V**, 492

Ward, A. Montgomery, credited with starting first mail-order house, **III**, 325

Ward, Artemas, and Washington's eight months army, **V**, 418

"Ward, Artemus," humorous lecturer, **III**, 260

Ward, John Quincy Adams, sculptor, **I**, 124

Ward, Nancy, "Beloved Woman" of the Cherokees, **I**, 176

Ward, Nathaniel, and Massachusetts Body of Liberties, **III**, 358

Warden, Frew and Company, and the Standard Oil Company, **V**, 156

Warder, Bushnell and Glessner Company, **III**, 140

Ware v. Hilton, **V**, 398

Warfield, B. B., and theological writings, **V**, 261

Waring, George, and "white wings," **V**, 188

Warmoth, H. C., and the Midnight Order (1872), **III**, 395

Warner, A. J., and the Silver League, **V**, 80

Warner, Seth, in battle of Bennington, **I**, 178; takes Crown Point, **II**, 93; and the Green Mountain Boys, **II**, 422; at Hubbardton, **III**, 54; **V**, 362

Warner, William, and Schuylkill Fishing Company, **V**, 43

Warner's Pass, **IV**, 221

Warren, Fort, as prison camp, **IV**, 347

Warren, G. K., and the Mine Run campaign, **III**, 406; and controversy with Sheridan, **V**, 69; and battle of Spotsylvania Courthouse, **V**, 150

Warren, John, and first military hospital, **III**, 51; as professor of anatomy and surgery, **III**, 51; describes influenza epidemic, **III**, 122

Warren, John Collins, founder of Massachusetts

General Hospital, **III**, 51; and operation under anæsthesia, **III**, 369

Warren, Joseph, at Bunker Hill, **I**, 253; and Masonry, **III**, 351; and Revere's ride, **IV**, 463; presents the Suffolk Resolves, **V**, 198

Warren, Lyman and Truman, fur traders of Chequamegon Bay region, **I**, 351

Warren, Peter, and the Louisburg expedition, **III**, 304

Warren, William A., and the Bellevue War, **I**, 176

Warren Act, or the Potato Act, **IV**, 322

Warren Gold Purchase Plan, **II**, 397

Warrington, Lewis, and the Mosquito Fleet, **IV**, 30; and *Peacock-Epervier* engagement, **IV**, 236

Warriors Path, Great, and Cumberland Gap, **II**, 96; joins Great Trading Path, **III**, 104; and Wilderness Road, **IV**, 494; part of Scioto Trail, **V**, 45

Warships, and national defense, **II**, 127; dreadnoughts as, **II**, 167; destroyers take place of dreadnoughts during World War, **II**, 167; and the United States fleet, **II**, 282; cruisers as, **II**, 284; destroyers as, **II**, 284

Warwick, Earl of, and the Providence Island Company, **IV**, 367; and Rhode Island charters, **IV**, 478; and renaming of Shawomet, **V**, 66

Warwick, R. I., established through efforts of Samuel Gorton, **IV**, 477

Warwick Commission, and British colonial policy, **I**, 421; and Lygonia, **III**, 317

Warwick Patent. *See* Connecticut, The Old Patent of

Washburn, C. C., builds first complete roller mill, **II**, 292

Washburn, Capt., and trapping, **V**, 311

Washburn-Langford-Doane Expedition, **V**, 506

Washington, Augustine, and the Principio Company, **IV**, 343; buys Wakefield, **V**, 391

Washington, Booker T., and Tuskegee Institute, **V**, 332

Washington, D. C., burned by British, **I**, 198; city directory appears in, **II**, 148; as a part of the District of Columbia, **II**, 153; burned by British, **II**, 387; **V**, 406

Washington, Fort (N. Y.), and building of Fort Lee, **III**, 260

Washington, Fort (Ohio), adds to the importance of Cincinnati, **I**, 375; and Harmar's expedition, **III**, 10; settlers confined to, **III**, 390; and St. Clair's defeat, **V**, 7; Wayne advances to, **V**, 427

Washington, George, and alfalfa, **I**, 47; and André's capture, **I**, 119; hears Arnold's plan for attacking Canada, **I**, 120; joins Forbes and Bouquet at Fort Raystown, **I**, 173; assumes command at Boston, **I**, 222; and Braddock's

expedition, I, 233; at Brandywine, I, 235; as brewer, I, 236; patents Burning Spring, I, 256; and the Senate as a council, I, 265; and camp followers, I, 279; elected President, I, 280; and laying the cornerstone of the Capitol, I, 311; and Chesapeake and Ohio Canal, I, 354; first president of the Society of the Cincinnati, I, 375; and the Confederation, II, 13; and ratification of the Constitution, II, 28; appointed commander in chief, II, 46; elected president of the Convention of 1787, II, 49; crossing the Delaware, II, 131; inaugurates practice of special agents for diplomatic missions, II, 148; owner of land in Dismal Swamp, II, 151; designates site for the National Capital, II, 153; and the rotation of crops, II, 154; mission to LeBœuf, II, 177; at Edge Hill, II, 185; and executive agents, II, 232; and the Indian factory system, II, 239; as "Father of his country," II, 254; careful with precedents he set, II, 259; and "First in war," etc., II, 276; and Forbes expedition, II, 298; and Franco-American Misunderstanding, II, 327; bids farewell to his officers at Fraunces Tavern, II, 330; and the French and Indian War, II, 342; and march of Rochambeau's army, II, 343; and gardening, II, 371; receives Genêt, II, 377; and battle of Germantown, II, 385; and Gist's travels, II, 390; and Great Meadows, II, 418; and Nathan Hale, III, 5; and battle of Harlem, III, 10; and the Highlands, III, 31; inauguration of, III, 82; and Indian policy, III, 105; and industrial research, III, 117; and insignia of rank in United States Army, III, 126; assailed by Jacobin Clubs, III, 166; fathers James River Company, III, 166; and Jay's Treaty, III, 169; encamps at Jockey Hollow, III, 177; visits Ticonderoga and Crown Point, III, 230; and western lands, III, 235; and land speculation, III, 239; mission to Fort LeBœuf, III, 259; orders building of Fort Lee, III, 260; and liberal construction, III, 268; papers of, purchased for the Government, III, 274; lifeguard for, III, 275; visits Logstown, III, 295; and the battle of Long Island, III, 299; favors lotteries, III, 303; and Masonry, III, 351; and the Mazzei Letter, III, 362; and the United States Military Academy, III, 398; and the Mississippi Company of Virginia, III, 421; and the battle of Monmouth, IV, 11; uses Nemacolin's path, IV, 12; recalls Monroe from France, IV, 15; and encampment at Morristown, IV, 28; and Mount Vernon, IV, 35; and introduction of the mule into the colonies, IV, 40; mentions passing Murdering Town, IV, 46; angered by *National Gazette's* attacks on Hamilton, IV, 59; and the idea of a National University, IV, 64; appointed commander in chief of the Army during naval war with France, IV, 72; and Navy of the United States, IV, 77; encamps at Neshaminy, IV, 86; and neutral rights, IV, 87; and neutrality, IV, 88; Farewell Address of, IV, 88; and Proclamation of Neutrality, IV, 91; occupies New York City, IV, 118; sworn in as first President, IV, 119; and the Newburgh Addresses, IV, 121; and oats, IV, 155; and Forks of the Ohio, IV, 162; and the Ohio Valley, IV, 165; rests at the Hermitage after battle of Monmouth, IV, 214; as incorporator and president of the Potomac Company, IV, 324; utilizes the Potomac Valley, IV, 325; subscribes to principle of separation of powers, IV, 327; and the Presidency, IV, 333; and the presidential title, IV, 334; and President's message, IV, 336; and battle of Princeton, IV, 342; protests against treatment on prison-ships, IV, 348; and public faith, IV, 371; establishes the Order of the Purple Heart, IV, 384; appointed commander in chief of the Revolutionary Army, IV, 472; transfers his army to New York, IV, 476; and riflemen, IV, 483; *Rights of Man* dedicated to, IV, 484; and mineral springs at Saratoga, V, 32; and massacre at Fort Seybert, V, 62; serves in House of Burgesses, V, 69; and appointment to office, V, 147; and capture of Stony Point, V, 185; and surveying, V, 210; frequent attendant at John Street Theater, V, 259; proclaims a day of thanksgiving, V, 259; and third-term doctrine, V, 263; and shift in trade routes and centers, V, 300; and the setting up of government factories and trading posts, V, 302; his first treaty negotiation, V, 315; uses trenches, V, 321; and battle of Trenton, V, 322; his commission and the name United States of America, V, 347; takes up winter quarters at Valley Forge, V, 355; visits the French at Venango, V, 359; and the battle of Virginia Capes, V, 376; born at Wakefield, V, 391; and Washington, D. C., V, 412; and Washington and Lee University, V, 416; and the Wayne campaign, V, 427; and West Point, V, 438; and the Whiskey Insurrection, V, 457; and the White House, V, 459; and battle of White Plains, V, 460; encamps at Whitemarsh, V, 461; and aloofness from Europe, V, 487; and Yorktown campaign, V, 509

Washington, John Augustine, acquires Mount Vernon, IV, 36

Washington, John W., and treaty with the Navaho Indians, IV, 68

Washington, Lawrence, and Mount Vernon, IV, 35; and the Principio Company, IV, 343

Washington, State of, organized, and admitted, V, 249

Washington, The, ship-of-the-line, V, 75

Washington, The, built by Henry Shreve, III,

423; and river navigation, **IV**, 489; built by Henry Shreve, **V**, 179

Washington, Treaties of 1837 and 1858, with Sioux Indians, **V**, 86

Washington, Treaty of (1871), and the Alabama claims, **I**, 41; abrogation of, **I**, 169; and Canadian-American relations, **I**, 300; and the fisheries question, **II**, 277; and Halifax fisheries award, **III**, 6; and international law, **III**, 141; and mixed commissions, **III**, 432; and treaties with foreign nations, **V**, 317; and the Welland Canal, **V**, 433

Washington and Lee University, endowed by Washington, **III**, 166

Washington Conference on the Limitation of Armaments (1921–22), and attitude toward China, **I**, 364; and national defense, **II**, 127; halts building of dreadnoughts, **II**, 167; and extraterritoriality, **II**, 238; and the Far Eastern policy, **II**, 243; and Five-Power Naval Treaty, **II**, 280; and Four-Power Treaty, **II**, 316; United States takes lead in calling, **III**, 142; and naval competition, **IV**, 69; Nine-Power Pact concluded at, **IV**, 134; and the Open-Door Policy, **IV**, 176; and position in the Pacific, **IV**, 196; and parity, **IV**, 217; and peace conferences, **IV**, 232; and treaties with foreign nations, **V**, 318; and Five-Power Naval Treaty, **V**, 414; and the Yap mandate, **V**, 503

Washington District, connected with Cumberland settlements by Avery's Trace, **I**, 142; organized by Wataugans, **V**, 243; established, **V**, 421

Washington *Gazette*, as political organ, **IV**, 128

Washington *Globe*, in campaign of 1836, **I**, 283; and removal of deposits, **IV**, 448

Washington Monument, **V**, 413

Washington *National Era*, publishes *Uncle Tom's Cabin*, serially, **V**, 337

Washington Naval Treaty (1922), and national defense, **II**, 127; and Five-Power Pact, **II**, 280; and London Naval Treaty of 1930, **III**, 296; denounced by Japanese government, **III**, 297; and Washington Conference on Limitation of Armaments, **V**, 417

Washington Navy Yard, **IV**, 79

Washington *Republican*, and the A. B. Plot, **I**, 1; as political organ, **IV**, 128

Washington Square Players, **III**, 286

Washington *Union*, replaces the Washington *Globe*, **II**, 392; official journal of Polk's administration, **II**, 403 f.

Washington's Eight Months Army, **III**, 414; **IV**, 476

Washita Campaign, and Camp Supply, **V**, 206

Washita Massacre, Arapaho participate in, **I**, 94; Cheyenne villages destroyed at, **I**, 355

Wasp, The, attacks Jefferson, **II**, 92

Wasp, The, sloop, **V**, 99

Watauga, backwoodsmen organize the Association, **I**, 145; Cherokees attack, **I**, 353; settlement at, **II**, 98; organization of the Association, **II**, 318; State of Franklin organized at, **II**, 329; and the Old Southwest, **V**, 132; Association set up, **V**, 242; settlement at, **V**, 450

Watauga, Fort, and the Wilderness Road, **V**, 465

Water Control District, as a political subdivision, **IV**, 299

Water Cure, as atrocity in war, **I**, 136

Water Mills, **III**, 52

Water Power, and the Ballinger-Pinchot controversy, **I**, 149; and conservation movement, **II**, 27; and utilization of electricity, **II**, 198; and the Federal Power Commission, **II**, 261; and machines, **III**, 320; and mill streams, **III**, 404; and Tennessee Valley Authority, **V**, 245

Water Routes and Portages, **IV**, 316

Water Supply, and aqueducts, **I**, 93; and use of bathtubs, **I**, 167; and hygiene, **III**, 64; and municipal ownership, **IV**, 43; New York City's, **IV**, 119; and public ownership, **IV**, 375; and sanitation, **V**, 28

Water Works, and engineering, **II**, 215

Waterhouse, Benjamin, introduces vaccination, **V**, 100, 355

Waterman, Henry, makes power elevator, **II**, 201

Waters, Walter W., and the Bonus Army, **I**, 211

Watertown, Mass., arsenal at, **I**, 122

Watervliet, N. Y., arsenal at, **I**, 122

Waterways, Great Lakes-St. Lawrence Project, **II**, 416; as internal improvements, **III**, 139; Lakes-to-Gulf Deep Waterways, **III**, 231; Nine-foot Channel, **IV**, 134; and Fort Peck Dam, **IV**, 238; and river and harbor improvements, **IV**, 488; and domestic trade, **V**, 291; and the Welland Canal, **V**, 433

Waterways Commission, Inland, **III**, 124; National, **IV**, 64

Watkins, Tobias, editor of the *National Journal,* **IV**, 128

Watling Island, Columbus' first landfall, **I**, 56

Watson, Elkanah, fosters first county fair, **II**, 73

Watson, James E., designated as party whip, **V**, 456

Watson, Thomas A., and the Bell Telephone Company, **I**, 66

Watson, Thomas E., nominated for Vice-Presidency, **III**, 395

Watson-Parker Act (1926), and industrial arbitration, **I**, 95

Watt, James, credited with laying foundation for industrial revolution with invention of steam engine, **III**, 117

Watterson, Henry, as newspaper editor, **IV**, 123

Watts, John, and the Pejepscot purchase, **IV,** 239

Watts Bar Dam, **V,** 245

Wave, The, races with the *Sylph,* **V,** 499

Waxhaws, and Southern campaigns (1780–81), **V,** 129

Way, George, and the Pejepscot purchase, **IV,** 239

Wayne, Anthony, and Arnold's raid in Virginia, **I,** 120; builds Fort Defiance, **II,** 127; and Lake Erie, **II,** 224; and the battle of Fallen Timbers, **II,** 241; gathers his army at Fort Fayette, **II,** 254; operations in Georgia, **II,** 380; and battle of Germantown, **II,** 385; builds Fort Greenville, **II,** 425; storms Stony Point, **III,** 31; and Hobson's Choice, **III,** 36; and Indians, **III,** 112; erects fort on site of Loramie's store, **III,** 301; final campaign against the Indians, **III,** 360; and the battle of Paoli, **IV,** 211; and Fort Recovery, **IV,** 428; and capture of Stony Point, **V,** 185; and Fort Washington (Ohio), **V,** 414

Wayne, Fort, and St. Clair's defeat, **V,** 7; built during Wayne's campaign, **V,** 427

Wayne, Fort, Treaty of (1803), **V,** 370

Ways and Means Committee, and the Speaker of the House, **V,** 142

"We cross the prairies as of old," **I,** 220

"We the People," Hamilton comments on, in *The Federalist,* **I,** 185; and the doctrine of sovereignty, **V,** 134

Wea Indians, and Algonquin family, **I,** 48; land cessions of, **III,** 100; division of the Miami, **III,** 390; and treaty of Fort Wayne, **V,** 370, 426

Weather Bureau, a division of the Department of Agriculture, **I,** 31; and balloons, **I,** 149; and Galveston storm, **II,** 368

Weatherford, William, leader of the Creeks, **II,** 184; surrenders to Jackson, **III,** 50

Weatherford's Town, destroyed by Claiborne, **II,** 86

Weaver, James B., Populist candidate for President, **I,** 288; and the Greenback party, **II,** 424; nominated for Presidency, **III,** 153; and the Populist party, **IV,** 313

Web Presses, **III,** 320

Webb, Daniel, refuses to rescue Fort William Henry (1757), **V,** 467

Webb, Fort, at West Point, N. Y., **V,** 438

Webb, George, first printer of South Carolina, **IV,** 346

Webb, James Watson, and the English Colony on the Rio Grande, **IV,** 486

Webb-Kenyon Act, **III,** 283

Webb-Pomerene Act, **V,** 327

Weber, Max, painter, **I,** 123

Webster, Daniel, and Bunker Hill Monument, **I,** 254; nominated for Presidency, **I,** 283; and Compromise of 1850, **I,** 442; and *Creole* slave case, **II,** 87; and the Dartmouth College case, **II,** 111; argues Gibbons v. Ogden case, **II,** 388; and Hülsemann incident, **III,** 58; and internal improvements, **III,** 139; and land speculation, **III,** 240; arouses indignation of the Masons, **III,** 352; and McCulloch v. Maryland, **III,** 364; and oratory, **IV,** 180; and sovereignty, **V,** 174; in Gibbons v. Ogden, **V,** 178; and the tariff, **V,** 222

Webster, John W., and the murder of George Parkman, **II,** 88; murder trial of, **V,** 323

Webster, Noah, and dictionaries, **II,** 146; and the first American survey of epidemiology, **II,** 221; editor of the *American Minerva,* **IV,** 123; and pamphleteering, **IV,** 202; author of *A Grammatical Institute of the English Language,* **V,** 40

Webster, Pelatiah, and pamphleteering, **IV,** 202

Webster, Timothy, Civil War spy, **V,** 146

Webster-Ashburton Treaty (1842), and Anglo-American relations, **I,** 75; and the Aroostook War, **I,** 121; and Canadian-American relations, **I,** 300; and the *Caroline* affair, **I,** 317; and Indian Stream Republic, **III,** 109; and the northeast boundary, **IV,** 147; and Rouse's Point boundary controversy, **IV,** 503; and slave trade, **V,** 104; and treaties with foreign nations, **V,** 317

Webster's *Blue-Backed Speller,* **I,** 180

Webster's *Dictionary,* distributed by New York *Tribune,* **I,** 214; and lexicography, **II,** 145; and early school books, **V,** 40

Webster's Spelling Book, **V,** 40

Weed, Thurlow, and anti-Masonic movement, **I,** 82; and the *Albany Evening Journal,* **IV,** 128; and printer's devil, **IV,** 344

Weeden, John, and Trevett case, **V,** 323

Weehawken, duelling ground, **I,** 258

Weekly Arizonian, **IV,** 126

Weekly News-Letter, **I,** 223

Weems, Mason L., author of *Life of Washington,* **I,** 180; and chapbooks, **I,** 341

Weiser, Conrad, and the treaty of Easton, **II,** 183; and the treaty of Lancaster, **III,** 232; visits Logstown, **III,** 295; and the Palatines, **IV,** 201

Weiss, C. A., shoots Huey Long, **I,** 129

Weitzel, Godfrey, and the White House of the Confederacy, **V,** 459

Welch, William Henry, and hygiene, **III,** 64

Weld, Theodore D., and the abolition movement, **I,** 3; and antislavery literature, **I,** 85; and antislavery movement, **I,** 86; and the Oberlin movement, **IV,** 155; and the Ohio State Antislavery Society, **IV,** 165; and the abolition movement, **IV,** 363; leads antislavery movement among church people, **V,** 97

Welfare Work, and pauperism, **IV,** 227

Welland Ship Canal, and Canadian-American waterways, **I,** 301

Welles, Gideon, and the Navy in the Civil War,

I, 389; and the *Monitor,* IV, 10; and the *Powhatan* incident, IV, 327

Wells, and city water supply, I, 93

Wells, French and Indian raids on, IV, 389

Wells, Butterfield and Company, I, 60

Wells, David A., and tariff commissions, V, 223

Wells, Fargo and Company, Holladay sells his properties to, III, 38; and Overland Mail, IV, 193; Louis McLane as western manager of, IV, 274; buys Holladay's stagecoach lines, V, 153; and stagecoach robberies, V, 153; carry the mails, V, 308

Wells, Henry, and the American Express Company, I, 60

Wells, Horace, and painless extraction, I, 71

Wells, John and William Charles, publish the *East Florida Gazette,* IV, 126; first printers in Florida, IV, 345

Wells, John I., press maker, IV, 346

Wells, Samuel Levi, and the Sandbar Duel, V, 27

Wentworth, Benning, and the New Hampshire grants, IV, 102; and Vermont, V, 362

Wentworth, John, and the Pejepscot purchase, IV, 239

Wentworth, John, grants charter for Dartmouth College, II, 110; driven out of New Hampshire, IV, 102

Wentworth, Paul, as a spy, V, 145

Werden, John, as a proprietary agent, IV, 361

Wesley, John, devises circuit riding, I, 376; and the Epworth League, II, 221; and the Methodists, III, 380; and Pietism, IV, 269; and the Anglicans in Savannah, V, 35; and Sunday Schools, V, 204

Wessagusset, Weston's settlers move to, V, 448

Wessells, Henry W., and Dull Knife's campaign, II, 175

West, Benjamin, painter, I, 123; V, 63

West Augusta, district of, I, 139; and the Pennsylvania-Virginia boundary dispute, IV, 249; and the Pittsburgh Resolutions, IV, 281

West Coast Hotel Co. v. Parrish, I, 10; III, 409; V, 161, 387

West Florida, and the Adams-Onís treaty, I, 9; and seizure of Baton Rouge (1810), I, 167; and Dunbar's Line, II, 176; development of, II, 287; establishment of, II, 290; boundary dispute, II, 290; and the Kemper raid, III, 203; boundary dispute, III, 305; and Louisiana, III, 309; and Mississippi, III, 420; and the Mobile Act, IV, 1; annexation of, IV, 220; and Pearl River, IV, 237; Pensacola becomes government seat of, IV, 250; and Spanish-American relations, V, 135; under Spain, V, 139; and territorial claims of the United States, V, 246; and the Yazoo-Chattahoochee Line, V, 503

West Indian Trade, and balance of trade, I, 146; and the livestock industry, III, 286; and mackerel fisheries, III, 321

West Jersey, and Penn's "Concessions," II, 2; and East Jersey, II, 182; and Laws, Concessions and Agreements, III, 254; a division of New Jersey, IV, 104; as a proprietary province, IV, 362

West Point, Arnold plans to betray, I, 73; military stores at, I, 112; defense set up at, II, 28; construction of works at, III, 31; silver deposits at, V, 82. *See also* Military Academy, U. S.

West Point and Montgomery Railroad, IV, 503

West Point Foundry, locomotives built at, III, 292

West Rexburg Community, I, 441

West Shore Railroad, IV, 118

West Virginia, Virginia v., V, 380

West Virginia Coal Fields, and martial law, III, 347

Westcott, E. N., author of *David Harum,* I, 180

Western Company, and Louisiana, I, 106; III, 305; and the Mississippi Bubble, III, 421

Western Design, and British colonial policy, I, 421

Western Engineer, The, makes first steamboat voyage up the Missouri to Council Bluffs, III, 152; and the Yellowstone Expedition, III, 300

Western Federation of Miners, I, 409; III, 21

Western Labor Union, IV, 174

Western Lands, and the Articles of Confederation, I, 125; and Jefferson's proposed states, III, 172; and colonial land grants, III, 235; and land speculation, III, 240; and Maryland, III, 349; New York cedes, IV, 116; and Ordinances of 1784, 1785 and 1787, IV, 181; cession of, and the public domain, IV, 369; V, 132; and state-making process, V, 171; North Carolina cedes, V, 243; and territorial claims of the United States, V, 246; Virginia first to cede, V, 373; and the Virginia Military Reserve in Ohio, V, 379; and distribution of wealth, V, 429; and the Western Reserve, V, 445; and the Yazoo fraud, V, 503

Western Missionary Society, III, 103

Western Reserve, and Cleveland, I, 397; and Connecticut's western lands, II, 24; Firelands of, II, 275; and Fort Industry, III, 120; and group migration, III, 397; and western lands, V, 444

Western Rural, edited by Milton George, II, 251

Western Separatism, and the Mississippi River, III, 424; becomes rampant, V, 435

Western Union Telegraph Company, and telephone patents, I, 66; comes into being, V, 238; and the telephone cases, V, 239; purchases telephonic devices, V, 441; and the Yukon, V, 512

Western World, exposes the Spanish conspiracy, V, 140

Westinghouse, George, perfects air brake, **I**, 7; and alternating current, **II**, 198

Westinghouse Electric and Manufacturing Company, failure of, and panic of 1907, **IV**, 210

Westinghouse Evening School, **III**, 115

Westminster, Treaty of (1655), and Maine, **III**, 326

Westminster, Treaty of (1674), makes Long Island part of New York Colony, **III**, 299

Westminster Confession, and the Cambridge Platform, **I**, 277; adopted by the Congregationalists, **II**, 16; adopted by Cumberland Presbyterians, **II**, 97; and the Edwardian theology, **II**, 189; and heresy trials, **III**, 27; and the Presbyterians, **IV**, 332

Westmoreland, Town of, and Pennsylvania-Connecticut boundary dispute, **IV**, 246; and settlement of Wyoming Valley, **V**, 498

Westmoreland County (Va.), creation of, **I**, 138

Weston, Thomas, and the Pilgrims, **IV**, 271

Westport, Mo., as starting point of caravan traffic, **I**, 312; Price caught at, **IV**, 339; and the Santa Fé Trail, **V**, 30

Westport Landing, **III**, 196

Westward Movement, and agriculture, **I**, 28; and the Alleghenies, **I**, 51; and army on the frontier, **I**, 117; and the "back country," **I**, 145; of production areas, **II**, 77; produces the frontier merchant, **II**, 352; and frontier oratory, **II**, 353; and Homestead legislation, **III**, 42; and Indian treaties, **III**, 89; and Indian removal, **III**, 106; and Jacksonian Democracy, **III**, 165; and merchant marine, **III**, 375; and group migration, **III**, 396; and military roads, **III**, 402; and the Mississippi Valley, **III**, 426; and the Pacific Ocean, **IV**, 196; and mountain passes, **IV**, 221; and the pioneers, **IV**, 274; and the Quakers, **IV**, 386; and River Towns of Connecticut, **IV**, 490; and American slang, **V**, 88; and transportation and travel, **V**, 307; and trapping, **V**, 311; and the West, **V**, 434

Wethersfield, Conn., attacked by the Pequot Indians, **IV**, 252

Wetzel, Lewis, hunter, **III**, 60

Weyerhaeuser, Frederick, and great fortunes, **II**, 312

Weyerhaeuser, George, kidnapping of, **III**, 209

Weymouth, George, and exploration of America, **I**, 57; visits the Maine coast, **III**, 203, 326; describes Monhegan Island, **IV**, 9

Whale Oil, used for lighting, **III**, 276

Whale Products, and foreign trade, **V**, 294

Whaleback Mound, **II**, 107

Whaling, and Cape Cod, **I**, 306; and Hawaii, **III**, 17; colonial industry, **III**, 119; off coast of Labrador, **III**, 225; and Nantucket, **IV**, 52; and the Pacific Ocean, **IV**, 196; and Ringgold-

Rodgers exploring expedition, **IV**, 485; and Sag Harbor, **V**, 4; and San Francisco Bay, **V**, 23; and the Spermaceti trust, **V**, 145; and Zwaanendael Colony, **V**, 515

Whalley, Edward, regicide in New England, **IV**, 438

Wharton, Edith, and fiction, **II**, 270

Wharton, Joseph, operates Lancaster Gap mine, **IV**, 132

Wharton, Richard, and the Pejepscot purchase, **IV**, 239

Wharton, Samuel, of the firm of Baynton, Wharton and Morgan, **I**, 170; and forming of Grand Ohio Company, **II**, 408; and the Indiana Company, **III**, 113; and land speculation, **III**, 239; and the Vandalia Colony, **V**, 357

Wharton, William H., and financing the Texas revolution, **V**, 253

"What hath God wrought!" **V**, 238

Wheat, and agricultural adaptation to the plains, **I**, 23; in New England, **I**, 27; governmental control of, **I**, 33; in Red River Valley, **I**, 208; and crop failures, **II**, 91; and agricultural diversification, **II**, 154; and grain elevators, **II**, 201; milling, **II**, 291; in Indiana, **III**, 112; and the National Nonpartisan League, **IV**, 139; and the Red River of the North, **IV**, 432; and the Southwest, **V**, 133; and foreign trade, **V**, 295

Wheat Director, appointment of, **II**, 297

Wheaton, Frank, and battles of Tule Lake, **V**, 329

Wheaton, Henry, and the Zollverein Treaty, **V**, 514

Wheaton, Lloyd, and the Philippine insurrection, **IV**, 261

Wheeler, Burton K., and campaign of 1924, **I**, 291; endorsed for Vice-Presidency by the LaFollette party, **III**, 227

Wheeler, Cyrenus, and the mowing machine, **IV**, 38; and the development of the reaper, **IV**, 419

Wheeler, Edward L., creator of the character "Deadwood Dick," **II**, 147

Wheeler, Etta Angell, and Society for the Prevention of Cruelty to Children, **V**, 112

Wheeler, G. M., and scientific exploration of the Colorado River, **I**, 427; railroad survey of, **V**, 283

Wheeler, John F., first printer of Oklahoma, **IV**, 346

Wheeler, Joseph, and Sherman's march to the sea, **V**, 71

Wheeler, W. A., nominated for Vice-Presidency, **I**, 286; elected Vice-President, **I**, 287

Wheeler, Wayne B., and the Anti-Saloon League, **I**, 84; and prohibition, **IV**, 357

Wheeler, William A., and the hot-air furnace, **III**, 23

Wheeler and Melick, develop a thresher-separator, **V**, 266

Wheeler Dam, construction of, V, 244

Wheeler-Howard Act (1934), and Office of Indian Affairs, III, 90; and Indian policy, III, 106

Wheeler-Lea Act (1938), and the Pure Food and Drug Acts, IV, 383; and trade practices, V, 299

Wheeler-Rayburn Act, or Public Utility Act (1935), IV, 377

Wheeling, W. Va., mail carried over Cumberland Road to, II, 97; Fort Henry at, III, 26; Clark mobilizes at, III, 291; and Zane's Trace, V, 512

Wheelock, Eleazar, establishes Moor's Indian Charity School, II, 110; works for Indians, IV, 330

Wheelock, John, deposed as president of Dartmouth College, II, 111

Wheelwright, John, and the Antinomian controversy, I, 83; and heresy trials, III, 27; founder of Exeter, IV, 101

Whig Party, in Alabama, I, 39; and anti-Masonic movement, I, 82; in campaigns of 1836 and 1840, I, 283; in campaigns of 1844, 1848 and 1852, I, 284; in campaign of 1860, I, 285; and the formation of the Constitutional Union party, II, 44; National Republicans change name to, II, 136; formed, III, 165; absorbs the National Republican party, IV, 62; as a political party, IV, 296; evolution of, IV, 454; and the Republican party, IV, 454; and spoils system, V, 148; and states' rights, V, 176; campaign slogan of 1840, V, 273

Whipping, as a colonial punishment, IV, 382

Whipping Post, II, 285

Whipple, A. W., conducts railroad survey, IV, 405

Whipple, Abraham, and burning of the Gaspee, II, 373

Whipple, Fort, original designation for Fort Myer, IV, 51

Whipple, George Hoyt, awarded Nobel prize in medicine, III, 370

Whipple, Squire, and bridges, I, 237; and engineering, II, 214

Whipple, William, signer of the Declaration of Independence, II, 123

Whips, provided by party caucus, I, 328; and Congress, II, 18

Whiskey, and the agrarian movement, I, 20; as a transportable agricultural product, I, 33; distilling of, II, 151; popularity of, II, 169

Whiskey Insurrection, and the Army, I, 113; Fort Cumberland occupied during, II, 96; as a protest against the excise, III, 132, 139; and the militia, III, 403; tarring and feathering during, V, 220; and treason trials, V, 313

Whiskey Ring, and political corruption, II, 64; trials of members of, V, 323

"Whiskey Trust," V, 326

Whistler, J. N. G., guards Northern Pacific Railway surveyors, IV, 480

Whistler, James McNeill, painter and etcher, I, 123

Whistler, John, commandant of Fort Dearborn, II, 115

Whitcomb, Chapman, and chapbooks, I, 341

White, Andrew D., and lecturing, III, 260

White, Anthony W., aids Wayne in Georgia, II, 381

White, Canvass, father of the American cement industry, I, 330; builder of Erie Canal, II, 226

White, E. D., and U. S. v. Trans-Missouri Freight Association, V, 349

White, Elijah, caravan of, I, 312; agent to the Nez Percé Indians, IV, 129

White, Ellen G., and the Seventh-day Adventists, V, 60

White, Henry, and the World War Peace Conference (1919), V, 490

White, Hugh L., nominated by Whigs, I, 283; and the Whig party, V, 455

White, James, and the Spanish conspiracy, V, 139

White, Jim, discovers Carlsbad Caverns, I, 314

White, John, as governor of Roanoke Island colony, IV, 144, 413

White, John, and the Dorchester Company, II, 161; and the Great Migration, II, 418; and the New England Company, IV, 99

White, Josiah, builds Lehigh Canal, I, 80

White, Stanford, murder of, II, 88; V, 323

White, Stewart Edward, describes thirst, V, 263

White, Thomas W., editor of the Southern Literary Messenger, V, 130

White, William, and the Protestant Episcopal Church, IV, 366; forms a Sunday School, V, 204

White Bird Canyon, Nez Percé Indians victorious at, IV, 129

"White Boys," or "Molly Maguires," IV, 6

White Eyes, Delaware chief, and treaty at Pittsburgh (1775), IV, 280

White House, early architecture of, I, 100; first bathtub installed in the, I, 167; Easter egg rolling at, II, 183

White League, organized, IV, 111

White Oak Swamp, battle of, V, 60

White Pine Acts, and British colonial policy, I, 422

White Sands National Monument, II, 178; IV, 19

White-Slave Traffic, and the Mann Act, III, 333; and sex relations, V, 62

White Squadron, and national defense, II, 127; beginning of, II, 283; and warships, V, 412

White Sulphur Springs, III, 406; IV, 460

White-Williams Foundation, II, 314

Whitefield, George, builds Bethesda House of Mercy, I, 181; and the Great Revival, II, 413;

and the New Lights, **IV**, 106; and revivals, **IV**, 464; sermons of, **V**, 59

Whitehead, Mortimer, and rural free delivery, **IV**, 508

Whiteman, Paul, and symphonic jazz, **V**, 120

White's Fort, Holston treaty signed at, **III**, 39

Whitewater Canal, **III**, 114

Whitlock, Brand, makes speech at tomb of Lafayette, **III**, 227; author of *On the Enforcement of Law in Cities*, **III**, 253

Whitman, Marcus, makes known much of the Northwest, **II**, 236; and the American Board Mission in Oregon, **IV**, 182; and Oregon missions, **IV**, 184; and wagon trains, **V**, 389; mission at Waiilatpu, **V**, 394

Whitman Massacre, Cayuse Indians participate in, **I**, 329; closes the Lapwai mission, **III**, 245

Whitmarsh, Thomas, founder of the *South-Carolina Gazette*, **IV**, 127

Whitney, Asa, and internal improvements, **III**, 139; and early government railroad surveys, **IV**, 405; and the Union Pacific Railroad, **V**, 342

Whitney, Eli, and the Colt six shooter, **I**, 428; invents cotton gin, **II**, 69; and interchangeable parts system, **II**, 248; **III**, 133; and great inventions, **III**, 148; and machines, **III**, 320; and mass production, **III**, 353; fills a contract for muskets, **IV**, 44; invents the cotton gin, **IV**, 284; **V**, 94

Whitney, Henry H., and message to Garcia, **II**, 370

Whitney, Horace K., printer of the *Deseret News*, **IV**, 127

Whitney, J. H., and wood engraving, **V**, 483

Whitney, William C., leader of the Cleveland Democrats, **I**, 398

Whitney, William Dwight, editor of *Century Dictionary of the English Language*, **I**, 335; **II**, 146

Whitney, Willis R., develops metallized carbon filament, **II**, 197; establishes industrial research laboratory of General Electric Company, **II**, 376; and the incandescent lamp, **III**, 232

Whitside, S. M., and the Messiah War, **III**, 380

Whittier, John Greenleaf, and antislavery literature, **I**, 85; and American hymns, **III**, 65

Whittlesey, Charles W., and the Lost Battalion, **III**, 302

Whole Booke of Psalmes, third product of the press in America, **IV**, 345

Wholesale Business, and the distribution of merchandise, **II**, 152; and domestic trade, **V**, 293

Whydah Negroes, imported as slaves, **IV**, 86

Wichita, on the Abilene Trail, **I**, 2; cow town, **II**, 79

Wichita Indians, Chouteau carries on trade with, **I**, 370; in Oklahoma, **IV**, 168; and Oklahoma openings, **IV**, 169; hold agency headquarters at Fort Sill, **V**, 79

Wickersham Commission on Law Enforcement, **II**, 89, 190; **III**, 253

Wickes, Lambert, and the Navy in the Revolution, **IV**, 471

Wickham, Henry, and the rubber industry, **IV**, 504

Wickham, W. C., and battle at Yellow Tavern, **V**, 506

Wickyups, **I**, 47

Widener, Peter A. B., and great fortunes, **II**, 312

Wigfall, L. T., and the Confederate Congress, **II**, 6

Wigglesworth, Edward, presents first American mortality tables, **III**, 129; and vital statistics, **V**, 381

Wigwams, birch-bark used for, **I**, 190

Wilbur, Parson, and the *Biglow Papers*, **I**, 184

Wilbur, Ray Lyman, and the All American Canal, **I**, 50; and Hoover Dam, **I**, 225; and Colorado River projects, **I**, 428

Wilcox, C. M., joins Shelby's Mexican expedition, **V**, 68

Wild Hog, Chief, arrest of, **II**, 175

Wild-Life Conservation, **I**, 137, 190

Wild Rice, takes place of maize among Indians, **III**, 87

Wildcat Banks, **I**, 156; **II**, 101, 229

Wilde, Richard Henry, poet, **V**, 123

Wilderness, Battles of the, and the Bloody Angle, **I**, 202; and campaign against Richmond, **IV**, 481

Wilderness Road, and the Alleghenies, **I**, 51; parties join for journey over, **I**, 184; Crab Orchard as station on, **II**, 82; goes through Cumberland Gap, **II**, 96; crosses Cumberland River, **II**, 97; Boone makes known, **II**, 235; an Indian path, **III**, 104; and mountain passes, **IV**, 221; passes through Powell's Valley, **IV**, 326; and road development, **IV**, 494; uses part of Scioto Trail, **V**, 45

Wiley, Calvin S., educational reformer, **V**, 122

Wiley, Charles, bookseller, **I**, 214

Wiley, Harvey W., and meat inspection laws, **III**, 367; and Pure Food and Drug Acts, **IV**, 383

Wiley, James W., co-founder of the *Columbian*, **IV**, 127; first printer of Washington, **IV**, 346

Wilkes, Charles, exploring expedition, **III**, 63; makes agreement with Samoan chiefs, **IV**, 76; exploration of the Pacific, **IV**, 77; claims Wake Island, **IV**, 195; surveys Puget Sound, **IV**, 380; arouses American interest in Samoa, **V**, 20; and the *Trent* affair, **V**, 321; and whaling, **V**, 452

Wilkes, John, and "ninety-two and forty-five," **IV**, 135

Wilkes-Barre, established by the Susquehannah Company, **V**, 211

Wilkinson, Benjamin, partner in St. Louis Missouri Fur Company, **V**, 12

Wilkinson, James, and treaty with the Choctaws, I, 9; directs building of Fort Bellefontaine, I, 176; and Burr Conspiracy, I, 208, 257; takes possession of Fort Charlotte, I, 345; and battle of Chrysler's Field, I, 371; at Fort Confederation, II, 13; at French Creek, II, 344; reaches French Mills, II, 346; and Fort Hamilton, III, 6; and battle of Lacolle Mill, III, 226; and Leech Lake Indian Council, III, 260; and the Louisiana Purchase, III, 308; takes possession of Mobile, IV, 1; and expedition against Montreal, IV, 18; obtains right of way on Natchez Trace, IV, 57; and Neutral Ground Agreement, IV, 87; and modification of Spanish policy with regard to the Mississippi, IV, 106; imposes martial law in New Orleans, IV, 110; and construction of Fort St. Clair, V, 7; and surrender at Saratoga, V, 32; and the Spanish Conspiracy, V, 139; leads expedition against Wabash Towns, V, 386; fails in campaign against Montreal, V, 405; and western exploration, V, 442; and western separatism, V, 447

Wilkinson, Jemima, founder of Jerusalem Community, I, 440

Wilkinson, T. S., Jr., perfects the mine, IV, 148

Wilkinson-Wayne Quarrel, V, 427

Willamette Valley, and Oregon, IV, 182; and Oregon Memorial of 1838, IV, 183; mission established in, IV, 184; and the Oregon Trail, IV, 186

Willard, Archibald M., paints "Spirit of '76," V, 146

Willard, Emma, encourages college training for women, V, 477, 480

Willard, Frances E., and the W. C. T. U., V, 479

Willard, Jess, prize fighter, IV, 353

Willard Clocks, I, 402

Willey Amendment, to the West Virginia statehood bill, V, 440

William, Fort, original name of Bent's Fort, I, 178

William, Fort, first structure of Fort Laramie, III, 245

William, Fort, trading post on the upper Missouri, IV, 29

William and Mary, College of, and higher education in the colonies, II, 185; gives first systematic legal instruction, III, 251; and Phi Beta Kappa Society, IV, 258; founded, V, 372; and colonial leaders, V, 375

William and Mary, Fort, attack on, IV, 102

William Henry, Fort, in French and Indian War, III, 229; captured by French and Indians (1696), IV, 240; capture of (1756), IV, 481

Williams, A. J., wins air trophy, I, 36

Williams, "Bill," unofficial explorer, II, 235; mountain man, IV, 37; scout, V, 46

Williams, David, helps capture André, I, 73

Williams, Ephraim, killed in battle of Lake George, III, 231; put in command of Fort Massachusetts, III, 354

Williams, Eunice Mather, taken prisoner after Deerfield massacre, II, 126

Williams, Francis, elected governor of Strawberry Bank, V, 188

Williams, George H., and the Treaty of Washington (1871), V, 416

Williams, Henry, and silhouettes, V, 78

Williams, John, and the Regulators of North Carolina, IV, 440; and the Transylvania Company, V, 309

Williams, Jonathan, first superintendent of the United States Military Academy, III, 398

Williams, Joseph, and treaty of Long Island of Holston, III, 299

Williams, R. G., edits antislavery newspaper, II, 206

Williams, Reelfoot, and first important stagecoach robbery, V, 153

Williams, Roger, witnesses purchase of Aquidneck Island, I, 93; and the Baptists, I, 161; and heresy trials, III, 27; attempts to Christianize the Indians, III, 103; banishment of, III, 147; as a liberal, III, 269; exile of, III, 357; among the Narragansett Indians, IV, 53; and philosophical thought and writings, IV, 263; and Providence Plantations, IV, 367; settles at Providence, IV, 477; secures the first charter of Rhode Island, IV, 478; minister of Congregational Church in Salem, V, 16; attacks slavery, V, 94; author of the tract, *G. Fox digg'd out of his Burrowes*, V, 291

Williams, S. Wells, and diplomacy, III, 415

Williams, William, signer of the Declaration of Independence, II, 123

Williams, William, and Spirit Lake massacre, V, 146

Williams and Company, and burning of the *Peggy Stewart*, IV, 238

Williams College, founded by the Congregationalists, II, 17

Williams Gap, IV, 221

Williams v. Mississippi, III, 422

Williamsburg, architecture of, I, 99; restoration of, I, 102; seat of government moved to, III, 167; restoration of, IV, 412; capital of Virginia established at, V, 372

Williamsburg Bridge, opened, IV, 119

Williamson, Charles, organizes the Levy, III, 265; and the Pulteney purchase, IV, 381

Williamson, David, and Gnadenhutten, II, 392; and Mingo Bottom, III, 408; and battle of the Olentangy, IV, 172

Williamson, Hugh, signer of the Constitution, II, 39

Williamson, William P., on the designing board of the *Virginia,* V, 414

Willing, James, and the *Rattletrap,* II, 367

Willing, The, used in Clark's Vincennes expedition, II, 367

Willing and Morris, and profiteering in the Revolution, IV, 475

Willis, Nathaniel, founder of the *Potowmac Guardian,* IV, 128; first printer of West Virginia, IV, 346; establishes the *Scioto Gazette,* V, 44

Willis, Nathaniel, founder of *Youth's Companion,* I, 363

Willis, Nathaniel P., dramatist, II, 166

Willis, Olympia Brown, enters the theological department of St. Lawrence University, V, 481

Willoughby, W. F., and Budget and Accounting Act of 1921, I, 247

Wills Creek, on the westward route, I, 51; beginning of Braddock's Road, I, 233; Gist starts his travels from, II, 390; Washington at (1754), II, 418; and the Ohio Company of Virginia, IV, 163

Willson, A. E., and Night Riders, IV, 134

Willys-Overland Motor Company, I, 140

Wilmington Courant, IV, 126

Wilmot Proviso, and the Alabama Platform, I, 41; Barnburners favor, I, 164; and Compromise of 1850, I, 442; favored by Conscience Whigs, II, 25; and the Missouri Compromise, III, 428; and popular sovereignty, IV, 309; and slavery, V, 96; and the Virginia Resolutions (1847), V, 379

Wilson, Allen Benjamin, invents a sewing machine, III, 148; V, 61

Wilson, Ernest H., and gardening, II, 371

Wilson, H. B., and the Navy in the World War, V, 493

Wilson, Jack. *See* Wovoka

Wilson, James, signer of the Constitution, II, 39; delegate to Convention of 1787, II, 50; and the Declaration of Independence, II, 121; signer of the Declaration of Independence, II, 124; and state sovereignty, V, 173

Wilson, James, serves as Secretary of Agriculture, III, 153

Wilson, James H., captures Jefferson Davis, I, 385; and engagement at Spring Hill, V, 150; and battle at Yellow Tavern, V, 506

Wilson, W. L., and the tariff, II, 401

Wilson, William B., appointed first Secretary of Labor, III, 220; and the Vare case, V, 358

Wilson, Woodrow, and Article Ten, I, 125; elected President, I, 290; and congressional regulation, II, 17; and making the world "safe for democracy," II, 136; and the diplomatic missions of Col. House, II, 148; and Dominican Republic, II, 159; and the Presidency, II, 259; and the adoption of closure rule, II, 272; and Flag Day observance, II, 280; directs design of presidential flag, II, 280; establishes exact proportions for United States flag, II, 281; and foreign policy, II, 305; and the Fourteen Points, II, 317; and Franco-American relations, II, 328; and freedom of the seas, II, 332; calls conference of governors and mayors, II, 406; and the phrase "He Kept Us Out of War," III, 21; and hyphenate groups, III, 65; and his Fourteen Points, III, 84; and the Inquiry, III, 124; and international law, III, 142; and the League of Nations, III, 255; and the Lodge Reservations, III, 293; and the sinking of the *Lusitania,* III, 315; and the Monroe Doctrine, IV, 14; upholds neutral rights, IV, 87; and "New Freedom," IV, 101; promotes antimonopoly laws in New Jersey, IV, 105; and nonrecognition, IV, 140; and open covenants, IV, 175; and oratory, IV, 180; and "peace without victory," IV, 236; and the Philippine Islands, IV, 262; political writings of, IV, 303; and preparedness, IV, 331; and the Presidency, IV, 333; and presidential absences from American soil, IV, 335; and special powers granted to Presidents, IV, 335; as president of Princeton University, IV, 343; and the United States Railroad Administration, IV, 399; recognition policy of, IV, 424; violates the Tenure-of-Office Act, IV, 448; and legislative riders, IV, 482; and the secret protocol, V, 52; urges the creation of a nonpartisan Tariff Commission, V, 223; asks for repeal of Tolls Exemption Act, V, 279; and "Too Proud to Fight," V, 281; popularizes his "New Freedom," V, 327; and the system of tutorial instruction, V, 332; and tyranny, V, 337; and Vera Cruz (1914), V, 360; student of University of Virginia, V, 375; vetoes the Volstead Act, V, 382; and declaration of war, V, 396; war powers of, V, 407; creates the War Trade Board, V, 407; and "Watchful Waiting," V, 421; whispering campaigns against, V, 458; supports the Nineteenth Amendment, V, 478; and the United States as a world power, V, 486; and World War Peace Conference (1919), V, 489; and the World War, V, 490 ff.; and the Yap mandate, V, 502

Wilson Act, liquor law, III, 283; and Original-package doctrine, IV, 188

Wilson Dam, construction of, V, 244; and Tennessee Valley Authority, V, 245

Wilson-Gorman Tariff Act. *See* Gorman-Wilson Tariff Bill

Wilson v. New, and railroad wages, I, 10; and emergency legislation, II, 210

Wilson's Creek, Price meets Lyon at, IV, 339

Winchell, James M., and American hymns, III, 65

Winchester, Elhanan, and the Universalists, V, 350

Winchester, James, and the Raisin River massacre, IV, 412

Winchester Rifle, IV, 483

Wind River Reservation, V, 497

Winder, Charles S., and battle of Cedar Mountain, I, 330

Winder, John H., and Libby prison, III, 268

Winder, William H., in battle of Bladensburg, I, 198; and battle of Stoney Creek, V, 185

Windmills, help to ameliorate effects of drouths, II, 170; and frontier transition, II, 351; and open range cattle period, IV, 177

Window Tax, as cause of Fries rebellion, II, 349

Wine, making of, II, 169; and pipe staves, IV, 276

Winegar, S. C., publisher of Frontier Scout, IV, 127; first printer of North Dakota, IV, 346

Wines, Enoch Cobb, and prison reform, IV, 348

Wingfield, Edward Maria, and founding of Jamestown, III, 166; elected president of Jamestown council, III, 167; leader in the Jamestown settlement, V, 372

Winnebago, Fort, building of, II, 320; V, 473

Winnebago Indians, and the Black Hawk War, I, 195; and Butte des Morts Council, I, 263; trouble with, compels restoration of Fort Dearborn, II, 115; removal of, III, 107; as mound builders, IV, 35; party to the treaty of Prairie du Chien (1825), IV, 329; and British attack on St. Louis (1780), V, 11; depend upon wild rice for their food supply, V, 464; and Wisconsin, V, 473

Winner, Septimus, popular songs of, V, 119

Winning of Barbara Worth, written by Harold Bell Wright, I, 180

Winona, and Maiden's Rock, III, 325

Winslow, Edward, explores Connecticut, II, 21; considered author of Mourt's Relation, IV, 38; and Plymouth Trading Post, IV, 291

Winslow, Edward, silversmith, V, 82

Winslow, Edward, Jr., and the formation of the Associated Loyalists, I, 131

Winslow, John, in French and Indian War, III, 229

Winslow, John A., and the Kearsarge and Alabama engagement, III, 202

Winslow, Josiah, and Great Swamp Fight, II, 420

Winsor, Justin, Narrative and Critical History of America, III, 35; and the American Library Association, III, 272

Winston, Joseph, and battle of King's Mountain, III, 212

Winter, John, and Lygonia, III, 317; and settlement of Saco Bay, V, 3; and the Trelawney plantation, V, 320

Winters, Aaron, discovers borax, I, 218

Winthrop, Adam, and the Pejepscot purchase, IV, 239

Winthrop, Fitz-John, in King William's War, III, 211; and early French and English clashes on Lake Champlain, III, 229

Winthrop, John, and the Antinomian Controversy, I, 83; Blessing of the Bay built for, I, 199; describes influenza epidemic, III, 122; and meaning of liberty, III, 270; and philosophical thought and writings, IV, 263; and scurvy, V, 47; launches the Blessing of the Bay, V, 72; and theocracy in New England, V, 260

Winthrop, John, The Younger, and the Atherton Company, I, 134; and industrial chemistry, I, 350; and Connecticut, II, 21; and Connecticut's Charter of 1662, II, 24; and industrial research, III, 116; and building of first furnaces and forges, III, 156; and mines, III, 407; succeeds in securing a charter which includes the New Haven Colony, IV, 104; establishes first observatory, IV, 156; and the River Towns of Connecticut, IV, 490; and settlement of Saybrook, Conn., V, 36

Winthrop, John, records astronomical phenomena, IV, 156

Winthrop v. Lechmere, and intestate estates, I, 89; III, 146

Winton, Alexander, and the automobile, I, 140

Winton Motor Carriage Company Case, V, 56

Wirt, William, nominated for Presidency, I, 82; author of Life of Patrick Henry, I, 189; nominated for Presidency, I, 283; argues Gibbons v. Ogden case, II, 388; and McCulloch v. Maryland, III, 364; in Gibbons v. Ogden, V, 178; Swiss immigrant, V, 215

Wirz, Henry, and Andersonville prison, I, 73

Wisconsin, dairying industry in, II, 105; and German immigrants, II, 384; organized, and admitted, V, 248

Wisconsin Heights, Battle of, V, 473

Wisconsin State Journal, and newspaper syndicates, IV, 123

Wisconsin Territory, Dakota becomes part of (1836), II, 106

"Wise, and Good and Rich," II, 135, 229; IV, 453

Wise, Fort, I, 179; III, 317

Wise, H. A., and the Raleigh Conference of Southern Governors, IV, 412

Wise, John, and the Compact Theory, I, 441; and the Ipswich protest, III, 153; political theories of, IV, 300; political writings of, IV, 302

Wise, John, balloonist, I, 149; pilots first dirigible flight, II, 148

Wister, Owen, author of The Virginian, I, 180

Witchcraft, hexing as, III, 28; in Massachusetts, III, 355; pressing to death for, IV, 337; in Salem, V, 16; and colonial laws, V, 203

Witheridge, John, trades at Pemaquid, **IV,** 239

Witherspoon, John, signer of the Declaration of Independence, **II,** 124; and philosophical thought and writings, **IV,** 263; president of College of New Jersey, **IV,** 343

Withington, Charles B., and the development of the reaper, **IV,** 419

Wittenmyer, Annie, president of the W. C. T. U., **V,** 479

Wolcott, Oliver, signer of the Declaration of Independence, **II,** 123

Wolf, Henry, wood engraver, **V,** 483

Wolfe, James, captures Quebec, **II,** 343; **IV,** 388; and colonial rangers, **IV,** 416

Wolfe, Samuel M., writes *Helper's Impending Crisis Dissected,* **III,** 25

Wolfskill, William, on the Spanish Trail, **V,** 142

Wolves, dogs purchased by towns for the destruction of, **II,** 157; and sheep, **II,** 294; **V,** 66, 483

Womack, Robert, discovers promising gold vein, **II,** 89; as a prospector, **IV,** 364

Woman Suffrage, a phase of the humanitarian movement, **I,** 2; in the campaign of 1920, **I,** 291; and the Nineteenth Amendment, **II,** 43; and Equal Rights party, **II,** 222; and feminism, **II,** 266; agitation for, **II,** 324; and the Greenback party, **II,** 424; and the Nineteenth Amendment, **IV,** 134; and the Seneca Falls Convention, **V,** 58; and the woman movement, **V,** 477; granted in Wyoming Territory, **V,** 497

Woman's Christian Temperance Union, **III,** 16, 290; **IV,** 356; **V,** 482

Woman's Relief Corps, and the Grand Army of the Republic, **II,** 407

Women, enfranchisement of, **II,** 193; rights of, and marriage, **III,** 346; enfranchisement of, **V,** 383; wages and hours of labor for, **V,** 387

Women of the Wilderness Community, **I,** 440

Women's Bureau, division of the Department of Labor, **III,** 221

Women's Clubs, and the woman movement, **V,** 477

Women's International League for Peace and Freedom, **IV,** 235; **V,** 395

Women's Peace Party, antiwar organization, **V,** 395

Women's Rights, a phase of the humanitarian movement, **I,** 2; agitation for, **II,** 265; and Seneca Falls Convention, **V,** 58

Wong Kim Ark Case, **V,** 349

Wood, A. B., discovers true nature of carbonate ore, **III,** 254

Wood, Abraham, sends out Batts-Fallam expedition, **I,** 168; commands Fort Henry, **IV,** 81; and early discovery of the Ohio River, **IV,** 164

Wood, Fernando, and the Copperheads, **II,** 58

Wood, Jethro, and the cast-iron plow, **II,** 247; **IV,** 287

Wood, Leonard, fosters the Citizens' Military Training Camp, **I,** 378; institutes reforms in Cuba, **II,** 94; as governor general of the Philippines, **IV,** 262; and Preparedness, **IV,** 331; and the Rough Riders, **IV,** 503

Wood, Samuel, and Sons, publishers of chapbooks, **I,** 341

Wood, William, granted right to coin copper pieces for the colonies, **I,** 411

Wood Engraving, **I,** 213

Wood Lake, and the Sioux uprising in Minnesota, **V,** 86

Wood Pulp, used for newspapers, **IV,** 212; and foreign trade, **V,** 295

Woodbury, W. P., founder of Fort Kearny on the Platte, **III,** 200

Woodruff, Wilford, and plural marriage, **IV,** 26; president of Mormon Church, **IV,** 27

Woodruff, William Edward, starts the *Arkansas Gazette,* **IV,** 126; Arkansas printer, **IV,** 345

Woods, Andrew, and Missouri Fur Company, **V,** 13

Woods, C. D., and the Pullman strike, **IV,** 381

Woods, Robert A., and wrong side of the railroad track, **IV,** 406; and social settlements, **V,** 109

Woodsdale, Kans., and county-seat wars, **II,** 74

"Woodstock Races," **V,** 280

Woodward, A. B., and his plan for Detroit, **II,** 144

Woodward, William H., sued by Dartmouth College, **II,** 111

Woodworth, Samuel, and the "Old Oaken Bucket," **IV,** 171

Wool, influence of cost of transportation on production of, **I,** 33; and rotation of crops, **II,** 154; and sheep raising, **V,** 66; and textiles, **V,** 258; and foreign trade, **V,** 295

Wool, John E., joined by Doniphan's expedition, **II,** 161; and Soldiers and Sailors Conventions, **V,** 117; and the Yakima Indian wars, **V,** 500

Wool Spinning, as household art, **III,** 53

Woolen Act (1699), and colonial commerce, **I,** 418; and British colonial policy, **I,** 422; restricts colonial manufacture, **III,** 335

Woolley, Edwin C., author of *Handbook of Composition,* **I,** 180

"Woolly Heads," **II,** 25

Woolman, John, attacks slavery, **V,** 94

Woolsey, Melancthon, and battle of Sandy Creek, **V,** 27

Woolson, C. F., and fiction, **II,** 270

Woolworth, Frank W., and Five-and-ten-cent stores, **II,** 279

Woolworth, F. W., Company, **I,** 336

Woolworth Building, built by Cass Gilbert, **I,** 101; introduces the "super-sky-scraper," **V,** 88

Wooster, David, and Tryon's retreat after burning of Danbury, **II,** 108; and the battle of Ridgefield, **IV,** 483

Worcester, Joseph E., publishes *A Universal and Critical Dictionary*, **II**, 146

Worcester, Noah, and the Massachusetts Peace Society, **IV**, 233

Worcester Polytechnic Institute, **III**, 114

Worcester v. Georgia, and Cherokee Nation v. Georgia, **I**, 352; and states' rights, **V**, 176

Worcester's Readers, **III**, 365

Worden, John L., commander of the *Monitor*, **IV**, 10

Work Projects, and relief, **IV**, 440

Workers' Alliance, and lobbying, **III**, 287

Workers International Industrial Union, **III**, 119

Workers (Communist) Party, **I**, 440; **II**, 251

Working Men's Advocate, Evans becomes editor of, **III**, 42

Workingmen's Protective Union, and consumer co-operatives, **II**, 56

Workman-Rowland Company, **I**, 269

Workmen's Accident Compensation, genesis of, **I**, 8; and labor legislation, **III**, 222; and *laissez-faire*, **III**, 229; and safety-first movement, **V**, 4; and social legislation, **V**, 107

Works Progress Administration, and airports, **I**, 37; continues work of the F. E. R. A., **II**, 257; created, **IV**, 96; and relief, **IV**, 440; and National Youth Administration, **V**, 511

World Affairs, **I**, 64

World Almanac, **I**, 52

World Court (Permanent Court of International Justice), and arbitration, **I**, 98; and the Democratic party, **II**, 137; replaces Permanent Court of Arbitration, **III**, 2; and international law, **III**, 142; and isolation, **III**, 163; and Ladd's peace plan, **III**, 226; establishment of, **IV**, 232

World Economic Conference (1933), and silver stabilization, **V**, 81

World of Tomorrow, architecture of, **I**, 102

World Peace Foundation, **IV**, 235

World Power, United States as a, **V**, 135

World War, American Expeditionary Forces in the, **I**, 59; and the Armistice of 1918, **I**, 108; and the United States Army, **I**, 113; and Army contracts, **I**, 115; and hospitalization, **I**, 116; and foreign trade, **I**, 147; and Balfour and Viviani-Joffre missions, **I**, 147; and Belgian relief, **I**, 174; battle of Belleau Wood, **I**, 175; treaty of peace with Germany (1921), **I**, 179; and blockade, **I**, 201; Americans attack at Cantigny, **I**, 305; Champagne-Marne Operation, **I**, 338; Americans at Château-Thierry Bridge, **I**, 348; and the churches, **I**, 374; use of convoys in, **II**, 53; and the Council of National Defense, **II**, 72; American Marines remain in Cuba after, **II**, 95; and public debt, **II**, 117; financing of, **II**, 128; demobilization after, **II**, 134; Dollar-a-Year Men in, **II**, 158; and dress, **II**, 169; and DuPont Company, **II**, 177; and the Emergency Fleet Corporation, **II**, 209; and farm prosperity, **II**, 249; Food Administration during, **II**, 296; and inflation, **III**, 121; and Liberty Loans, **III**, 271; and Declaration of London, **III**, 296; Marines in the, **III**, 343; Meuse-Argonne Offensive, **III**, 381; mine sweeping during, **III**, 406; mobilization for, **IV**, 2; Montdidier-Noyon Operation, **IV**, 16; and munitions, **IV**, 45; National Army in, **IV**, 58; Navy in, **IV**, 78; and freedom of the seas, **IV**, 87; and neutrality, **IV**, 90; Northern Mine Barrage, **IV**, 148; Oise-Aisne Operation, **IV**, 167; and the packing business, **IV**, 199; and peace movements, **IV**, 235; and operations on the Piave River, **IV**, 266; and the explosive industry, **IV**, 326; and Preparedness, **IV**, 331; price fixing during, **IV**, 338; and propaganda, **IV**, 359; and the American Red Cross, **IV**, 429; and retaliation in international law, **IV**, 461 f.; St. Mihiel operations, **V**, 14; and sea power, **V**, 48; and sex relations, **V**, 62; and shipbuilding, **V**, 72; and ocean shipping, **V**, 74; Somme Offensive, **V**, 119; and suspension of specie payments, **V**, 144; and Trade with the Enemy Acts, **V**, 300; trench in the, **V**, 321; and army uniforms, **V**, 341; and settlement of War Claims Act, **V**, 400; debts, **V**, 401; cost of, **V**, 409; loss of life in, **V**, 410; and the United States as a world power, **V**, 486; Ypres-Lys Operation, **V**, 511

World War Peace Conference (1919), and freedom of the seas, **II**, 338; and the Inquiry, **III**, 124; and the International Labor Organization, **III**, 140; and the League of Nations, **III**, 255; and the Monroe Doctrine, **IV**, 14; and the League of Nations, **IV**, 232; and trading with the enemy, **V**, 301; and the Yap mandate, **V**, 502

World's Columbian Exposition, and architecture, **I**, 101; advertises Chicago, **I**, 356; Ferris Wheel featured at, **II**, 267; reveals industrial advance, **III**, 337; and the Midway Plaisance, **III**, 396; and postage stamps, **IV**, 318; and the Wild West Show, **V**, 464

Worth, W. J., and the battle of Chapultepec, **I**, 342; and "headquarters in the saddle," **III**, 21; and capture of Mexico City, **III**, 389; and battle of Molino del Rey, **IV**, 6

Worthington, Thomas, member of the Chillicothe Junto, **I**, 364; and military tracts, **III**, 402; and Ohio, **IV**, 160

Wounded Knee, Battle of, **III**, 380; **V**, 87

Wovoka (Jack Wilson), originator of the Ghost Dance, **II**, 388

Wray, John, and the Raystown Path, **IV**, 418

"Wreck of the Hesperus," and Norman's Woe reef, **I**, 306

Wrenn, John H., book collection of, I, 212

Wrenn, Robert D., tennis player, V, 245

Wright, Benjamin, builder of Erie Canal, II, 226

Wright, Carroll D., and slums, V, 99

Wright, Edward, revises Mercator's map, III, 340

Wright, Fanny, and the Working Man's party, V, 484

Wright, Frances, lecturer, III, 260; establishes Nashoba, IV, 54

Wright, Frank Lloyd, architect, I, 102

Wright, George, forces the Yakima Indians to submission, V, 500

Wright, Harold Bell, author of *The Winning of Barbara Worth*, I, 180

Wright, Hendrick B., opposed by the Copperheads, II, 58

Wright, Henry C., and formation of the New England Non-Resistance Society, IV, 234

Wright, Horatio G., commands Army of the Ohio, IV, 162; and battles at Sailor's Creek, V, 5; and battle of Spotsylvania Courthouse, V, 150

Wright, James, and the treaty of Augusta (1773), I, 138; appointed governor of Georgia Colony, II, 379

Wright, Luke E., first ambassador to Japan, I, 54; governor-general of the Philippines, IV, 262

Wright, Moses, and the Holland Patent, III, 38

Wright, Orville, and airplane disasters, I, 35; and aviation, I, 142; invents the airplane, III, 149; constructs Kitty Hawk airplane, III, 214

Wright, Patience, first American wax modeler, V, 426

Wright, Wilbur, and aviation, I, 142; invents airplane, III, 149; constructs Kitty Hawk airplane, III, 214

Wrightson, William, publisher of the *Weekly Arizonian*, IV, 126

Writings on American History, compiled by Grace G. Griffin, II, 405

Writs of Assistance, Otis argues against, IV, 300; and the American Revolution, IV, 465; and the rum trade, IV, 507; and taxation without representation, V, 229; and unreasonable searches and seizures, V, 351

Wyandot Indians, and Brodhead's campaign, I, 242; Crawford sets out to attack, II, 83; and treaty of Greenville, II, 425; and Fort Harmar treaty, III, 10; and Hull treaty, III, 58; in the Revolution, III, 88; land cessions of, III, 100; and treaty of Logstown, III, 295; and treaties of Fort McIntosh, III, 366; and treaty at Pittsburgh (1775), IV, 280; in Upper Sandusky, V, 352; and Great Warriors Path, V, 408. *See also* Huron Indians

Wyant, Alexander, landscape painter, I, 123

Wyatt, Francis, and potatoes, IV, 322

Wyeth, Nathaniel J., and the fur trade, II, 362; builds Fort Hall, III, 6; and Oregon fur trade, IV, 182; on the Oregon Trail, IV, 185; and battle of Pierre's Hole, IV, 269

Wyllys, Fort, at West Point, N. Y., V, 438

Wyman, Seth, and Lovewell's Fight, III, 310

Wynehamer v. New York, and the due process clauses, II, 172

Wynne, James, and vital statistics, V, 382

Wyoming, organized, and admitted, V, 249; gives women the vote, V, 478

Wyoming Massacre, and Butler's Rangers, I, 263; and Forty Fort, II, 313; and Harris' Ferry, III, 13; and the Clinton-Sullivan-Brodhead expeditions, III, 88; Lazarus Stewart is killed in, IV, 229; Susquehanna settlers defeated in, V, 210

Wyoming Stock Growers' Association, I, 325

Wyoming Territory, creation of, II, 106

Wyoming Valley, and land grants, III, 235; land speculation in, III, 239; and the Susquehanna settlers, V, 210; and the Susquehannah Company, V, 211; and the Yankee-Pennamite wars, V, 502

Wythe, George, delegate to Convention of 1787, II, 50; signer of the Declaration of Independence, II, 124

X

XIT Ranch, on the Staked Plains, V, 154

XY Company, and the Five Villages, II, 280; builds fort at Grand Portage, II, 409; and liquor in the Indian trade, III, 91

XYZ Affair, and diplomatic missions, II, 148; and the Franco-American misunderstanding, II, 327; and origin of "Hail Columbia," III, 3; and "Millions for defense, etc.," III, 405

Y

Yachting, I, 70; V, 148

Yakima Indian Wars, and the Walla Walla settlements, V, 394; and the State of Washington, V, 415

Yale College, and the Congregationalists, II, 16; and higher education in the colonies, II, 185; and football, II, 298; and Latin America, III, 248; and foreign exchange students, V, 191

Yale Divinity School, and revivals, IV, 464

Yamacraw Indians, and settlement of Savannah, V, 35

Yamasee War, and the Carolina proprietors, I, 316; Catawba Indians in the, I, 323; and Spaniards, V, 126

Yancey, William L., and the Alabama Platform, I, 41; and Civil War diplomacy, I, 392; and recognition of the Confederacy, II, 5; and the Confederate Congress, II, 6; advocates secession, II, 275; creates League of United South-

erners, **III**, 256; and oratory, **IV**, 180; educational reformer, **V**, 122; organizes League of United Southerners, **V**, 131

Yankee Notions, **II**, 48

Yankee-Pennamite Wars, and Connecticut's western lands, **II**, 24; and land grants, **III**, 235; Lazarus Stewart engages in, **IV**, 229; and Pennsylvania boundary, **IV**, 243; and Pennsylvania-Connecticut boundary dispute, **IV**, 246; and the Susquehanna settlers, **V**, 210; and the Susquehannah Company, **V**, 211; and settlement of Wyoming Valley, **V**, 498

Yankee Sound, explored by Palmer, **IV**, 201

Yankton Indians, a division of the Sioux, **V**, 85

Yankton Reservation, **V**, 127

Yap Island, and Washington Conference on Limitation of Armaments, **V**, 417

Yates, Robert, publishes proceedings of Convention of 1787, **II**, 50

Yates Pool, and oil production, **III**, 394; **IV**, 167

Yazoo Claims, and the Georgia Compact, **II**, 381

Yazoo Companies, and the Old Southwest, **V**, 132

Yazoo Indians, Jesuit missions among, **III**, 175

Yazoo Land Frauds, connected with the Blount Conspiracy, **I**, 203; and Fletcher v. Peck, **II**, 284; and the Georgia Compact, **II**, 380; and the Georgia-Mississippi Company, **II**, 381; and land scrip, **III**, 238; and land speculation, **III**, 239; and western lands, **V**, 444

Yazoo River, and Florida boundary, **II**, 290

Yeardley, George, and first legislature at Jamestown, **V**, 372

Yellow Creek Massacre, **II**, 87

Yellow-Dog Contract, and Coppage v. Kansas, **II**, 57

Yellow Fever, and calomel, **I**, 276; conquered in Cuba, **II**, 94; wiped out, **II**, 150; epidemic of, **II**, 221; prevalent on *Jersey* prison-ship, **III**, 174; studied by Rockefeller Foundation, in Latin America, **III**, 249; eliminated in Louisiana, **III**, 306; and medicine, **III**, 369; in Mississippi, **III**, 421; and mosquitoes, **IV**, 30; in New York City, **IV**, 118; in Norfolk, **IV**, 142; and the Panama Canal, **IV**, 205; and sanitation, **V**, 28; in Savannah, **V**, 35

Yellow Hand, killed on War Bonnet Creek, **V**, 400

Yellow Journalism, origin of term, **I**, 431; and news reporting, **IV**, 122; and the tabloids, **V**, 216

"Yellow Kid," controversy over comic strip, **I**, 431

Yellow Peril, and Japanese exclusion, **III**, 168

Yellowstone, The, Catlin travels in, **I**, 324; Chouteau ascends Missouri River in, **III**, 430

Yellowstone Expedition, S. H. Long commands, **III**, 300

Yellowstone Park, first seen by John Colter, **II**, 235; **III**, 335; as a national park, **IV**, 217

Yerkes, Charles T., art collection of, **I**, 125

Yerkes, R. M., and army intelligence tests, **III**, 133

Yerkes Observatory, **IV**, 156

Yick Wo v. Hopkins, and equal protection of law, **II**, 222; and doctrine of equality, **II**, 223

Yogoda Sat-sanga, Hindu cult, **IV**, 187

York (Toronto), and capture of Fort George, **II**, 379

York, Duke of, proprietary of the, **II**, 132; and Iroquois treaty (1684), **III**, 160; granted all of Long Island, **III**, 299; grants New Castle to Penn, **IV**, 95; granted New Netherland, **IV**, 104; claims New Netherland, **IV**, 109; proprietary of the, **IV**, 240, 362; and the New Hampshire Grants, **V**, 362; proprietary, and the Western Reserve, **V**, 445; proprietary, and settlement of Wyoming Valley, **V**, 497

York, Me., settlement of, **I**, 20

Yorkshire County, **III**, 327

Yorktown Campaign, and battle of Chesapeake Capes, **I**, 354; won by French aid, **II**, 13; Rochambeau's part in, **II**, 343; French forces in, **II**, 345; Cornwallis defeated in the, **IV**, 477; and sea power, **V**, 48; and the battle of Virginia Capes, **V**, 376

Yosemite National Park, **IV**, 217

You Bet Mining Camp, **I**, 171

Young, Bennett H., raids St. Albans (Vt.), **V**, 5

Young, Brigham, chosen governor of State of Deseret, **II**, 140; furnishes Mormon battalion, **IV**, 24; leads Mormon expedition, **IV**, 24; and the Mormon Trail, **IV**, 24; presiding officer of the Mormons, **IV**, 26; and the Mountain Meadows massacre, **IV**, 36; not of the Reorganized Latter Day Saints, **IV**, 449; founder of Salt Lake City, **V**, 19; and Utah, **V**, 353

Young, Brigham H., printer of the *Deseret News*, **IV**, 127; first printer of Utah, **IV**, 346

Young, Ewing, early trapper and pioneer, **II**, 236; and the fur trade, **II**, 362; at Taos, **V**, 219

Young, Harry, Sheridan's chief spy, **V**, 146

Young, McClintock, and the development of the reaper, **IV**, 419

Young, Owen D., and General Electric Company, **II**, 376

"Young America," **III**, 387; **V**, 511

"Young Charlotte," ballad, **II**, 293

Young Communist League, **I**, 440

Young Men's Association for Mutual Improvement, **IV**, 20

Young Men's Christian Association, stresses Bible study, **I**, 181; and philanthropy, **IV**, 260; and religion, **IV**, 442; and social settlement work, **V**, 109; and World War relief, **V**, 488

Young Plan, and the Bank for International Settlements, **I**, 154; replaces Dawes Plan, **II**,

113; and Lausanne Agreement of 1932, **III**, 251; and the Reparation Commission, **IV**, 450

Young Women's Christian Association, stresses Bible study, **I**, 181; and philanthropy, **IV**, 260; and religion, **IV**, 442; and social settlement work, **V**, 109; and World War relief, **V**, 488

Younger, Thomas Coleman, and the Northfield Bank robbery, **IV**, 149

Younger Gang, robbers, **I**, 152

Youth's Companion, founded by Nathaniel Willis, **I**, 363

Youth's Friend and Scholar's Magazine, **I**, 363

Yukon, gold discovered in, **II**, 396

Yuma Indians, in Arizona, **I**, 104; and Fort Yuma, **V**, 512

Yung Wing, foreign exchange student to Yale, **V**, 191

Z

ZMC-2, construction of the, **II**, 149

ZR-1, airship authorized by Congress, **II**, 148

ZR-3, construction of the, **II**, 149

ZRS-4, construction of the, **II**, 149

ZRS-5, construction of the, **II**, 149

Zamorano, Agustin V., California printer, **IV**, 345

Zane, Ebenezer, settles the site of Wheeling, W. Va., **V**, 455

Zane's Trace, first road built in Ohio, **II**, 97; and the National Road, **IV**, 63

Zanesville, capital of Ohio, **IV**, 160

Zavala, The, and the Texas navy, **V**, 256

Zeisberger, David, establishes Schoenbrunn, **V**, 38

Zenger Trial, and rules of evidence, **II**, 92; and freedom of the press, **II**, 337; and libel, **III**, 268; **IV**, 115; and news reporting, **IV**, 122

Zenoni, John B., and Missouri Fur Company, **V**, 13

Zimmerman Note, and the World War, **V**, 491

Zinzendorf, Count Nikolaus Ludwig, and the Moravians, **IV**, 22; and Pietism, **IV**, 269

Zion National Park, **IV**, 218

Zoar Community, **I**, 440; **III**, 397

Zollicoffer, F. K., at Camp Wild-Cat, **I**, 280; killed at Mill Springs, **III**, 404; and Swiss origin, **V**, 215

Zoning, and housing, **III**, 53

Zouaves, **II**, 204

Zukor, Adolph, and motion pictures, **IV**, 32

Zuñi, Chamuscado expedition to, **IV**, 500

Zwaanendael Colony, establishment of, **II**, 132

DICTIONARY OF AMERICAN HISTORY